In memory of my parents, Joseph and Jeanmarie

DREAMER OF THE DAY

FRANCIS PARKER YOCKEY AND THE POSTWAR FASCIST INTERNATIONAL

BY KEVIN COOGAN

*All men dream: but not equally. Those who dream
by night in the dusty recesses of their minds wake in
the day to find that it was vanity: but the dreamers
of the day are dangerous men, for they may act their
dream with open eyes, to make it possible.*

—*T. E. Lawrence,* Seven Pillars of Wisdom

Autonomedia

Library of Congress Cataloging in Publication Data
Coogan, Kevin.
Dreamer of the day: Francis Parker Yockey and the postwar fascist
    international / by Kevin Coogan.
p. cm.
Includes bibliographical references (p.) and index.
ISBN 1-57027-039-2 (pbk.)
1. Yockey, Francis Parker, 1917–1960. 2. Fascists—United States—Biography.
3. Right-wing extremists—United States—Biography. 4. Fascism—History—
20th century. I. Title.
HN90.R3Y633 1998
320.53′3′092—dc21
[b]
98-18591
CIP

Autonomedia
POB 568 Williamsburgh Station
Brooklyn, NY 11211-0568 USA
Phone & Fax: 718-963-2603
http://www.autonomedia.org

Book design: Dave Mandl

Printed in the United States of America

TABLE OF CONTENTS

ACKNOWLEDGEMENTS

When I began working on *Dreamer of the Day*, I never imagined the cooperation that I would receive from so many people. I am particularly grateful to H. Keith Thompson and Peter J. Huxley-Blythe for their invaluable help. I would also like to thank Willis Carto for sharing with me his memories of meeting Yockey. Tom Francis's insights into Yockey's writing of *Imperium* proved eminently helpful in understanding the overall construction of the book, and Adam Parfrey provided some important early leads. The late Keith Stimely's archives contributed several otherwise inaccessible interviews with some of Yockey's closest collaborators.

I am grateful to Nicholas Goodrick-Clarke for his foreword. Jeff Bale's phenomenal knowledge of postwar fascism helped me situate "Yockeyism" in the spectrum of the modern radical right. Kurt Tauber's monumental book *Beyond Eagle and Swastika* also proved invaluable.

I especially wish to thank Gail Gans for giving me access to Anti-Defamation League archives from the 1950s. The librarians at Columbia University, the Hoover Institute, and the Research Division of the New York Public Library all deserve thanks for their assistance in tracking down much obscure material.

Above all, I must thank two Autonomedia comrades, Jordan Zinovich and Dave Mandl. Jordan fearlessly edited a much longer manuscript into an actual book, while Dave did an incredible job of copy editing and text design. Without them, *Dreamer of the Day* would not exist. (The less said about Dave's bus driver, the better.) Autonomedia's Jim Fleming believed in the project from the very beginning. I am further indebted to Alex Trotter for heroically indexing the book, Robert Egert for his cover, and Chiaki Fukuda for design ideas.

Despite such valuable assistance, any inaccuracies in the book are mine alone.

FOREWORD
BY NICHOLAS
GOODRICK-CLARKE

Francis Parker Yockey was one of the most shadowy and enigmatic figures in the American far right in this century. As a student in the 1930s he fell under the spell of Oswald Spengler's cultural pessimism and rejection of liberalism. He despised the liberal-capitalist culture of America; his hopes for a fascist future were always focused on the creation of an authoritarian European superstate. He outlined his vision of Europe's future in his book *Imperium*, first published in London in 1948.

A restless and obsessive conspirator who spent almost a decade being hunted by the FBI, Yockey may have already been involved in pro-Axis espionage in the United States during World War II. After the war he served briefly as a lawyer in the "second-string" war crimes trials held in Wiesbaden, West Germany, but soon devoted himself to the career of an underground fascist agent. While most neo-Nazis continued to see Soviet communism as the great enemy, and the chief motive for their continued demands for a fascist revival, Yockey was driven by his anti-Semitism and anti-Americanism to forge new and uncharted alliances between the far right, communism, and the new nationalist regimes of developing countries.

Kevin Coogan's study of Yockey and the postwar fascist international presents an in-depth look at these surprising alliances in Europe, the Middle East, the East Bloc, and Cuba from the late 1940s right up to the present in postcommunist Russia. Coogan's research also sheds extraordinary new light on the activities of the American right from the 1930s to the present. His meticulous research into the obscure corners of the far-right support system, their shifting alliances and mysterious undercover operatives, shows not only how the network functions but how it interacts with intelligence services, state interests, and diplomatic "gray areas" in order to foster its ideological growth and identity. His book also provides an extraordinary portrait of the conspiracy theorists, extremists, conmen, occultists, and bearers of false identity in cheap hotels, rented rooms, and *poste restante* offices across the world.

Mr. Coogan shows particularly clearly how Yockey's own brand of radical pro-Soviet fascism owes a significant intellectual debt to inter-war German right-wing thought in two important respects. The first concerns geopolitics. Although divided by the rival treaties of the Entente and Central Powers and the ensuing hostilities of the First World War, Russia and Germany found new ground for alliances after 1918. Both nations were pariahs in the postwar world. The fledgling Soviet Union had overwhelming financial and military problems due to withdrawal from the war, the Russian Revolution and Civil War, and Western intervention on behalf of the Whites in 1919. With the exception of many artists, intellectuals, and a few canny businessmen (like Armand Hammer), the bourgeois West generally regarded the new state with fear and revulsion throughout the 1920s. But Germany was possibly the greater outcast due to the lost war followed by the Versailles Treaty, with its war-guilt clauses, occupation by foreign troops (1919–1930), strict control of armaments and armed forces, loss of territories, and massive reparations. Mutual aid followed on this shared outcasting in the international system. Only thus can one understand the improbable deals and agreement between the German government and Soviet Russia. The Rapallo Treaty (1922) led to the construction of German armament plants (tanks, aircraft, chemical warfare), covert airbases, and military training camps in Russia.

The German-Russian tilt received further impetus from right-wing ideologues and publicists. Militant nationalists like Franz Schauwecker, Edwin Erich Dwinger, and Werner Beumelburg created a cult of classless frontline brotherhood to compensate for defeat and death. Others, like Arthur Moeller van den Bruck, Ernst Jünger, and Ernst von Salomon, took this further with a Prussian-Russian "spiritual axis" against liberalism, bourgeois society, and the West. The Strasser brothers kept the socialism of National Socialism alive in a domestic context in Berlin and North Germany (Goebbels was an apostate from this movement) against the Bavarian mainstream of the Nazi Party from 1925 to 1934. Meanwhile, the National Bolsheviks (Richard Scheringer's Aufbruch circle, Ernst Niekisch's Widerstand movement, and Karl O. Paetel) developed the Prussian-Russian axis into a militant national-communist synthesis against the "bourgeois" Nazis (and the "Catholic, plutocratic puppet" Adolf Hitler!).

In the later Cold War era, Yockey's anti-American and anti-Semitic ideology drove him in a similar direction. With Europe and Germany herself divided between the superpowers, Yockey preferred to conceive of a new Euro-Imperium which would eventually pacify or even absorb the Soviet Union, thereby creating a new Eurasian superpower to challenge American hegemony in the Western hemisphere. To his mind, this was infinitely preferable to the maintenance of Western Europe as a mere colony of American vassal-states in the name of liberal capitalism.

But if geopolitics suggested a Eurasian imperium, Yockey and his followers also had ideological reasons for a pro-Soviet tilt. Anti-Semitism can easily manifest itself as anti-capitalism, reminiscent of the Strasserist line within National Socialism. To Yockey, the closed economic system of the Soviet Union appeared to defy Jewish-owned banks, trusts, and corporations. In November 1952 Yockey greeted the Soviet-sponsored show trials of Rudolf Slanksy and other leading Jews in the Czech communist regime as a long-awaited sign of Soviet anti-Semitic policy. Yockey's flirtation with the new nationalist regime of Egypt and his other contacts in the Middle East were also part of his tireless odyssey to find new friends in his war against America and Jewry. He even regarded Fidel Castro as a potential ally in his campaign to reach out towards any enemies of America.

Kevin Coogan ultimately provides a study of postwar fascist ideology which admirably complements Zeev Sternhell's pioneering works on its radical origins. With his books *Neither Right Nor Left* (1983) and *The Birth of Fascist Ideology* (1989), Sternhell showed how fascism, with its roots in French and Italian syndicalism and populism, grew up alongside Marxism in a common assault on late–19th century liberalism. After the defeat of the Third Reich and the division of Europe, Yockey appeared as the radical who would combine the two in order to defeat the liberal-(Jewish)-capitalist order of America and so resurrect an authoritarian Europe for the new millennium.

Let there be no illusions: Fascism was always a radical political movement. There is a far greater likelihood of its return in an unfamiliar guise than in the flags and uniforms of its 20th-century experiments. Kevin Coogan's important book helps us to understand both the protean nature of fascism and its perennial capacity to tap popular feelings of anger and frustration in the visionary projection of an alternative political order.

INTRODUCTION:
INTO THE
LABYRINTH

An eight-year FBI manhunt ended on the afternoon of 6 June 1960, when Francis Parker Yockey, one of the most mysterious figures ever to emerge from the American far right, was arrested in Oakland, California. The United States government first became interested in Yockey in the early 1950s, after it received reports that he had been advocating an alliance between the far right and the Soviet Union against America. There were even rumors that he had visited Russia. After his arrest, the government discovered that he had recently been in Havana, Cuba, where he had reportedly tried to meet Castro.

Born in Chicago in 1917, Yockey was a *cum laude* graduate of Notre Dame's law school. After a brief stint in the Army during World War II, he served as an assistant district attorney in Detroit. Then, in 1946, he went to Wiesbaden, West Germany, as a U.S. government attorney assigned to the war crimes trials. Disgusted with what he saw, he abandoned his position and journeyed to the south of Ireland. Under the pseudonym "Ulick Varange," he wrote his magnum opus, *Imperium: The Philosophy of History and Politics,* in just six months. A massive neo-Spenglerian tome that called for the formation of a new European superpower, *Imperium* was first published in London in 1948. It is still sold today in right-wing bookstores in Europe and America.

Yockey's importance was underscored by one law enforcement official, who told the *San Francisco Examiner* shortly after the arrest that Washington was "very, very interested" in the case.[1] The San Francisco director of the Anti-Defamation League of B'nai B'rith proclaimed to the press that Yockey was "the most important figure in world fascism we now know."[2]

The euphoria surrounding Yockey's apprehension ended abruptly. Early on the morning of 17 June 1960, Yockey was found dead in his high-security cell in the San Francisco city jail. Underneath his pillow he left a cryptic note: "I shall write no message which I know will not be delivered—only this, which will be: 'You will never discover who helped me, for he is to be found in your multitudinous ranks, at least outwardly.'" An autopsy would reveal that he had committed suicide by ingesting a capsule containing .2 grams of potassium cyanide—double the lethal dose.

The local newspaper headlines about Yockey have long faded. One man, however, still vividly remembers Yockey's last days. He is Willis Carto, *Imperium*'s American publisher and founder of the Liberty Lobby, one of the most influential far-right organizations in America. Under Carto's guidance, the Liberty Lobby's popular weekly newspaper, *The Spotlight*, has become the *New York Times* of the far right. He also founded, and for many years personally controlled, the Institute for Historical Review (IHR), the most important publisher and distributor of Holocaust-denial literature in the world.[3]

At the time of Yockey's arrest, Carto was living in San Francisco, where he helped publish a small journal called *Right*. In the mid-1950s he had been given a rare copy of the original two-volume London edition of *Imperium* and had been dazzled by its brilliance. After reading about Yockey's incarceration in the local papers, Carto visited him in jail just a few days before his suicide to see if he could help rally support for him.

After Yockey's death, Carto continued to keep his memory alive. In November 1962, Carto helped arrange the publication of the first American edition of *Imperium*. He then brought out his own Noontide Press edition of the book in 1963, and the first paperback edition in 1969. A third Noontide Press paperback edition appeared in 1991. *Imperium* has sold well over 20,000 copies in the United States. It has also been translated into German and Spanish. Yet despite the book's influence on some of the leading thinkers and far-right activists in both the United States and Europe, almost nothing is known about Yockey's life. To acolytes and critics alike, he remains a highly mysterious figure.

Yockey operated in an unmapped world, a mysterious Atlantis whose contours are barely visible under ever-shifting seas of time and deceit. His was a world of false identity, deep cover, and relentless travel throughout the United States, Europe, Canada, the Middle East, and Latin America. Because he was most at home in the twilight land of the fascist diaspora, a careful examination of his life can serve as an Ariadne's thread through the labyrinth-like history of postwar fascism.

An intellectual with a reported near-genius IQ, Yockey was inspired by the writings of Oswald Spengler, the German philosopher of history best known for *The Decline of the West*. Spengler's ideas helped midwife a generation of rightist intellectuals in Weimar Germany, inflamed with the desire for a "Conservative Revolution." The writings of the Conservative Revolutionary legal theorist Carl Schmitt would have a significant influence on Yockey, whose thinking would also be shaped by the arguments of Major General Karl Haushofer, founder of a German school of geopolitics in Munich in the 1920s and a top advisor to the German General Staff.

Yockey's intense identification with Europe was symbolized by his pseudonym, "Ulick Varange." Ulick is an ancient Irish name meaning "reward of the mind," while Varange refers to the Varangians, ninth-century Vikings who first brought Western influence to Russia and helped found the first Russian state in Kiev. "Ulick Varange," then, symbolized the ideal of a united Europe stretching from Galway to the Urals.

The name also had a prophetic meaning unknown to its creator. As Revilo P. Oliver, a far-right Classics Professor and Yockey admirer, points out:

> [The] Varangians are best known as the Norse mercenaries who founded the elite corps of Byzantine armies, and Ulick is the great Erse [Irish] adaption, from the Latin *Ulixes*, of the name of the great Aryan hero [Ulysses], celebrated for his courage and practical wisdom, who, at the very beginning of the epic, is described as having wandered for many years after the fall of the sacred city of Ilium, which his fellow Greeks destroyed, and having seen many foreign cities and observed the character of many tribes of men. Both names, therefore, connote a stranger in a strange land.[4]

Yockey was a stranger most of all in his native America. His true homeland existed only as a vision. His Xanadu was a new united Europe, an Imperium powerful enough to expel the "occupying forces" of its two great "outer enemies": the United States and Russia. Ulysses-like, he wandered ceaselessly in pursuit of his dream.

Yockey wanted most of all to create a resistance movement against American military and financial domination of the Continent. Even the specter of Russian hegemony over Europe was acceptable, as long as Russia first agreed to enter into an alliance with a reconstituted fascist elite. He believed such an alliance would ultimately culminate in the formation of a new Imperium from the North Atlantic coast to the foothills of Asia.

Yockey greeted evidence of Soviet anti-Semitism with special joy. In December 1952, while living clandestinely in New York, he wrote an article called "What Is Behind the Hanging of the Eleven Jews in Prague?," which examined the downfall of leading Czech Jewish Communists in a Moscow-directed purge. In it, he praised the execution of the Jewish Communist leader Rudolf Slansky as proof that Great Russian nationalists (not Jewish Marxist "culture distorters") now ruled the Kremlin. His article was particularly astonishing since just a few months earlier he had been living in Washington, D.C., secretly working for Senator Joseph McCarthy!

With the rise of the non-aligned states in the Third World, like Nasser's Egypt, Perón's Argentina, and Castro's Cuba, Yockey saw another geopolitical weapon against American hegemony. He met Nasser in Cairo in 1953 and, shortly before his death, tried to arrange a meeting with Castro. The nagging suspicion that Yockey was working with *both* the Nazis and the Communists to encourage the spread of anti-American sentiment in Europe and the Third World is what led Washington to become so concerned with him.

A skilled conspirator with a magician's bag of false passports, forged identity papers, and phony names, Yockey eluded arrest for many years. Yet it was a surplus, not a dearth, of false identities that led to his capture. To understand his downfall, we must focus our thoughts not on the image of Yockey as either a lofty neo-Spenglerian philosopher or a Nazi James Bond, but on a far more mundane picture. Conjure in your mind a drab baggage-room in a hot Texas airport in the middle of the afternoon of an ordinary Saturday in early June 1960. In that room lay the bomb that would destroy Yockey.

Bombs were very much in the headlines that June fourth. A few days earlier, a powerful bomb planted to protest the Israeli capture of Adolf Eichmann had destroyed a synagogue in Uruguay. The Texas bomb, however, was constructed not of dynamite but of paper—paper neatly packed into the modest frame of a single gray Samsonite suitcase.

Notes:

1. *San Francisco Examiner,* 9 June 1960.

2. *San Francisco Chronicle,* 23 August 1960.

3. For a good introduction to Carto and the Liberty Lobby, see Frank Mintz, *The Liberty Lobby and the American Right: Race, Conspiracy and Culture* (Westport, CT: Greenwood Press, 1985).

4. Revilo P. Oliver, "The Enemy of Our Enemies," commentary/introduction to Francis Parker Yockey, *The Enemy of Europe* (Reedy, WV: Liberty Bell Publications, 1985), p. 5.

JAILHOUSE RAGNAROK (JUNE 1960)

The greatest happiness known to man is to be sacrificed.

—Ernst Jünger

1
LOST AND FOUND

On Friday the heat wave broke. The day before, the Bay Area had reached a record 95 degrees. But when American Airlines flight 47 landed at San Francisco International Airport on the night of 3 June 1960, the air was cool. One of the flight's departing passengers, an attractive, slender man in his early 40s, around 5'8" with dark hair and brown eyes, especially enjoyed the weather. The passenger, who despised the heat, had spent another June seven years earlier in Cairo, Egypt, sweltering under a cruel sun. A few minutes after landing in San Francisco, however, the man who called himself "Richard Hatch" would be confronted with a man-made disaster: His luggage, a large gray Samsonite suitcase, had been lost in transit.

An experienced traveler, Hatch had been flying for hours. Booked out of Washington on an American Airlines flight to Oakland with a transfer in Dallas/Fort Worth, Texas, he had been rerouted through Chicago because of a mechanical delay. In the confusion, he had been unable to transfer his suitcase in time. Local San Francisco airline personnel asked Hatch to give them a phone number or forwarding address where he could be contacted once his luggage finally arrived. He explained that he would regularly check in by phone because he had not yet decided on where he would be staying. Once his bag had been located, he said, he would return to claim it. Then he disappeared into the night.

The suitcase was resting safely in the American Airline lost-and-found room at Amon Carter Field, Fort Worth, Texas. By Saturday afternoon, the puzzle of its rightful owner had grown too strong for the Texas baggage handlers. They decided to open it. The baggage room's decor could not have been more drab. But if the scenery was dull, the irony was thick: The workers, who opened the suitcase to learn its true owner, instead discovered a cornucopia of owners, each with a different name and passport. Yet all the passports bore the photograph of the same man.

The most recent passport was Canadian and carried the name "Charles Montague Taylor," an art appraiser by profession, who was born in 1913 in Niagara Falls, Ontario. It had been issued by the Canadian embassy in Washington, D.C., on 31 May 1960, just four days before Hatch's flight west. There was also a U.S. passport for a teacher named "Edward Max Briceman," who had been born in Richmond, Virginia, in 1916. Yet another passport (this one British) belonged to a "Michael Joseph Taylor" and had been issued by the British consulate in San Francisco on 10 August 1959. Finally, there was a German identity card in the name of "Franz Yorck," along with press credentials listing Franz-Ludwig Yorck as a staff member for the German magazine *Quick.*

Along with more prosaic items like clothing and a typewriter, the suitcase yielded a salmagundi of other personae, as well as $850 worth of American Express travelers checks and a Diner's Club credit card for a "Barry R. Brannon," which the FBI later learned had been altered from "Harry F. Shannon." Other Harry Francis Shannon documents included a photocopy of a birth certificate along with a California driver's license, a Bank Americard, and a voter registration card. The voter registration card revealed that Shannon, a professional photographer who lived at 925 Geary Street in San Francisco, had been a supporter of the ultra-right Constitution Party. Another photocopied birth certificate obtained from the county clerk of Cook County, Chicago, was for a "Jack Peter Forest," whose driver's license gave his residence as 6360 Bryn Mawr, Hollywood, California. His public library card, however, was from Bellingham, Washington.

The mystery took a new twist when the baggage handlers found documents for "Patricia Lagerstrom" of 925 Geary Street in San Francisco (although she also maintained a post office box in Baltimore, Maryland). A marriage certificate documenting the union of Michael Joseph Taylor and another woman named "Ofelia Rodriguez" on 3 September 1959 at Virginia City, Nevada, also turned up. Two more photocopied birth certificates, one for an "Ivy Louise McLeod," and the other for a child born in 1930 in San Francisco to Julian and Luz Harrara, were next. And still the documents kept on flowing, in a steady stream of birth certificates and false IDs.

That Saturday evening, Dallas FBI agent Alfred C. Ellington received a phone call from American Airlines alerting him to the find. That the FBI learned about the mysterious suitcase at all was a stroke of luck, since just a few hours after the bag had been opened a wire arrived from San Francisco naming Hatch its rightful owner and ordering that it be sent immediately to California.

Hatch's suitcase finally left Fort Worth that Sunday afternoon on an American Airlines flight that arrived in San Francisco around 9:00 P.M. Earlier that day the Dallas FBI had sent a teletype labeled "Urgent" to "Director, FBI" as well as to FBI field offices in Baltimore, Los Angeles, New Orleans, San Francisco, Seattle, and Washington, D.C., informing them of the discovery. Early Sunday evening, American Airlines contacted the local FBI to report that Hatch had again called to inquire about his luggage. Around 10:15 that night, the FBI began planning Hatch's arrest.

Although his suitcase had already reached the Bay Area, American Airlines told Hatch it was not scheduled to arrive until early Monday morning and that he was more than welcome to come to the airport and pick it up. He instead requested that the bag be brought to the residence of Alex Scharf at apartment #23, 465 Bellevue Avenue, in Oakland. He explained that he was temporarily staying with Scharf, the educational director of a Hebrew school associated with a local Oakland synagogue, Temple Beth Abraham.

Around 10:30 A.M. on Monday, 6 June 1960, FBI agents Keith Teeter, Robert Leonard, and Alfred Miller drove to the small Spanish-style apartment building overlooking Oakland's Lake Merritt Park where Scharf lived. Hatch, however, was nowhere to be found. After a few minutes' wait he phoned the apartment to ask if his bag had been delivered safely. With three FBI agents standing next to him, Scharf assured his friend that all was well.

When Hatch returned to the apartment, he must have been delighted at the sight of his suitcase, though the delight would quickly fade once he was introduced to his three visitors. After agreeing to answer a few questions, he was interrogated for three and a half hours. He told the FBI that he had been born in Santa Ana, California, in 1923. After graduating from Santa Ana High, he had served in the U.S. Army from 1942 to 1943 and received an honorable discharge. Since then he had pursued a career as a self-employed photographer, mostly in Mexico, although he had been in New Orleans for the last few months. Most recently, he had been staying in Baltimore, Maryland.

The FBI agents then asked Hatch if he had registered under the 1948 Selective Service Act. He replied that he didn't think so, since he had already registered under the 1940 Act while living in South Bend, Indiana. What he didn't know was that the FBI had already searched for a draft card in his name and knew that one didn't exist. By asking him about his draft status, the agents were merely establishing the legal basis for an arrest.

Finally, the conversation came around to the gray suitcase. Hatch was asked if he could describe its contents. He said that it contained some clothes, a typewriter, a pin-sized "work of art," and a small bag. He denied any knowledge of passports, birth certificates, or other documents. According to the official FBI report, "Hatch was then asked if there were possibly articles in the suitcase that he was not aware of." "Possibly," he replied. He then told the agents that, shortly before leaving the Washington airport, "he had been met by a friend, whose name he did not know," who had given him a small bag that he had placed in the suitcase. He was then asked if he had a key to the suitcase and, if so, would he mind opening it?

The suitcase was unfastened and once again the flurry of passports and birth certificates appeared. After he "expressed surprise" at seeing all the documents, Hatch asked if he was now under arrest. The agents told him no, but politely inquired whether he could provide them with any personal identification. He was only too eager to help: If he had one thing in abundance, it was identification. First, he showed a statement from the National Bank of Commerce in New Orleans indicating that he had about $1,000 in the bank as of 26 January 1960. On 11 February 1960, he had deposited another $1,300 and, a few days later, a further $500. On the back of the bank statement were two cryptic handwritten notes: "RNTA-7, Al Fondo de u 3rd Estacion, Dragones y Sulotta-6-7100" and "605 Walter, 2—James White." He next showed the agents a smallpox vaccination certificate from the Laredo Quarantine Station on the Texas-Mexico border that had been issued on 19 March 1960. He also supplied them with a Los Angeles library card and a 1959 voter registration card that listed his address as 765 Sutter Street, San Francisco.

Hatch carried over $2,000 in cash. Asked why he had such a large amount, he replied that he had intended to give Alex Scharf a personal loan. At that point Scharf asked if he could get his money. "That would no longer serve any purpose," Hatch replied. "I no longer have any interest in your problems."

Hatch then requested a private interview with agent Keith Teeter in another room of the apartment. He still refused to give any explanation for the passports and other papers; he claimed that a logical explanation existed, but that he couldn't give it just now because he might be misunderstood. Around 2:15 P.M., while Hatch and Teeter were conversing in private, agent Miller left the apartment and headed for a pay phone to call headquarters. He reached FBI agent Edward M. Cunningham and briefed him about Hatch's story. With Miller still on the phone, Cunningham contacted Assistant U.S. Attorney William P. Clancey and conveyed to him the developments unfolding at 465 Bellevue. Faced with Hatch's inability to explain what he had been up to, Clancey authorized the filing of a complaint against Hatch for draft evasion.

Around 2:40 P.M., after returning to the apartment, Miller told his fellow agents that the legal green light had been given for a bust. Five minutes later, Hatch was officially informed that he was now under arrest. He was casually standing in the hall close to the kitchen door when he heard the news. Suddenly he bolted, raced through the door, out another door, and down the back porch. Although agent Leonard grabbed his left coat-sleeve and wrist, Hatch managed to catch Leonard's right hand in a door jamb. As Leonard screamed in pain, Hatch slammed the door shut, cutting Leonard's hand and leaving a wound that required five stitches to close. Enraged, Leonard continued his pursuit with Teeter close behind.

Hatch's options were limited. Since the apartment building's back steps ended in a contained parking area, he was forced to run up a driveway toward Bellevue Avenue and Lake Merritt Park. Rather than run toward an exposed picnic area in front of the lake, and thinking that all three FBI men were behind him, he wheeled left and headed a short way down a hill leading to Grand Avenue and possible freedom. Agent Miller, however, had gone out the apartment building's front door in a flanking action. Just as Hatch made his turn onto Bellevue, Miller came barreling out the front door and literally ran into him. A few seconds later, Leonard and Teeter caught up with the two men. Seeing Leonard's hand, Hatch said: "Oh, I'm sorry, I didn't mean to do that." He was then unceremoniously thrown into a car and taken to Oakland County Jail to be booked on a charge of draft evasion.

While Hatch commemorated the 16th anniversary of D-Day in the slammer, the FBI worked hard to determine who he really was. A copy of his fingerprints was quickly sent to the FBI's Identification Division in Washington. By the next day, Washington had conclusively identified Hatch as Francis Parker Yockey. A successful match had been made to prints taken by the Washington, D.C., police on 18 December 1945 after Yockey had been arrested on a minor shoplifting charge.

Once Yockey's identity was known, the government quickly moved to prevent him from making bail. Prosecutors dropped the draft evasion complaint and replaced it with charges of passport violation and assaulting a federal agent. Although normal bail for passport violation was just $5,000, the government initially asked for $10,000, a figure that jumped in just a few days to an extraordinary $50,000.

Washington wanted Yockey badly. Now that he had finally been captured, it seemed possible to answer a mystery that had long defied solution. Throughout the 1950s, the government had regularly been hearing reports that Yockey had somehow been involved in an anti-American far-right underground movement with ties to Russia. For years the FBI, the State Department, and Army Intelligence had searched for him in both Europe and the United States. In the spring of 1953 the FBI had been legally authorized to pick him up for questioning on the charge that he had used a false passport when leaving the United States in January 1953. Despite these efforts, Yockey had roamed freely across Europe, the United States, Latin America, and the Middle East. Now he sat trapped in Cell 2 of the Oakland municipal jail.

2
PAPER
TRAIL

Early Monday evening Yockey made a phone call to his older sister, Alice Louise Spurlock, who lived in Gilroy, California, south of San Francisco. For appearance's sake, he told his jailers that he wished to speak to his sister, "Louise Hatch," who happened to be staying with Spurlock. Receiving no answer (Spurlock was vacationing in Hawaii at the time), he waited for almost an hour and a half before telling authorities he wanted to contact a Washington lawyer named Perry Patterson, whom he had known from his student days at Georgetown University. At the last minute, however, he decided not to make the call. Finally, around 8:30 P.M. California time, he called his oldest sister, Vinette Coyne, who lived in Bethesda, Maryland, with her husband William, a U.S. Navy officer. They spoke for seven minutes.

Yockey spent the rest of his first night in jail contemplating suicide. Within a week, the FBI would learn about his plan. On 13 June 1960 the FBI's Keith Teeter visited the Santa Rita Rehabilitation Center in Pleasanton, California, to talk with an accused rapist. The rapist, who had shared a cell with Yockey on the night of his arrest, said that Yockey had revealed his real name and told him that he was an attorney. Yockey claimed that he needed his many false identities to escape the FBI, which had been hounding him because of his links to Communists. He then explained that he had been interested in forming a political party to get rid of "Boss Tweed" types and, to further this objective, had innocently associated with Communists. He added that the FBI had first come across his trail while he was in Canada meeting an important person whose room had been surreptitiously bugged.

Yockey's real purpose that Monday night was to draw up a last will and testament. As his cellmate watched, he wrote out two copies of a two-page will. He told the man that he had over $2,000 and would use part of the money to help him make bail if, in return, he made sure that one copy of the will was delivered to his brother-in-law, William Coyne. The other copy was to go to his yet-to-be-appointed attorney. Yockey then said "that he had prepared the will because he intended to commit suicide . . . by removing the teeth from a comb and sharpening the remaining part of the comb to form a weapon."[1]

The next night Yockey woke another prisoner, in a cell across from his, who had been booked for burglary. In a conversation with the man in the jail's exercise yard earlier that afternoon, he had learned that he was a former art student. That night he interrogated the man about his knowledge of human anatomy. The prisoner recalled that Yockey "wanted to know where he could inflict a wound which would cause his death." He also "spoke of using his tie to hang himself" and said that "he had complained of being ill in the hope that he would be taken to a hospital where he could get a surgical instrument with which to kill himself."[2]

The accused rapist and the accused burglar officially witnessed Yockey's will before the three men were relocated to different parts of the jail. Before they were moved, Yockey gave the accused rapist the copies of his will, which the man hid under the mattress of his new cell. Although he had promised the man money, all of Yockey's cash had been seized as evidence, and with no financial reward forthcoming the man simply forgot about the will. On 10 June, after he was sent to Santa Rita, the prison cleaning staff threw the scraps of paper away. Both prisoners, however, remembered the will's contents. According to their separate statements, Yockey left all the belongings in his suitcase to the Coyne family. The $2,276 in cash was to go to his sister Alice, no doubt in part to help with funeral expenses.

Once his will had been taken care of, Yockey told his cellmates about his love for Nazi Germany. He also discussed Adolf Eichmann, the Nazi war criminal seized by Israeli agents in Argentina less than a month earlier, and whose capture had been made public by Israeli Prime Minister David Ben-Gurion on 23 May. Yockey, who clearly identified with Eichmann's plight, said that his abduction was contrary to international law and only made possible because of Jewish money power. America, too, was run by the "great Jewish political machine." He expressed "great fear" at the possibility of imprisonment, especially in a mental hospital. The accused burglar told the FBI that Yockey "felt that imprisonment . . . or commitment to a mental institution" would be "disgraceful and undignified" and "would detract from his stature in the eyes of associates whom he did not identify."[3]

While Yockey languished in his cell, the government began tracking his fraudulent identities. The final FBI count showed that, along with his three bogus passports and fake German identity card, he had eight birth certificates and photocopies of 16 others.[4] Of the myriad names Yockey used, "John Priapus" was the one least expected by the FBI. As John Priapus, he had penned a series of overtly sado-masochistic short stories. "The Misfortunes of Yvonne," a 48-page typed manuscript, was one Priapus piece; another was a 3-page story called "John's Wife." A third 18-page tale was entitled "Strange Iris." On the pages of two stories, he had stapled photos of nude women from pornographic magazines. He also had a 62-page booklet called *Arduous Figure Training at Bondhaven*, published by the Nutrix Company of Jersey City, New Jersey. *Arduous Figure Training*, according to the FBI, "contained numerous sketches of partially clad females and . . . was of a masochistic or sadistic nature."[5] Yockey's erotica was sent to Washington after the Bureau's San Francisco office requested FBI headquarters to "compare these pornographic documents with available obscene data in the Bureau's files," since "the possibility exists that he may have engaged in the writing of pornographic material, either commercially or as a matter of personal desire."[6]

Yockey's choice of reading material was eclectic to say the least. Along with *Arduous Figure Training*, he was studying a German edition of Schopenhauer's translation of the sayings of a 17th-century Spanish philosopher and Jesuit priest named Balthasar Gracián. He also carried with him a list of occult-sounding book titles including *Reincarnation, Your Second Body, Chemical Action of Light*, and *Cosmic Rays*, as well as a copy of an unidentified article from the 1937 issue of *Theosophical Forum*, a journal published by the American branch of Madame Blavatsky's Theosophical Society. Most mysterious of all was a collection of Yockey's own essays with titles like "Thoughts on Polarity Relating to the Calculus of Polarities" and "The Polarity of the Psyche," as well as one page called "Gedanken" (Thoughts) that began with remarks on "One Aspect of Feminism." His suitcase included two pages of material from *Social Justice in England and America* by H. G. Wells and *Sex and Character* by Otto Weininger, an obscure turn-of-the-century Viennese philosopher. He had also clipped an article by J. Robert Moskin concerning the domination of the American male by the American female; another article by George B. Leonard, Jr., called "U.S. Men Give Up Individuality for Conformity"; and a William Attwood essay entitled "Does He Work So Hard?"

While FBI headquarters scrutinized the Bureau's porn files for clues, other G-men tried to reconstruct Yockey's movements before his arrest. For someone with no visible means of support, Yockey certainly got around: His paper trail showed incessant travel up and down the west coast of North America, from Alaska to California, as well as visits to Texas, New Orleans, and the Baltimore/Washington area. His address book was filled with cryptic entries, numbers, and notes.

27

San Francisco, it turned out, was an excellent place to begin retracing Yockey's activities. On the night of 6 June, even before fingerprint analysis confirmed his identity, the San Francisco FBI was buzzing with rumors about him that began after his calls to Alice Spurlock and Vinette Coyne. The local FBI office had repeatedly interviewed both Spurlock and the Coynes during its hunt for Yockey. In the mid-1950s William Coyne had worked as an executive officer at the U.S. Navy's Postgraduate School in Monterey, California. William and Vinette Coyne had repeatedly lied to the FBI about Yockey's whereabouts. The Bureau also strongly suspected, but could not conclusively prove, that Alice Spurlock had helped her brother get a U.S. passport under the name "Edward Price" in May 1954. The passport, later altered to read "Edward Briceman," was found in the gray suitcase.

The FBI investigation had actually begun on 5 June, one day before Yockey's capture, when the Bureau started examining addresses sent to San Francisco from Dallas. That Sunday, the San Francisco FBI spoke with the landlord of an apartment building at 925 Geary Street and learned that Francis Shannon and his girlfriend Patricia Lagerstrom had spent almost seven months at that address, starting around late May or early June and continuing to 1 December 1959.[7] Shannon told the other tenants that he was a writer and said that he received $1,000 a month for work published in South America. He showed one of his pieces to a neighbor who thought it "anti-American." Shannon and Lagerstrom (described by the landlord as being about 5'4" and 105 pounds, with blue eyes and blond hair) spoke German to each other when strangers were around.[8] The couple had had no visitors that the landlord could remember except for two people whom he described as "Latin types."

In late November 1959 Shannon announced that he was moving to Stinson Beach, California. Before leaving 925 Geary he informed a representative of a credit agency that it would be a waste of time to answer any questions because he was about to go on an extended tour of Latin America. Then, in February or March 1960, he checked back in at 925 Geary to see if there had been any mail for either himself or Lagerstrom. He also told the landlord that Lagerstrom was in Mexico City looking after her sick mother.[9]

A month and a half after leaving 925 Geary, Shannon and Lagerstrom resurfaced in New Orleans as "Richard and Pat Hatch." The Hatches first checked into the De Soto Hotel on Baronne Street on 17 January 1960.[10] The next day, they left the De Soto; four days later they registered at the Baronne Hotel just across the street.[11] The Hatches stayed at the Baronne for a little over a month, from 22 January to 25 February 1960. Hatch told the hotel manager that he had come to New Orleans to conduct historical research on the city. While Pat Hatch left the hotel every day (claiming that she was baby-sitting for a sick friend), Richard spent his time alone in his room writing. Each day he mailed the previous night's work to an unidentified address. Curious, the manager asked a housekeeper to recover any papers that might have been thrown into the wastepaper basket. Hatch, however, always made sure that no evidence of his writing remained in the trash.

Although they checked in with 10 bags of new luggage, the Hatches wore the same clothes almost every day. Richard was usually attired in a white shirt and dark tie. Pat's uniform included a white leather coat, white shoes, and a white beret. Her description also differed somewhat from San Francisco's Pat Lagerstrom. The Geary Street landlord said that Lagerstrom was around 5'4" and 105 pounds with blond hair and blue eyes. Pat Hatch was described by the Baronne's manager as "Garboish," around 5'6" and 120 pounds with chestnut brown hair and "a little on the gawkish side." In New Orleans the Hatches spoke to each other in French, not German. After the manager commented that Pat was quite fluent, Richard explained that although his wife was American, she had been born in Belgium.

The Hatches also seemed to have plenty of money.[12] Despite their apparent wealth, however, the couple lived quite frugally right up to the day that they announced they were checking out of the Baronne and leaving New Orleans. On 25 February the Hatches took a cab to the New Orleans airport. The hotel manager thought that their destination was Washington, D.C., because a man later called the hotel to request that their mail be forwarded to a Washington address. The New Orleans post office then received a note asking that all mail be sent to 316 North Charles Street in Baltimore. But if Hatch's ultimate destination was the Washington-Baltimore area, he made at least two sidetrips: one to Miami and one to Havana.

Yockey's Miami–Havana trail surfaced shortly before his death in a most unlikely way. On 8 June he was moved from Oakland to the main jail in San Francisco. One week later, while waiting in a holding area before being shuttled to court, he encountered a fellow prisoner, a 41-year-old career criminal named Mark Kirstead whom he had first met four months earlier in Miami.[13] Kirstead, who had a criminal record dating back to 1938, was being held on grand theft charges arising from the sale of two stolen television sets.[14]

On 6 July 1960, a few weeks after Yockey's death, the FBI learned about Yockey and Kirstead from an Immigration and Naturalization Service investigator. Kirstead gave the INS an affidavit about a jailhouse conversation he had had with Yockey between noon and 1 P.M. on 15 June. Kirstead reported that he and Yockey had first met in Miami Beach, Florida, in late February or early March 1960, shortly after Yockey left New Orleans.[15] His affidavit continued:

> On June 15, 1960, I was sentenced to 90 days in the San Francisco County Jail. At that time I was ordered transferred to County Jail #2 at San Bruno. While in the process of being transferred, I was moved from the east side of

29

the jail to the west side to await the bus that transports the prisoners to San Bruno.

While waiting for this transfer, I was approached by one of the inmates and he asked me if I remembered him. Right at that moment I did not. Then he went on to explain to me that we had met at a cocktail lounge in Miami Beach, Florida, in the early part of this year. After he reminded me of this I did recall this meeting and also recalled meeting this man at that time. This inmate turned out to be Mr. Francis Yockey.

Kirstead said that he did not recognize Yockey at first because he had worn horn-rimmed glasses in Miami and had called himself "Mr. Blair." He then recalled that Blair and "his associates" had been staying at the Nelson Hotel in Miami Beach. However, Kirstead (who was then calling himself "Dale Marcus") met Blair at the cocktail lounge of Miami's famous Flamingo Hotel:

> These three people were sitting at the bar at this time. In some way we got into a conversation about Havana. After we talked about this for some time we introduced ourselves, bought each other drinks, and became quite friendly. I told them I intended to go down to Havana for a weekend and so Mr. Yockey gave me his card and told me to call him when I got there. I spent approximately two hours as near as I can remember with these people at that time. Two nights later I went back into this place and these same people were there, only they were sitting at a piano bar and Mr. Yockey was playing the piano. At this time I stayed in their company for an hour or so. I left them and never saw them again until I met Mr. Yockey in the county jail here in San Francisco.

Kirstead also described Yockey's two companions. Like the visitors to Geary Street, they were "Latin types." In Miami, Blair was with two Spanish-speaking journalists: a man named Emmanuel, who was associated with Cuba's well-known *Bohemia* magazine, and a woman named Shena Diaz,[16] who was introduced as an employee of a newspaper called *El Mundo*. Emmanuel was a heavy-set man in his early 40s, about 5'6" with glasses and a mustache. Diaz was around 30, 5'7" and very attractive, with dark hair and a buxom figure.

Yockey, however, did not identify himself to Kirstead just to reminisce. He desperately wanted him to return to Havana on a secret mission for him:

> He told me that he needed help badly and asked me if I would help him. I said I would and so he gave me the following information that he wanted to deliver to Emanual in the editor's office of the *Bohemian* [sic] magazine in Havana, Cuba. He (Mr. Yockey) gave me this address: A-63-27 Calle—Entre 2 y 4th Calle, Vedado, Havana, Cuba. I was to give this address to Emanual and tell him to pass it on to someone by the name of Alferd [sic]. He would no [know] what to do.

Mr. Yockey appeared to me to be very desperate about this message and told me that if I would do this the people there would take care of me financially and also see that I met the right people.

To make sure that he remembered the address correctly, Kirstead wrote it down on the back of a newspaper.

When Kirstead then asked Yockey why he couldn't deliver the message himself, he replied: "You will read it in the newspapers." The two men never spoke again.

Notes:

1. Report of FBI Special Agent Keith Teeter and Officer Tom Cannizzaro, 13 June 1960.

2. Teeter report, 14 June 1960. Teeter interviewed the man the day after his trip to Santa Rita.

3. Ibid.

4. On Tuesday, 7 June, the State Department's San Francisco office also became involved in the passport forgery investigation.

5. FBI document SF 105-1769.

6. SF FBI office Airtel to FBI laboratory, 20 June 1960.

7. On 7 June, the landlord identified Yockey as Shannon from FBI photos.

8. Lagerstrom also received a Christmas present mailed from Germany.

9. While it is impossible to know whether Yockey visited Mexico City, he undoubtedly spent time in Mexico. Recall the smallpox vaccination certificate issued to Richard Hatch on 19 March 1960 at the Laredo, Texas, Quarantine Station on the U.S.-Mexico border.

10. They also made a call to a Rosa Bella Pierce at 2332 Seminole Lane. Just who Pierce was is not explained in the FBI documents.

11. Yockey's whereabouts from 18 to 22 January are unknown. Before moving into the Baronne Hotel he notified the New Orleans post office that letters to him could be sent to 1716 Charles Street. After moving to the Baronne, he had his address changed to the hotel. The 1716 Charles Street note mystified the FBI because it was the address of a popular restaurant called the Corrine Dunbar. None of the restaurant's employees recognized Yockey.

12. Recall that on 26 January 1960 Yockey deposited $1,000 in an account at the National Bank of Commerce in New Orleans. Then on 13 February 1960 he deposited another $1,300, and a few days later he added $500 more.

13. Kirstead used the alias "Dale Marcus," but the 27 July 1960 *San Mateo Times* (citing an AP wire) provided his real name.

14. *San Francisco Chronicle*, 27 July 1960.

15. From the 7 July 1960 SF SAC memo to J. Edgar Hoover transmitting the Marcus/Kirstead affidavit, which San Francisco had obtained a day earlier.

16. Kirstead thought her first name could also have been "Cina" or "Cena" and her last name may have been "Diece" or "Dietz."

3
"PASSPORT MYSTERY MAN KILLS SELF"[1]

In the weeks before Yockey's arrest, San Francisco's papers had been filled with stories about Nazis, Israeli spies, CIA lies, and Cold War intrigue in Cuba. Adolf Eichmann's abduction by Israeli secret agents continued to generate headlines. In Washington, CIA Director Allen Dulles repeatedly dodged questions about an American U-2 spy plane shot down over Soviet territory one month earlier. The U-2 affair had thrown Soviet Premier Nikita Khrushchev into a frenzy. After lambasting President Eisenhower as unfit to "run a kindergarten," he warned that the Soviet military was prepared to use nuclear rockets against countries housing U-2 bases. On 4 June, one day after Yockey arrived in the Bay Area, the Soviet leader again made news by announcing that he was soon going to pay his first state visit to Fidel Castro's Cuba. To the local media, Yockey's capture was tabloid heaven. Here was a hometown mystery whose cast of characters included Nazis, Reds, Feds, a mysterious Hebrew school principal, and even a Cuban connection.

After Yockey's first brief appearance before U.S. Customs Commissioner (and ordained rabbi) Joseph Karesh, the 9 June *San Francisco Examiner* began its front-page story: "A sullen, silent mystery man, with passports showing he had flitted throughout the Western world under assumed names, caused the wires to hum between here and Washington last night." The rival *San Francisco Chronicle* quoted a government official as saying:

"This is definitely a security matter. Both the State Department and the Department of Justice are interested in this man" . . . And the FBI would only say, "We have orders not to say anything at all about the case." But it was learned that Yockey—the name he is currently using—is a matter of "great interest" to the Federal government's investigative branches . . . "This is not a small fish," a government source said last night. "This is a man that we are very, very interested in."

Although Yockey was an attorney, his court case began disastrously. His initial counsel, Carl Hoppe, was a family friend of the Coynes. A patent lawyer by profession, he had no experience trying criminal cases. On 9 June he threw both his case and his client into a frenzy when he told Commissioner Karesh: "I'd like to have Mister Yockey examined by a psychiatrist to determine whether he is sane. I do not believe he has all of his senses." In a stage whisper, Yockey hissed at Hoppe: "That's a dirty trick." He then told the astonished Karesh: "I'm sorry—I'd like to dismiss the attorney. This comes as a complete surprise to me." Karesh allowed Yockey and Hoppe to consult privately for 20 minutes. When they returned, Hoppe sheepishly withdrew his motion.

Hoppe's doubts about his client's mental health were no trick. Yockey spoke openly and frequently about suicide. Emmet Hagerty, a leading San Francisco criminal attorney called in to advise Hoppe, told the *San Francisco Examiner* that Yockey had talked freely about "the suicide of Göring and Himmler, but I told him that suicide was nonsense and immoral."

Neither Hoppe nor Hagerty had the slightest knowledge about Yockey. Both were unaware that in *Imperium* he had written:

If someone says that to admit the fact that Life is fulfilled in Death is pessimism, he shows something about *himself*. He shows his own cowardly fear of death, his entire lack of heroism, of respect for the mysteries of Being and Becoming, his shallow materialism . . . This is their valuation of life: The longest life is the best. To this mentality, a short and heroic life is *sad*, not inspiring. Heroism generally is thus merely foolish since indefinitely prolonged life is the aim of "Progress." . . .[2]

The great ethical imperative of this age is individual truth-to-self, both for the Civilization and its leading persons. To this imperative, an unfavorable situation could never bring about an adaptation of one's self to the demands of the outsider, merely in order to live in slavish peace. One asserts himself, determined on personal victory, against whatever odds exist. The promise of success is with the man who is determined to die proudly if it is no longer possible to live proudly.[3]

Prepared to live up to *Imperium*'s brave words, Yockey began plotting a daring escape that could only result in either freedom or death. The government discovered his plot on 13 June after the mother of Jack Fambrough, a 21-

year-old inmate, contacted the FBI and said that her son had an important story to tell. Fambrough, who had been charged with attempted robbery at the Oakland Army Base, told the FBI that Yockey was trying to involve both himself and an Italian-American forger named Philip Galati in a wild escape.

Yockey had been moved from Oakland to the San Francisco County Jail on 8 June. From there he was regularly transported to the Federal Courthouse under the escort of U.S. Marshals. His escape plan hinged on his instructing his attorney to make bail for Galati, who had convinced Yockey that he had access to two .38 revolvers, a shotgun, and a 1957 pink and black Lincoln. After making bail, Galati was to return the next day to Dumbar Alley behind San Francisco's Hall of Justice. When Yockey and Fambrough were led out by the Marshals, they would pretend to get into a fistfight, causing enough confusion for Galati to "hold court" on the lawmen. Once the Marshals were neutralized, the three men would abscond in Galati's Lincoln.

Yockey promised his co-conspirators that they could either join his ring or he would help them escape to Cuba, where his contacts would richly reward them.[4] He said he was well connected in Cuba and had been in Havana just a few months earlier to see Castro. Although he had not met Fidel personally, he told Fambrough that he had discussions with one of Castro's personal secretaries.

Yockey made it clear that, should the escape fail, he was intent on suicide. If the plot fell apart while they were still in jail, he intended to race to the third tier of the prison and jump to his death. He also said that on the day of the planned escape he wanted one of Galati's revolvers so that he could shoot himself if anything went wrong. If the escape broke down in Dumbar Ally, he begged Galati to kill him with a shotgun blast.

Yockey also proselytized Fambrough and Galati on the virtues of fascism. Both men said they came to despise him because he was so "anti-U.S.," "anti-Negro," "anti-Jewish," and, basically, "anti-everything." Fambrough told the FBI: "Yockey does not have a criminal mind and small details escape him. He is a brilliant man but has no practical intelligence and I do not believe Yockey would get four feet out of the city in an escape attempt by himself." One example of his lack of "practical intelligence" proved especially telling: Fambrough was a light-skinned African-American, but Yockey assumed that he was Cuban-American and spoke candidly to him about his horror at being trapped in a jail filled with blacks!

After hearing Fambrough's story, the FBI paid a call on Galati. He confirmed the details of the plot but claimed that he was just conning Yockey, whom he labeled "brilliant" but "nuts." As soon as the FBI confirmed the details of Yockey's scheme, the information went straight to the U.S. attorney, who used it to bolster the government's request for high bail. U.S. Assistant Attorney Clancey revealed both the escape plot and Yockey's talk of suicide at the end of a tumultuous court session on 14 June, the day of the planned escape. After hearing Clancey speak, Yockey snapped: "Not a word of truth."

Yockey's two sisters were also in the courtroom. Vinette arrived in the Bay Area first. On Saturday, 11 June, she met her brother for 20 minutes inside the prison. On 14 June, he managed to have a 40-minute conversation with his sisters in Commissioner Karesh's office during a court recess. Outside the court building, the sisters told reporters that Yockey was a brilliant philosopher who had been unjustly persecuted by the government because of his beliefs. "Why did he have three passports?" one newsman asked Vinette. "Maybe he thought three passports were better than one," she replied. Vinette made more news when she jumped up in the middle of court proceedings and began waving a copy of the U.S. Constitution while shouting: "According to the Constitution no one shall be held upon excessive bail. And there is nothing in the Constitution about a mental examination." On cue, Alice Spurlock began waving her own copy of the Constitution. Yockey also interrupted that day's proceedings, loudly proclaiming that the FBI was a bunch of liars and that, as a lawyer, he knew his rights. Barely heard above the din was Yockey's attorney, Carl Hoppe, who begged the court for permission to withdraw. "I'm a patent lawyer without any experience in this matter at all," he pleaded. The court agreed. By day's end, Emmet Hagerty had become Yockey's temporary counsel.

The chaos surrounding the case extended to the street outside the court, where shouting reporters begged the mystery man for a scoop. At first Yockey tried to ban TV cameras from filming him. Then a voice in the crowd called out to him in German, "It's all right. You are among friends." Delighted, Yockey bestowed exclusive photo rights upon a local KPIX-TV cameraman named Bernie Rausch, cryptically described by the *San Francisco Examiner* as a "former ground crewman for the German Luftwaffe . . . who fled Germany under a Nazi death sentence and is now an American citizen."[5]

The most important journalist to speak with Yockey came from a highly obscure San Francisco–based mimeographed monthly tract called *Right: The National Journal of Forward-Looking Americanism*. He was Willis Carto, the future head of the Liberty Lobby, the Institute for Historical Review, and Noontide Press. Although Carto had acquired a rare copy of the original two-volume London edition of *Imperium* in 1955, he knew next to nothing about its author. Yockey had been underground for so long that Carto had assumed he was dead. Only after the FBI questioned him about Yockey in 1959 did he suspect that he was still alive. Picking up a local paper one day, Carto was stunned to learn that "Ulick Varange" himself was in a jail cell not far from his apartment.

On 10 June 1960 Carto showed up outside the San Francisco jail to interview Yockey for *Right*. After receiving permission from Yockey's attorney, Carto talked with Yockey for 15 minutes, from 2:30 to 2:45 P.M. Separated by a thick wire mesh screen in the jail's dingy visiting room, he could barely see the mystery man.[6] Yockey bitterly criticized Hoppe's insanity plea, saying, "They want to make me a zombie. My lawyer did the worst thing he could have done." He also complained about being forced to wear the same shirt for a week in a filthy jail filled with Negroes. Still, he thought that a jury trial might be an opportunity to publicize his ideas. When Carto pointed out that a jury trial could be rigged, Yockey replied that he was willing to be a martyr and was not afraid to die for his ideals.[7]

At Yockey's suggestion, Carto wrote a memo to three rightists about his plight. They were Fred Weiss, an elderly Manhattan-based German national who was Yockey's closest American collaborator; Russell Maguire, publisher of the *American Mercury*; and Conde McGinley, publisher of *Common Sense*. In his memo, Carto reported:

> Yockey was picked up in Oakland the day before yesterday. Three passports in his possession; different names, his picture. Seven birth certificates.
>
> The FBI has been hunting for him for years. He is being held in the San Francisco County Jail No. 1 for $50,000 bail. The papers say that this bail is demanded by the FBI. The FBI says differently—that the State Department demands it.
>
> According to the FBI, they are not very interested in him any more but were, some months back, when they contacted nationalists all over the U.S. giving the excuse that they were looking for him. The papers note the FBI head here, Richard Auerbach, as saying that he is very important, etc., but refused to give details.
>
> We interviewed Yockey in jail today. He says that he plans to make a big stink and get a lot of publicity. He hopes that all nationalist papers will follow his case and help him. His lawyer, a friend of the family, Carl Hoppe, has good instincts but [is] ignorant of things. He even suggested yesterday that Yockey be given a psychiatric examination. This, of course, would mean a lobotomy if they can get away with it. We suggested that this might be a way for him to get out if he wanted to; claim insanity, and that if he had a lot of friends on the outside, "they" would not be able to make a zombie out of him. He, however, wants to fight it out with a jury trial, publicity, etc. We told him that he won't get publicity if the Jews don't want to give him any; witness the Atlanta trials. He knew nothing about this except he had read some passing references to it in the paper.[8]
>
> (This and other things indicate that he was out of the country for a long while. He seems out of touch with things. For instance, he had never heard of *Right*.)

It has been persecution that forced him to violate the law by getting the false passports. He has been hounded simply for his opinions. A flagrant case of violation of civil rights, which led him to take illegal actions.

The outrageously high bail has no relation to his passport fraud. Auerbach, FBI head, you remember, says that this has been set by the demand of the State Department. He told this to us personally. But the papers play it up as if this bail is the result of the FBI(?).

Yockey thinks that all American nationalists are cowards and self-seekers. Yet he hopes for publicity. We assured him that we would do our best to publicize his case and his disgusting persecution and treatment. He asked us to notify the above-named nationalists, with the exception of *Women's Voice*, which we are adding on our own.[9] He feels that these are the ones most likely to help him.

Right feels that Yockey is a genius. His book, *Imperium*, proves that. In spite of the fact that there are many points in it with which we do not agree (for instance, Yockey is not a scientific racist, which *Right* is), we will help him all we can and try to use his case to dramatize Jewish terrorism. Incidentally, the U.S. Commissioner who has charge of Yockey's case, Joseph Karesh, is an ordained rabbi.[10]

Carto's brief talk with Yockey had some unexpected consequences. After word leaked out about their conversation, the local papers, desperate for leads, transformed Carto into Yockey's co-conspirator. Reporters from the *San Francisco Chronicle* even staked out Carto's apartment in San Francisco's Mission district.[11]

Along with the FBI, the Anti-Defamation League, which had a long-standing interest in Yockey, was closely monitoring the case. Stanley Jacobs, the ADL's regional director, was a regular at Yockey's court appearances. Jacobs told reporters that Yockey was "the most important figure in world fascism we now know."[12] During Yockey's underground years, the ADL regularly supplied the FBI with leads pertaining to him. After his arrest, the ADL circulated to the press the rumor that he may have secretly visited the Soviet Union. When a reporter tried to ask him if there was any truth to the Russia story, an irate Yockey exploded: "You dirty swine, get out of here."

Even as the media brouhaha escalated, the U.S. Attorney's Office continued to methodically build its case. The paper trail from Yockey's suitcase helped prosecutors determine that Yockey's "Edward Max Briceman" passport was doubly false. Yockey had taken an earlier "legitimate" U.S. passport, which he had obtained in 1954 by falsely swearing that he was "Edward Max Price," and later altered it to read "Edward Max Briceman." The government also knew that Alice Spurlock had been a witness for the Edward Max Price passport. A subpoena was issued to Spurlock on 15 June demanding that she testify about her role in the passport forgery.

Another subpoena went out that same day to Alex Scharf, the Hebrew-school educator at whose apartment Yockey had been staying when he was arrested. Prosecutors badly wanted to talk with Scharf after learning that Yockey's "Michael Joseph Taylor" passport had listed "Alex Scharf" as his witness.[13] Scharf, however, had told the FBI that he only knew Yockey as "Richard Hatch," a casual acquaintance whom he had met by accident one day in 1959 when they were both gambling in Reno, Nevada. But when agents of the court returned to 465 Bellevue to deliver the subpoena, they discovered that Scharf had disappeared for parts unknown. His vanishing act, however, would quickly be overshadowed by an even more stunning development.

On the night of 16 June 1960 Yockey prepared for death over a game of checkers. Adam Nieman, his checkers opponent and cellmate, said that Yockey told him during their game that "he was the No. 1 leader of some sort of organization. He said he had knowledge of people he loved and thought he'd be forced to reveal it." Again Yockey discussed committing suicide, this time by placing a weight on his throat. Yockey and Nieman's conversation took place in Cell 20 on the ground floor of the San Francisco County Jail, where Yockey had been transferred to prevent him from jumping to his death.

As the lights went out that night, Yockey turned strangely sinister. "You'll sleep all night, of course," he told Nieman. He then "kept looking over the edge of the bunk at me," Nieman later told the press. "I got quite concerned but finally I fell asleep." When he awoke the next morning, he found Yockey's dead body. Sometime in the early morning hours of 17 June, Francis Parker Yockey had swallowed a capsule filled with potassium cyanide.

Notes:

1. Headline in the *San Francisco News Call Bulletin*.

2. From *Imperium: The Philosophy of History and Politics* by Ulick Varange (Francis Parker Yockey) (Torrance, CA: The Noontide Press, second paperback printing, April 1983), p. 50. All my citations from *Imperium* are from this edition.

3. Ibid., p. 57.

4. Yockey complained to Fambrough and Galati that the government's seizure of his address book meant he could no longer contact his West Coast network. However, he told Galati about a man in St. Louis, Missouri, named Robert McGuire and said that Galati should contact McGuire after he made bail with a message from Yockey.

5. *San Francisco Examiner*, 14 June 1960.

6. Carto begins his introduction to the Noontide Press edition of *Imperium*: "Dimly, I could make out the form of this man—this strange and lonely man—through the thick wire netting."

7. I would like to thank Willis Carto for giving me a copy of his original note.

8. Carto was referring to the successful acquittal of members of the far-right National States Rights Party (NSRP) who had been charged with bombing an Atlanta synagogue.

9. *Women's Voice* was a far-right publication based in Chicago.

10. The *Right* memo is from the H. Keith Thompson collection at the Hoover Institute in Stanford, California.

11. Years later a reporter for the *Chronicle* named Denne Pettitclerc recalled: "We thought Willis Carto was the only one who had the key to everything." See "Yockey: Profile of an American Hitler" by John C. Obert in the September 1981 issue of *The Investigator.*

12. *San Francisco Chronicle,* 23 August 1960.

13. On 26 June a San Francisco postal inspector named James Conway identified Scharf's handwriting on the application. *San Francisco Chronicle,* 29 June 1960.

4
AFTERSHOCKS

Yockey's suicide infuriated the FBI, the State Department, and the U.S. Attorney's Office. It also sent San Francisco prison officials scrambling for cover. Although prison administrators were well aware of Yockey's suicide threats, Sheriff Mat Carberry quickly declared that his men were not at fault. But if they weren't, who was? In a 23 June 1960 memo to Washington, the San Francisco FBI office commented: "Bureau's attention is directed to the fact subject [Yockey] was permitted to be interviewed by a variety of individuals, such as press, photographers, and miscellaneous persons as well as family from whom he could have received poison powder."[1]

While the way Yockey engineered his death remains a mystery, his motive for killing himself was clear. On 13 June his worst fears had come one step closer to realization when the U.S. Attorney had introduced a motion asking for a determination of his sanity. Commissioner Karesh added that if the government didn't push for a psychiatric examination, he might insist on it himself. That same day a federal grand jury was convened to further investigate his activities.

With the shift to federal court, Judge William T. Sweigert took the case over from Commissioner Karesh. On 15 June, Yockey, acting as part of his own defense team, cross-examined Commissioner Karesh in Judge Sweigert's court. Karesh, who had been called to bolster the case for a psychiatric exam, told the court that Yockey was "the most unusual of any accused person who has ever appeared before me." During his cross-examination, Yockey asked Karesh if he were prejudiced because the papers had called him an anti-Semite. At that point Judge Sweigert cut off his line of questioning. Prosecutors, however, were delighted to let Yockey continue speaking for as long as he wanted, convinced that he only helped strengthen their case.

Over defense objections, the government introduced evidence that Yockey had received an honorable medical discharge from the U.S. Army in 1943 after being diagnosed as mentally ill.[2] On 15 June, Judge Sweigert ruled that Yockey would have to undergo a psychiatric exam and that the results must be available by 11 July. That same day Yockey told Mark Kirstead that Kirstead would read about his fate "in the papers."

Although Yockey had every reason to feel desperate, was his situation hopeless? After the Hoppe debacle, his family hired a top criminal attorney named Jake Erlich to defend him. With Erlich on his side, there was no question that the government's $50,000 bail figure would come under fierce assault. Yet it was clear that Yockey's decision to kill himself in the event of capture had been long thought out. He also felt sure that the charges against him would soon escalate, telling his cellmates that the case was "nothing" compared to what it could soon become. Mark Kirstead thought that Yockey "was deathly afraid of something" and seemed particularly worried that "his associates in the United States would be discovered and the work they were engaged in would be destroyed."[3]

On 21 June 1960 Yockey's sisters arranged his burial in Gilroy, California, where Alice Spurlock lived. In 1982, David McCalden, a far-right Holocaust-denier and a former director of Willis Carto's Institute for Historical Review, became curious about Yockey's final days. In the September 1982 issue of his *Revisionist Newsletter*, McCalden described a visit he had paid to Gilroy to examine Yockey's grave in the cemetery of St. Mary's Catholic Church. To his astonishment, he found that there was no tombstone. Church records revealed that the remains had been exhumed on 23 July 1964, cremated at the local Oakhill crematorium, and then reburied in the same grave. In a follow-up story in the October 1982 *Revisionist Newsletter*, McCalden reported: "Alice Spurlock (who lived in Gilroy) [next] ordered that the ashes should be exhumed and scattered at sea by the U.S. Navy (?)."

McCalden was right to be puzzled, since Yockey was never in the U.S. Navy. The only mention of Yockey in Freedom of Information Act material released by the Navy was from an interrogation of Yockey's brother-in-law, William Coyne, by the Office of Naval Intelligence (ONI).[4] If Yockey *was* reburied at sea, the most likely culprits are the Coynes. On 20 July 1965 William Coyne became the commanding officer of the USS *Compass Island*, his last assignment before his retirement in July 1967.[5] If McCalden's facts are correct, Yockey's sisters probably reburied him at sea after his ashes were exhumed by Spurlock in anticipation of Coyne's new position as Captain of the *Compass Island*.

The Coynes and Spurlock continued in their deceptions about Yockey even after his death. According to McCalden, St. Mary's records listed Yockey's place of death as "Brooklyn, NY." This particular bit of chicanery was most likely an attempt by the sisters to obfuscate the circumstances surrounding his death, since suicides could not receive a Catholic burial. But why did Spurlock have Yockey's ashes reburied after his cremation?

The answer to that question may be linked to another important unsolved riddle: How did a man under such close surveillance manage to acquire a cyanide capsule? The most likely explanation would be that he had the capsule hidden in his possessions at the time of his arrest but couldn't get to it because his clothes and other belongings were being held as evidence.[6] He seems to have hinted as much to his cellmate Philip Galati during a discussion of escape plans, when he said, "If I don't find a way out, I've always got an ace in the hole."[7] Perhaps some prison guard or trustee who felt sympathetic to him, or was promised a reward, brought Yockey some of his possessions without knowing that he was bringing the poison as well. Yockey's taunting suicide note ("You will never discover who helped me, for he is to be found in your multitudinous ranks, at least outwardly") is deliberately ambiguous. It is also possible that an outsider managed to smuggle the poison to him either in prison or during the courtroom proceedings

Yockey's death triggered a period of angry finger-pointing among the various law enforcement agencies. Sheriff Carberry of the San Francisco jail was publicly accused by Assistant U.S. Attorney William Clancey of bungling the case. Clancey claimed not only that Yockey had asked another prisoner about the possibility of getting "some poison," but that after the prisoner had informed prison authorities, they ignored the warning. The prisoner, Yockey's Miami acquaintance Mark Kirstead, told the U.S. Attorney's Office that as soon as he was moved to the County Jail in San Bruno, he immediately notified two prison officials about Yockey's request but that they failed to take his statements seriously.[8]

Some four years after his suicide the mystery surrounding Yockey's death continued to trouble the Israeli government. I stumbled upon the Israeli connection through a most unlikely source: Willis Carto, who had given me copies of old press clippings he had saved about the case. At the bottom of Carto's clip file was a 1964 column by Herb Caen of the *San Francisco Chronicle*. Caen's 21 July column was dominated by chit-chat about the Republican National Convention, which had just left San Francisco after nominating Barry Goldwater for president. In a brief aside, Caen wrote:

> The strange case of Francis Yockey, the neo-Nazi who committed suicide in a jail cell here in 1960, might be back in the headlines soon. A private eye (Al Gilstein) hired by a private group is almost ready to close in on the man who smuggled in the cyanide.

That was it. According to Carto, there was never any follow-up article. Neither the late Herb Caen nor his long-time assistant could recall any details about the *Chronicle* item. There was also no mention of any Gilstein exposé about Yockey in the paper's morgue that the *Chronicle*'s economics editor, Jonathan Marshall, examined for me. As for Al Gilstein (H. Allen Gilstein), he was long dead.

To unravel at least part of the puzzle, I spoke with two top Bay Area private investigators, David Fecheimer and the late Hal Lipset. Both men had known Gilstein and remembered him well. Gilstein, it turned out, was no run-of-the-mill P.I. A lifetime bachelor with a taste for Saville Row suits, he spent his vacations relaxing in elegant European spas. What was most unusual about him, however, was that he did not drive a car. The joke was that if you discovered that you were being tailed by a San Francisco bus, chances were excellent that Gilstein was on the case.

Gilstein's reason for not driving a car was most significant: As a young man he had fought in Israel's 1948 war for independence and had badly injured his back. The Israelis continued to maintain close ties to him, and the Israeli consulate in San Francisco regularly used his services to arrange security for visiting dignitaries.[9] If Gilstein didn't work directly for the Mossad, he was certainly close to people who did. He also maintained strong ties to Jewish groups in the Bay Area.

Did Gilstein stumble upon a conspiracy? Or had he been given a false lead that never panned out? Why was the case apparently never mentioned again after it had been leaked in the most widely read newspaper column in San Francisco? For that matter, did Gilstein feed the information to Caen? Or had the story been planted by someone intent on disrupting the investigation? And, finally, was there any relationship between Gilstein's probe and Alice Spurlock's decision to cremate Yockey's remains? Herb Caen's column appeared on 21 July. Two days later, Spurlock had Yockey's body exhumed for cremation and reburial.

Two months after Yockey's suicide, Willis Carto's *Right* mourned his death in an August 1960 cover story entitled "ADL Closes File on Yockey: Creative Genius Driven to Suicide." *Right*'s lament began: "Frustrated and driven to despair, hounded and persecuted like a wild beast, deserted and ignored by the easy-living cowards for whom he had fought so hard—a great creative genius committed suicide in the San Francisco County Jail." After stating that "the world already owes a great debt to Francis Parker Yockey," *Right* concluded its eulogy: "Oh God, may his great, troubled soul, purged now of the self-assumed burden of responsibility he bore, at last find the peace and rest he never thought of seeking in life."

In his introduction to *Imperium*, Carto returned to the moment when he first learned of Yockey's death:

Friday morning, June 17, I arose as usual. I heard the radio announcer pronounce words that stunned me.

Yockey was dead.

"I'll sleep through 'til morning" was the cryptic message he gave his cellmate, last night. Was the morning he anticipated the dawn of a new age? A garbled note was found. The coroner declared it suicide and said the poison was potassium cyanide. No one knew where he had gotten it.

The case was closed.

Carto remembered one detail incorrectly. Yockey did not say "I'll sleep through 'til morning." In fact, he had told his cellmate Adam Nieman in no uncertain terms, "You'll sleep all night, of course." His implied threat suggests that he wanted Nieman asleep when he took the cyanide capsule from some secret hiding place or when an unknown individual delivered it to him later that night.

Still, Carto was essentially correct. With Yockey's suicide, the puzzling case of the mystery man with too many passports had come to a close.

Notes:

1. The memo also noted that "subject's sister, Alice Spurlock, is a nurse in a Salinas, California, hospital," implying that she would have had easy access to poison.

2. At the time, the medical discharge had actually helped Yockey escape prosecution for desertion, and he later liked to brag about how he "snowed" the Army's psychiatrists. It is also worth recalling that Yockey's first lawyer, Carl Hoppe, had raised the issue of his mental health. Hoppe and Vinette Coyne had discussed such a motion, and Hoppe said that Vinette was willing to sign papers placing her brother in a mental hospital. As I shall show later in this book, her support for an insanity defense had its likely origin in the World War II incident.

3. *San Francisco Chronicle*, 27 July 1960. In this article, Kirstead is also cited as saying that the man he met with Yockey in Miami was Emmanuel Diaz. In his INS affidavit, however, he clearly stated that he did not know Emmanuel's last name.

4. I found it impossible to locate Alice Spurlock or even to determine whether she was still alive. Yockey's daughter, Dr. Francesca Yockey, also did not know whether Vinette Coyne or Alice Spurlock were still living.

5. Details of William Coyne's career are from the Naval Historical Center in Washington.

6. Recall that Yockey bitterly complained to Carto about having to wear the same shirt for an entire week.

7. "Sheriff Disputes U.S. Yockey Poison Story," *San Francisco Examiner*, 21 June 1960.

8. *San Francisco Chronicle*, 27 July 1960. The jailers' lack of interest in Kirstead's story was easy to understand. They had already heard so many reports

about Yockey's different plans to kill himself that one more example made little impact on them.

9. I was given the name "David Ben-Dove" as one of Gilstein's close contacts inside the Israeli Consulate in the 1960s.

GENEALOGY OF MORTALS (1917-1938)

At its peak, bourgeois nihilism is also the wish to annihilate the bourgeois.

—*Theodor Adorno,* In Search of Wagner

5
GRAVE
MYSTERIES

Francis Parker Yockey was born in Chicago on 18 September 1917, to Louis Francis and Rose Ellen Yockey. The youngest of four children, he had an older brother, James, as well as two sisters, Vinette and Alice. The Yockeys were Catholics and the family seems Swiss or southern German in origin (Yockey being an American variant of Jäggi or Jägi).[1] The family was upper-middle class, and Louis, although trained as a lawyer, made his living as a stockbroker. The Yockeys also maintained strong cultural ties to Europe, particularly Paris. After their 1911 wedding Louis and Rose Yockey lived in Paris, where both James and Vinette were born. After the family returned to Chicago they continued to maintain an interest in European culture, especially classical music. Yockey's mother studied at the Chicago Music College, while Francis was a musical prodigy who could have had a career as a concert pianist. Years later, Yockey's English comrade John Anthony Gannon recalled that he "was a wonderful pianist, excelling in Chopin, Liszt, and Beethoven. I never saw him play by music, but then neither do the great concert pianists. His playing was accepted as brilliant by all who heard him, and all were moved by it."[2] Yockey's exceptional musical skills, brilliant intellect, almost photographic memory, and strong artistic temperament gave him the sense that he was a natural member of an intellectual and cultural elite.

Although the Yockeys lived in Chicago, the family's roots were in the small town of Ludington, Michigan, where both his father and mother had grown up. Yockey's German-born grandfather, Valentine, came to Michigan in 1858 to serve as a foreman at a lumber mill. Six years later, he and his Irish-born bride Eleanor settled in the small town of Ludington on the western shore of Lake Michigan, where Valentine helped manage a lumber mill.

Shortly after he settled in Ludington, Valentine Yockey contracted typhoid fever, an illness from which he never completely recovered. Still, the Yockeys prospered enough in the lumber business to move to Chicago. There disaster struck after Valentine "was persuaded to sign a note for a man who called himself a friend. There was the usual result. Their savings were swept away."[3] The family then returned to Ludington, where Eleanor ran a boarding house. On 22 December 1883 Valentine Yockey died at age 51. His funeral (the largest in Ludington at the time) was conducted under the auspices of the Masonic and German Aid Society.

Eleanor, who was 17 when she married, remained one of Ludington's best-known residents, serving as both a midwife and a doctor to men injured in the mills. Her own life was not without hazard. One New Year's day, while trying to reach the home of a dying friend, she fell through a hole in the ice on Pere Marquette lake. Only with great difficulty did her youngest son Louis Francis manage to pull her out of the freezing water. Perhaps in part because of this incident, Louis Francis and his mother remained especially close.[4]

Louis Francis's relationship to his father, however, remains unknown. What is clear is that he could not have been Valentine Yockey. The mystery of Francis Parker's grandfather begins with Louis Francis's tombstone at Ludington's Pere Marquette Cemetery. The legend on the stone reads: "Louis F. Yockey, 1886–1936."[5] Valentine Yockey died in 1883, three years before Louis was born. The one mention of Yockey's grandfather in the FBI files confirms the fact that Valentine could not have been Francis's grandfather. On 27 March 1953 the FBI interviewed Fred and Alice Yockey (Yockey's unmarried aunt and uncle) at their home in Chicago. Alice told the FBI that "her nephew is very pro-German, and she is of the opinion that this pro-German attitude was brought about by the influence Yockey's grandfather, who was a German, had on Yockey." Since Francis clearly knew his grandfather, he could not have been Valentine Yockey.[6]

Without knowing the identity of Yockey's grandfather, it is impossible to either confirm or deny a strange claim about Yockey, namely that he was part Jewish. In December 1965, James Madole, the head of the far-right National Renaissance Party (NRP), published a long essay in the NRP's *Bulletin* called "The Historical and Metaphysical Roots of the Conflict between Jew and Gentile." Although Madole had met Yockey, his article was inspired by the suicide of a young NRP member named Daniel Burros, who was notorious for being an almost psychotic anti-Semite. After a *New York Times* story revealed that Burros was himself Jewish, he shot himself in the head. In his article, Madole defended Burros as a genuine National Socialist despite his Jewish origin. In passing, he mentioned that Yockey, "author of the immortal right-wing classic *Imperium*," was also "one-quarter Jewish."

What makes the issue of Yockey's origins particularly interesting is that he passionately and repeatedly argued that "blood" did not determine character. In a chapter of *Imperium* called "Subjective Meaning of Race," he wrote:

> Every race, no matter how transitory it may be contemplated from the viewpoint of History, expresses a certain idea, a certain plane of existence by its life, and its idea is bound to be attractive to some individuals outside it. Thus in Western life we are not unfamiliar with the man who, after associating with Jews, reading their literature, and adopting their viewpoint, actually becomes a Jew in the fullest sense of the word. It is not necessary that he have "Jewish blood." The converse is also known: Many Jews have adopted Western feelings and rhythms, and have thereby acquired Western race. This process—contemptuously called "assimilation" by the Jewish leaders—threatened during the 19th century the very existence of the Jewish race by its ultimate absorption of its total racial body into the Western races.[7]

While Yockey claimed that "the hierarchy of races is a *fact*," he also believed that attempts to interpret history in terms of race were absurd and had to be abandoned. To Yockey:

> The 20th-century viewpoint in this matter starts from facts, and the observed fact is that all strong minorities—both within and without a High Culture—have welcomed into their company the outsider who was attracted to it and wished to join it, regardless of his racial provenance, objectively speaking.[8]

Yockey took his concept of race directly from his intellectual mentor Oswald Spengler, who in his book *The Hour of Decision* said of race:

> It is not intended in the sense in which it is the fashion among anti-Semites in Europe and America to use it today: Darwinistically, materially. Race purity is a grotesque word in view of the fact that for centuries all stocks and species have been mixed, and that warlike—that is healthy—generations with a future before them have from time immemorial always welcomed a stranger into the family if he had "race," to whatever race it was he belonged. Those who talk too much about race no longer have it in them.[9]

While Spengler defined Yockey's views on race, what remains unknown is the extent to which his embrace of Spengler was rooted in his own family's genealogy.[10]

For the first 15 years of his life Yockey lived in Chicago as the brilliant, seemingly apolitical son of well-off parents. He seemed to have had little contact with his oldest brother James, who later became a schoolteacher in Ludington. He also had a terrible relationship with his mother.[11] With both his sisters, particularly Vinette, the story was much different. Elsa Dewette, Yockey's Belgian mistress, told a far-right potential biographer of Yockey named Keith Stimely:

> You *must* before anything else try and get a hold of Vinette Coyne: It was *she* who "brought him up" (he had *no* sentimental links *at all* with his mother). Vinette was his real mother, and took care of him from his very tender years. She did *everything* for him, and till 1950 she sent him cheques so that he would not starve in Europa. She even sold her jewels for him. I believe she *taught* him when he was very young.[12]

Another glimpse into Yockey's youth comes from a woman named Janet Arnold. In 1954, as "Richard Allen," Yockey briefly married (and then abandoned) Arnold. She later told the FBI that Yockey had been "a child genius who was spoiled by his family. Years ago his father lost all his money during the market crash and following that the father began drinking." She then said:

> At the time his father lost his money, Richard [Yockey] was about 14 years of age and this made a definite impression upon him. He was a child genius and would have developed . . . into a concert pianist, but about the same time his father lost his money, Richard had an accident which injured his hand, cutting the tendons and definitely spoiling his chances of ever becoming a concert pianist.[13]

Elsa Dewette disputed this story:

> F. did *not* suffer an injury to his hand: *fiddlesticks*—a pure invention on his part. He used this argument (as other pianists I have known also did) to enable him to refuse to play, when he did not feel like it, or when the piece asked for proved to be too difficult for his technical possibilities . . . (A very well-known trick amongst professionals too.) He never had the intention of becoming a concert pianist—this was just wishful thinking, all "bla-bla"— to impress his naive "conquests."[14]

Yet Yockey told Dewette that he had been in a major car accident in his youth and said that some black motorists in the other car nearly beat him to death after the crash. They knocked out his front teeth and for the rest of his life he had to wear dentures. He also told his college friend Perry Patterson that the car accident had so damaged the tendons in his arm that a concert career was impossible. He said that while he could play as well as ever, the injury had ruined his stamina.[15]

The trauma surrounding the car accident and subsequent fight stayed with Yockey all his life. According to John Gannon: "Most Americans can drive a motor car, and I always had a motor car, but FPY never showed any inclination to drive, or to refer to driving."[16] When he did drive, he seemed to deliberately tempt fate. When he went on a tour of Germany with Elsa Dewette, she recalled that:

> We travelled in my small second-hand car. I drove. F. was a bad driver (too nervous) and consequently reckless. We nearly got killed in the Bavarian Alps (the only time he drove) . . . F. insisted on driving. The roads in the mountains were very narrow. F. drove much too fast—I was, as usual, beyond caring and kept my mouth shut. There were many bends. Suddenly, there appeared a huge military truck (also driving too fast I must say)—the left door of my car (where F. was sitting) was grazed—F. of course did not want to stop for an explanation . . . so he drove on full-speed, turn after turn. That truck was so large, I do not think it could possibly have turned around in that narrow road to pursue us. It was an extremely narrow escape, but F.'s hour had not come, and nor had E.'s. We felt pretty shaken.[17]

The Depression also took a terrible financial toll on Yockey's family. They were forced to leave Chicago in 1932 and return to Ludington. They moved into a house that James Foley, Rose Ellen's father, had built in 1895.[18] His stockbroker days long over, Louis Yockey worked as a clerk for the State of Michigan's auditor general's office.[19]

Louis Yockey died in 1936 at age 51 under circumstances that remain a mystery. Samuel Sonenfield, Yockey's immediate superior in Wiesbaden, Germany, when Yockey worked for the war crimes tribunal, believed that Yockey's father died in the same car crash that had badly injured his son. Elsa Dewette thought this nonsense, telling Keith Stimely:

> I was amazed at the Sonnenfeld [sic] version of F.'s father's death. I heard quite a different story from F. himself: You remember I told you F. lost his front teeth in a fight. He told me he had a car-crash with some niggers, that these nearly beat him to death; and that was how he lost his teeth. There was no mention at all of his father's presence in this incident.

Dewette also said:

> F. told me that his father was a "noceur" [reveler, debauchee] . . . "qui aimait beaucoup les petites femmes." He was off to Paris four or five times a year, very elegant: top hat, spats, and all: quite the Fred Astaire type. F. seemed secretly to admire this rogue of a father. He did indeed dilapidate the family's fortune and I seem to remember F. telling me that he died in Paris after a night of debauchery, but that this had been a great scandal in the family, and kept quiet . . . Where lies the truth? I distinctly remember F. laughing heartily when telling me of the prowess of his father. So you see, the two versions are very, very different.[20]

Ludington's chief of police had a more prosaic explanation. He told the FBI that Yockey's father drank himself to death.

Samuel Sonenfield thought that Yockey's hatred of America was emotionally linked to his father's collapse. Keith Stimely later summarized Sonenfield's view this way:

> F. told him [Sonenfield] that he resented—while at the same time *admiring* (a kind of dualism)—his father, Louis Yockey. But he especially *resented America for having destroyed* his father. Louis Yockey lost a lot of money in the Depression, and turned to drink . . . [Sonenfield] had the feeling that F. somehow, deep in his psyche, blamed "America" and its decline for having killed his father.

Unlike his father, Francis did not drink alcohol. Elsa Dewette recalled that "he positively hated the taste of strong alcohol, especially whiskey, and *never* used strong drinks. I debauched him enough to make him appreciate a glass of good old red Bordeaux with his steak." He also did not smoke.[21]

Yockey chose as *Imperium's* motto Nietzsche's: "*Was mich nicht umbringt, macht mich starker*" (What does not destroy me makes me stronger). Yet Nietzsche's observation in *Beyond Good and Evil* might have been more apt for the youth who would transform himself into an avatar of "Western Imperialism" while still in his teens: "A great man, did you say? All I saw was an actor creating his own ideal image."

Notes:

1. Information on the name Yockey from the genealogy journal *The Lost Palatine*, #4, 1983.

2. From a 7 December 1980 letter from John Anthony Gannon to Keith Stimely. The quality of Yockey's musical talent was also acknowledged by his political critics. In a 27 March 1953 letter to H. Keith Thompson, A. Raven Thomson, one of Oswald Mosley's aides, remarked:

> He (Yockey) then broke with us [the Union Movement] and has been generally found to be so conceited and unstable in personal relations (he is a musical artist of no mean ability) that it is almost impossible to work with him even allowing for his extremist views, which are, however, stated in most brilliant terms.

3. From a local Ludington newspaper profile of Eleanor Yockey. For this and other background material, I am indebted to Mary McDonald from the Ludington–Mason County District Library.

4. When Louis and Rose Ellen Yockey made their 1911 European tour they took Eleanor with them to visit her native Ireland.

5. I am indebted to Jim Cabot, Ludington's local historian, who examined the Yockey and Foley family tombstones.

6. Yockey's mother's background is equally opaque. Yockey's daughter Brünnhilde (who later legally changed her name to Francesca) told me that Rose Ellen Foley was adopted. James and Lavina Foley, who lived in Ludington, adopted her two years after the death of their biological daughter.

7. *Imperium*, pp. 296–97.

8. Ibid., p. 301. On p. 282 of *Imperium*, Yockey summarized his views this way:

Race is *not* group anatomy; race is *not* independent of the soil; race is *not* independent of Spirit and History; races are *not* classifiable, except on an arbitrary basis; race is *not* a rigid, permanent, collective characterization of human beings, which remains always the same throughout history.

9. Oswald Spengler, *The Hour of Decision* (New York: Knopf, 1934), p. 219.

10. It should be noted that there were also variations in Yockey's name. On his 1934 application to the University of Michigan, he gave his name as "Francis Foley Yockey." He was also listed in the local Ludington phone book as "Yockey, Francis Foley." In 1936, however, he used the name "Francis Parker Yockey" in his application to transfer from the University of Michigan to Georgetown. He also once listed his father as Louis Yockey but his mother as "Nellie Parker" on a German police permit.

11. Vinette's husband William Coyne also told the FBI: "YOCKEY definitely did not get along with his own mother." Summary report of the FBI investigation of Yockey by FBI agent Lloyd Bogstad, 20 February 1956.

12. Letter from Elsa Dewette to Keith Stimely, 15 May 1982.

13. Janet Arnold's 20 August 1959 interview with the FBI.

14. Letter from Elsa Dewette to Keith Stimely, 31 March 1982.

15. Perry Patterson interview with me.

16. Letter from John Anthony Gannon to Keith Stimely, 7 September 1980.

17. Letter from Elsa Dewette to Keith Stimely, 14 July 1982.

18. James Foley died in 1926.

19. The 1935 Ludington phone directory lists his occupation as "clerk."

20. Letter from Elsa Dewette to Keith Stimely, 15 May 1982.

21. Letter from Elsa Dewette to Keith Stimely, 22 March 1982.

6
THE HOUR OF DECISION

Yockey began his freshman year at the University of Michigan at Ann Arbor in the fall of 1934. Years later, Yockey's friend Perry Patterson recalled hearing that during his time at Ann Arbor, he had been "strongly pro-Communist." He even got into trouble by playing the Communist "Internationale" on the piano at a school party. The flirtation with Marxism, however, did not last long. According to Patterson, while at Michigan Yockey "turned to Nazism and became a believer in the supremacy of the German race and their political future."[1]

Yockey's shift to the extreme right was inspired by Oswald Spengler, the German philosopher of history. He first read Spengler's *The Decline of the West* while on a school break in the library of Ludington Circuit Court Judge Hal Cutler, a family friend who especially admired Francis for his brilliance.[2] In *The Decline of the West* Spengler developed what he called a "morphology of history." All the world's great cultures, from Babylon, Egypt, China, and India up to the modern West, went through the same inevitable process of rise and fall in a series of vast organic historical life cycles. In its ascendent stage a society was best described as a "Culture." This was a time of self-confidence, growth, and optimism, when both art and religion flourished and day-to-day life was infused with a sense of higher spiritual purpose and meaning.

Inevitably, Culture was superseded by a state of decay that Spengler called "Civilization," an age dominated by money, greed, materialism, and a widespread sense of spiritual exhaustion and ennui. Europe (Spengler's "Faustian culture") entered the age of Civilization in 1789, the beginning year of the French Revolution. The inevitable last stage of Civilization was "Caesarism," a time when society becomes increasingly dominated by totalitarian strong men who overcome outworn forms of liberal parliamentary democracy. Given its unstable nature, Caesarism would inevitably lead to a series of horrific wars heralding the extinction of the culture's life-cycle. Rather than deny or run away from the inevitable, the great challenge facing modern man was how to live a heroic and meaningful life in the violent "wintertime" of the West.

When *The Decline of the West* was published in America in the 1920s, it became an overnight sensation.[3] Even critics of the book like Charles Beard (who called it "majestic nonsense") and Oliver Wendell Holmes ("a stimulating humbug of a book") acknowledged its extraordinary intellectual achievement. Because *The Decline of the West* so challenged "Roaring '20s" optimism, its American reviewers almost unanimously scoffed at its pessimistic conclusions. How much more powerful, then, to discover Spengler's masterpiece as a teenager at the height of the Great Depression!

Around the time that Yockey read *The Decline of the West*, Knopf also published the first English-language edition of Spengler's 1933 book-length manifesto, *The Hour of Decision: Part One—Germany and World-Historical Revolution. The Hour of Decision* was an overtly political work; Yockey begins *Imperium* with a quote from it that reads: "The individual's life is of importance to none besides himself: The point is whether he wishes to escape from history or give his life for it. History recks nothing of human logic."[4]

Yockey never wavered in his belief that Spengler was "The Philosopher of the Twentieth Century." Convinced that he was Spengler's intellectual heir, he would later visit Spengler's niece in Germany to gain more personal insight about his mentor. In virtually all of his published writings, and *Imperium* in particular, he repeatedly paraphrased Spengler (at times to the point of plagiarism), used Spenglerian jargon, and employed Spengler's ideas to explain current events. He also delighted in making subtle references to obscure passages in Spengler known only to the cognoscenti.[5] Spengler's extraordinary impact on Yockey suggests that Yockey had an almost religious experience while reading him. To understand how that might be possible, it should be recalled that Yockey had come to Spengler from a background as a classical pianist and aesthete and may have first been interested in Spengler for artistic, rather than political, reasons.

In 1931 Knopf published a three-volume book called *A Cultural History of the West* by Egon Friedell, an Austrian-Jewish actor associated with Max Reinhardt's Vienna Theater. First published in Germany in 1928 as *Kulturgeschichte der Neuzeit* (Cultural History of the New Age), Friedell's now-forgotten opus took America's intelligentsia by storm, going into a second printing in January 1933. A historian of ideas, Friedell analyzed the cultural development of the West from a strong Spenglerian viewpoint. (His

German publisher, C. H. Beck, was also Spengler's publisher.) *A Cultural History* was translated into English by Charles Francis Atkinson, the extraordinary translator of both *The Decline of the West* and *The Hour of Decision*.

Friedell, who committed suicide in Vienna in 1938 after the Nazis occupied the city, had a profound impact on Yockey. Like Friedell, Yockey strongly believed that ideas, not material causes, were the decisive factors in history. Many of Yockey's cultural references in *Imperium* also came from Friedell.[6]

The question of the role, as well as the future, of art was of great importance to Spengler, who argued that the Culture phase in the West had exhausted itself forever. He believed that the continued glorification of Art and Culture in the age of Civilization was little more than effete escapism. According to Spengler:

> I would sooner have the fine mind-begotten forms of a fast steamer, a steel structure, a precision-lathe, the subtlety and elegance of many chemical and optical processes, than all the pickings and stealings of present-day "arts and crafts," architecture and painting included. I prefer one Roman aqueduct to all Roman temples and statues.[7]

In the age of Civilization, genius was to be expressed not by painting, poetry, or music but through war, engineering, and bridge-building. Spengler most famously demanded the abandonment of Culture in his introduction to *The Decline of the West*, when he wrote: "I can only hope that men of the new generation may be moved by this book to devote themselves to technics instead of lyrics, the sea instead of the paint-brush, and politics instead of epistemology. Better they could not do."[8]

In 1921, Spengler concluded his essay "Pessimism?" with a discussion of the artist of the future:

> Hardness, Roman hardness is taking over now. Soon there will be no room for anything else. Art, yes; but in concrete and steel. Literature, yes; but by men with iron nerves and uncompromising depth of vision; religion, yes; but take up your hymnbook, not your classy edition of Confucius, and go to church. Politics, yes; but in the hands of statesmen and not idealists. Nothing else will be of consequence. And we must never lose sight of what lies behind and ahead of us citizens of this century. We Germans will never again produce a Goethe, but indeed a Caesar.[9]

Spengler converted Yockey from an aesthete into a practitioner of an aesthetic form of politics, a politics infused with the grandeur of art and open only to a small spiritual elite.[10] Spenglerism, however, was a difficult banner to rally round. As Eric Heller observes in *The Disinherited Mind*, the age of Caesarism reduced society to "a strict and rigid order" of human "molecules" trapped inside warring totalitarian states. Whether in victory or defeat, these societies would remain as sterile as Rome under the Caesars until this spiritually dead mass finally collapsed.[11] Spengler summed up his bleak vision in the conclusion to his book *Man and Technics*:

> We are born into this time and must bravely follow the path to the destined end. There is no other way. Our duty is to hold on to the lost position, without hope, without rescue, like that Roman soldier whose bones were found in front of a door in Pompeii, who during the eruption of Vesuvius, died at his post because they forgot to relieve him. That is greatness. That is what it means to be a thoroughbred. The honorable end is the one thing that cannot be taken from a man.[12]

For Yockey, however, the coming of the Caesars heralded a potential rebirth for the West. In *Imperium* he even claimed that "Europe stands at the *beginning* of a world-historical process"—not at its end.[13] Perhaps this is why he dedicated *Imperium* not to "The Philosopher" but to "The Hero of the Second World War"—Adolf Hitler. Using Spengler's spectacles, but with a different prescription, Yockey saw Hitler as Napoleon reborn. Like Napoleon (whom Yockey also hero-worshipped), "The Hero" tried to realize the European Imperium and, again like Napoleon, fell victim to the barbarian Slavs. Yet by unwavering dedication to a "suprapersonal Destiny" that demanded the creation of a unified European Imperium as the last great supernova of the West, both Napoleon and Hitler became Hegel's "history on horseback," the Zeitgeist made flesh.[14]

Although Yockey came to Nazism through *The Decline of the West*, Spengler was not a Nazi. *The Hour of Decision* was even suppressed by the Nazis shortly after they took power.[15] Because Spengler's peculiar and complex relation to Nazism affected Yockey, "The Philosopher's" own encounter with "The Hero" must briefly be examined.

As one of Munich's leading right-wing thinkers, Spengler was intimately familiar with the Nazis. He was even inside the Munich Beer Hall on the evening of 8 November 1923, when Hitler launched his abortive putsch. Spengler, however, was essentially a political monarchist, and his encounters with Hitler convinced him that the Nazi movement was composed of the worst sort of proletarianized street-rabble. In 1927 he wrote about the Nazis: "I have not only stood aloof from the National Socialist Movement which led to the Munich putsch, but actually, unfortunately in vain, done my utmost to prevent it . . . I am of the opinion that politics should be based on sober facts and considerations and not on romanticism of the feelings."[16]

Although Spengler cultivated an aura of delphic detachment, he was highly political. As early as 1919, in his extremely influential *Prussianism and Socialism*,[17] he openly engaged in political struggle against Russian-style Marxism, German social democracy, and Weimar liberalism. He even acted as a bagman and transmitted funds from a right-wing German politician and former Krupp director named Alfred Hugenberg to one of the Bavarian paramilitary leagues known as the Kampfbunde.[18]

To Spengler's mandarin mind, real government must be aristocratic, since every nation in history was led by an aristocratic minority. Although he voted for Hitler in the 1932 elections as part of a broad conservative electoral bloc, he believed that movements like Nazism were symptoms of Europe's decline. Hitler's populist rhetoric, as well as the Nazis' hooliganism and pandering to the masses, reflected Germany's problem rather than its solution. His attacks on the political left in *The Hour of Decision*, both for "noisy agitation at the street corners and in public meetings" and for its "enthusiasm for the mass in general as a foundation for one's individual power," could equally be applied to Ernst Roehm's Stormtroopers. Spengler even joked that the Nazis were best described as "a party of the unemployed led by the work-shy."

In *The Hour of Decision* Spengler criticized Italian fascism in a way equally applicable to Nazism:

> For Fascism is also a transition. It had its origin in the city mobs and began as a mass party with noise and disturbance and mass oratory; Labor-Socialist tendencies are not unknown to it. But so long as a dictatorship has "social service" ambitions, asserts that it is there for the "worker's" sake, courts favor in the streets, and is "popular," so long it remains an interim form. The Caesarism of the future fights solely for power, for empire, and against every description of party.[19]

Fascism lacked "the Caesarian skepticism and contempt for humanity, the deep sense of the fleetingness of all phenomena." Although Mussolini's "creative idea was grand" and "a possible form for the combating of Bolshevism," fascism still trafficked in "revolution from below." Fascism's weakness was its "tendency to subordinate intellectual and economic leadership to executive working-out because of inability to understand it; to disregard other's property, to confuse the conceptions of nation and mass—in a word, the Socialistic ideology of last century."

Yet, if a movement like Nazism could just be used to destroy the Communists, Socialists, and liberal Weimar democrats, it might help usher in a Germany led not by beerhall brutes but by an aristocratic and intellectual elite committed to the preservation of the state in an era of increasing social breakdown. Spengler dubbed his Teutonic version of Plato's Guardians "Prussian socialism," and saw himself as the new state's *éminence grise*, if not philosopher-king.

The Hour of Decision was published in Germany in early 1933, just as Hitler took power. Spengler tried to placate the Nazis in a quickly written introduction that began: "No one can have looked forward to the national revolution of this year with greater longing than myself. The sordid Revolution of 1918 I detested from its first day." But he also could not resist criticizing Germany's new rulers:

> The danger with enthusiasts is that they envisage the situation as too simple. Enthusiasm is out of keeping with goals that lie generations ahead. And yet it is with these that the actual decisions of history begin. The seizure of power took place in a confused whirl of strength and weakness. I see with misgiving that it continues to be noisily celebrated from day to day ... Sound ideas are exaggerated into self-glorification by fanatics, and that which held promise of greatness in the beginning ends as tragedy or comedy.[20]

After Hitler became chancellor in January 1933, the Nazis at first actively courted Spengler. While Goebbels begged him to speak on the radio, Hitler held a long private meeting with him. Spengler, however, was less than impressed, writing that while the Führer seemed "a very decent fellow," sitting opposite him "one doesn't feel for a second that he's significant."[21]

Although Spengler volunteered his services as an advisor to the Reich (even sending Hitler a copy of *The Hour of Decision*), the NSDAP wasn't buying. After *The Hour of Decision* became an instant bestseller, Hitler's minions tried to halt the sale of the book. Nazi critics lashed out at Spengler's "ice-cold contempt for the people," his worship of aristocratic and monarchist society, his pessimism, and his denial of race. In *The Myth of the Twentieth Century*, Alfred Rosenberg wrote about Spengler: "He does not see racial-spiritual forces forming the world, but fabricates abstract schemes to which we are all subjected 'fatally.' Ultimately this brilliantly presented doctrine denies race, personality, intrinsic value, every real, culturally productive impulse of the 'heart of hearts' of the Germanic mind."[22] Some critics even raised the issue of "Jewish blood" after Hitler's archivists uncovered the fact that Spengler's great grandfather, Frederick Wilhelm Grantzow, was partly Jewish. Spengler was also too close to Germany's old ruling classes, which included wealthy business magnates and right-wing nobles like former German chancellor Franz von Papen. He was equally guilty of another grave sin: He was not an anti-Semitic conspiracy theorist. Like many educated Germans, Spengler thought that Judaism was an exhausted belief system that had played out its historic vitality many centuries ago and only survived in Europe's ghettos like a fossil preserved in amber. Because Judaism (like Islam and early Christianity) was world-denying, escapist, and anti-historical, the Western ("Faustian") antipathy to it was cultural, not racial.

Spengler identified Judaism as a "Magian" form of society with a cave-like conception of space that was intermediate between the classical Greek ("Apollonian") idea of the Gods having human characteristics and the West's Faustian concept of an infinite universe. Magians were dualists who believed in an unrelenting struggle between good and evil. In such a belief system, the separation of politics and religion was theoretically impossible and intellectually meaningless. *The Decline of the West* argued that the late Romans, Jews, Mohammedans, and early Christian theologians like Saint Augustine were all Magian.

In the Nazi glorification of the Volk, Spengler detected a kind of "Magian" distortion of the West's notion of a free, individual, self-willed "I" in favor of the collective herd. In *The Hour of Decision* he lashed out:

> The urge to be released from one's own will, to be submerged in the lazy majority, to know the happiness of a lackey's soul, to be spared the master's anxieties—all this is here disguised under big words. The Romanticism of the insignificant! The apotheosis of the herd-feeling! The last final way to idealize one's own dread of responsibility! This kind of hatred of individualism, arising out of cowardice and shame, is a mere caricature of that of the great 14th–15th century mystics, with their anti-egoism . . . Today there is a simpler method: One turns "Socialist" and runs down the "I" of other people . . . One's own "I" gives no more trouble. The levelling-out of brains is complete: One meets "in the masses," wills "in the mass," thinks "in the mass." Those who do not think with it, who think for themselves, are felt to be enemies. It is now the mass, and not the godhead, in which the lazy, stupid "I," suffering from all manner of inhibitions, "submerges" itself: and that, too, is "release." It is almost mystical.[23]

Although Spengler's polemic was ostensibly directed against the left, his words did not endear him to the National Socialist German Workers Party.

"The Philosopher" became openly hostile to the Nazis after Hitler's 29 June 1934 "Night of the Long Knives" purges, when Himmler's SS murdered not just the thuggish leaders of Ernst Roehm's SA, but also friends of Spengler's like the Bavarian rightist leader Gustav von Kahr and Gregor Strasser, Hitler's chief factional opponent inside the NSDAP. In a panic, Spengler burned his correspondence with Strasser. His own death in 1936 was for the Nazi hierarchy a most welcome development, although they continued for ideological reasons to glorify him as a German Virgil who had prophesied Hitler's coming.

Yockey's quasi-religious conversion to Spengler's high-culture brand of right-wing radicalism meant that he was no sycophant of Adolf Hitler's personality cult. As a self-proclaimed elitist, he always maintained an aristocratic disdain for the Volk, whose only role was to serve the ruling elect, or what he called the "culture-bearing stratum." For Yockey, Hitler was "The Hero" not because of but in spite of his plebian racial musings. He was Spengler's long-prophesied new Caesar come to lead the rebirth of the West out from under the rubble of the old liberal order.

61

Notes:

1. FBI file to Director (105-8229) from SAC, WFO (100-26536), 16 December 1954, based on a 6 December interview with Perry Patterson.

2. From my interview with Dr. Francesca Yockey, Yockey's daughter.

3. Volume one of *The Decline of the West, Form and Actuality* was first published in America in 1926 by Alfred A. Knopf. Volume Two, *Perspectives of World History,* appeared in November 1928. By 1940 Volume One had sold over 26,000 copies and Volume Two had sold 21,000 copies; impressive numbers for such a difficult book.

4. Oswald Spengler, *The Hour of Decision* (New York: Knopf, 1934), p. 21; *Imperium*, p. 1.

5. In the closing section of his 1949 *The Proclamation of London,* Yockey writes:

> Washington's program is to conscript the Europeans—what it cynically calls the "manpower" of Europe—and thus to spare the jitterbugs of North America the losses of arduous campaigns against Russia . . . No, Europe is no more interested in this projected war than in a struggle between two Negro tribes in Sudan.

Only the most devout Spenglerian would recall that in *The Decline of the West,* "The Philosopher" wrote:

> A battle between two Negro tribes in the Sudan, or between the Chesrusci and Chatti of Caesar's time, or—what is substantially the same—between anti-communities, is merely a drama of "living nature." [Oswald Spengler, *The Decline of the West,* Vol. Two (New York, Knopf, 1928) p. 48.]

6. The influence of Friedell's *A Cultural History of the Modern Age* is also mentioned in Willis Carto's introduction to *Imperium*.

7. Spengler, *The Decline of the West,* pp. 43–44.

8. Ibid., p. 41.

9. Oswald Spengler, *Selected Essays* (Chicago: Henry Regnery, 1967), pp. 153–54.

10. While attending Notre Dame, Yockey wrote a brief essay called "Life as an Art." See the appendix "The Devil and Francis Parker Yockey."

11. Eric Heller, "Oswald Spengler and the Predicament of the Historical Imagination," in his *The Disinherited Mind* (London: Bowes and Bowes, 1952), p. 183.

12. Oswald Spengler, *Man and Technics* (New York: Knopf, 1933), p. 104.

13. *Imperium*, p. 409.

14. One of Yockey's prized possessions was the *Maxims of Napoleon.* Throughout *Imperium,* Yockey cites Napoleon ("Imagination rules the world" is one quotation). Yockey clearly saw Napoleon as the political founder of the Imperium and quotes Napoleon as writing:

> I wanted to prepare the fusion of the great interests of Europe, as I had accomplished that of the parties. I concerned myself little with the passing rancor of the peoples, for I was sure that the results would lead them irresistibly back to me.

Europe would in this way have become in truth a united nation, and everyone would have been, no matter where he traveled, in the same Fatherland. This fusion will accomplish itself sooner or later through the pressure of facts; the impulse has been given which, since my downfall and the disappearance of my system, will make the restoration of balance possible in Europe only by merger and fusion of the great nations. [*Imperium*, p. 245.]

15. Part two of *The Hour of Decision* was abandoned by Spengler because of Nazi pressure.

16. Alastair Hamilton, *The Appeal of Fascism* (London: Anthony Blond, 1971), p. 118.

17. Yockey wrote a now-lost 60-page commentary on *Prussianism and Socialism* in the late 1940s.

18. Walter Struve, *Elites Against Democracy* (Princeton, NJ: Princeton University Press, 1973), pp. 236–37. One of Spengler's closest political allies was Dr. Paul Reusch, the general representative of the enormously wealthy Haniel family. Reusch played a central role in organizing the Ruhrlade, a shadowy association of heavy industrialists that Yale historian Henry A. Turner (author of *Big Business and the Rise of Hitler*) has dubbed "the secret cabinet of heavy industry" in the Weimar Republic. Spengler and Reusch also belonged to the Gaa Gesellschaft, which Struve identifies as "an exclusive, secretive right-wing group that included politicians, writers, businessmen, and officers." Spengler even attempted to create a press network to disseminate propaganda for German big business.

19. Spengler, *Hour of Decision*, p. 186.

20. Ibid., pp. xii–xiii.

21. Hamilton, *The Appeal of Fascism*, p. 155.

22. Ibid., p. 118.

23. Spengler, *The Hour of Decision*, p. 200.

7

BLACKBOARD JUNGLE

In the fall of 1936 the 19-year-old Yockey transferred from the University of Michigan to Georgetown University's School of Foreign Service. He entered the Jesuit institution a devout Spenglerian. Perry Patterson, Yockey's closest student friend, still remembers his ability to quote page after page from *The Decline of the West* virtually verbatim. He also recalled going with him to local cafes, where Yockey would entertain the crowd with his musical skill, excelling at Chopin in particular. Yockey (who called everyone by their last name) exhibited a wry sense of humor and had a fondness for W. C. Fields. Yet he always remained an intensely serious, highly political individual who could describe Adolf Hitler as an "effective instrument in terms of history."[1]

Yockey was also close to Walter Jaeger, a charismatic 34-year-old Georgetown professor of law and international relations. Best known as the editor of the 23-volume *Williston on Contracts*, Jaeger was one of Georgetown's outstanding professors.[2] Patterson told me that Yockey and Jaeger "had similar politics, sentiments, and feelings." Jaeger's intense interest in Europe began in his youth, when his father was a European correspondent for the Hearst International News Syndicate. After graduating from Columbia with honors in 1923, he received a doctorate in political science from Georgetown in 1926. He was then appointed graduate assistant to Jesuit Father Edmund Walsh, the Regent of Georgetown's School of Foreign Service. After further studies at the University of Paris's Faculty of Law and the École Libre des Sciences Politiques under a Carnegie teaching fellowship, Jaeger returned to Georgetown and received his law degree in 1932. He also worked with James Brown Scott, then solicitor of the State Department, on a casebook on international law.[3] (He also taught at the U.S. Naval Academy in Annapolis.[4]) Politically, Jaeger was an outspoken isolationist: On 3 November 1937 the *Washington Post* reported on one Jaeger speech where he demanded that the United States stay out of any conflict in Asia and warned that Russia and Great Britain both wanted America to fight Japan. The United States, however, should "let the Orient alone" and "stay in our own hemisphere."

Like Jaeger, Yockey was especially interested in the relationship between international law and foreign policy. Many of his ideas on statecraft were derived from former Major General Karl Haushofer, a professor at the University of Munich and the doyen of 20th-century German geopolitical theory, who published a journal called the *Zeitschrift für Geopolitik*. German geopolitical ideas had also been popularized by Colin Ross, a Haushofer collaborator and the Nazi "America expert," who often lectured to foreign policy groups in the United States.

Georgetown's School of Foreign Service was one of the few American academic institutions devoted to a careful analysis of German geopolitical doctrines.[5] No American studied Haushofer more closely than Father Walsh.[6] After World War II, Walsh was chosen by the U.S. government to interrogate Haushofer. His discussions ended abruptly on 11 March 1946, when the elderly general and his wife, Martha, committed suicide.

In *Imperium*, written not long after Haushofer's suicide, Yockey commented:

> It is therefore not surprising when the materialists persecute, by maligning, by conspiracy of silence, cutting off from access to publicity, or by driving to suicide, as in the case of Haushofer, those who think in 20th-century terms and specifically reject the methods and conclusions of 19th-century materialism.[7]

Yockey's complaint was especially curious since Father Walsh had denounced Haushofer for being too materialist! Haushofer's ice-cold *Machtpolitik* (power politics) terrified Walsh, a highly conservative Catholic exponent of international law who looked to the Holy Roman Empire with nostalgia. In 1944 Walsh attacked Haushofer in an essay called "Geopolitics and International Morals."[8] In it, he wrote:

> No informed European or thoughtful American should fail to recognize that the German geopolitik is precisely what its name signifies—the politics of a wholly earthly conception of life and human destiny. It was the logical culmination of a process of secularization both of the mind and of cultural institutions which had been in progress since the Renaissance and the Industrial Revolution ... this one-sided, distorted Humanism introduced a paganism of taste, charm, and refinement which, coupled with personal depravity in high places, cancerous morals, simony, and nepotism, weak-

ened respect for ecclesiastical authority and hastened the religious revolt of the northern nations in the 16th century. In statecraft it produced Machiavelli and justified the Haushofers.[9]

Father Walsh was not only an expert on Haushofer. An adamant foe of Bolshevik Russia, he authored *The Fall of the Russian Empire* (1927) and *The Last Stand: An Interpretation of the Soviet Five-Year Plan* (1931). Walsh knew that Lenin's first major diplomatic breakthrough was Russia's 1922 Rapallo Treaty with Germany. He also knew that Haushofer was convinced that Soviet Russia and Germany were natural geopolitical allies. In his book *Total Power,* Walsh observed: "A rapprochement between Germany and Soviet Russia was consistently advocated [by the German geopoliticians] because of Russia's spatial mass, richness of raw materials, and the hinterland of security which its friendship would assure to the Reich."[10]

Geopolitics arose in the late 1800s, in part as a by-product of conflicts generated by the European powers as they competed against each other in Africa and Asia.[11] The founder of modern geopolitical theory, Friedreich Ratzel, taught geography at the Universities of Leipzig and Munich. To Ratzel, states were biological organisms engaged in continual Darwinian struggle: A state either moved to higher forms or devolved into decadence, since "to remain static meant loss of character and vitality." He grounded his vitalistic political doctrine in geography and believed that the territory and location of a state, and how well it adapted to its geographical challenge, determined its future. He saw *Raum* (space) as a political force of prime importance and argued that healthy states naturally gravitated toward territorial expansion.

Haushofer, a brilliant linguist whose languages included Chinese, Japanese, Korean, and Russian, literally learned geopolitics at Ratzel's knee. Ratzel was a close friend of Haushofer's father, Max, who taught economic geography at the Munich Polytechnicum. As a youth, Haushofer often participated in his father's discussions with Ratzel.

One of Haushofer's favorite quotations came from Ovid: "*Fas est ab hoste doceri*" (It is one's duty to learn from the enemy). One of his most important enemies was the American admiral Alfred Thayer Mahan. In his 1890 classic *The Influence of Sea Power upon History, 1660–1783,* Mahan argued that control of the seas (the "great highway") meant control of the world. His ideas soon came under attack from Halford Mackinder, then a reader in geography at Oxford and later the director of the London School of Economics. In a 1904 essay entitled *The Geographical Pivot of History,* Mackinder portrayed world history as "a recurring conflict between the landsmen and the seamen." He also highlighted the coming strategic importance of Eurasia, Russia's vast heartland. In the past, Mackinder noted, the primitive social and nomadic condition of Eurasia had given advantage to seafaring powers. For hundreds of years nations that dominated the sea lanes dominated the globe. Power in the 20th century, however, would inevitably shift from sea to land once Russia developed the vast natural fortress of Eurasia. As Russian industrialization spread, the Eurasian heartland (not Mahan's sea lanes) would become "the pivot of the world's politics." By complacently concentrating on sea power, Mahan had missed the coming Russian challenge. In Mackinder's famous dictum: "Who rules East Europe commands the Heartland; who rules the Heartland commands the World Island; who rules the World Island commands the world."

What Mackinder saw as a threat to British hegemony, Haushofer interpreted as an opportunity for Germany to shatter its geopolitical "encirclement" by the British Empire. The extent of British power was burned into Haushofer's psyche in 1908 when the Bavarian General Staff sent him on a special mission to study the Japanese army. Sailing to Japan, he could not help noticing that wherever his ship stopped—at Cyprus, Alexandria, Aden, India, and Singapore—there flew the Union Jack. "It was with immense relief," he recalled years later, "that we finally saw the flag of the Rising Sun waving over Formosa."[12]

There was only one blade sharp enough to cut the Gordian knot of British encirclement: Russia. Mackinder had made it clear: If Germany were ever to become a world power, she must ally with Russia. Failing such an entente, Germany's only other option was to come to some sort of understanding with England, permanently condemning the Fatherland to second-rate status as a land-based power denied the vast riches of overseas empire.

In *Imperium,* Yockey attacked American followers of Mahan for failing to grasp the importance of Mackinder, Haushofer, and Homer Lea, Mahan's most powerful American opponent. In a veiled attack on Georgetown, he commented:

> No American university has heard of geopolitics, or anything resembling it. Mahan's sea-power theories are the last word on grand strategy, and the eventuation of the First and Second World Wars—which Americans are taught to regard as "victories"—only reinforce the sea-power idea, despite the fact that world-shaking events have fundamentally altered the relationship between continental power and sea power.[13]

Mackinder's critique of Mahan showed that the British Lion rested on legs of water. Following his lead, Haushofer became the "anti-Mahan" of geopolitics. As Robert Strausz-Hupé remarks in *Geopolitics: The Struggle for Space and Power,* "Haushofer's own doctrine of landpower is the most extreme negation of Mahan's theories."[14] To Strausz-Hupé the "kernel of Geopolitic" was the doctrine of landpower, since the British were invincible at sea. But if "Britain's seapower could be crushed by the destruction of its bases," then "the bastions of the British Empire could be outflanked by gigantic pincer movements across the mainland of Europe."[15]

In World War I, Germany violated geopolitical fundamentals when it failed to either ally with Russia or come to terms with England. Haushofer was determined to make sure that Germany did not repeat the blunder. After the first world war, he wrote: "Germans and Russians finally recognized that both of them had been the victims, and, by fighting each other to the death, had only pulled the chestnuts out of the fire for the sake of the imperialistic aims of the neighboring Western Powers."[16] His ideas also enjoyed the support of the head of the German General Staff, Colonel General Hans von Seeckt. Although a bitter anti-Communist, he was nicknamed "Red Seeckt" for his pro-Russian foreign policy views. Nor was the idea of an alliance between the German military and the Bolsheviks terribly new. In 1917 the German General Staff had helped make it possible for Lenin to topple the Allied-backed Kerensky government, and by so doing almost changed the outcome of World War I.

Throughout the 1920s the German and Soviet militaries maintained the closest of ties. To escape Allied restrictions on German military growth, a hidden wing of the German military (dubbed the "Black Reichswehr") regularly carried out secret training maneuvers on Soviet soil. Postwar discussions between Bolshevik foreign policy expert Karl Radek and German military officers first began in Berlin in 1919. In the spring of 1921 Lenin formally requested German aid to help reorganize the Red Army. In anticipation of Lenin's request, Seeckt established a secret unit called *Sondergruppe R* (Special Group R), headed by Colonel Walter Nicolai, the former chief of military intelligence, to work out areas of cooperation with the Red Army. In the summer of 1921 a German military mission headed by Colonel Oskar von Nidermayer met Lenin in Moscow. The 1922 Rapallo Treaty between Berlin and Moscow was just one public indication of a more covert relationship between the two powers.[17]

In its struggle to break British dominance, German military intelligence also looked to nationalist independence movements in the Middle East, Asia, and Ireland. After World War I Haushofer continued to support these anti-British groups. In the 1930s, Indian nationalist leader Subhas Chandra Bose (whose Indian National Army later received military support in World War II from both Germany and Japan) was a correspondent for the *Zeitschrift für Geopolitik*.[18] Haushofer's closest Third World ally, however, was Japan. Some of the most important decisions concerning Japanese-German relations were first negotiated in his living room.[19]

In July 1942 foreign policy expert Hans Weigert profiled Haushofer's "Eurasian liberation front" policies in *Foreign Affairs*. Weigert pointed out that Haushofer actually welcomed "the rise of the colored world," even writing that "the struggle of India and China for liberation from foreign domination and capitalist pressure agrees with the secret dreams of Central Europe." Haushofer also mocked the idea of an alliance of the white race against the colored world: "It is not up to the Germans to create a white bloc. This bloc was smashed by those who used colored troops in the Rhineland to keep down a white race. The opposite postulate, 'Oppressed peoples of the world unite!' can be much better justified on ethical grounds."

To unite what he called the "Eurasian continental organization from the Rhine to the Amur and the Yangtze," Haushofer tried for years to persuade Japan to come to terms with both China and the USSR. He also tried to convince the Nazis to live in peace with the Soviet Union. To the editors of the *Zeitschrift für Geopolitik*, the idea of a crusade against Russia was absurd.

Haushofer was in essence a brilliant and supremely daring gambler playing the ultimate high-stakes game with a series of skilled bluffs. He wanted to restore German power through an intricate and many-layered foreign policy balancing act, which would avoid another disastrous war with England as well as the uncontrolled rise of Soviet Russia. Like Spengler, he also had an unusually complex and strained relationship with Hitler. They first met in Munich in the early 1920s through Haushofer's protégé Rudolf Hess, who was a member of Munich's influential far-right Thule Society.[20] After the collapse of the Beer Hall Putsch, Hess briefly hid from the authorities in Haushofer's summer home in the Bavarian Alps. While visiting Hess in Landsberg prison, Haushofer again met Hitler. Given the Haushofer-Hess-Hitler connection, it would be easy to assume that Corporal Hitler simply channeled the expansionist desires of Major General Haushofer. In reality the situation was far more complex, especially given the fact that Haushofer's wife and intellectual collaborator, Martha, was half-Jewish.[21]

Equally important, at least on paper, Adolf Hitler was a devout Anglophile who in *Mein Kampf* repeatedly expressed his deep admiration for the British empire.[22] Hitler argued that Germany's drive for *Lebensraum* (living space) in the East was the best way to avoid any future conflict with England. He also denounced anti-British foreign nationalist groups that had worked closely with German intelligence during World War I.[23]

Far from being the work of an isolated madman, *Mein Kampf*, albeit crudely, articulated a popular current of Western eugenic and "biopolitical" thought that saw the world's "colored" nations (including Russia) as the ultimate threat to the West. A similar argument had been advanced in the United States in tomes like Madison Grant's *The Passing of the Great Race*, which was published in Germany in 1925 by the volkish, Munich-based house J. F. Lehmann. Hitler was so impressed by the book that he sent Grant a note calling it his Bible.[24]

An equally important biopolitical work was Lothrop Stoddard's *The Rising Tide of Color Against White World Supremacy*, first published by Scribners in 1920. In it, Stoddard predicted a coming massive Third World revolt: Japan's stunning military defeat of Czarist Russia in 1905 was an ominous portent of things to come. He was also outraged by German attempts to appeal to the "colored" world during World War I:

> German imperialism was plotting even deadlier strokes at white race-comity, not merely by preparing war against white neighbors in Europe, but also by ingratiating itself with the Moslem East and by toying with schemes for building up a black military empire in central Africa . . . [P]roposed German alliances with Pan-Islamism and Japan preached by disciples of *Machtpolitik* were strenuously opposed as race-treason by powerful sections of German thought.[25]

Now it was time for Germany to unite with the rest of the West to crush Bolshevism,

> the arch-enemy of civilization and the race. Bolshevism is the renegade, the traitor within the gates, who would betray the citadel, degrade the very fibre of our being, and ultimately hurl a rebarbarized, racially impoverished world into the most debased and hopeless of mongrelization.[26]

Stoddard and Grant were no street-corner cranks. Stoddard had gotten his Ph.D. from Harvard, while Grant was chairman of the New York Zoological Society, a trustee of the American Museum of Natural History, and a councillor to the American Geographic Society. All their works were widely reprinted in Germany, and in late 1939 Stoddard met with Hitler, Himmler, and other Nazi dignitaries.[27] Spengler, too, was influenced by Stoddard. In the "Colored World Revolution" section of *The Hour of Decision* (where he footnoted *The Rising Tide of Color*), Spengler posed the "great historical question": "whether the fall of the white powers will be brought about or not?"[28]

Yet if it was objectively in the interest of the "white world" to forge a Pan-Nordic International against the "Yellow Peril," why were Europe's powers continually engaged in such self-destructive wars? Here we return to geopolitics, where states continually struggle against each other for power in an utterly Hobbesian world. A "White International" was virtually impossible in such a geopolitical jungle because, as Spengler himself remarks in *The Hour of Decision*: "Man is a beast of prey. I shall say it again and again."[29]

After World War II it was not the "colored" world but "white" powers like the United States, England, and France that had again occupied Germany while allowing the Russian seizure of Eastern Europe. Following Haushofer, Yockey would look East after 1945 for allies in the struggle to "liberate" Germany from a second Allied occupation.

Notes:

1. My interview with Perry Patterson.

2. Jaeger died in 1982 at age 80.

3. Scott was also chief editor of the prestigious *American Journal of International Law*, as well as the author of *The Catholic Conception of International Law*.

4. Yockey maintained his ties to Jaeger well after World War II. The FBI even discovered a letter he had written from Washington on 22 January 1952 that mentioned that he was "counting heavily upon old Jaeger" to help him find "some base economic employment." He also listed Jaeger as a reference on an undated employment form.

5. Yockey's interest in geopolitics is evident in a student paper he wrote at Georgetown called *Philosophy of Constitutional Law*, where he makes a passing reference to the Swedish geopolitical theorist Rudolf Kjellen, writing: "*no* state (in Rudolf Kjellen's understanding of that word) has even been contained in form or restrained in action by a written constitution." An intense Germanophile and professor of government at Sweden's Göteborg University, Kjellen is credited with the invention of the term "geopolitics."

6. The first part of Walsh's book *Total Power: A Footnote to History* (New York: Doubleday, 1948) was a detailed critique of Haushofer.

7. *Imperium*, p. 29.

8. Walsh's essay appears in *Compass of the World: A Symposium on Political Geography*, edited by Hans W. Weigert and Vilhjalmur Stefansson (New York: Macmillan, 1944).

9. Walsh, "Geopolitics and International Morals," in *Compass of the World*, pp. 26–27. Compare his ideas to Haushofer's description of geopolitics:

> Geopolitik is the doctrine of earth relations of political developments. It is based on the broad foundations of geography, particularly political geography, as the doctrine of political space organisms and their structure.
>
> The findings of geography as to the character of the earth's spaces furnish the frame for Geopolitik. Political developments must take place within this frame if they are to have permanent success. Those who shape political life will occasionally reach beyond this frame, but sooner or later the earth-bound character of political developments will always prevail. Thus Geopolitik becomes the doctrine of an art. It is to guide practical politics to that point where it must take the step into the unknown. Only if inspired by geopolitical knowledge can this step be successful. Geopolitik must and will become the geographical conscience of the state. [Cited in *The World of General Haushofer: Geopolitics in Action*, by Andreas Dorpalen (New York: Farrar & Rinehart, 1942), p. 23.]

10. Walsh, *Total Power*, p. 7.

11. The following discussion draws on Geoffrey Parker's *Western Geopolitical Thought in the Twentieth Century* (London: Crown and Helm, 1985).

12. Dorpalen, *The World of General Haushofer*, p. 3.

13. *Imperium*, p. 518.

14. Robert Strausz-Hupé, *Geopolitics: The Struggle for Space and Power* (New York: G. P. Putnam, 1942), p. 246.

15. Ibid., p. 243.

16. Hans W. Weigert, *Generals and Geographers: The Twilight of Geopolitics* (New York: Oxford University Press, 1942), p. 140. In 1925 an editor of the *Zeitschrift für Geopolitik* wrote:

> Germany will have to decide where she stands: Does she want to be a satellite of the Anglo-Saxon powers and their super-capitalism, which are united with the other European nations against Russia, or will she be an ally of the Pan-Asiatic union against Europe and America? . . . No nation is closer to Russia than is Germany; and only Germany can understand the Russian soul; Germany and Russia have been friends for centuries; their economic structures are complementary; they must hang together. [Cited in Hans Weigert's profile of Haushofer in the July 1942 issue of *Foreign Affairs*.]

17. By the mid-1920s, the USSR was producing weapons for the Reichswehr. On 2 December 1926 the *Manchester Guardian*'s Berlin correspondent reported on Soviet military aid and caused a brief political scandal.

18. Haushofer called Bose the great "Hindu fighter against the Anglo-American domination of Asia."

19. In the 1930s one of Haushofer's top military collaborators, Eugen Ott, became German Ambassador to Tokyo. Ott, in turn, was a close friend of the Tokyo correspondent for the *Zeitschrift für Geopolitik*, the German journalist and famous Soviet spy Richard Sorge.

20. On the Thule Society, see Nicholas Goodrick-Clarke, *The Occult Roots of Nazism* (Wellingborough, Northamptonshire: The Acquarian Press, 1985). See also Reginald H. Phelps, "'Before Hitler Came': The Thule Society and the Germanen Order," in *The Journal of Modern History*, Vol. XXXV, No. 3, Sept. 1963; Georg Franz, "Munich: Birthplace and Center of the National Socialist German Workers' Party," in *The Journal of Modern History*, Vol. XXIX, No. 4, December 1957; and René Alleau, *Hitler et les Sociétiés Sécrètes* (Paris: B. Grasset, 1969), which includes a list of Thule Society members.

21. According to Hans Weigert, before 1933 the *Zeitschrift für Geopolitik* avoided any discussion of National Socialism. Between 1924 and 1933, Hitler's name appeared not more than a dozen times. Haushofer mentioned him only once or twice. For a recent assessment of Haushofer and the Nazis, see a series of articles in *Political Geography Quarterly*, Vol. 6, No. 2, April 1987. Also see Bruno Hipler, *Hitlers Lehrmeister: Karl Haushofer als Vater der NS-Ideologie* (St. Ottilien: EOS Verlag, 1996), which is strongly critical of attempts to minimize Haushofer's Nazi ties. Given Haushofer's importance, an English-language biography of him is long overdue.

22. Adolf Hitler, *Mein Kampf* (Boston: Houghton Mifflin, 1943), p. 145.

23. Ibid., pp. 656–58. Also see my appendix "Secret Societies and Subversive Movements."

24. Stefan Kühl, *The Nazi Connection: Eugenics, American Racism, and German National Socialism* (New York: Oxford University Press, 1994), p. 85.

25. Lothrop Stoddard, *The Rising Tide of Color* (New York: Charles Scribners' Sons, 1920), pp. 204–05.

26. Ibid., p. 221.

27. Kühl, *The Nazi Connection*, p. 61. Also see Charles C. Alexander, "Prophet of American Racism: Madison Grant and the Nordic Myth," *Phylon*, Vol. XXIII, No. 1, 1962.

28. In *The Hour of Decision* (p. 208) Spengler defines the colored world as including "Not only Africa, the Indians—as well as the Negroes and half-breeds— of the whole of America, the Islamic nations, China and India extending to Java, but, above all, Japan and *Russia*, which has again become an Asiatic, 'Mongolian' State." He also comments (p. 175) that the mass of colored nations includes "Russians, South Spaniards, and South Italians, and the peoples of Islam just as much as the Negroes of English-speaking America and the Indians of Latin America."

I shall discuss Spengler's views of Russia in more detail later.

29. Ibid., p. 21. Spengler here is also referring to Nietzsche's idea of mankind. See Roger Woods, *The Conservative Revolution in the Weimar Republic* (New York: St. Martin's Press, 1996), p. 53.

8

CONSERVATIVE
REVOLUTION

Yockey was particularly interested in questions of international law, especially as it related to Germany. In the late 1930s, as "Francis Parker," he even lectured on the topic at rightist meetings. While at Georgetown, he was introduced to the ideas of Carl Schmitt, Germany's leading Catholic international and constitutional law theorist, whom Father Walsh described as "the outstanding legal authority of the Nazi regime."[1] During the Weimar period Schmitt had served as an advisor to German chancellor Franz von Papen, a Vatican Knight of Malta and the leader of the Catholic Center Party.[2] On 1 May 1933 Schmitt joined the NSDAP and was made a Prussian State Councillor by Göring. In June 1934 he became editor of Germany's leading law journal, the *Deutsche Juristen-Zeitung*. His prominence caused one leftist journal to dub him "the Crown Jurist" of the Third Reich.[3]

In *Imperium*, Yockey freely plagiarized from Schmitt. For example, in his chapter "The 20th-Century Political Outlook," he writes:

This was described as Machiavellian, but obviously Machiavelli was a political thinker and not a camouflager. A book by a party-politician does not read like *The Prince*, but praises the entire human race, except perverse people, the author's opponents.

Actually Machiavelli's book is defensive in tone, justifying politically the conduct of certain statesmen by giving examples drawn from foreign invasions of Italy. During Machiavelli's century, Italy was invaded at different times by Frenchmen, Germans, Spaniards, and Turks. When the French Revolutionary Armies occupied Prussia, and coupled humanitarian sentiments of the Rights of Man with brutality and large-scale looting, Hegel and

Fichte restored Machiavelli once again to respect as a thinker. He represented a means of defense against a foe armed with a humanitarian ideology. Machiavelli showed the actual role played by verbal sentiments in politics.[4]

In 1926, Schmitt had written in his book *The Concept of the Political:*

This misfortune occurred to Machiavelli, who, had he been a Machiavellian, would sooner have written an edifying book than his ill-reputed *Prince.* In actuality, Machiavelli was on the defensive as was also his country, Italy, which in the 16th century had been invaded by Germans, Frenchmen, Spaniards, and Turks. At the beginning of the 19th century the situation of the ideological defensive was repeated in Germany—during the revolutionary and Napoleonic invasions of the French. When it became important for the German people to defend themselves against an expanding enemy armed with a humanitarian ideology, Machiavelli was rehabilitated by Fichte and Hegel.[5]

Yockey's debt to Schmitt is equally apparent in Yockey's 1953 book *Der Feind Europas* (The Enemy of Europe), whose title hints at Schmitt's distinction between "enemy" and "foe." (In German, *feind* can mean either.) In Schmitt's argument, an enemy is in a temporary position of political antagonism, like two 18th-century European dynastic states fighting over contested territory. A foe, however, was a far more fundamental friend/enemy grouping. The Crusades, as a clash between Islam and Christianity, was a friend/foe distinction. *Der Feind Europas* could also be translated as "The Foe of Europe" because it tries to determine whether America or Russia was Europe's foe as opposed to its enemy.

In *The Concept of the Political*, Schmitt claimed that "the specific political distinction to which political actions and motives can be reduced is that between friend and foe."[6] He stressed the "friend/foe" antithesis to distinguish it from the liberal parliamentary tradition. For Schmitt, "the friend, enemy, and combat concepts receive their real meaning precisely because they refer to the real possibility of physical killing." War then became "the existential negation of the enemy."[7] In the moment of confrontation, the test, or the "staking life itself," the political was defined.

In his critical commentary on *The Concept of the Political*, the conservative philosopher and former Schmitt protégé Leo Strauss writes:

"Foe" takes precedence over "friend" because "the concept of foe"—as distinguished from the concept of friend—implies "the real possibility of a struggle," and because, from the possibility of war, from the *"Ernstfall,"* from "the most extreme possibility," "human life takes on its specifically political tension."[8]

After explicitly attacking Schmitt's friend-enemy distinction in *Total Power*, Father Walsh comments: "As another German revolutionist, Karl

75

Marx, long before had divided all humanity into two classes, bourgeois and proletarian, so Schmitt insisted on the militant distinction: 'We and they.'"[9] Nor was Walsh's comment mere rhetoric, since Schmitt had read Lenin and admired him as a political theorist. He also shared Lenin's contempt for parliamentary chatter.

Schmitt's assault on liberal notions of political discourse had its roots in a Weimar intellectual current inspired by Spengler that has been dubbed "the Conservative Revolution." Like other Conservative Revolutionaries, whose ranks included the novelist Ernst Jünger and the philosopher Martin Heidegger, Schmitt believed that liberalism, democracy, individualism, and Enlightenment rationalism were the products of a superficial and materialistic capitalist society.[10] Out of the collapse of liberal order there would arise a new virile man of adventure, a kind of Western *ronin*, willing to risk all and imbued with an almost mystical belief in the state.

Schmitt particularly despised Weimar parliamentary democracy. In the 1920s he developed his famous theory of "the state of exception" for the overcoming of constitutional rule (what he called "legal positivism") through the suspension of the Constitution during a crisis. He also thought that the end of constitutional order opened up the path for a new heroic "politics of authenticity."[11]

Like Spengler, Schmitt saw the state as supreme. In his book *Political Theology* he argued: "The *existence of the state* is undoubted proof of its superiority over the validity of the legal norm." Therefore, "the decision [on the state of exception] becomes instantly independent of argumentative substantiation and receives an autonomous value."[12] He also believed that government proceeded "in three dialectic stages" from "the absolute state of the 17th and 18th centuries, through the neutral state of the liberal 19th century, to the totalitarian state in which state and society are identical."[13] Commenting on this passage, Father Walsh observed that the final stage of Schmitt's idea "was the monopoly of all power, all authority, all will in the Führer, conceived and accepted as Messiah endowed with unlimited legal prerogatives in a state under perpetual martial law."[14]

Yockey was extraordinarily influenced by Schmitt's contempt for constitutional order and his sense of politics as a high-risk existential art best played in life-or-death situations of ultimate confrontation, or *Ernstfall*. Yet like Spengler, Haushofer, and many of his Conservative Revolutionary contemporaries, Schmitt's relationship with the Nazis was highly ambiguous. In the 1920s he had justified the suspension of Weimar legality by arguing that threats from *both* the right and the left necessitated the declaration of the state of exception. Schmitt even dedicated one of his important works to a Jewish friend killed in World War I.

In 1933 Schmitt's position changed radically. After Hitler's elevation to chancellor, radical rightists like Schmitt hoped to unite the nation, eliminate the Communist threat, abolish the hated Weimar Republic, and restore aristocratic rule with Corporal Adolf as their front man. The Night of the Long Knives, when Hitler liquidated the more proletarian wing of the NSDAP represented by the SA, was legally rationalized by Schmitt as a necessary act that took precedence over conventional legal norms.

Although Schmitt endorsed Hitler's bloodletting, the Night of the Long Knives cut many ways. Hitler also used the purge to intimidate his potential rivals in the old military and political establishment who had given him political respectability, even murdering one of Franz von Papen's closest aides. The Nazi challenge to the old guard was spelled out by Joseph Goebbels in a June 1934 speech, when he thundered:

> If we had relied upon those suave cavaliers [the reactionaries], Germany would have been lost. These circles sitting in armchairs in their exclusive clubs, smoking big cigars and discussing how to solve unemployment, are laughable dwarfs, always talking and never acting. If we stamp our feet, they will scurry to their holes like mice. We have the power and we will keep it.[15]

In 1936, after the SS began investigating Schmitt's "non-Aryan" (Yugoslavian) wife, the Nazi juggernaut turned on Schmitt. He soon found himself being regularly threatened in the pages of the SS organ *Das Schwarze Korps*. The SS attack was not motivated by Schmitt's unwillingness to ingratiate himself with Hitler (he had written a legal defense of Nazi racial theory in his *Staat, Bewegung, Volk*); his troubles were simply a by-product of a power play by Himmler to seize total police and judicial power.

In the face of the SS attacks, Schmitt wisely abandoned any ambition to become Hitler's "Crown Jurist." Instead, he turned his attention to international law. On 1 April 1939, shortly after the German takeover of Czechoslovakia, he gave a speech before the Institute of Politics and International Law at the University of Kiel. In both his speech and his subsequent book, *Völkerrechtiche Grossraumordnung*, he argued for the legitimacy in international law of the idea of a *Grossraumordnung* (an extraterritorial order, literally a "great space order").

Schmitt claimed that the traditional nation-state system had broken down. The British, Soviet, and American empires, as well as Japan's Greater East Asia Co-Prosperity Sphere, dwarfed older concepts of "nation." Enormous shifts in state power demanded corresponding shifts in international law. In this context, Grossraum should be understood as an area dominated by a power not as the result of organic geopolitical expansion but rather as a zone primarily defined by a "political idea." A German-dominated central Europe was just such a Grossraum in that it was a political idea distinct from its two universalist opponents, the laissez-faire ideology of Anglo-Saxon capital and the equally universalist Communist ideology.

Schmitt pointed out that Grossraum was not an imperial state, since classic imperial states like the Hapsburg Empire tried to subsume all territories and nationalities under a universalist order. Equally important, Grossraum was not a legalistic attempt to justify a "greater Reich" since that concept was defined by the unification of German racial minorities with the Fatherland. If anything, Grossraum was best understood as a German version of the American Monroe Doctrine. Under Grossraumordnung, national groups would still be preserved as individual nations, although they would be subsumed under Berlin's political, economic, and military hegemony.

Schmitt's ideas were quickly picked up by the German press, and by the prestigious *Frankfurter Zeitung* in particular. The *Times* of London and the *Daily Mail* (which labelled Schmitt "the leading international lawyer in Germany") also gave Grossraum theory widespread attention. In a speech to the Reichstag on 28 April 1939, Hitler alluded to the Monroe Doctrine and declared: "We Germans support a similar doctrine for Europe."

Schmitt's introduction of Grossraum theory into international law was intimately related to German geopolitics. When British Prime Minister Neville Chamberlain reached an understanding with Hitler over Eastern Europe in their infamous 1939 "Munich Agreement," he essentially endorsed the legitimacy of a German Grossraumordnung in the East. In his book *When Nazi Dreams Came True*, historian Robert Herzstein notes that "by building upon the theories of Haushofer and the concept of the Reich as a central historical and geographical force," Schmitt had provided the Nazis with an argument that could be used to legally rationalize the domination of continental Europe.[16]

In *Imperium*, Yockey critiques traditional notions of geopolitics along lines suggested by Schmitt. In an otherwise laudatory section on Haushofer, he writes:

> These fundamental geographical facts are the basis of all large-scale political thinking. The *basis*, but not the *source*, for the origin of grand thinking of any kind whatever in a High Culture, making itself effective through a Culture-bearing stratum of human beings. The science of geopolitics was itself a knowledge-system created by a High Culture which had arrived at the stage of unlimited Imperialism, the Age of Absolute Politics. It bore, however, within it a remnant of materialistic thinking which led to the error of placing the origin, determination, or motivation of politics in physical facts. This was an absolute error, since all Materialism, as a description of facts, is an absolute error. The origin of ideas, impulses, experience, is the soul. The origin of politics itself is the human soul. The origin of grand cre-

ative politics is the soul of a High Culture . . . The error of geopolitics was in thinking that the outer could determine the inner. But the soul is always primary, and the use made of material, or of geographic position, is a mere reflex of the type of soul . . . Geopolitics, as developed before this time, was not founded on the 20th-century view of history and politics, but on tacit materialistic ideas left over from the 19th century. The researches of this science have, however, permanent value, and its assertion of large-space thinking was an historically essential development. The name of Haushofer will remain honored in Western thought.[17]

Although Yockey chastised Haushofer for failing to spiritually conceptualize Grossraum, Schmitt had Haushofer's full support. As far back as 1931, in his book *Geopolitik der Panideen*, Haushofer had written: "Without ideological content, imperialism soon dies off." He argued that Europe needed a concept like Pan-Slavism, or Pan-Asianism; a new *Panideen* or "supernational all-englobing ideas seeking to manifest themselves in space."[18]

Grossraum was just such a Panideen, and it met with Haushofer's complete approval. In the March 1940 issue of *Zeitschift für Geopolitik*, he went into rapture over Schmitt's theory, calling it "a planetary outlook . . . keen formulations . . . world-spanning demands of spatial-political justice: a high goal of mankind and the highest of German geopolitiks."[19] It was the Nazi racialists, not proponents of geopolitik, who attacked Grossraum. In the December 1940 issue of *Nationalsozialistische Monatshefte*, Schmitt's critics pointed out that since any state could use Grossraum theory to rationalize expansion, the concept of the "German Reich" would lose its specific racial justification.[20]

Schmitt's notion of Grossraum also helps explain why Yockey felt it was so important to write *Imperium*. He believed it was vital to the future of postwar fascism to create a pan-European vision not weighed down by Nazi racialism. *Imperium* was his attempt to provide Europe's defeated fascist elite with a new Panideen appropriate to a radically new geopolitical situation.

In a 1953 letter to the German rightist Wolfgang Sarg, Yockey said about *Imperium*: "My doctrine, whose principles are entirely superpersonal, is called 'Imperialism' . . . I arrived at its fundamentals in the year 1936, before I had ever visited Europe." Given Yockey's intellectual encounters with both Haushofer and Schmitt at Georgetown, his claim may well be true.

Notes:
1. Father Edmund Walsh, *Total Power: A Footnote to History* (New York: Doubleday, 1948), p. 242. Schmitt's prominence as a Catholic legal theorist meant that he was particularly studied in Catholic law schools. For example, when Yockey was at Notre Dame's law school in 1940, one of Notre Dame's experts on

international law was a Schmitt protégé named Waldemar Gurian. A half-Jewish Catholic priest, Gurian broke with Schmitt over his mentor's turn to the Nazis.

2. Papen had his own connection to Georgetown, having sent his son to study there.

3. Gary Ulman, review of Joseph Bendersky's book *Carl Schmitt: Theorist for the Reich*, *Telos*, Spring 1984, p. 208.

4. *Imperium*, pp. 221-23.

5. Carl Schmitt, *The Concept of the Political* (New Brunswick, NJ: Rutgers University Press, 1976), p. 66. Other examples include Yockey's discussion of Benjamin Constant in *Imperium* (pp. 211-12), which rewrites pages 74-76 of *The Concept of the Political*. Yockey's "The Two Political Anthropologies," in *Imperium* (pp. 204-07) is also from Schmitt.

I must thank Tom Francis for first making me aware of just how much Yockey took from Schmitt. Francis believes that Yockey may not have cited Schmitt directly because Schmitt had come under interrogation by Allied authorities for his role with the Nazis. My own feeling is that Yockey wanted to approximate Spengler's notion of a "symbol" in *The Decline of the West*. Spengler felt that laws of causality could not apply to a culture's felt "deep wordless understanding," which was beyond rational dissection. This was analogous to what Goethe called "the Idea, of which the form is immediately apprehended in the domain of intuition, whereas pure science does not apprehend but observes and dissects." (*The Decline of the West*, Vol. I, p. 61.)

Yockey wrote *Imperium* not as a logical argument but a kind of prose poem which would articulate the inner feelings of what he called "Europe's elite." As he put it in the Foreword to *Imperium* (p. xivii): "The real author is the Spirit of the Age, and its commands do not admit of argumentation." He also wrote for an audience that he knew would recognize the ideas of a Spengler or Schmitt. Although Yockey "plagiarized" from Schmitt, the point is virtually irrelevant to a critique of *Imperium*, whose style was deliberately meant to be vatic and inspirational, not scholarly.

6. Schmitt, *The Concept of the Political*, p. 26.

7. Ibid., p. 33.

8. Leo Strauss, "Comments on Carl Schmitt's *Der Begriff des Politischen*," in *The Concept of the Political*, p. 86. Strauss, who was Jewish, had to leave Germany after the Nazis came to power.

9. Walsh, *Total Power*, p. 233.

10. Richard Wolin, "Carl Schmitt: The Conservative Revolution and the Aesthetics of Horror," in *Labyrinths: Explorations in the Critical History of Ideas* (Amherst, MA: University of Massachusetts Press, 1995), p. 106.

11. Ibid. According to Wolin (p. 119):

Following the well-known definition of sovereignty [Schmitt's statement that "Sovereign is he who decides over the state of exception"] . . . he immediately underscores its status as a "borderline concept"—a *Grenzbegriff*, a concept "pertaining to the outermost sphere." It is precisely this fascination with the "extreme" or "boundary situations" (what Karl Jaspers calls *Grenzsituationen*)—

those unique moments of extreme peril or danger that become a type of existential "proving ground" for "authentic" individuals—that stands as one of the hallmarks of the sweeping critique of "everydayness" proffered by *Lebensphilosophie* in all its variants. In the *Grenzsituationen*, "*Dasein* glimpses transcendence and is thereby transformed from possible to real *Existenz*." By according primacy to the "state of exception," as opposed to political normalcy, Schmitt tries to invest the emergency situation with a higher, existential significance and meaning.

12. Ibid., p. 111.

13. *Total Power*, p. 242. Yockey concludes *Imperium* with an almost identical notion, describing the West as following a "Triadic development" from unity under medieval Catholicism to the "antithesis" of political nationalism and materialism, and a final "Synthesis" which "is the period of the Future" and which existed in "crude provisional form" during World War II. See *Imperium*, p. 612.

14. Walsh, *Total Power*, p. 242.

15. From a speech by Goebbels cited in the 22 June 1934 *New York American*.

16. Robert Herzstein, *When Nazi Dreams Came True* (London: Sphere, 1982), p. 22.

17. *Imperium*, pp. 562–64.

18. Geoffrey Parker, *Geopolitical Thought in the Twentieth Century* (London: Crown and Helm, 1985), p. 73.

19. Max Weinrich, *Hitler's Professors* (New York: YIVO, 1946), p. 74.

20. The Nazis tried to work through these differences. In January 1941, Schmitt wrote *Das Reich und Europa*, and that same month he became part of the Society for European Economic Planning and Greater Space Economy headed by Werner Daitz of Rosenberg's Foreign Affairs Office. Daitz dreamed of a "biological Monroe Doctrine" combined with "European socialism." See Weinrich, *Hitler's Professors*, pp. 124–25.

9
SECRETS OF
ASSOCIATION

The first written evidence of Yockey's turn to the right comes from his time at Georgetown. It is a 15-page, single-spaced student paper entitled "Philosophy of Constitutional Law." In it he attacks the Weimar Constitution, calling it a prime example of how Constitutionalism "on the Continent" was the "focal point of all anti-traditionary forces" and the "quintessence of all nationalistic efforts to destroy the state." Echoing Spengler's *Prussianism and Socialism,* he writes: "The Prussian Constitution of 1850 and *a fortiori* the Weimar Constitution of 1919 were outright denials of the Prussian soul."[1]

In America, however, the struggle between "traditional" and liberal forces was played out in legal interpretations of the Constitution. Yockey praises the Federalist interpretation of the Constitution because the Federalists had some conception of a strong dirigist State:

> Just as the personality of Hamilton was decisive for the political party of Federalism, so was that of Marshall decisive for what we may call the spiritual tradition of Federalism, meaning by that the tacit feeling, always effective among at least a few men throughout our whole nation and today experiencing a powerful spiritual implementing, that we are one nation, one historical unit, and hence should be represented in history by one state instead of being shut out from history by the provincial policies of federation. The defeat of the Federalists was not the defeat of one party by another: it was the defeat of the incipient American state-idea by the spirit of Party. It was the defeat of Blood by Money, of political by economic.

With the decline of the Federalists, America grew into two separate societies. While the South became "a patriarchal, aristocratic society with an economic basis of agriculture and a technical basis of muscle-energy," the North turned into "a plutocratic society based on manufacturing and commerce with a technical basis of coal energy." The Dred Scott decision "was the last time that Blood spoke; since then our constitutional law has been the law of Money." After the Civil War, "the nation passed finally under the complete and undisputed control of a plutocracy." Today, America was ruled by "the lords of the trust."

While belief in constitutional rule still remained strong in America, in Europe it was rapidly becoming obsolete:

> In Italy and Germany, inwardly the strongest of the world-powers, no one any longer mentions constitutional law; it is no longer a legal discipline, nor is it even taught in the law academies.[2] In France, always two steps away from another Reign of Terror, no one pretends that constitutional law will afford any more precedents or impose any limitations on the coming annihilation-conflict.

Because constitutional law "was indissolubly wedded" to parliamentarianism, "in the face of powerful extra-parliamentary forces it suddenly became no longer efficacious." World War I "marked the inevitable decline of the bourgeoisie and its peculiar political institution." Since then:

> Western nations have known either proletarian governments, national governments, or military dictatorships, the latter being frankly temporary and provisional. In Rome the course of events was from Patricians and Plebeians, through Optimates and Populares to Pompeians and Caesareans. We stand now at the epoch leading to the last period.

Real politics must therefore become extra-parliamentary:

> When a group drops its Party garb and organizes itself for extra-parliamentary political activity, it is suicide for the opposing group to carry on the game of majorities and rules. This is the significance of the arising in Western Europe of *followings of individuals* instead of the historically dead party formations.

The streets, not the courtrooms, would soon become the centers of the coming struggle:

> Anti-constitutional feeling in the United States comes at present from the Left, as does most of the extra-parliamentary activity. This administration [Roosevelt] has stepped beyond the bounds, not of this or that decision, but of the whole idea of imposing legal limitations on internal political activity. There is yet no focus of resistance to the bolshevization of the nation. May I step once more into the role of vaticinator and say that any effective resis-

tance to it must of necessity be extra-legal and extra-constitutional. An unconstitutional attack demands an unconstitutional defense, and in the struggle the Constitution, even though it be a slogan for one side or the other, will be quietly interred in the vault of History.

For this reason Yockey applauded the formation of right-wing militias like Michigan's Vigilantes, who fought strikers in Detroit's great auto factories. "The cheering example of the quickly formed 'Vigilantes' in the proletarian uprising of last winter" was for Yockey just the kind of extra-parliamentary political activity America needed. He concluded his essay: "Although the slogan of the Vigilantes is 'Law and Order,' it will soon cease to mean the old law, the old order. My last word on the Law of the Constitution thus is: *Requiescat in pace.*"

Yockey's obituary fused Spengler's belief in the coming of Caesarism and Carl Schmitt's contempt for bourgeois "legal positivism" with the gritty reality of Michigan's class struggle, where reasoned debate came perilously close to giving way to a dictatorship of shotguns and baseball bats. In a 29 June 1937 *New York Times* article, F. Raymond Daniel portrayed Michigan as being on the brink of civil war as an army of volunteer strikebreakers and vigilantes made up of merchants, white-collar workers, and farmers led by the American Legion and Veterans of Foreign Wars (VFW) prepared for action against auto workers and left-wing militants. "Baseball bats, shotguns, and rifles have become almost standard equipment of restaurants, filing stations, stores, and bars in many parts of the state," Daniel reported. He noted that "in scores of cities and towns" committees of vigilante leaders held weekly secret meetings to plan strategy. Both the unions and the vigilantes had also developed "elaborate espionage systems, and plotting and intrigue is everywhere."

The vigilantes worked closely with Henry Ford's private security force. Ford was also the most admired American in Nazi Germany for his authorship of *The International Jew* and his role in circulating the bogus *Protocols of the Learned Elders of Zion*. On 5 July 1937 Nazi Propaganda Minister Joseph Goebbels used the pages of *Der Angriff* (Attack) to endorse Ford's fight against the leftist Congress of Industrial Organizations (CIO). He also called upon Fritz Kuhn's German-American Bund to help Ford smash communism and the CIO. Bundists even held joint meetings with the Michigan VFW to support the vigilantes. The sight of superpatriotic VFW members shaking hands with Kuhn's Nazis led *New York Times* reporter Daniel to comment: "It is a strange liaison, this reputed combination of patriots and followers of an alien philosophy with whom are allied a horde of heterogeneous organizations."

"Philosophy of Constitutional Law" was no abstract academic exercise. Yockey spent his summers in Michigan. He even attended an ROTC course one summer at Michigan's Camp Custer. Therefore it is particularly intriguing to wonder how closely Yockey was already tied to the American right and the Bund at the time he wrote his essay.

Yockey left Georgetown in 1938 without graduating. According to his daughter Francesca, the family moved to Arizona for about a year because one family member (most likely Alice, whose nickname was "Wheezer") suffered badly from asthma. According to the FBI's examination of his academic records, Yockey actually graduated from the University of Arizona at Tucson. He then left Arizona and moved to Chicago, where he enrolled in Northwestern's law school, where his Georgetown friend Perry Patterson was also studying.

While in Chicago, Yockey served as a kind of aide-de-camp to a lawyer and important right-wing activist named Newton Jenkins. Born in Ohio, Jenkins was educated at Ohio State and Columbia University's Law School. After serving in World War I, he returned to the Midwest and became legal counsel to many farm groups and agricultural cooperatives. He also began working closely with the Progressive Party. By 1932 Jenkins had established enough of a presence to garner over 400,000 votes in his senatorial bid in that year's Republican primary. He also used his Chicago radio program to support Franklin D. Roosevelt for President.[3] No simple nativist, Jenkins came to fascism from the progressive movement.

The Yockey-Jenkins connection came to the FBI's attention in a curious way. On 31 March 1954, in his "Washington Merry-Go-Round" column, Drew Pearson launched an attack on Soviet ties to the far right. Pearson wrote that the FBI "is most interested in Varange, a mystery man who also goes by the name of Francis Yockey and Frank Healy. He is known to be the author of a book on fascist strategy, urging anti-American, but not anti-Soviet activities."[4]

Pearson's story caught the attention of a former acquaintance of Yockey's from the late 1930s, who then contacted the FBI.[5] The source reported that he had first met Yockey in 1938 in Newton Jenkins' Chicago law office:

> _____ recalls that Yockey was an intense, secretive, bitter individual who did not tolerate anyone who would not wholeheartedly agree with his solution to world problems. He stated that while Yockey would not talk about his own ideas, his actions indicated that he was "completely opposed to people of the Hebrew faith and followed the philosophy of the German Nazis wholeheartedly." _____ stated that Yockey had his own ideas on some of these matters, and that Yockey was "power hungry" and gave the impression that he would not stop until he became the most powerful individual in the world. _____ believes that Yockey will not succeed in this because he creates too many enemies. _____ feels that Yockey will go along with any program whether it stemmed from Moscow, Buenos Aires, Yorkville,

Tokyo, or Washington, D.C., as long as he can be the leader. _____ stated that Yockey believed that the world capitalist structure was about to crumble and that fascism was the only solution, but he insisted that it be the Yockey form of fascism and none other.[6]

The informant also said he

visited Yockey's home one time in 1938. This was his only visit with Yockey and that subject invited him to discuss the German language. _____ stated that Yockey gave the impression that he was testing him on his knowledge of German. _____ made no other visits to Yockey's home. He cannot recall what Yockey's room looked like or where it was located, but recalls the impression that Yockey was living out of a suitcase in a furnished room. He recalled that Yockey had a home in Michigan, where he was supposed to have two sisters, one of whom was engaged to a graduate of the United States Naval Academy at Annapolis. _____ stated that in all his investigations he was unable to discover where Yockey was born, where his parents lived, what his parents' names were, where he got his money, and what his ultimate aim in life was.

As for Newton Jenkins:

He [informant] met subject [Yockey] in Chicago in 1938 through one NEWTON JENKINS (deceased) in JENKINS' office at 39 South La Salle Street, Chicago, Illinois. _____ stated that JENKINS was a "JENKINS progressive," stating that JENKINS' followers were interested primarily in seeing Russia defeated. _____ and JENKINS were active in promoting the America First Committee, the Keep America Out of War Committee, and similar organizations working for the defeat of Russia and Communism.
_____ placed YOCKEY's name on a mailing list of what he described as Nationalist publications but was unable to recall the names of any of these publications, and stated that they were in line with the aims of the followers of NEWTON JENKINS.

Jenkins also maintained extensive ties to the German-American Bund. In his 1940 book *The Fifth Column Is Here*, George Britt noted that Jenkins had built up "one of the most extensive political records of pro-Hitler commitments." Jenkins' attempt to unite fascist and Nazi groups into a third political party led the Bund to christen him *"Der Führer der Dritten Partei"* (The Leader of the Third Party).[7]

Jenkins began his right turn from the reformist left. In 1934 he formed "The Third Party" under the slogan "U.S. Unite!" Party headquarters was 39 South La Salle Street, the same office where the FBI informant met Yockey. Jenkins' new party had its roots in his experience working for the Progressive Party's Robert M. La Follette, the Wisconsin political leader who had received nearly five million votes in his 1924 presidential campaign.[8] In his 1934 pamphlet *The Third Party*, Jenkins portrayed himself as a progressive opposed to big business. He explained that he was founding his new organization because Franklin Roosevelt had backed down on implementing the more radical aspects of the New Deal.[9] In a section called "NATION BETRAYED BY FALSE PROPAGANDA," he warned that the British Empire had too much influence over American foreign policy.[10]

Jenkins made no secret of the fact that he favored active government intervention into the nation's economic affairs, and looked to Mussolini's Italy and Hitler's Germany as models for America. To help build his Third Party, he began making overtures to Hitler's supporters in the "Friends of the New Germany," which soon became the German-American Bund. One of the first Bundists he contacted was Fritz Kuhn. On 16 August 1939, while testifying before the House Committee on Un-American Activities, Kuhn said that he had first met Jenkins in 1935. He helped get Jenkins' party registered in Michigan, where Kuhn was then living. Jenkins also participated in a 1935 meeting with a number of pro-Nazi, pro-Fascist, and nativist "superpatriots" to discuss the formation of a third party. Silver Shirt leader William Dudley Pelley, anti-labor union operative Harry Jung, and Bund leaders Walter Kappe and Fritz Gissibl were prominent attendees. Jenkins regularly held public rallies, including a 30 October 1935 talk at the Lincoln Turner Hall in Chicago. While stormtrooper types with swastika armbands guarded the meeting, Jenkins denounced Jewish control of America.[11]

Jenkins' efforts met with remarkable success, and in 1936 he became campaign manager for the most significant third-party challenge to Franklin Roosevelt. That year, three of America's most important populist leaders met in Cleveland to form the Union Party. They were Father Charles Coughlin, head of the National Union for Social Justice (NUSJ) and the most listened-to radio personality in America; Gerald L. K. Smith, a close associate of the recently assassinated Louisiana Governor Huey Long; and Dr. Francis Townsend, originator of the Townsend plan to help the elderly cope with the Depression financially.

The Union Party nominated former North Dakota Congressman William Lemke as its candidate for President. After the convention ended, some 80,000 to 100,000 people turned out for an outdoor Union Party rally in Chicago to hear Father Coughlin speak.[12] According to Coughlin biographer Sheldon Marcus, Jenkins "was entrusted with a great deal of responsibility" in running the Union Party's day-to-day operations, even though Dr. Townsend considered him too pro-Hitler.[13]

After the Union Party's defeat, Jenkins continued to maintain excellent relations with the Bund and spoke at the Bund's 1937 National Convention at Camp Siegfried in New York.[14] He then launched his own paper, *American Nationalism*, which served as the propaganda arm of yet another Jenkins organization, the American Nationalist Political Action Clubs. The ANPAC aimed to unite over 125 rightist groups into a coordinated movement.[15]

Given Jenkins' prominence inside the Midwest right, it is quite possible that Yockey entered Jenkins' network before he came to Georgetown. He may even have been encouraged to transfer to Georgetown in order to place a brilliant young sympathizer of the new Germany in the School of Foreign Service. As much as he generally hated Georgetown, Yockey's two years there transformed him into a sophisticated exponent of German geopolitics. His attraction to both Spengler and Conservative Revolution theorists like Carl Schmitt also made him virtually unique in the American far right. American supporters of Nazi Germany were usually German-Americans, crude anti-Semitic nativists, or staunch conservatives who viewed Hitler as a heaven-sent bulwark against Bolshevism. Yockey was none of these. His was a case of ideological conversion to a Nazified version of the Weimar "New Right" Conservative Revolutionary current. His time at Georgetown had sharpened his intellectual understanding. Now his political commitment would be tested on the mean streets of Chicago.

Notes:

1. Echoing both Karl Marx and Carl Schmitt, Yockey argues:

> A law conflict is a power conflict, and it can only be settled in the way in which political power conflicts can be settled, i.e., by the sword . . . The constitution idea is an expression of a minority and the conflicts it engenders are conflicts of two minorities. These are class conflicts just as surely as the struggle between Emperor and First Estate, Kings and Parliament (17th and 18th century), are class conflicts. The class which wins gives the law to the rest. Every law is established by a few in the name of the generality.

He then adds: "I most emphatically do not mean to imply that class law in this sense has any similarity to the materialistic stupidities of the valiant class-warriors of the gutter. Economic distinctions rarely by themselves determine a law, and even insofar as they are a factor at all they only have weight within a definite historical period—in our case beginning c. 1820."

2. Although Yockey makes no direct reference to Carl Schmitt in his essay, he does cite a German book on constitutional law.

3. Biographical information on Newton Jenkins from his privately published book *I've Got the Remedy* (Chicago, 1940).

4. Pearson's article was written to call attention to a major exposé of ties between Russia and the far right that was published in the 13 April 1954 issue of the *Reporter* magazine, a well-known liberal investigative journal.

5. The FBI interview took place at Hyattsville, Maryland, on 5 April 1954. Although the informant's name is blacked out, he undoubtedly had some connection to the military. Hyattsville is not far from Andrews Air Force Base, and there

is a note at the end of the interview mentioning the FBI's forwarding a copy of it to the commander of the OSI (Office of Special Investigations) office at Andrews.

6. FBI report BA 105-643.

7. George Britt, *The Fifth Column Is Here* (New York: Wilfred Funk, Inc., 1940), pp. 112–13.

8. See Newton Jenkins' pamphlet *The Third Party* (Chicago, 1934).

9. Jenkins' support for Roosevelt was not an uncommon pattern for other populists who later embraced Hitler. In 1932 Father Coughlin declared: "Roosevelt or Ruin!" and "The New Deal is Christ's Deal!"

10. In *The Third Party*, Jenkins wrote:

All of the present political parties in our country are permeated and directed by insidious international propaganda. Prominent leaders among the republicans, the democrats, the progressives, and socialists are all committed to world citizenship. International propaganda is largely European propaganda. European propaganda is directed almost wholly by the British Empire. The average American would be shocked if told that the British Empire is better represented in all of the existing American political parties than is this, our own country.

Anti-British rhetoric was also regularly used by Chicago Mayor William ("Big Bill" or "Kaiser Bill") Thompson to appeal to German-American and Irish-American voters.

11. Sheldon Marcus, *Father Coughlin: The Tumultuous Life of the Priest of the Little Flower* (Boston: Little, Brown, 1973), pp. 126–27. In *Secret Armies: The New Technique of Nazi Warfare* (New York: Modern Age Books, 1939), pp. 122–23, John Spivak reports that Jenkins told the crowd: "The trouble with this country now is due to the money powers and Jewish politicians who control our Government."

12. Franz Schulze, *Philip Johnson: Life and Work* (New York: Knopf, 1994), pp. 123–24.

13. Marcus, *Father Coughlin*, pp. 126–27.

14. On Jenkins and the Bund meeting, see Marvin Miller, *Wunderlich's Salute* (Smithtown, NY: Malamud-Rose Publishers, 1983), p. 32.

15. See the House Committee on Un-American Activities testimony of John Metcalfe on 5 October 1938.

UNDER VESUVIUS (1938-1945)

The secret of the greatest fruitfulness and the greatest enjoyment of life is: to live dangerously! Build your cities under Vesuvius!

    —*Friedrich Nietzsche*, The Gay Science

The revolver in the hip-pocket is an American invention.

    —*Oswald Spengler*, The Hour of Decision

10
"THE TRAGEDY
OF YOUTH"

Once he was back in Chicago, Yockey quickly established close ties to the
German-American Bund, Father Coughlin's Christian Front, and William
Dudley Pelley's Silver Shirts. His affiliations were no doubt helped by his
association with Newton Jenkins.[1] Although Yockey had returned to Chicago
to attend Northwestern University's law school, he was far more interested in
political action than case law. During his time at Northwestern, he made just
average grades. He was also unhappy with the school's political climate, and
later claimed that it "was nothing but a group of Negroes, Jews, and
Communists."[2] In June 1939 he transferred to De Paul Law School for the
1940 term.[3]

Yockey spent much of his time in the dangerous world of far-right politics.
During the 1930s fierce battles regularly took place in Chicago's streets and
meeting halls, where Bundists fought Jewish and left-wing activists from
tough ethnic neighborhoods.[4] Some of the most active far-right street fighters
came from the Silver Legion, more popularly known as the Silver Shirts
because of the group's distinctive uniform.

The Silver Shirts had been formed in January 1933 by William Dudley
Pelley, a popular spiritualist turned far-right agitator.[5] In 1933 Pelley
approached the German-American Bund (then called the Friends of New
Germany) to form a political alliance. He then began pouring out tracts
denouncing the Illuminati and blaming Jewish merchants for the black slave
trade. He even claimed that "demon" spirits inhabited Jewish bodies.[6]

The Silver Legion reached its peak in 1934 with some 15,000 members. By
1938, the organization had shrunk to 5,000 believers, who were split between

two tendencies: Pelley's more "new age" supporters saw the organization primarily as an extension of its founder's metaphysical theories, while the group's political wing stressed the need for more "action"-oriented political tactics.[7] The action faction was particularly strong in Chicago. Chicago *Daily Times* reporter John Metcalfe attended a Silver Shirt rally on 8 August 1938, where he heard the group's "Field Marshall," Roy Zachary, tell some 200 followers that the Roosevelt administration was on the brink of setting up a full-scale Communist dictatorship. Zachary claimed that the day was soon coming "when the Silver Shirts will succeed to the point that no orthodox Jew will be permitted to testify in a court or cast a ballot in America," and advised his supporters "to go out and get guns" and "plenty of ammunition" to "prepare for the Communist revolution that is coming to America."[8]

The ties between the Bund, the Silver Shirts, and Newton Jenkins became especially evident after Jenkins took up the cause of four Chicago Silver Shirts who had been arrested in late October 1939 for painting swastikas and smashing windows at a Jewish-owned department store. The incident generated considerable notoriety because it reminded many Americans of the horrors of *Kristallnacht* ("The Night of Broken Glass," when German mobs destroyed Jewish stores in a pogrom-like outburst) just a year earlier. In his book *I've Got the Remedy*, Jenkins minimized the department store incident as a late-night prank that occurred after the men had attended "some sort of an anti-Jewish Halloween dance."[9]

Homer Maerz, the leader of the arrested fascists, had served as a liaison between the German-American Bund and the Silver Shirts. He was bailed out of jail by William Wernecke, a leading Chicago Bundist and the former head of the Bund's local security unit, the *Ordnungdienst* (Order Service).[10] Wernecke, who knew Yockey well, was also a member of Newton Jenkins' inner circle.[11] According to left-wing journalist John Spivak, Wernecke could "usually be found at 30 North La Salle Street, Chicago, where he poses as a broker. Most of his time is spent in the office of Newton Jenkins."[12]

In the late 1930s, Yockey became a regular speaker at far-right functions in the Chicago area. In a 13 December 1951 FBI summary of Yockey's activities, an informant (described as "having considerable contact" with the Bund), reported that in 1940 Yockey "traveled under the name of Francis Parker and lectured under that name and posed as an international law authority at meetings where he lectured."[13] The source also said that in 1939 he

had attended a meeting of the Silver Shirts at WILLIAM A. WERNECKE's farm near Chicago at which meeting FRANCIS PARKER YOCKEY was the speaker. This source advised that YOCKEY had told him that he was the author of several articles for *Social Justice*.[14]

Yockey's first known political article, "The Tragedy of Youth," appeared in the 21 August 1939 issue of Father Coughlin's *Social Justice.* "The Tragedy of Youth" was subtitled "Their Generation, Now Unemployed, Must Fight the War then Become Slaves in the Red State that Follows," and the article proved as leaden as its subtitle. In it Yockey described á "Left Army, an army which now includes labor unions, WPA workers, those on relief, organized Negroes, the teachers and professors, and the greater part of youth." He then warned "those serious-minded youths, who are genuinely interested in the tremendous problems now facing us" about an "insidious attack":

Books have been written, plays have been staged, and an unending train of lecturers have mounted the platform—all to convey to these thinking youths the same message of class war and international hatred . . . The result of this campaign to destroy Christian Americanism among the youth is that *every periodical, 95 per cent of the books, and all the lecturers are Leftists.* Leftist ideas are a part of the very atmosphere which American youth breathes.

"Unless a powerful Christian nationalism arises," liberals would use a new war with "foreign governments which have liquidated class war within their nations" to impose a "repressive war-dictatorship" on America.[15]

"The Tragedy of Youth" also included a *de rigueur* attack on Jewish ("alien-minded minority") control of the media:

The alien-minded minority in control of the cinema, the radio, and the newspaper and magazine press has poured out a constant stream of propaganda with the intent of gaining complete spiritual power over the minds of young Americans emerging into maturity. With what success the attempt has met everyone knows who has talked on their own level to representative American youths from the ages of 19 to 27. One and all their worldviews have been cut out for them in New York, Hollywood, and Washington.

Thanks to FDR and MGM,

appalling numbers of youth have been led into a cynical ultra-sophisticated attitude which regards drinking as a badge of social aptitude, which makes a fetish of sport, and professes eroticism as a way of life. A perverted and insane pictorial art, lewd exhibitionist dancing, and jungle music form the spiritual norm of this sector of America's youth.

Despite Yockey's fervent "Is American youth to wait supinely, absorbed in picture magazines, for the butchers to start their blood bath here?" and his call to arms ("Youth of America—*Awake!*"), "The Tragedy of Youth" was significant not for the originality of its message but as evidence that its author was an up-and-coming star in the far right.[16]

A few weeks before "The Tragedy of Youth" was published, *Social Justice* devoted a great deal of coverage to a group called the Christian Front.[17] Founded in Brooklyn in 1938 by a law student named John Cassidy, the Christian Front was attempting to expand into the Midwest.[18] In its 17 August 1939 issue, *Social Justice* carried words of praise for the Christian Front from Father Coughlin himself. "The Tragedy of Youth," then, may have been part of a Christian Front recruitment drive.

Just as "The Tragedy of Youth" appeared, American politics was thrown into turmoil with the announcement of a non-aggression treaty between Germany and the Soviet Union. The Hitler-Stalin Pact paved the way for Germany's invasion of Poland on 1 September 1939, and the subsequent division of Polish territory between Berlin and Moscow. The Hitler-Stalin Pact stunned the right as much as the left. Since the early 1930s, nativists had ceaselessly denounced Roosevelt for being in league with Communism. Yet it was Hitler who had now openly embraced Stalin. An article in the 21 August 1939 Silver Shirt publication *The Weekly Liberation* summed up the common reaction to news of the Pact: "Consternation that bordered on stupefaction was general throughout the world."

The Hitler-Stalin Pact opened up strange new possibilities in American politics. Communist speakers began denouncing the imperialist British Empire, praising Hitler's political realism, and declaring that "the Yanks aren't coming" to fight in another European "inter-imperialist war." Although Roosevelt easily defeated Wendell Willkie (a foreign policy interventionist like FDR) in the 1940 presidential campaign, there was a tremendous undercurrent of voter unease over America's becoming again caught up in a war in Europe. Many German-Americans and Irish-Americans voted Republican. Only the overwhelmingly Democratic "solid South" kept the election from being close.[19] By a very large number, Americans also opposed large-scale Jewish emigration to the United States.

Many progressives, pacifists, and idealistic college students began looking to a new isolationist and anti-war organization called America First, officially launched in September 1940, to keep America out of any future war. America First supporters included such leading liberals as Protestant theologian Harry Emerson Fosdick, Adam Clayton Powell, Sr., and Dorothy Detzer, head of the Women's International League for Peace.[20] To attract liberal and moderate elements, America First expelled Silver Shirts from its local chapters and asked the FBI to investigate any Nazi infiltrators.[21] At an America First rally in New York's Madison Square Garden, the liberal journalist and rally chairman John Flynn denounced a leading Coughlinite agitator in the audience named Joe McWilliams (dubbed "Joe McNazi" by the press). "I repudiate the support of the Bund, the Communists, and the fascist parties," Flynn shouted.[22] His outburst, however, did not end right-wing connections to

America First, because the nativists (and Father Coughlin's forces in particular) were too important to completely ignore.[23]

With Charles Lindbergh, America First found a perfect candidate to court the right. "Lucky Lindy" toured Germany in the 1930s and liked what he saw. Back in America, he began sounding like Oswald Spengler with a midwest twang. In a *Reader's Digest* article called "Aviation, Geography, and Race" that could have come from the "White World Revolution" chapter of Spengler's *The Hour of Decision*, Lindbergh wrote:

> Racial strength is vital—politics, a luxury. . . . It is time to turn from our quarrels and to build our White ramparts again. This alliance with foreign races means nothing but death to us. It is our turn to guard our heritage from Mongol and Persian and Moor, before we become engulfed in a limitless foreign sea. Our civilization depends on a united strength among ourselves; on a strength too great for foreign armies to challenge; on a Western Wall of race and arms which can hold back either Genghis Khan or the infiltration of inferior blood.[24]

America First also received support from Philip La Follette, Wisconsin's three-time governor and Progressive Party leader, who regularly appeared at its rallies. While he never joined the organization, La Follette saw America First as the seed crystal of a new third-party challenge to the Democratic and Republican parties.

The rise of America First to political respectability (combined with Hitler's stunning military victories) made Roosevelt's political future look bleak.[25] According to historian Saul Friedländer, if it had not been for the Japanese attack on Pearl Harbor, "the American isolationists might have succeeded in keeping the United States from intervening in the conflict."[26] As German victories continued to multiply, a new third party could challenge Roosevelt during the 1942 races for the U.S. House and Senate.[27] By 1944, such a party could be in a position to field a serious candidate for president, something that the Union Party had been incapable of accomplishing in 1936.

Newton Jenkins could hardly wait, so bedazzled had he become with the "two beacon lights," Hitler and Mussolini:

> The influence of the two beacon lights has perhaps only begun. The Hitler light shines brightly down toward the Black Sea . . . The beacon lights from Rome already shine far down into the heart of Africa. A new power is abroad in the heart of the Nile. New hope stirs the hearts of the people in the hot lands throughout Africa. Then over in Asia the teeming millions see the lights of Mussolini. He is becoming the white hope of the people of Arabia and India. The old British Empire is in jitters in both Arabia and India. For the British Empire, unless she cuts loose from Jewish influences, the sun is sinking toward the horizon. For Mussolini the beacon light leads his way toward these new fields where millions dwell.

Hitler likewise hears the call of the East. His light is apparently being seen far from home in the East. He has worked out an economic arrangement with Turkey. Down toward the Persian Sea the people are calling to him. The Blue Danube is to be deepened to the Black Sea. Far beyond, the Hitler light has reached Baghdad. Don't be surprised to see a new route to India stretching all the way from the North Sea.[28]

After the Union Party's defeat in 1936, Jenkins continued to maintain its national headquarters in Chicago, while its former presidential candidate William Lemke ignored reports that Jenkins was allowing Bundist and pro-Nazi groups to use the Party apparatus. But with the dissolution of the Union Party in 1938, Jenkins was driven into semi-clandestine activity.[29] Now the "two beacons" seemed ready to illuminate his own return to political power.

While the Hitler-Stalin Pact had the potential to radically change American politics, it also caused major disruptions inside the far right. What were Father Coughlin's supporters, many of whom were Catholic anti-Communists from Eastern Europe or the Ukraine, to make of Hitler's helping Stalin murder their relatives? One would-be American Führer named Raymond Joseph Healy became so disgusted by the German-Soviet alliance that he completely turned against his former comrades, including Yockey. In September 1940, Healy publicly chronicled the sub-rosa world of the Chicago right. If Chicagoans had missed "The Tragedy of Youth," they could now read about its author in one of their major local papers.

Notes:
1. By the late 1930s Jenkins had become a figure of considerable prominence on the right. He had run for mayor of Chicago in 1936 on the Union Party ticket (in Illinois, the Union Progressives) with strong backing from the Bund. The Union Progressive candidate for Illinois governor, former Chicago mayor William Hale ("Big Bill") Thompson, also courted Bund support. Thompson, however, only managed to attract a little over one hundred thousand out of the almost four million votes cast for governor. See David Bennett, *Demagogues and the Depression* (New Brunswick, N.J.: Rutgers University Press, 1975), pp. 245–46.

In Chicago, the Union Progressives were formed as a merger of Coughlinite groups with Harrison Parker's Cooperative Party and Jenkins' Unionists. See Lloyd Wendt and Herman Kahn, *Big Bill of Chicago* (Indianapolis: Bobbs-Merrill, 1953), pp. 343–44. Also see Reinhard Luthin, *American Demagogues* (Boston: Beacon Press, 1954). The Union for Democratic Action in 1942 put out a pamphlet entitled *The People vs. the Chicago Tribune*, which reported that a Chicago political figure named Curly McCarthy had ties to Jenkins. Jenkins is also mentioned in Richard Rollins, *I Find Treason: The Story of an American Anti-Nazi Agent* (New York: William Morrow, 1940), pp. 77–78. In his book *In Hitler's Shadow* (Port Washington: Kennikat Press, 1973), Leland Bell reports that the Bund held a meeting on 4 December 1936 in Chicago to unite Italian, German, Polish, Ukrainian, and Russian organizations in an anti-Communist front. This meeting may have been organized by Jenkins, who worked tirelessly to form a united right.

2. Yockey complained about Northwestern to James Haritage, an assistant field director of the American Red Cross who met Yockey in June 1951 and was interviewed by U.S. Army intelligence on 4 October 1951.

3. Yockey's sister Vinette had also attended De Paul.

4. One Jewish street fighter, Jack Rubenstein, later achieved fame as Jack Ruby.

5. Arthur Schlesinger, Jr., has described Pelley's magazine *Liberation* as "a mad mixture of astrology, spiritualism, radiotherapy, anti-Semitism, and Nazism." (Schlesinger, *The Age of Roosevelt: The Politics of Upheaval* [Boston: Houghton Mifflin, 1960], p. 81.) For a detailed discussion of Pelley's mix of mysticism and fascism, see Leo Riboffo, *The Old Christian Right: The Protestant Far Right from the Depression to the Cold War* (Philadelphia: Temple University Press, 1983). For an interesting discussion of some of Pelley's occult ideas, see Michael Barkun, *Religion and the Racist Right: The Origins of the Christian Identity Movement* (Chapel Hill: University of North Carolina Press, 1997). After World War II Pelley became interested in UFOs. For a literary satire that mocked "the National Revolutionary Party" or "Leather Shirts," see Nathaniel West's 1930s novella, *A Cool Million* (New York: Noonday Press, 1963).

6. Pelley also reported that Jesus would return soon. The Silver Shirt publication *Liberation* even published photos of the "materialized Jesus" sent in by "responsible persons."

7. Riboffo, *The Old Christian Right*, p. 65.

8. Cited in a report on the Silver Shirts in the John Metcalfe collection in the Hoover Institute.

9. Newton Jenkins, *I've Got the Remedy* (Chicago, December 1940), p. 37.

10. Maerz was found guilty of malicious mischief and spent about a year in prison. After being freed, he immediately founded a Nazi propaganda agency in Chicago called the Pioneer News Agency. In the fall of 1941, in a raid on Maerz's residence, congressional investigators reportedly found more than half a ton of "anti-Semitic, pro-fascist, pro-German, and pro-Japanese literature." See Michael Sayers and Albert Kahn, *The Plot Against the Peace* (New York: George Braziller, 1945), pp. 175–76.

11. The far-right author Eustace Mullins, who knew Wernecke, told me that Wernecke was independently wealthy thanks to his mother, a former secretary to the president of Standard Oil. According to Mullins, Wernecke's mother stole some Standard Oil charts and sold them for a considerable amount of money that she then invested in the Chicago real estate market. Her son later took over the business.

12. John Spivak, *The Shrine of the Silver Dollar* (New York: Modern Age Books, 1940), p. 156. Spivak called his book *The Shrine of the Silver Dollar* because Father Coughlin, who was dedicated to returning the United States to the silver standard, used contributions to his radio program to speculate on silver. Spivak says that Newton Jenkins was close to Walter Baertschi, the president of Coughlin's Social Justice publication house. Spivak also claimed to have an affidavit from someone

who had spoken to Wernecke at a 8 February 1939 Bund meeting in Chicago quoting Wernecke as saying that he had just returned from an important meeting with Father Coughlin in Michigan.

13. The source may well have been a former rightist named Ray Healy, who knew Yockey.

14. From an FBI report by Agent John E. Moore, 3 July 1952, Chicago, "Internal Security—Canada—Security Matter—X" 100-25647. This report is a major FBI summary of Yockey's activities and is based in part on Army Intelligence files.

15. The notion that Roosevelt was planning a dictatorship was standard right-wing rhetoric. During the Union Party campaign in the fall of 1936, Father Coughlin "predicted that if Roosevelt were re-elected, 'the red flag of Communism would be raised in this country by 1940 . . . The Communists are coming out for Mr. Roosevelt and he lacks the courage to denounce them.'" See Geoffrey Smith, *To Save a Nation: American Countersubversives, the New Deal, and the Coming of World War II* (New York: Basic Books, 1973), p. 47.

16. When "The Tragedy of Youth" appeared in *Social Justice*, it was advertised on the front page.

17. On Coughlin's role in creating the Christian Front, see Smith, *To Save a Nation*, pp. 132–33.

18. For a critical analysis of the Christian Front, see Theodore Irwin, *Inside the Christian Front* (American Council on Public Affairs, Washington D.C.). Irwin writes:

> While outside New York what is known as the Christian Front is wholly a membership setup, perhaps affiliated with or screened by State Social Justice clubs and superpatriotic bodies, at headquarters it also serves the more ominous function of a loosely knit coalition acting for a score or more groups openly Fascist in sympathies. . . . Full blown in New York, the movement more recently has sprouted in key cities throughout the nation. Organization meetings of the Front, scheduled for the fall in many cities, became "neutrality" rallies when the arms-embargo issue arose.

19. See Robert Herzstein, *Roosevelt and Hitler* (New York: Paragon House, 1989), p. 353, for an analysis of the vote.

20. Yockey was also involved in America First and convinced Perry Patterson to join the group.

21. See Justus Doenecke's introduction to the papers of America First in *In Danger Undaunted: The Papers of America First* (Stanford, CA: Hoover Institute Press, 1990), fn. 49, p. 71.

22. John Roy Carlson, *Under Cover* (New York: E. P. Dutton, 1943), pp. 251–52. On behalf of America First, Flynn wrote a letter to the Bund asking Bundists not to join America First.

23. See Wayne Cole's analysis in his book *America First* (Madison, WI: University of Wisconsin Press, 1953).

24. Quoted in O. John Rogge, *The Official German Report* (New York: Thomas Yoseloff, 1961), p. 281. After Lindbergh made a speech that identified the "Jews"

as one American group opposed to isolationism, he was criticized by other elements inside America First.

25. German success in Russia was seen as a pivot to break the interventionist forces in America. From a note in the journal in the German naval general staff of 8 July 1941:

> Since the Führer hopes that the imminent collapse of the Soviet Union will have an important effect on the attitude of Great Britain and the United States, it is absolutely essential that all incidents with the United States should be avoided. [Quoted in Saul Friedländer, *Prelude to Downfall: Hitler and the United States/1939–1941* (New York: Knopf, 1967), p. 255.]

26. Ibid., p. 303.

27. America First was also seen as a potential stalking horse for a new third party. See Ladislas Farago, *The Game of Foxes: The Untold Story of German Espionage in the United States and Great Britain During World War II* (New York: David McKay, 1971).

28. Newton Jenkins, *The Republic Reclaimed*, p. 78. Jenkins' vision reinforces Arthur Schlesinger, Jr.'s observation in *The Age of Roosevelt: The Politics of Upheaval* (p. 95), that to "the intelligent pro-fascist" the lesson was clear that if fascism was to come to America, "it would not do so under its own steam. It could happen here only as a by-product of fascist triumph in the world. Insofar as the American fascists had a serious existence after 1935, it was only as agents, conscious or inadvertent, of Adolf Hitler."

29. Ibid. Jenkins even had to create his own semi-clandestine political movement. From *The Republic Reclaimed* (pp. 10–12):

> On a hot night in July in 1939 on the fourth floor of an old dilapidated building in the heart of the Chicago loop, three or four hundred women and men, sweating and fanning away through a three-hour session, adopted a proclamation which concerned their country . . .
>
> In view of the repeatedly demonstrated weakness of many men and women in public office . . . their abject stultification to Jewish influence and power . . . there shall be no rolls or rosters kept and there shall be no memberships in this movement until such time as this provision may be modified. We take this precaution not to operate secretly but because we have no right to contribute the names of innocent patriots to the organized witch-hunters who infest our country.
>
> In view of the high standing of Newton Jenkins . . . we hereby request and urge him to accept the national chairmanship of this movement through its formative period until such time as in his judgment it shall appear appropriate to him to set up a permanent organization.

Jenkins' movement also voted to deny membership to Jews.

11

"I DID HITLER'S DIRTY WORK IN CHICAGO"

On 17 September 1940 the *Daily Times* of Chicago published the first install-
ment of "I Did Hitler's Dirty Work in Chicago," a series of insider exposés on
the Chicago far right by Raymond Joseph Healy. At 26, Healy had extensive
fascist credentials. In 1934 the self-proclaimed "Irish-American Hitler"
attended training sessions at a Bund-sponsored "Aryan university" in the
Yorkville section of Manhattan.[1] With Bund support, Healy organized a series
of front groups that included the Irish-American Patriots, the Gentile Workers
Party, the American Business Men's and Consumers' Defense, the American
Mothers Against War and Communism, and the American Federation of
Youth.[2] The Bund also financed *The Key*, Healy's anti-Semitic paper.[3] Healy's
Damascus turn came after the Hitler-Stalin Pact ruined his faith in fascism.[4]

Healy's defection also came at a time when the Bund was collapsing.
Although Fritz Kuhn's Amerikadeutscher Volksbund was loyal to the Third
Reich, the German government, particularly the Foreign Ministry, despised
the "Blunderbund."[5] With U.S. congressional committees regularly making
sport of blackjack-toting Bundists, Berlin decided in 1937 to build a new and
far more sophisticated propaganda apparatus in the United States.[6] Hans
Thomsen, the German chargé d'affaires, organized a complex campaign to
neutralize (if not win) the hearts and minds of America.[7] Under his leadership
a series of propaganda outlets, including the New York–based German Library
of Information, the Flanders Hall publishing house, the American Fellowship
Forum, and Manfried Zapp's Trans-Ocean news service, helped encourage the

growth of "Fortress America" isolationism. Thomsen worked closely with George Sylvester Viereck, a well-known German-American poet, novelist, and essayist who had been Germany's main American propagandist in World War I. Together, they coordinated a propaganda and lobbying effort that had the multi-talented Viereck virtually writing speeches for isolationist congressmen.

In January 1938 Berlin ordered all German nationals to leave the Bund. The Bund was also forbidden to use the Party insignia, and Kuhn was warned that, if he chose to visit Germany, he would only be received by a low-level delegate from the *Volksdeutsche Mittelstelle* (the German People's Central Authority). Nor could he publicly discuss Bund affairs while in Germany.[8] When Kuhn did return to the Fatherland in February 1938, he was virtually ignored.

In the fall of 1938 the Bund began a series of desperate attempts to reach out to "patriotic" networks inside the nativist right to prove its continued usefulness to Berlin. Kuhn even flirted with the idea of merging the Bund with the Italian Black Shirts, Anastase Andre Vonsiatsky's Russian Nationalist Revolutionary Party, Donald Shea's National Gentile League, and similar groups. Bund gatherings now included "anti-British working-class Irish, Russian emigrés, Italian ex-servicemen, Coughlinites, and lower-middle-class and working-class nativist Americans."[9] At Bund rallies, pictures of Hitler and George Washington were prominently displayed side by side.

With the announcement of the Nazi-Soviet Pact in late August 1939, Kuhn's "American turn" exploded like a trick cigar. How could Ukrainians, Czechs, Poles, and Irishmen who worshiped the Pope, the Virgin Mary, General Franco, and Adolf Hitler, in that order, accept Germany's entente with the Red Devil Stalin? Fights broke out between Bundists and Christian Mobilizers.[10] The Bund also faced opposition from the covert intelligence wing of the United States government.[11] FDR asked Army Intelligence (G-2) in 1937 to launch an investigation of the Bund's paramilitary training camps. The Army, in turn, sent the problem to the Justice Department, which put the FBI on the case. Although the Department of Justice concluded that the Bund was *not* engaged in illegal activities, a renewed government investigation began in June 1939, under the pretense of enforcing the Foreign Agents Registration Act. This time the FBI coordinated its activity with both G-2 and the Office of Naval Intelligence (ONI).[12]

On 5 December 1939 Fritz Kuhn was convicted on larceny and forgery charges and sent to Sing Sing. Ten days later, the Bund's new leader, Gerhard Wilhelm Kunze, abandoned any plans to merge the Bund with other groups. He also withdrew Bund funding from Ray Healy's *The Key*. With encouragement from Berlin, many former Bundists chose to return to Germany.[13]

Meanwhile, a new, more sophisticated organization called the German-American National Alliance (GANA—also known as the *Einheitsfront* or United Front) attempted to repair the damage caused by the Bund. According to Sander Diamond, the most prominent historian of the Bund, as far as Berlin was concerned, "GANA had taken the place of the Bund in the Midwest."[14] In its bid for respectability, GANA purged its first secretary, Homer Maerz, the Chicago Silver Shirt later arrested for smashing windows at a Jewish-owned department store.[15]

By late 1939 a strange series of events, including the Hitler-Stalin Pact and the intensified campaign by *both* the German and American governments to break the Bund, had led to the marginalization of action-oriented fascists like Ray Healy and Homer Maerz. Still, hard-core Bund organizers like William Wernecke, who headed the Chicago Bund's paramilitary organization and intelligence service, the Ordnungdienst, tried to help out jailed comrades like Maerz.

Yockey was a member of Wernecke's network, and his name first appeared in Ray Healy's final *Daily Times* article, on 22 September 1940, in this context. Healy wrote:

Wernecke, through his "Joint Committee of Patriotic Organizations," attempted last year [1939] to arrange a mass meeting at which Father Coughlin was to speak. The meeting never was held but preliminary plans for it were made...I became chairman of an organization we called the "Friends of Father Coughlin" and spoke at meetings to protest against the arrest and conviction of the men involved in a department store window-breaking. The handbills called me "author, lecturer, editor, and political authority." Meetings arranged by Wernecke were held at Link's Hall, 3435 N. Sheffield, and at the Swiss club house, 639 Webster.

Another speaker was billed as "Francis Parker, University of Virginia, noted international law authority." Actually he is an anti-Semite named Yockey, a law student who was a busboy at the Arcade Cafeteria, 32 S. Clark.[16]

Healy reported that Mrs. Lois de Lafayette Washburn, the leader of the National Liberty Party (NLP) and a prominent figure on the nativist right, was much taken by Yockey.[17] According to Healy, when Washburn tried to get the NLP organized in Chicago in April 1939, "she suggested that 'some orator like Yockey read the NLP book' at a meeting."

Less than two weeks before Healy's first article was published, Yockey left Chicago for Notre Dame's law school. Notre Dame's records show that he applied for admission for the fall term on 5 September 1940. South Bend was to prove the last and happiest stop on Yockey's ramshackle tour through American academia.[18] He later said that Notre Dame was the only school he had ever enjoyed.[19] While there, he met Charles MacFarlane, an undergraduate from San Antonio, Texas, whose father had been a Texas Supreme Court Justice. When Yockey visited the MacFarlane family over the 1941 Easter break, he met his future wife, Alice; like her brother and future husband, she was a committed fascist.[20]

After graduating *cum laude* from Notre Dame's law school on 1 June 1941, Yockey passed the Michigan law board. He then returned to Chicago. On 31 January 1941, his oldest sister Vinette married William Coyne, a Chicago-born engineer and graduate of the U.S. Naval Academy at Annapolis.[21] Yockey lived with his brother-in-law and two sisters at 6341 North Greenview in Chicago throughout the fall of 1941. He also studied for the Illinois bar and, on 9 March 1942, became eligible to practice law in Illinois.

While they were living on North Greenview, the family became involved in a bizarre personal dispute that marked the first known entry of the FBI into Yockey's life. Incredibly, it was the Yockeys who went to the FBI, with a strange tale of an evil tormentor who had accused them of being "Nazi spies." Equally incredible was the fact that the object of their wrath was not Ray Healy but William Wernecke, one of the leaders of the Chicago far right who had worked closely with Yockey!

In a 1952 summary of the Yockey case, FBI Agent John Moore noted: "On November 15, 1941, a WILLIAM COYNE, 6341 North Greenview, Chicago, Illinois, appeared at the Chicago Office of the FBI with his wife and one ALICE YOCKEY to make a complaint against one WILLIAM WERNECKE." Then, on 26 November 1941, Yockey sent a letter to the State Bar of Michigan that shed some light on the content of the Coynes' conversation with the FBI. He told Bar officials:

> I have reason to suspect that a certain person in Chicago has recently sent you a letter concerning me and concerning vicious libels on my character. My reasons for the suspicions are these: My sister, ALYCE LOUISE YOCKEY,[22] who is an X-ray technician, incurred the hatred of this man by befriending a certain young lady whom he was persecuting. When he discovered this, he called my sister's employer and slandered my sister viciously, saying he was a representative of the Federal Bureau of Investigation, and that my sister was an agent of the German government and a peddler of narcotics. He also slandered, in the presence of many witnesses, the character of my other sister and my brother-in-law W. D. COYNE. He further called the employer of my brother-in-law, who is a graduate of the United States Naval Academy and working as an engineer on defense contracts—and, again saying he was an agent of the Federal Bureau of Investigation, said that my brother-in-law was stealing plans and transferring them to the Japanese Government. He further slandered all of us by saying that we were dope addicts, peddlers of narcotics, kidnappers, and keepers of a house of ill fame.

From the above you will no doubt understand why I suspect that this man may have written to you. The members of my family and I are going to pursue our legal remedies, and therefore, if you have received any libelous matter concerning me, I request that you send it to me for evidentiary purposes, or at least a copy of it. The man in question is WILLIAM WERNECKE. When we notified the Federal Bureau of Investigation of these instances, we learned that they have a thick file on this man's subversive activities, but that so far he has eluded the law.

I passed the bar examination given last June in Ann Arbor, but as I understand it, I am not a full member of the Michigan Bar Association until January, when the dues are payable. Nevertheless, I suspect that this man has written to you in the hope of damaging my character.[23]

The Yockeys took Wernecke's attacks so seriously that they apparently tried to get him arrested for impersonating an FBI agent. But why would Wernecke lash out so violently against the Yockeys, and Alice in particular? Alice Yockey's name surfaces in the FBI files in a most unusual way. One mention comes from the FBI informant who first met Yockey in Newton Jenkins' Chicago office. The informant reported

that one of YOCKEY's sisters was interested in the Keep America Out of War Committee in Chicago in 1940 or 1941. He recalled that he was told that one of YOCKEY's sisters came to a meeting of this organization with Herbert Hans HAUPT, one of the eight German saboteurs who was executed by the United States as an espionage agent. _____ did not know the names of Yockey's sisters.[24]

The FBI learned that Alice Yockey had ties to Herbert Haupt just two days after Haupt's arrest in Chicago on charges of being a German agent. According to FBI document CG 100-25647: "On June 29, 1942 _____ advised SA H. E. SPLENDORE that HERBERT HANS HAUPT, convicted German saboteur, had been friendly with YOCKEY and his sister, ALICE YOCKEY."

The appearance of Herbert Hans Haupt leads us into the difficult question of Yockey's ties to a German sabotage operation ironically code-named "Operation Pastorius," after the leader of the first German settlement in America, Franz Daniel Pastorius. Operation Pastorius began in the summer of 1942 when eight Nazi saboteurs, including Haupt, were sent by U-boat to America to carry out a campaign of economic sabotage and terror.

Haupt was the youngest member of the team. Born in Germany in 1919, he came to America when he was five years old. After finishing high school, he became extremely active in the Chicago Bund. He also became a friend of William Wernecke, who led the Bund's uniformed mini-Gestapo, the Ordnungdienst. Wernecke had a small armory of rifles, shotguns, and other weapons that he kept on his farm just outside Chicago (the same farm where

Yockey spoke in 1939). Haupt and Wernecke regularly visited the farm for target practice.

In 1939 Haupt became involved with a woman named Gerda Stuckmann Melind, who worked at a local beauty salon. Melind first met Haupt either at the Germania club or the Haus Vaterland, the local Bund headquarters, where Wernecke ran the Aryan Bookstore.[25] Although Haupt and Melind became engaged, their relationship came to an abrupt end in June 1941, when Haupt suddenly disappeared from Chicago. Melind later recalled that on several occasions Haupt had mentioned wanting to go to Mexico, "but changed his mind several times. The last time I saw him he said he was not going to Mexico, that he wanted to stay in Chicago." She only discovered that he had abandoned her after getting a card from St. Louis reporting that he was on his way to California.[26] Haupt's decision must have seemed particularly harsh since Melind was pregnant with his child.[27]

Alice Yockey was a friend of Herbert Haupt. But what was her relationship with Gerda Melind? It is possible that she may have befriended Melind after Haupt left her. In his letter to the Michigan Bar, Yockey calls the lady in question "a certain young woman." Melind was three years younger than Alice Yockey, and both women may have blamed Wernecke for ordering Haupt to leave Chicago and abandon Melind.

What seems beyond dispute is that Haupt's decision to disappear from Chicago was linked to the Bund underground. In October 1942 Haupt's former friend William Liebl told a Chicago court that was trying Haupt's parents for treason that his vanishing act was tied to a sub-rosa war between the Bund and the FBI. According to the 29 October 1942 *Daily Times* of Chicago:

> Herbert Hans Haupt, the executed Nazi saboteur, escaped death by gunfire from FBI agents as he swam the Rio Grande in an escape to Mexico before going to Berlin, a surprise witness revealed today at the treason trial. It was the first revelation that FBI agents were onto Haupt's trail even before he became a secret agent trained by the German high command. The witness was William Liebl, a native Chicagoan and a Marine private stationed at San Diego, Calif., who testified Haupt had revealed to him in Stuttgart, Germany, that the FBI had been "trailing him for spreading propaganda."

The 20-year-old Liebl was born in Chicago but had moved with his family to Germany in 1935, after his father was offered a job there. He returned to the United States in June 1942 "through diplomatic exchange" and enlisted in the Marines. He recalled Haupt telling him

> that he and two buddies ditched their car at the border to escape agents who were "trailing him for spreading Nazi propaganda." Haupt and one other, Wolfgang Wergin . . . got away with their lives. The other, reported to be Hugo E. Prouskin, was killed.

Haupt then told Liebl that he had contacted the German consul in Mexico City after leaving the United States, and was given money to charter a plane to South America. He and Wergin later went to San Francisco "and with funds obtained from the German consul there went to Yokohama, whence they were taken on a blockade runner around Africa to Germany." Haupt was a lieutenant in the German army when he contacted Liebl. He said that he had been instructed to meet with him by Walter Kappe, a former Bund newspaper editor turned German officer who directed the spy school that trained Haupt.[28]

The story behind the covert war between Haupt and the FBI, like the origin of the feud between Wernecke and the Yockey family, may never be fully known. In the case of the Yockeys and Wernecke, however, it is worth noting that it took place in late November 1941, a time when the Chicago right must have been feeling extremely confident about the future. Each day brought new headlines about spectacular German military victories. By late November, when advance Wehrmacht units could literally see the spires of Moscow in their field glasses, Hitler seemed on the verge of creating an invincible new empire. No one could know that Pearl Harbor was less than two weeks away.

Despite the turmoil inside the far right, Yockey, on the surface at least, pursued a normal career for a young man just out of law school. For a few months he worked as an attorney at the Thompson and Lannin law firm in Mount Vernon, Illinois. In September 1952 the FBI visited Mount Vernon to investigate this period in Yockey's life. One source told the Bureau that Thompson and Lannin had been active before World War II and that, shortly before his death, Thompson formed a partnership with Lannin. After Thompson died, Lannin "had another attorney in the business for about two or three months" named Yockey, who lived with Lannin in an apartment building. The source described both men as "odd characters."

On 16 September 1952 the FBI interviewed John Lannin. He told the agents that he had met Yockey in "approximately" 1938 at Northwestern. He gave some details about the Yockey family, including the fact that Yockey's father had been a stockbroker in Chicago. He also thought that the family had some investments "in various oil stocks" inasmuch as Yockey's mother "had a very large sum of money."[29]

Yockey's legal career came to a halt on 20 May 1942, when he enlisted in the U.S. Army at Kalamazoo, Michigan. Private Yockey then spent part of his basic training at Camp Custer, Michigan, where he had taken ROTC classes in the summer of 1936. Enlistment, however, did not signal a change in Yockey's political convictions. One FBI report noted that a "confidential informant" had met "a FRANCIS YOCKEY . . . at Camp Custer, Michigan, while on a tour of duty," and remembered him as "a young radically minded individual who was constantly stirring up discord and was an admirer of WILLIAM DUDLEY PELLEY."[30]

Army Intelligence was also aware of Yockey. From an FBI summary of information on Yockey dated 13 December 1951:

> In February 1943 another government agency prepared a list of disloyal or subversive persons who were suspected Nazis in the Sixth Service Command. In this list was included Francis Yockey, Loyola University [sic], Chicago, Illinois. (100-42328-362) (Army)[31]

Yockey's military career took a remarkable turn on 21 September 1942, when he was reported AWOL. Two months later, on 22 November 1942, he voluntarily turned himself over to Army control at Fort Gordon, Georgia. Why he went AWOL, and what he did during these two lost months, again leads us back into the world of Operation Pastorius.

Notes:

1. The Irish-American community was particularly sympathetic to Bund attacks on England. In *Stormy Weather: Crosslights on the Nineteen Thirties* (New York: G. P. Putnam, 1977), J. G. Furnas estimates that almost 40 percent of the Bund's supporters were Irish-American.

2. Two Healy organizations, the American Business Men's and Consumers' Defense group and the American Mothers Against War and Communism, were founded in New York in 1935 with the aid of a leading Bundist named Walter Kappe.

3. In September 1939 Healy (representing the "American Nationalist Youth") also helped organize a Bund-supported rally to celebrate "Gentile Day." Other scheduled speakers included George Deatherage of the Knights of the White Camelia; William Wernecke, chairman of the Joint Committee of Patriotic Organizations; a delegate from the United Hetman Organization of Ukrainians; and Otto Willumeit, head of the Chicago branch of the German-American Bund. Although tickets were sold for the meeting at the Chicago Bund headquarters, the rally was canceled because of bomb threats.

4. Newton Jenkins, however, supported the Pact. In *I've Got the Remedy* (privately published in 1940) he wrote:

> Now what about Communism? . . . A strange, strange thing recently happened, when the bulk of Jewry suddenly decided to move out of Communism . . . When Hitler and Stalin decided to refrain from gutting each other for the pleasure and profit of the ruling classes in England, World Jewry got the biggest jolt it suffered since the Munich Conference.

5. On tensions between the Bund and the German Foreign Ministry, see Sander Diamond, *The Nazi Movement in the United States, 1924–1941* (Ithaca, NY: Cornell University Press, 1974), p. 289.

From its origin as the Friends of New Germany (FONG), the Bund maintained close organizational ties to Rudolf Hess who, with his lieutenant Ernst Wilhelm

Bohle, ran the Auslands-Organization der NSDAP (AO), that represented the Nazi Party in relations with foreign sections of the party. Another group in Nazi Germany that had ties to the Bund was the Deutsches Ausland-Institut (DAI), whose primary function was to gather information on Germans and people of German descent living abroad. While under the control of Goebbels' Propaganda Ministry, the DAI also received funding from the Ministry of the Interior. On the DAI, see "The Kameradschaft USA" by Arthur L. Smith, Jr., in the *Journal of Modern History,* December 1962, Vol. XXXIV, No. 4, as well as Smith's *The Deutschtum of Nazi Germany and the United States* (The Hague: M. Nijhoff, 1965).

6. The policy shift led to increased power for the *Volksdeutsche Mittelstelle* (VDM—better known as VoMi), which was headed by SS Lieutenant General Werner Lorenz. It gradually took over the management of Nazi activity in America from Hess's NSDAP-AO, a change that General Karl Haushofer helped coordinate. On Haushofer and VoMi, see O. John Rogge, *The Official German Report* (New York: Thomas Yoseloff, 1961) and Donald McKale, *The Swastika Outside Germany* (Kent, OH: Kent State University Press, 1977), pp. 142–43. In December 1938 Haushofer, working closely with Hess, became president of "another organization which contacted Germans in foreign countries, the 'Volksbund für das Deutschtum in Ausland' (VDA)." See Henning Heske, "Karl Haushofer: His Role in German Geopolitics and in Nazi Politics," in *Political Geography Quarterly,* Vol. 6, No. 2 (April 1987), p. 142. In 1932 Hess and Richard Walther Darré had formed the "Geopolitics Study Group" (Arbeitsgemeinschaft für Geopolitik), which also worked with Haushofer.

7. Thomsen also served as Germany's de facto ambassador after Ambassador Dieckhoff was recalled to Berlin in 1938 in the wake of *Kristallnacht.*

8. Diamond, *The Nazi Movement in the United States,* p. 296.

9. Ibid., p. 320.

10. Ibid., p. 343. In the 28 August 1939 issue of *Social Justice,* Father Coughlin distanced himself from the Bund.

11. Roosevelt asked the FBI in late 1936 to accumulate files on members of American fascist and communist movements and to keep such investigations hidden from Congress. The FBI also compiled a "custodial detention" index of individuals with strong Nazi or Communist inclinations whose "presence at liberty in time of war or national emergency would constitute a menace." See Leo Riboffo, *The Old Christian Right* (Philadelphia: Temple University Press, 1983).

12. Don Whitehead, *The FBI Story* (New York: Random House, 1956), pp. 163–68.

13. Their decision was made easier by the fact that the Bund and other rightist groups were losing the battle for control of the streets in cities like Chicago. For example, on 28 November 1938 there was a spectacular attack on a major Silver Shirt rally during which Silver Shirt national leader Roy Zachary was knocked unconscious. (See the Silver Shirt magazine *Liberation* for a discussion of the attack in its 28 January 1940 issue.) The attack may have been a payback for *Kristallnacht,* which began on 10 November 1938.

14. Diamond, *The Nazi Movement in the United States*, p. 302.

15. A report on Maerz in the files of the Non-Sectarian Anti-Nazi League (NSANL) archives at Columbia University's Butler Library discussed

> the *Deutsche Amerikanische Einheitsfront* (The German-American National Alliance or United Front) in Chicago. At the first meeting Maerz was elected one of the directors of the group, which then proposed to adopt a constitution and by-law. Later, Maerz was also made secretary of the organization. In February 1939 Maerz was removed from his offices by the other directors because his name was bringing the group too much undesirable publicity—this despite the fact that the alliance was a pro-German organization.

The German-American National Alliance (GANA) and Maerz's removal were also discussed in Appendix 7 to the House of Representatives Special Committee on Un-American Activities, 78 Congress, First Session (*Report on the Axis Front Movement in the United States*), Part VII of the *Investigation of Un-American Activity in the United States* (1943).

16. The Arcade Cafe was the site for many of Newton Jenkins' meetings. See the 11 November 1939 issue of *The Hour* for a reference to the Arcade Cafe.

17. In 1938 Washburn, aided by an ex–Silver Shirt named Frank Clark and Jeremiah Stokes, a Salt Lake City attorney and pamphleteer, created the National Liberty Party. Washburn was later a defendant in the Mass Sedition Trial during World War II. Washburn is profiled in John Roy Carlson (pseudonym for Avedis Derounian), *Under Cover* (New York: E.P. Dutton, 1943).

18. By examining Northwestern, De Paul, and Notre Dame records in 1952, the FBI reconstructed Yockey's academic past. Yockey entered the University of Michigan during 1934–35 and then transferred to Georgetown, where he stayed until the spring of 1938. He then moved to Arizona, where he attended the University of Arizona at Tucson. He next enrolled in Northwestern Law School from February 1938 to June 1939. That September, he entered De Paul Law School and stayed until the end of the school year. He then transferred to Notre Dame and graduated from its law school on 1 June 1941.

Later in life, Yockey would list the University of Michigan and Georgetown for his undergraduate education, but he never graduated from Georgetown (a fact I confirmed with Georgetown). It seems most likely that he graduated from the University of Arizona. A summary of Yockey's school record comes from an official at Northwestern University interviewed by the FBI on 20 October 1952. She told the FBI that Yockey attended Northwestern from February 1938 to June 1939.

> _____ stated the subject had attended the University of Arizona, Tucson, Arizona, prior to the time he began his studies at Northwestern University Law School. She further advised records of her office reflect the subject attended Michigan University during 1934 and 1935 and Georgetown University until the spring of 1938. She also stated a transcript of the subject's work was sent to De Paul University in Chicago on September 16, 1939. [From FBI agent Tony Smilgin's report from the Chicago FBI on 31 October 1952.]

It remains unclear how much time Yockey spent in Arizona. I confirmed with Georgetown that he left the school in 1938 and was not expelled. Perry Patterson told me that he had left that same year because he had an arrangement with Northwestern whereby after he finished his last year there he would have guaranteed placement in Northwestern's law school. Yockey may have had a similar arrangement with the University of Arizona.

One FBI report, by Agent John F. Sheik, dated 16 September 1952, is from Phoenix, Arizona. It states that an investigation was made of an address at 1303 North Park, Tucson, Arizona, "where subject [Yockey] had stayed in 1939." My suspicion is that the FBI made an initial error in recording the dates of Yockey's attendance in Northwestern and that the error was copied to other documents. One guess is that the family moved to Arizona sometime in 1938 and remained until 1939 or 1940, and that Yockey moved by himself to Chicago most probably in the fall or winter of 1938 (or possibly early 1939) to register for the spring session of Northwestern's law school. Perry Patterson also recalled his surprise at seeing Yockey at the school, suggesting that he had assumed that Yockey was still in Arizona. Yockey's official residence, however, may have been Arizona. Recall that the FBI informant who first met Yockey in Newton Jenkins' office said that he was living in a furnished room.

19. James Haritage told military intelligence that "SUBJECT [Yockey] claimed to have attended nine universities in the United States, including Notre Dame and Northwestern, and expressed contempt for all of them, except Notre Dame." I count only six schools: Michigan, Georgetown, Arizona, Northwestern, De Paul, and Notre Dame.

20. Details on Yockey and the MacFarlanes come from an interview with Dr. Francesca Yockey, the daughter of Francis Parker Yockey and Alice MacFarlane.

21. According to a 1959 Navy record on Coyne, he was born 25 March 1915 in Chicago. According to records from the Naval Historical Center, Coyne graduated from the U.S. Naval Academy in 1939 and was commissioned as an ensign on 6 July 1942. Coyne first met Yockey in the fall of 1939, when he began dating Vinette.

22. For reasons that are not clear, Alice Yockey is at times spelled Alyce.

23. Yockey received a reply from the Michigan Bar telling him that Wernecke had not contacted the Bar.

24. FBI document BA 105-643.

25. In the summer of 1940 the building was almost destroyed by a bomb. See James Schneider, *Should America Go to War? The Debate over Foreign Policy in Chicago, 1939–41* (Chicago, IL: University of Chicago Press, 1989), p. 109.

26. Melind testified twice, once at Haupt's treason trial in Washington and once in Chicago at the trial of Haupt's parents. The testimony cited here is from the Chicago trial; Melind is responding to questions from Assistant U.S. Attorney Earle C. Hurley. See "Haupt Kept Own Secrets, Says Fiancee" by Frederick Seaberg, the *Daily Times* of Chicago, 1 November 1942.

27. On Melind's pregnancy, see Eugene Rachlis, *They Came to Kill* (New York: Random House, 1961).

28. The details of Liebl's testimony come from the 31 October 1942 *Daily Times* of Chicago article, "Haupts Knew of Sabotage, U.S. Charges."

29. Lannin is the only source to suggest that Rose Ellen Yockey had money invested in oil stocks. At the time Lannin was speaking, Rose Ellen Yockey lived with the Coynes. William Coyne (before returning to the Navy during Korea) was an engineer working in the Shell Oil Company's refinery in Roxanna, Illinois, next to Alton, Illinois, where the Coynes lived. (See FBI report of Agent John Granfield, Springfield, Illinois, 14 October 1952.) It is possible that Lannin confused Coyne's involvement with Shell Oil with oil wealth in Yockey's family. The Yockey family's financial status remains a mystery.

30. 8 January 1952 memo from the FBI's SAC in Detroit (100-20737) using Army Intelligence records.

31. The note "(Army)" was handwritten next to the number cited by someone in the FBI.

12

KAMERADSCHAFT USA

Operation Pastorius began in early 1942, after Hitler demanded that Admiral Canaris's *Abwehr* (Defense) espionage service launch sabotage operations on American soil. Canaris then assigned Colonel Lahousen-Vivremont, head of Abwehr II, and Captain Wilhelm Ahlrichs, the chief of the Abwehr's American section, to plan the attack.[1] Together they came up with Operation Pastorius, a series of assaults on major war-related aluminum production plants in New York, Tennessee, and Illinois, as well as on a railroad line that supplied coal for war factories on the East Coast.

Although the Abwehr was charged with implementing Hitler's orders, the plan's real enthusiasts came from the Nazi Party's Foreign Organization, the Ausland Organization (AO), headed by Ernst Wilhelm Bohle. Bohle had managed to maintain power after his boss Rudolf Hess's mysterious trip to England by reaching an understanding with the SS. He sent the Abwehr one of his top deputies, a 37-year-old former high-ranking Bundist named Walter Kappe, to manage Operation Pastorius. In 1925, two years after joining the NSDAP, Kappe emigrated to the United States and began working with Fritz Gissibl, founder of the pro-Nazi Teutonia Society. A skilled journalist, Kappe edited the Teutonia Society's *Vorposten: News of the German Freedom Movement in the United States*.

After the Nazi seizure of power, Gissibl headed the Bund's precursor organization, the Friends of New Germany (FONG), while Kappe served as its chief propagandist. Gissibl returned to Germany in 1936 to head the *Amerika Abteilung* (the American Bureau) of the *Deutsches Ausland-Institut* (DAI— German Foreign Institute).[2] Kappe rejoined him in 1937 at the American

Bureau.[3] He also edited the DAI's *Deutschtum und Ausland/Der Auslanddeutsche* (The German Abroad).[4] Although under the control of Goebbels' Propaganda Ministry, the DAI worked closely with the Ausland Organization.

Newton Jenkins knew Fritz Gissibl and Walter Kappe extremely well.[5] His relationship with Kappe was particularly evident during the Union Party campaign. The Bund had backed the Union Party ticket throughout 1936. A few weeks before the election, however, when it was clear that the Union Party was going nowhere, Fritz Kuhn returned from Germany with "Bund Command 2," ordering his men to support the Republican candidate, Alf Landon. Kappe, who had been the Bund's chief organizer of political work in America, opposed the decision.[6] On 5 March 1937 the *New York Post* reported that Kappe had been dismissed as editor of the Bund's New York–based *Deutschen Weckruf und Beobachter* (Awakening Call and Observer) over the Union Party dispute.[7]

Along with their DAI work, Gissibl, Kappe, and Sepp Schuster—another ex-Bundist living in Germany—founded a "private social club" called the *Kameradschaft USA* (Comradeship Group), which was headquartered in the DAI's Stuttgart office.[8] As an ostensibly private organization, the Kameradschaft USA did not violate any diplomatic restrictions on links between the German government and the Bund.[9] The Kameradschaft's main task was to help German nationals from America (the *Rückwanderers*, or returnees) resettle in the Fatherland. It also served as a kind of shadow intelligence agency. In his book *Nazi Germany and the American Hemisphere*, Alton Frye reports that the Kameradschaft "sent a secret agent to the U.S. for eight months during 1938 and 1939 to work out plans for cooperation with the Bund."[10] Bundists also supplied the Kameradschaft with information "about their activities, the extent of anti-Semitism in the States, the nature of the non-intervention movement, and other current events."[11] The full extent of Kameradschaft activity will never be known, since a substantial part of the files concerning Rückwanderers from around the world "was either destroyed or has never been recovered."[12]

After the outbreak of war in Europe, Walter Kappe entered the German military as a regular soldier.[13] In January 1941, after Gissibl went to Poland to help resettle returning German nationals in the East, Kappe was reassigned to head the Kameradschaft.[14] Kappe continued his intelligence activity and the Abwehr was astonished to learn that he and Bohle had already selected 10 of their most fanatical men for Operation Pastorius. They even made an independent arrangement with the German navy to get the men to America.[15]

In April 1942, Kappe (now an SS officer) began training his first unit of saboteurs at a special school in Brandenburg, near Berlin. The youngest of the eight men chosen for the first wave of Pastorius was the 22-year-old Herbert

Hans Haupt. When Edward Kerling, another member of the unit and a holder of the Nazi Party Gold Emblem, complained that he was too young, Kappe replied "that Herbert Haupt broke the blockade and he was decorated with an Iron Cross, and we knew he was a hero."[16]

But was Haupt selected for Pastorius simply for breaking the blockade? Again we are led back to his decision to leave Chicago in June 1941. Was he working for the Kameradschaft even then?[17] U.S. intelligence suspected that two of Haupt's comrades, Bundists Edward Kerling and Herman Neuberger, had been involved in clandestine operations *before* returning to the Fatherland. In 1939 Kerling bought a yawl called the *Lekala*, which he and Neuberger said they intended to sail to Germany. The Coast Guard seized the vessel after it became waterlogged near Wilmington, North Carolina. Kerling and Neuberger were then accused of planning to use the boat to secretly supply U-boats with fresh provisions. Both men denied the charge and insisted that they were only trying to circumvent the British blockade.[18]

The FBI stumbled upon Operation Pastorius after one of Kappe's agents, George Dasch, voluntarily contacted the Bureau shortly after his arrival in America. Kappe's men had been divided into two units. Haupt's team was transported by U-boat to Ponte Vedra Beach, 25 miles southeast of Jacksonville, Florida, where they landed in the early morning of 17 June 1942. The next day Haupt and another agent took a train to Chicago.

Dasch's unit was landed by U-boat off the coast of Amagansett, Long Island, on the night of 12 June 1942. They immediately ran into trouble after being spotted and questioned by a 21-year-old Coast Guard patrolman named John Cullen. After returning to his station, Cullen rounded up more Guardsmen and went back to hunt for the mysterious visitors. Although they failed to find them, they discovered the spot where Dasch's team had buried their uniforms and equipment. One day later, Dasch panicked and called the New York FBI. On 19 June 1942 he invited the FBI to his New York hotel room and poured out the details of Pastorius to the stunned G-men.[19] After Haupt and the other saboteurs were identified by Dasch, the FBI, "using records of previous investigations made of persons who had returned to Germany before the war . . . located relatives and friends of the saboteurs and kept them under surveillance."[20] The Feds even had a photo of Haupt taken "months earlier by tiny cameras held in the palms of G-men shadowing German-American Bund activists."[21]

Haupt's role in Operation Pastorius is particularly interesting. One of the captured German agents, Ernest Peter Burger, told the FBI that Haupt was instructed to find regular employment.[22] Specifically, he was ordered to get back his old job at the Simpson Optical Company in Chicago, which manufactured parts for the Norden bombsight. Berlin believed that Andreas Grunau, superintendent of the company, would be willing to rehire Haupt with no questions asked. So did the FBI. The 13 November 1942 *Washington Post* grimly noted: "Grunau is in Federal custody."

Rather than participate in any direct sabotage mission, Haupt was given $16,000 and told to set up a series of safe houses for the next wave of Pastorius agents. The FBI believed that Kappe also planned to return to America to personally direct the Pastorius underground once the safehouse system was secure.

Because he had to function above ground, Haupt was ordered to visit the FBI's Chicago office to fix any draft registration problem by claiming that he had been in Mexico since June 1941.[23] He was also instructed to recontact William Wernecke: Wernecke was supposed to fix Haupt up with a Chicago doctor who would give him pills to speed up his heart rate so he would flunk his Army physical.[24] Haupt's link to Wernecke again suggests that his Mexico adventure had been carried out at the behest of a pre-existing underground.

There are at least two slightly different versions of Haupt's Mexico trip. William Liebl testified that Haupt told him that he had contacted the German consul in Mexico City and was given money to charter a plane to South America. He then said that Haupt went to San Francisco and, again with funds obtained from the local German consul, went to Japan, where he joined a blockade runner around Africa to Europe.[25] In his book *They Came to Kill*, Eugene Rachlis states that Haupt was virtually penniless when he arrived in Mexico City on 14 June 1941. He then contacted a man named Hans Sass, who put him in touch with the German consulate, which sent him to Japan.[26] Whatever the exact sequence of events, the German government clearly went to some trouble to bring him back to Germany. But what had Haupt done to merit an Iron Cross *before* his recruitment to Pastorius? Had he played an active part in the Kameradschaft underground in Chicago? And was he specifically chosen by Kappe to incorporate some of his old comrades into the Pastorius support network?

Two days after Haupt's arrest, the FBI learned of his connections to the Yockey family:

> On June 29, 1942 _____ advised SA H. R. SPLENDORE that prior to a trip to Mexico by HERBERT HANS HAUPT (also mentioned in re blind memorandum), HAUPT was very friendly with a girl by the name of ALICE YOCKEY, 6341 North Greenview Avenue, who was a nurse at the St. Francis Hospital. According to _____, Miss YOCKEY had a brother, FRANCIS, who lived at the same address. This source furnished no further details concerning FRANCIS YOCKEY.[27]

After his arrest, Haupt refused to cooperate with the FBI. In early August 1942, a little more than a month after his arrest, Haupt and five of his comrades were electrocuted. One month later, on 21 September 1942, Yockey was officially reported AWOL from the Army.

Although we know very little about Yockey's two months underground, what we do know is striking. An FBI document, "To: DIRECTOR, FBI, From: SAC, ST. LOUIS (105-281), Subject: FRANCIS PARKER YOCKEY; EGIDIO BOSCHI SECURITY MATTER 5-8-52," detailed a conversation between Yockey and a mysterious Italian fascist named Egidio Boschi. In it, both men boasted about their service to the Third Reich during World War II. According to the report:

> On November 7, 1951, _____ overheard a conversation between two men, later learned to be the two mentioned above. The gist of the conversation was that they were and had been spies for the Nazis and Fascists during World War II. Mr. BOSCHI stated he was an artist and that during the war he had a rooming house in Santiago de Chile and certain connections on the waterfront. These connections directed American Naval Captains to his rooming house when they sought information as to where they could be entertained; that from information he obtained from women he introduced to them, he was able to learn the departure dates of their respective ships; that he would then wire this information to German submarines and boasted that he had supplied information resulting in the sinking of 12 American and British ships. They were familiar with all events of the war and were on intimate terms with high-ranking Nazis and Fascists, mentioning many names, events, and places in connection with their espionage activities.

Boschi was helping U-boat commanders destroy Allied shipping. But what was Yockey's wartime contribution to the Reich? There is exactly one page in the FBI's files on Yockey's missing two months. On 7 July 1952 the special agent in charge of the San Antonio, Texas, office of the FBI sent a report to "DIRECTOR, FBI, on Subject: FRANCIS PARKER YOCKEY IS [internal security] CANADA." The report begins with a discussion of Yockey's estranged wife Alice. After their marriage broke up in 1947, Alice returned from Germany to Texas , where she applied for a government job on a military base. The FBI ran a routine security check on her, which turned up the following information:

> For the possible assistance of Chicago there is enclosed one copy of the report of SA JOSEPH E. JONES dated 6/29/48 at San Antonio concerning ALICE O'REAR YOCKEY, LGE, containing the background and results of investigation concerning the subject's estranged wife.
>
> The espionage case on _____ was opened in the San Antonio office in October, 1942, on a rather vague suspicion that _____ might possibly be engaged in some espionage activities. This case was ultimately closed on October 12, 1943, upon _____ entry into the U.S. Army. There is a great

deal of information concerning _____ contained in the file and it doesn't appear that any of the information would be particularly pertinent to Chicago's current investigation. The file reflects that YOCKEY and _____ about October 1942 made a trip to Mexico City endeavoring to locate one "HANS, the German sailor boy" and to inquire about transportation to Spain from San Antonio or Mexico. The file indicates that YOCKEY, with alias TORQUEMADA, while in San Antonio, registered at the St. Anthony Hotel on October 3, 1942, using the alias GEORGE PATTERSON, 714 Henison or 714 Kenesaw, Chicago, Illinois. At the time of YOCKEY's marriage to ALICE on July 6, 1943, he gave his address as 810 North Street, Mt. Vernon, Illinois. His marriage certificate also bears the address 722 Junior Terrace, Chicago, Illinois.

YOCKEY is reported to have been in the U.S. Army and discharged prior to his marriage. The espionage file further reflects that information furnished by the St. Louis office indicates that YOCKEY was in deserter status at the time of his trip to Mexico with _____.

Yockey's presence in San Antonio suggests that he was meeting with Charles and Alice MacFarlane. The San Antonio FBI's investigation may have been aimed at Charles MacFarlane and dropped when he entered the Army. The report also correctly identified Yockey's alias as "Torquemada." Yockey's English friend John Anthony Gannon confirmed Yockey's alias in a letter to Keith Stimely, when he asked: "Why did he [Yockey] often assume the name of Torquemada when writing anonymously?"[28] Elsa Dewette also verified the Torquemada alias, telling Keith Stimely: "F. nearly always signed his letters to me Torquemada (you know who that gentleman was). He seemed to have a great admiration for this personage and also a sort of secret longing to be a little Torquemada himself one day."[29]

On 16 October 1942, a few weeks after Yockey went AWOL, Newton Jenkins was found dead at his home of a heart attack at age 55.[30] Two weeks later the U.S. government announced that it was launching a treason trial against Herbert Haupt's parents (Haupt's father, Hans Max Haupt, was also a Bundist); his uncle and aunt, Mr. and Mrs. Walter Froehling; and the parents of his closest friend, Mr. and Mrs. Otto Richard Wergin.[31] The government charged that the Haupts and Wergins were part of their son's conspiracy because they had failed to turn him over to the FBI after they learned that he had returned from Germany. On 16 November 1942 a Chicago jury convicted the Haupts, Wergins, and Froehlings of treason for "sheltering and assisting" Herbert. One week later the male defendants were sentenced to death by electrocution, while their wives were given 25 years in jail.[32]

Yet the attack on Pastorius was far from over. On 17 November, one day after the Haupt convictions, the FBI flooded the nation with photos of Walter Kappe.[33] The FBI warned that Kappe, "alias Kappel" ("a stocky man, 5 feet 10 inches tall, who weighs about 230 pounds" with "gray eyes, blond hair, and fair complexion"), was under orders "to take charge of a proposed Nazi sabotage ring, which was to have its headquarters in Chicago."[34]

Two weeks before Yockey disappeared from the Army, the FBI arrested a Chicago attorney named Newell McCartney for sending seditious material through the mail.[35] That same day, J. Edgar Hoover came to Chicago to announce another arrest that must have caught Yockey's attention. Hoover reported that William Wernecke had been charged with violation of the Selective Service Act and was being held for investigation.[36] Wernecke had come under FBI scrutiny after agents tailed Haupt to his farm shortly before Haupt's arrest.

Wernecke was indicted on draft evasion charges on 13 November 1942, with the FBI claiming that he had created his own "Episcopal Evangelical Church" to avoid the draft. The FBI also discovered a weapons arsenal, along with 2,100 rounds of ammunition and two cans of black powder, on his farm. On 21 September 1942, 15 days after Wernecke's indictment and a month after Haupt's execution, Yockey went AWOL.

Was Yockey a Nazi spy? Had he been ordered to go to Mexico on some kind of mission? Or had he simply panicked, and if so, what had he done that made him so concerned about his safety? The most one can say is that Yockey occupied a gray area. Given his involvement with Wernecke, Haupt, and Jenkins, he clearly had ties to the Kameradschaft USA, which itself operated in a gray zone somewhere between a social club and a spy network. He seems to have been less a spy in the usual sense of the term than a textbook "Fifth Columnist."

Yockey's friend H. Keith Thompson recalled an incident from the early 1950s, when Yockey was living in New York. He said that "in a talk once with GSV [George Sylvester Viereck] the matter of the saboteurs came up, in FPY's presence, but he never said anything to indicate that he knew one of them."[37] Yet eight years after Operation Pastorius, Yockey, as Ulick Varange, mentioned Haupt in an article called "America's Two Ways of Waging War" for the December 1950–January 1951 issue of his European Liberation Front journal, *Frontfighter*.[38] He noted that while Washington was arresting Russian spies during the Korean War, there was no comparison to the popular hysteria surrounding the Haupt case.[39] Criminals sometimes really do return to the scene of the crime. Was "America's Two Ways of Waging War" one of those times?

Notes:

1. An intelligence professional, Ahlrichs had been involved with many successful Abwehr operations in America. See E. H. Cookridge, *Gehlen: Spy of the Century* (New York: Random House, 1971), p. 243. Neither Ahlrichs nor Canaris

wanted anything to do with Pastorius, which they considered a hopelessly amateur attempt doomed to failure.

2. Arthur Smith, Jr., "The Kameradschaft USA," in the *Journal of Modern History*, December, 1962, Vol. XXXIV, No. 4. Sander Diamond gives a somewhat different profile of Gissibl in *The Nazi Movement in the United States* (Ithaca, NY: Cornell University Press, 1974), fn. 13, p. 215: "Upon his return to Germany, Gissibl was considered for a position at the DAI. Through never a full-time member of the staff, he worked with the leadership of the Institute and established the Kameradschaft-USA in 1938. He also held a position in the Tarnungsverlag (Stuttgart), a Nazi publishing house; in 1937, he was appointed SS *Hauptsturmführer* [captain], and after 1941 he was an SS *Obersturmbannführer* [lieutenant colonel] (SS number 309,051)."

3. Kappe became a propaganda director of the Berlin radio station DJB, according to the 26 July 1942 *Washington Post*. On p. 220 of *Wunderlich's Salute* (Smithtown, NY: Malamud-Rose Publishers, 1983), Marvin Miller reports that one of the future German saboteurs, George Dasch, worked for Kappe in the DJB monitoring American programs.

4. Ibid., p. 136.

5. John Metcalfe testified before the House Committee on Un-American Activities (HCUA) that Jenkins told him:

> At one time the Bund did have a great leader. He was Fritz Gissibl, brother of Peter, and a dynamic personality. He knew how to organize. But the Government got after him after several years. And when he could not get citizenship papers, he went back to Germany.

Also see the John Metcalfe collection at the Hoover Institute for an interview between Metcalfe and Jenkins.

6. There is an interesting discussion in *Wunderlich's Salute* (p. 20) about the Union Party. At a 1936 Bund rally

> fascist Newton Jenkins urged support for the Union Party at Camp Sigfried in his effort to get Congressman William Lemke (R-N.D.) elected President in 1936 . . . Herman Schwarzmann, the militant leader of the Bund's Astoria, Queens, unit, lauded Jenkins' plan to unite more than 122 groups behind the Union Party, but Kuhn reacted to this campaign with Bund Command 2, which urged support for • Alf Landon (R-Kan.) because the other plans seemed too communistic.

7. The *Post* acknowledged its dependence on information from anti-Nazi German language papers in the U.S.

8. Miller, *Wunderlich's Salute*, p. 136. *Wunderlich's Salute* reports that the DAI "was created in 1917 to thwart the propaganda efforts of the British and the French. It became a depository of foreigners' names, addresses, and biographies from which Kappe selected most of his recruits for sabotage" (p. 136). Arthur L. Smith, Jr., also says that the DAI's primary function was the gathering of "information of all kinds on Germans and people of German descent living abroad." According to *Wunderlich's Salute*, the Kameradschaft USA was under the control of the

Hess/Bohle AO (although the DAI was part of the Propaganda Ministry) because it maintained liaison with U.S. Bundists.

9. In *The Nazi Movement in America* (fn. 12, p. 92), Sander Diamond explains the Kameradschaft USA this way:

> Some explanation of the Zentrale der Kameradschaft-USA is in order at this juncture. This organization was founded in Germany in 1938 by Fritz Gissibl, who served as the Bund leader of the Friends of the New Germany in the 1930s. The Kameradschaft was located in the German Foreign Institute headquarters in Stuttgart (House of Germanism) and was loosely affiliated with the DAI and the AO der NSDAP. Its functions were to help resettle members of the American Nazi movement who had been repatriated by Germany or had returned to Germany on their own in the late 1930s, and to perpetuate the memory of the Nazi movement in the United States by unifying former Bundists, many of whom were naturalized Americans. In all, an estimated 450 to five hundred Bundists returned to the Reich and belonged to the Kameradschaft branches (after 1941, it was renamed the Amerikadeutsche Kameradschaft) in Braunschweig, Frankfurt, Hanover, Düsseldorf, Leipzig, Hamburg, Stuttgart, Berlin, and Munich. The applications for membership in this group are rich in data concerning the origins of the Bund and the fate of many of its members.

10. Alton Frye, *Germany and the American Hemisphere, 1939–1941* (New Haven: Yale University Press, 1967), p. 92. SS presence in Bund matters is also cited in Sander Diamond, *The Nazi Movement in America* (p. 287). Diamond reports that the Foreign Ministry was upset that "some Nazi agencies, including the German Foreign Institute (DAI) and the *Volksdeutsche Mittelstelle* (VoMi— Ethnic German Office [also translated as the Central Agency for Racial Germans]) under SS *Obergruppenführer* [Lieutenant General] Werner Lorenz, had retained limited contact with the Bundists in spite of existing prohibitions."

11. Miller, *Wunderlich's Salute*, p. 136. Kappe, for example, sent Carl E. Krepper to the U.S. in 1941 "to collect intelligence" (p. 222). Kappe would also have been interested in questions of American politics and morale as part of his task as a propagandist.

12. Smith, "The Kameradschaft USA."

13. Kappe was a private first class on the Polish front. He then took part in the invasion of France and rose to sergeant. Next he was promoted to lieutenant and transferred back to Berlin to work in the Foreign Office. (It was most likely that at this time he took over the leadership of the Kameradschaft USA.) One month before Pearl Harbor, in November 1941, he joined the SS. In January 1942 he began creating the Pastorius sabotage units. (The main source on Kappe is the Walter Kappe file from the U.S. Department of State, Berlin Document Center.) See *Wunderlich's Salute*, p. 220.

14. Gissibl was elevated to an SS Lieutenant Colonel and sent to Poland as part of the Nazi plan to resettle racial Germans in the East. In *The Nazi Movement in the United States* (Appendix III), Gissibl is listed as being in Poland from 1941 to 1944.

15. Charles Wighton and Günther Peis, *Hitler's Spies and Saboteurs* (New York: Holt, 1958), pp. 44–45.

16. From the transcript of Ernest Peter Burger's testimony in the trial of Haupt's parents, as reported in the 23 October 1942 *Chicago Sun*.

17. The suspicion that German intelligence was active in Chicago dated back at least to February 1938, when Chicago homicide detectives suspected German involvement in the murder of a German-Jewish refugee named Dr. Max Bernhard Sammet. On Sammet's death, see Richard Rowan, *Secret Agents Against America* (New York: Doubleday, 1939), p. 205. Rowan also identifies Lieutenant General Paul von Lettow-Vorbeck as an important figure in German intelligence operations in America.

18. In 1940 Kerling would return to Germany from Lisbon, Portugal. On the *Lekala*, see Leon Prior, "Nazi Invasion of Florida," in the *Florida Historical Quarterly*, October 1970.

19. The exposure of Operation Pastorius infuriated Hitler:

> When, on June 30, Hitler was told of the disaster which had overtaken "Operation Pastorius," he flew into a rage and summoned Canaris to his headquarters at the Wolfschanze. "What is your intelligence service good for," he yelled, "if it causes such catastrophes?" Canaris replied that the agents had been caught because one of them had betrayed the operation. He calmly added: "This man [meaning Dasch] was an old member of the National Socialist Party and a bearer of the Party's 'Order of the Blood.' He was recommended to me by the Party's foreign department of *Reichsleiter* Bohle . . . " This only enraged Hitler even more and he shouted at Canaris: "All right, if you do not like good Party members then you should employ criminals or Jews in the future!" [From E. H. Cookridge, *Gehlen: Spy of the Century* (New York: Random House, 1971), p. 65.]

Even more incredibly, the FBI (with some reason) believed that Dasch may have been a Soviet agent! See Weighton and Peis, *Hitler's Spies and Saboteurs*, pp. 47–49.

20. Don Whitehead, *The FBI Story* (New York: Random House, 1956), p. 204.

21. William Brewer, *Hitler's Undercover War: The Nazi Espionage Invasion of the U.S.A.* (New York: St. Martin's Press, 1989), p. 282.

22. *The Chicago Sun*, 28 October 1942. Burger also said that Haupt was told not to contact his parents. His statement sounds strange, since Haupt was supposed to reintegrate himself back into his past life. Whatever his orders, after his return to Chicago Haupt not only saw his parents but he also proposed marriage to Gerda Melind.

23. Whitehead, *The FBI Story*, p. 204.

24. Haupt's father said that Wernecke had known that Haupt was planning to return to Chicago. *The Washington Post* of 11 November 1942 reported that Haupt told his father (who allegedly repeated it to the FBI when the elder Haupt was arrested in late June 1942) "that spy Haupt's submarine voyage to this country was also known to William Wernecke, Chicago Bund leader now facing draft charges, and Andreas Grunau, superintendent of the Simpson Optical Co., which manufactured parts for the Norden bombsight."

25. *Daily Times of Chicago*, 30 October 1942.

26. On 13 July 1942 the *Washington Times* noted: "Haupt, it was learned, went to Japan after he left this country . . . Before going to Japan, Haupt slipped into Mexico and then made his way to Tokyo. Later, through the aid of Japanese authorities, he obtained passage on a 'blockade runner' to Bordeaux, France."

27. Memo to Director, FBI, from SAC, Chicago, 2 January 1952. There is also another FBI report about Yockey and Haupt: "On June 30, 1941, _____ advised that Francis Parker Yockey was a friend of Herbert Hans Haupt, convicted Nazi saboteur, prior to Haupt's departure from the United States to Germany. (98-10280-241)" This information comes from a collection of reports sent by the FBI to "Director, Central Intelligence Agency, 2430 E Street, N. W." on 5 January 1952.

It seems odd that the FBI got information about Yockey and Haupt on 30 June 1941 and Alice Yockey and Haupt on 29 June 1942. FBI files are often filled with typos; if one of the years was mistyped it means that the FBI followed up on its lead from the day before. It is also possible that—if the FBI had been following Haupt, and since Haupt did in fact disappear from Chicago in early June 1941—Yockey's name may have surfaced as part of an FBI follow-up to its earlier Haupt investigation.

28. John Anthony Gannon, letter to Keith Stimely, 15 February 1981.

29. Elsa Dewitte, letter to Keith Stimely, 22 June 1982. In light of the questions about Yockey's background, it is interesting to note that Torquemada, famed head of the Spanish Inquisition, was conventionally believed to have had "Jewish blood." It is also worth mentioning that Yockey had a close friend codenamed "Saint Ignatius." In a 2 April 1980 letter to Keith Stimely, Gannon asked if he knew of a "St. Ignatius." Then, in a 15 February 1981 letter, Gannon returned to "St. Ignatius":

> Before I answer your questions, I must put one to you, again, which you have failed to answer, so far, or you have missed noting in the mass of other things: Do you know the identity of "St. Ignatius"? Whomsoever stands behind this mask in FPY's life—or stood behind it—was the repository of FPY's complete trust to an extent equal to my own. He was an American or lived in America. Strangely, ED [Elsa Dewette] never seems to have heard of him.

When Stimely failed to discover "St. Ignatius," Gannon again returned to him in a 24 November 1981 letter:

> Before answering your numbered questions, here are . . . addresses for you . . . Thrasher Hall, 158 Borteau Avenue, Chicago, who may have been the "St. Ignatius" often spoken of by Y with the deepest affection. I think TH sent Y money from time to time, and he was on the FRONTFIGHTER mailing list.

Who "Thrasher [Thatcher?] Hall" was, or if "Thrasher Hall" was a real name or an address, is unknown. Perry Patterson told me that he was not "St. Ignatius." It is possible that Charles MacFarlane was "St. Ignatius." Another possibility is that Yockey's friend from Northwestern, John Lannin, was "St. Ignatius." Lannin was close to the Yockey family, even getting a personal call from Yockey's sister Vinette in 1955 when he was living in Illinois and the Coynes were in Boston.

Yockey listed Lannin in a résumé he submitted, which falsely claimed he had worked for him in an "import-export" business in London in 1948. Lannin also wrote a letter of recommendation when Yockey applied to the Red Cross in 1950.

30. In the *New York Times* obituary of Jenkins on 17 October 1942, it was reported that he had had a heart ailment and was found dead at home. Jenkins had also been called before a federal grand jury in Washington investigating the far right. Henry Hoke mentions Jenkins in a list of grand jury witnesses on p. 29 of *It's a Secret* (New York: Reynal & Hitchcock, 1946).

31. Recall that Wergin's son Wolfgang went with Haupt to Mexico City in June 1941.

32. The Haupts successfully appealed the verdict. The U.S. Circuit Court of Appeals unanimously reversed the lower court's decision because statements by the defendants had been improperly admitted; the joint trial had caused evidence against one defendant to prejudice the others; and the judge had given improper instructions to the jury.

33. Miller, *Wunderlich's Salute*, p. 220.

34. *Washington Post*, 26 July 1942. Kappe never did make it to the U.S. After the Pastorius disaster, he wound up on the Eastern Front.

35. McCartney had circulated anonymously written anti-war pamphlets that were mailed from Chicago and Michigan.

36. *New York Times*, 6 September 1942.

37. H. Keith Thompson, response to my questionnaire.

38. The article, "America's Two Ways of Waging War," was reprinted in the leading postwar Nazi propaganda journal, the Argentina-based *Der Weg* (Vol. V, No. 7).

39. Because copies of *Frontfighter* are so rare, I read Yockey's article in *Der Weg*. In it, he says:

> Ueberführte russische Spione werden nach Russland deportiert. Dies alles steht im schärfsten Widerspruch zu der Volkhysterie, die anlässlich des Falles Haupt hervogerufen wurde. Hierbei wurden von acht Europäern, die sich in Sabotage-Mission in Amerika aufhielten, sechs getötet.
>
> Während des zweiten Weltkrieges wurden alle Deutschen in den USA in Konzentrationslagern interniert.

My rough translation is:

> Convicted Russian spies were deported to Russia. This all stands in sharpest contrast to the popular hysteria that was aroused on the occasion of the Haupt affair. Here were eight Europeans apprehended on a sabotage mission in America, six died.
>
> During the Second World War, all Germans in the USA were interned in concentration camps.

13
"DEMENTIA
PRAECOX"

On 22 November 1942, two months after he went AWOL, Francis Parker Yockey voluntarily returned to the United States Army's Camp Gordon in Georgia. Years later Yockey's brother-in-law William Coyne gave a written statement to the Office of Naval Investigations (ONI) describing his return:

I did not see him [Yockey] again until the fall of 1942, at which time I was on active duty as an Ensign in the Navy and serving as an instructor in the Pre-Flight School in Athens, GA. Shortly after his appearance at my home in Athens, GA (at which time he was AWOL), I persuaded him to turn himself in, and actually drove him to Camp Gordon, GA, for this purpose. A few months later he received a medical discharge from the Army and became a resident in my home (about two months). In March of 1943, I was transferred to the U.S.S. *New Jersey* and saw no more of him until after my return from the Pacific to civilian life in 1946.[1]

Army Intelligence (G-2) was also aware of Yockey. In February 1943 his name appeared on a G-2 list of Army personnel who were suspected Nazis. On 4 March 1943, G-2 interviewed a source who recalled hearing Yockey speak at a 1939 Silver Shirt meeting at William Wernecke's farm outside Chicago.[2] Yet a full inquiry into Yockey's activities never took place. Shortly after returning to military control, he suffered a "nervous breakdown" and was placed in the U.S. Army Hospital at Camp Gordon. The FBI summarized this period as follows:

There is contained in the file the proceedings of a Board of Medical Officers which convened in order to determine whether YOCKEY should be discharged under a Certificate of Disability. The psychiatric examination indicated marked delusions of persecution in which he involved many people in his environment. There were ideas of grandeur present and he said that he was better than anyone else. He involved prominent people in his delusional system. He admitted auditory hallucinations and stated that he heard the voice of his father talking to him from time to time. It was recommended by the Board that YOCKEY be discharged by reason of Certificate of Disability due to Dementia Praecox [premature or incipient], Paranoid type, cause undetermined.[3]

On 15 January 1943 Yockey was transferred to Allen Hospital, a private sanitarium in Milledgeville, Georgia. He spent just 10 days there before being released on 25 January 1943. His freedom came after he was rediagnosed as a "paranoid state–psychopathic personality." Yockey's paranoia was now said to be stress-induced, not biological. According to the FBI, the sanitorium doctor felt that

> subject did not have as severe a mental disease as dementia praecox, in which a patient generally becomes worse. _____ stated that there is a temporary mental illness which arises because a person with an inadequate personality is placed in a difficult situation. In Subject's case, _____ suggested he was probably unable to cope with the fact that he was not an officer and had to take orders from people he considered of inferior intelligence.[4]

Based on his "medical condition," Yockey was given an honorable discharge from the Army on 13 July 1943.

Yockey was quite proud of how he had "snowed" the Army. He even reenacted his performance for Elsa Dewette, who later wrote: "the 'dementia praecox' affair (a hilarious *fake*); (F. told me all about it, and made me roll with laughter, he was such an actor)."[5] His fate was in sharp contrast to that of William Wernecke. On 5 June 1943 Wernecke was convicted of making false statements to government officials as well as falsely assuming the role of a minister to avoid the draft. He was sentenced to five years in jail and fined $10,000.[6]

On 6 July 1943, shortly before his release from the Army, Yockey married Alice MacFarlane in San Antonio, Texas. The couple then moved to Detroit, where Yockey worked for the Dykoma, Jones, and Wheat law firm. On 9 May 1944 he was accepted for membership in the Detroit Bar Association. The Wagner-loving Yockeys had two daughters, Isolde and Brünnhilde, whom they nicknamed "Lollie" and "Bruni."[7]

Yockey next become an assistant prosecutor for Wayne County, a job he held from 18 September to 31 December 1944. He was a political appointee of Detroit D.A. William E. Dowling, who may have chosen him as a favor to

Ludington Judge Hal Cutler.[8] He was assigned to the criminal division, and only resigned after Dowling's electoral defeat.[9]

Yockey made an enormous impression on a young woman named Leona Farah, who also worked in the Detroit court system. (She became such an ardent fan that she even followed him to Germany in 1946.) Leona introduced him to her brother George, who had just returned from the war in the Pacific. George Farah had enrolled as a student at Wayne State University intent on studying gestalt psychology, and Leona insisted that he meet Yockey, whom she considered extraordinary. Although George Farah lost track of Yockey in 1946, he still vividly remembers their conversations, which often occurred while they were playing chess. He unhesitatingly calls Yockey a "genius" with a "very aristocratic view of political life." Farah (who holds a Ph.D. in psychology) says that Yockey was an artistic personality par excellence whose intensity bordered on paranoia. He describes Yockey as being infused with a kind of "sickness, like a magnificent obsession. He could only see north, not northwest or northeast."[10]

After leaving the D.A.'s office, Yockey worked for the Detroit branch of the Office of Price Administration (OPA). (He applied for the OPA job on 22 March 1945, and was hired on 2 April.) While at the OPA, he began openly propagandizing for Germany—so much so that one of his fellow workers complained to the FBI. On 8 October 1945 the Detroit FBI office learned that "YOCKEY is alleged to have made remarks such as the following: 'The United States had no business in the war. The war was started by the Jews, and Germany should have won the war.'" Yockey was also described as "a radical and an atheist."

Although the Detroit FBI ignored the complaint, in June 1948 the Bureau interviewed William J. Cody, the Circuit Court Commissioner for Michigan, and again Yockey's name came up. The interview seems to have been part of a routine background check on a job applicant for a government position (although given FBI deletions, it is impossible to know for sure). After Judge Cody told the FBI about Yockey's pro-Hitler ideas, the Bureau interviewed a woman who had met Yockey in Judge Cody's courtroom in October 1945. According to the FBI report:

> MR. WILLIAM J. CODY, Circuit Court Administrator, State of Michigan, furnished SA JOHN C. DOIG in June 1948 the following information:
> YOCKEY was employed in the Office of Price Administration. Mr. CODY never had much to do with YOCKEY until a woman whose name is believed to be _____ contacted CODY, stating that a man named YOCKEY was seeing her daughter against her wishes. _____ advised that YOCKEY was a frequent caller on her daughter and would always bring pro-German literature with him when he called.

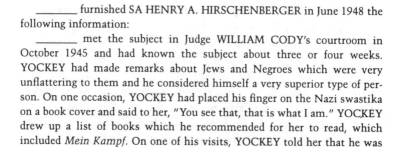

_____ furnished SA HENRY A. HIRSCHENBERGER in June 1948 the following information:

_____ met the subject in Judge WILLIAM CODY's courtroom in October 1945 and had known the subject about three or four weeks. YOCKEY had made remarks about Jews and Negroes which were very unflattering to them and he considered himself a very superior type of person. On one occasion, YOCKEY had placed his finger on the Nazi swastika on a book cover and said to her, "You see that, that is what I am." YOCKEY drew up a list of books which he recommended for her to read, which included *Mein Kampf*. On one of his visits, YOCKEY told her that he was almost shot for treason when he was in the United States Army.[11]

During Yockey's time in Detroit, his marriage fell apart. Elsa Dewette offered her view of the marriage in a letter to Keith Stimely:

> The experience of Matrimony. This . . . ended in disaster. The second year of his marriage, he wrote on the flyleaf of the *Maxims* of Napoleon (his hero) which I have, "the average American revolves around the cash-box, the stomach, and two children . . . " Poor meek Mrs. FPY must have had the shock of her life when she discovered that the dove she had married turned out to be a ferocious eagle . . . Mrs. Y sincerely believed that her spouse was a raving lunatic . . . She was *terrified* of him.[12]

Despite his narrow escape two years earlier, Yockey slowly began edging back into a life of intrigue. Incredibly, he decided to become a lawyer with the Nuremberg war crimes tribunal and, on paper, he seemed an excellent candidate. A former assistant prosecutor, he was a *cum laude* Notre Dame Law School graduate with a medical discharge from the Army. He knew German, had a strong interest in international law, and had studied at Georgetown's prestigious School of Foreign Service. Most important, he was volunteering for an overseas assignment during a desperate manpower shortage, as GIs began returning from Europe en masse.[13]

Yockey left his OPA post on 26 October 1945, and headed for Washington. On 26 December 1945 he applied for a passport "for travel in Germany on official business for the War Department," and was issued his papers on 3 January 1946.[14] Just before he left, a strange incident almost wrecked his plans. On 18 December 1945 he was arrested in a Washington store and charged with "grand larceny"—shoplifting a black negligee. A brief mention of his arrest appeared in press reports after Yockey's 1960 capture in Oakland. Years later, Willis Carto decided to investigate. He sent a man named Bob Duke to see whether "Richard Hatch" (Yockey's cover name in 1960) had ever been picked up by the Washington police. After a futile records search, Duke asked the clerk handling the matter to see if a Francis Parker Yockey had ever been arrested.[15] The clerk soon returned with two documents. One was a warrant charging Yockey with grand larceny in the theft of a black rayon crepe negligee. This charge, a felony, was then dismissed, and a second warrant was issued for a shoplifting misdemeanor. Yockey was found innocent and released after a 20 December hearing. The negligee affair had a strange coda. On 7 June 1960, fingerprints taken from the 1945 arrest led the FBI to conclusively identify Richard Hatch as Francis Parker Yockey.

Notes:

1. ONI report on William Coyne, dated 28 July 1955 by R. W. Hufnagl.

2. The reference to Yockey may have come from an investigation of Wernecke.

3. SAC St. Louis to Hoover, 28 December 1951. (St. Louis was a major depository for Army records.) The FBI also learned that "a summary of the United States Army medical record indicates YOCKEY stated that 'he should have been an officer instead of being made to scrub floors.'"

4. From a 70-page summary report about Yockey prepared on 7 July 1960 at the San Francisco FBI office by Agent Wayne K. Welch, Field Office File 105-1769.

5. Elsa Dewette, letter to Keith Stimely, 12 October 1981.

6. Eustace Mullins told me that the failure to charge Wernecke with espionage made some members of the Chicago right suspect that he had made a deal with the government.

7. As an adult, Bruni legally changed her name to Francesca. When I am discussing Yockey's daughter as a girl, I shall refer to her as Bruni. Isolde Yockey disappeared in the mid-1970s while her sister was studying in Europe. If she is still alive, her current whereabouts are unknown to her sister.

8. In an interview with the FBI, Dowling (whose name was blacked out) said he had hired Yockey "just at the time the Subject graduated from law school." When Judge Cutler was interviewed by the FBI, he said he had helped obtain "a position for the Subject with a law firm in Detroit after he graduated but that the Subject left this position." Yockey may have briefly worked for Dowling in Detroit while he studied for the Michigan law boards.

9. *Detroit News*, 9 June 1960.

10. My interview with George Farah.

11. Chicago FBI summary of Yockey's activity by Agent Lloyd O. Bogstad, 8 July 1954.

12. Elsa Dewette, letter to Keith Stimely, 12 October 1981.

13. It would be interesting to know whether Walter Jaeger wrote Yockey a letter of recommendation. In 1943 Jaeger co-wrote the *United States Army Officers' Handbook of Military Law and Court-Marshall Procedure: "Army Officers' Blue Book,"* which appeared with a foreword by the Judge Advocate General of the Army.

14. From a report by FBI Agent William Mc Devitt, Jr., dated 29 September 1953.

15. Willis Carto gave me a copy of Duke's report.

ON
THE
EDGE

America always did fill me with a terrible feeling that I didn't know where I was, a feeling of being on the edge of the world, of being isolated.

—From a letter by Francis Parker Yockey
dated 9 August 1950

The adventurous man can conceive care only as a weakness and annoyance since he only thinks subjectively, i.e., metaphysically, and ostensibly loves severity. If this fails he takes flight into some kind of intoxication, be it only the intoxication of blood.

—Martin Heidegger

14

EMPIRE OF
THE SENSELESS

"Ulick Varange" was made in America, not Europe. But what was America? In *The Hour of Decision*, Oswald Spengler wondered: "What *is* 'hundred percent Americanism?' A mass existence standardized to a low average level, a primitive pose, or a promise for the future?"[1] He concluded that America, with its "intellectually primitive upper class, obsessed as it is by the thought of money," lacked that "element of historic tragedy, of great destiny, that has widened and chastened the soul of Western peoples through the centuries." America was little more than "a boundless field and a population of trappers, drifting from town to town in the dollar-hunt, unscrupulous and dissolute; for the law is only for those who are not cunning or powerful enough to ignore it."[2] The United States even had

> an almost Russian form of State socialism or State capitalism, represented by the mass of trusts, which, like the Russian economic administrations, systematically standardizes and controls every detail of production and marketing. These are the real lords of the land in both cases. It is the Faustian will-to-power, but translated from organic growth to soulless mechanization.[3]

A society adrift, Spengler's America was no longer dominated by those who "inwardly" belonged to the "ruling Anglo-Saxon type." "Quite apart from the Negroes," the immigration of "no less than 15 million Poles, Russians, Czechs, Balkan Slavs, Eastern Jews, Greeks, inhabitants of Asia Minor, Spaniards, and Italians" had created "an alien, foreign-thinking, and very prolific proletariat with its spiritual home in Chicago."[4] America had become so alien to its European roots that *The Decline of the West* portrays it as a new form of society:

> Men migrate, and their successive generations are born in ever-changing landscapes; but the landscape exercises a secret force upon the plant nature in them, and eventually the race-expression is completely transformed by the extinction of the old and the appearance of the new one. Englishmen and Germans did not migrate to America, but human beings migrated thither *as* Englishmen and Germans, and their descendants are there *as* Americans.[5]

Yockey devoted over a hundred pages of *Imperium* to describing an America incapable of "destiny thinking." A vast, formless swamp, America failed to qualify as a nation, which by his definition

> *is an Idea.* Its material manifestations are the actualization of this Idea as it fulfills itself. We can, for purposes of understanding, divide the Nation into three strata. On top is the Idea itself. It is incapable of expression in words, for it is not an abstraction, not a concept, but is a soul. It can only be expressed in lives, deeds, thoughts, events. Under it is the minority which embodies the Idea at high potential, the nation-bearing stratum. It represents the Idea in History. For *practical* purposes it is the nation. It is, as actuality, what the mass of the population, the body of the nation, is as possibility. The lowest level is the mass. It widens out toward the base, becoming ever less differentiated as one goes down. Finally one reaches the level where an eternal stratum is reached, that takes no part whatever in the national Idea, which does not experience the History which is playing its drama higher up on top.[6]

A nation, in short, is "a people containing a Cultural Idea."[7] Because America lacks a Cultural Idea, America, by definition, is not a nation.[8]

Yockey traces America's failure to its geographical origin. Blessed with a vast, nearly empty frontier, the country failed to develop "the consciousness of political tension which arises from a true frontier."[9] Thus, "there has been no State in America," since "State is a unit of opposition—there were no other States on the North American continent, and thus no American State could arise." Therefore, "there was no Nation," "no Genius in politics," "no ruling class," "no Tradition," and "no idea in whose service the population-stream of the continent lived."[10]

America's physical vastness was just part of the problem. Equally alarming was the Founding Fathers' "religion of Rationalism," which

> dominated America in a way that it was never able to dominate Europe. Europe always had resistance against Rationalism—based on tradition until the middle of the 19th century, and after that based on anticipation of the coming anti-rationalist spirit of the 20th century—as exemplified in Carlyle and Nietzsche. But America did not possess the first because it had no tra-

dition, and had not the second, because Cultural impulses and Culture-for-warding phenomena come from the Mother-soil and are thence radiated outward, as the Rationalist religion of America came from England, through France.[11]

Rationalist and materialist ideology also made America vulnerable to domination by the Jewish "culture-distorter." Following Spengler, Yockey considered Judaism an "Arabian Culture," a self-contained "Church-State-Nation-People-Race." He argued that the Jews would have remained on the fringes of Western society, subject to pogroms and legal/religious sanctions, but for the "triumph of economics, opposition to absolutism, opposition to the religious unity of the West, freedom of trade, and usury."[12]

The Enlightenment, in particular, opened up the West to Jewish influence: "Without Western materialism, money-thinking, and liberalism, the entry of the outsider into Western public life had been as impossible as the mastery of Talmudic casuistry would have been to a Westerner."[13] Because America was founded on Enlightenment principles, it was especially vulnerable to Jewish capture.

Liberalism, materialism, and rationalism were more than political distortions. Spengler called liberalism "the form of suicide adopted by our sick society."[14] Yockey also saw liberalism as a sign of gender breakdown, "an escape from hardness into softness, from masculinity into femininity, from History to herd-grazing, from reality into herbivorous dreams, from Destiny into Happiness." What was feminism if not "a means of feminizing man? . . . transforming man first into a creature whose only concern is with his personal economics and his relation to 'society,' i.e., a woman." "Society," the realm of women, was "static and formal," and freed "from the possibility of heroism and violence." Such "liberalistic tampering with sexual polarity only wreaks havoc on the souls of individuals, confusing and distorting them."[15]

For the right in general, feminism was against the natural order. But what *was* natural? Unlike the clerical and monarchist right, which still saw man as made in God's image, the Conservative Revolutionaries often glorified the irrational, the wild, and the violent. They especially despised the Enlightenment argument that man was essentially a rational being who had been blinded by centuries of priestly superstition. Against the notion that men were created equal and endowed with inalienable rights, Spengler claimed that man was best described as "a beast of prey."[16]

Yet for all their celebration of natural impulses, the Conservative Revolutionaries saw the pursuit of pleasure as a sign of weakness and degeneracy, an ignoble substitute for the heroic life. In *The Mass Psychology of Fascism*, Wilhelm Reich wanted to understand the fear of pleasure and craving for authority that had led so many to embrace fascism. Spengler's problem with mass man was the opposite of Reich's. To Spengler, the West was a "late civilization" too infatuated with bread and circuses to notice the barbarians surging ever-closer to the gate. Yockey also felt that America's love of "happiness" was its great vice:

> For happiness one will compromise anything, give anything, sell anything. Happiness becomes synonymous with pursuit of economic and sexual motives. It absolutely excludes any profitless struggle against odds, merely in order to be one's self.[17]
>
> The "happy-end" is the ideal of [American] life and literature. There is no thought of bearing up under the bitterest and most crushing blows of Fate. These are overcome by avoiding one's glance. The lucky man, and not the man who has suffered in silence and becomes stronger, is the central figure in the happy-end literature.[18]

In the "America" section of *Imperium*, the Negro becomes a kind of paradigm for the nation in general. Yockey's Negro is incapable of the tragic, being only a pleasure-seeking, pain-avoiding, childlike creature. In the chapter "The Negro in America," he asserts: "The soul of the Negro remains primitive and childlike in comparison with the nervous and complicated soul of Western man, accustomed to thinking in terms of money and civilization."[19] Yet throughout *Imperium*, he celebrates instinct, rhythm, race, blood, and irrationality—categories traditionally associated in the West with so-called primitive peoples. He even argues that "Race in the subjective sense is thus seen to be a matter of *instinct*. The man with strong instincts has race, the man with weak or bad instincts had it not" because the "center of gravity of ascendent Life" is on the side of "instinct, will, race, blood."[20]

Yockey was an intense, visceral racist, and he included encomiums to the KKK in *Imperium*.[21] His hatred and fear of black people may have had its origin in the physical beating he reportedly took at the hands of some African-Americans after his youthful car accident. His racism also had ideological roots in German philosophy—in particular, Hegel's idea that blacks were a *Kindernation* (child nation). In *The Philosophy of History*, Hegel claimed that Africans had never achieved "the sense of human personality—their spirit sleeps, remains sunk in itself, makes no advance, and thus parallels the compact, undifferentiated mass of the African continent."[22] Hegel's black is "natural man," incapable of abstraction, and existing outside the movement of the World Spirit, outside historical time itself.

The notion that certain societies existed outside the form-shaping nature of historical time was equally important to Spengler. All of Spengler's great cultures proceed along an organic, historical time curve of rise and fall. As Northrup Frye observes about Spengler's method: "If we try to write a history of Patagonians or Zulus or Mongols, we can produce only a series of events or incidents." Eighteenth-century Lapland is much like 13th-century Lapland. "We do not feel, as we feel when we compare 18th-century with 13th-century England, that it is five centuries *older*."[23]

For a classically trained pianist like Yockey, the ultimate Negro assault on time was jazz. He bitterly complains in *Imperium* that "music is seldom heard in America, having been replaced by the cultureless drum-beating of the Negro."[24] Behind such "cultureless drum-beating" lurks African lust and Hebrew cunning:

> The Western erotic, grounded in the chivalry of Gothic times, with the concomitant honor-imperative of the centuries of Western history, has been driven out. The ideal of [Frank] Wedekind, the Culture-distorter who preached compulsory Bohemianism in Europe around the turn of the 20th century, has been realized by the Culture-distorting regime in America . . . In this effort, jazz music is a useful appurtenance, for this primitive beating is nothing but the expression of lust in the world of sound, a world which is capable of expressing all human emotions, both higher and lower.[25]

Spengler also loathed jazz. In *The Hour of Decision*, he denounced "the 'happy ending' of an empty existence, the boredom of which has brought in jazz music and Negro dancing to perform the Death March for a great Culture."[26]

How was it possible, then, that so many whites participated in Negro, pleasure-seeking, "anti-heroic" behavior? Although Yockey was quick to claim the mantle of "blood" and "instinct" against sterile rationalism, it was the very chaos of emotion that he feared, its indulgent, overflowing, formless, anarchic nature.[27] Spengler was equally terrified of "formlessness"; in *The Hour of Decision*, he remarks: "Thus we get the 'democracy' of the century—not form, but formlessness in every sense as a principle—parliamentarianism—constitutional anarchy—the republic—the negation of every kind of authority."[28]

The Conservative Revolutionaries, aesthetically as well as politically, glorified the austere, the stern, and the heroic—the Holy Trinity of Sparta, Rome, and Prussia. In their resistance to the pleasures of the body, to the threat of luxury and indulgence, we see a shift in psychic geography away from the Roaring Twenties, Weimar Berlin, and Paris, the jazz capital of Europe.[29] The British scholar C. S. Lewis first felt the new paradigm while looking at an illustrated edition of *Twilight of the Gods*, when suddenly, "pure Northernness engulfed me: a vision of high clear spaces hanging above the Atlantic in the endless twilight of Northern summer, remoteness, severity . . . the same world as Baldur . . . something cold, spacious, remote."[30]

Bohemian Paris, the mythic City of Lights eternally liberated from Babbitry and Puritanism, had enchanted Louis Francis Yockey. His son, however, only heard the siren call of Berlin; a cold, hard, dark Berlin; a Berlin of denial, conquest, struggle, war, and blood.

Notes:

1. Oswald Spengler, *The Hour of Decision* (New York: Knopf, 1934), p. 67.

2. Ibid., p. 67.

3. Ibid., p. 68.

4. Ibid., p. 70.

5. Oswald Spengler, *The Decline of the West* (New York: Knopf, 1928), Vol. II, p. 119. For Yockey's almost verbatim repeat of this paragraph, see *Imperium*, p. 275.

6. *Imperium*, p. 331.

7. Ibid., p. 328.

8. Again Yockey borrows from Spengler, who wrote in *The Hour of Decision* (p. 36):

With the 19th century the powers pass from the form of dynastic states into that of national states. But what, exactly, does this mean? Nations—that is, civilized peoples—had of course been there long before. Moreover, on the whole they coincided with the sphere of authority of the great dynasties. These nations were *ideas*, in the sense in which Goethe speaks of the idea of his existence: the inward form of a significant life which, unaware and unobserved, inspires every deed and every word. But *"la nation"* in the sense of 1789 was a *Rationalistic* and *Romantic* ideal, a wish-picture of expressly political, not to say social tendency. In this shallow age no one is able to distinguish the two. An ideal is the product of reflection, a conception or proposition which has to be formulated before one can "have" it. Accordingly it shortly becomes a catchword which one uses without spending any more thought on it.

Ideas, on the other hand, are wordless. Their vessels are seldom, if ever, aware of them, and for others they can hardly be conveyed in words. They must be *felt* in visualized happenings, *described* in actual realizations. Definitions they defy. Neither wishes nor aims concern them. They are the obscure urge which attains form in a human life and soars fatefully and directionally over the individual existence: thus the *idea* of Romanness, the *idea* of the Crusades, the Faustian *idea* of striving after the infinite.

9. *Imperium*, p. 445.

10. Ibid., p. 485. America's failure to create an elite especially upset Yockey. "There is no level of the populace, no American group, which feels any higher task than self-enrichment. There is no Samurai, no Comintern, no Black Dragon Society, no nobility, no Idea, no Nation, no State." *Imperium*, p. 593.

11. Ibid., p. 396.

12. Ibid., p. 421.

13. Ibid., p. 437.

14. Spengler, *The Hour of Decision*, p. 122.

15. *Imperium*, pp. 222–23. Also see *Imperium*, pp. 298, 387, and 528.

16. Spengler, *The Hour of Decision*, p. 21.

17. *Imperium*, p. 508.

18. Ibid., p. 507. Attacks on "happiness" were a long-standing theme of the German right. Werner Sombart, the economic historian whose *Jews and Modern Capitalism* is cited by Yockey in *Imperium*, wrote an influential pamphlet in 1915 entitled *Merchants and Heros*. In it, he denounces the Merchant's quest for happiness and the "peaceful co-existence of merchants," as opposed to the Hero who lives to "fulfill a task." Sombart's Merchant asks "What canst thou give me, O Life?" The Hero implores: "What can I give thee, O Life?"

19. Ibid., p. 524.

20. Ibid., pp. 294–95.

21. Ibid., p. 497, p. 555.

22. Sander Gilman, *On Blackness Without Blacks: Essays on the Image of the Black in Germany* (Boston: C.W. Hall, 1982), p. 94. On the Nazi fear of blacks, see Jost Hermand, *Old Dreams of a New Reich: Volkish Utopias and National Socialism* (Bloomington, IN: Indiana University Press, 1992).

23. Northrup Frye, "Spengler Revisited," in *Spiritus Mundi* (Bloomington, IN: Indiana University Press, 1976), p. 184.

24. *Imperium*, p. 504.

25. Ibid., p. 505.

26. Spengler, *The Hour of Decision*, pp. 227–28. Jazzphobia was alive and well in the Third Reich. See Michael Kater, "Forbidden Fruit: Jazz in the Third Reich," in *American Historical Review*, Vol. 94, No. 1, Feb. 1989.

27. Sander Gilman argues that Nietzsche's celebration of the instinctual and the body first challenged Hegel's category of the primitive.

28. Spengler, *The Hour of Decision*, p. 38.

29. Inside the left, the Weimar period also became viewed as decadent. In the late 1940s the Soviet Union launched a major campaign against jazz.

30. Anna Bramwell, *Blood and Soil: Walther Darré and Hitler's "Green Party"* (Bourne End, Buckinghamshire: Kensal Press, 1985), p. 40.

15
THE UNIVERSE
OF THE
PARTICULAR

Visions of hierarchic order inspired right-wing aesthetics as well as politics in the 1930s. Historian George Mosse argues that Yeats, Pound, Wyndham Lewis, and T. S. Eliot favored a turn away from Romanticism to a classical tradition that identified beauty with order. Both the Stalinist left and the fascist right felt the need for a new absolutism that would exclude "all chaos in art and lead to unwavering moral decisions. These decisions had to be in favor of harshness, struggle, and leadership, opposed to compromises and prevarication in art as well as politics."[1]

But what kind of absolutism? In the not-so-distant past, the European right grounded its critique of modernity in the solid cedar of Biblical bunkum and hoary tradition—arguments that the Conservative Revolutionaries strongly rejected. Living in Nietzsche's shadow, they felt his acute sense of a world "perpetually creating and destroying itself."[2] While valorizing fixed opposition, they were also hierophants of strife, struggle, and the decentering of the bourgeois "I." Unlike the Conservative Revolutionaries, the Nazi "I" was static, its boundaries biologically defined.[3] The Conservative Revolutionary "I," however, was a zone of constant contention. Weaknesses that the Nazis ascribed to the ritually polluted "other" (Jew/Communist/Liberal) could be found in the heart of everyone living in the "wintertime" of the West.[4] Escape from the *necessary* inner experience of "late civilization" was impossible. Chiaroscuro was the color of a world at twilight.

Spengler looked to Heraclitus in particular as a kind of master thinker because he argued that without strife, "all things would cease to exist."[5] The idea that the world is based on the clash of opposites was of great importance to Spengler, who was devoted to the concept of static polarities.[6] Yockey was also entranced by Heraclitus, and carried with him a study of the philosopher by a German historian of ideas named Zeller.

Yockey's fascination with opposites reached a point of overflow in his 1953 book *Der Feind Europas* (The Enemy of Europe), when, under two general opposing categories—"Imperialism/Capitalism" and "Ascendent instincts/ Decadent instincts"—he lists no less than 34 polarities, including:

- Faith/Rationalism
- Primacy of the Spirit/Materialism
- Idealism/Sensualism
- Will-to-Power/Will-to-Riches
- World as Object of Organization/World as Object of Plunder
- Rank as Social Distinction/Society as a Collection of Individuals
- Fulfillment of Duty/"Pursuit of Happiness"
- Absolute Will to Biological Fertility/Race-Suicide, Birth Control, Puritanism, Bohemianism
- Absolute Will to Increase Power/Surrender of the World Hegemony of the West
- Hierarchy/Equality
- Discipline/Freedom, Ethical Laissez-faire
- Authority/Parliamentarism
- Aristocracy/Plutocracy
- Society as Organic Unity/Class War
- Sexual Polarity/Feminism
- Europe as Imperium/Petty Statism
- Europe as Nation/Chauvinism
- Europe as Fatherland/Petty Nationalism
- Order/Freedom
- Stability/Constant Motion, Business Cycles
- Art Practiced in Conformity with the Cultural Task/"L'Art pour l'Art"
- Politico-Military Expansion/Financial-Military-Economic Expansion

And on and on.[7]

Yockey's interest in polarity also had a mystical element. Recall that when his belongings were seized, the FBI discovered a series of his essays with titles like "Principles of Polarity," "The Polarity of the Psyche," "Thoughts on Polarity Relating to the Calculus of Polarities," and "The Limits of Polarity." His mysticism is equally evident in *Imperium*, where he predicts the coming triumph of a new religiosity over rational thought. He writes that the 20th century sees the end of Rationalism. Even now—1948—it is pale and emaciated. Scientists and philosophers are falling away. Mysticism is reappearing, both in its authoritative religious form and in the form of theosophistic fads. Mechanism in biology has yielded to Vitalism. Materialism fights desperately, hopelessly, against the resurgence of the Soul of Culture-Man.[8]

Yockey concludes the "Cultural Vitalism" section of *Imperium:* "Since the new State negates Rationalism, the enemy of the soul of Culture-man, it has an affirmative attitude toward the spiritual development, the Rebirth of Religion which accompanies the arising of the new State."[9]

In his 1930 essay "Total Mobilization," the Conservative Revolutionary theorist Ernst Jünger argued that World War I marked the death of what he called "the 19th century's great popular church"—the cult of progress, individualism, and secular rationalism.[10] To Jünger, one of the most decorated German soldiers in World War I, the sheer monumentalism of modern war had buried the idea of "individualism" itself under a vast "storm of steel." Even battlefield heroics were meaningless in a world where a little man sitting far behind the front lines could push a button and annihilate the fiercest band of warriors.

Modern war and technology, logical outgrowths of scientific progress, had begun to undermine popular faith in reason. To Jünger the real question was how to live in a new age of myth and titanium first midwifed in the blood-drenched trenches of Europe. Futurism built its mythology around speed, airplanes, and cars. Bolshevism gloried in an ecstatic vision of huge hydroelectric power plants stretching across the Urals. America saw the birth of the cult of Technocracy that viewed engineers as a new caste of high priests.[11] Jünger wrote his famous essay *Der Arbeiter* (The Worker) to herald the coming of the new god-men of technology and total state organization in both the West and the Soviet Union.

The crack-up of the "ideas of 1789" had strange consequences. As bourgeois (*bürgerlich*) constitutional democracy was surpassed and the idea of "civil society" grew obsolete, politics took on an increasingly mythological form. Even in "atheist" Russia, Stalin became a human god. The rebirth of the mythic in the heart of the modern led to what the historian of religion Mircea Eliade has called "a revolt against historical time." To Eliade, the writings of T. S. Eliot and James Joyce were "saturated with nostalgia for the myth of eternal repetition and, in the last analysis, for the abolition of time."[12] In 1934 the Marxist philosopher Herbert Marcuse wrote an essay examining the German new right entitled "The Struggle Against Liberalism in the Totalitarian View of the State."[13] Like Eliade, Marcuse was struck by the right's "devaluation of time in favor of space, the elevation of the static over the dynamic ... the rejection of all dialectic"; in short, "the depravation of history."[14]

The turn to myth was intimately related to the quest for a new kind of post-Christian absolutism, since the new right rejected "God." "Blood," not faith, was at war with reason; honor fought profit; "organic totality" clashed with "individualistic dissolution"; Blutgemeinschaft (the community of blood) struggled against Geistgemeinschaft (the community of mind). The Conservative Revolutionaries set as their task the creation of a new virile warrior mythology. Right-wing Sorelians, they hoped that such a mythology would slow, if not reverse, Germany and Europe's perceived decline.

Belief in universal truth also came under assault. If "Man" did not exist, neither did his universal rights. Only Germans, Frenchmen, Japanese, and Russians existed. Each culture had its own unique "wordless" inner spiritual truths that could not be shared with other cultures. Within individual cultures, what was "true" was not subject to rational analysis. Truth was the articulation of the inner spirit of a particular culture. Each culture's truths (not Truth) were revealed in its science, music, mathematics, painting, and architecture as well as in its political structures, military tactics, ways of dress, gods, and myths.

The assertion of the autarky of historical/cultural/natural truths above examination before the court of reason came under fierce assault from the left as a glorification of irrationalism. The left felt that the Enlightenment was tactically worth defending because Marxism was seen as the logical heir of Enlightenment ideals. In The Destruction of Reason, the philosopher, literary critic, and erratic Stalinist Georg Lukács stresses the particular importance of antinomies for both "dialectical" and "irrational" thought. Antinomy can mean a contradiction between equally valid principles or it can mean a clash between principles or ideas that is insoluble in the light of current knowledge. Antinomies are common in thinking, since creativity begins at the point when the mind's previous level of understanding is no longer adequate to resolve the challenge posed by the new antinomy. Specific antinomies, then, can be viewed as historical and subject to being resolved, at least on the conceptual level, by potential future advances in knowledge.

Lukács argued that irrationalism begins at the same point of antinomy. Irrationalism, however, deliberately "absolutizes the problem" and "hardens the limitations of perception" from the understanding into "perceptual limitations as a whole." In other words, it calls into question the power of reason to ever know. By so doing, it "mysticizes into a 'supra-rational' answer the problem thus rendered artificially insoluble."[15] Faith and myth now return to center stage.

To Herbert Marcuse, the phrase "Reality does not admit of knowledge, only of acknowledgment" was the classic formulation of irrationalist theory.

In such an argument, "Life" is the "primal given," an existential or ontological state of affairs which the mind cannot penetrate. Reason was actually *lebensfeindlich* (hostile to life), and the modern world *Entseelung* (desouling). What Marcuse thought decisive was "that irrational givens ('nature,' 'blood and soil,' 'folkhood,' 'existential facts,' 'totality,' and so forth) are placed prior to the autonomy of reason as its limit in principle (not merely in fact), and reason is and remains causally, functionally, or organically dependent on them."[16] Reason, in short, must always be servant to Blood.

With such a paradigm, "existential facts" became new absolutes, and as outside time as myth itself. Antinomies were beyond the world of discourse and above historical mediation. In such a world conflict between opposites (Schmitt's friend/enemy distinction writ large) could only be mediated by "decisionism"—that is, by the stronger will.[17] Will became to fascism what Reason was to the Enlightenment.

Yockey's aristocratic radicalism was grounded in just such a mythical construction of the world. "Ideas," timeless symbols of the soul of a specific High Culture, governed everything. It didn't matter that only "250,000 Europeans" by his own estimate actually wanted to implement the Idea of Imperium.[18] It was the elite's task to bend the will of the mass to the emanation of the supra-rational Idea:

> The populations are stratified and specialized, and the human beings live out their lives and destinies in ways entirely subordinate to the higher organism. The latter compels these humans with *ideas*. Only a small spiritual stratum of each human population is adapted to this kind of compulsion, but those who belong to it remain in the service of the Idea, once it is felt. They will live and die for it, and in the process they determine the destinies of the population whence they spring. These *ideas*—not mere abstractions, strings of concepts, but living, pulsating, wordless necessities of being and thinking—are the technic by which these higher beings utilize human beings for their purpose.[19]

In the extreme of polarity lay what the Catholic philosopher Aurel Kolnai called the "all-important Nazi idea of limits." According to Kolnai such limits were "not conceived as means of organization and communication within the moral Universe of Mankind but, so to speak, as 'biological' hedgelines—extensible at will—around a totalitarian living unit, the 'Universe of the Particular.'"[20]

In the 1920s, in his book *England, Europe and the World*, General Haushofer put forth a geopolitical vision of German autarky in a European trading zone.[21] With his theory of Grossraumordnung, Carl Schmitt advanced a similar view of a self-contained German Universe of the Particular that incorporated Central Europe. But how was such a Universe to be achieved during the Caesarist "Age of Absolute Politics" except through war? The more categories were polarized, the more cultures were labeled incompatible, the closer they approached the condition of "the Political," or Schmitt's moment of Ernstfall, when politics was reduced to an existential "kill or be killed."

In "Soul of the City," one of the most brilliant chapters in *The Decline of the West*, Spengler writes: "Civilization is nothing but tension. The head, in all the outstanding men of Civilizations, is dominated exclusively by an expression of extreme tension." But what was that tension but a vision of shapelessness, of a world in constant flux as it perpetually creates and destroys itself?

One of Spengler's high civilizations, Babylon, felt the deepest need for its priestly caste to enact the exact same rituals to ensure the return of the sun and the coming of the rain year after year, century after century. Without such repetition, all would pass over into formlessness and chaos. Outside the gates of the vast walled city, just beyond the horizon, lay shifting sand and swirling sea. Marduk's priests knew: Forever on the edge lurks Tiamat.

Notes:

1. George L. Mosse, *Germans and Jews: The Right, the Left, and the Search for a "Third Force" in Pre-Nazi Germany* (New York: Howard Fertig, 1970), p. 158.

2. Roger Woods, "The Radical Right: The 'Conservative Revolutionaries' in Germany," in *The Nature of the Right*, edited by Roger Eatwell and Noël Sullivan (London: Pinter, 1989), p. 136. For a survey of the Conservative Revolutionaries, see Armin Mohler's essay in *Nouvelle Ecole*, No. 23 (Autumn 1973). For an excellent discussion in English, see Alastair Hamilton, *The Appeal of Fascism* (London: Anthony Blond, 1971). Also see Jeffry Herf, *Reactionary Modernism: Technology, Culture, and Politics in Weimar and the Third Reich* (New York: Cambridge University Press, 1984).

3. Karsten Harris remarks in *The Meaning of Modern Art* that Hitler operated through the language of Platonism "when he opposes the flux of appearance to true being." His trick was to make his own "pseudo-biological conception of race or people" identical with being, in other words "to put the finite in the place of the transcendent." Cited in Alice Yaeger Kaplan, *Reproductions of Banality: Fascism, Literature, and French Intellectual Life* (Minneapolis: University of Minnesota Press, 1968), fn. 14, p. 160.

4. For example, in *Prussianism and Socialism*, when Spengler is discussing the appeal of capitalist democracy and parliamentarianism to German supporters of the liberal 1848 Revolution, he calls it the "inner England" in German society.

5. Heraclitus was also the subject of one of Spengler's two dissertations.

6. Klaus Fischer, *History and Prophecy: Oswald Spengler and the Decline of the West* (Frankfurt: Peter Lang, 1989), p. 86.

7. Francis Parker Yockey, *The Enemy of Europe* (Reedy, WV: Liberty Bell Publications, 1985), pp. 51–52. See also p. 617 of *Imperium* for another listing of opposites.

8. *Imperium*, p. 349.

9. Ibid., p. 366. Here Yockey follows Spengler, who saw the linking of a new culture zone with the birth of a new religion. Spengler thought the new religion might appear in Russia. For other examples of Yockey's celebration of religion and denigration of mechanistic rationalism, see pp. 111, 237, 371, and 414 of *Imperium*.

10. Ernst Jünger, "Total Mobilization," in *The Heidegger Controversy* (Boston: MIT Press, 1993), edited by Richard Wolin, p. 124. Also see Jeffrey Herf, "Paradoxes of Cultural Pessimism: Spengler as a Reactionary Modernist," in *Der Fall Spengler* (Koln: Böhlau Verlag, 1994), edited by Alexander Demandt and John Farrenkopf.

11. For an excellent discussion of technocracy, see J. G. Furnas, *Stormy Weather* (New York: G. P. Putnam, 1977).

12. Mircea Eliade, *The Myth of the Eternal Return* (Princeton, NJ: Princeton University Press, 1991), p. 153. Eliade also attacks Heidegger from the right for Heidegger's showing that "the historicity of human existence forbids all hope of transcending time and history" (p. 150). Criticizing both Heidegger's "temporality" and Nietzsche's notion of "destiny," Eliade remarks: "It is by no means mere fortuitous coincidence that, in this philosophy, despair, the *amor fati*, and pessimism are elevated to the rank of heroic virtues and instruments of cognition" (pp. 152–53). Here Eliade is arguing against Spengler's famous notion of "pessimism" because Spengler felt the modern age was ultimately irreversible.

13. Marcuse's essay is reprinted in *Negations* (Boston: Beacon Press, 1968).

14. Ibid., p. 24.

15. Georg Lukács, *The Destruction of Reason* (Atlantic Highlands, NJ: Humanities Press, 1981), p. 97.

16. Marcuse, *Negations*, p. 15.

17. Yockey also celebrates the end of dialogue in the foreword to *Imperium:* "The real author [of *Imperium*] is the Spirit of the Age, and its commands do not admit of argumentation" (p. xvii).

18. Yockey's estimate in *Imperium*, p. 258.

19. Ibid., p. 5.

20. Aurel Kolnai, *The War Against the West* (New York: Viking Press, 1938), p. 537. In *Imperium* (p. 198), Yockey makes a passing reference to the German word *zwischenstattlich*, which means something "occurring between States, as self-contained impenetrable units."

21. One World War II book on geopolitics by Johannes Mattern was tellingly called *Geopolitik: Doctrine of National Self-Sufficiency* (Baltimore: The Johns Hopkins Press, 1942).

16

DREAMER OF
THE DAY

In the early 1950s the American rightist H. Keith Thompson wrote a brief
memoir about his experience with Yockey in New York. He recalled that
Yockey

> was a strange person. At first, he would only consent to periodically con-
> tacting me, using the name "Oswald Spengler" . . . Little by little, Yockey
> made certain revelations about himself . . . He told me of his poor economic
> background, his broken home life, and his struggle to attend law school in
> the American Midwest. But I was shocked when he pointed out that as a
> young lawyer, he deliberately lost the cases of several clients just to prove
> that he could do it—to "strengthen himself" against human weakness.[1]

Casual, even random, encounters with Yockey could quickly turn explosive. His British colleague John Anthony Gannon noted that

> in moments of personal tension, Yockey would often engage others in star-
> ing-out contests, prosecuted to the point where the other party would avert
> his gaze. Such contests could arise anywhere, even on an Underground train
> with a complete stranger, and [British rightist] Guy Chesham and I often had
> to intervene and hurry Yockey away before the engazement ended in possi-
> ble violence.[2]

Even Yockey's obsession with domination had roots in Spengler. In his
analysis of volume two of *The Decline of the West,* the Marxist critic Theodor
Adorno observed that what was decisive for Spengler was "domination . . .
His entire image of history is measured by the ideal of domination."[3] The
issue of domination had strong roots in German thought. Carl Schmitt, for

example, derived his "concept of the political" from the famous master/slave dialectic in Hegel's *Phenomenology of Mind*. In his analysis of this section of the *Phenomenology*, Herbert Marcuse notes that in Hegel, when "mere consciousness reaches the stage of self-consciousness," it discovers itself "as *ego*, and the ego is first *desire:* It can become conscious of itself only through satisfying itself in and by an 'other.'" At this stage, satisfaction can only be derived by the negation of the other, "for the ego has to prove itself by truly 'being-for-itself' *against* all 'otherness.'" Such a self "can exist only by incessantly winning and testing his existence *against* something or someone which contests it." To this form of consciousness, freedom "depends on being 'recognized,' 'acknowledged' as master" by another self-conscious subject because "self-consciousness can attain its satisfaction only in another self-consciousness."[4]

The master/slave dialectic for Hegel came down to a question of life and death when the master proved himself fit to rule by his willingness to die:

> Freedom involves the risk of life, not because it involves liberation from servitude, but because the very content of human freedom is defined by the mutual "negative relation" to the other. And since this negative relation affects the totality of life, freedom can be "tested" only by staking life itself. Death and anxiety—not as "fear for this element or that, not for this or that moment of time," but as fear for one's "entire being"—are the essential terms of human freedom *and* satisfaction. From the negative structure of self-consciousness results the relation of master and servant, domination and servitude.[5]

The moment of "staking life itself" defined Schmitt's concept of Ernstfall—"the most extreme possibility"—which, as Leo Strauss and others have noted, had its intellectual origin in the *Phenomenology*. Critic Martin Jay also makes it clear that Schmitt's use of the master/slave dialectic (a moment that is overcome in the *Phenomenology*) has nothing in common with dialectical thinking precisely because Schmitt poses "an existential, ahistorical distinction between friend and foe."[6]

To Yockey, the idea of danger as spiritual possibility, the quest for Ernstfall, was so central that he chose as *Imperium*'s motto Nietzsche's famous "*Was mich nicht umbringt, mach mich starker*" (What does not kill me makes me stronger). An authentic life could only be lived under Vesuvius. Nor was Yockey unique in his fascination with both the presentness and Eros of danger. The Conservative Revolutionary theorist Ernst Jünger began his 1931 essay "Über die Gefahr" (On Danger):

> Among the signs of the epoch we have now entered belongs the increased intrusion of danger into daily life. There is no accident concealing itself behind this fact but a comprehensive change of the inner and outer world.

We see this clearly when we remember what an important role was assigned to the concept of security in the bourgeois epoch just past. The bourgeois person is perhaps best characterized as one who places security among the highest of values and conducts his life accordingly.

Jünger then observed:

The supreme power through which the bourgeois sees security guaranteed is reason. The closer he finds himself to the center of reason, the more the dark shadows in which danger conceals itself disperse, and the ideal condition which it is the task of progress to achieve consists of the world domination of reason through which the wellsprings of the dangerous are not merely to be minimized but ultimately to be dried up altogether. The dangerous reveals itself in the light of reason to be senseless, and relinquishes its claim on reality. In this world all depends on the perception of the dangerous as the senseless, then in the same moment it is overcome, it appears in the mirror of reason as an error.

This can be demonstrated everywhere and in detail within the intellectual and actual arrangements of the bourgeois world. It reveals itself at large in the endeavor to see the state, which rests on hierarchy, as society, with equality as its fundamental principle and which is founded through an act of reason ... It reveals itself further in the many and very entangled efforts to understand the life of the soul as a series of causes and effects and thus to remove it from an unpredictable into a predictable condition, therefore to include it within the sphere in which consciousness holds sway.[7]

Danger, however, and not security had become the defining experience of postwar Europe, and Germany in particular. The masters of this brave new world "like salamanders," had "gone through the school of danger." Only they would hold their own when "things 'the likes of which were only possible in South America,' are now familiar to us." Jünger dubbed his new man a *Vanbanquespieler* (a player of dangerous games), an adventurer willing to stake all on the throw of the dice.

Yockey was just such a Vanbanquespieler. Yet, as unusual as he was, he was not completely unique. Philip Johnson, today the doyen of American architectural modernism, once traveled a path remarkably similar to Yockey's.[8] As artistic personalities who had been heavily influenced by Spengler and Nietzsche, both men felt a strong link between rightist political revolution and aesthetic order.

Johnson abandoned the art world of cosmopolitan New York in the early 1930s and returned to the Midwest. He worked with Father Coughlin and campaigned furiously for the Union Party's 1936 presidential campaign. He most likely knew Newton Jenkins, because at one point Johnson joined the Union Party's national entourage. Like Yockey, Johnson focused on youth organizing; he even co-founded a group called "Youth and Nation" that was featured in the 27 March 1937 issue of Father Coughlin's *Social Justice*. In the summer of 1939, Johnson became a European correspondent for *Social Justice*. One of his articles on Europe appeared in the 24 July 1939 issue, just a month before Yockey's "The Tragedy of Youth" appeared in that same publication. During the German invasion of Poland, he toured the front lines at the invitation of Goebbels' Propaganda Ministry.

Like Yockey, Johnson came very close to being investigated by the U.S. government as a possible German agent. As early as May 1940, the Office of Naval Intelligence was wondering whether Johnson was a Nazi spy. That October, *Harper's* exposed him as a fascist. *Harper's* appeared on newsstands in the beginning of September, around the time that Ray Healy's attack on Yockey appeared in Chicago. The FBI only closed its file on Johnson in August 1944, after he returned to Harvard.

Unlike Johnson, Yockey couldn't walk away from the game. He writes almost imploringly in *Imperium:*

> What would be a world without politics? Nowhere would there be protection or obedience, there would be no aristocracy, no democracy, no empires, no fatherland, no patriotism, no frontiers, no customs, no rulers, no political assemblies, no superiors, no subordinates. For this world to come about or to continue to exist, there would have to be a total absence of men with lust for adventure and domination. No will-to-power, no barbarian instincts, no criminals, no superiority feelings, no Messianic ideas, no unpeaceable men, no programs of action, no proselyting, no ambition, no economics above the personal level, no foreigners, no race, no ideas.[9]

To deny politics was to deny the heroic, to substitute bourgeois domesticity for aristocratic radicalism, to choose comfort over quest. Alongside a series of quotes Yockey compiled from Spengler, Goethe, Napoleon, and Count Keyserling, he wrote: "The ambition to rule souls is the strongest of all passions. Self-interest is only the key to commonplace transactions." He then cites Napoleon, who asked: "Where is the man who would not gladly be stabbed, if in exchange he could be Caesar?"[10] Elsa Dewette also captured something fundamental about Yockey's need for the heroic when describing a journey they took in 1949:

> In Ulm, as elsewhere, we visited the Cathedral. F. was strangely attracted by a large tombstone, i.e., a Medieval Knight, *grandeur nature,* complete with sword and his lady—holding hands. F. said we too would one day be laying together like that (he wasn't far from the truth either . . .). When I was in Burgos, Spain—I saw the large tombstone, in the Cathedral, of EL CID lying there, holding the hand of his lady JIMENA. I sent a large photographic reproduction of this to F.: He was *delighted*—but I think he must have burnt it when he went "underground."[11]

Notes:

1. H. Keith Thompson manuscript, Hoover Institute.

2. John Anthony Gannon, "A Remembrance of the Author of *Imperium*," p. 5, from the H. Keith Thompson archives at the Hoover Institute.

3. Theodor Adorno, "Spengler after the Decline," in *Prisms* (Cambridge, MA: MIT Press, 1981).

4. Herbert Marcuse, *Eros and Civilization: A Philosophical Inquiry into Freud* (New York: Vintage Books, 1962), p. 103.

5. Ibid., pp. 103–04.

6. Martin Jay in *Telos*, No. 71, Spring 1987, p. 73. Of course Marxism, with its concept of class struggle, anointed the proletariat as its agent of forceful change. As Marx put it: "The weapons of criticism are no match for the criticism of weapons."

7. Ernst Jünger, "On Danger," *New German Critique*, No. 59 (Summer 1993).

8. See Franz Schulze, *Philip Johnson, Life and Work* (New York: Knopf, 1994).

9. *Imperium*, p. 203.

10. Yockey's notes supplied with a comment by Marie Urbas Weiss.

11. Elsa Dewette, letter to Keith Stimely, 11 February 1982.

IN THE
IMPERIUM
(1946-50)

Under the debris of our shattered cities, the last so-called achievements of the middle-class 19th century have been finally buried . . . Together with the monuments of culture there crumble also the last obstacles to the fulfillment of our revolutionary task. Now that everything is in ruins, we are forced to rebuild Europe. In the past, private possessions tied us to bourgeois restraint. Now the bombs, instead of killing all Europeans, have only smashed the prison walls which held them captive . . . In trying to destroy Europe's future, the enemy has only succeeded in smashing its past; and with that, everything old and outworn has gone.

—Joseph Goebbels, 1945

17

GRAVEYARD

OF EUROPE

When Yockey arrived in Germany in January 1946, he could hardly believe his eyes. The Thousand Year Reich that once stood on the brink of ruling all Eurasia now lay shattered; its streets reduced to rubble; its armies in tatters; its political leadership dead, jailed, or in exile; its population shivering and starving.

Yockey was assigned to the 7708 War Crimes Group in Wiesbaden (a suburb of Frankfurt) as a civilian employee of the War Department. The 7708 investigated and prosecuted lower-level accused war criminals; Yockey was appointed as a post-trial review attorney who evaluated clemency petitions. He lived in the Hotel Taunus, which had been given over to American personnel as officers' quarters. After getting a piano installed in his room, he amused himself by playing tunes like "Deutschland über Alles." He also found a new fraulein, the 24-year-old Gisella Kuehn, whom he first met in the summer of 1946 at the State Opera House in Wiesbaden.

Yockey's immediate superior was Samuel Sonenfield. During World War II, Sonenfield had been posted to the Military Justice branch of the Army Judge Advocate General's Corps, and served in both Washington and the Pacific Theater. In the autumn of 1945, he was redeployed to the War Crimes Group. In a letter to the *National Review*, he recalled:

> I was put in charge of the Post Trial Section, which is where, before long, I ran into Mr. Yockey. A lot of the lawyers ... were being discharged and going home, and the Army was filling slots with civilian lawyers, who were arriving to take their place. Some of them were not too sound as lawyers. Among them was Francis P. Yockey.

He was a very strange and uncommunicative person, but my attention was quickly drawn to him. The most notable thing about him was that he never could be found. His absenteeism was chronic. As I remember it, what finally happened was that he was assigned to one of our outlying detachments, such as Dachau, perhaps, or Heidelberg—and that he just disappeared. He probably melted into the gray area of the AWOL soldiers (and civilians) who were absent from their units, but scraped a living by all sorts of conniving and finagling in a badly disrupted economy.[1]

Yockey *was* involved in the black market. On 10 November 1949, agents from the 66th Detachment of the U.S. Army's Counter-Intelligence Corps (CIC) interviewed a Mr. A. W. Gaedertz, Jr., about Yockey. Gaedertz, whose father was a director of General Motors Opel A.A., told the CIC

that he had known YOCKEY since autumn 1946; that YOCKEY was introduced to him by one HERBERT KAISER, a black market operator; that YOCKEY sought to obtain a new Opel automobile in exchange for black market cigarettes through GAEDERTZ's family connections.

Bruno Buchna, owner of the Reichert Hotel in Wiesbaden, was also involved in the cigarette operation and was said to have received the sum of 100,000 Reichsmarks from Yockey in 1947.[2]

Yockey was at the same time involved in business even more hazardous to his health than cigarettes. Gaedertz told the CIC investigators that at their first meeting

YOCKEY sought to enlist him in an underground "resistance" movement. According to GAEDERTZ, YOCKEY was searching for young Germans, preferably ex-Wehrmacht officers who were not totally disillusioned, who would "stand up" against the occupation authorities, counteract the obsequy of U.S.-installed public officials, and thereby establish a fitness to rule Germany upon the withdrawal of the Allied Occupation.

Yockey's most important military connection in Wiesbaden was Martin Becker. The CIC records disclose

that MARTIN BECKER is known to his neighbors as an extreme nationalist, a *Ritterkreuztraeger* [holder of the Knight's Cross] and former Captain in the Luftwaffe, a member of the NDP, and is allegedly in close contact with the STRASSER group.[3] BECKER is considered suspicious by some of his neighbors because of his frequent (almost weekly) trips to the East Zone, ostensibly to procure pharmaceutical glass for his business. Neighbors say that an American civilian [Yockey] had lived with BECKER, but no longer resided there.

When Yockey was talking about organizing underground "resistance" cells, he was on dangerous ground. Well after Germany's surrender, acts of sabotage continued against Allied personnel. The United States military headquarters in Bremen was destroyed by explosives in June 1945. In September of that same year, 40 men were arrested in Thuringia and accused of plotting to blow up military installations.[4] Three months later, British and American authorities arrested eight hundred members of a Werewolf resistance group. While Yockey was in Wiesbaden, Werewolf leaders Erwin Fisher and Hans Pietsch each received seven-year jail sentences for trying to revive the organization in the Frankfurt area.[5]

The Werewolves were the most colorful component of an underground created before Germany's surrender. This parallel world swore allegiance to Grand Admiral Karl Dönitz, the former chief of the German navy whom Hitler had appointed as his successor. Dönitz's chancellory was a small jail cell in Spandau prison, where he remained until 1955, serving a sentence for war crimes.

While in Wiesbaden Yockey wrote at least one pamphlet, entitled *Why the Americans Did Not Go to Berlin*. According to the CIC report:

GAEDERTZ stated further that YOCKEY, then residing at the Taunus Hotel, an American Officer and Civilian Bachelor Billet, courted the friendship of Germans who he sought to impress as a person of culture through his ability to play the piano, his seemingly profound knowledge of German music and literature, and his Nazi political and philosophical views. GAEDERTZ stated that he had translated into German a pamphlet written by YOCKEY entitled *Why the Americans Did Not Go to Berlin*. Such pamphlet, according to GAEDERTZ, purported to expose the Jewish-Communistic-Capitalistic influences that were directing American military policy.

When CIC investigators interviewed Yockey's former maid, Mrs. Matilda Steinhof, she also reported that "YOCKEY did much writing on political matters which was incomprehensible to her."[6]

If Yockey did produce other propaganda, it would almost certainly have included an attack on the legitimacy of the Nuremberg war crimes trials process.[7] Propaganda denouncing the trials began appearing throughout Germany immediately after the war, much of it valorizing the German army. One such pamphlet claimed to be (and most likely was) a collection of letters that Colonel General Alfred Jodl, the former chief of operations of the German Armed Forces High Command, had written to his wife from death row.[8] Although *Personal Witness of a German—Alfred Jodl's Letters from His Imprisonment in Nuremberg* appeared without an imprint, it was believed to have been produced by a group called Natinform.[9] Before the outbreak of World War II, Natinform had established a number of cells, particularly in Argentina and Brazil, to disseminate Nazi ideology throughout Latin

America. After Germany's defeat became inevitable, Natinform served as the NSDAP's propaganda apparatus in exile. By late 1944 the group had transferred key documents and funds to a secret headquarters near Göteborg, Sweden;[10] at the end of the war, the documents and money were sent to Latin America.

Through the Natinform apparatus, manuscripts written in Europe were sent to Latin America and printed by Erasmus Verlag in Brazil, or by either the Prometheus or Dürer Verlag houses in Argentina, and smuggled back into Germany.[11] *Why the Americans Did Not Go to Berlin* may have been intended for Natinform. It is worth noting that, starting in 1949, Yockey's writings (as "Ulick Varange") were published in the magazine *Der Weg* (The Way), which was part of the Natinform/Dürer Verlag group in Buenos Aires.

While Yockey's connections in the underground grew, his marriage crumbled. In the middle of 1946 Alice Yockey and their two children, Isolde and Brünnhilde ("Lollie" and "Bruni"), came to Wiesbaden in a last attempt to save the marriage. Samuel Sonenfield recalled Alice this way:

> I do remember that he [Yockey] had brought his wife over to join him after he arrived and that she and their two small children were on our hands for a while. I met him and her on the street in Wiesbaden once, before he bolted, and he introduced me to her. She was a mousy little creature, pale and grey, and seemed completely cowed by him. My brief impression of him had been that those whom he could dominate, he would.

The Yockeys moved into a flat at 86 Lahnstrasse. After Yockey vanished from Wiesbaden in late 1946, Alice moved to a new building at 48 Mossbacherstrasse, where she stayed from 13 December 1946 to 16 December 1947, when she left Germany and returned to Texas. During her stay in Wiesbaden, she kept Matilda Steinhof as her maid. Steinhof later told the CIC that

> YOCKEY had deserted his wife and children immediately prior to Mrs. ALICE YOCKEY's removal to the Mossbacherstrasse address; that YOCKEY thereafter made occasional uninvited and unwelcome visits to the Mossbacherstrasse house; that in 1947 the Counter-Intelligence Corps made frequent unsuccessful raids at the premises at all hours in an attempt to apprehend YOCKEY.

Although Steinhof says that Yockey deserted his family, Elsa Dewette thought that Alice had actually thrown her husband out of the house. She also commented:

> F. deeply loved his children. Twice I saw this proud man bitterly crying because Mrs. FPY had forbidden him to enter either house or garden to get a glimpse of his children. Each time she saw him approaching the place, she

155

began to shout blood and murder, and call hysterically for the M.P. Each time, F. had to flee for dear life, as he was convinced, once the authorities got hold of him, he would be placed in a mental hospital. He told me all this himself; also many touching details about his children.[12]

Dewette believed that the combination of the Nuremberg trials, Germany's physical devastation, and the breakup of his marriage had left Yockey spiritually wounded:

When I knew F., there was already something "old" in his nature, something *abîmé* [ruined, damaged] in him. It took me some time to find out how this had come about. F. had been marked by two tragedies: The worst one was what he had been brought to watch at the Nuremberg trial, and in the streets of vanquished Germany—the second, the tragic breaking-up of his marriage, and the forced separation from his children whom he very deeply loved . . . So something had been murdered in him at an early age. As I said: Sometimes he appeared to be a wizened little old man. I believe I helped to heal these scars, for as much as they already were old scars.[13]

While Alice kept the children, Francis kept Alice's land and money. Again Elsa Dewette:

F. told me that the family had owned a large citrus ranch in Texas. But the whole thing was ruined (plus the family) because of an unexpected spell of severe frost destroying all the plants. I think this happened in the spring of 1949, but am not quite sure of the date, although F. did tell me (story also followed by the legendary "hollow laugh").[14]

Dr. Francesca Yockey ("Bruni") said that Yockey convinced her mother to use her inheritance both to buy the citrus grove and to sign the property over to him. Alice went to A. W. Gaedertz, Jr., in the autumn of 1947 and asked him to help her recover "some $30,000 in negotiable shares of a California [Texas] citrus venture (name not recalled) which YOCKEY allegedly obtained by fraud from ALICE YOCKEY."[15]

On 26 November 1946 Yockey was officially fired from his position with the war crimes tribunal due to "abandonment of position." On 27 December 1946, he showed up at the American Consular Service in Zurich to get a one-year extension on his passport, which was granted. He claimed at the time that he was living at Ptatterstrasse 48 in Zurich and was a student at the Institute Minerva.[16] After spending an unknown period using his updated passport to travel in Europe, he returned to the United States and stayed with Vinette and William Coyne in Illinois. He also sent his German girlfriend Gisella Kuehn regular food packages. His time with the Coynes lasted for about five months, before he left for Ireland in the fall of 1947 to write *Imperium*.[17]

The best indication of Yockey's state of mind at this time comes from a pledge he wrote while in Wiesbaden. It was modeled on Ivan's pledge to his brother Alyosha in Dostoyevski's *The Brothers Karamazov*, a passage that Spengler analyzed in volume two of *The Decline of the West*. Yockey wrote:

> I will go from one end to the other of my beloved Europe. I know well that I shall be going only to a churchyard, but I know, too, that the churchyard is dear, very dear, to me. Beloved dead lie buried there. Every stone over them, every bomb-crater containing the pulverized bones of these dead, tells of a life once so ardently lived, so passionate a belief in its own achievements, its own truth, its own battles, its own knowledge, that I know, even now I know, that I shall fall down and kiss these stones, these endless ruins, this blood-drenched, sacred earth, and weep.
>
> But I surely also know that then, despite a convulsive rage at the perpetrators of this crime, I will again stand erect over this European graveyard and swear the solemn oath that to my last breath I will fight tooth and nail against those who attempted, in vain to be sure, to destroy the cradle of our Western Culture, with its unmatched accomplishments, with its deeds unique in the annals of Humanity. This I, Francis Yockey, do solemnly swear![18]

Notes:

1. Sonenfield's letter appeared in the 8 October 1971 *National Review*; it was inspired by a *National Review* cover story on Willis Carto and the Liberty Lobby by C. H. Simonds, published on 10 September 1971. The article discussed Yockey at some length.

2. Buchna told investigators from the CIC's 66th Detachment on 9 November 1949 that he was attracted to Yockey because he was a man of great culture, but that their friendship fell apart after Yockey had asked him to pay for some books that he had earlier given him. Buchna said he last saw Yockey in June 1949. In fact, the Army learned that Yockey stayed at the Reichert Hotel in mid-November.

3. The NDP, one of the first postwar political parties in Germany, was quickly penetrated by the far right. The reference to "the STRASSER group" is presumably to Otto Strasser's Black Front, which had broken from the NSDAP in the late 1920s on the grounds that Hitler had sold out to big business and the German nobility. On Strasserist currents in the postwar German right, see Perry Biddiscombe, "Operation Selection Board: The Growth and Suppression of the Neo-Nazi 'Deutsche Revolution,' 1945–47," in *Intelligence and National Security*, Vol. 11, No. 1 (January 1996).

4. Wellington Long, *The New Nazis of Germany* (Philadelphia: Chilton Book Company, 1968), p. 39.

5. E. H. Cookridge, *Gehlen: Spy of the Century* (New York: Random House, 1971), p. 100.

6. In his 1960 essay *The World in Flames*, Yockey also mentions writing in October 1946 an unpublished essay entitled "The Possibilities of Germany" "in a

quiet garden in Wiesbaden." "The Possibilities of Germany" seems to have been a geopolitical essay, because in it he speculates about the power balance between "the Anglo-Saxon-Jewish combine and the Russian empire."

7. In this context it is worth mentioning what may be the first far-right attack on the legitimacy of the war crimes trials in English. This was an anonymous pamphlet entitled *The Nuremberg "Trial"* that appeared in 1946. It is possible that Yockey had something to do with this pamphlet, which appeared during his stay in Wiesbaden. Although I have not seen it, I learned of its existence while examining the *Revisionist Bibliography* compiled by Keith Stimely and published in 1981 by the Institute for Historical Review (IHR). Stimely says that it attacks war crimes Justice Robert H. Jackson in particular. In Yockey folklore there is a legend that he got into a shouting match with Justice Jackson. The August 1960 issue of *Right* claims that during "an angry exchange with Justice Jackson," Yockey quit the war crimes tribunal. In fact, he was fired for desertion. Samuel Sonenfield, who surely would have heard of such an incident, was unaware of any confrontation. There is also no mention of it in either the FBI or Army files. And finally, Justice Jackson was based in Nuremberg, not Wiesbaden.

8. Jodl was executed on 16 October 1946.

9. In this book I shall discuss two organizations called Natinform. The first was the propaganda group based in South America. The second was a British-German group created in the early 1950s. For clarity, I shall refer to the South American organization as "Natinform" and the British-German group as "NATINFORM."

10. The British anti-fascist journal *Searchlight* thought Natinform was initially based in Malmö, Sweden.

11. Long, *The New Nazis of Germany*, pp. 41–44.

12. Elsa Dewette, letter to Keith Stimely, 12 October 1981.

13. Elsa Dewette, letter to Keith Stimely, 15 May 1982.

14. Elsa Dewette, letter to Keith Stimely, 31 March 1982.

15. Gaedertz told the CIC that he had telephoned Leona Farah (the Detroit clerk who followed Yockey to Germany) at the U.S. Occupation Military Government in Berlin in an attempt to locate him. Gaedertz also said that Farah gave Yockey money.

16. I was unable to learn anything about the Institute Minerva.

17. In his introduction to *Imperium*, Willis Carto says that after his time in Wiesbaden, Yockey "returned to America for five months," which sounds correct.

18. Yockey's pledge is reprinted in *The World in Flames*, which was published after his death by H. Keith Thompson and Fred Weiss.

18
MEETING
MOSLEY

Yockey arrived in Dublin, Ireland, on 18 September 1947, his 30th birthday.[1]
He then headed to Brittas Bay in County Wicklow, where he wrote *Imperium*
on an old typewriter he dubbed "the devil machine," and dated his introduction "Brittas Bay, January 30, 1948." Elsa Dewette recalled Yockey telling her
that

> he chose to stay in Brittas Bay only because he liked the look of the place:
> It was quiet, beautiful, and remote: an ideal corner of his beloved Europa. I
> never heard of any contacts to help him get settled. He told me that he had
> just rented a room in a boarding house (or was it a private one?), settled
> down, and started to write, just like that . . . I am convinced that, before
> starting on the task, he had the construction of it all planned in his head—
> and for both volumes at that. It stood there, clearly before him. And he
> wrote it without hesitation (or even corrections).[2]

Imperium was not the only project that occupied Yockey's time. He also
became involved in a business transaction that involved his German girlfriend, Gisella Kuehn. Kuehn later told U.S. Army CIC investigators that she

> heard from YOCKEY from BRITTAS BAY, Ireland, from where he asked her
> to buy books for him, particularly the work *Untergang des Abendlandes* by
> SPENGLER. KUEHN stated that she attempted to procure books; that she
> had asked her employer, Dr. WEIT, who has a large library, to sell her some,
> which request was refused. According to KUEHN, YOCKEY had told her to
> offer cigarettes for books and that cigarettes would be provided by BRUNO
> BUCHNA.

Kuehn then mentioned another financial enterprise that involved Buchna: the acquisition of a plot of land at one of Nazi Germany's most sacred sites, Hitler's retreat at Berchtesgaden. She told the CIC

> that during the winter of 1947–48 she had received a letter from YOCKEY from BRITTAS BAY, Ireland, telling her to buy, in her name, a plot of land (*Grundstueck*) in the vicinity of Berchtesgaden. KUEHN stated that through her friend, one HEINZ ERICH KRAUE, a contract was made with the farmer JOSEF KURZ and the attorney HEINRICH FROELICH, for the sale of a piece of land for the sum of 25,000 RMs. KUEHN stated that she returned to WIESBADEN, obtained the money from BUCHNA, and telegraphed the stated amount to JOSEPH KURZ; that KURZ refused to deed the property, came to WIESBADEN, and demanded 25,000 RMs more of her. KUEHN stated that she advised BUCHNA of KURZ's demand; that BUCHNA told her he would communicate it to YOCKEY. KUEHN stated further that the money reform occurred; that BUCHNA took her to the office of BECK-MANN [a lawyer and close friend of Yockey] where she signed papers authorizing BECKMANN to begin action for the recovery of the money paid KURZ or for specific performance; that in February 1949, upon the advice of her employer, Dr. WEIT, she advised BECKMANN that she was withdrawing from the transaction; that BECKMANN prepared for her signature an assignment of her interest to BRUNO BUCHNA.

Yockey visited England sometime in the autumn of 1947 to meet with Sir Oswald Mosley, the pre-war leader of the British Union of Fascists (BUF), who had been jailed under the "preventive detention" order known as Defense Regulation 18B in the spring of 1940.[3] Mosley took his first tentative step back into politics in 1946 with *My Answer*, a book that denied any charge of treason. One year later, he published his own *Imperium*-like opus called *The Alternative*.[4] Like Yockey, he argued that the narrow nationalism of pre-war fascism was obsolete and that a new United Europe must be created as a third force between the Soviet threat and American capitalism.

As Mosley edged closer to the spotlight, small groups like the Order of the Sons of St. George, the Mosley book clubs, and Jeffrey Hamm's British League of Ex-Servicemen and Women, eagerly prepared for their paladin's return. One Manchester-based pro-Mosley grouping was John Anthony ("Tony") Gannon's Imperial Defence League. Gannon had joined the BUF in 1935 at age 14, and later became an assistant district leader for propaganda in Manchester as well as a regional speaker.[5] In June 1940 he was detained under Defence Regulation 18B for six months.[6] His initial meeting with Yockey took place shortly before the official founding of Mosley's postwar Union Movement (UM).[7] Gannon later recalled:

> I first met FPY—Yockey to all and sundry—in the autumn of 1947 at the London bookstore headquarters of the Union for British Freedom, this being

one of the regional organizations preparing for the return of Sir Oswald Mosley to active politics. Yockey was introduced to me by A. Raven Thomson—pre-war director of policy in the British Union of Fascists—with the comment that I would find him an interesting companion.

In appearance he was somewhat bohemian, wearing a dark green jacket, navy blue roll-top sweater, and corduroy trousers. Some five feet seven inches tall, of slim but wiry build, dark brown hair and eyes, and pale complexion. One noticed those deep-set eyes, and the intensity of their expression combining both intelligence and authority. We spoke together for a long time in compete agreement on what had happened to Europe and what needed to be done to restore its position, ending only when it became time for me to leave for the railway station to take my train for Manchester. It was agreed that we would meet again in the natural course of events, but no precise arrangement was made.[8]

Yockey told Gannon that he "had come to Europe to meet others in the service of the Idea, in particular, Sir Oswald Mosley, before writing a book." But even at their first meeting, intrigue swirled about him, as Gannon reports:

As I was prepared to leave, I was approached by another man with an American accent, whom I had noticed in a general sort of way whilst speaking with Yockey, because he seemed to be taking some interest in our conversation. He asked if I was leaving, and I replied that I was bound for Euston station; to which he at once rejoined that he was also going in that direction, and that it would be a good idea to share a taxi together, to which I agreed.

My new acquaintance enquired if I knew Yockey, and I replied that I had met him for the first time that evening. He then warned me against having anything further to do with Yockey, stating that he was sure that Yockey was working for the FBI and the ADL. There then followed the routine request for my name and address so that we could keep in touch, which I declined on the grounds that I was going abroad for an indefinite period. By this time we had arrived in Euston, and I left Yockey's accuser with the certain conviction that HE was an agent of the ADL, and that his denunciation of Yockey confirmed the latter's bona fides as one of us.[9]

Yockey also met Guy Chesham, another leading Mosleyite who, like Gannon, would become a founding member of Yockey's European Liberation Front (ELF). According to a critical report on Yockey issued in 1953 by the joint German-British fascist group NATINFORM:[10]

In 1946–47 YOCKEY made his way to London after leaving the U.S. Army, and immediately commenced his political activity. The first object of his attention was OSWALD MOSLEY, who in 1947 launched the so-called Union Movement. YOCKEY was able to establish a satisfactory contact with MOSLEY and became a paid member of the organizing staff of the Union Movement. His work for same was in the European Contact Section and his closest colleague in this section was the leading functionary, GUY CHESHAM.

Although I have been unable to learn whether Yockey did, in fact, become a paid member of the European Contact Section of the Union Movement, Gannon thought it possible that Yockey may have spoken at some Union Movement meetings and received a few pounds from Mosley.[11] Lady Diana Mosley also remembers Yockey's visiting them when she and her husband were living in Wiltshire after the war.[12]

In the early spring of 1948, after completing *Imperium*, Yockey returned to England. While living in London, he continued his secret campaign against the war crimes tribunal, a campaign begun in Wiesbaden when he turned over legal files to the Nazi underground.[13] Confirmation of his covert activity comes from the French fascist and literary critic Maurice Bardèche.[14] In 1947 Bardèche published *Lettre à François Mauriac*, which defended the Collaboration. He also denounced the postwar *epuration* (purification or purge) and, in particular, the execution of his close friend and intellectual collaborator Robert Brasillach for treason.

Lettre was an enormous success.[15] Bardèche's next book, *Nuremberg ou la Terre Promise* (Nuremberg or the Promised Land), appeared in 1948 and was soon translated into six or seven languages.[16] *Nuremberg* attacked the French Resistance and argued that the German military had little alternative but to loyally follow orders and fight for the German nation (*patrie*). *Nuremberg* was also one of the earliest attempts to deny the Holocaust. It claimed that at least some of the evidence about the concentration camps had been falsified and that deaths attributed to Nazi genocide were primarily the result of war-related illness and starvation. As for the gas chambers, they were actually used to disinfect the inmates, not kill them. He even claimed that when the Nazis proclaimed the "final solution of the Jewish problem," they really meant relocating the Jews to ghettos in the East.[17]

In 1948, the same year of *Nuremberg*'s publication, Yockey published *Imperium*, which may have been the first attempt by an American to deny the Holocaust in print. Yockey writes:

> Photographs were supplied in millions of copies. Thousands of the people who had been killed published accounts of their experiences in these camps. Hundreds of thousands more made fortunes in postwar black markets. "Gas-chambers" that did not exist were photographed, and a "gasmobile" was invented to titillate the mechanically minded.[18]

Yockey's denial appeared in a chapter called "Propaganda," and followed a paragraph criticizing "the cinema-factories of Hollywood [which] ground out lying plays and newsreels." Bardèche also attacked concentration camp photographs in *Nuremberg*, and claimed that the camps were being transformed into Holocaust museums "decorated" with "reconstituted torture chambers in places where they never existed . . . like for a film set."[19]

After *Nuremberg*'s publication, Bardèche recalled that

> Yockey had entered into correspondence with me under the name of Ulick Varange while sending me a certain number of extremely valuable documents coming from the archives, of which he had knowledge, and which were intended for the headquarters of General McCloy, concerning the requests for clemency for a certain number of the persons condemned by the International Military Tribunal. I made use of that documentation in the second book that I did on the Nuremberg Trials under the title *Nuremberg 2 or the Counterfeiters*.[20]

In his 1993 memoir, *Souvenirs*, Bardèche revealed that Yockey had sent him documents to aid in the defense of accused war criminals like SS Lieutenant General Otto Ohlendorf.[21] A lawyer and economist, Ohlendorf played a prominent role in the SS's espionage service, the *Sicherheitsdienst* (Security Service), better known as the SD. He also commanded an *Einsatzgruppe* (Action Group) in the Ukraine that murdered some 90,000 people between 1941 and 1942. Sentenced to death in 1948, he spent three and a half years in detention before being executed on 8 June 1951.

Resistance to the war crimes process in England was led by Mosley, who "from the start of the proceedings at Nuremberg" had "publicly denounced" both the trials and "the pursuit of vengeance against a whole people."[22] As he recounts in his autobiography, *My Life*:

> I particularly resented . . . the treatment of soldiers whose only crime was to obey orders. Some of these men were doomed from the start; if they did not obey when the order was given, they were shot on the spot by existing authority, and if they did obey they were subsequently executed by the victorious Allies. Postwar prosecution was even extended in less degree to men who could not conceivably be connected with any crime.[23]

He also expressed special sympathy for members of the Waffen SS:

> At an earlier stage, young Germans fresh from the army, and particularly from the SS regiments, were passionately European and entirely supported my advanced European ideas. I had heard from many of them long before I was free to travel and had an insight into what they were then thinking, which is perhaps almost unique.

The Waffen SS included volunteers from France, Italy, Belgium, Holland, Spain, and other nations. Many of them were highly political and idealistic and saw war against Bolshevik Russia as a pan-European knightly crusade. Mosley believed that these Waffen SS veterans were the natural leaders of a new post-Hitler European fascism freed from the "old nationalism" that he attacked in *The Alternative*.

Both Yockey and Mosley worked to save a host of convicted war criminals from the gallows. Yockey was particularly active in the defense of SS Lieutenant Colonel Fritz Knoechlein. During the 1940 battle for France, Knoechlein commanded a unit of the 2nd *Totenkopf* (Death's Head) Regiment. During the fighting his unit surrounded a hundred British troops holed up in a farm. Even after the British ran up a white flag, Knoechlein claimed that they continued to fire on his men. Enraged, he marched the captured Tommies to a barn wall and had them machine-gunned, leaving the dead and wounded in one large heap.[24]

According to John Gannon, Yockey managed to secure a top British barrister and Labor member of the House of Commons named Reginald Paget for Knoechlein's defense.[25] Gannon also recalled that both Mosley and Raven Thomson intervened on Knoechlein's behalf.[26] Yockey also worked with two leading British military men, retired Major General J. F. C. Fuller and the military historian Captain Basil Lidell Hart, both of whom would later write glowing reviews of *Imperium*.

Yockey's anti–war crimes trials activism may have served as his introduction to Mosley's Union Movement. As an American lawyer with direct knowledge of the war crimes bureaucracy, Yockey would have been an invaluable liaison between the British right and those on the Continent working against the trials. This might help explain his close ties to Guy Chesham, who worked for the Union Movement's European Contact Section.

Yet despite their efforts, neither Yockey nor his friends could save Knoechlein. After the massacre, two badly wounded British soldiers were discovered by a different German unit and sent to the hospital. One Tommy, Private Pooley, lived to testify at Knoechlein's trial. On 25 October 1948 Knoechlein was convicted of war crimes. Three months later he was hanged.

Notes:

1. While in Ireland, Yockey may have dabbled in a bit of passport fraud. He applied for a new passport in Dublin on 22 September 1947, claiming that he had lost his old one while coming through customs. "A new passport renewal series No. 826, Passport No. 22-FS-211938, was issued to the subject on November 6, 1947, at Dublin, Ireland." (From a long FBI review of the Yockey case by Lloyd Bogstad dated 8 July 1954 [CG 100-25647].)

If Yockey had lied, it would mean that he now had two passports. He may have forged the dates on one of these passports in 1949. CIC agent Lieutenant Robert W. Lewis noticed that there was something odd about Yockey's passport and his military entry permit:

No person contacted could or would furnish any information concerning SUBJECT's ability to enter and depart Occupied territory. Information from the Combined Travel Board, HERFORD, is not clear and possibly in error with respect to dates. According to the Combined Travel Board, SUBJECT was issued a U.S. Passport at DUBLIN, Ireland, on 6 November 1949, which date fell on a Sunday, likewise the date, 28 August 1949, an application date for a military Entry Permit also fell on a Sunday. [From a 25 January 1950 CIC report.]

2. Elsa Dewette, letter to Keith Stimely, 31 March 1982.

3. Mosley used his time in jail to further study Spengler's *The Decline of the West*. See Richard Thurlow, "Destiny and Doom: Spengler, Hitler and 'British Fascism,'" in *Patterns of Prejudice*, Vol. 15, No. 4, 1981. Thurlow also discusses Yockey's influence on the British far right.

4. Political analyst George Thayer thought *The Alternative* a "pretentious and wordy book, full of such phrases as 'transcending the diurnal politics of normality,' 'The Great Negation,' 'Doer versus Deniers,' and 'Hierarchical Synthesis.'" (George Thayer, *The British Political Fringe* [London: Anthony Blond, 1965], p. 41.) Mosleyites thought differently: Some saw *Imperium* as indebted to *The Alternative*. Mosley lieutenant Jeffrey Hamm told the American rightist Keith Stimely that Mosleyites "tended to regard it [*Imperium*] as an imitation of O.M.'s *The Alternative*."

5. Above that rank were only the national speakers and Mosley himself.

6. John Anthony Gannon, letter to Keith Stimely, 13 July 1980.

7. Mosley reemerged on the political scene when he gave a speech at a 15 November 1947 conference of the Mosleyite book clubs. The Union Movement was officially launched on 8 February 1948.

8. John Anthony Gannon, remembrance of Yockey. From the H. Keith Thompson collection in the Hoover Institute.

9. Ibid.

10. Recall that NATINFORM was not related to the South America–based organization also known as Natinform.

11. "I have never heard FPY speak in public, but I did hear that in his early days in London he had spoken for UM." John Anthony Gannon, letter to Keith Stimely, 7 September 1980.

12. Lady Diana Mosley, letter to Keith Stimely, 29 June 1982.

13. In a section of *Imperium* entitled "The Terror," Yockey calls the war crimes process "a huge and inclusive program of physical extermination and politico-legal-socio-economic persecution . . . instigated against the defenseless body of Europe" (p. 598).

14. Born 1 October 1909, Bardèche became the friend of Robert Brasillach, a French literary critic and collaborator who was executed in February 1945 for his role in helping Germany during the Occupation. Bardèche married Brasillach's sister Suzanne in July 1934. In the 1930s, he co-wrote with Brasillach a book on cinema and a book on the war in Spain. Bardèche would later achieve fame for his writings on Stendahl, Balzac, and Proust. (His book on Proust won the *Grand Prix de la Critique Literaire* in 1971.)

15. Alice Yaeger Kaplan, *Reproductions of Banality: Fascism, Literature, and French Intellectual Life* (Minneapolis: University of Minnesota Press, 1986), Chapter 7 ("The Late Show: Conversations with Maurice Bardèche"), p. 177.

16. Ibid., p. 178. It also resulted in Bardèche being briefly jailed.

17. See Deborah Lipstadt, *Denying the Holocaust: The Growing Assault on Truth and Memory* (New York: The Free Press, 1993), p. 50, for a brief summary of Bardèche's argument.

18. *Imperium*, p. 533.

19. Quoted in Kaplan, *Reproductions of Banality*, p. 167.

20. Correspondence from Maurice Bardèche to Keith Stimely, summer 1982. *Nuremberg II ou Les Faux Monnayeurs* (Paris: Les Sept Couleurs, 1950) also appeared in German as *Nurnberg oder die Falschmünzer* (Wiesbaden: Priester, 1957).

21. Bardèche wrote about Yockey: "Il était venu me voir après mon livre sur le procès. Il savait beaucoup de choses, beaucoup trop de choses et me transmit des documents établis par la défense pour les recours en grâce d'Ohlendorf et de plusieurs autres accusés. Ces documents donnaient des faits une tout autre vision que celle de l'accusation." *Souvenirs* (Paris: Buchet/Chastel, 1993), p. 252.

22. Sir Oswald Mosley, *My Life* (New York: Thomas Nelson, 1968), p. 443.

23. Ibid., p. 439.

24. On the Knoechlein case, see Gerald Reitlinger, *The SS: Alibi of a Nation, 1922–1945* (New York: Viking, 1957), pp. 148–49.

25. Paget (later Lord Paget of Northampton) successfully defended German General Erich von Manstein on war crimes charges.

26. In a 1953 letter to Keith Thompson, former ELF member Peter J. Huxley-Blythe suggested that Yockey did not have support from Mosley. According to Huxley-Blythe: "Yockey first met Mosley when he tried to solicit the latter's aid for certain German officers condemned to death: Mosley refused to help."

Huxley-Blythe was wrong. Although he met Yockey in Gannon's company very briefly in London during a Union Movement convention, his one serious conversation came in 1949, after Yockey had broken with the Union Movement. When I interviewed him, he said that Gannon and Guy Chesham were the real experts on Yockey and Mosley. The man who knew the most was Guy Chesham, as Gannon explains:

> On several occasions in 1948 I was in the company of Y and OM, but not on those where they crossed swords. For this sort of information you must seek out Guy Chesham, for he did witness such encounters, which were usually in OM's flat in London over a meal. Chesham moved to London from Sheffield, did a certain amount of work for OM as an employee of sorts, and had, thereby, opportunities to witness these domestic scenes.

John Anthony Gannon, letter to Keith Stimely, 1 March 1981. Gannon tried without success to locate Guy Chesham so that he could be interviewed by Keith Stimely. I also was unsuccessful in my attempt to find Chesham.

19

THE EUROPEAN
LIBERATION
FRONT

First published in London in 1948, *Imperium* tried to imagine fascism after Hitler, a fascism no longer dominated by German race doctrine. In "the period of the future," Yockey claimed, no "European 'nation' of the older type" would exist. Already, the idea of a united Europe could be found "everywhere in the minds of the Culture-bearing stratum of the West, and for a while it was actualized in its first crude provisional form during the Second World War."[1] Once the idea of Imperium was fully established, "no force within the Civilization" could resist the coming "Cultural Reunion" that would unite "North and South, Teuton and Latin, Protestant and Catholic, Prussia, England, Spain, Italy, and France, in the tasks now waiting."[2] Yockey concludes *Imperium:*

> The West has two centuries and tens of millions of lives of the coming generation to give to the war against the Barbarian and the distorter. It has a will which has not only emerged unbroken from the Second World War, but is now more articulate all over Europe, and is gaining in strength with every year, every decade. Merely material superiority will do them little good in a war whose duration will be measured, if necessary, in centuries. Napoleon knew, and the West still knows, the primacy of the spiritual in warfare. The soil of Europe, rendered sacred by the streams of blood which have made it spiritually fertile for a millennium, will once again stream with blood until the barbarians and distorters have been driven out and the Western banner

waves on its home soil from Gibraltar to the North Cape, and from the rocky promontories of Galway to the Urals.

This is promised, not by human resolve merely, but by a higher Destiny, which cares little whether it is 1950, 2000, or 2050. This Destiny does not tire, nor can it be broken, and its mantle of strength descends upon those in its service.[3]

Copies of *Imperium* were sent to rightist leaders around the world. In Germany, General Otto Remer, Luftwaffe aces Heinz Knoke and Hans-Ulrich Rudel, and former Hitler Youth leader Karl-Heinz Priester praised the book, while in Italy, Movimento Sociale Italiano (MSI) leader Giorgio Almirante, the fascist theorist Julius Evola, and Princess Pignatelli of the MSI-allied Women's Social Movement endorsed its message. Maurice Bardèche recalled that *Imperium* "interested me a great deal and to such a point that I began the translation of it which is still in my files."[4] *Imperium* was also distributed to leading British universities as well as the Library of the House of Commons. Retired Major General J. F. C. Fuller called it the most prophetic book since *The Decline of the West*, while military historian Captain Basil Liddell Hart labeled it a "work of genius."[5]

The enthusiasm for *Imperium* reflected a strongly felt need for a new kind of fascism. The call for a united Europe was also being forcefully articulated by Sir Oswald Mosley.[6] In *The European Situation: The Third Force*, Mosley commented: "In 1948 I stated the policy—Europe a Nation—because it seemed to me at this point in history to be both the deep desire of the European and the practical necessity of the present situation." This new Europe would be "a great unity imbued with a sense of high mission, not a market state of jealous battling interests." A united Europe would insure that

> Europeans shall never be slaves either of West or East; either of finance or of bolshevism. We shall neither be bought by Wall Street nor conquered by the Kremlin. We will neither serve beneath the yoke of usury nor suffer beneath the knout of communism. We in Europe have deeper roots, a higher culture, a greater tradition, a longer and more tested strength, a harder vitality, a finer purpose, and a further vision than any other power on earth.

Italy's Movimento Sociale Italiano first took up the practical task of realizing a new postwar fascist order. In Rome in March 1950 the MSI organized a meeting to discuss the future of Europe, the participants including Mosley, Bardèche, Anna Maria Mussolini, and Sweden's Per Engdahl.[7] A follow-up gathering that October attracted delegates from France, England, Spain, Italy, Sweden, Denmark, Norway, Germany, Belgium, Switzerland, and Portugal. Former Hitler Youth leader Karl-Heinz Priester spoke for many at the conference when he stressed the notion of Europe as a "third force":

While Russia is trying to bolshevize Europe, the West is colonizing us. We who have been defamed for years because of our soldierly stand against Bolshevism are being asked to defend a foreign world as dishonored mercenaries! This the front generation is not in the least inclined to countenance. In order to offer resistance to the oppressors of Europe and Germany, the front generation is holding out its hands to the nationalist forces of all countries to work together to make Europe a third great force in the world. To do this the front generation in all countries must destroy the barriers of parochial nationalism and of alien interpretations of democratic principles.[8]

In May 1951, another MSI-supported pan-European congress in Malmö, Sweden, created the *Europäische Soziale Bewegung* (ESB or European Social Movement), commonly known as the "Malmö International."

Given both the ferment for a united Europe and their similar ideas for Europe's future, Yockey was shocked when Mosley, whom he counted on most to support *Imperium*, strongly turned against him. Elsa Dewette described Yockey's disillusionment with Mosley this way:

This is exactly what happened between Mosley and F.: I have it from F. himself and I tell you that many ridiculous and complicated things have been written about this, although the matter was quite simple. F. had this manuscript of *Imperium*. He thought—naturally—that Mosley was the most obvious person to go to, to help him have it printed and publicized. First, F. had to beg several times to have an interview. At last his *Grandeur* (M.) accepted to see him. He treated him very offhandedly. But F. was obstinate, and not to be baffled. He left the manuscript with M. begging him to read it. A few days later he returned to M.'s office and F. told me he had the impression that M. had only glanced at a few pages, and certainly not read it through. F. got so desperate he then offered M. to renounce all rights on the book, and not only that, but that *M. could sign his name under it, as the author* (I was so shocked at this, I nearly cried). M. refused this also. When F. told me this, he ended by laughing this terrible bitter laugh. It still echoes in my ears and gives me the shivers. That is the story F. told *me* . . . M. treated F. with disdain and irony. He never at any moment took him seriously . . . Anyway, after the way he had been treated, F. hated Mosley.[9]

Mosley did more than just decline to publish *Imperium*. Guy Chesham, Mosley's Oxford-educated lieutenant, said that he even blocked a promised review of *Imperium* in the Union Movement paper. In his *Memorandum of Dissociation* (Chesham's resignation statement from the Union Movement), he lashed out at Mosley:

This significant book [*Imperium*] was not even reviewed by you, contrary to your promise; paper was not provided to the author, contrary to your promise, and in spite of the fact that you were using up political paper to publish politically useless aesthetic works.[10] Moreover, the character of the author was assailed with a bitterness and fury of the order usually reserved for the heroic William Joyce.[11]

It was therefore necessary to listen to you explaining at tedious length why you could not review the book. These reasons were in inverse proportion to the force of the attacks on the author. A philosophical quibble on some difference between Goebbels and Spengler was, I recollect, your official excuse.[12]

How ironical that your group should set itself up as the keeper of the National Socialist conscience! It has no point of contact whatsoever with the Nazi Movement, spiritual, ideological, organizational, traditional, or cultural. It is not decent for people to take the name of Spengler and Goebbels in vain: The former, were he alive today, would be declared a war criminal, the Jews aver. The latter would have banned the anti-Nazi scribblings of *Union* in their entirety and have made short shrift of your own pretensions at the present time.

Chesham continued:

With this book you acquired a heaven-sent opportunity to supply your group with a granite-like ideology. It is true that your treatment of the author underlined your well-known inability to tolerate men of intellect and imagination about you, but it was your failure to adopt the ideology of the book which displayed the full extent of your purely social-economic activity and your incredible delusions of grandeur. You hated *Imperium* because it was a summons to action, because it demanded a shattering of illusion and a manly facing of political facts.[13]

"Take note," he concluded, "the acceptance of *Imperium* among political and intellectual circles at home and abroad is now *a political fact*."[14]

John Gannon thought that Mosley distanced himself from *Imperium* from a loss of nerve:

In this period, FPY, Chesham, and I were active in the UM of O.M., but becoming ever more skeptical as to the prospects of it ever being a REAL political force. Whereas the imprisonment of Hitler in Landsberg forged the steel of personal resolution and dedication, O.M.'s sojourn in Holloway gaol proved to be the opposite. His confidence had been shaken, he was older, less decisive, more opportunistic . . . Like many before us, however, we did not find it easy to make a final judgment on O.M., and put if off for as long as possible.[15]

Peter J. Huxley-Blythe also recalled that the Union Movement had been divided between "many people from the past" who remembered Mosley with nostalgia and "younger ones like myself who wanted more dynamic leadership. We didn't want to have to apologize for the past." But Mosley "was not the man of action that he [once] was and, upon reflection, he may never have been."[16]

In his brief discussion of Yockey, Mosley biographer Robert Skidelsky comments: "Although at the time the period 1947–50 looked like a simple revival of fascism, one can now see it as a process of [Mosley's] extrication from the dead hand of pre-war fascism and a rededication to a new, and more moderate, crusade."[17] Mosley's "more moderate crusade" meant coming to terms with American hegemony over Western Europe; a view Yockey fiercely opposed. While still in Mosley's circle, he had extensive discussions with A. Raven Thomson, one of Mosley's closest aides, about the American question. In a letter to H. Keith Thompson, Raven Thomson remarked:

> Yockey is a brilliant young intellectual American expatriate with a strong anti-American phobia, as have so many expatriates living here, taking the view that the present American influence in Europe is more damaging to European culture than the direct but alien threat of communism from the East.
>
> He joined our Movement at the time of its formation in 1948, obviously in the hope of getting our Chief [Mosley] to finance his book, which he refused to do because it was full of Spenglerian pessimism and was quite unnecessarily offensive to America. He then broke with us and has been generally found to be so conceited and unstable in personal relations (he is a musical artist of no mean ability) that it is almost impossible to work with him, even allowing for his extremist views, which are, however, stated in the most brilliant terms.[18]

I suspect that a good part of the reason for Mosley's hostility to Yockey can be found in Raven Thomson's remark that Yockey was "unnecessarily offensive to America." Recall that the political climate in Europe in 1948 had become extraordinarily dangerous, with the Berlin Crisis raising the possibility of imminent war. Suddenly the once-self-evident fascist "third way" was radically called into question.

Yockey advanced a clear line around the East-West issue. He argued that there were only three ways to restore fascism. The most unlikely option was an American "Nationalist Revolution." The second way, almost as implausible, was the ascension to power of an "Imperialist" in one or more European nations who would shatter the American "occupation." The third way, however, "would follow the invasion and conquest of American-occupied Europe by Russia, in the process of which Europe would be united against this alien force and the struggle for liberation would begin."[19]

Yockey's neutralist position was opposite Mosley's. In *The European Situation: The Third Force*, Mosley argued that

> Europe lies helpless between the powers of America and Russia; and it is chiefly occupied or controlled by the former. Until Europe is free, some are indifferent which is the occupying power. That attitude reveals an inability to grasp realities and an error in tactics. Let us regard facts and nothing but

facts. Under Russia, European freedom is killed, and under America, European freedom can still exist and even grow. That is the basic difference which must determine the question of attitude.

The more Mosley tilted West, the more Yockey tilted East. He did so at the side of Baroness Alice von Pflugl, a mysterious older woman who became his lover in 1948. Although Pflugl financed the publication of *Imperium*, information on her is hard to come by. Elsa Dewette reports that

> F. was slightly ill at ease when he spoke of her, which was seldom. I do not recall his exact words. He referred to her as "that German woman" . . . From what I gathered, she was probably a kind of *exaltée*, who liked to see herself as the center of a political movement, or even a political plot—perhaps a kind of "heroine." God knows . . . I also had the strange feeling that she irritated him in some way, but he never mentioned this in so many words.[20]

John Anthony Gannon was summoned to Pflugl's mansion near Regent's Park in April or May 1948 to begin serious political talks with Yockey and Guy Chesham.[21] He recalled that she lived in "a large mansion-type HOUSE (not an apartment) and, as it was a Crown property, it is likely to be still standing . . . The furnishings were good and completely in keeping with a house of considerable prestige. A full grand piano was included."[22]

As for the Baroness, Gannon found her "a neurotic woman, good-intentioned, a fringe-fascist, wealthy, but inclined to let subjective matters take precedence over objective issues." He thought she got her money from "her former husband, the Baron (not, reputedly, any title of great age or significance in Austria)."[23] During 1948, "Y. was her lover, and when he ceased to be such, this brought about the disjunction."[24]

It was while he was with Pflugl that Yockey began advocating the idea of far-right cooperation with the Russian conquest of Europe. In November 1948, during the preparation of the European Liberation Front, a hard-line British National Socialist named John Gaster and his German-born girlfriend Elizabeth Schnitzler met with Yockey to discuss politics.[25] The anti-Yockey British-German group NATINFORM (the Nationalist Information Bureau) later issued a remarkable account of their meeting

> in the house of the Baroness von Pflugl—Park Gate West, London. Both our co-operators were known to be opposed to the Union Movement. YOCKEY, therefore, immediately launched an attack on the Union Movement, which he described as the instrument of U.S. policy. Speaking in German fluently, he began to praise the Soviet Policy in Germany, in particular referring to the so-called Army of Seydlitz and Paulus.[26] *"Ich will nur mit Deutschen redern, die sich nicht bemicheln lassen."* [I will speak now only to the Germans who are not Michels.][27] He then asked our co-operator to help him organize secret partisans in Western Germany who would be prepared to

collaborate with the Soviet Military Authorities in action against the WESTERN Occupying Powers.

Yockey, small, dark, of unknown mixed races, pale and intense, walked up and down in the large apartment whilst the Baroness sat on a sofa—speaking of the soul of Germany and its orientation eastwards. Yockey claimed that if his proposals were accepted we would be initiated into a vast and worldwide secret organization, working to establish an authoritarian state ("the real National Socialism"!). Yockey claimed that this organization was already millions-strong and that he was the representative of the leader whose name he kept secret.

Yockey stressed that "to start with" he did not contemplate the use of anti-Jewish propaganda and also stressed the "ZWEIGLEISIGKEIT" [two-tier nature] of his political tactic. First of all he wanted to found a sensational newspaper, specializing in anti-American agitation. *"Die Nord-Amerikanner sind die gefährlichsten Bolschewiken."* [North Americans are the most dangerous Bolsheviks.] He quoted in rapid succession passages from [Spengler's] "PRUSSENTUM UND SOZIALISMUS," etc. and also quoted a statement of MOELLER VAN DEN BRUCK: *"Die Umlagerung der europaischen Krafte, die einst nach Westen hin sich vollzog, vollzieht sich heute nach Osten. Un abermals ist Deutschland ihr Mittelpunkt."* [The storage place of European power that once carried out toward the West, today is carried out toward the East. And once again Germany is its center.] Also much else of this kind. It was obvious that, due to his association with the Union Movement, Yockey did not expect to be meeting with persons who could evaluate the political implications of Spengler, Moeller, etc. However, this was his misfortune, and both our co-operators immediately warned all nationalist comrades against this political infiltration behind the mask of Spenglerism.

Nor was this the only attempt to ally the radical right with the USSR. In another section of the report, NATINFORM stated:

In 1950, our agent[28] was approached by GUY CHESHAM with an invitation to a private meeting at his home (77 Elgin Mansions, London, W6). As the Yockey-Chesham relationship and its significance was already known to our agent, it was decided to cultivate this contact with a view to obtaining information. Preliminary discussions with Chesham revealed the fact [that] he was now promoting a definite line of policy and seeking collaborators. The main trend of this policy was based on *Imperium* and the concept of Yockey, although Chesham claimed to be acting independently of Yockey, [Huxley-] Blythe, and Baroness von Pflugl.

Later, a special private meeting at which our agent was also present (July 1950) was arranged. CHESHAM outlined a policy of infiltrating into all Nationalist groups with a view to seizing control from within or organizing sabotage. The political direction of this activity was to be violently anti-

American, avoiding all anti-Bolshevist conceptions. No anti-Jewish propaganda was to be permitted [at] first.

It was furthermore suggested that forces could be raised in England for direct action against American military bases in England. The Communist Party in England—as Chesham stated—has come to a standstill where it is making no progress—therefore—if we organized successfully an anti-American front with popular support—it would become possible to obtain financial support from the Soviet embassy in London.

This statement was amplified by reference to an organization of a similar nature being set up in Germany. This organization in Germany was to be the concern of YOCKEY (at that time said to be in Germany) and it was also mentioned that agreement had been reached between F. YOCKEY and ALFRED FRANKE-GRICKSCH for collaboration and for publishing a German translation of the *Imperium*. It was also stated that KAUFMANN (Hamburg) and BECK-BROICHSITTER had been approached but these persons were not actively concerned in the plan as they had not agreed with all of the proposals made to them by Yockey.[29] Chesham stated that Adolf Hitler and Alfred Rosenberg had "distorted" the real National Socialism. "Real National Socialists" believed in Spengler and van den Bruck.

Later in the same week GANNON arrived from Fleetwood to report on his work with HUXLEY-BLYTHE. Chesham attempted to create the impression that all these persons were acting quite independently and that his "personal project" was something quite new. Of course Yockey had not told Chesham about his previous approach to our agents and this was not mentioned by same so Chesham continued to believe that we had no information about Yockey and Baroness v[on] P[flugl]. Later, he admitted to knowing the Baroness. He also stated that Yockey had large connections in Italy and worked in connection with an Italian Politician—STASSI, editor of the monthly journal *Imperium*. Special stress was laid on building contact with all EX-SOLDIER organizations as the most important channel for future political activity.[30]

With Mosley against them (and now without money from the Baroness), Yockey, Gannon, and Chesham launched the European Liberation Front (ELF) sometime in late 1948 or early spring 1949.[31] To mark the ELF's official creation, Yockey wrote *The Proclamation of London*. Although the manifesto was actually composed in Belgium in April 1949, Gannon said that the ELF backdated it to 1948 to evoke the memory of another political pamphlet then celebrating its centenary: *The Communist Manifesto*.

Gannon explained the ELF this way:

The ELF, along with *Imperium* and *The Proclamation of London*, was intended to mark a symbolic turning-point in the development of the final period of the Western Imperium, providing the philosophical basis, milestones, and finger-posts for those who came after. We, FPY, Chesham, and myself, were realists, and we knew there was NO chance of a mass movement succeeding in the prevailing political/economic situation at that time, or of the near or midterm future . . . It was our aim to create an elite nucleus in each of the lands of the western Imperium, to accept THE BOOK and its situation-estimate as the basis for future action whenever possible, and to maintain contact in the interim. That is why FPY traveled endlessly within the IMPERIUM, and outside of it, in search of gold to finance the future . . .

We had the idea of founding an Order, secret of necessity, of the elite of our Idea within the Imperium which would work to secure the adherence of highly-placed people in all Western lands, knowing that all revolutions are made from above and not below . . . My own position in the ELF in England was not, formally, created in other parts of the Imperium, but I feel sure that the basis was made by FPY in Italy, and possibly in Germany. FPY had no organizational position of command, nor did he seek such. He recognized that his work lay in writing The Book and establishing its acceptance, in which he succeeded completely, with the Elite of the Imperium.[32]

Even at its height the ELF had only about 150 supporters. Its main task seems to have been the production of anti-American neutralist propaganda. It also published a mimeographed monthly called *Frontfighter* that began in early 1950 and continued until 1954, when Gannon left England for South America.[33] *Frontfighter's* circulation was approximately five hundred copies a month, which the group distributed to contacts around the world through its extensive mailing list.[34] Gannon and Chesham were the ELF's actual organizers, while Yockey remained behind the scenes. Although it was never intended to be a mass organization, the ELF held public meetings in London and in the north around Manchester.

One of the ELF's first recruits was Peter J. Huxley-Blythe, who as a student in the late 1930s had become interested in Mosley. After serving on a Royal Navy battleship in the Pacific, he left the service in 1947. Returning to the north of England, he hooked up with Gannon, who briefly introduced him to Yockey at the Second Union Movement Conference in London in 1948.[35] After Huxley-Blythe quit the Union Movement in 1950, he again met Yockey at Gannon's Manchester home. He later recalled:

I think that the message I first got from Yockey was that the Americans (I now talk about the United States, not about the American people but the American government), the American financial center, the American attitudes, government attitudes, and financial attitudes were far more dangerous at that time than the Soviets. The Soviets, at least I thought, one could deal with. There were still resistance movements behind the Iron Curtain, they hadn't all been crushed, there were still people who were very well organized . . . and therefore when Yockey said, "Look, what we should do, yes we should look at the Soviets but the real enemy is Washington and New York," that made a lot of sense, particularly the way he put it over . . . He put this over extremely well, Yockey did, when I met him, and that really the main enemy was the United States. Europe would defeat Russia anyway.[36]

After their conversation, Huxley-Blythe became the first editor of *Frontfighter*. Its mailing address was his home in Fleetwood.[37]

Whatever political hopes were held for the ELF, they essentially ended after Huxley-Blythe was called back into the Royal Navy during the Korean War and Chesham quit the group. Chesham, Yockey's closet collaborator, left after a bitter personal clash with him in either late 1949 or the early 1950s. Gannon said the falling-out occurred when Chesham "would not endure the breakup of his marriage, largely being brought about by Y.'s unreasonable behavior, insults to Frau Chesham, orders to G.C. to leave the 'bitch,' and to follow Y. into the dreamland of Bohemia."[38]

The ELF's most important piece of propaganda was a 32-page Yockey pamphlet called *The Proclamation of London*. Its cover was deep red and featured the ELF's symbol, a red flag with a white center circle inside of which was a black sword. The back of the pamphlet listed twelve ELF demands, including "Liberation of Britain and Europe from the reign of the inner-Traitor and the outer-Enemy"; "Integration of liberated Britain into the sovereign European People–Nation State"; "Immediate expulsion of all Jews and other parasitic aliens from the Soil of Europe"; and "Establishment of the Organic State."

The Proclamation began: "Representative adherents of the Front, from all the former nations of Europe, have gathered together in London for the purpose of documenting their outlook, their aim, and their position in the world." In fact, the Front's only representatives were Yockey, Gannon, and Chesham, and they met not in London but in Gannon's living room in Manchester. In *The Proclamation of London*, Yockey attempted to summarize *Imperium* in pamphlet form but with an even harder anti-American edge. He argued that by controlling America, the Jews had infected Europe with

> materialism, atheism, class-war, weak happiness-ideals, race-suicide, social-atomism, racial promiscuity, decadence in the arts, erotomania, disintegration of the family, private and public dishonor, slatternly feminism, economic fluctuation and catastrophe, civil war in the family of Europe, planned degeneration of the youth through vile films and literature, and through neurotic doctrines in education. They have sought to rot Europe, to attenuate its racial instincts, to devirilize it, to deprive it of honor, heroism, and manliness, of the sense of its World-Mission, of its sense of Cultural unity, even of its chivalrous military code. They have sought to paralyze the will of Europe and destroy its will-to-power by bringing in the ethical syphilis of Hollywood to poison the sacred soil of Europe.

Thanks to America's political, cultural, and financial domination of the continent:

The outer enemies are today the arbiters of Europe. They have set up their alternative to the natural, destined Europe of Authority and Faith: Europe as a source of booty for extra-European forces; Europe as a reservoir of manpower for the disposition of the American generalate; Europe as a loan-market for the New York financier; Europe as a beggar-colony watching for crumbs from the table of rich America; Europe as a historical sight for visiting colonials, a place where once there were great happenings; Europe as a museum, a mausoleum; Europe as a moribund collection of petty states and squabbling peoples; Europe as an economic madhouse where every tiny unit is against every other; Europe as a backward population waiting for reeducation by the American world-clown and the sadistic Jew; Europe as a laboratory for gigantic social experiments by Moscow and for the genocide experimentation of New York and Tel Aviv; Europe as a Black Mass of scaffold-trials, backward-looking persecution, treason, terror, despair, and suicide.

The United States was also at fault for allowing the Russian domination of East Europe. Yet Russia was not completely lost:

European possibilities still exist within Russia, because in certain strata of the population adherence to the great organism of the Western Culture is an instinct, an Idea, and no material force can ever wipe it out, even though it may be temporarily repressed and driven under.

Yockey then attacked the American effort to rally a divided Europe against Russia:

The Liberation Front does not allow Europe to be distracted by the situation of the moment in which the two crude Bolshevisms of Washington and Moscow are preparing a Third World War. In these preparations, the Culture-retarders, the inner enemies, the liberal-communist-democrats are again at their posts: With one voice the Churchills, the Spaaks, the Lies, the Gaulles, croak that Washington is going to save Europe from Moscow, or that Moscow is going to take Europe from Washington. There is nothing to substantiate this propaganda. . . . Russia is only a threat to a divided Europe; a united Europe can destroy the power of Russia at the moment of its choosing. It is a crass lie to say that Europe cannot defend itself against Russia. Do they think it is possible for Europe to forget the knowledge that it has just purchased with the blood of millions of its sons? Do they believe that Europe can forget that the Jewish-American regime, and it alone, brought the Red Armies into the heart of Europe? Is it possible that they think Europe can forget that the inner enemy with his liberal-communist-democracy led Europe into this abyss?

Yockey particularly opposed any European participation in NATO:

Washington's program is to conscript the Europeans—what it cynically calls the "manpower" of Europe—and thus to spare the jitterbugs of North

America the losses of arduous campaigns against Russia. Abysmal stupidity motivates this wish-thought. Do they really think that Europeans will accomplish military wonders fighting against one enemy of Europe on behalf of another? Do they think an American-Jewish High Command inspires the feelings necessary in a European officer-corps to elicit its heroic instincts?

No, Europe is no more interested in this projected war than in a struggle between two negro tribes in the Sudan.

Against Washington, Yockey advocated neutralism:

The European struggle is the fight for the liberation of our sacred soil and our Western soul. It is a horizontal struggle, against all enemies of Europe, inner enemies, and extra-European forces, whoever they are. Before Europe can fight a vertical war, it must be constituted as the Imperium of Europe, the organic Culture-State-Nation-Race-People of the West. And when Europe makes war then, it will be against the political enemy of its own choosing, and at the time of its choosing. In these decisions, Jew, Moscow, and Washington figure not at all. The propaganda of the American-Jew and the Jewish-American deceives no one.

The Proclamation of London was a remarkable document. By fusing anti-Semitism with anti-Americanism, it clearly identified the United States, not Russia, as Europe's main foe. It also added fuel to rumors already swirling throughout the British far right that the mysterious Yank who called himself Ulick Varange had crossed over to the red side of the Iron Curtain.

Notes:

1. *Imperium*, pp. 612–13.
2. Ibid., p. 615.
3. Ibid., p. 619.
4. Maurice Bardèche, letter to Keith Stimely, summer 1982. Other *Imperium* enthusiasts included the Canadian fascist leader Adrian Arcand and Oswald Pirow, the founder of South Africa's New Order Party. In Argentina, Emilio Gutierrez Herrera, the leader of the Union Civica Nacionalista, also endorsed the book.
5. Liddell Hart and Fuller's comments are cited in Johann von Leers' review of *Imperium* in *Der Weg* (Vol. 5, No. 9, 1951).
6. Robert Skidelsky writes in his biography *Oswald Mosley* (London: Macmillan, 1975), p. 488:

Mosley's Europe had its origins in the kind of fascist solidarity which led William Joyce to Berlin and which had thrown up "collaborators" all over Europe. Although Mosley . . . was not prepared to accept European unification on German terms, his postwar idea was already foreshadowed in Marcel Déat's proclamation in 1943 of a "solidary community of European nations," a "European socialism," and a "European duty against the evils of bolshevism and capitalism," and in the manifesto of Mussolini's ill-fated Republic of Salò the same year, which called for the "realization of a European Community, with a federation of all nations."

7. The MSI had earlier created its own European Study Center that published a journal called *Europa Unità*.

8. Kurt Tauber, *Beyond Eagle and Swastika: German Nationalism since 1945* (Middletown, CT: Wesleyan University Press, 1967), Vol. 1, pp. 208–09.

9. Elsa Dewette, letter to Keith Stimely, 22 March 1982.

10. At the margin of the page, Mosley wrote: "Absurd falsehood: Why should we?"

11. William Joyce (Berlin Radio's "Lord Haw-Haw") was executed after World War II for his collaboration with Nazi Germany.

12. This may be a reference to Goebbels' attack on Spengler after the publication of *The Hour of Decision*.

13. Again in the margin, Sir Oswald wrote of *Imperium*, "A very dull re-hash of Spengler."

14. Chesham's memo with Mosley's handwritten notes were sent to Keith Stimely by Nicholas Mosley.

15. John Anthony Gannon, letter to Keith Stimely, 13 July 1980.

16. Peter J. Huxley-Blythe's reply to my questionnaire.

17. Skidelsky, *Oswald Mosley*, p. 491.

18. Letter from A. Raven Thomson to H. Keith Thompson dated 27 March 1953, sent from Union Movement headquarters in London.

19. John Anthony Gannon, "Remembrance of the Author of *Imperium*," in the H. Keith Thompson archives at the Hoover Institute.

20. Elsa Dewette, letter to Keith Stimely, 22 March 1982.

21. John Anthony Gannon, letter to Keith Stimely, 13 June 1980.

22. Along with the piano, Gannon reported that Pflugl also had a manservant, "a 'Vichy' Frenchman, collected by VF [von Pflugl] out of practicality and nostalgia. It could be that he was a minor 'wanted man,' sought by anti-European forces; in which case, he would be 'cheaper,' and this would have merited consideration by VF." John Anthony Gannon, letter to Keith Stimely, 24 November 1981.

23. NATINFORM claimed that Pflugl was also the grand-daughter of "a Jew named Alexander—now deceased." From Wolfgang Sarg's 28 January 1953 letter to H. Keith Thompson in the H. Keith Thompson archives in the Hoover Institute.

24. After their split, Pflugl formed Ostropa Press in response to Westropa Press, the imprint house for *Imperium*. She called her press Ostropa because she believed "that the new message would come from the EAST, and she would be the Mother of the Idea!" John Anthony Gannon, letter to Keith Stimely, 13 June 1980.

As for *Imperium*'s printing history: It came out in 1948 in two volumes. Volume one had 405 pages and volume two had 280 pages. Volume one was printed by C. A. Brooks & Co., Ltd. and volume two by Jones & Dale—both London-based. Approximately 1,000 copies of volume one but just 200 copies (possibly 300 according to Tony Gannon) of volume two appeared with a deterioration of quality in volume two that suggests financial problems. As for the publisher BCM/WESTROPA (BCM meant British Commercial Monomarks—a paid-for post-box), all communications were sent to Gannon's home in Manchester. According to the NATINFORM report on Yockey, C. A. Brock, the publisher of volume one, was a commercial firm "undertaking work for Marxist associations." Gannon described C. A. Brock as "a semi-crook printer, who had done work for O.M. At a price, he would print anything. Of Brooks & Dale, volume two, I know nothing." [Information based on description of *Imperium* in Willis Carto's introduction as well as references by Gannon. Note that Carto spells volume one's publisher as C. A. Brooks while Gannon has it C. A. Brock. Also Gannon has it as Brooks & Dale while Carto lists it as Jones & Dale.]

25. I shall discuss Gaster and Schnitzler in more detail later in this book.

26. This was a reference to the Free German movement, which was created in the USSR out of captured German troops and led by Field Marshall Friedrich von Paulus, head of the Sixth Army Group that surrendered at Stalingrad.

27. A "Michel" was a term of contempt applied by Spengler to liberal Germans. In more general terms it means a naive, trusting type of person.

28. This was John Gaster.

29. I will discuss Yockey's German connections later in this book.

30. The initial draft of the NATINFORM report is included in a letter from Wolfgang Sarg to H. Keith Thompson, dated 28 January 1953, in the H. Keith Thompson archive at Hoover. Thompson also showed the report to the FBI when it questioned him about Yockey. A long summary of the report that quotes at great length from the Sarg letter is in the FBI file.

31. Gannon recalled: "In the autumn of 1948, FPY, Chesham, and I parted company with O.M., each writing a personal letter of farewell, intended to serve as landmarks for posterity. We founded the European Liberation Front." (John Anthony Gannon, letter to Keith Stimely, 13 June 1980.) The NATINFORM report on Yockey also lists an Oliver Grose and R.G. Lowe as part of the early ELF group.

32. John Anthony Gannon, letter to Keith Stimely, 15 February (most likely 1981). Yockey's hope that *Imperium* would become "THE BOOK" was also expressed in *Imperium* (p. 438) where he wrote: "The Western was always esoteric: When Goethe's *Collected Works* were published in 1790, only 600 copies were subscribed. Yet this public was enough for his fame over all Europe. Buxtehude, Orlando, Gibbons, Bach, and Mozart wrote for a small public, including no Culture-distorters. Napoleon's policy was understood in its last ramification by few persons in his contemporary Europe."

33. Peter J. Huxley-Blythe believes that the first *Frontfighter* actually appeared early in 1950.

34. Because copies of *Frontfighter* are so scarce, it is impossible to get an exact list of what articles Yockey did write and what were some of the journal's other connections. Some articles from *Frontfighter*, however, were reprinted in other fascist journals, including *Der Weg* in Argentina.

35. From a 1953 letter from Peter J. Huxley-Blythe to H. Keith Thompson.

36. Huxley-Blythe's September 1994 taped response to my questionnaire.

37. Huxley-Blythe also spoke at ELF meetings.

38. John Anthony Gannon, letter to Keith Stimely, 24 November 1985. After quitting the ELF, Chesham became an important figure in Arthur Keith Chesterton's League of Empire Loyalists (LEL), which pursued a vigorously anti-American policy. I shall discuss Chesterton's LEL in more detail later.

20

EX ORIENTE LUX[1]

When Yockey began his turn East, he was not acting alone. Around the time of *Imperium's* publication, the right-radical *Sozialistische Reichspartei* (Socialist Reich Party) was founded in Germany. The SRP's call for a pro-Eastern neutralist Germany was almost identical to Yockey's position, and the ELF was in some respect the SRP's British cousin.

Some clues to Yockey's thinking are provided in the "Russia" chapter of *Imperium*, where he argues that there are really two Russias. The first Russia, symbolized by Peter the Great, wished to imitate the high culture of the West. But neither Peter nor his successors could implant "Western ideas below the surface of the Russian soul," since

> the true, spiritual Russia is primitive and religious. It detests Western Culture, Civilization, nations, arts, State-forms, Ideas, religions, cities, technology. This hatred is natural, and organic, for this population lies outside the Western organism, and everything Western is therefore hostile and deadly to the Russian soul.[2]

The Russian Revolution was both a revolt of the Marxist, Western-oriented intelligentsia and an uprising of the anti-Western underclass:

> The actual form of the Revolution when it did occur was dual: There was a revolt of the primitive Russian soul against the Western Romanov regime and all that it represented, and there was a simultaneous assumption of the leadership of this revolt by the Jewish Culture-Nation-State-Race . . . The duality of the Bolshevik Revolution meant that the one side of it was a failure, the primitive, Asiatic, instinctive side. The aim of the Russian side of

the rising was to sweep away *all* Western institutions, ideas, forms, and realities. Thus it wished to extirpate the Western technology and economic forms as well as the other aspects of the Westernization of Russia.[3]

The Bolsheviks, however, had advanced technology "in preparation for a series of wars against hated Europe." Even after the American development of the atomic bomb, Yockey maintained that Russia still held a "vastly superior" strategic position, since it did not hesitate to use "terror, military occupation, kidnapping, and assassination" to control its territory.[4] While "revolts in the American spheres in Europe" might end U.S. domination, any uprising in Russian-controlled territory "would be drowned in blood."

Russia was brutal because its barbarian soul was "outside the West"; so much so that Russia

> is thus purely destructive as far as the West is concerned. Russia is the bearer of no Utopian hopes for the West, and anyone who believes it is [is] a Cultural idiot . . . By virtue of its physical situation, on the border of the West, Russia will, and must always, remain the enemy of the West, as long as these populations are organized as a political unit.[5]

While Europe would ultimately be united "from the rocky promontories of Galway to the Urals," Yockey was also clear that, for the next 25 years at least, Russia was a *lesser* enemy than America:

> These powers [America and Russia] differ for Europe's purposes in that the true America belongs to the Western Civilization, and the true Russia can never possibly belong there. But in the *immediate*, short-range view, extending over only the next quarter of a century, one of them is more dangerous than the other.
>
> Russia's total alienness is realized all through Europe, horizontally and vertically. Under a Russian occupation of Europe, even the European Communists would soon be in the great never-ending revolt against the Barbarian. The European Michel element, with its weak urge toward parliamentary babbling and money-loving, and its detestation of the firm, strong, Prussian-European will-power, would find itself cleansed of its spiritual sickness under the lash of the Mongolian. It would become European. Nor could a Russian occupation hope forever to hold Europe down . . .
>
> America, on the other hand, is not generally understood in Europe. Even in the Culture-bearing stratum of the West there is no clarity that America under Culture-distorting leadership is Europe's total enemy . . . The differing relationship between Russia and America to Europe is thus simply that Russia, even though it tries to split Europe, can only unite it. The effect of American occupation, however, is to split, for it appeals to the sub-Europeans, the Retarders, the Michel elements, the money-worshippers, the lazy and the stupid, and to the worst instincts in every European . . . What difference does it make to Europe whether the Russians move a factory to

Turkestan, or the Americans blow it up into the air? The difference between the spiritual effect of the two occupations makes the Russian less harmful.[6]

Yockey's 1953 book *Der Feind Europas*, originally an unpublished section of *Imperium*, is even more explicit in its desire to reach accommodation with Russia:[7]

The effect that a Russian occupation of Europe would have on Western Culture is not yet equally well-known, and can be determined only by uncovering its organic basis. The Russian is a barbarian; the European is a Culture-man in his late-Civilization phase ... The barbarian comes to destroy and he stays to learn. The belief that a Russian-barbarian occupation of the whole of Europe would be similar to the Russian occupation of half of Germany after the Second World War is a complete false estimate of the possibilities.[8]

According to *Der Feind Europas*, Russia had just two strategic choices:

The first possibility is an endless series of European uprisings against Russia that could result only in the expulsion of the demoralized barbarians. The second possibility would result from Russia's introducing a clever regime and according Europe extensive autonomy and magnanimous treatment. Within a few decades, this Europe would naturally aim at infiltrating horizontally the whole Russian seat of origin, its technical, economic, social, and, finally, military and political life. Instead of the Russification of Europe, as Dostoevski and Aksakov dreamt of it, would result the Europeanization of Russia once again, and this time in far stronger degree ... An attempt by Russia to integrate Europe into its power-accumulation peacefully would eventually result in the rise of a new Symbiosis: Europe-Russia. Its final form would be that of a European Imperium.[9]

Yockey returns to this argument a few pages later:

Should Russia aim at a lasting incorporation of Europe into its Empire, it could succeed only if it granted Europe significant concessions. The first of these would have to be administrative autonomy for Europe as a unit, for that is the desire of all Europeans—the Michel-stratum and its leaders, the senile Churchills, of course, excepted.

Should Russia attempt to terrorize Europe, it would summon forth in the European People the will to counter-terror. Faced with the barbarian, all Europeans, even the simplest-minded liberals, would learn the necessity of inner firmness, of a stern will, the virtues of Command and Obedience, for these alone could force the barbarian to accept demands, or else retreat to his tundras and steppes. All Europeans would realize that not parliamentary babble, class-war, capitalism, and elections, but only Authority, the Will-to-Power, and finally, the military spirit could ever drive out the barbarians.[10]

Yockey's ideas about Russia cannot simply be reduced to pure Machtpolitik. His arguments had their intellectual origin in a 1920s emigré White Russian intellectual movement called "Eurasianism." Eurasian themes were echoed by both Oswald Spengler and Arthur Moeller van den Bruck, a German literary critic who founded the "left wing" of the Conservative Revolutionary movement.

Eurasianism emerged from a coterie of exiled White Russian intellectuals headed by Prince Nicolai Trubetskoi, a Russian literary theorist and linguistics scholar.[11] In 1920 Trubetskoi wrote the Eurasian manifesto *Europe and Mankind*, which has been described as "an out-and-out indictment of Western imperialism."[12] *Europe and Mankind* attacked all forms of Western thought, including Marxism, as reflecting the prejudices of European universalist "Romano-Germanic thinking." "Romano-Germanic" did not mean Indo-European: The German tribes (originally "Scythians" from the Russian steppes) were equally victims of the Romano-Germanic juggernaut. The term "Romano-Germanic" referred to an unholy alliance between the universalizing theology of the hated Roman Catholic Church and the military power of the medieval Teutonic Knights. Together they had colonized Russia's soil and soul under the banner of Catholic universalism. Romano-Germanic thinking could only view Russia as a primitive backwater of Europe. Trubetskoi, however, insisted that Russia, as a unique combination of Europe and Asia, was an autochthonous culture zone.

Bolshevism was the last artificial attempt to impose Western universalist ideology on Russian soil. The revolution, however, wore a Janus face. In one respect it was the disastrous culmination of the Westernizing trend in Russian history; just under the surface, however, the revolution offered the possibility of a messianic transformation of Russian society once Bolshevism had exhausted itself, since it had forever destroyed the old Europhile ruling elite.[13] For that reason the Eurasians, unlike the vast majority of White exiles, did not entirely reject the revolution, and instead adopted a "constructive" attitude toward the new state.[14] October 1917, then, was both a final spasm of the old European order and a sign that the world was finally entering a new age where organic, spiritual culture would obliterate sterile Romano-Germanic universalism.[15] Seen in this light, Lenin's revolt could serve as a beacon for a broader "Colored World Revolution."

The Eurasian worldview, especially as applied to the concept of Eurasia itself, was rooted more in Karl Haushofer's Germany than Czar Nicholas II's Russia. Professor David Riasanovsky, a leading expert on the Eurasians, argues that in its geopolitical formulation, Eurasianism "can be considered a product of . . . [the] application of European, especially German, geopolitical theories to Russia."[16] One influential German variant of Eurasianism was advanced by Oswald Spengler. In *The Decline of the West*, Spengler examined historically "young" cultures that had their natural development artificially altered by an older, alien culture that "lies so massively over the land" that the new culture "cannot get its breath." Under such circumstances, the new culture begins to "hate the distant power with a hate that grows to be monstrous."[17]

Russia was Spengler's textbook case. He argued that, beginning with the founding of Petersburg in 1703, Peter the Great "forced the primitive Russian soul into the alien mold, first of full Baroque, then of Enlightenment, and then of the 19th century."[18] The "soul of Old Russia," however, could never understand "late-period arts and sciences, enlightenment, social ethics, the materialism of world-cities." Dostoevski was right when he wrote that "Petersburg is the most abstract and artificial city in the world." To old Russia, Moscow was holy, Saint Petersburg satanic.[19]

Russia was the Russia of *both* Tolstoy and Dostoevski. Tolstoy spoke for the Westernizing spirit of the upper class, while Dostoevski gave voice to the peasant mass. Therefore, "Tolstoy is the former Russia, Dostoevski is the coming Russia."[20] Spengler then explained:

> Tolstoy . . . is essentially a great understanding, "enlightened" and "socially minded" . . . Tolstoy's hatred of property is an economist's, his hatred of society a social reformer's, his hatred of the State a political theorist's. Hence his immense effect upon the West—he belongs, in one respect as in another, to the band of Marx, Ibsen, and Zola.
>
> Dostoevski, on the contrary, belongs to no band, unless it be the band of the Apostles of primitive Christianity. His "Demons" were denounced by the Russian Intelligentsia as reactionaries. But he himself was quite unconscious of such conflicts—"conservative" and "revolutionary" were terms of the West that left him indifferent . . .
>
> Dostoevski, like every primitive Russian . . . lives in a second, metaphysical world beyond. What has the agony of a soul to do with Communism? A religion that has got as far as taking social problems in hand has ceased to be a religion. But the reality in which Dostoevski lives, even during this life, is a religious creation directly present to him . . . Tolstoy, on the other hand, is a master of the Western novel—*Anna Karenina* distances every rival—and even in his peasant's garb remains a man of polite society.[21]

Dostoevski was "a saint"; Tolstoy "only a revolutionary." As Tolstoy's heirs, the Bolsheviks were as alienated from Russia as he had been. Spengler concluded his extraordinary analysis:

> The real Russian is the disciple of Dostoevski. Although he may not have read Dostoevski or anyone else, nay, perhaps *because* he cannot read, he is himself Dostoevski in substance; and if the Bolshevists, who see in Christ a mere social revolutionist like themselves, were not intellectually so nar-

rowed, it would be in Dostoevski that they would recognize their prime enemy. What gave this revolution its momentum was not the intelligentsia's hatred. It was the people itself, which, *without hatred*, urged only by the need of throwing off a disease, destroyed the old Westernism in one effort of upheaval, and will send the new after it in another. For what this townless people yearns for is its own life-form, its own religion, its own history.[22]

The notion that the soul of Russia was Dostoevskian was first introduced to the European intelligentsia by Arthur Moeller van den Bruck, who in 1906 organized the first complete (23-volume) German edition of Dostoevski.[23] Moeller spent World War I in army headquarters in Berlin as a member of the Press and Propaganda Department for the eastern front.[24] After the war, the German Foreign Office sponsored a book he wrote that tried to convince President Wilson to offer Germany favorable peace terms.[25] After the Versailles Treaty (signed in Paris in June 1919) imposed a harsh peace, Moeller and his friend Baron Heinrich von Gleichen established the Juniklub to protest it. The June Club, whose members included some of Germany's leading industrialists, adopted the slogan "No enemy to the East."

Moeller counterposed the tactic of an opening to the East to Spengler's famous "theory of pessimism." He argued that Germany and Russia were both vigorous young peoples and that the outcome of World War I "had separated them with finality from the decaying West."[26] Given the political will, cultural regeneration—or what Moeller called *Anderskehrbarkeit*, in opposition to Spengler's idea of historical irreversibility (or *Unumkehrbarkeit*)—was now possible.[27]

Spengler and Moeller argued out their differences in a debate at the June Club in the summer of 1920. Otto Strasser, who with his brother Gregor later created the "left" or Strasserist tendency in Hitler's NSDAP, was in the audience. In his autobiography *History in My Time*, Strasser said he would "never forget that fruitful discussion" when "the Pessimist and the Optimist of the West expounded their versions of the coming decades." Although "the two conceptions were opposed to each other," Spengler and Moeller were "yet attuned to each other and complementary to each other, so that all of us, moved by this moment, solemnly swore to devote our lives to the realization of these visions."[28]

Karl Haushofer and Rudolf Hess arranged for Hitler to meet Moeller at the June Club in 1922. After Moeller failed to convince Hitler that Germany and Russia shared a common destiny (or *Schicksalsgemeinschaft*), it was up to the Strassers to implement Moeller's vision inside the NSDAP.[29] The historian Konrad Heiden writes that "the Strassers and Goebbels [then a "left" Nazi] now founded a Strasser party in the Hitler party. Its program was anti-capitalistic, even nihilistic."[30] Like Moeller, the Strassers advocated a German alignment with Bolshevik Russia, Gandhi's India, and Chiang Kai-shek's then-Soviet-supported Kuomintang so that Germany could form an alliance with "the 'young,' in part colored, peoples of the East against the declining West; with Bolshevism against capitalism; with—as Houston Stewart Chamberlain would have put it—the Tartarized Slavs against Wall Street, with world doom against Versailles."[31]

The Eurasian call for a grand anti-colonial revolt and Moeller's alliance of "young peoples" were remarkably similar. Some Eurasians also seem to have been actively involved in a complex alliance between Soviet and German military intelligence. In *The Secret Road to World War II*, espionage expert Paul Blackstock says that in the 1920s elements of the Eurasian movement came under the control of a Soviet general named Aleksandr Langovoy. (Langovoy also helped create the "Trust," the famous Soviet-controlled "monarchist" movement that caused havoc with Western secret services.[32]) Blackstock was most likely referring to the Gutchkov Circle, a 1920s salon headed by Alexander Gutchkov, the former chairman of the czarist Duma, who had come into contact with Eurasian exiles in Berlin. Former Soviet General Walter Krivitsky reported that the Gutchkov Circle worked closely with General Bredow, the chief of military intelligence for the German Army until he was murdered by Hitler.[33]

Yockey's call for an understanding with Russia, then, had deep historical roots. In its report on Yockey, NATINFORM accused him of quoting from Moeller van den Bruck. Although Yockey later denied mentioning Moeller, it seems clear that Moeller's "optimism" helped guide Yockey's turn to the East.

Notes:

1. "Light from the East."
2. *Imperium*, pp. 578–79.
3. Ibid., p. 580.
4. Ibid., pp. 584–85.
5. Ibid., p. 586.
6. Ibid., pp. 594–95. Yockey also makes a curious observation about the Russian view of the war crimes process, writing: "America conducts a gigantic hanging holiday called 'war crimes,' which is aimed at settling old Semitic-vengeance scores. Russia values subject individuals according to their *present* and *future* value to Russian plans, and is not interested in their past actions." (*Imperium*, p. 585.)
7. Yockey says in his introductory note to the book that it was originally meant as part of *Imperium* but that personal reasons made it impossible. This could be a reference to the loss of Baroness von Pflugl's financial backing.
8. *The Enemy of Europe* (Reedy, WV: Liberty Bell Publications, 1981), pp. 80–81.
9. Ibid., p. 82
10. Ibid., p. 84.

11. Trubetskoi later held the chair of Slavonic Studies (Linguistics) at the University of Vienna in the 1930s.

12. David Riasanovksy, "The Emergence of Eurasianism," in *California Slavic Studies*, Vol. IV, 1967, p. 55. Also see Riasanovksy's "Prince N.S. Trubetskoy's 'Europe and Mankind,'" in *Jahrbuecher für Geschichte Osteuropas*, July 1964. For a more recent mention of the Eurasians, see Richard Herzinger and Hannes Stein, *Endzeit-Propheten oder Die Offensive der Antiwestler* (Reinbek bei Hamburg: Rowohlt, 1995), pp. 133–42.

13. Spengler felt the same way. In a 14 February 1922 address entitled "The Two Faces of Russia and Germany's Eastern Problems," he said: "Even Lenin's creation is Western . . . Some day, in some way or other, it will perish. It is a rebellion against the West, but born of Western ideas."

14. As Professor Riasanovsky observes, while "all other Russian emigrés tried to deny the reality of the October Revolution and to turn the clock back, to 1861, 1905, or the Provisional Government of 1917," the Eurasians "faced reality and looked ahead." (From "The Emergence of Eurasianism," pp. 53–54.)

15. As Professor Robert C. Williams puts it: "By interpreting the Bolshevik revolution as a cultural or religious event, rather than a political one, the Eurasians made it seem not only logical and earth-shaking, but even worthwhile." Robert C. Williams, *Culture in Exile: Russian Emigrés in Germany, 1881–1941* (Ithaca, NY: Cornell University Press, 1972), p. 261.

16. Riasanovsky, "The Emergence of Eurasianiam," p. 62.

17. Oswald Spengler, *The Decline of the West*, Vol. 2, p. 189. The Eurasians later borrowed from Spengler's analysis of Russia. See Williams, *Culture in Exile*, p. 259.

18. Spengler, *The Decline of the West*, Vol. 2, pp. 192–93.

19. Ibid., p. 193.

20. In this context Spengler introduces Ivan's pledge to his brother Alyosha from *The Brothers Karamazov*, the same pledge Yockey alluded to in his 1946 Wiesbaden oath.

21. Spengler, *The Decline of the West*, Vol. 2, pp. 194–95.

22. Ibid., p. 196.

23. In his introduction to the series, Moeller portrayed Dostoevski as the prophet of Russia's destiny; his later support for a German alliance with the Soviet Union also had its roots in his understanding of Dostoevski. See Fritz Stern, *The Politics of Cultural Despair: A Study in the Rise of the Germanic Ideology* (Berkeley, CA: University of California Press, 1961).

24. Ibid., p. 208.

25. Ibid., p. 223.

26. Ibid., p. 239.

27. From a profile of Moeller by Alain de Benoist in *The Scorpion*, No. 12, Winter 1988/89.

28. Klemens von Klemperer, *Germany's New Conservatism: Its History and Dilemma in the Twentieth Century* (Princeton, NJ: Princeton University Press, 1957), p. 174. Otto Strasser is quoted in Stern, p. 239.

29. Strasser said that the popular use of the term "Third Reich" (the title of Moeller's last major book before he committed suicide) came through the Strasserist influence in the Nazi Party.

30. Konrad Heiden, *Der Fuehrer: Hitler's Rise to Power* (Boston: Houghton Mifflin, 1944), p. 286.

31. Ibid.

32. Paul Blackstock, *The Secret Road to World War II: Soviet versus Western Intelligence, 1921–1939* (Chicago: Quadruple, 1969). In 1924 the OGPU began to infiltrate the Eurasian movement, so much so that by 1926 Langovoy became *"persona grata"* in Eurasian emigré circles. See Geoffrey Bailey, *The Conspirators* (New York: Harper and Brothers, 1960), fn. 5, pp. 276–77.

33. After Bredow was executed in 1934, his foreign operations were absorbed into the Gestapo and Heydrich's SD section of the SS.

21

THE STRASSER
QUESTION

Given his political views, was Yockey a "Strasserist"? In the early 1950s Arnold Leese, the grand old man of the British far right, denounced both Yockey and the ELF as Strasserists. The American Nazi leader George Lincoln Rockwell would also label "Yockeyism" a Strasserist perversion of true National Socialism.[1]

"Strasserism" is not an easy term to define. Used historically, it refers to the northern wing of the Nazi Party, led in the mid-1920s by the brothers Gregor and Otto Strasser. Intent on recruiting factory workers in the industrial north, the Strassers insisted that the Nazis were socialists who would break up the domination of big capital and the vast landed estates. They also called for an alliance with Russia and the "East" against England and France, the hated enforcers of the Versailles Treaty. The Strassers' radical propaganda, as well as their independent power base, angered Hitler, who drew his strength from the far more conservative Bavaria. "Strasserist" can also be used to describe the "Black Front" that Otto Strasser created after he quit the Nazi Party, in July 1930 (with the cry, "The socialists are leaving the NSDAP!"), to protest Hitler's alliance with big business and aristocratic elites symbolized by the Krupps and the Papens. His brother Gregor stayed inside the party, only to be murdered by Hitler during the Night of the Long Knives in 1934.[2]

In a strictly historical sense Yockey was not a Strasserist. But if by Strasserist one means someone who held "national bolshevist" foreign policy views[3] and rejected biological determinism,[4] then he was a kind of small-*s* "strasserist." He was also strasserist in his hatred of capitalism. In *Der Feind*

191

Europas he described capitalism as "the Inner Enemy . . . whereby the word is used in its total meaning of a cultural-spiritual-ethical-economic principle."[5] Finally, he maintained important ties with Alfred Franke-Gricksch, a key leader of the postwar German far right and a former member of Otto Strasser's Black Front. (Gregor Strasser had served as the witness at Franke-Gricksch's wedding.[6]) Like Yockey, Franke-Gricksch advocated close cooperation between the far right and the East Bloc.

According to the 1953 NATINFORM report, while Yockey was still working with the Union Movement, he created his own ring (later the European Liberation Front) "linked to the activity of Alfred Franke-Gricksch, then the leading German advisor to the Union Movement. Through Franke-Gricksch, Yockey established relations with an organization referred to as the *Bruderschaft* (Brotherhood) in Germany."

The Bruderschaft was one of the most important groups in Germany's postwar fascist elite. Using its intelligence and organizational contacts with fascist movements around the world, it played a critical role in the Nazi underground railroad that smuggled war criminals to South America and the Middle East. In the early 1950s, elements from the Bruderschaft also helped create the Freikorps Deutschland, a paramilitary organization later outlawed by Occupation authorities.[7]

The Bruderschaft was founded in 1945–46 in a British POW camp in Germany by Major Helmut Beck-Broichsitter, an ex–staff officer of the Grossdeutschland Division. He was soon joined by Franke-Gricksch, who brought to the group a detailed plan to recapture power "through slow, methodical insinuation into governmental and party positions, under cover of such secrecy or camouflage as might be necessary for the success of the operation."[8]

Alfred Franke-Gricksch had been heavily involved in far-right political intrigue since the late 1920s, when he joined the Strassers' northern wing of the NSDAP. He also became a founding member of the Black Front. After Hitler took power, he went into exile with Otto Strasser, first in Vienna and later in Prague.[9] He then deserted Strasser and returned to Germany. After reaching an understanding with Himmler, he joined the SS and eventually rose to the rank of lieutenant colonel. Shortly after his defection, "the Gestapo succeeded with ease in what it had previously failed to achieve: the penetration and liquidation of the tight, hitherto-well-concealed underground apparatus of the Black Front."[10]

In a 1990 letter to Willis Carto's Institute for Historical Review, Ekkehard Franke-Gricksch explained his father's pre-war activity this way:

> My father, my mother, the Strassers, and Himmler had known each other since about 1927. They were dedicated National Socialists, and thus fol-

lowed Hitler. My father joined the party in 1928 and left it in 1930. Gregor Strasser was the witness at my parents' wedding . . .

When Hitler took control of the government in 1933 and distanced himself from his original National Socialist goals . . . my father fled the country with Gregor [actually Otto—K.C.] Strasser . . . The Reich Supreme Court sentenced my father to death in absentia for treason—that is, because he was a member of the Strasser organization . . . [However] my father came to an understanding with Himmler about the Party's betrayal of the National Socialist revolution. Himmler and my father came to an agreement, and my father joined the Waffen SS under the name Alfred Franke—behind the back of the Party. Himmler only asked that he refrain from political activity for the time being, until the time was right for that.[11]

In *Hitler and the Final Solution*, British historian Gerald Fleming gives a thumbnail sketch of Franke-Gricksch's career taken from his SS personnel file:

1934 reconnoitering of the radio stations "Schwarze Front"/Otto Strasser near Prague; report on this to Heydrich, which led in January 1935 to the murder of Rudolf Formis, who serviced the illegal station in Dobris near Prague from a room in the Hotel Zahori; 1935–1939 SS *Hauptsturmführer* [captain] in the Death's Head formations in Dachau; October 1939 until March 1941, as Intelligence Officer in the Death's Head Division (SS); March 1941–July 1942 in SD Main Office and Section SD–England; August 1942 to end of the year, active service in the SS Police Division; from January 1943 until the end of the war in SS Personnel Main Office.[12]

Franke-Gricksch first served as an officer in the SS *Totenkopfverbande* (Death's Head Unit) from 1935 to 1939, where he was responsible for indoctrinating concentration camp guards. After the Totenkopfverbande was transformed into the Totenkopf Division of the Waffen SS, he became one of its intelligence officers.[13] He was then transferred to the Main Office of Heydrich's Sicherheitsdienst (SD) until August 1942, when he joined an SS Polizeidivision on the Eastern front. After illness forced him to return to Berlin, he was assigned to the SS *Personalhauptamt* (Central Personnel Office) in January 1943.[14]

It is Franke-Gricksch's activity at the end of World War II, however, that concerns us most. Imagine Berlin in April 1945. The thunder of continual Soviet artillery bombardment is relentless. The Thousand Year Reich is in ruins. Yet Franke-Gricksch, by that time head of the Personnel Section of Himmler's RSHA (the Reich Security Main Office), Nazi Germany's CIA, spent the last days of the war preparing a blueprint for a postwar fascist Europe which he titled *The German Freedom Movement* (*Popular Movement*). Drafted on 3 April 1945, *The German Freedom Movement* demanded a Nazi Party purge to free it "from a degenerate Party bureaucracy and the ubiquitous corrupt Party bosses, from a ruling caste in State, Party, and Party organizations which has deceived itself and others for years." It also denounced "a biased, un-German Führer cult within the country and an empty arrogance of power in foreign policy." Franke-Gricksch then demanded that Germany be preserved "from reversion to the obsolete concept of capitalism, politically active clergy, the divisive party wrangling of parliamentary democracy, narrow Austrian, Bavarian, Rhineland, or other particularism, and communist class warfare which divides a people."[15]

The German Freedom Movement outlined a new pan-European foreign policy program, which included a 12-point "European peace settlement" and the creation of a new "Sworn European Community" of peoples who would retain their "individual existence" and right "freely to form their own political organization." A "European arbitration system" would also be created to secure some form of voluntary allegiance to a "Germanic Reich." One scholar aptly described Franke-Gricksch's plan for a new Europe as being based on the "call of the blood," but tempered "by the introduction of a federal system and excluding any claim to sole leadership by Germany."[16]

Three years before *Imperium, The German Freedom Movement* envisioned a post-Hitler Europe freed from the biological exaltation of the German race.[17] A similar concept had been developed by a top clique of SS technocrats whose ranks included SS Brigadier General Franz Alfred Six. An intimate of Heydrich, Six presided over a propaganda empire that included the RSHA's Amt VII (Office VII), which was in charge of Ideological Research (*Weltanschauliche Forschung*).[18] Six was also involved in SS planning for the invasion of England and would have been in charge of all "police action" during the occupation.[19] After Six became head of the German Foreign Policy Institute, he actively promoted the idea of a united Europe through books like *Europe's Civil Wars and the Present War of Unification* and *Europe: Tradition and Future*. As the fighting in the East grew desperate, Six escalated his pan-European propaganda throughout the occupied territories.[20]

SS Lieutenant General Werner Best was another strong advocate of pan-European fascism. A former Conservative Revolutionary and Ernst Jünger fan, he became the first director of the RSHA's Personnel Office (Amt I), where Franke-Gricksch later served. A counter-intelligence expert with a doctorate in law, Best later became a director of Amt II, which supervised administrative, economic, and judicial matters for the RSHA. His first AMT II assistant was Franz Alfred Six.[21] Best was next put in charge of civil administration for all of occupied France from 1940 to 1942. Then, in December 1942, he became Reich Plenipotentiary to Denmark.

Best used his power to rehabilitate Carl Schmitt inside the SS. He became Schmitt's patron and protector because he saw that Grossraumordnung theory could serve a useful role in the legal reconstruction of Europe. Thanks to

Best, Schmitt was allowed to lecture to elite audiences throughout occupied Europe and Spain. During his interrogation at Nuremberg, Schmitt explained how his new SS connection came about:

> After my public defamation [by the SS] in December 1936 I obtained the possibility of lecturing abroad again only in 1942, when Himmler and those around him began to feel unsure about foreign countries . . . The SS only took up the theme of Grossraum after 1940, most likely owing to [Dr. Werner] Best, who came across it in France and later in Denmark and, in typical SS style, sought to overpower this interesting new subject. In addition to Best, the editors of this new journal [*Reich, Volksordnung, Lebensraum*] were a few other SS leaders whose names I no longer remember.[22]

Schmitt said that Best's circle

> had the ambition to become an intellectual elite and to form a kind of German "brain trust" in this field. At the same time, however, they were compelled to present themselves as representatives of true Hitlerism. Since that was difficult to reconcile with intellect and "brain-trust," an inner contradiction arose for which the concept of Grossraum was a kind of touchstone . . . From the winter of 1941/42 a growing inner uncertainty became recognizable and with it the need for better ideological supports than either the backwoods orthodoxy of Hitlerism or the literary holdovers of 19th-century Rosenbergism could provide.[23]

After Hitler's suicide, technocrats like Best, Six, and Franke-Gricksch were free to reinvent fascism.

Franke-Gricksch's postwar plans were interrupted when he was seized by the British authorities and placed in a POW camp in Colchester, England. He would remain a British prisoner until his release in the autumn of 1948. While in England, he maintained his leadership position inside the Bruderschaft; after his return to Germany he became the group's acknowledged ideological leader.

The Bruderschaft's mission, as preached by Franke-Gricksch, was to midwife the creation of a new kind of elite rule now that "the era of the masses has passed." This elite would fight "moral vacuum" and "value nihilism" with total dedication to a higher morality and with the conviction that the masses would eventually accept "a personally experienced (*gelebt*) hierarchy of values" as the basis for a new moral order. Once a materialistic, mechanistic view of society had been vanquished, a new elite-led organismic German socialism would overcome social alienation.[24]

When Yockey was helping to develop military "resistance" networks in Wiesbaden, was he acting in concert with the Bruderschaft? One of his closest friends in Wiesbaden was a highly decorated ex-Luftwaffe man named

Martin Becker. In one CIC report, Becker was described as "allegedly in close contact with the STRASSER group." He was also reported to take weekly trips to the Russian-controlled East Zone for supposed business reasons. Was Becker really linked not to Otto Strasser (then in exile in Canada) but to a "Strasserist" tendency inside the Bruderschaft identified with Franke-Gricksch?[25] There was also an active "Strasserist" current in the early postwar German right led by Dr. Bernhard Gericke (who later helped found the SRP); this group may have had ties to Franke-Gricksch.[26]

All that is known for sure is that Yockey began publicly arguing that Russia was the lesser of two evils in London sometime in 1948. Then, in 1949 (after Franke-Gricksch had returned to Germany), Yockey, Guy Chesham, and John Gannon founded the ELF. NATINFORM suggests that the convergence of Yockey's and Franke-Gricksch's views was more than ideological and that they had been involved in the same political network. There is also no question that they were in personal contact by the early 1950s at the very latest.

When Yockey visited England in 1947, he told Gannon that he had come "to meet others in the service of the Idea" before writing *Imperium*. Had he also come with an introduction from the Bruderschaft?

Notes:

    1. I shall describe Leese's and Rockwell's attacks on Yockey later in this book.

    2. Recall that Gregor Strasser also had ties to Oswald Spengler, who destroyed his correspondence with him after Strasser's murder.

    3. The term "national bolshevik" was first used to describe a wing of the early German Communist Party, which supported the Russian Revolution but did not want to be under the total diktat of Moscow. It was later applied to those elements inside the German right who wanted to pursue a foreign policy orientation to the East. For a discussion of national bolshevism, see Klemens von Klemperer, "Towards a Fourth Reich? The History of National Bolshevism in Germany," in *The Review of Politics*, No. 13, 1951. One recent book on the subject is a two-volume work by Louis Dupeux entitled *National Bolchevisme: Strategie Communiste et Dynamique Conservatrice* (Paris: Editions Champion, 1979).

    4. In *Nemesis?* (Boston: Houghton Mifflin, 1940), Otto Strasser's biographer, Douglas Reed, recounts a series of discussions Strasser had with Hitler on 21 and 22 May 1930. Strasser told Hitler:

> I hold your racial theories to be entirely false. In my view, the "race" is but the original raw material, and in the case of the German people four or five races contributed to make this. Political, climatic, and other influences, together with pressure from without and assimilation within, made of this mixture a people; and the processes of history evolved the third and highest form, that which we call "a nation."

Hitler replied:

What you say is pure Liberalism. There *are* no other revolutions but racial revolutions. There are no economic, political, or social revolutions, there is the struggle of the racially inferior lower class against the ruling upper race . . . Precisely because you lack this knowledge of race, your foreign policy is so wrong. For instance, you have often spoken openly in favor of the so-called Indian freedom movement, although this is obviously nothing but a rebellion of the inferior Indian races against the high-quality English-Nordic race. The Nordic race has the right to rule the world and we must make this right the guiding star of our foreign policy . . . For these reasons, we can never go together with Soviet Russia, where a Jewish head rests on a Slav-Tartar body. I know the Slavs from my own homeland. Earlier, when a Germanic head sat on a Slav body, co-operation with Russia was feasible, and Bismarck said this. Today it would be simply a crime.

See pages 97–113 of *Nemesis* for the full Hitler-Strasser encounter.

5. *The Enemy of Europe*, p. 51.

6. His name is also sometimes given as Franke-Grieksch. In Wellington Long, *The New Nazis of Germany* (Philadelphia: Chilton Books, 1968), p. '79, it is reported that Gregor Strasser was Franke-Gricksch's brother-in-law.

7. Kurt Tauber, *Beyond Eagle and Swastika* (Middletown, CT: Wesleyan University Press, 1967), Vol. 1, p. 122.

8. Ibid., Vol. 1, p. 123.

9. Ibid., Vol. 1, p. 122. Franke-Gricksch's relations with Strasser are also mentioned in Patrick Moreau's *Nationalsozialismus von links: Die "Kampfgemeinschaft Revolutionärer Nationalsozialisten" und die "Schwarze Front" Otto Strassers 1930–35* (Stuttgart: Deutsche Verlags-Anstalt, 1985), where Franke-Gricksch is cited both under his real name and his then-pseudonym "Hildebrand."

10. Tauber, *Beyond Eagle and Swastika*, Vol. 1, p. 123. One writer on Franke-Gricksch says: "During this Czech [exile] period, he received from Heydrich safe conduct to Berlin in order to close a deal with the SD chief for his rehabilitation at the RSHA [Reich Security Main Office] so that he could become an SS captain, executive officer (Ic) in a Totenkopf division and department chief in the SS personnel office—[all] at the price of betraying the personnel and . . . connections of the Strasser emigration." See *Beyond Eagle and Swastika*, Vol. 2, fn. 11, p. 1035.

11. Cited in "The Franke-Gricksch 'Resettlement Action Report': Anatomy of a Fabrication," by Brian A. Renk, in the Fall 1991 issue of *The Journal of Historical Review* (published by Willis Carto's Institute for Historical Review), p. 275. Later in this book I shall explain the IHR's interest in Franke-Gricksch.

12. Gerald Fleming, *Hitler and the Final Solution* (Berkeley, CA: University of California Press, 1984), fn. 7, p. 142. Franke-Gricksch's role with SD-England in 1942 is of particular interest for our purposes. Did he accumulate lists of potential collaborators in the British right, and Mosley's British Union of Fascists (BUF) in particular?

13. The Death's Head Division lived up to its name. In the Russian campaign the unit developed "a lust for killing Russians." Hallmarks of the unit's stay in Russia "included the burning of villages, the murder of prisoners, and the sum-

mary execution of captured commissars and politruks." From C. Sydnor, *Soldiers of Destruction* (Princeton, NJ: Princeton University Press, 1977), p. 316.

14. Ibid., p. 337. Franke-Gricksch was with the SS Polizeidivision from August to the winter of 1942.

15. Marlis G. Steinert, *Capitulation 1945: The Story of the Dönitz Regime* (London: Constable, 1969), p. 5.

16. Ibid., p. 6. A partial translation of *The German Freedom Movement* appears as an appendix in T. H. Tetens, *Germany Plots with the Kremlin* (New York: Henry Schuman, 1953).

17. Franke-Gricksch was temperamentally suited to just such a task. As early as 10 February 1941, he wrote a memo to Himmler attacking SS indoctrination policy:

> The memorandum is subtly critical of the crude and harsh emphasis upon hatred of racial enemies and obedience to orders that Franke-Gricksch describes as the staple of political indoctrination inside the SSTK [SS Totenkopf (Death's Head) Division]. The document concludes with an appeal that Himmler revise the ideological training in the SS to include an emphasis upon what Franke-Gricksch calls the great political, economic, and geographical issues the SS soldier needed to know to be a convinced National Socialist. [C. Sydnor, *Soldiers of Destruction*, fn. 6, pp. 315–16.]

18. Robert Hertzstein, *When Nazi Dreams Came True* (London: Sphere, 1982), p. 188.

19. Tauber, *Beyond Eagle and Swastika*, Vol. 2, fn. 60, p. 1043.

20. Hertzstein, *When Nazi Dreams Came True*, pp. 42–44.

21. On Best, Six, and the structure of the RSHA, see Appendix I of André Brisaud, *The Nazi Secret Service* (New York: Norton, 1974).

22. *Telos*, No. 72, Summer 1987, pp. 107–16.

23. Ibid., p. 114.

24. Tauber, *Beyond Eagle and Swastika*, Vol. 1, pp. 130–31. Tauber also notes: "The Bruderschaft's ideology was obviously greatly indebted to Conservative Revolutionary and National Socialist thought."

25. I shall discuss Franke-Gricksch's relations with the East Bloc later in this book.

26. Perry Biddiscombe, "Operation Selection Board: The Growth and Suppression of the Neo-Nazi 'Deutsche Revolution,' 1945–47," in *Intelligence and National Security*, Vol. 11, No. 1 (January 1996).

22
LIFE WITH FRANZ

After *Imperium*'s publication Yockey traveled throughout Europe to promote its message. While visiting Belgium in the spring of 1949, he met a beautiful Flemish choreographer named Elsa Dewette who, at 46, was 14 years older than he was. In a series of letters to the American rightist Keith Stimely, Dewette recalled her relationship with the man she called Franz.[1] Because her letters give such an extraordinary and rare glimpse into Yockey's personal life, I shall quote extensively from them.

Born in Ghent in 1903, Dewette became mesmerized by dance after seeing Isadora Duncan perform.[2] A talented artist and designer, she also won awards in oil painting and native costuming from the Brussels Academy of Fine Arts. In 1932 she founded her own dance troupe, which specialized in traditional Flemish "*Eurythmische Spiele*" (Eurythmish Games).[3] Her German-educated father was the head of the Brussels Telephone Centrale. "From the first days," she recalled, "[my father was] a great admirer of the Hero [Hitler]."[4] Her father's closest German friend was a professional military officer. During the war:

> This man happened to be an officer of very high rank in the German Army during the occupation of Belgium. Of course, my father was delighted to see him again, and he often came to dine at our house. When the war ended, the neighbors (some had been in the "Resistance") had noticed this man's uniform, and nearly put fire to my parents' house. They had to go into hiding for some time.[5]

Belgium dealt more harshly with collaborationists than almost any other European nation: Over four thousand fascists were given death sentences. With good reason, Dewette felt she was a marked woman:

The day the "Allies" arrived in Brussels, the door of my house was covered with huge painted swastikas . . . I was a marked woman. I had a list of hotels where people of "our kind" fled to sleep at night. For many days I had to use impossible stratagems to remain invisible . . . When the first weeks of the bloodhunt were over, I slowly dared to show myself at the [dance] school. I was, however, after that brutally interrogated by the police, my apartment was visited CIA-style—but nothing was found—I have previously also to experience what it was to burn papers . . . It was decided that I would go and visit my aunt, who had emigrated to California in 1912, and who had been begging to see one of the family "from Europe."

When I returned to Brussels, the school was still going strong, thanks to my two devoted monitrices. I was full of ideas, and soon I had many engagements, also in television, which had just started its activities. My artistic inspiration was as fresh and as strong as it had ever been. One triumphal creation followed another. And in 1949, I met FPY: a milestone in my life.[6]

Dewette and Yockey met at a small soiree organized to discuss *Imperium:*

The little gathering of Europeans was nothing more than a drab little tea party, the purpose of which I have as yet not quite understood; but I suppose it took place for the following reason: I think F. had been in contact with two obscure journalists who had come into possession of some volumes of *Imperium*, but did not quite know what to do with FPY himself when he arrived from England a few days previously. So, I suppose, on impulse and, not knowing any better, they took him to the house of this (not very good) Flemish painter, probably a friend of theirs, who had vague "European" ideas. The house of this painter was situated in a village (now a suburb of Brussels) called Watermaal-Bosvoorde, one street away from my parent's house.

I, *zufällig* [by chance], was visiting my parents that afternoon, and as my Father had also been asked to that little gathering (he knew this painter), I was asked to come to help translate whatever had to be translated. The people present were: the two journalists, the painter and his wife, my Father, myself, and FPY, that was all. After the first appropriate noises of introduction, F. was introduced as the author of *Imperium* (no one had heard of either him or the book). The book was passed around, there was an attempt at wise and appreciative conversation, tea was drunk; to me it seemed all very miserable and even grotesque. The painter knew neither French nor English, F. knew hardly any French, so my Pa and I were alone to present a book which we had never heard of. Poor F. realized what was happening and shut up like a clam. Knowing him as I did later, it was lucky that he did not burst out in a violent scene! But I think my presence acted as a lightning-conductor that day.

My first impression of him? He looked a mixture of terrorist and illuminated preacher! Dangerous-magnetic, with his somber look, his (almost) emaciated face, and his disdainful haughty air. As the would-be conversation followed its course (who is this bloke coming to tell us about Europe?), F. was now completely disinterested and stared unblinkingly at me. I felt very uncomfortable as this went on, and the others were beginning to notice . . . Suddenly F. got up and said he would like to go for a little walk with my Father and myself, just to talk in English about his book. He did not care a damn about the journalists. He only used this as pretext to be alone with me, and my Father was no fool. After the "little walk" (the weather was radiant), F. asked if I could give him a lift to town—poor F.—I wondered where to? In reality he had nowhere to go. Nor had he any money: This is absolutely true—so what could poor Elsa do: Take him along of course.[7]

When they were finally alone, Dewette saw that he looked "ill and disappointed."

I asked him what was the matter; he finally flapped out that he had not eaten properly for two days. (In that period and later, he lived on small cheques which his sister, Mrs. Coyne, sent him—and this money had not arrived when expected.) The first thing to do was to take him home and feed him. He was so ravenous: I remember staring at him, unbelieving. After that he was silent and very tired. Then we began to talk about *Imperium*. He talked and talked—he was like a flame—he could hardly believe there was a woman there who understood what he was talking about! But I also became aware of the fact that, having been rejected everywhere for months, he was in a terribly depressive mood, even near to a self-destructive mood maybe. I had met with these dangerous moods in artists. The only thing to get them to snap out of them is to try and get them to work.[8]

I had a grand piano. He was attracted to it as to a magnet. He started to play. And the next few days, he played and played and played. I was amazed at his genuine musical gifts: one can be a virtuoso and yet never possess this gift. He did. He seemed like a man risen from the dead. He was transformed.[9]

Dewette and Yockey quickly became infatuated with each other:

Soon we lost all sense of reality. I cannot explain that kind of exaltation that took possession of us. I had never experienced this before, nor—I am convinced of that still—had he. To cut a long story short, he expressed the need to write again, and to get away from it all, if possible, to the country. In spite of my desire to be near him, I knew he should be alone to write. So I thought of a plan: Why shouldn't he ask the journalist—if there was still time—the loan of his cottage for a few days. I promised to stay near him (we were nearing the Easter holidays, also in my school), at an inn in the village, at his beck and call until he felt like seeing me . . . This was on 11 April 1949. (My birthday was on the 12th.) I heard nothing from him for three days and three nights. I thought: Perhaps he has gone . . . Perhaps he has killed himself . . . etc. Well, I got a phone call on 14 April at 9 P.M. He said "COME." I rushed (with car) to the cottage and rang the bell. Out he came, looking as white as a sheet. I said: How do you feel? He said: terrible—very, very bad, and he looked it too. His hands were shaking. We got into the car, and he thrust a bundle of papers into my lap. He said: this is for you. It was the *Proclamation* [of London].

That night, we became lovers.[10]

Dewette described her experience with Yockey this way: "To our relationship itself, nothing could ever be changed: It started with such spiritual intensity (it was almost a mystical experience)—it developed into a mutual passion, and it almost ended in tragedy."[11] But as for marriage:

Of course F. proposed marriage. Several times in 1949. But all the while I knew this was a desperate attempt to prevent a separation. I found this even sad but, of course, I did not tell him so. (No woman should marry a soldier and I always did think of him as a soldier fighting for a holy cause.) To me, marriage means children, a home, a quiet life, and great responsibilities. This was not my Destiny, although I love children. I waited for the propitious moment to have the matter definitely out with F. At last the moment came: I explained to him gently that our relationship was something so exceptional, whatever happened we must not lower it down to another level, a level that was not for us, the level of the daily grind that would inevitably destroy all that had been, and still was, so precious between us. He cried. And said, of course I was right, he had known all along that it was an impossible proposition. He even asked me to forgive him for having been so weak. (And between us . . . he as usual had completely overlooked the fact that he was still married.) So that was that. And our dramatic meetings went on as before.[12]

Dewette portrayed Yockey's relationship with women this way:

FPY was never the gay little conquering hero. First, he was very curious about these strange animals: women. He wanted to dissect them (all in him always started in the mind—he was not a simple sensual man)—to understand the way they functioned, mentally and physically, and he perpetually also wanted to exert his "will to power," to get more confidence in himself, in his virility, in his power as a man. But believe me or not, he was shy, and even gauche in his approach to women. But his "conquests" were not too difficult: Instinctively the female species was invariably attracted to him by what I called his ever "romantic-hungry-Hamlet-look." They felt that he was poor, defenseless, interesting, and their motherly protective instinct immediately set at work. (This happened to me too!) So FPY did not have much trouble as a "conqueror." Alas, there were three attributes which he hated in women: (a) their possessiveness, (b) their eternal craving "to be happy," (c) their eventual stupidity, by which he meant their lack of culture or other things. And so, if one or several of these female faults began to be too much to be borne by his frayed nervous system he just walked out, and that was the end of that, never mind the tears and the broken hearts left behind. That was, as I said before, F. all over. I am afraid to confess that I am made of the same stuff: We creative artists, creative philosophers, etc., visionaries, etc., are monsters as people. Monstrously egotistical. I could cite a thousand examples.[13]

Life with Franz was seldom dull:

To say it in a vulgar way: F. was always a damn nuisance to "go out" with. When I first knew him, we went to some restaurant or other, generally because I had no time to cook a meal. But each time that venture became a disagreeable farce: "The service was rotten, the waiters were (all and always) idiots, the quality of the food was bad" (all untrue: Belgium is renowned for its fine cuisine)—"only a fascist regime could correct this slovenly situation, etc." The whole venture always ended up as a mini-political meeting, in the midst of a horrified and hostile public. I wanted to crawl under the table. Well, from then on, I flatly refused to "go out" with him anymore.

But the worst incident was yet to come: it happened in the Central Post Office (now demolished), a large hall with wickets all around. F. wanted some stamps but he had to wait in a queue. I felt the temperature of his temper rising. When at last it was his turn at the wicket, the clerk, who was an elderly man and did look half asleep, was too slow for F.'s liking. F. shouted: "Imbecile, in a fascist country you would no more be allowed to show your stupid face here"—insult upon insult were flung at this poor man's face, who, shaken out of his torpor, looked so amazed that it was almost like a vaudeville. F. went on shouting—people rushed to where we were standing. I heard shouts of: "*C'est un fou, il faut l'arrêter, appelez la police . . .* " ("It's a lunatic, stop him, call the police"). I felt something must be done at once . . . and found nothing better than to pretend to faint, sprawled on the floor. Attention was at once (as I hoped it would be) diverted to me. F. came down to reality and bent over me. The tension fell. And we walked out of that place slowly and, I thought, looking rather sheepish. I heard murmurs of "*Pauvre femme . . . Avec un fou pareil*" ("Poor woman . . . With a madman like that") (never a truer word was said!)[14]

Unlike the Belgian postal system, Dewette was more than a match for Yockey:

He once slapped my face because I was mad because he had tormented my cats . . . but by God, in a flash he got a formidable slap back in his face. I bet he never got that from any other woman he ever knew! He stared at me in shock and amazement (it was so comical: I had to force myself hard not to laugh!). He said quietly: "I'm sorry." This kind of incident never happened again. As I told you before, the great, the genius, could behave as an insufferable child. I had neither the time nor the strength to stand for such tantrums.[15]

Dewette thought that Yockey was at his happiest during a trip they took to Bavaria in June 1949:

Here is a true story: When in Germany, one of our dreams was to visit the castle Schwansee, a gift of King Louis of Bayern to his idol Wagner, after the creation of *Lohengrin*. So to Schwansee went these two romantic Wagnerites. Holding hands, and in a state of musico-religious fervor, we went inside that holy shrine. But the more we saw of it: painted swans, swans carved in wood, large porcelain swans with flowerpots in them, embroidered swans, walls full of swans (I believe there were even some in the lavatory): well it was evident: it was all frightful "KITSCH." I did not dare to look at F., wondering if his romantic illusions still held. But when I did catch his eye, we both "exploded" and could not stop our hysterical fits of laughter, much to the horror of the other German visitors. We fled out of that castle, followed by rude remarks about "those American barbarians!" That of course was the funniest part of all! Well, we ran all the way downhill to take refuge in a *bier-stube,* and to drown our disillusion in two pints of Lowenbrau. F. was very drunk, and more comical than ever. I was pleasantly tipsy too, and it was one of the happiest days of our lives.

During the whole of that trip, F. was in an ecstatic mood. I had never seen him like that: he sang, he whistled, he danced like a tight-rope dancer on the curb of the street, he even shouted something comical at a traffic policeman, who did not seem to appreciate this at all: I shouted at once: "*Wir sind nur zwei Tage verheiraten—er ist verrückt.*" ["We're just married two days— he's crazy."] I was pretty and the policeman laughed and let us go.

The lovers even had their own Wagnerian moment:

In the mountains at Oberstdorf, we had an idyllic time—it was unreal. The real world was far away: We were only just discovering each other; and also we liked more and more what we discovered. We also felt, as the condemned aristocrats in the Bastille must have felt, there could be but oblivion for us in the end. It was a strange time. We came "back to normal," descended towards Bregenz on the shores of the Bodensee; it was then only a very small watering-place (now huge and invaded by the usual cohorts of tourists). One afternoon we wanted to go swimming; the weather was gorgeous. We swam very far out (we were both strong swimmers)—we had such a good time, we had not noticed that the sky had gradually become very black. Suddenly a violent storm broke out (as it is wont to do in those parts). There was thunder, there was lightning . . . large waves began to crash over our heads, and the spray was blinding us. We turned back, F. swimming alongside of me. The din was terrible. Suddenly, I heard him shout: "Elsa, if we have to die here, at least we shall die together." Finally we did reach the shore, and fell

flat on our faces, thoroughly exhausted. In later years I often wished I had
died that afternoon in the lake at Bregenz.

We returned to Belgium. Nearing Brussels, our hearts sank with each
mile. The dream—the only one—allowed to us, was at an end. When we
were back in Brussels, F. made one comment on this trip. He said: "The
things we did in Germany must have caused a number of earthquakes all
over the world." I liked that![16]

As Yockey moved deeper underground, he and Dewette stopped seeing
each other. She also thought that he had begun to change:

After our "parting in the flesh," so to speak, there followed again a series of
frantic telephone calls, and an avalanche of letters: sometimes I received
three letters a week, sometimes only one in 10 days. F. was deeply
depressed. I remarked (and I deplored) that his letters became more and more
bitter, harder, very cynical. It was as if he was full of resentment, full of hate
against this fate which had deprived him of the only human being who
could "deliver him from his own self-tormenting self" (his own words).
There was a feeling of revenge in him—and I have often wondered whether
this might not have been one of the reasons for his ultimate cruelty to
women: You know how he was—taking them—using them for a couple of
months—and then dropping them without a tinge of conscience. To me this
is still incomprehensible. I had known him [to be] kind, sensitive, generous,
tender, and completely trustful.

There came a long lull in our correspondence until the end of 1951, as I
was abroad [her dance troupe was in the Belgian Congo]—then in 1952 and
1953 he wrote more or less regularly and sent me books and records. I am
sorry to disappoint you, but he rarely mentioned anything about the people
he met, or what exactly he was doing. The letters were very personal, as if
he wanted to get away and forget for a little while the disillusions and dis-
appointments he was eternally meeting with. He was sad, lonely, misunderstood, hated. My heart bled for him (as it does now when I recall all this).
I believe it was at the end of 1953 [more likely 1954—K.C.] that he told me
in a telephone call that he was "getting in a dangerous situation" and there
was nothing more for him to do than to "go underground." He would go on
calling me, but I must not write anymore. (Probably the complication of his
"false names.") I understood . . . I always felt myself to be the wife of a soldier more than anything else. And my duty was to keep my mouth shut
eventually, and to obey.[17]

After Yockey went "underground," Dewette said: "I knew nothing of him,
or of his activities, for six years." Then, incredibly

in June 1960, I received a long letter from him, also of a purely private
nature, revealing nothing of the difficulties which he must have felt coming.
The letter was typed, dated if I remember well June sixth or seventh. The

envelope bore the address of the YMCA in San Francisco. At the bottom [of the letter] were also the letters DESTROY (which alas I did).

Yockey's letter was postmarked from San Francisco on 14 June, two days before his death. After that letter, she heard nothing at all about him for 15 years. Then, in 1975, one of her friends saw a copy of *Imperium oder Chaos*, the Grabert Verlag edition of *Imperium*, in a bookstore. Although it did not include Carto's introduction, Dewette gathered that Yockey was dead. Five years later, in November 1980, she was contacted by John Anthony Gannon. After coming across her address in an old *Frontfighter* subscription list, Gannon wrote her on behalf of Yockey's would-be far-right biographer Keith Stimely. When Gannon visited her later that month, she finally learned the grim details of her lover's fate.[18]

After her affair with Yockey, Dewette went on to achieve considerable artistic success. She won the Belgian TV equivalent of an Emmy in 1961 for her work as a choreographer. She also became a professor in the Drama Section of the Belgium State Royal Conservatory of Music. Still an ardent fascist, she turned to Spain, and bullfighting in particular, for solace:

> Do you remember I went to Spain for 30 consecutive years? I know a great deal about Spanish music, and also bullfighting: that sublime "ballet with Death" where no cheating is possible. I have seen 305 bullfights with the best matadors in Spain but it is said one ought to see five hundred before knowing anything about the great and noble art of the *tauromaquia*. People who know me and even admire me think this passion for bullfighting is a black spot on my character: They think I am a sadist. So much the better, I say.[19]

Notes:

1. All told, there are almost 80 pieces of correspondence between Elsa Dewette and Keith Stimely. The two became good friends, and only their early letters really concern Yockey. Stimely died in 1992, with his biography of Yockey not even begun. When I contacted his family, they sent my request for his material to H. Keith Thompson, who had copies of the Stimely–Dewette letters. With the permission of the Stimely family, Thompson sent me the bulk of Stimely's archives, including the letters. He did so only after writing to Dewette's last known address and receiving no reply. The Stimely–Dewette correspondence ends in the late 1980s. Dewette wrote her letters with the intention that they would be used in a biography. I have only slightly edited the material for readability.

2. Besides Duncan, she was also influenced by the work of Rudolf van Laban and Kurt Joos.

3. Dewette had been briefly married during the war, to a painter named Darciel. After her divorce, she continued to use the name Darciel professionally.

4. "My father, besides being an engineer and having studied in Germany, was also a philosopher and a musician—as from the age of 14 I was nurtured on

Nietzsche, Schopenhauer, later Spengler etc., and Wagner. F. and I were mad Wagnerites!" (Elsa Dewette, letter to Keith Stimely, 27 January 1981.)

5. Elsa Dewette, letter to Keith Stimely, 15 December 1985.

6. Elsa Dewette, letter to Keith Stimely, 21 December 1981.

7. Elsa Dewette, letter to Keith Stimely, 12 February 1982.

8. Elsa Dewette, letter to Keith Stimely, 15 February 1982.

9. Elsa Dewette, letter to Keith Stimely, 27 January 1981.

10. Elsa Dewette, letter to Keith Stimely, 19 February 1982.

11. Elsa Dewette, letter to Keith Stimely, 27 April 1984.

12. Elsa Dewette, letter to Keith Stimely, 15 May 1982.

13. Elsa Dewette, letter to Keith Stimely, 11 November (year not noted).

14. Elsa Dewette, letter to Keith Stimely, 27 April 1984.

15. Elsa Dewette, letter to Keith Stimely, 12 October 1981.

16. Ibid.

17. Elsa Dewette, letter to Keith Stimely, 7 April 1982.

18. In a 24 November 1981 letter, Gannon gave Keith Stimely his impression of the then-73-year-old Dewette:

I know that you will be interested in the physical appearance of E.D. She is a tiny woman, no more than five feet high IN SHOES; birdlike in movement; her skin is now akin to parchment, but not excessively so; she is neat in dress, without being elegant; somehow, an impression is conveyed that here is a woman who has lived for many years in darkened rooms; her taste in furniture runs to black oak in the heavy Spanish style, some of it being genuine, old pieces; likes cats . . . She is cautious in meeting people to rather a paranoid degree, raising detailed questions as to the purposes involved in preliminary. [I] feel that here is a woman in self-imposed mourning for Y., even BEFORE she knew he was dead—with few, if any, real friends—but self-sufficient in her loneliness, and NOT unhappy in it.

19. Elsa Dewette, letter to Keith Stimely, 15 December 1985.

23

THE TROUBLE
WITH "CLARENCE"

Imperium especially appealed to the most radical wing of Italy's Movimento Sociale Italiano (MSI), the largest and best-organized fascist movement in postwar Europe. Yockey seems to have visited Italy at least twice, first in 1949 after *Imperium's* publication, and again in 1951. Thanks in part to John Gannon's extensive connections, he "met the leaders of the MSI in Italy, and was financed in his personal expenses by Princess Pignatelli, a heroic noblewoman of Naples, devoted to Il Duce, and who had tried to save his life, in vain."[1] Pignatelli was active in the MSI's women's division, the *Movimento Italiano Femminile* (MIF). Yockey helped organize an MIF congress in Naples in the autumn of 1951. He also spoke at the meeting.[2] He later commented on the experience in a letter dated 3 October 1951:

> I am staying in one spot for about three weeks . . . I am in Naples organizing the foreign part of a Fascist convention to be held 25–28 October. As you know, I do not believe in conventions, I believe in the lonely agonies of superior men, but I have ulterior motives, not the least of which is the fact that my expenses of living are being paid during this month, and thus for a short while I am relieved from the terrible pressure of economics.[3]

Yockey's unhappiness with conventions was shared by MSI founder Giorgio Almirante, who praised *Imperium* after its publication.[4] A former official in the Ministry of Popular Culture in Mussolini's Salò Republic, he spoke for MSI hardliners opposed to turning the group into a purely parliamentary organization.

The postwar divisions inside the MSI dated back to 1943, when the Fascist Grand Council deposed Mussolini. After the Nazis freed him from an Italian jail, Mussolini established a new government known as the Salò Republic in the Nazi-held north of Italy. Believing that his downfall had been caused by the old Italian elites, Il Duce returned to fascism's radical socialist roots and demanded the nationalization of Italian industry. After the war his Salò Republic supporters like Almirante continued to represent a kind of northern "Strasserist" tendency inside Italian fascism. At its June 1950 convention, the Salò radicals were defeated by a more moderate wing of the party, and Almirante was replaced as MSI party boss. By the time of Yockey's second sojourn to Italy, in the fall of 1951, the MSI had reversed its earlier opposition to Italian participation in NATO.

Yockey's co-thinkers in the anti-MSI hard right were grouped around journals like *Imperium*, coincidentally the title of Yockey's opus. According to the NATINFORM report, in July 1950 Guy Chesham "stated that Yockey had large connections in Italy and worked in conjunction with an Italian politician—Stassi, editor of the monthly journal *Imperium*." *Imperium* managed to produce four issues in 1950 before being suppressed by the police.[5]

Imperium was one of the journals that supported the ideas of Baron Julius (Giulio) Evola, the leading rightist theorist in postwar Italy.[6] *Imperium* also published Evola's first major postwar political statement, *Orientamenti* (Orientations), in 1950.[7] Here, Evola argued against all forms of "national fascism" (including the Salò Republic), demanding instead a new "*Gemeinschaft Europas*" (European Community) best symbolized by the Waffen SS.[8]

The similarities between Evola and Yockey were known inside the far right, as evidenced by Felix Schwarzenborn's article "Imperium Europaeum," which appeared in the Argentina-based Nazi publication *Der Weg*.[9] In his review of *Orientamenti*, Schwarzenborn cited both *Frontfighter* and the European Liberation Front as proof that the idea of Imperium was in the air ("*Dass diese Dinge in der Luft liegen*") throughout all Europe, not just Italy. The ELF was also well aware of Evola: In the April 1951 issue of *Frontfighter* he was labeled "Italy's greatest living authoritarian philosopher."

On 1 June 1951 the Italian authorities jailed Evola and 20 other neofascists and charged them with plotting the overthrow of the Italian state. The trial, which lasted from June to November 1951, was still underway when Yockey attended the MIF's Naples meeting. (Evola, who later described the trial as a "comic episode," was eventually acquitted.)

The arrest of Evola was just one example of the complex political situation that existed in Italy in the late 1940s and early 1950s. Italy's Christian Democrat–led government, and its supporters inside both the Vatican and the CIA, needed the far right to oppose the Communists. Many MSI members, however, strongly objected to any cooperation with the state. The MSI had only two real options: It could continue to maintain a revolutionary "anti-bourgeois" stand while having some parliamentary presence, or it could accept the status quo and become a full parliamentary organization. A second great choice involved foreign policy: Which superpower was Italy's main enemy—Russia or America?

Neither question was academic, since in 1948 the MSI had won six seats in the Italian Chamber of Deputies and one in the Italian Senate. Advocates of the parliamentary road generally accepted the postwar order, which included Italian support for NATO. Rejectionists insisted on anti-American neutrality, with some even open to a tactical tilt East. The MSI's founders, supporters of the Salò Republic, held radically anti-bourgeois "left" corporatist fascist views. MSI founder Almirante, for example, had earlier helped create the Fasci di Azione Rivoluzionaria (FAR) in 1946.[10] FAR member Mario Tedeschi best expressed the group's outlook when he commented that

> real Fascism, that is to say radical, nationalist, and socialist Fascism, had been subverted by conservative forces during the *ventennio* [twenty years] of power. The monarchy and the plutocratic bourgeoisie had conspired to bring down Mussolini in 1943. Members of the Grand Council who had voted against the Duce were guilty of treason.[11]

Although FAR violently opposed the Italian Communists, it also hurled bombs at the U.S. embassy in Rome.[12] Even after FAR and other groups moved away from "direct action," they continued to take pride in remaining true to the radical ideals of Salò.

The MSI's overriding fear of Italy's Communist Party (the PCI), however, led it to form anti-PCI electoral blocs with the Christian Democrats in Rome and other cities. Its biggest electoral base was also in the conservative south: The more pragmatic and traditional "southerner" Augusto De Marsanich defeated Almirante in January 1950 for the position of MSI general secretary. One key to Almirante's downfall was his opposition to NATO. Under Almirante, the MSI had voted in the spring of 1949 against any Italian role in NATO. After a bitter debate at the party's congress that June, the group reversed itself and accepted NATO membership. Not long after the vote, De Marsanich took power. Hard-right splinter groups around publications like *Imperium* were then formed to oppose the MSI majority.

To make matters even more complicated, the Italian Communist Party began aggressively courting the MSI's anti-NATO wing. As early as the spring of 1947, PCI leader Giancarlo Pajetta opened talks with several Salò veterans, including Concetto Pettinato, head of the main fascist paper during Salò; Giorgio Pini, Salò vice-minister of the Interior; Admiral Ferruccio Ferrini, vice minister of the Navy; Lando Dell'Amico, a war hero decorated by Field Marshall Kesselring for his bravery; and Stanis Ruinas, an influential newspaperman. The PCI then began financing a magazine called *Il Pensiero Nazionale*, edited by Ruinas and written by and for Salò fascists.[13] Ruinas was later replaced as editor by Dell'Amico, whom Ignazio Silone called "one of the boldest and most tireless of the neofascist militants."[14] Dell'Amico's main task was "to enlist other fascists in a united front against America."[15] The PCI also utilized Stalin's attacks on "Zionism" and "cosmopolitanism" in the early 1950s to bolster its ties to the right.[16] Dell'Amico's last mission for the Communist apparat, then headed by PCI chief Palmiro Togliatti's brother-in-law Paolo Robotti, was to establish contact with an anti-Semitic group that published a weekly called *Asso di Bastoni* (The Ace of Spades).[17]

In the war between the "left" and "right" wings of Italian fascism, many young radicals desperately tried to escape the embrace of either the Christian Democrats or the Communists, both of whom were seen as surrogates for the Americans or the Russians. The violent *veroniani*, followers of the Salò Republic's Charter of Verona, which had been partly adopted by the MSI in 1947, were most committed to "third way" neutralism. In the early 1950s, *veroniani* like Pino Rauti, Clemente Graziani, and Mario Gionfrida organized gang-like paramilitary groupings with names like *Legione nera* (Black Legion), *I Figli del sole* (Children of the Sun), and *La Sfida* (Defiance). Convinced that democracy was a "disease of the soul," they turned to Baron Evola for inspiration.[18]

Evola argued that it was absurd to identify the right with capitalism. Fascism, properly understood, was the antithesis of bourgeois society, not its avatar. Since fascist values like blood, sacrifice, and heroism were far more pagan than Christian, fascism was also in opposition to the Catholic Church.[19] He was equally relentless in his condemnation of the Salò left. To Evola, Marxism, with its stress on material issues, was merely a further extension of bourgeois ideology, not its negation. Any movement primarily inspired by economic concerns was intrinsically anti-heroic.

Evola wrote an important review of Yockey's *Imperium* in the spring of 1951 for the first issue of a fascist journal called *Europa Nazione*.[20] Before examining his analysis, it is important to understand how much he and Yockey had in common. Besides being admirers of Spengler (Evola translated parts of *The Decline of the West* into Italian), they held similar views on the question of race. Like Yockey, Evola rejected "biological" anti-Semitism for a higher, more "spiritual" form of anti-Jewish hatred. In a 1942 article entitled "*L'equivoco del razzismo scientifico*" (The Misunderstanding of Scientific Racism) he argued:

> We would like to make it clear . . . what in better times the wellborn have always said were the marks of race: namely, straightforwardness, inner unity, character, courage, virtue, immediate and instant sensitivity for all

values, which are present in every human being and which, since they stand well beyond all chance-subjected reality, they also dominate. The current meaning of race, however, which differs from the above by being a construction of "science" and a piece out of the anthropological museum, we leave to the pseudointellectual bourgeoisie, which continues to indulge in the idols of 19th-century Positivism.

In his anti-Semitic *Tre aspetti del problema ebraico* (Three Aspects of the Jewish Problem), Evola also refused to reduce European history to conspiracy theory:

In the concrete course of development of modern civilization, the Jew can be seen as a power, who collectively with others has worked to create our "civilized," rationalistic, scientist, and mechanistic modern decadence, but on no account can he be marked as its single, far-reaching cause. To believe such a thing would be very stupid. The actual truth is that one would rather fight against personified powers than against abstract principles or universal phenomena, because you can also fight them practically. So the world has turned en masse against the Jew, as he seemed to show in his being a typical form that one finds, however, in much wider regions and even in nations that are practically untouched by Jewish immigration.

Even in his introduction to an Italian edition of the *Protocols of the Elders of Zion* (!), Evola wrote: "We must say at once that in this matter we personally cannot follow a certain fanatical anti-Semitism, especially that which sees the Jews everywhere as *deus ex machina* and by which one finally leads oneself into a kind of trap."

Given the similarity of his views to Yockey's, it is not surprising that Evola thought *Imperium* important; the questions he posed to its author were also addressed to a whole generation of fascist youth. Evola argued that "Varange" had fundamentally misread Spengler by not taking seriously enough Spengler's emphasis on the difference between Kultur and Zivilization. Civilization could only be a time of decline ("*la fase autunnale e crepuscolare*"). Yockey, however, wanted to build the Imperium at a time when the formation of a supernational and organic united Europe was inconceivable: "*Il fatto è che unità supernazionale dai tratti positivi ed organici non è concepibile in un periodo di 'civilizzazione.'*" He had further confused the age of Caesarism with the coming of the Imperium. To ardently argue, as Yockey did, that the breakup of the Third Reich now cleared the way for the emergence of a new pan-European mass fascist movement was romantic nonsense. The defeat of the NSDAP (to Evola a highly problematic political formation to begin with) could not now be easily transformed into a harbinger of a coming victory.

While agreeing with *Imperium*'s vision of a united Europe, Evola believed that now, more than ever, that message could only be grasped, and certainly only acted upon, by a tiny elite of superior men operating behind the scenes. *Imperium* had underestimated the profundity of the crisis now confronting Europe. Yockey's problem was not that he had failed to supply the correct political road map; rather, he seemed unaware of how useless roadmaps were when the road itself was hopelessly flooded.

After his death in 1974, Evola was lauded by MSI founder Almirante as "our Marcuse, only better." It was an extremely perceptive remark. Like Herbert Marcuse in *One Dimensional Man*, Evola argued that the postwar system was so strong, both materially and ideologically, that resistance was only possible by a handful of Übermenchen operating outside the normal channels of power. Such a situation was in some ways actually welcomed by Evola, who had extreme contempt for all mass organizations.

The divisions over the future orientation of the far right extended beyond the Italian Alps. The MSI-initiated *Europäische Soziale Bewegung* (European Social Movement, or ESB, more popularly known as the "Malmö International") was largely a paper organization because of these divisions. ESB leaders like Mosley, Bardèche, and De Marsanich were incapable of creating a viable pan-European fascist movement. While preaching "third force" neutralism on Sunday, they spent the rest of the week praising NATO and damning Russia. Such rhetoric failed to ignite the passions of a new generation of action-oriented fascist youth who remained unapologetic about the past.[21]

The Malmö International split in the fall of 1951 after the more radical wing of the organization walked out. Between 28 and 30 September, a group of ESB dissidents led by the French fascist René Binet and the Swiss Guy Amaudruz created the New European Order (*Neue Europäische Ordnung*, or NEO) at a Zurich conference.[22] It is possible that Yockey attended the NEO conference, because that September he was en route from Germany to the MIF meeting in Naples. Yockey also knew René Binet, whom he had first met at the home of Maurice Bardèche in Paris a year earlier.

Born in 1914, Binet had been a member of the Jeunesses Communistes until he was expelled from the group in 1934. He then joined the Trotskyist Groupes d'Action Révolutionnaire, but eventually drifted more and more to the right. After spending part of World War II in a German POW camp, he volunteered in 1944 to fight in the all-French Waffen SS Charlemagne Division. After the war ended, he published a clandestine journal called *Le Combattant Européen* directed at former members of the Waffen SS. He also spent time in jail for trying to build a new National Socialist movement in France.

Binet advocated a new form of racial "biopolitics" that he tirelessly promoted in underground journals like *La Sentinelle* (1949–52) and *Le Nouveau*

213

Prométhée. He also worked closely with Bardèche to lay the foundations of the ESB before breaking with it over its lack of radicalism and failure to endorse biopolitical theory. His militancy may have led to his death: He was killed in a car crash near Pontoise on 16 October 1957, and there were rumors that he may have been murdered.[23]

While Binet and Bardèche were still in close collaboration, Bardèche arranged a meeting between Yockey and Binet. Although they had been in contact for some time, Bardèche's first meeting with Yockey took place in Paris at Bardèche's home at 10 Rue du Bouloi in the winter of 1950/1951, while he was serving as the French representative to the ESB. Bardèche later recalled his impression of Yockey in a letter to Keith Stimely:

> I had the impression of finding myself in the presence of a man whose talent I knew from his book but who had an absolutely unrealistic mind. We had been able to measure by the reports of our correspondents in the European Social Movement how difficult the moral recovery of Europe would be in the wake of the policy of reeducation and of police set up by the Americans. Varange saw himself on the eve of taking power in the principal European countries, and from his point of view it was only a question of discussing with René Binet the supreme command of the new European order. This absolutely unreal dialogue set one against the other two persons who were equally authoritarian and equally completely blinded by Utopian hopes . . . Varange allowed absolutely no criticism of his ideas. He was convinced that he was the repository of an absolute, undebatable truth, and that the methods that he thought to be able to use allowed no discussion. I had absolutely abstained from taking a position and in fact the discussion, often passionate and violent, took place only between Varange and René Binet. I even refused to arbitrate between two adversaries whose personalities were equally opposed and intolerant and impermissible to all arbitration.[24]

The real-life encounter between Bardèche, Binet, and Yockey led to a hilarious chapter in Bardèche's novel *Suzanne et le Taudis* (Suzanne and the Slums) called "Le Fascisme International."[25] In it, Yockey is "Ulrich Clarence" and Binet is "René Vinay":

> Clarence, muffled up in his overcoat, lying in the armchair in the room that served me as a study, gulped down his ninth cup of coffee, and every 15 minutes turned the half of the coal scuttle into an apocalyptic fireplace which resembled the firebox of a locomotive. Having taken the time to note on a piece of paper the number of the local fire department, I followed the conversation of Clarence (who was speaking in German) as best I could, red, sweating, my hand fan-shaped behind my ear. Fortunately, that monologue was interrupted every 10 minutes, because Clarence, suffering from a bladder ailment, frequently had need of a moment of solitude. He got up, heroically braved the corridor, stepped over the tricycle, the children, and the

hobby horse, and left me thus some minutes of respite. Then he returned, fed the fireplace, took up the coffee and continued at the point where he had left the exposition of the organization of the party that he wished to found. That organization very simply reduced itself to an absolute obedience under pain of death to Ulrich Clarence, founder and president: The sanction was automatic in case of lack of discipline.

In honor of Clarence, I had called René Vinay, a fascist of the puritan type, who spent his life founding parties and publishing mimeographed flyers. He entered courageously into the furnace and the conversation took a more animated turn. Vinay thought that Clarence ought to obey Vinay, and Clarence stupidly persisted in maintaining that Vinay ought to obey Clarence. Consoled by the liveliness of that philosophical conversation, I disappeared to go to my dentist . . .

When I came back two hours later none of the speakers had eaten any of the others, but the session had not adjourned.

Bardèche then sighed:

One of the great misfortunes of men who do not like democracy is surely that Hitler began his political action with nine comrades in the basement of a beer hall. Too many excellent young men have concluded that with a half-dozen pals and a mimeograph machine they were also going to seize power. Clarence, in spite of his excess enthusiasm as a neophyte, was a courageous and estimable young man. He had dared to sacrifice his career and his comfort in order to protest violently against the Nuremberg trial, an indignation which was unwise at that time. He gave himself over entirely, without money, without support, to a difficult and hopeless apostolate. One does not meet very often men of that stamp. Why is it necessary that nearly all of them have in themselves a predisposition to a jealous and implacable despotism? I have known, after Clarence, very many "fascists," for the race is not dead. Some of them had boots, they were familiar with the runes, and they camped out on the night of the solstice in order to sing under the stars the beautiful solemn songs of their ancestors. The others did not have boots, they held up their skinny reformers' heads severely, they wore glasses, they collected cards, and they made furious speeches. All were poor, they believed, they fought, they detested lying and injustice.

In his 1961 book *Qu'est-ce que le Fascisme?*, Bardèche commented: "We seek in vain the *book* of Fascism," although "no such bible exists" because "fascism is not a doctrine" but "an obscure and remote longing written in our blood and in our souls." Fascists are men "who feel more deeply and more desperately than other men" that the ideal of fascism "is a means of salvation, the secret of life and well-being which every zoological species preserves like an instinct in the depths of its conscience."[26] But how were "those who feel more deeply and desperately" to survive in the wintertime of the West?

Notes:

1. John Anthony Gannon, letter to Keith Stimely, 13 July 1980.

2. 8 July 1954 report by Lloyd Bogstad of the Chicago FBI. The report also cites an unidentified German source on Yockey: "During the Italian Women's Movement Congress, the subject [Yockey] tried to convince a German guest of his idea to recreate Germany as a military power, which should seek to subjugate the world and establish a Germanic empire." The report also noted: "The subject's repeated criticisms of the Italians for their 'lack of order' seemed to have gained him few friends in Rome, Italy."

3. FBI file 105-643, report of FBI Agent Donald H. Holland, dated 2 March 1953. The FBI also found a telegram date-stamped "1951 OTT 24 PM" addressed to Ulick Varange: "ULICK VARANGE COMITATO ORGANIZZATORE CONGRESSO NACIONALE MIF NAPOLI ACCEPTADA INVITACION LIEGARE NAPOLES DIA VENTICUATRO TREN VEINTE QUINCE CON ELISA LARA PUNTO RUEGO RESERVEN ALOJAMIENTO PUNTO SALUDOS EIROA." The FBI translated this as "Ulick Varagne Organizational Committee of the National Congress Naples Accept invitation will arrive Naples the 24th day train 2015 with ELISA LARA stop request reserve lodging stop greetings EIROA." The FBI translator did not know that MIF stood for the Movimento Italiano Femminile.

4. Gannon includes Almirante in his list of fascist leaders favorably impressed by *Imperium*.

5. Christopher Boutin, *Julius Evola dans le Siècle (1898–1974)* (Paris: Editions Kime, 1992), fn. 10, p. 353. I have not been able to identify "Stassi," who was named in the NATINFORM report as editor of the journal *Imperium*.

6. For an excellent analysis of Evola, see Franco Ferraresi, "Julius Evola and the Radical Right," in *Archives of European Sociology*, XXVIII (1987).

7. *Imperium* was then being edited by Enzo Erra and published out of 13, Via Parta, Castello, Rome.

8. Franco Ferraresi explains that for Evola

> concepts like those of nation and fatherland are rejected because of their natural-istic-collectivistic origin . . . they indicate a "matter" which must be "formed" by the State. Furthermore, in modern Western history, nations have been responsible for the disruption of the European imperial order. ["Julius Evola and the Radical Right," p. 124.]

9. *Der Weg*, No. 9, 1951.

10. From Almirante's biography in Philip Rees, *Biographical Dictionary of the Extreme Right since 1890* (New York: Simon & Schuster, 1990).

11. Tedeschi's views as summarized in Leonard Weinberg, *After Mussolini: Italian Neo-Fascism and the Nature of Fascism* (Washington, D.C.: University Press of America, 1979), p. 15.

12. *The Recent Growth of Neo-Nazis in Europe*, a 1951 report by the American Jewish Committee.

13. Claire Sterling, "Italy: The Co-Operation of Extreme Left and Far Right," in the 13 April 1954 *Reporter*. This issue also included an attack on Yockey.

14. Ignazio Silone, "A Vignette of the Red-Fascist Alliance," in the 13 April 1953 issue of *New Leader*.

15. Ibid.

16. When Dell'Amico asked if this meant the CP had abandoned its anti-racist policy, Robotti (whose wife was Jewish) replied, "No, but since Zionism came under American influence, a new historical situation has arisen."

17. *Asso di Bastoni* was an excellent example of Italian "universal fascism." In its 18 December 1955 issue, a writer for *Asso di Bastoni* commented:

> There is no place in the world where a fascist movement has not developed, from the ices of the Island of Olafur Thors, head of the "National Front," to the "Tierra del Fuego," where Perón commanded, to the islands of the Persian Gulf where a section of the MSI exists . . . to the rice plantations of nationalist Thailand of the ex-collaborationist Luang Pibul Songram; from the land of the Pharaohs and of the Pyramids where the dictator Nasser is developing his doctrine of the nationalist and authoritarian corporativism to the state of Azerbaigian where the memory of the deeds of Fatalibayli Dudanginsky are still remembered, to the Balkans with the Ustaches and the Iron Guards, and to the Mountains of the Phalange; from the English castles of Sir Oswald Mosley to the Russian steppes of Vlassov and to the Black Forest of the "Steel Helmets" and of the "Werewolves"; from Budapest on the Danube with the *"Croci Frecciate"* to the Islands of Indonesia of the ex-collaborationist Soekharno; from the slopes of Fujiama, the sacred mountain of the Japanese, where the nationalist sect of the "Black Dragon" of Ichiro Midori is working; to the Indies where the faithful followers of Chandra Bose meet; from the Ireland of the "Blue Shirts" to Tunis of ex-collaborationist Habib Burghiba; from the Parisian Montmartre with the young cohorts of Doriot and the journalists of *Rivarol* to the fertile plains of Wang-Ching-Wei's China; from the deserts of the Middle East of Daoud Monchi Zadegh and of the Grand Mufti to the quiet and limpid waters of the Swiss lakes of Amaudruz; from the Norwegian fjords of Hamsun and Per Enghdal and Sven Hedin's Stockholm to the Lisbon of the "Portuguese Legion"; the Slovakia of Tiso and Cernak and the Bolivia of Paz Estenssoro; from Mannerheim's Finland to the islands of the West Indies where nationalist and phalangist movements are active in black shirts to Israel and the extreme rightist party "Herut," everywhere, in every place and country of the world, the fascist approach has found and finds fanatic supporters.

18. Weinberg, *After Mussolini*, p. 24.

19. Ibid.

20. Evola's strategy for the right was further outlined in his 1953 book *Gli uomini e le rovine* (Men Among the Ruins), a book of particular importance because he devoted an entire chapter ("Europa Una: Forma e Presupposti") to Yockey's *Imperium*. This chapter was a reprint of Evola's earlier review. See *Gli uomini e la rovine* (Rome: Edizioni dell'Ascia, 1953).

21. Angelo Del Boca and Mario Giovana, *Fascism Today* (New York: Pantheon, 1969), p. 84.

22. The conference was ostensibly a meeting of the Fourth Plenary Session of the "national pioneers." Among the attenders was Fritz Rossler of the SRP. See

Jeffrey Bale's 1994 Ph.D. thesis from the University of California at Berkeley entitled "The 'Black' Terrorist International: Neo-Fascist Paramilitary Networks and the Strategy of Tension in Italy, 1968–1974," pp. 98–99.

23. Rees, *Biographical Dictionary of the Extreme Right Since 1890*.

24. Maurice Bardèche, letter to Keith Stimely, summer 1982.

25. Maurice Bardèche, *Suzanne et le Taudis* (Paris: Plon, 1957), pp. 123–30.

26. Del Boca and Giovana, *Fascism Today*, p. 179.

BEHIND
ENEMY LINES
(1950-JANUARY 1953)

I am back on the wrong continent again.
—Francis Parker Yockey

24

CONTINENTAL

HOPSCOTCH

In either late 1949 or early 1950 Yockey returned to America hoping to find political and financial support for the ELF from the Christian Nationalist Crusade (CNC), the largest American far-right group in the immediate postwar period. The group's founder, the Reverend Gerald L. K. Smith, was a flamboyant demagogue and fanatical anti-Semite who began his career as an advisor to Louisiana Governor Huey Long. After Long's assassination, Smith helped co-found the Union Party with Father Coughlin and Doctor Francis Townsend.[1] Smith lived in Detroit during World War II and enjoyed the patronage of Henry Ford. In 1947 he created the Christian Nationalist Crusade/Christian Nationalist Party as the postwar continuation of his America First party.[2] He also published an influential magazine called *The Cross and the Flag*.

After staying with the Coynes in Roxanna, Illinois, Yockey visited the CNC's national headquarters in nearby St. Louis.[3] Don Lohbeck, his main CNC contact, had been a skilled classical pianist before turning to a full-time career in rightist politics. After working for the America First Committee, he joined forces with Smith in 1944.[4] Yockey and Lohbeck shared an apartment in St. Louis during the summer of 1950. As "Ulick Varange," Yockey gave a series of talks on the Nuremberg trials under CNC auspices. He addressed one CNC meeting on 13 June 1950. The FBI later obtained a memorandum from the St. Louis Police Department about the meeting:

> The speakers were DON LOHBECK, candidate for congressman of the 11th Missouri District, who was chairman of the meeting; JOHN W. HAMILTON, candidate for senator from Missouri; and ULICK VARANGE, residing

at Roxanna, Illinois, who has recently returned from Europe, who described the underground working of the party in France, Germany, England, and also in Belgium.

All remarks at meeting were directed against the Communists, Jews, Negroes, and Republican and Democratic Parties . . . VARANGE stated that he attended the trials at Nuremberg and other places and spoke of the unfairness of the trials and the importance of the testimony of the Jews. He also stated that we will have a Nuremberg trial in this country some day . . .

_____[5] flier announcing a program at the St. Louis House, 2345 Lafayette Ave., St. Louis, Mo., on 6/29/50. The flier indicates ULICK VARANGE, "Representative of the European Liberation Front," will speak on the topic "Is Europe Dead?" . . . The flier also indicates that there will be a discussion concerning the "Secret Jewish Government in Washington."

_____ attended a meeting sponsored by the Christian Nationalist Party on 6/29/50. The speakers included ULICK VARANGE, who stated that he just returned from Europe in order to meet the leaders of the "party" and to contact its members and then he planned to return to Europe. He ridiculed the Nuremberg trials saying they were controlled by the Jews, and that thousands of "white Christian Germans" were actually convicted before being tried. He contended that the Jews control the world today.[6]

Yockey, Lohbeck, and Hamilton then drove from St. Louis to Los Angeles for the CNC national convention held on 20–23 July 1950. Yockey seems to have been one of the convention's featured speakers. In a letter dated 31 July 1950 and postmarked from Roxanna, he discussed both his speech and his increasing difficulties with Smith. According to the FBI summary of the letter:

Subject YOCKEY describes a "tremendous speech" he had recently made in California. He referred to one SMITH and states that SMITH does not want to have anything to do with him, since the talk he gave. YOCKEY stated that he, SMITH, puts out an excellent information service magazine, etc., "but personally I do not think he will get anywhere as his line is all wrong."[7]

Yockey eventually decided that Smith was little more than a huckster. When Keith Stimely interviewed H. Keith Thompson about Yockey's relations with Smith, Thompson reported that

Yockey knew what the Americans were, and he was particularly contemptuous of the American "right-wing," because he had first-hand experience in the Gerald L. K. Smith organization, and found out what a racket that was.

Q: Could you tell me what you know about Yockey's experience with Gerald L. K. Smith? I believe, if I'm not mistaken, that this was before your involvement with Yockey, I believe in 1950 or thereabouts. Did he ever tell you what his experience had been?

A: Not specifically, except that he obviously had written, and maybe even delivered some talks, for that organization. But he was particularly put off by a woman named "Pearl" something-or-other, who I think . . .

Q: Opal? Opal Tanner White?[8]

A: Yes, that's the broad. And the general forces around Smith, and came to consider Smith just a financial opportunist using the whole *Cross and Flag* structure to achieve self-promotion. But Yockey was with him I think probably for just a few months at one point, and may have written some of their material.[9]

Realizing that his relationship with Smith was going nowhere, Yockey tried to recruit Lohbeck away from the CNC in much the same way that he had split Guy Chesham and John Gannon from the Union Movement. During the car ride back to St. Louis from Los Angeles, Yockey and Lohbeck held a series of intense political conversations. Lohbeck was so stunned by what he heard that he became convinced that Yockey was really a Communist!

A decade after their conversation (and long after his own break with Smith), Lohbeck contacted the FBI after hearing a 9 June 1960 radio report about Yockey's arrest in California. He told the Bureau that

on an unrecalled date in 1949 YOCKEY called on him in his office at St. Louis, Missouri, and expressed an interest in the Christian Nationalist Party of America and *The Cross and the Flag*. Yockey told him he had just come to the United States from France, and Yockey accepted [Lohbeck's] invitation to reside at the Informant's house. _____ during his association with Yockey, he learned that Yockey's real name was Yulick Varange, and that he had a sister, name unknown, who resided in Wood River, Illinois. Yockey accompanied _____ [John Hamilton], described by Informant as a former member of the Communist Party, who was in 1949 an active member of the Christian Nationalist Party of America, to the Christian Nationalist Party of America's national convention in Los Angeles, California. At this convention, and during the return trip to St. Louis, Missouri, Yockey made statements leading [Lohbeck] to believe he was not sincerely interested in nationalism; that Yockey was using him, and, accordingly, on their arrival in St. Louis, Missouri, [Lohbeck] suggested that Yockey move from his residence, which Yockey did. [Lohbeck] could furnish no information as to Yockey's itinerary after he left Informant's residence, other than Yockey left St. Louis.

Yockey _____ had only a few personal belongings on his arrival in St. Louis, but did not appear to want for funds. Informant stated that later in 1949, and during 1950, he received unrecalled political publications from various countries in South America and Italy, which, because of the contents, he believed were mailed to him by Yockey. [Lohbeck] said he had no further contact with Yockey. [Lohbeck] described Yockey as extremely intelligent but completely unscrupulous; a person who is well educated and who has traveled extensively throughout the world. He related that he could furnish no information regarding Yockey's birth date and/or citizenship, and volunteered that, based on his conversations and associations with Yockey in 1949, he believed Yockey to have been at that time a Communist.

His attempt to gain American support a failure, Yockey spent the fall of 1950 preparing to return to Europe. That December he applied for a job with the American Red Cross (or, as he put it, the "Red Cross Steamship Line"), whose national headquarters was in St. Louis. He wrote on his application that he was practicing law in Carbondale, Illinois,[10] and made it clear that he would only take a European assignment.[11] He was then sent to Fort Custer, Michigan, for Red Cross training.[12]

Going to Europe with the Red Cross held considerable advantages. As an assistant Red Cross supervisor, Yockey would hold a government rank equivalent to that of a U.S. army major.[13] With Red Cross credentials, he would also have a perfect cover as well as a steady source of income. In a letter from Battle Creek, Michigan, dated 17 March 1951, he wrote that he was using the name "Frank" with his fellow Red Cross workers because: "With Frank one can be frank. I have the Americans in my environment call me FRANK. It blurs their impression of me and that is precisely as it should be." His Red Cross colleagues were equally frank in their assessment of him. One woman who worked with him in Michigan later told the FBI

that she was employed _____ by the American Red Cross from 1950 to November 1952. She said that the Subject was Assistant Field Director for the Red Cross from December 1950 to June 1951 at Fort Custer. _____stated that the Subject was transferred in June 1951, with the First [actually Second—K.C.] Armored Division in his Red Cross capacity to Fort Hood, Texas. _____ also stated that during the few months that she was acquainted with the Subject he impressed her as being very cultured, specifically enamored with classical music. She said that the Subject had many feminine tendencies and that others who had worked with him were "suspicious regarding his activities," although she stated "no one ever had any definite proof of these suspicions."

_____ went on to say that YOCKEY had told her that he had visited Europe during the summer of 1950[14] and that the only reason he joined the Red Cross was to get transportation back to Europe, where he stated he knew many ways to make money other than what he could make in this country ... She said that the Subject continually extolled the advantages of living in Europe to such a degree ... that his talk along that line was unbearable ... _____ stated that YOCKEY on numerous occasions expressed a hatred of Jews and Negroes and praised the way in which the Germans exterminated the Jews during World War II.[15]

After completing his training, in June 1951 the Red Cross sent Yockey to Fort Hood, Texas, to prepare for his assignment with the Second Armored Division in Germany. Fort Hood was near San Antonio, and Yockey visited his children using his Red Cross railroad pass. An Army intelligence report concerning this period states:

SUBJECT, while in FT HOOD, Texas, had many disagreements with ARC [American Red Cross] Director Clifford GIBBS. SUBJECT also got into difficulties there for unauthorized use of his tax-exempt railroad transportation permit. SUBJECT claimed tax exemption in his personal trips to SAN ANTONIO, Texas. Interviewee did not know the details but believed their departure for Europe was all that prevented prosecution.[16]

While at Fort Hood, Yockey met James Haritage, who was slated to become the assistant field director of the Second Armored Division in Germany. They sailed to Germany on the same ship. Haritage later told U.S. Army intelligence that Yockey was "the most brilliant screwball" he ever met. He also recalled that:

SUBJECT [Yockey], through his actions and conversations, was well remembered by his fellow passengers. SUBJECT expressed himself as being anti-American in everything from automobiles to women. SUBJECT, who classified himself as a European, was an outspoken pro-German. SUBJECT tried to impress everyone with his education and self-proclaimed culture. SUBJECT continually expressed contempt for the American Army, usually referring to officers as lion tamers and the enlisted men as monkeys . . . Subject claimed to have been born Catholic, but to have since disavowed himself from all religion. SUBJECT liked to argue for hours at a time with the Chaplains aboard ship . . . SUBJECT claimed to own citrus fruit interests in the Rio Grande Valley of Texas, near McALLEN or MISSION. Income prior to the heavy freeze of 1949 was sufficient for SUBJECT to live as a man of leisure . . .

SUBJECT claimed previous service in Germany as a U.S. civilian. He claimed CIC and the MPs had caused him difficulties inasmuch as they tried to make him leave Germany after he was fired; however, that he was able to evade them after he had his passport altered.

SUBJECT claimed to have been able to live in Europe on his fraudulent passport for two years after he evaded the CIC. He spent this time in England, where he had a rich mistress [Baroness von Pflugl] some years his senior, who kept him, but of whom he grew tired and left; in Belgium where he had another mistress [Elsa Dewette]; and in France.

As soon as Yockey stepped off the boat in Bremerhaven, West Germany, he was involved in intrigue. CIC files report that:

Upon arrival in BREMERHAVEN, the Red Cross personnel was met by ARC Field Director John SOUTHGATE. SOUTHGATE escorted the personnel while in BREMERHAVEN and looked after their needs. SUBJECT persuaded SOUTHGATE to drive them by an address in BREMERHAVEN so that SUBJECT could look up a friend, an ex-Nazi Submarine Commander. The friend was found not to be at home.

The CIC later filed a report on Yockey's mysterious side-trip, based on an interview with Southgate. He told the CIC that after stopping off in a local tavern

> YOCKEY asked SOUTHGATE if he could take them [the three Red Cross men] to 18 Dionysus Strasse, BREMERHAVEN. After asking the waiter for the direction, SOUTHGATE took the three . . . to the given address . . . From their conversation en route to this address, Source was led to believe that SUBJECT had a letter for a person at this address. Source stated that this person was a former German submarine man, who had been a prisoner of war in the United States or that the person who had written the letter that SUBJECT was to deliver to the German submarine man knew him while he was a prisoner of war in the United States. Upon inquiring at the above address, they were informed that the person had moved.[17]

The CIC identified Yockey's contact as a German sailor named Erick Steinbrinck. Born in 1918, he had lived at 18 Dionysus Strasse from 13 August 1948 until July 1951. Local police records showed that he had spent some time as an English prisoner of war and had only left England on 2 November 1949. He was said to be fluent in French, English, Spanish, Danish, Swedish, and Norwegian.[18]

After Bremerhaven, Yockey and his co-workers proceeded to Stuttgart, where the Red Cross had its main headquarters. They spent the next 10 days in Mannheim:

> Upon arrival in MANNHEIM, SUBJECT became a "lone wolf" and was spending all of his free time, and part of the time he should have been working, contacting old friends. SUBJECT during his 10-day stay in MANNHEIM visited FRANKFURT and WIESBADEN, on more than one occasion. SUBJECT claimed that he had wanted to contact an old mistress in WIESBADEN [Gisella Kuehn] . . . but on arrival there was met by her husband, who had intercepted his message. The incident went off with no particular difficulties ensuing.[19]

Yockey spent the night of 28 July 1951 at the Rose Hotel in Wiesbaden.[20] He then returned to Mannheim and was assigned as the Red Cross representative to the Second Armored's replacement center at Baumholder. In a letter dated 1 August 1951 he moaned: "I am in a God forsaken village named Baumholder, or rather in a camp above it. It is not too far from the French border in the Hunsrück Mountains."

Two weeks in the Hunsrück was more than enough time for Yockey to get into trouble. A CIC report dated 25 February 1952 notes:

> SUBJECT had no apparent respect for authority of any kind and in the two-week period at BAUMHOLDER, he succeeded in making enemies with all persons in authority. SUBJECT was openly very pro-German and his entire attitude seemed to be against the government of the United States. On several occasions, SUBJECT reportedly stated that he had come overseas on "The Red Cross Steamship Line" and it was apparent that he had used the Red Cross only as a method of getting back to Germany. SUBJECT had no interest in his work and would not even maintain office hours. He tried to take advantage of every possible loophole he discovered and made the statement that he had traded Red Cross supplies for free meals at one of the Army messes. . . . On one occasion, when SUBJECT should have been on duty, he took an army vehicle and driver and went on a personal week-end trip to FRANKFURT.
>
> Upon being relieved in BAUMHOLDER [on 8 August 1951], SUBJECT was transferred to Seventh Army Headquarters to work under a Mr. Robert SHOUTEN, after which SUBJECT was permitted to "resign" from the Red Cross.

While at Seventh Army headquarters in Stuttgart, Yockey stayed in the Graf Zeppelin Hotel, his room and board paid by the Red Cross. Every night he seemed to have another prostitute in his room. Red Cross director Robert Shouten—who first thought him "slightly queer"—quickly changed his mind after seeing the parade of "Bahnhof types" visiting his room.[21]

While in Stuttgart, Yockey landed a new job as a review attorney with the Judge Advocate Office of the Seventh Army. After Judge Advocate Colonel Stanley Jones told him that the job was his, he handed in his resignation to the Red Cross. There was just one hitch: The job required a routine security check. In a letter dated 20 August 1951 Yockey wrote:

> I do not yet know whether my new position will mature. Two different sets of secret police have to clear me for it and a certain section of one of the two I know has me listed as an undesirable. It is frightful that I have to expose myself in this stupid fashion. No one can simultaneously try to do big things and be obligated to devote all his time and energy to the little, little thing of earning his living.

Yockey had to be cleared by two U.S. security agencies. Although the Provost Marshall's office of the European Command (EUCOM) turned up nothing negative, EUCOM's Intelligence Division was a different story. One CIC report noted: "A confidential TWX was received from EUCOM Intelligence stating that derogatory information was contained in the files of this Intelligence Division, and that a complaint-type investigation was being conducted on SUBJECT."[22]

Yockey's troubles dated back to 1949, when he had gone on a continental tour to promote *Imperium*. The EUCOM files contained a long report on a CIC investigation that had been undertaken in mid-October 1949, after a director of the Hessian Landes Zentral Bank in Frankfurt named Dr. Weit complained that Yockey had been spreading anti-American and "national bolshevist" propaganda.[23] Weit's secretary, Gisella Kuehn, was Yockey's old girlfriend, and Army intelligence suspected that Weit, a married man, was having an affair with her. Weit contacted the CIC after he and Kuehn had unexpectedly run into Yockey at the Wiesbaden State Opera on 15 October 1949. Whatever Weit's motive, EUCOM now knew that the same man who had spent the fall of 1949 spreading anti-American propaganda was about to get an important post at Seventh Army Headquarters. The CIC then began backtracking Yockey's activities starting with his arrival in Bremerhaven.[24]

As the investigation mushroomed, Yockey realized the game was up. He checked out of the Graf Zeppelin on 29 August 1951 and headed south. On a postcard dated "Garmisch, September 4," he wrote:

> I am en route to Rome today. I had a disaster and lost my job. I resigned [from the Red Cross] in the expectation—more, assurance—of having another at once, twice as good financially. But the secret police told the prospective employer (Judge Advocate, 7th Army) that they wanted to investigate me for six months and he became frightened.

The CIC traced Yockey to a cafe in Innsbruck, Austria, where he had struck up a conversation with a uniformed Red Cross employee named Emerson Lamb. Yockey told Lamb that he was heading to Italy. After that point, the trail went cold.

Yockey did in fact go to Italy, where he helped organize the international section for a conference of the MSI's women's division in Naples. What is not known is whether he also visited Switzerland to attend the founding conference of the New European Order in Zurich in late September 1951.

After arriving in Naples, Yockey learned that the CIC agents were not the only ones on his trail. A mysterious 48-year-old Italian artist named Egidio Boschi had tried to locate him in England earlier that year. He finally caught up with Yockey in Naples. Their encounter led Yockey to return almost immediately to North America.

Notes:

1. After the Union Party presidential campaign failed to catch fire, Smith became so disruptive that Newton Jenkins had to kick him out of the campaign.

2. See Glen Jeansonne, *Gerald L. K. Smith: Minister of Hate* (New Haven: Yale University Press, 1988).

3. According to John Gannon, he was instrumental in arranging Yockey's entry into Smith's circle. "Also through me, he [Yockey] visited Gerald L. K. Smith of the

Christian Nationalist Crusade in the U.S., but this was not a great success for FPY, who resented GLK [Smith]'s wealthy apparatus and felt it was not being used to finance a world-revival of neo-fascism; and was, in turn, resented by GLKS as an upstart." John Anthony Gannon, letter to Keith Stimely, 13 July 1980.

4. Jeansonne, *Gerald L. K. Smith*, p. 84.

5. This source was almost certainly the St. Louis branch of the ADL.

6. FBI report from St. Louis to Washington dated 13 July 1960.

7. From the FBI summary of letters by Yockey supplied to the FBI by Doctor Warren Johnson. I shall discuss Johnson's relations with Yockey later in this book.

8. Opal Tanner White was a longtime Smith backer. She used an inheritance from the estate of her former boss, a right-wing businessman named Carl H. Mote, to purchase a building in St. Louis that she leased to Smith at a nominal sum for use as his headquarters. Yockey most likely approached her in an attempt to get money.

9. 13 March 1986 Keith Stimely–H. Keith Thompson interview contained in the H. Keith Thompson collection at the Hoover Institute.

10. Yockey was undoubtedly using John Lannin's law firm as a reference.

11. CIC report, dated 17 December 1954, by Special Agent Richard Quinn, Jr.

12. On 8 January 1951 Yockey wrote: "I am at Ft. Custer, Michigan, with the American Red Cross. If in a few months I am not on my way I would feel that my transportation idea failed, and I shall leave this thing and proceed alone."

13. After Yockey left the Red Cross in Germany in 1951, the CIC noted that he failed to register as a tourist for a necessary entry-exit permit from the *Amt für Oeffentliche Ordnung* (Office for Public Order).

14. In fact, he visited America from Europe in the winter of 1949 or spring of 1950.

15. From an FBI interview from a source in Augusta, Michigan, in a report from the Detroit office dated 2 March 1953.

16. 66th CIC Detachment Agent Wehland G. Steenken's report on Yockey dated 4 October 1951, File: II-5538; D-267264. The interviewee was James Haritage.

17. CIC report dated 7 November 1951.

18. CIC report by Special Agent William Brenner dated 7 November 1951.

19. CIC report dated 4 October 1951. The Army report on Yockey was prepared by First Lieutenant Robert L. Lewis and was sent to the headquarters of the 66th CIC Detachment.

The Army learned that Yockey's lawyer friend Heinz Beckmann (who had been involved with the Berchtesgaden land deal) was introduced to Yockey through Martin Becker, whom Beckmann had known since 1939, when they were in the military together. Yockey had been staying with Becker just three weeks earlier in October 1949. The CIC also learned that Yockey had attempted to contact Becker in the middle of August 1951 but Becker denied meeting him.

20. CIC report dated 5 October 1951.

21. Yockey stayed in the hotel from 9 to 29 August 1951.

22. 1 October 1951 report by CIC agent Kenneth Baldon.

23. CIC report on Yockey dated 25 January 1950.

24. The CIC also learned from Haritage that Yockey may have been involved in currency speculation. The CIC report states:

SUBJECT after his arrival in Germany was involved in some financial transactions. SUBJECT claimed to urgently need a large sum of money and did request some of his sister. At the same time SUBJECT sent money to the United States. Interviewee did not know any of the details and could not interpret the transaction except that he doubted its legality.

25
MONTREAL
WINTER

Egidio Boschi, who spent the fall of 1951 searching for Yockey, was a veteran of Mussolini's famous 1922 march on Rome.[1] After moving to Santiago, Chile, in 1927, he spent the next 30 years involved in fascist movements in Chile and Argentina. A tall man with brown eyes, he had one extraordinary talent: Using a microscope, he painted art works on the heads of pins. According to John Gannon, Boschi (who almost went blind in the process) "succeeded in painting REAL micro-miniature works of art, in oils, on the heads of ordinary pins, portraits and landscapes." These were "REAL paintings, of detail and character, and were regarded as new wonders of the world by all who saw them." He exhibited his pins in cities like Montreal, Atlantic City, London, Paris, Rome, and Brussels as well as in South America.[2] Boschi discovered *Imperium* during one of his European tours. His inquiries led him to Gannon, who arranged for him to meet Yockey at the Naples MIF conference.

Although Boschi painted a portrait of Argentina's President Juan Perón on the head of one of his pins, he was considerably to the right of Perón, and worked closely with the Union Civica Nacionalista (UCN), led by Emilio Gutierrez Herrera. After Perón attacked the UCN for being too extreme, the April 1951 issue of *Frontfighter* ran an editorial strongly defending Herrera.[3]

Soon after they finally met, Yockey agreed to become Boschi's "business manager." The two men left Italy separately in late October or early November 1951.[4] They then regrouped in Montreal, where Boschi had apparently arranged an exhibit of his pins. In a postcard from Montreal dated 3 December 1951, Yockey explained:

I am back on the wrong continent again. The strangest thing has brought me back here. I am managing an enterprise for an artist. This chap is an Italian from South America. He came to Europe last year with his paintings to exhibit them, and he visited Gannon, having heard of *Imperium*, etc. When he learned I was in Naples he came down there to see me, qua author of *Imperium*, which he regarded as a bible. He is also a very sick man: cardiac, pleurisy, bronchitis, high blood pressure. Write me care of Coyne at Roxanna. I am in Canada because Boschi is waiting still for a visa to go to U.S. Perhaps he won't get it.[5]

Yockey and Boschi had not gone to Canada in November just to exhibit pins. They also planned to meet Adrian Arcand, Canada's top fascist and head of the Montreal-based National Christian Social Party. Arcand had maintained close ties to the Nazi International during the 1930s and had been a featured speaker at a massive German-American Bund meeting in Madison Square Garden.[6]

Shortly after Yockey and Boschi regrouped in Montreal, the U.S. government learned of their presence. The Canadian police may have picked up Yockey's trail during a routine surveillance of Arcand and alerted American authorities.[7] It is also possible that the State Department or some other U.S. government agency had been following Yockey after he acquired his last legitimate American passport in Naples on 15 October 1951.[8]

Whatever the sequence of events, on 7 November 1951 Yockey and Boschi had a conversation in their hotel room that was "overheard" by two unidentified "American citizens temporarily in Montreal."[9] After the secret listeners heard the two men boast about their aid to Germany during World War II (Boschi was especially pleased at how he had given German U-Boat commanders the location of Allied ships), they concluded that Yockey and Boschi "were and had been spies for the Nazis and fascists during World War II." The two also seemed

> familiar with all events of the war and were on intimate terms with high-ranking Nazis and fascists, mentioning many names, events, and places in connection with their espionage activities. They were in Montreal for the purpose of opening a Fourth Front magazine and mentioned a contact that they were here to make with a person later ascertained to be Adrian Arcand, a well-known Canadian fascist.
>
> They mentioned that they were both wanted by the authorities, but did not worry as long as they were in Canada, where they knew they would be safe due to the inefficiency and stupidity of the Canadian intelligence service, and that they were free to avoid American Customs and Immigration regulations due to the stupidity of members of these two services. They also mentioned that they had witnessed part of the Hitler extermination program and had the greatest admiration for Hitler. Mr. Boschi mentioned to

Mr. Yockey that it was a pleasure to meet a high-ranking official of the party and they made frequent mention of an underground movement. They also spoke of one of their members connected with a New York City newspaper, *Little Italy*, which was encouraging their readers to write letters to the President and to members of Congress to further their cause.

What Yockey and Boschi meant by a "Fourth Front" magazine was never clear. However, in a dispatch dated 9 December 1951, local U.S. Consul General Albert W. Scott informed the State Department:

> In the near future Mr. Yockey plans to establish a large center in Paris, France, for the purpose of distributing propaganda against the occupation of Germany by the United States. He continues to express very strong anti-American sentiments.

The reference to Paris is particularly interesting, since the New European Order (NEO) did set up a European Liaison Service of the National Forces (*Europäische Verbindungsstelle* or EVS) in Paris in May 1952. The service was finalized at the third NEO conference in Paris in January 1953.[10] EVS propaganda attacked the American presence in Europe as an imperialist occupation and denounced the European Defense Community as a prime example of U.S. colonial domination.[11] This possible NEO connection also suggests that either Yockey or Boschi (whose passport showed travel in Switzerland) may have attended the NEO's founding meeting.

After Yockey and Boschi finished their conversation: "This matter was reported _____. The next morning, November 8, 1951, they informed us that the two suspects were coming to the Consulate General for visas. They appeared shortly afterwards."

The report continues:

> On November 9, 1951, _____ reported to this office that they had overheard conversations between Boschi and Yockey to the effect that they were members of the fascist organization but that they were willing to transfer their services to the Russians but in no case would they work for the United States or Great Britain—that they were in Canada for the purpose of opening a Fourth Front magazine—that they had made contact with Adrian Arcand . . . Mr. Yockey remarked that he had traveled considerably in Germany, Italy, and Switzerland; that the last time he was in Germany he was wanted by the military police, but succeeded in evading them and returned to the United States where he expected to be held on arrival, but entered the country without any difficulty.[12] He also mentioned that he had married a German girl in Germany, but was now divorced.[13] He said he was well acquainted with German officials and ex-officials, among them von Papen.[14]

The secret listeners then paid a visit to their hotel room:

232

A search was made of their room and two microscopes, one pair of powerful field glasses and a very expensive German camera were found. Both men are under surveillance by _____ who believes they are engaged in subversive activities and are probably endeavoring to revive the fascist movement in Canada which was very strong at the beginning of World War II. (Subjects have moved to the Windsor Hotel.)

Surveillance broke down after Arcand discovered that he and Yockey were under observation. Arcand later told H. Keith Thompson:

He [Yockey] had registered at the Windsor Hotel in Montreal, and when I went there to spend a night with him, the desk office clerk (a friend and "member") warned me that the combination of FBI–Canadian Intelligence had installed a tape recorder in the adjoining room; so that we had the fun of our lives in giving the FBI and Canadian Intelligence improvised messages in most loud talk, about the Zionists being masters of our mutual governments, FBI, RCMP, and what not.[15]

After the U.S. Consulate was informed, Boschi's request for an American visa became bogged down in paperwork. A frustrated Yockey left Montreal on 20 November 1951 and flew to New York (where he would meet Fred Weiss and H. Keith Thompson for the first time). He also tried to arrange an exhibition of Boschi's pins at a New York department store before returning to Canada.[16]

Boschi's inability to legally enter America led to a breakdown of his partnership with Yockey.[17] In a postcard from Montreal dated New Year's Day, 1952, Yockey wrote: "I am in great difficulties with this artist mad man, this pin painter. He is in a terrible state of moral deterioration, not to say physical and mental as well." Yockey again checked out of the Windsor on 6 January 1952 and headed back to New York.[18] The U.S. Consulate General in Montreal reported on 28 February 1952 that he had written a postcard to Boschi stating that he was staying at the Hotel Milner at Broadway and 31st Street.

While he was in Montreal, Yockey gave Boschi some money and in return took six of his pins. According to Gannon:

FPY joined in the [Boschi] venture, but fairly soon quarrelled with Boschi and departed holding six of the pins! This was not a theft, but FPY's idea of a financial settlement, as Boschi owed his partner FPY a little money. In this quarrel, I have no sympathy with FPY, for Boschi was one of the best men I have ever met, but being an artist by temperament, despised money until he had none left! FPY was REALLY also an artist by temperament, certainly NOT a politician, and the clash was perhaps inevitable.[19]

Despite numerous delays, Boschi persisted in his attempt to enter the United States. The U.S. consulate finally informed him on 24 March 1952 that his visa request had been denied because he was now considered "a person whose admission would be prejudicial to the interests of the United States." Copies of an FBI report on Boschi were also sent to G-2 and "Director, Central Intelligence Agency."[20]

On that same day, a Chicago-based State Department agent named Miles Briggs questioned Yockey's aunt and uncle, Alice and Fred Yockey, in the hope of locating their nephew. The State Department also requested FBI help in the search. The FBI notified its Chicago and Detroit offices on 9 April 1952:

> You are instructed to immediately institute an investigation to ascertain subject's whereabouts in the United States and his past activities in your area ... You are also instructed to set out appropriate leads to other offices to ascertain the Subject's activities.[21]

While the State Department hunted Yockey in Chicago, their prey was living literally a block away from State Department headquarters in Washington, D.C. In a letter dated 22 January 1952, he wrote:

> I come hither to find myself some base economic employment, after my Boschi enterprise showed itself no longer feasible. I was counting heavily upon old Jaeger ... and I learned with one telephone call that he is in Florida until the end of the month.
>
> I shall be here all week, at least up to Saturday staying at the YMCA Hotel, 18th and G Streets, a block away from the infamous State Department.

"Jaeger" was Georgetown law professor Walter Jaeger, Yockey's friend from the 1930s.[22] He also contacted his old Georgetown classmate Perry Patterson, who was now a high-powered lawyer in the Washington office of the Chicago-based firm Kirkland Ellis. While in Washington, Yockey carried out legal research on various war crimes cases for H. Keith Thompson, and helped Thompson draft a letter to Secretary of State Dean Acheson concerning the treatment of convicted German war criminals in Spandau prison. He also gave Thompson legal advice about becoming a registered agent for the German Socialist Reich Party.[23] Then, through his Washington connections, Yockey landed a job considerably different from the one that he had held with Boschi.

Notes:
1. A 28 May 1952 FBI report said that Boschi was the son of Joseph and Angela Podesta; his birthday was given as 6 June 1903. He lived at Calle Lord Cochrane, 538 Santiago de Chile with his wife Magda. Boschi applied for a passport at the Italian consulate in Santiago on 21 October 1949. His passport showed that he had recently been in Italy, France, Switzerland, and England.

2. John Anthony Gannon, letter to Keith Stimely, 13 July 1980.

3. Gannon reported that because the UCN continually attacked "the triple, satanic creations of Jewry—Masonry, Communism, and Finance-Capitalism," Herrera was arrested and exiled from Argentina.

4. Yockey went to America, where he most likely visited the Coynes. Boschi went directly to Canada.

5. From the collection of Yockey letters obtained by the FBI from Doctor Warren Johnson.

6. Arcand also had ties to William Dudley Pelley's Silver Shirts: The 21 November 1937 issue of the Silver Shirt publication *The New Liberation* extensively praised him.

7. The problem comes from the fact that there are two reports on the conversation and it is not clear if the second report is a further summary of the first report or if there were two conversations, one taking place on 7 November 1951 and the other on 9 November 1951. It may be that the 7 November conversation was reported to the consul general on 9 November. If this is the case, it seems likely that Yockey and Boschi had already made contact with Arcand. If they had not yet made contact but only did so on 8 or 9 November, then it is more likely that the initiative for the investigation came from outside normal security procedures.

8. EUCOM intelligence may have alerted American consulates in Italy to be on the lookout for him.

9. Due to FBI deletions it is impossible to determine the identity of the two eavesdroppers or whether they were recording the conversations for the American government.

10. A permanent secretariat of the EVS was formed in Lausanne under the direction of Guy Amaudruz. In the Winter 1962/63 issue of *Prevent World War III*, Nehemiah Robinson reported that the EVS had been set up in Paris in May 1952 through Amaudruz.

11. Kurt Tauber, *Beyond Eagle and Swastika* (Middletown, CT: Wesleyan University Press, 1967), Vol. 2, fn. 41, p. 1091. On the official founding of the EVS, see *Beyond Eagle and Swastika*, Vol. 1, p. 212.

12. Yockey may have thought that his visit to the U.S. consulate in Naples would tip off the government, and he may have been right.

13. This could be Gisella Kuehn. It is possible that Yockey did technically marry her, although such a marriage would have been a farce since he was still legally married to his American wife.

14. Spelled "von Pappen" in the summary. During World War I, Papen, a German military attaché in Washington, was intimately involved in planning sabotage operations against American industry. See Jules Witcover, *Sabotage at Black Tom* (Chapel Hill: Algonquin Books, 1989).

15. Adrian Arcand, letter to H. Keith Thompson, 16 July 1961. (After his arrest, Yockey also made a passing reference to the wiretap in a jailhouse conversation.) Arcand and Yockey became good friends. After learning of Yockey's death, Arcand told H. Keith Thompson:

> I consider it an honor that he [Yockey] spent a whole week with me in Lanoraie and Montreal. How he could play a Bach prelude on my miserable piano is

beyond words! And he certainly was (as he boasted) *un grand artiste* at making mashed potatoes, as he taught my wife when he was here.

16. U.S. Consulate report by Albert Scott to the State Department dated 9 November 1951 (Confidential Dispatch No. 112).

17. Before leaving New York in December 1951, Yockey sent a luggage case by train to the Coynes' home in Illinois. My guess is that he spent Christmas at the Coynes' before returning to Montreal.

18. State Department Office of Security report, dated 13 March 1952, by Donald L. Nicholson to J. Edgar Hoover.

19. John Anthony Gannon, letter to Keith Stimely, 13 July 1980. In a 13 September 1987 letter to Stimely, Gannon wrote: "Of course, in my FPY piece [Gannon's reminiscence of Yockey] I did NOT go into the Boschi episode, which was within my direct knowledge, and where I find FPY to be completely at fault." In another letter to Stimely (this one dated 24 November 1981), Gannon wrote: "In any dispute between B(oschi) and Y, I would be on B's side. Both were artist-types, but B had done plenty of fighting as well as thinking." When Yockey was arrested in June 1960, the FBI found one of Boschi's pins in Yockey's suitcase.

20. FBI Ottawa Liaison Office to Director, FBI, 17 April 1952. Other blacked out FBI reports on Boschi were sent to Donald L. Nicholson of the Division of Security, Office of Security and Consular Affairs at State.

21. Because the FBI thought that Yockey may have been staying with his aunt and uncle (he had listed their address in a résumé), Chicago became the lead office in the investigation.

22. Jaeger had spent World War II as a director of research for the Industrial College of the Armed Forces. He also worked with the U.S. Army's Judge Advocate's Office.

23. Yockey had already been in contact with the SRP through the ELF. According to Gannon he introduced Yockey to the SRP. Gannon told Keith Stimely in a 24 November 1981 letter: "I was the SRP contact, and I introduced Y to it. SRP had won seats in Lower Saxony for Rudel and Remer, Rudel being in Argentina at the time, but neither were allowed to take up their seats. Heinz Knöke, ex–Luftwaffe fighter ace, visited me in Cambridge, possibly 1952, where he, LFS [L. F. Simmons, the man who replaced Huxley-Blythe as editor of *Frontfighter*], and I discussed full co-operation."

26

THE GHOST OF
JOE McCARTHY

In late January 1952, Yockey moved into the home of Dr. Warren Johnson, a Baltimore-area psychiatrist who lived with his wife, Virginia, in Towson, Maryland. The Johnsons first met Yockey in 1947 in St. Louis when he was visiting the Coynes.[1] For legal advice on his passport problem, Yockey turned to Perry Patterson. Patterson later told the FBI that he

> had not seen or heard of YOCKEY until about two or two and a half years ago when YOCKEY came to Washington, D.C., seeking employment. He came to see _____ [Patterson] and borrowed $10 which has not been repaid. After staying in Washington a week or two, YOCKEY went to Baltimore and stayed with friends there for about two months . . . YOCKEY also revealed to [Patterson] that he had been in Canada or had returned to the United States from Germany through Canada and was having troubles concerning his passport. The State Department was attempting to pick up YOCKEY's passport and YOCKEY did not want to return his passport to the State Department because he would then be unable to leave the United States.[2]

Yockey stayed in Washington for about three months. When he left in May 1952, he took Virginia Johnson with him.[3] After his wife's desertion, Dr. Johnson discovered letters that Yockey had written her from Europe. "Portions of the correspondence," the FBI noted, "are of an obscene nature and should be handled accordingly."[4] The letters made it clear that Yockey and Virginia had begun their affair five years earlier in St. Louis.

As part of his divorce action, Dr. Johnson contacted the FBI about Yockey's activity. On 22 September 1952 the FBI received a letter from Yockey found by Johnson, dated 5 February 1952. It read:

I called on [Perry] Patterson, who arranged an appointment for me with Senator McCarthy for Saturday P.M. He wanted me to write a speech for him, based on a whole batch, a huge corpus of material, to have it ready by Monday.

There are still several things to settle with him but it looks as though I have a job. Really quite unbelievable that it should be this particular job. Everything else orally.[5]

The FBI also discovered the manuscript of a speech that Yockey had ghost-written for McCarthy called "America's Two Ways of Waging War."[6] In it, he had McCarthy contrast America's demand for Germany's unconditional surrender with Washington's attempt to negotiate a peace with the Communists in Korea:

First of all what was the objective of the Second World War? It was given to the world as UNCONDITIONAL SURRENDER. They wanted total victory, and they said so. But what is the objective in the Chinese war now going on? In Acheson's words, it is "a just truce." Not even peace! Much less victory. No question of unconditional surrender. Marshall as Secretary of Defense visited the battlefront and there announced to the press that the American mission in Korea is "to prevent the enemy from coming below the 38th parallel." Did he make a similar announcement when America was fighting Germany and Italy? No, when he wanted victory, he said so, and he subscribed to the "Unconditional Surrender formula."

Next, during the present Chinese war, the whole regime in Washington says we must prevent the conflict from spreading, we must localize the conflict. What did they want in the Second World War? They wanted a continual extension of the front, continual involvement of other powers. They exerted every conceivable pressure to bring other powers in on their side. When they had two fronts, they wanted a third, and when they had that, they wanted a fourth. They wanted to *win* that war.

Next, did they refuse any offers of troops in the Second World War? On the contrary, they used every pressure on neutrals to extract troops from them to use against Germany and Italy. But in the present war against Red China they have refused Chiang Kai-shek's standing offer of 500,000 combat-ready troops. Not only do they refuse his offer but they have ordered the American Navy to blockade Chiang Kai-shek so that he can not strike the Chinese Communists. Yes, tonight, as we meet here, the American Navy is protecting Red China.

Yockey then contrasted the reluctance of the Truman administration to enact an internal security law banning the Communist Party with government policy in World War II:

> During the Second World War the Washington regime was not faced with a great problem of an inner enemy. Nevertheless it interned and uprooted all the Japanese on the West Coast and numerous German-born men and women all over the land. The vast majority of all the internees were American citizens, but nobody worried much about their "civil liberties."
>
> During the present war with Red China, however, everything is different. The inner enemy is numerous, highly organized, thoroughly indoctrinated, with a literature of class war, proletarian dictatorship, and world conquest going back a century. At the very narrowest, the inner enemy includes the Communist Party and affiliated organizations; more realistically it includes also the Communist sympathizers and backers of Communist-front organizations, many of whom are in high positions in the Executive, Legislative, and Judicial branches of the Federal and State governments...
>
> The war in which America is now engaged is being waged not for American victory, but for Communist victory, and those in America who are ultimately responsible for the conduct of this war are guilty of black, damnable treason.

After a call to use the A-bomb in Korea, Yockey concluded "America's Two Ways of Waging War" with an *Imperium*-like flourish:

> America has only written its first pages in history, and not its last. I believe in the future of the Western Civilization, of which America is an integral, organic part . . . It is not a part of the divine plan that a great superpersonal force working for order and creativeness in the world, like the Western Civilization, is to be overcome by an onslaught of barbarians against an America weakened by corruption and betrayed by a horde of Achesons . . . We shall liberate our land from the domination of traitors and then, by the help of the Almighty God, we shall restore the word *America* to its old meaning in the world before all nations. By the deluge of our votes, by the irresistible storm of our organized protest, we shall sweep America clear of its inner enemies and onward to its God-given Destiny.

As Yockey's 5 February 1952 letter makes clear, Perry Patterson played an important role as his go-between to McCarthy. Patterson in the early 1950s served as legal counsel to the Washington *Times Herald*, owned by the Patterson newspaper clan. While *not* related to their lawyer, the Pattersons were part of a family newspaper empire headed by the right-wing Chicago press magnate Colonel McCormick. The papers in the McCormick chain, which included the *Chicago Tribune* and the New York *Daily News*, were extremely conservative. Colonel McCormick particularly hated the Nuremberg trials and once refused to have lunch with Roosevelt's Attorney

General Francis Biddle, a member of the Nuremberg tribunal, on the grounds that he would not dine with a "murderer."[7]

As the *Times Herald*'s attorney, Patterson had to defend the paper against a libel action after Senator McCarthy's secretary placed a picture in the paper showing Maryland's Democratic Senator Millard Tydings, a leading McCarthy critic, shaking hands with Earl Browder, the onetime head of the American Communist Party. The photo became famous after it was shown that McCarthy's staff had crudely faked it.[8]

Another likely Yockey link to McCarthy was his Georgetown friend Walter Jaeger. As a Catholic anti-communist, McCarthy had excellent connections to Georgetown's School of Foreign Service and knew Father Walsh. Jaeger's ties with McCarthy, however, may have been more direct. McCarthy was a member of the Senate Committee on Expenditures in Executive Departments headed by Senator Clyde Hoey, another conservative opposed to the Nuremberg trials.[9] Throughout 1951 and 1952 the Committee investigated violations of the Ship Sales Act of 1946 that regulated the sales of surplus U.S. military equipment to civilians.[10] Jaeger was on a three-man panel headed by Vice Admiral Edward Cochran that had been formed in October 1950 to study shipping subsidies given by the Federal Maritime Board.

The most startling revelation of a Yockey-McCarthy connection, however, comes from a casual statement by Yockey's British comrade, John Anthony Gannon. According to Gannon, Yockey and McCarthy had been in contact well before their February 1952 meeting. He told Keith Stimely:

> After his move to England, FPY continued to work for the freeing of "war criminals" . . . Senator Joe McCarthy was involved with this work, having made visits to Germany with parties from Congress, and FPY was in touch with him . . . Yes, I know that FPY had a considerable relationship with Joe McC, and found him well informed on the Culture-Distorters issue.[11]

Was Gannon right about Yockey's "considerable relationship" with McCarthy? Reconstructing direct links between McCarthy and Yockey before 1952 is almost impossible. Still, some important facts should be noted. By early 1948, McCarthy had become actively involved in the plight of German POWs held by Russia. He even wrote a letter calling for the repudiation of the Yalta and Potsdam agreements due to Russia's refusal to release German troops captured in World War II.[12] He then threw himself into a 1949 congressional investigation of alleged mistreatment of German POWs accused of war crimes during the Battle of the Bulge. The most infamous war crime, the "Malmédy Massacre," occurred after a unit of the First SS Panzer Regiment Leibstandarte Adolf Hitler was accused of murdering 83 American POWs. Some 73 SS men were convicted of the killings, and 43 were sentenced to hang.[13]

The prisoners' first lawyer, Lieutenant Colonel Willis M. Everett, Jr., filed a petition with the U.S. Supreme Court claiming that the soldiers had been subjected to brutal torture and compelled to confess. The U.S. Army then created a three-man commission headed by Texas Supreme Court Judge Gordon Simpson to investigate the charges. One panel member was Judge Edward LeRoy Van Roden, a colonel in the Officers' Reserve Corps and a Judge in a Pennsylvania Orphans Court. Yockey's friend H. Keith Thompson, who knew Van Roden, credits him for McCarthy's involvement in the case.[14]

Van Roden claimed to have examined the records of some one thousand war crimes cases before concluding that the entire legal process was wrong. He expressed his views in a widely noticed article in the well-known liberal publication *The Progressive*, although his credibility took a nose-dive after it was revealed that the article had been ghost-written by James Finucane of the National Council for the Prevention of War (NCPW).

The NCPW was founded in 1921 by a Quaker named Frederick J. Libby as a pacifist lobbying group. It later received considerable financial backing from William H. Regnery, a wealthy Chicago-based Catholic isolationist whose son Henry, creator of the conservative journal *Modern Age* and founder of Regnery Books, also became Libby's good friend and benefactor.[15] The NCPW worked closely in the 1930s with isolationists on both the left and right, including America First.[16] According to historian Justus Doenecke, the NCPW "supported many isolationist activities, supplying research, speech writing, and informal liaison to such anti-interventionists as Senator William L. Langer."[17] It also played a key role in organizing opposition to the war crimes trials, and was particularly active in distributing statements from German Catholic and Protestant clerics from the Munich-based Committee for Christian Aid to War Prisoners, which had been established in 1948.

Rudolf Aschenauer, the chief lawyer for Christian Aid, was a kind of William Kunstler for accused Nazi war criminals. He served as the legal advisor to Bishop Johann Neuhausler, the Roman Catholic bishop of Munich, as well as to the Protestant Church Council in Bavaria.[18] Aschenauer also published a journal in defense of accused and convicted war criminals called *Die Andere Seite* (The Other Side), whose U.S. agent was H. Keith Thompson.[19] The NCPW's links to Aschenauer became public after the Senate Committee on Armed Services appointed Senator Raymond Baldwin to head a subcommittee to investigate the Army's handling of the Malmédy trials. McCarthy, a guest member of the subcommittee, found its final report supporting the Army an outrage.[20] McCarthy critics, however, charged that the senator had regularly been fed misleading information from Aschenauer.[21] When the subcommittee then questioned Aschenauer in Munich, it learned that he had actually sent his material to the NCPW's James Finucane who, in turn, circulated the information to McCarthy and other Army critics.

Finucane's boss, Fred Libby, also served as chairman of the Committee for Return of Confiscated German and Japanese Property. The committee lobbied for the passage of congressional legislation to return property confiscated by the United States during and immediately following World War II to Germany and Japan. Finucane was executive secretary of the committee, whose members included the Holocaust-denier Dr. Austin App, the historian Harry Elmer Barnes (who later became a Holocaust-denier as well), and other luminaries, including Henry Regnery and the Honorable Learned Hand.[22]

Despite the Baldwin Subcommittee's report defending the Army, the negative publicity generated by the Malmédy case ruined the war crimes trials process. According to historian Tom Bower, the Malmédy controversy was "the biggest calamity to befall the attempt to punish the individual murderers," so much so that serious attempts at denazification "collapsed in the wake of the debacle."[23] Many at the Pentagon, including Secretary of the Army Kenneth Royall, were more than happy to see the war crimes process end, since they were now far more concerned with the quick remilitarization of Germany against Russia. To this wing of the Pentagon, aggressive denazification only antagonized potential friends in the Wehrmacht, blocked full German cooperation with NATO, and encouraged Communist-backed anti-American and neutralist propagandists.[24]

Given the military's interest in stopping denazification, Judge Van Roden may have been chosen for the Simpson panel because he held right-wing views. Van Roden had endorsed a 1948 book entitled *The Crime of Our Age* by a former Lutheran pastor named Ludwig Adolphus Fritsch, who described his text as an attempt to show how "the Jews and the Anglo-Saxons succeeded in uniting the nations of the world into an unholy alliance in order to destroy Germandom."[25] Van Roden said of Fritsch's opus: "I think it should have a wide distribution not only to clergy but to all Americans."[26] Van Roden was also a close friend of Colonel Willis Everett, the man who first launched the entire Malmédy case against the government. When Van Roden was appointed to the Simpson Commission, it was not known that he had shared a room in Frankfurt with Colonel Everett after the war. While in Germany for the Simpson Commission, he regularly received letters from Everett containing his most extreme allegations. According to Tom Bower, Van Roden shared Everett's biases and prejudices and believed that "Jewish refugees were using their new American nationality as a cloak for vengeance against the Germans."[27]

Yockey was posted to Wiesbaden, a suburb of Frankfurt, in 1946 during his stay with the 7708 War Crimes Group. He could not have met Van Roden, since Van Roden was back in Pennsylvania by January 1946. It is quite possible, however, that he knew Everett, who was a defense lawyer at a time when Yockey was assigned to hear clemency petitions. Yockey also acted as an organizer for Rudolf Aschenauer's legal defense network in the late 1940s, while he was living in London.[28] There is another intriguing connection as well: Maurice Bardèche. Bardèche was well informed about the postwar American isolationist right: His 1951 book *L'Oeuf de Christophe Colomb* (The Egg of Christopher Columbus) was dedicated to Senator Robert Taft, the Grand Old Man of the GOP and a strong critic of the Nuremberg trials.

Around the time Yockey began working directly for McCarthy, the senator had tentatively decided to enhance his identification with pro-German elements of the far right, so Yockey's speech may have been deliberately crafted to appeal to German-Americans in particular. It may even have been written in anticipation of a talk that McCarthy was scheduled to give in New York City.

Posters began appearing in New York in mid-April 1952, proclaiming that Senator McCarthy would speak at the Yorkville Casino at 210 East 86th Street on Sunday, 4 May 1952, at 8:30 P.M. The posters explained that the affair "will be dedicated to strengthening relations between the United States and Germany and to voice our belief in a just peace treaty for Germany in which we especially espouse the cause of the expellees and their lost homelands." Also scheduled to speak were *The Crime of Our Age* author Ludwig Fritsch; Dr. Austin App, a college professor and Holocaust-denier who wrote for *Common Sense*; rally chairman Edward A. Fleckenstein, the head of the far-right German-American Voters Alliance and a friend of H. Keith Thompson; Father E. J. Reichenberger, a Catholic priest whose passport was lifted by the State Department for speeches he gave in Germany attacking the U.S. Occupation policy; "Baron" W. F. Von Blomberg (born William Frary), a former press agent who had been adopted at age 26 by an elderly German countess; and Henry C. Furstenwalde, formerly on the staff of the U.S. embassy in Berlin, who had also worked in the Office of Alien Property Custodian in the Department of Justice.[29]

The announcement of McCarthy's scheduled appearance caused an uproar. *The Daily Compass* ran a front-page exposé on 14 April 1952 which began: "Senator Joseph R. McCarthy, Republican of Wisconsin, will speak at a rally in Yorkville on Sunday evening, May 4th, organized by elements of the German-American Voters Alliance, successor to the German-American Bund." Other attacks appeared in the *New York Post*. The negative publicity caused McCarthy to drop out of the rally, claiming that he had another speaking engagement in the midwest. With H. Keith Thompson acting as "floor manager," the rally took place on schedule with the other listed speakers.

Although Yockey had managed to get himself into McCarthy's entourage, he remained highly critical of the American military's "soft line" regarding Germany; he felt that the U.S.-sponsored remilitarization meant that Germany would be a prime target for Soviet nuclear attack in a future war. He published a two-part essay on this question in the March and April 1952 issues of *Frontfighter*, entitled "America's Two Political Factions." The essay, written while he was in Washington,[30] states that the American "inner-political scene" was split between "the Jewish or Communist faction" and the "military faction." He was most interested in the military faction's significance for Europe:

> The military faction has no *political* objective whatsoever; its purely military objective is preparation of a successful war against Russia, securing in the process all possible strong-points and bases and utilizing to bring about its victory the manpower of Europe. In its official doctrinal publications, this faction has referred to the former nations of Europe as "pawns" in the war-front against Russia.

Despite the rollback of the war crimes process by the "military faction," he concludes that

> both factions mean the subjection of Europe, both mean the thwarting of its organic destiny, both are animated by jealousy of Europe and the wish to prevent the coming Imperium of Europe ... Let no misguided European beguile himself into an utterly misplaced sympathy with the American generalate as an American *nationalist* group, for this it most certainly is not ... in the political realm, it cannot be repeated too often, the American generalate is unconscious. It would as soon fight Europe as China ... These generals are not men of the stamp of Moltke, Schlieffen, and Clausewitz, but rather of the stamp of Henry Ford. Their contribution to warfare is the assembly line; their military faith is not in morale, love of Fatherland, and iron discipline, but the belief that with enough industrial production Destiny itself can be set aside and History made to come out the end of a tube ... The arrogant products of America's human assembly line who call themselves at present the Allied High Command have no past, they contain no unifying Inner Imperative, no Idea, they represent no Nation and no State, they have no future.
>
> *At this moment both of America's factions are the enemy of Europe. Europe will not fight under the banner of its enemy.*

Notes:

1. It is unclear how the Johnsons met Yockey, but a blacked-out FBI document indicates that they may have been introduced socially through the Coynes. There is an indication in one FBI document that Doctor Warren Johnson may have at one point been dating Alice Yockey, who worked either as an X-ray technician or as a nurse.

2. From a 16 December 1954 FBI WFO (Washington Field Office) report on a 12 December interview with Perry Patterson by FBI agent William Muncy. Virginia Johnson also told her aunt and uncle that Yockey had "sent his passport to a friend at Sandy Spring, Maryland." This was Perry Patterson, who owned a farm in Sandy

Springs, where Yockey spent a weekend. Only in late 1954, when the FBI thought Yockey might be back in America (and after the Army-McCarthy hearings), did it question Patterson.

3. H. Keith Thompson vaguely recalls the FBI telling him about a physical altercation between Yockey and Warren Johnson. Yockey most likely had to flee Washington in haste after Johnson found out about his affair with Virginia.

4. FBI Baltimore office report dated 23 December 1952.

5. Report from the Baltimore FBI office by FBI agent Ronald Holland (BA 105-643), dated 2 March 1953. The FBI also reported that Dr. Warren Johnson was granted a divorce from his wife on 17 March 1953.

6. Yockey first used this title in a two-part *Frontfighter* article in the December 1950 and January 1951 issues. This article was reprinted in *Der Weg*.

7. Justus Doenecke, *Not to the Swift: The Old Isolationists in the Cold War* (Lewisburg, PA: Bucknell University Press, 1979), p. 142.

8. Patterson was involved in yet another lawsuit involving McCarthy, this time with Drew Pearson. From *The Drew Pearson Diaries* of 22 April 1952:

Perry Patterson, attorney for Col. McCormick, got in touch with Bill Roberts yesterday and hinted at a settlement of the McCarthy suit. He begged that McCarthy be let off the hook from answering questions. Bill was adamant and refused. It appears that the *Tribune* crowd is sore at McCarthy. [Drew Pearson, *Diaries, 1949–1959* (New York: Holt, Rinehart and Winston, 1974).]

9. See the discussion of Hoey in Tom Bower, *Blind Eye to Murder* (London: Andre Deutsch, 1981), pp. 290–91. Hoey and McCarthy at one point wanted to create their own special committee to investigate charges that German prisoners accused of the Malmédy massacre had been mistreated.

10. On this panel, see Jim Hougan, *Spooks* (New York: William Morrow, 1978), p. 304.

11. McCarthy's German connections were alluded to in an interesting undated letter from the Hamburg Nazi Rolf Kempcke to a member of the far-right National Renaissance Party. Kempcke wrote:

I would give you an important communication about a certain Mr. Richard Topp, whose address is Ahrensburg near Hamburg, Hansdorfer Strasse 5. This man is not only the confidential person to Sen. McCarthy, but he works also as Agent for the U.S. Secret Service and for the Soviet Headquarters in Berlin-Karlshorst. I know this by several sources which are absolutely trustworthy, for a less part from himself [Topp] and also from one of his collaborators. I think it would be right that you transmit this notification as soon as possible to Sen. McCarthy.

I came in touch with the Topp organization at the first time when I participated in Summer 1951 in a instructing course of the U.S. Army, who was lasting 10 days on the exercise field of Grafenwoehr in Bavaria. I become this instructing as an anticommunist fighter of resistance given by German-sympathetic American Officers, by the intervention of the *"Bund Deutscher Jugend* [BDJ]." Since this time I was informed about the activities of Dr. Richard Topp in the most exact manner. Therefore: Be careful!

Topp headed the Hamburg League of Independents. See Kurt Tauber, *Beyond Eagle and Swastika* (Middletown, CT: Wesleyan University Press, 1967), Vol. 2, fn. 66, pp. 1290–91. The BDJ was part of the CIA's "Operation Gladio" network in Europe.

12. Richard Reeves, *The Life and Times of Joe McCarthy* (New York: Stein and Day, 1982), p. 162.

13. In the late 1940s some McCarthy critics pointed to a Wisconsin German-American industrialist family, the Harnischfegers, as the key influence on McCarthy in the Malmédy case. Richard Reeves, however, interviewed a college friend of McCarthy's named Tom Korb, who came to Washington to work for McCarthy from the Harnischfeger Corporation at McCarthy's request. Korb said that he told McCarthy to stay away from the case in no uncertain terms, but that McCarthy had already made up his mind.

14. Van Roden described his background for H. Keith Thompson's book *Doenitz at Nuremberg* (New York: Amber Publishing Corp., 1976), which was co-edited with Henry Strutz and later reprinted by Willis Carto's Institute for Historical Review.

15. After World War II the Regnerys and Libby created the isolationist Foundation for Foreign Affairs as a rival to the New York Council on Foreign Relations (CFR).

16. In his memoirs Libby writes about hearing a Charles Lindbergh speech "which gave me a new conception of the power of absolute honesty and purity of heart." See p. 160 of Libby's *To End War: The Story of the National Council for the Prevention of War* (Nyack, NY: Fellowship Publications, 1969). For an excellent account of the postwar isolationists that discusses the NCPW, see Justus Doenecke's *Not to the Swift: The Old Isolationists in the Cold War.*

17. Justus D. Doenecke, "Toward an Isolationist Braintrust: The Foundation for Foreign Affairs," in *World Affairs*, Vol. 143, No. 3, Winter 1980/81, p. 265. The NCPW's activity overlapped the same Congressional circles then being courted by George Sylvester Viereck and the German embassy in Washington.

18. Reeves, *The Life and Times of Joe McCarthy*, p. 183.

19. After Adolf Eichmann's capture, Aschenauer even published a document written by Eichmann while he was living in Argentina entitled *Ich, Adolf Eichmann, Ein Historicher Zeugenbericht.* See Pierre Vidal-Naquet, "Theses on Revisionism," in *Unanswered Questions* (New York: Schocken Books, 1989), edited by François Furet, fn. 33, p. 377.

20. See Tom Bower, *Blind Eye to Murder,* on the case. Also see Richard Reeves, *The Life and Times of Joe McCarthy.* Aschenauer published a long pamphlet in English entitled *Truth or "Clever Strategy" in the Case of Malmédy?* (Nuremberg, February 1950) to refute the Baldwin subcommittee.

21. On this charge and for part of the subcommittee's questioning of Aschenauer in Munich, see Tauber, *Beyond Eagle and Swastika*, Vol. 2, fn. 65, pp. 1303–05.

22. See *Seven Reasons for Return,* a Committee pamphlet written by Finucane. The group was headquartered in the National Press Building.

23. Bower, *Blind Eye to Murder*, p. 268.

24. The surreal nature of the early Cold War was summed up in a joke popular in Germany at the time. Two American officials booked on the same plane to Germany meet each other in a New York airport and discover they are both working for the U.S. High Commissioner in Germany. "What's your job?" one of them asks. "Demilitarization." "That's odd," the other replies. "Mine is remilitarization."

25. Doenecke, *Not to the Swift*, fn. 52, p. 150. The 14 April 1952 *Daily Compass* reported that Fritsch's book included chapters with titles like "Roosevelt's Satanism" and "Germany: Protector of the White Race."

26. Van Roden quoted in an undated news release from *Prevent World War III*, most likely December 1953.

27. Bower, *Blind Eye to Murder*, p. 282. One of Everett's charges was that the SS men had been mistreated by vengeance-seeking German Jewish refugees who worked for the war crimes tribunal.

28. Recall that Yockey was involved in the unsuccessful defense of SS General Otto Ohlendorf, whose lawyer was Aschenauer. The FBI also discovered a copy of Aschenauer's magazine *Die Andere Seite* from Yockey's time with the Johnsons. Also recall that Yockey was advising H. Keith Thompson on war crimes–related issues.

29. According to H. Keith Thompson, McCarthy had agreed to speak at the rally after being approached by Blomberg.

30. The first part of the essay comes from a summary by FBI agent Lloyd Bogstad dated 20 July 1953. The second complete part comes from Keith Stimely's photocopy of the April 1952 issue (No. 23) of *Frontfighter*.

27

ON THE RUN

Yockey hastily left Washington in early May 1952, after Dr. Warren Johnson discovered his affair with Virginia. Yockey and Virginia headed north to Atlantic City, New Jersey. Incredibly, Yockey spent part of May and June 1952 exhibiting the pins he took from Egidio Boschi at the Million Dollar Pier on Atlantic City's boardwalk. The FBI files report:

> _____ Million Dollar Pier, Boardwalk, Atlantic City NJ, stated that the Subject arrived in Atlantic City, NJ, about the middle of May 1952, with an exhibit of landscape paintings on pinheads which he desired to exhibit.
> _____ stated that the Subject told him that this exhibit had been very successful at the Festival of Britain[1] and that he, _____, invested about $500 in fixing up the exhibit. _____ advised that the exhibit ran for about a month but never took in more than a dollar or two a day and that on 6/18/52 he found it necessary to discontinue it and devote the space to something more lucrative.[2]

On the night of 24 May 1952, following the advice of his divorce attorney, Dr. Johnson and an unidentified friend showed up at Atlantic City's Endicott Hotel, where he had learned that Yockey and Virginia were staying.

> _____ of the Endicott Hotel . . . stated that the hotel records indicate that F. YOCKEY, Roxanna, Ill., checked in on 5/9/52 and his room was declared vacant 5/25/52. They stated that the records indicate he was joined by his wife the nights of 5/12/52 and 5/24/52. They related that on 5/24/52 two men came to the hotel about midnight to see the YOCKEYS and the night man, ED GLANCY, showed them to the hotel lounge and advised the YOCKEYS of the presence of visitors. They stated that GLANCY informed

them that the men stayed a short while and, immediately upon their leaving, the YOCKEYS paid their bill and checked out. GLANCY stated the two men returned in the early morning hours of 5/25/52 and were informed that the YOCKEYS had checked out.[3]

Low on funds, "Mr. and Mrs. Francis Downey" next moved into the Lyric motel, where they stayed from 28 May to 18 June 1952.[4]

Having failed to confront Yockey in Atlantic City, Doctor Johnson contacted Virginia's parents and told them that she had run off with a man wanted by the FBI and who, in his professional opinion, was a "paranoid psychotic."[5] When the Seattle office of the FBI interviewed Virginia's father, on 18 June 1952, he told the agents that he had seen copies of letters from Yockey supplied to him by Dr. Johnson that "seemed to indicate the subversive nature" of his activities.

Virginia went to New York on 23 June to visit her aunt and uncle, possibly with the hope of borrowing money. She told them that

> the man she had run away with had given her a new concept on political views, on living, etc., and that although the exact nature of his political views must be kept completely confidential, she was only able to say that they were entirely new to most people's way of thinking. She had indicated they were definitely not communistic, but just the "opposite." According to _____ their daughter indicated to _____ that the Subject was attempting to get a passport to travel in Europe but was having some difficulty due to his political beliefs. She also spoke of some papers which her husband had found and which were being used by her husband to hold over her, the insinuation being that those papers were subversive in nature and implicated both _____ and the Subject.[6]

Virginia also said that Yockey "was presently in New York in an effort to set up a concession at Coney Island displaying pictures engraved on the head of a pin."[7]

The New York office of the FBI received a phone call on 25 June from Virginia's aunt, who reported that Yockey and Virginia had been living in Atlantic City. She also revealed that Yockey was now staying at the YMCA's Sloane House on 34th Street and Eighth Avenue. A 25 June teletype labeled "Urgent" then went out to FBI headquarters advising that Yockey was at Sloane House. The telegram concluded: "THE BUREAU IS REQUESTED TO ADVISE NY IF YOCKEY IS WANTED BY THE BUREAU OR THE STATE DEPARTMENT, AND ALSO ADVISE NY WHAT ACTION IS TO BE TAKEN BY THE NYO [New York Office], IF ANY."

The next day, 26 June 1952, K. Balinkoff, a Special Agent from the Security Division of the U.S. State Department, showed up outside Yockey's room at Sloane House, only to find him not at home:

BALINKOFF stated he was going to await YOCKEY's return, but upon instructions from his superiors he left a note for YOCKEY telling him to call the State Department, New York City. This YOCKEY did on June 28, and advised that he was positive it was a case of mistaken identity and that he, in fact, never held a United States passport. BALINKOFF requested that he appear at the State Department office on that date, and YOCKEY stated that he would if he could be accompanied by his lawyer. To this BALINKOFF agreed, but he stated that YOCKEY never appeared and several hours thereafter he checked at the Sloane House and found out that YOCKEY had checked out without leaving a forwarding address.

After fleeing Sloane House, Yockey found new sanctuary thanks to H. Keith Thompson, who took him to his parents' apartment in Chatham, New Jersey, where they shared a room. Yockey also stayed in Thompson's apartment at 433 East 82nd Street in Manhattan and at Fred Weiss's farm in Middletown, New York.[8]

Thompson later described day-to-day life with Yockey at his parents' unwitting hideaway:

> Well, in general he accompanied me in to New York, I went to my business activities and he went to whatever activities he had planned for the day, and we would meet late-afternoon and then come back out on the commuters' train back out to New Jersey. Neither of us spent much time at my parents' apartment . . . Yockey had his own appointments, his own connections; he probably ran off to Virginia [Johnson] as soon as he got off the ferryboat to Manhattan in those days, from the Lackawanna train, which had taken us to Hoboken. I would go to my office, and he would go off somewhere on his own, meeting God knows whom. I never interrogated him about his business, nor he about mine.[9]

During that summer the two men became friends. When I asked Thompson about his warmest memory of Yockey, he returned to this period:

> Probably the fondest memory is insignificant for your purposes. We went a number of times to the NJ shore, which he enjoyed a bit "off-season" before the hordes of ground apes descended.[10] Then, too, remember that this was some 40 years ago, when things were different in all respects. Anyhow, he liked to walk the boardwalks late at night, and the beach too. On those long walks beside the ocean, we talked of everything: politics, the law, *Imperium*, personalities in the political realm, etc. On those deserted beaches, we would sometimes—temperature permitting—strip down and take a swim, like at 3 A.M. I vividly remember one occasion when we watched the sun rise over the Atlantic . . . I think on those few occasions he let down his natural guard and we talked for hours, quite freely. We discussed the great men of the 20th century: Hitler, Mussolini, William II (a visionary of the Yockey class), Himmler, Franco, lesser figures like Perón,

Stroessner, the emigré Germans (Rudel, Skorzeny, von Leers, Remer, many more)—and mourned the judification-internationalization of the world, the destruction of Europe, the rise of the colored races, etc.[11]

Quiet moments like these would not last long.

Notes:

1. Yockey is no doubt referring to Boschi's earlier trip to England.

2. 8 August 1952 report from Paul Alker of the FBI's Newark office.

3. Ibid. Johnson said he had presented Yockey and Virginia with evidence from the letters and informed them that they had been given to his attorney for a divorce action. As the testimony of the night clerk suggests, Yockey apparently never met Johnson. It is possible they spoke over the house phone or that Johnson left them a letter.

4. Ibid.

5. Johnson also said that Yockey was a responsible person "in that he knows what he is doing and is firmly convinced that his beliefs are genuine." From Johnson's first interview with Baltimore FBI Agent Holland on 12 September 1952.

6. 8 August 1952 Newark FBI office report. FBI deletions make it impossible to be sure if Virginia was speaking to her parents or her aunt and uncle. The FBI met with Virginia's parents in Seattle on 18 June 1952.

7. 18 August 1952 report by FBI agent Lawrence Bracken of the New York office. Virginia's aunt was interviewed in the NY FBI office on 7 July 1952, when she gave her story in more detail and again told the FBI about the letters that Dr. Johnson had discovered.

8. See the H. Keith Thompson interview with Keith Stimely in the Hoover archives. I shall describe Yockey's relationship with Fred Weiss in the next chapter.

9. Ibid.

10. A favorite Yockey insult was to call someone a "ground ape."

11. H. Keith Thompson's reply to my questionnaire.

28

FRIENDS

OF FRANZ

Yockey spent the fall and winter of 1952 living clandestinely in New York City, trying to find a way back to Europe without being detected by the U.S. government. Fearing that his passport would be confiscated, he turned to Frederick Charles Weiss and Harold Keith Thompson for help.

Both of his benefactors had been involved in pro-German activities for years and maintained particularly close relations with the *Der Weg* network in Argentina. The 66-year-old Fred Weiss was also quite active in the New York right.[1] The son of a prosperous German industrialist, he was born in Pforzheim, Germany, in 1886, and claimed to have been a patent lawyer with a Heidelberg-Sorbonne education.[2] He first came to the U.S. in 1910, but later returned to Germany, where he served as an artillery captain during World War I. He provided his military resume in one of his pamphlets:

> After four years of continuous service in the trenches of World War I, I fought in 1918–19 as a volunteer in the "Baltikum" outfit against the Trotskyites. In World War I, I fought with Field Artillery Rgt. 29 and Heavy Artillery Rgt. 13 at Ypres, the Somme, St. Quentin-Montmorency, Champagne, and Lorraine. I also served as Divisions-Observer (Inf. Reg. 241 under General von La Chevallerie).[3]

Weiss also claimed to an ADL investigator that

> I was on the World War I list of German war criminals, last name from the bottom. For shooting up a French village; I was an artillery captain . . . When the French seized the Ruhr in 1920, I fled. But they caught me in Düsseldorf. I spent 11 months in prison.[4]

H. Keith Thompson heard that Weiss had married a Jewish woman while in Germany. He had a daughter from the marriage named Ruth, who once visited Weiss in New York in the 1950s.[5]

After returning to the United States in 1930, Weiss became active in the New York real estate market and owned an apartment house in White Plains. He lived, however, in the heavily German Yorkville district of Manhattan as well as on his farm in Middletown, New York. While he was in Yorkville, he met Marie Urbas, who owned a hairdressing business. Marie had strong mystical leanings, and Thompson recalls her telling him more than once about the time Wotan himself appeared to her in a cave. Fred and Marie lived together as common-law husband and wife until his death in the mid-1960s.

Weiss's political activity before World War II is unclear. It seems likely, however, that he worked with Kurt Mertig, a Yorkville rightist who founded the Citizens Protective League and the German-American Republican League in 1936. After Pearl Harbor, Mertig was banned from living within three hundred miles of the East Coast by the Army Exclusion Board.[6] As a German national who knew "the wrong people," Weiss was declared an "enemy alien" and spent time on Ellis Island.[7] "But I never joined the Bund and never became a Nazi Party member," he later explained. "That's why the U.S. government was never able to pin anything on me even though they held me for investigation for many months."[8]

Once World War II ended, Weiss began attending right-wing functions, including a 31 August 1946 meeting of the Christian Veterans Political Council.[9] That same year he published *Quo Vadis America: When Will Bolshevism Take Over?*[10] He issued a follow-up pamphlet in 1947 called *Germania Delenda Est!*[11] He also formed the Le Blanc publishing house (*blanc* being French for white, as *weiss* means white in German) to produce his English-language pamphlets as well as anti-Semitic material meant for distribution inside Germany.[12] Some of his writing also appeared in *Der Weg*.

Like Yockey, Weiss was an avowed Spenglerian. As early as 1946, in *Quo Vadis America*, he defined postwar politics in Spenglerian jargon as a struggle of "Orient vs. Occident or Magian vs. Faustian Culture."[13] In his *Germania Delenda Est!*, he critiqued Nazi "blood theory" and pointed out that the destruction of two-thirds of the German population during the Thirty Years' War so altered the "Nordic" genetic type that when the U.S. entered the war, "the balance of 'pure' Nordic blood was certainly against the Axis."[14] He even began the introduction to Part II of *Quo Vadis America* with a Spenglerian note about race:

Whenever I speak of "race," I mean it in an ethical, not in a Darwinian or zoological sense. When I speak of "colored" races, I do not mean this literally since, besides Africans, Indians, Negroes, and half-breeds, of the whole of America, the Islamic nations, Chinese and Japanese, I include above all "Russia," which again has become an Asiatic "Mongolian" State and which now is the sovereign of all colored nations.[15]

Well before he met Yockey, Weiss presented the Jewish conspiracy in a way that sounds almost identical to Yockey's description. In *Quo Vadis America*, he warned against a Magian Jewish consensus that

> to all appearances has traveled unaltered through millennia, cemented together not by deliberate organization but by a wholly metaphysical impulse; a consensus not like we Western men bound up with the soil of our country—but landless, timeless and boundless, to us utterly alien and incomprehensible . . . This consensus, after having achieved his aim: the Classless, Stateless, World Chaos, would then remain the only COHESIVE power in the world, well equipped with a Machiavellian intelligence.

Weiss, however, insisted that "Asiatic" Russia was no longer under Jewish control. In a September 1950 pamphlet called *The Untouchables* he divided communism into a Western, Jewish-controlled Trotskyism and the Eurasian form known as Stalinism that, he believed, reflected the true soul of Russia. He then argued that the Jewish "alien nation" or "consensus" always supports

> the aims . . . most nearly comparable with the essence of his boundless, landless nation. Hence, "by nature," he is today a "communist" of the Trotsky brand; a One-World-Apostle . . . And, if he does no longer possess the material power to enable him to act in the cadre of his own Culture (as we see it today in Stalin's "Russia"); if he no longer can ignore or manipulate the destiny of the Russian peoples (as he did in Trotsky's time); he stands helpless in the midst of events and his cohesion falls apart. Hence, it is quite natural that today he subtly professes to be an "Anti-Communist" . . . by which he, naturally, means only to be opposed to "Stalinism" (which he regards today—and righteously so—as his most deadly enemy).

Weiss repeatedly raised the specter of German technological genius allied with the vast material resources of Eurasia—an alliance that he believed would soon make Russia the world's dominant power. His Russian orientation became so pronounced that his numerous critics inside the New York right claimed that he was being secretly funded by the Communist Party.[16] Although Weiss denied the charge, he did not hide his "East orientation," and in a 1953 interview he frankly explained just why he supported a German-Russian axis. According to the ADL-sponsored book *Cross-Currents*, Weiss

> quite freely admitted that he would prefer, under some situations, to see Germany tie in with the USSR rather than with the United States. This notwithstanding his all-too-frequent tirades against "Jewish-manipulated

bolshevism" and "Asiatic hordes." "We Germans must find out whether we can get more out of the East or the West. I've come to the conclusion—and this is disclosing my innermost thought—that we can work out a better deal in going along with the East rather than the West. With our know-how and with our experience, we can get ahead faster with the USSR than with the West. Furthermore, the USSR has much more to offer us."[17]

Weiss also played a pivotal behind-the-scenes role in the creation and financing of the National Renaissance Party (NRP), the first neo-Nazi organization in postwar America.[18] The NRP was formed in January 1949, after Kurt Mertig's German-American Republican League and his Citizens Protective League merged with the Philadelphia-based Nationalist Action League, headed by William Henry MacFarland.[19] The NRP took its name from Hitler's *Political Testament*, where the German dictator proclaimed: "I die with a happy heart" because "from the sacrifice" there would spring up "the seed of a radiant renaissance of the National Socialist Movement."

Although Mertig became the first chairman of the NRP, his health was poor and he soon turned his position over to MacFarland. A young member of MacFarland's Nationalist Action League named James Madole then took over the day-to-day management of the NRP. Yet Weiss remained the real power behind the tiny group during its early years and regularly used it for a host of tasks that included mailing Weiss-produced propaganda around the world.

Yockey's other New York benefactor was a 32-year-old Yale graduate and former U.S. naval officer named Harold Keith Thompson. Born in 1920, he was exactly three years younger than Yockey, both men having been born on September 17. In the August 1954 issue of a paper called *Exposé*, he described his early years:

> Raised in Maplewood, New Jersey, by devoted, thoroughly American parents in moderate circumstances, I reached my adolescence at the zenith of Adolf Hitler's Third Reich . . . Nearby, in New York City and Irvington, NJ, were the militant activities of the German-American Bund. I could not resist the temptation . . . My personal political indoctrination had by chance occurred at distinguished hands. Even as a teen-aged boy, I maintained a correspondence with Kaiser Wilhelm II, whom I admired, and became a friend of Carol II of the Hohenzollern, King of Romania, and of Prince August Wilhelm of Prussia, Brigadier General in Hitler's SA and the German Hohenzollern most dedicated to National Socialism.[20] Through "Auwi" [Prince August Wilhelm] an approach was made to Hitler's adjutant and a signed photograph of Adolf Hitler was forthcoming which adorned my desk at home until U.S. entry into World War II made this inappropriate. King Carol remained my friend in exile, to the interest of Military Intelligence, until his untimely death last year.[21] Prince August remained my friend

through, and in spite of, the war, until his death in 1949 as a result of imprisonment by the Allies for "denazification."

Thompson's devotion to Germany led a former director of Willis Carto's Institute for Historical Review named David McCalden to claim that he had been appointed an SS *Sturmbannführer* (major) in July 1941.[22] What is beyond dispute is that Thompson did enter into a close personal and political relationship with George Sylvester Viereck before World War II. A poet, novelist, and German agent of influence in both world wars, Viereck helped coordinate a highly sophisticated propaganda and lobbying network in the late 1930s with German chargé d'affaires Hans Thomsen. While living in New York, Viereck helped direct organizations like the German Library of Information, whose publication *Facts in Review* he edited.

The outbreak of war came as a shock to the German diplomatic corps, which had been furiously trying to encourage "Fortress America" isolationism. It was also highly traumatic for Thompson. After consultation with individuals who had his deepest respect, he decided to enlist in the U.S. Naval Reserve on 12 June 1942. A year later Thompson was recommended for direct commission as an ensign in the Naval Reserves. The Navy instead assigned him to the reserve officers training program, first at Drew University and then at Yale. After graduating from Yale in 1946, he joined Admiral Byrd's Antarctic Expedition (Operation Highjump) and served aboard Byrd's flagship, the USS *Mount Olympus*. He later worked in the Naval Personnel and Training Division in Washington until January 1948, when he resigned from the Navy.

Returning to New York, Thompson became involved in various businesses, including a fabric wholesaler called E. M. Latson Co. He worked as a salesman for the company in Texas and the Southwest, a position he used for frequent visits to Mexico to see his friend King Carol II of Romania. He then joined his father as a partner in a printing firm called Cooper Forms in lower Manhattan.

Thompson best remembered his time in New York in the early years of the war. In a 9 June 1995 letter to me, he cheerily reported:

> My file-burning is proceeding well... You'd be amused to know that I burned this week blueprints, deck and cargo plans, and related materials pertaining to SS *Normandie*. They were yellowed, brittle, and disintegrating. But such old memories! At my age only memories are left.

On the afternoon of 9 February 1942, a fire totally destroyed the SS *Normandie* (renamed the SS *Lafayette* during the war). The *Normandie* was a huge ship, some 83,400 tons. The blaze that engulfed it was so intense that smoke spread from the West 49th Street pier where the ship was docked down to 18th Street and over to Fifth Avenue. After the smoke finally cleared, one man was dead and over 250 sailors, workers, Coast Guardsmen, and firemen were injured. At a time when ships were desperately needed, the Navy had lost its largest auxiliary vessel.

After the disaster, various investigations tried to pin the blame on the company in charge of converting the *Normandie* into a navy transport for gross carelessness. Others pointed to the incompetence of the New York Fire Department. It also turned out that the company in charge of hiring workers and guards for the *Normandie* was the Oceanic Service Corporation. One of Oceanic's organizers, William Drechsel, a former marine superintendent of the North German Lloyd Steamship Line, had previously helped out various Bundists with bail money. However, two congressional committee investigations into the fire, one in the House and one in the Senate, concluded that the blaze had been caused by careless workmen.[23]

While continuing to act as the now-elderly Viereck's protégé, Thompson decided to take on a more visible role in the early 1950s. He became the registered agent for both the Socialist Reich Party (SRP) and Rudolf Aschenauer's *Die Andrere Seite*, as well as the New York agent, U.N. correspondent, and occasional writer for *Der Weg*/Dürer Verlag. He also represented Hans-Ulrich Rudel, the famous Luftwaffe ace, SRP supporter, and *Der Weg* activist, in literary matters involving the publication of Rudel's book *Stuka Pilot*.

Thompson recalled that he met Fred Weiss in the summer of 1951 thanks to Rudel:

> Rudel sent me a letter which he had received from Weiss, a curious mixture of German, Latin, and English which Rudel didn't really understand. He asked me to set up contact with Weiss and give some impressions of his operation, i.e., what was he really all about. First contact was by telephone, and thereafter we met in NYC, a beginning of countless confabs in Manhattan cafeterias, diners, and small cafes where he preferred to talk business. Some months thereafter I made my first visit to the Weiss farm.[24]

Like Yockey, both Weiss and Thompson clearly saw themselves less as American rightists than as German agents operating behind enemy lines. Both men had spent many years in the pro-German underground. Yet even for such skilled conspirators, protecting their new comrade for long was still a high-risk proposition.

Notes:

1. See the November 1954 *ADL Bulletin* for a report on Weiss.

2. A report on Weiss from the archives of the Non-Sectarian Anti-Nazi League (NSANL) says that he was in partnership with the firm of Lutz and Weiss, which was involved in gold and silver plating. It also said that Weiss held various patents.

3. From Fred Weiss's pamphlet, *How West Hooker Smears Honest Patriots.*

4. Arnold Forster and Benjamin Epstein, *Cross-Currents* (New York: Doubleday, 1956), p. 207.

5. Weiss apparently told the ADL that he was close to some Jewish thinkers in Germany. "If he [Weiss] still cherishes his early associations with German-Jewish philosophers (and still seeks out Jewish attorneys to handle his legal affairs), Weiss is nonetheless a confirmed anti-Semite." From the October–November 1954 issue of the ADL publication *Facts*.

6. See a profile of Kurt Mertig in the 15 December 1948 *Friends of Democracy Battle*.

7. H. Keith Thompson's reply to my questionnaire.

8. Foster and Epstein, *Cross-Currents*, pp. 207–08.

9. ADL files.

10. This was a three-part series. Weiss dates part one of *Quo Vadis America* to January 1946.

11. Weiss printed 100,000 copies of copies of *Germania Delenda Est!*, 70,000 in German and 30,000 in English. He also mailed copies to every name on his list of ex–Afrika Korp men. See Forster and Epstein, *Cross-Currents*, p. 211.

12. Weiss's propaganda operation surfaced in March 1953, after the German police raided the homes of leaders of an illegal neo-Nazi movement called the German Rally. During the raids the police seized a large collection of Nazi and anti-Semitic literature that had been printed outside Germany. One confiscated item was a four-page German language pamphlet decrying West Germany's cooperation with the United States as "happiness for the Star of David"; it had been printed at Weiss's New York–based Le Blanc Publishing House. (From *The ADL Bulletin*, November 1954.) Yockey also had a copy of this leaflet, which is reproduced in his FBI files. It was part of the cache of material found by Dr. Warren Johnson in May 1952.

13. *Quo Vadis* ends with the line "*Ducunt Fata Volentem Nolentem Trahunt*" (Destiny leads the willing, it pulls the unwilling), the same quote Spengler used to conclude volume two of *The Decline of the West*.

14. In the same pamphlet Weiss again emphasizes: "Race purity is a grotesque word in view of the fact that for centuries all stocks and species have been mixed and that certainly the German peoples are no exception."

15. Weiss, however, was very much a racialist. In a Le Blanc pamphlet distributed by the NRP in the early 1950s entitled *Hang on and Pray*, Weiss accuses the British historian Arnold Toynbee of betraying the white race. Weiss writes:

He [Toynbee] is opposed to white "race consciousness," but he glows with pleasure to see colored faces in his audience of students. Colored "race-consciousness" is not bad, and Saint Arnold feels it himself, even though his skin is unfortunately white. "Islam remains," he says, "and has a great spiritual mission." The African Negroes, he says, "have a pure and lofty conception of the nature of God, and of God's relation to man. They may be able to give mankind a fresh start." The presence of the atomic bomb generates the thought in Toynbee that the extreme catastrophe is that we might succeed in exterminating the African Negroes.

16. The attack on Weiss for getting CP money was made by several New York rightists, including DeWest Hooker and Edward Fleckenstein.

17. Foster and Epstein, *Cross-Currents*, p. 208.

18. On the origins of the NRP, I am relying on William Goring's December 1969–January 1970 report on the NRP published in the National Information Center's *Newsletter*. I also used a press release from the NSANL on the NRP, which was published on 11 August 1954.

19. MacFarland published two small journals, *National Progress* and *IMP's Bulletin*. In June 1949 he united his Nationalist Action League with the Loyal American Group of Union, New Jersey, which was sponsoring Conde McGinley's hate sheet *Common Sense*. MacFarland later renamed his Nationalist Action League the American Flag Committee.

20. Thompson also claimed that his family was descended from a Scottish-German line that included Frederick the Great's military advisor and very close friend, Field Marshall Keith.

21. U.S. intelligence suspected King Carol II of being a courier for Nazi funds. In reply to my question about King Carol, Thompson said that he was

> a friend of mine from the late '30s; served him as agent in various matters, philatelic, art, commercial (U.S. properties), and some public relations . . . Carol II died in 1953, in Estoril, Portugal. He had lived in Spain, Mexico ('40s), and Brazil, until finally settling in Estoril. One of my fondest memories as a very young man: dancing most of the night with Magda Lupescu (later Carol's wife as Princess Eleana of Romania) in a Mexico City nightclub, Carol chatting with friends at the table, smoking and drinking. A great man in many ways and a friend (he gave me the rank of commodore on his staff). I was glad to further his relationship with Wenner-Gren. But this is all aside from the Yockey matter, on which it has no bearing.

"Wenner-Gren" was the Swedish industrialist and suspected Nazi collaborator Axel Wenner-Gren.

22. McCalden made his claim in the June 1983 issue of his *Revisionist Newsletter*. After being dismissed by Willis Carto, McCalden attacked anyone involved with the IHR, including Thompson, who had become a friend and mentor to Keith Stimely. (Stimely, Yockey's would-be biographer, took over part of McCalden's old job.) According to McCalden, Thompson's activities

> so much impressed the German government that on 27 July 1941 Thompson was appointed a special agent of the Nazi government's SD/Overseas Intelligence Unit. The appointment was signed by Hitler himself and I have a photocopy here for those who would like to check out the signature.

In his July 1983 newsletter, McCalden stated that:

> HKT's appointment by Adolf Hitler as SS *Sturmbannführer* [major] of the *SicherheitsDienst* (Section AMT VI, *Abteilung II, Auslandische Sicherheitsstelle*) dated 27 July 1941 could of course be construed as treason, if it could be shown that the appointment continued after America's entry into the

war later that same year . . . The original document was captured by the U.S. 222nd Infantry Regiment and is now lodged at Interpol headquarters.

Rather than deny the story outright, Thompson said he had a "modest role" in the SS and told me that I could describe him this way: "Recruited for SD as a teenager in 1938, commissioned 1940, and at it ever since and still at it." He believes that the McCalden document is authentic, although it might have been issued in 1944 and backdated to 1941. He also enclosed a souvenir log from the North German Lloyd Breman ship SS *Columbus* ("a great ship") recording a July 1939 trip to the West Indies and South America. There are rumors that Thompson had secretly visited Germany, and his enclosure of the souvenir log *may* be a hint that he had transferred from the boat to another ship bound for Europe.

23. Francis MacDonnell, *Insidious Foes: The Axis Fifth Column and the American Home Front* (New York: Oxford University Press, 1995), p. 131.

24. H. Keith Thompson, letter to me dated 14 November 1995.

29

ESCAPE FROM
NEW YORK

In September 1952 Yockey and Virginia Johnson ("Mr. and Mrs. Frank Healy") checked into the Blake Hotel, at 142 West 44th Street.[1] Yockey remained at the Blake until 28 December 1952.[2] That fall, H. Keith Thompson introduced him to George Sylvester Viereck, who nicknamed him "The Orange Boy" because Varange sounded a little like "orange" in French. The elderly poet maintained a literary and political salon in his apartment at the Hotel Belleclaire on 77th Street and Broadway.[3] His circle included the rightist theorist Lawrence Dennis, Georgetown historian Charles Callan Tansill, and Harry Elmer Barnes, an influential historian and isolationist who took up the banner of Holocaust-denial late in life.[4] More literary figures, like Charles Jackson, author of *The Lost Weekend*, were also regulars. Thompson still remembers Yockey and Virginia sitting on the floor of Viereck's living room chatting about books, politics, and the New York literary scene. Keeping up his deception, Yockey introduced Virginia as his "sister" to Viereck's friends.

Along with art and politics, sex was very much part of Viereck's world, and he made no secret of his own bisexuality, believing he was in good company with Plato, Socrates, and Oscar Wilde. From his youth onwards he also had a fondness for orgies.[5] Viereck's fascination with sex led him to champion the work of Dr. Magnus Hirschfeld. A German Jewish doctor, early gay-rights activist, and founder of the Institute for Sexual Science, Hirschfeld was so despised by the German ultra-right that they tried to kill him at least twice. Viereck, however, considered Hirschfeld the "Einstein of sex" because he had shown that sex was "relative."[6] He was also a good friend of Dr. Alfred Kinsey, head of the Institute for Sex Research.[7] H. Keith Thompson met both

Kinsey and his assistant Dr. Wardell Pomeroy at Viereck's salon, and he thought that Yockey may have been introduced to Kinsey as well.

Another leading sexologist, Dr. Harry Benjamin, was Viereck's personal physician as well as one of his oldest friends. A highly cultured German Jew who had come to the United States in 1913, Benjamin started out as an endocrinologist studying gerontology and glands. In the early 1930s, after discovering that one of his patients was a transvestite, he became fascinated by the phenomenon. He later expanded his interest to transsexuals and became a world expert on the subject.[8] In the 1940s he began working with Kinsey, and introduced him to a famous San Francisco madam named Mabel Malotte, who let Kinsey take her history.[9]

Harry Benjamin also played an important role in Virginia Johnson's life. She first met him in Atlantic City in the summer of 1950, when she and her then-husband Warren heard him speak at a medical convention. While living with Yockey in New York she approached Benjamin and asked for help. Benjamin offered her a job as his part-time assistant. Because Virginia was pretending that Yockey was her "brother," one ADL informant reported that a "Dr. Blumenthal" [sic] mentioned Virginia's "incestuous" relationship to Kinsey.

Another Harry Benjamin project was the study of prostitution. Possibly as a result of her association with Benjamin, rumors began circulating that Virginia had quit a job as a model to become a high-class call girl.[10] One informant told the ADL that Fred Weiss

> developed a contact with a prostitute who is the girlfriend of Dr. Benjamin, a psychiatrist who goes in for all kinds of sex orgies. The good doctor used his girlfriend to participate in some of the orgies held by Viereck in his room at the Belleclaire Hotel.[11]

The ADL informant met both Virginia and Fred Weiss at the Drake Cafeteria on 45th Street and Sixth Avenue in 1953. Over coffee, Virginia explained her devotion to Yockey:

> He opened up a new world to me, helped me to understand the why and wherefore of international conflict and gave me an aim to work toward. I suppose I was what you would call a cockeyed nationalist. As a school kid, when I put my hand on my heart and swore allegiance to the flag, I really believed and was moved by it . . . [Yockey] helped me to understand all this and to tie it in with the need for a world order with determined leaders. To me, he is the greatest thinker of our time. Spengler was his teacher, but he thinks and writes better than Spengler. He is selfless and devoted to the cause. He is really indifferent to physical comforts. When he gets discouraged because a lot of stupid people don't seem to want to be saved, I give him courage. I take him in my arms and tell him how wonderful he is. I go out

and get material for him, I snoop for him. I go to any lengths to get money for him when he needs it. I'm now staking him for the completion of his big book [*Der Feind Europas*, published in late 1953]. Several times he would have given up writing if I didn't keep after him. I'll see that he gets the money he needs for years to come. If he should fall in love with somebody else, he knows I'll still be there to stake him. He is more to me than a lover—he gave me an outlook and purpose in life.

Yockey also became briefly involved with Hazel Guggenheim McKinley, an heiress to the Guggenheim family fortune. Hazel made headlines in 1928 when her two young children (one four years old and the other 14 months) fell from the roof of a 13-story New York apartment building while she was watching them. Although she had a long history of emotional instability, she escaped police investigation, a fact widely attributed to the Guggenheim fortune.[12] H. Keith Thompson, who introduced Yockey to Hazel, later recalled:[13]

Hazel was a friend of mine and on the "occasional" list in the Viereck circle (not Benjamin's). She was a grand lady. Tall, bosomy, and on the heavy side (not fat), she wore purple mascara, bleached her hair blonde, and smoked from a long cigarette holder. Sort of a cafe society figure of the '20s . . .

She wanted me to introduce her to some other young men, "particularly fascists," a type she admired. (Although I never discussed politics with her, I recall that she admired Mussolini and blackshirts.) One fine day I took Yockey to her apartment (elegant) as I remember it at the corner of 72nd and Fifth or thereabouts, blue-and-gold silk draperies everywhere, beautifully furnished, etc. We had a light supper there—the three of us—and then I left. I believe she enjoyed FPY quite a bit. I had hinted to Hazel that the guy never had any money, etc. and I'm sure she gave him something. I never asked her or him. One just did not discuss such matters with FPY.[14]

Former IHR director David McCalden claimed that Yockey's interlude with Hazel had a sado-masochistic twist. Fred Weiss and Thompson were both aware of Yockey's S/M interest, and after he vanished in Germany in 1955, Weiss joked that if the U.S. or West German government had not killed or captured him, Yockey's sexual practices may have finished him. Weiss was quoted in the ADL files as saying: "Because of his peculiar sex practices—whipping girls—Yockey may have run into one who didn't relish this kind of play, and had him done in." H. Keith Thompson also commented:

I think most of his relationships (sexual) were of the normal variety, but he did like a tinge of S&M. To one young lady I knew, Yockey gave a mild spanking with a soft cloth belt, turning both on . . . But to portray Yockey as any sort of pervert would be very wrong. He was utterly normal, in the '40s and '50s meaning of that term.[15]

Although Yockey clearly seemed to have enjoyed at least part of his stay in the Big Apple, it was obvious that the longer he remained in New York, the more vulnerable he was to capture. H. Keith Thompson was also coming under FBI scrutiny because of his role as the American agent for the Socialist Reich Party. He recalled that

> there was frequently some government agent following me around. The FBI shadowed me on a junket with GSV to attend a meeting of the Manuscript Society in the rectory of a Brooklyn church. This came to light because a few days later the FBI visited the minister who hosted the event and he wrote me about it. The same would have been the case had FPY accompanied. They might have identified him (tho' more likely not as they are really stupid).

Some remarkable developments in Europe that November made Yockey especially eager to return to the Continent. Fourteen leading Czech Communists (11 of them Jews) were tried and convicted in a Prague show trial of being spies for Zionist organizations like the Joint Distribution Committee, as well as the freemasons, the CIA, and British intelligence. The defendants included Czech Communist Party secretary general Rudolf Slansky, the Czech foreign minister, the Czech delegate to the Cominform, the deputy secretary-general of the Communist Party, the deputy minister of defense, the deputy minister of national security, two deputy foreign ministers, the deputy finance minister and ambassador to East Germany, the secretary general of the Communist Party in Brno, and the editor of the Prague CP paper, *Rude Pravo*.[16]

The Prague Trials were a test run for the brutal anti-Jewish "anti-cosmopolitan" campaign launched by Stalin in the last year of his life. The Russian dictator's offensive included the infamous phony "Jewish Doctors' Plot" against his life as well as the planned deportation of Russia's Jews to a new Siberian "homeland." In Poland, Hungary, and Czechoslovakia, native anti-Semitism was manipulated in the hope that unpopular Soviet occupation policies would be blamed on the misdeeds of a clique of Zionist spies.

Yockey saw the Slansky trials as a defining political moment, as the Russians now appeared to be moving into an overtly "communist" form of anti-Semitism. His interest in Czechoslovakia may also have had an espionage angle. In a 13 March 1986 interview with Keith Stimely, H. Keith Thompson said that Yockey had done a job for Czech intelligence in the mid-1950s. During the interview, Stimely asked:

> In line with your comment about communist associations of both [Frederick Charles] Weiss and Yockey, you once told me that you had the idea, and you hold it to this day, that Yockey was involved with the Eastern Bloc in some

way as a courier, specifically with Czechoslovakia. Could you please tell me why you believe this, what the evidence is?

Thompson replied:

Only what he told me ... He once mentioned that he had a paid job as a courier for a Czech intelligence officer or agency; he didn't know what he was transporting and it was simply a matter of taking papers of some sort from Europe to the United States, and perhaps in the other direction. It's very common that East Bloc countries have courier services for sensitive papers; the CIA has such services all over the world, and there's no reason to expect that the Eastern Bloc countries did not have these services. Their services of course were on behalf of the Soviet Union, their principal; little Czechoslovakia itself was not much interested in anything, but they operated a service at the request of the KGB.[17]

When I asked Thompson about Yockey's East Bloc links, he said: "He did a brief courier job for the Czechs, but it did not involve going further than Vienna."[18] In a letter dated 14 October 1994 he elaborated:

FPY asked me if I needed anything done in Austria. He was running a paid errand for the Czechs and that was his transfer point (Vienna). I did not cross-examine, and he made it clear that this was a matter of earning some money and a one-time deal. I brought up the "risks" but he considered them no more than usual. I gather that it was for a "friend of a friend." He did not know the contents of the "small packet" and did not care.

Thompson also recalled: "When we talked about the Czech matter he was glad not to have to cross the border." Yet just a few months before he first met Thompson, while attending the MIF convention in Naples, Yockey *may* have expressed an interest in travel behind the Iron Curtain. According to FBI files:

On October 17, 1951, the subject applied for a passport at Naples, Italy, and Passport No. 1893 was issued [on] this date. The subject planned to visit countries in the Eastern hemisphere, with limitations.[19]

Instead, Yockey returned to North America to work with Boschi.

If Yockey had a relationship with the Czechs, he wasn't the first rightist to do so. The Czech Department of National Security (SNP) actively recruited fascists and ex-Nazis.[20] Nor was Soviet Bloc recruitment limited to Prague. In Poland, for example, the Soviet NKVD made Boleslaw Piasecki, Poland's leading pre-war fascist, the leader of a Russian-backed "Catholic" organization called PAX.[21]

The Prague Trials were also the subject of the most controversial article Yockey ever wrote: "What Is Behind the Hanging of the Eleven Jews in Prague?" First published anonymously, in December 1952, in the *Bulletin* of Fred Weiss's National Renaissance Party (and republished in *Frontfighter* and

Der Weg),[22] it circulated throughout the far right in Europe, the Middle East, and the Americas. When the article appeared in the NRP's December 1952 "Special Edition," it came with this introduction:

> This entire issue of the National Renaissance *Bulletin* has been paid for by a group of important gentlemen recently arrived from Germany. It is their wish to provide the American people and fascist sources in Europe, South America, and Africa with a vital and detailed report emanating from Europe. The author of this report is well known but for obvious reasons his identity cannot be divulged. We have also been supplied with a large mailing list covering nearly every important pro-fascist leader and newspaper in Europe, Africa, and South America. Any of these sources of information have our permission to reprint "What Is Behind the Hanging of the Eleven Jews in Prague?" We are sending out an exceptionally large number of this issue throughout the world because the cost has been underwritten.[23]

The essay begins:

> On Friday, November 27, 1952, there burst upon the world an event which, though small in itself, will have gigantic repercussions in the happenings to come. It will force a political reorientation in the minds of the European elite. This monumental event was the conclusion of the treason trial of the Jews in Prague and their condemnation to death by the Soviet authorities.

Yockey argued that the Soviet turn against the Jews was a significant intensification of a broader crisis in East-West relations that began early in 1947, when Russia refused to accept United Nations control over atomic-weapons projects. After Russia's refusal, "the next policy of World Jewry's leadership was to persuade the Stalin regime by the encirclement and pressure of the 'Cold War' that it was hopeless to resist." In response

> the Stalin regime began its inner policy of dropping numerous Jews from the highest governmental positions, then slowly purging them from the lesser positions as well. Elastically the Stalin regime tried every approach in attempting to appease Jewish leaders. It offered aid to Israel, it then withdrew the offer and shut off emigration to Israel. Stalin tried every policy but still the Jewish-inspired encirclement policy of Russia continued. Wooing the Arabs did not change the mood of American Jewry, nor did spurning the Arabs.

Therefore:

> The treason trials in Bohemia are neither the beginning nor the end of a historical process, they are merely an unmistakable turning point . . . The talk concerning "the defense of Western Europe against Bolshevism" belongs now to yesterday. Nearly every square inch of European soil is controlled militarily or financially by International Jewry, the deadly enemy of

European Culture, which seeks the political, cultural, and historical extinction of Western Civilization.

The Prague Trials were also a signal for Europe's "fascist elite" to move away from U.S. control:

The Prague Trials have gone off with an explosive roar to waken this European fascist elite to active resistance against the death plans being hatched for European Culture in Washington by American Jewry. The fact is: The Russian leadership is killing Jews for treason to Russia, for service to the Jewish entity. Nothing can gainsay or reverse this fact. The European elite will perforce note this fact and act accordingly.

Yockey then argues that the right should play the "Russian card":

Henceforth, the European fascist elite can emerge more and more into world affairs, and will force the leadership of American Jewry to render back, step by step, the custody of European Destiny to the people of Europe. If the Jewish-American leaders refuse, the new fascist leaders of Europe will threaten them with the Russian bogey. By thus playing off Russia against the leadership of American Jewry, Europe can bring about its own liberation from the perils of Jewish Democracy imposed by American bayonets . . .

To us in Europe, the Prague Trials are welcome, they clear the air . . . As far as Europe is concerned, America's political hacks may as well haul down the Stars and Stripes and run up the Star of David . . . A second inevitable development of the Prague Trials is the intensification of the American diplomatic offensive against Russia, the "cold war" . . . Russia will naturally retaliate: Today *Pravda* says "Zionism is a tool of American imperialism." Tomorrow it will say "American imperialism is the tool of Zionism."

In early January 1953 Yockey safely returned to Europe. When Fred Weiss was interviewed by the FBI on 23 September 1954, he was asked about Yockey's departure.[24] Weiss claimed that Yockey had left for Europe on the SS *United States*. He also said that Yockey had asked him in January 1953 to make a sworn declaration to help him get a passport but that he had refused. He then hinted that Yockey may have obtained a forged passport from a Middletown, New York, contractor named Spinelli. Weiss mentioned that he "was only casually acquainted" with Spinelli, whom he described as a "gangster," but that Yockey had expressed an interest in meeting him.[25]

January 1953 was also a turbulent month for Virginia Johnson. From 21 to 28 January, she was hospitalized in New York's Mount Sinai Hospital. When FBI agent Lawrence Bracken questioned one Mount Sinai doctor on 10 March 1953, he was told that Virginia indicated "that she had recently had what appeared to be a criminal abortion" and that "severe complications had set in." The government learned of Virginia's medical problems after Dr. Warren

Johnson received a bill from Mount Sinai for her treatment. Virginia and Warren Johnson were legally divorced on 17 March 1953.[26]

After Yockey left New York, H. Keith Thompson concocted a draft of a few pages of a phony "memoir" that purported to expose Communist infiltration of the U.S. right. Thompson's piece was supposedly part of a novel that he and Lyle Stuart (the left-wing publisher of *Exposé*) were going to write. The real purpose behind the "sample chapter," however, was to take some FBI heat off Thompson by showing how he had been "duped" by Yockey and Weiss. Thompson and Weiss also spread rumors that they were now bitter enemies. The ADL even picked up a report that Virginia Johnson ("Madelaine Jockay") and Weiss had paid $50 to have a gangster beat up Thompson because he knew too much about Yockey. Thompson's memoir was very much part of this same deception game.[27] In his story, Thompson included real information about Yockey while carefully distancing himself from him. According to Thompson:

Yockey liked to tell of eluding State Department and other federal investigators "who wished to question him about his passport." Apparently some department of government was keeping a periodic watch on the homes of his Midwest relatives because, through various mail drops, he would be informed of visits of such investigators and warned to keep away. Little by little, I came to feel that Yockey's difficulties were not mere passport technicalities as he maintained, but that this man was actually "wanted" by this government. I discussed this apprehension with Weiss, stating that it would be unwise to become involved with fugitives, international or otherwise. Weiss confirmed this point of view, stating that he was anxious to have Yockey leave our circle at the earliest possible moment. I told Weiss that I felt his close association with Yockey was hazardous for us all, charming as the man could be and as brilliant a writer as he most certainly was. Weiss agreed. But I ascertained that Weiss remained closely associated with Yockey.

Events moved swiftly. The press attacks upon me were strong and I was the center of much attention from every manner of investigative agency. It became almost impossible to meet anyone, except by pre-arranged and devious methods. Yockey sensed this and drew into his shell. He did not intend to be spotted.

My contact with Yockey had been, during the Fall of 1952, at a telephone number, LU2-4524. Investigation showed this to be a midtown hotel where he and a girlfriend were living as Mr. and Mrs. Frank Healy. One day in late November[28] Yockey came to me and said that he had surprised "hotel personnel" installing "wires" in his room without any satisfactory explanation of the wires. He had also discovered someone lurking in the hallway outside his room in the middle of the night.[29] These things, coupled with the investigations centered around my foreign-agent status, would necessitate his moving, and leaving the country as soon as possible. A few days later, when

I called the hotel, I was informed that Healy had checked out and left no address.[30]

But how did Yockey manage to return to Europe undetected? When Thompson became a partner with his father in the Cooper Forms printing company, he did more than just work for commercial clients. Besides printing some Weiss pamphlets, he said that he used his printing operation to create documents for fugitive war criminals because he could always get "foreign paper" for those who met his standards, "i.e., never for money; it was not a business but a political service."[31] It seems clear that Thompson, Weiss, Viereck, and Virginia Johnson all had strong connections to underground New York that were employed to help Yockey make his escape.

Notes:

1. Yockey took the name Healy from a tombstone near the Weiss farm.

2. 8 April 1954 report by FBI Agent Edward Brandt.

3. H. Keith Thompson said that Viereck was really an old-time German monarchist when it came to politics, in part because Viereck believed that his father was an illegitimate child of one of the Hohenzollern princes, who had an affair with his actress mother. Also see Phyllis Keller, *States of Belonging* (Cambridge, MA: Harvard University Press, 1979).

4. For a profile of Barnes, see Justus Doenecke's article "Harry Elmer Barnes," in the summer 1973 issue of the *Wisconsin Magazine of History*.

5. One Viereck biographer writes that "In his sophomore year at college, Viereck knew an elderly physician who sought to renew, vicariously, his own love life by creating amorous opportunities for young people. Viereck was one of his beneficiaries and became an observer of many blends and variations of love, curious comminglings and perversions of all kinds." Elmer Gertz, *Odyssey of a Barbarian* (Buffalo, NY: Prometheus Books, 1978), pp. 85–86. Also see Keller, *States of Belonging*, pp. 121–29.

6. As Hirschfeld put it:

> Because of the duality of sex, there is oneness. Every male is potentially a female and every female potentially a male. If a man wants to understand a woman, he must discover the woman in himself, and if a woman wants to understand a man, she must dig in her own consciousness to discover her own masculine traits. [From John Lauristen and David Thorstad, *The Early Homosexual Rights Movement (1864–1935)* (New York: Time Changes Press, 1974), p. 75.]

7. It was Viereck who told Kinsey about Aleister Crowley, the bisexual British "sex magician" who had worked with Viereck in a German propaganda network in New York during World War I. Kinsey became so fascinated by Crowley that he went to Europe to purchase Crowley's diaries. See Wardell Pomeroy, *Dr. Kinsey and the Institute for Sex Research* (New York: Harper and Row, 1972).

8. One of Benjamin's patients was Christine Jorgensen. Benjamin also wrote *The Transsexual Phenomenon*.

9. Benjamin's own book on the subject is called *Prostitution and Morality* (New York: Julian, 1964).

10. The FBI heard that Virginia had a job as a professional model at the Bonomo Studios at 1841 Broadway in the Times Square area. When the FBI interviewed an employee at the Bonomo Studios he could not confirm that Virginia had worked there, since no record was kept of professional models hired on a daily basis.

11. The ADL source also said that Virginia was married to someone whose name sounded something like "Yokay" and that Yokay was then (late 1953) living in Munich on a passport provided by Weiss. Yokay was reported to be working for Weiss "on espionage jobs" in France and Egypt. Virginia was said to be doing odd jobs for the Egyptian military attaché through Weiss's connection in New York.

12. John H. Davis, *The Guggenheims: An American Epic* (New York: William Morrow, 1978).

13. In the ADL files there are also references to Thompson's ties to Hazel Guggenheim.

14. H. Keith Thompson's reply to my questionnaire.

15. Ibid.

16. The case began in the autumn of 1951, when Slanksy was arrested. On 3 December 1952 Slansky was executed. A decade later the Czech Supreme Court announced that the trial was a fabrication by the Czech Ministry of the Interior. See Paul Lendvai, *Anti-Semitism Without Jews* (New York: Doubleday, 1971), which also has an interesting discussion of "anti-Zionist" activities in Communist Poland. Also see *The Protocols and the Purge Trials*, a report by the Anti-Defamation League on the Prague trials.

17. From Keith Stimely's interview with H. Keith Thompson in the H. Keith Thompson archives in the Hoover Institute.

18. H. Keith Thompson's reply to my questionnaire. Vienna seems to have served as a crossover point for postwar SS dealings with the East Bloc. In *The Black Corps* (Shepperton: Ian Allen, 1992), Robin Lumsden writes:

> ODESSA derived additional funds from its illegal trade shipping scrap metal to Tangier and Syria, and its transfer to the Middle East of weapons stolen from U.S. ammunition depots in Germany. Its contact men also procured import and export licenses and sent strategic goods through holes in the Iron Curtain, particularly Vienna, which acted as a gateway to Czechoslovakia [p. 158].

19. 8 July 1954 FBI file No. 100-25647 by FBI Agent Lloyd Bogstad. Of course, by "Eastern hemisphere," the report may have been referring to the Middle East.

20. One such spy, Joroslav Zajicek, said that "the Communist spy masters, in their search for competent agents, were ready to employ former Nazis and Gestapo agents." Zajicek had used his old Gestapo cronies in the West to spy on the American military. E. H. Cookridge, *Gehlen: Spy of the Century* (New York: Random House, 1971), p. 191.

21. Before World War II, Piasecki organized paramilitary gangs (the ONR-Falanga) to attack Jews and leftists. He was also involved in a 1937 plot by right-wing colonels in the Polish military to seize power. A strong admirer of Mussolini, Piasecki fought the Germans during the invasion of Poland and was only released

by the Gestapo through the intervention of Mussolini. Under the direction of the NKVD, Piasecki and his old colleagues from the Falanga days ran PAX and a related business operation called I.N.C.O., the largest private enterprise group in the East Bloc. On Piasecki, see his entry in Philip Rees, *Biographical Dictionary of the Extreme Right* (New York: Simon and Schuster, 1990), as well as L. Blit, *The Eastern Pretender* (London: Hutchinson, 1965).

22. Yockey's article appeared in *Der Weg* under the title "Stalin und die Juden."

23. Reading the essay, it is clear that Yockey also intended the piece for *Frontfighter*, since he cites from *Imperium*, quotes *The Proclamation of London*, and writes: "The trials have made easier the task of the European Liberation Front."

24. FBI interview with Fred Weiss dated 4 November 1954.

25. Thompson told me that Weiss did have some knowledge of mob types through the real estate business.

26. According to an ADL report, Virginia later became the girlfriend of another man, whom she eventually married. She had dropped out of Yockey's life by the spring of 1954.

27. Much of Thompson's story repeats testimony he gave to the FBI on 14, 23, and 30 September 1953, when he was interviewed about Yockey by FBI agents James P. Martin and Edward A. Brandt. Thompson is listed as "T-2" in the FBI report. When the FBI asked him how Yockey had obtained his false passport, Thompson said that it "had been secured for YOCKEY through an acquaintance _____. Informant stated _____ [Weiss] indicated that_____ [Spinelli] is associated in some way with 'gangsters.'"

28. Actually December. Recall that Yockey only checked out of the Blake Hotel on 28 December 1952.

29. Whether the FBI or some other agency did try to wire Yockey's hotel room cannot be determined. The FBI files make no reference to such an operation. However, such files may have been part of the group of files deleted in their entirety.

30. From an untitled H. Keith Thompson manuscript in the Hoover Institute. Thompson goes on to report his great shock at seeing the publication of Yockey's defense of the Prague Trials, and blames Yockey and Weiss for it.

31. H. Keith Thompson's reply to my questionnaire.

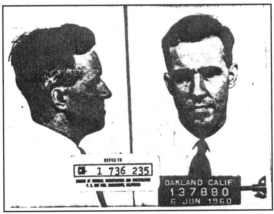

1. A handcuffed Yockey in court after his arrest. 2. Yockey's mugshot photos, taken the day of his arrest.

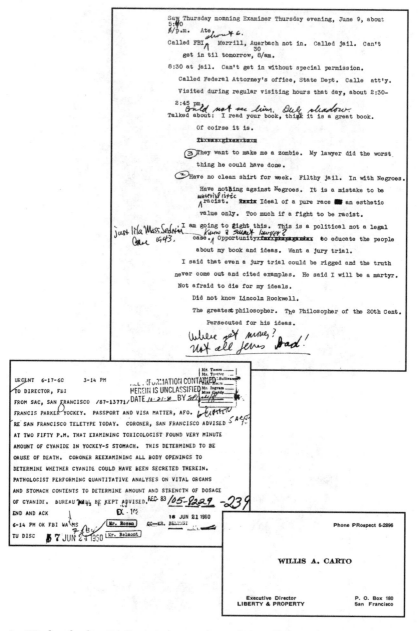

Saw Thursday morning Examiner Thursday evening, June 9, about
8:40 p.m. Ate, *about 6.*

Called FBI *Merrill,* Auerbach not in. Called jail. Can't
get in til tomorrow, 8/am. 30

8:30 at jail. Can't get in without special permission.

Called Federal Attorney's office, State Dept. Calle att'y.

Visited during regular visiting hours that day, about 2:30-
2:45 pm. *Could not see him. Only shadow.*
Talked about: I read your book, think it is a great book.

Of coirse it is.

~~Ixxxxxgixxxxxx~~

③ They want to make me a zombie. My lawyer did the worst
thing he could have done.

② Have no clean shirt for week. Filthy jail. In with Negroes.

Have nothing against Negroes. It is a mistake to be
materialistic
racist. ~~Xxxxx~~ Ideal of a pure race █ an esthetic
value only. Too much if a fight to be racist.

Just like Mass Sedini I am going to fight this. This is a political not a legal
Case 1943. case. *Know a smart lawyer?* Opportunity~~xfxxxpxxpxgxnxx~~ to educate the people
about my book and ideas. Want a jury trial.

I said that even a jury trial could be rigged and the truth
never come out and cited examples. He said I will be a martyr.
Not afraid to die for my ideals.

Did not know Lincoln Rockwell.

The greatest philosopher. The Philosopher of the 20th Cent.
Persecuted for his ideas.

Where get money?
Not all Jews. Dad!

URGENT 6-17-60   3-14 PM
TO DIRECTOR, FBI
FROM SAC, SAN FRANCISCO /87-13771/

FRANCIS PARKER YOCKEY. PASSPORT AND VISA MATTER, AFO.
RE SAN FRANCISCO TELETYPE TODAY. CORONER, SAN FRANCISCO ADVISED
AT TWO FIFTY P.M. THAT EXAMINING TOXICOLOGIST FOUND VERY MINUTE
AMOUNT OF CYANIDE IN YOCKEY-S STOMACH. THIS DETERMINED TO BE
CAUSE OF DEATH. CORONER REEXAMINING ALL BODY OPENINGS TO
DETERMINE WHETHER CYANIDE COULD HAVE BEEN SECRETED THEREIN.
PATHOLOGIST PERFORMING QUANTITATIVE ANALYSES ON VITAL ORGANS
AND STOMACH CONTENTS TO DETERMINE AMOUNT AND STRENGTH OF DOSAGE
OF CYANIDE. BUREAU WILL BE KEPT ADVISED.
END AND ACK
6-14 PM OK FBI WA MS
TU DISC

ALL INFORMATION CONTAINED
HEREIN IS UNCLASSIFIED
DATE 11-21-8 BY

REC-83 105-8229 -239

18 JUN 21 1960

Phone PRospect 6-2896

WILLIS A. CARTO

Executive Director   P. O. Box 180
LIBERTY & PROPERTY   San Francisco

---

1. "Only shadow": Carto's notes from his jailhouse interview with
Yockey. 2. "URGENT: To Director FBI": The FBI telegram reporting
Yockey's death. 3. Willis Carto's Liberty & Property business card.

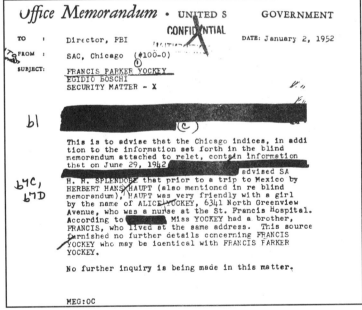

Office Memorandum • UNITED S   GOVERNMENT

TO : Director, FBI   DATE: January 2, 1952

FROM : SAC, Chicago (#100-0)

SUBJECT: FRANCIS PARKER YOCKEY
EGIDIO BOSCHI
SECURITY MATTER - X

b1

(C)

This is to advise that the Chicago indices, in addi
tion to the information set forth in the blind
memorandum attached to relet, contain information
that on June 29, 1942

advised SA
H. R. SPLENDORE that prior to a trip to Mexico by
HERBERT HANS HAUPT (also mentioned in re blind
memorandum), HAUPT was very friendly with a girl
by the name of ALICE YOCKEY, 6341 North Greenview
Avenue, who was a nurse at the St. Francis Hospital.
According to   Miss YOCKEY had a brother,
FRANCIS, who lived at the same address. This source
furnished no further details concerning FRANCIS
YOCKEY who may be identical with FRANCIS PARKER
YOCKEY.

No further inquiry is being made in this matter.

MEG:OC

1. Oswald Spengler, the German philosopher of history who inspired Yockey. 2. FBI report on Yockey, his sister Alice, and the German spy Herbert Hans Haupt.

1. A bookish H. Keith Thompson holds court in his apartment while Adolf looks on. 2. Three generations of fascists: Matt Koehl, H. Keith Thompson, and George Sylvester Viereck.

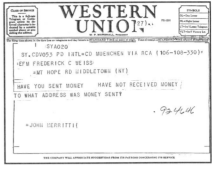

1. Fred Weiss in Yorkville in the late 1940s. 2. Yockey's "John Merritti" telegram from Munich (ca. 1953) asking Weiss for money. 3. Johann von Leers, the editor of *Der Weg*. 4. A Dürer Verlag letter authorizing H. Keith Thompson to serve as *Der Weg*'s U.N. correspondent.

1. A photograph of Yockey taken around 1949. 2. The Italian rightist theorist Julius Evola.

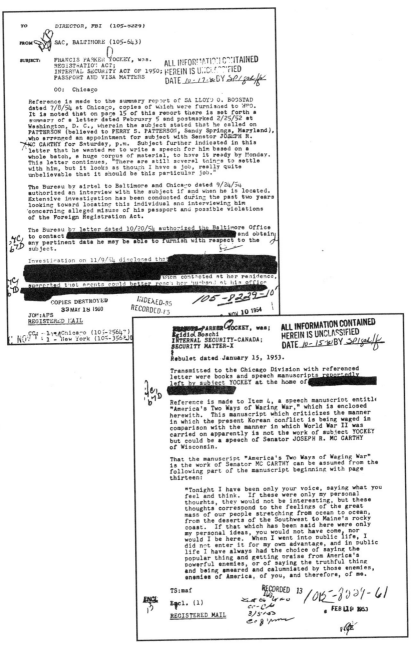

TO   DIRECTOR, FBI (105-5229)

FROM   SAC, BALTIMORE (105-643)

SUBJECT: FRANCIS PARKER YOCKEY, was.
          REGISTRATION ACT;
          INTERNAL SECURITY ACT OF 1950;
          PASSPORT AND VISA MATTERS

          OO: Chicago

Reference is made to the summary report of SA LLOYD O. BOGSTAD
dated 7/8/54 at Chicago, copies of which were furnished to WFO.
It is noted that on page 15 of this report there is set forth a
summary of a letter dated February 5 and postmarked 2/25/52 at
Washington, D. C., wherein the subject stated that he called on
PATTERSON (believed to PERRY S. PATTERSON, Sandy Springs, Maryland),
who arranged an appointment for subject with Senator JOSEPH R.
MC CARTHY for Saturday, p.m. Subject further indicated in this
letter that he wanted me to write a speech for him based on a
whole batch, a huge corpus of material, to have it ready by Monday.
This letter continues, "There are still several things to settle
with him, but it looks as though I have a job, really quite
unbelievable that it should be this particular job."

The Bureau by airtel to Baltimore and Chicago dated 9/24/54
authorized an interview with the subject if and when he is located.
Extensive investigation has been conducted during the past two years
looking toward locating this individual and interviewing him
concerning alleged misuse of his passport and possible violations
of the Foreign Registration Act.

The Bureau by letter dated 10/20/54 authorized the Baltimore Office
to contact ███████████████████ and obtain
any pertinent data he may be able to furnish with respect to the
subject.

Investigation on 11/9/54 disclosed that ███████████████
███████████████████████ when contacted at her residence,
suggested that agents could better reach her husband at his office.

COPIES DESTROYED   INDEXED-85
   33 MAY 18 1960   RECORDED-15   105-8229-10
JOM:APS
REGISTERED MAIL
NOV 1   NOV 10 1954
CC - 1 - Chicago (105-25647)
   1 - New York (105-3562)

FRANCIS PARKER YOCKEY, was;
Egidio Boschi
INTERNAL SECURITY-CANADA;
SECURITY MATTER-X

Rebulet dated January 15, 1953.

Transmitted to the Chicago Division with referenced
letter were books and speech manuscripts reportedly
left by subject YOCKEY at the home of ████████████

Reference is made to Item 4, a speech manuscript entitle
"America's Two Ways of Waging War," which is enclosed
herewith. This manuscript which criticizes the manner
in which the present Korean conflict is being waged in
comparison with the manner in which World War II was
carried on apparently is not the work of subject YOCKEY
but could be a speech of Senator JOSEPH R. MC CARTHY
of Wisconsin.

That the manuscript "America's Two Ways of Waging War"
is the work of Senator MC CARTHY can be assumed from the
following part of the manuscript beginning with page
thirteen:

    "Tonight I have been only your voice, saying what you
    feel and think. If these were only my personal
    thoughts, they would not be interesting, but these
    thoughts correspond to the feelings of the great
    mass of our people stretching from ocean to ocean,
    from the deserts of the Southwest to Maine's rocky
    coast. If that which has been said here were only
    my personal ideas, you would not have come, nor
    would I be here. When I went into public life, I
    did not enter it for my own advantage, and in public
    life I have always had the choice of saying the
    popular thing and getting praise from America's
    powerful enemies, or of saying the truthful thing
    and being smeared and calumniated by those enemies,
    enemies of America, of you, and therefore, of me.

TS:maf   RECORDED 13   105-8229-61
Encl. (1)
                                               FEB 18 1953
REGISTERED MAIL

1. Yockey reports on his "really quite unbelievable" job. 2. An excerpt
from the speech Yockey wrote for Senator Joseph McCarthy.

SENATOR McCARTHY
will speak at the
YORKVILLE CASINO

FELLOW AMERICANS:

YOU ARE CORDIALLY INVITED TO ATTEND THE

AMERICAN-GERMAN
FRIENDSHIP RALLY

ON SUNDAY EVENING, MAY 4th, 1952, AT 8:30, AT YORKVILLE CASINO,
210 East 86th Street, New York City

This affair will be dedicated to strengthening relations between the United States and Germany and to voice our belief in a just peace treaty for Germany in which we especially espouse the cause of the expellees and their lost homelands. We have set aside this evening to honor two leading civilizations, the American and the German.

OUR GUEST SPEAKER WILL BE AN OUTSTANDING AMERICAN LEADER, THE DYNAMIC U. S. SENATOR

Hon. JOSEPH R. McCARTHY

IN ADDITION YOU WILL BE ENTERTAINED BY A
BAND CONCERT

The German Americans of New York and New Jersey are particularly urged to attend this rally as it will be the first large meeting of its kind. Senator McCarthy will be the only scheduled guest speaker — he has an important message to give you. On this evening leading individuals active for German rehabilitation will appear on the stage, including:

PROF. AUSTIN J. APP   HENRY C. FURSTENWALDE

BARON W. F. VON BLOMBERG   FATHER E. J. REICHENBERGER

REV. L. A. FRITSCH, D.D.   EDWARD A. FLECKENSTEIN,
                                                          Chairman of Rally

The band will play after the meeting and the hall will remain open to the public for the rest of the evening.

AMERICAN—GERMAN FRIENDSHIP RALLY COMMITTEE
218 East 86th Street, New York 28, N. Y.

ADMISSION PRICES:

General Admission
(Unreserved seats and standing room) ....$1.20 (inc. tax)
Reserved Section .... 1.50 .
Balcony 1.80

TICKETS CAN BE PURCHASED NOW AT:

NEWSSTAND   *In New Jersey:*
200 East 86th Street   KRUEGER'S TRAVEL BUREAU
New York 28, N. Y.   6505 Bergenline Avenue
                                                          West New York, New Jersey

GET YOUR TICKETS NOW!

After the controversy caused by this announcement, Senator McCarthy was forced to cancel his appearance.

INSTITUTE FOR HISTORICAL REVIEW
POST OFFICE BOX 1306 ● TORRANCE, CALIFORNIA 90505 ● U.S.A.

Welcome to the IHR's
Fifth International Revisionist
Conference, 3-5 September 1983

Master of Ceremonies: KEITH STIMELY

● *Please have your identification badges with you during all conference activities.*
● *Please be on time. All conference events will begin as scheduled.*
● *A question and answer period will follow each lecture.*
Please keep your questions and comments relevant and for the appropriate time.
● *Be sure to check with the hotel desk regarding shuttle bus departure times to the airport.*

SATURDAY 3 SEPTEMBER

7:00-7:15pm	Call to Order and Welcoming Remarks: TOM MARCELLUS and KEITH STIMELY.
7:15-8:15	DR. JAMES J. MARTIN: Dedication of Conference to Francis Neilson.
8:15 on	Social, No-Host Bar.

SUNDAY 4 SEPTEMBER

7:00-8:45am	Buffet Breakfast.
9:00-10:30	DR. WILLIAM B. LINDSEY: Auschwitz, Zyklon B, and the Trial of Dr. Bruno Tesch.
10:30-10:45	Coffee Break.
10:45-12:30pm	DR. ROBERT JOHN: Behind the Balfour Declaration: Britain's Great Promise to Lord Rothschild.
12:30-2:30	Lunch.
2:30-4:00	FRIEDRICH P. BERG: Diesels, Gas Vans, and Zyklon B.
4:00-4:15	Coffee Break.
4:15-6:00	DAVID IRVING: Uprising: Hungary Revolts Against Communism.
7:00-10:00	Revisionist Dinner. WILLIS A. CARTO, and Guest Speaker DR. MARTIN A. LARSON: A Brief History of Monetary Crimes Against America.

MONDAY 5 SEPTEMBER

7:00-8:45am	Buffet Breakfast.
9:00-10:30	H. KEITH THOMPSON: Grand Admiral Doenitz, Last Legitimate President of Germany: His Succession Government, the Nuremberg Proceedings and Their Aftermath, Some Personal Experiences and Observations.
10:30-10:45	Coffee Break.
10:45-12:30pm	DR. ROBERT FAURISSON: Four Years of Proceedings Against French Revisionism
12:30-2:00	Lunch.
2:15-3:45	DR. WILHELM STAEGLICH: "The Auschwitz Myth": A Book and Its Fate in the German Federal Republic.
3:45-4:00	Announcements and Adjournment.

The Staff of the Institute for Historical Review wishes to extend a special thanks to all the speakers and attendees who have helped make this conference a success. Orders for cassette tapes of these lectures can be placed at the book display table.

Publisher of The Journal of Historical Review

1. "Master of Ceremonies" Keith Stimely, Willis Carto, and H. Keith Thompson at the 1983 IHR convention. 2. H. Keith Thompson: Still keeping the faith.

1. Jean-François Thiriart's December 1967 Christmas message to America. 2. Thiriart and Russian rightist Aleksandr Dugin in Moscow in 1992.

KALI-YUGA
(OCCULTISM,
SECRET SOCIETIES,
AND POSTWAR
FASCISM)

We have been concerned with a cultural phenomenon which cannot be subsumed under the traditional canons of political theory. For it was not constructed as a logical and coherent system that could be understood through a rational analysis of philosophical writings. The phenomenon which has been our concern was a secular religion, the continuation from primitive and Christian times of viewing the world through myth and symbol, acting out one's hopes and fears within ceremonial and liturgical forms.

—George L. Mosse,
The Nationalization of the Masses

Well-nigh 2000 years and not a single new god!
—*Friedrich Nietzsche,* The Antichrist

30

CHILDREN OF
THE SUN

Perhaps the most significant review of *Imperium* appeared in a 1951 issue of
Der Weg, the Buenos Aires–based literary mouthpiece of the Nazi diaspora.[1]
Der Weg called the book *"ein Lichtblick in der tiefen Dunkelheit unserer
Tage"* (a ray of light in the deep darkness of our time),[2] and concluded that
Imperium would become the *"Bekenntnisbuch der nächsten grossen
europäischer Revolution"* (the bible of the next great European revolution).

Yet what was most important about the review was the reviewer's initials:
"v.L." This was Professor Johann von Leers, *Der Weg's* editor. Born in 1902,
Leers studied law at the universities of Kiel, Berlin, and Rostock. A skilled linguist who spoke fluent Japanese, he worked for a time in the German Foreign
Office. After joining the Nazi Party in 1929, he became the ideological training chief of the Nazi Student League and later served as the director of the
Department of Foreign Studies of the prestigious *Deutsche Hochschule für
Politik* (the German High School for Politics). He then became editor in chief
of Goebbels' *Wille und Weg*.[3] Leers was best known, however, for producing
a seemingly endless stream of anti-Jewish hate literature.[4]

After Germany's defeat, Leers helped organize Nazi escape routes to Latin
America.[5] "There is little doubt," writes historian Kurt Tauber, "that from
the very beginning von Leers played a considerable part in the organization
and running of the underground railroad which permitted the flight of threatened Nazis."[6] He left Europe for Argentina to become *Der Weg's* editor in
1950.

Der Weg was supported by a group of German industrialists including
Ludwig Freude, whose son Rodolfo was private secretary to Juan Perón.

Freude was one of four financiers who controlled much of the wealth sent from Germany to Argentina in the last years of the war in an operation code-named Aktion Feuerland. He worked closely with Ricardo Staudt, a German-Argentine businessman; Dr. Heinrich Dorge, a former aide to Hitler's one-time finance minister Hjalmar Schacht; and Ricardo von Leute, an officer of the Banco Aleman Transatlantico. The Nazi loot was deposited in vaults in the Banco Germanico and Banco Tourquist in the name of Eva Duarte, later Eva Perón.[7]

In 1946 Freude opened a small bookstore called Dürer Haus. The store was managed by Eberhard Fritsch, who was also helping to organize Nazi escape routes to South America.[8] A branch of Dürer Haus called Dürer Verlag began publishing *Der Weg* in June 1947, and by 1948 the magazine's circulation had reached 6,000.[9] (Dürer Verlag also issued the first German edition of Maurice Bardèche's *Nuremberg ou la Terre Promise*.[10]) In his book *Beyond Eagle and Swastika*, Kurt Tauber describes Dürer Verlag as "the source of the most virulent and the boldest Nazi writings then extant."[11] It also appears to have been a central component of the Natinform network created by Goebbels' Propaganda Ministry in South America.[12] As *Der Weg*'s editor, Leers was continuing in his post as a Propaganda Ministry official.

To have *Imperium* so glowingly reviewed by Leers was no small endorsement. What makes Leers particularly interesting, however, is not just his praise for *Imperium* or the fact that he regularly printed German translations of *Frontfighter* stories in *Der Weg*—what is most striking is that he viewed Russia along the same national bolshevik/Eurasian lines as Yockey.[13] In one *Der Weg* essay, entitled "Östliche Prophetie," which introduced two essays by Dostoevski,[14] he even invoked Spengler's "Pseudomorphosis" concept to explain Russia's soul.[15]

Leers also used his essay to attack what he called the "Rosenberg Clique" (the Baltic White Russian Alfred Rosenberg was the Nazi minister for Eastern Affairs during World War II) and its mistaken view of German policy for occupied Russia.[16] He specifically meant Rosenberg's support for the balkanization of the Soviet Union into smaller states under German hegemony. Such a policy had outraged many anti-Bolshevik White Russian exiles who opposed any fracturing of the Russian Empire. Leers later repeated his attack on Rosenberg in a letter to H. Keith Thompson:

> Referring to statements . . . that I have been a friend and collaborator of Rosenberg. I may say that this is indeed an absurdity. It is well known that our opinions were completely opposite in the Russian question. He hated Russia and I have considered every conflict with Russia a catastrophe for Germany, because Russia is too strong for us to be our enemy. Besides that, I have always been convinced that a German-Russian collaboration in the same way of Bismarck is preferable for my country. Because of this so-called

russphily, I have been dismissed on instigation of Alfred Rosenberg and of his anti-Russian assistant Braeutigam,[17] who has even today a high position in Western Germany, by Dr. Goebbels from my position as chief of the Academical Department of the High School of Politics in Berlin, dismissed without a moment's notice! Historical development has demonstrated that I was right.[18]

Tension between Rosenberg and Leers dated back to the 1920s, when Rosenberg became the leading critic of the foreign policy of the Strasser wing of the Nazi Party. Konrad Heiden points out that while the Strassers "wanted to incite all the colored peoples—Chinese, Indians, Persians, Egyptians—against the City of London," Rosenberg regarded the non-Jewish English elite as "the born Aryan ruler of colored 'sub-humanity'" with whom Germany must "systematically and peacefully" divvy up world domination.[19] As director of the Nazi Party's Foreign Affairs Department (*Aussenpolitische Amt*), Rosenberg also struggled to discredit Moeller van den Bruck's influence.[20] He published an article in the 8 December 1933 *Völkischer Beobachter* entitled "*Gegen Tarnung und Verfalschung*" (Against Disguise and Falsehood) lambasting Moeller. Another article in *Wille und Macht* by a Rosenberg supporter attacked Moeller's "obsession with the East."[21]

Leers' turn to the East was intertwined with an intense belief in the occult. A pagan sun-worshipper,[22] he contributed an article for *Der Weg*'s 10th-anniversary issue called "The New World Age," in which he predicted: "It will soon be impossible for people performing miracles with hypnotism, spiritual healing, telepathy, and occultism to be fobbed off with the tribal god Jehovah and to force their new piety into old bottles."[23]

Leers played a leading role in the 1920s Nordic religious revival, along with Professor Jacob Wilhelm Hauer of the German Faith Movement, race theorist Hans F. K. Günther, and Count Ernst Reventlow.[24] His occult connections included his friendship with his fellow sun-worshipper Professor Herman Wirth. Leers devoted a 1951 *Der Weg* article to Wirth: "*Die Forschungen von Herman Wirth*" (The Researches of Herman Wirth).

An academic who had initially specialized in the history of German folksongs, Wirth first achieved prominence in 1928 with an enormous work called *Der Aufgang der Menschheit* (The Rise of Mankind). He argued that Nordic man's original homeland was neither India nor the Russian steppes but a far-north Arctic/Atlantic "solar" culture. Using arguments about continental drift derived from the geologist Alfred Wegener, he claimed the shifting of continents and polar drift had driven the original inhabitants south. Remnants of this primal Nordic people, however, still survived in the blond, bearded Eskimos found by Knud Rasmussen on his 1906–07 Thule Expedition.[25]

Wirth led the *Forschungs-und Lehrgemeinschaft "Das Ahnenerbe"* (The Heritage of Our Ancestors' Group for Research and Teaching). Originally a private study group (the Herman Wirth Gesellschaft), the Ahnenerbe later came under the personal control of Heinrich Himmler. In a sense Leers was the "founder" of the Ahnenerbe, because he first put Wirth in touch with Himmler.[26] He may have done so in part to counter the influence of Alfred Rosenberg's think tank, the Kampfbund für deutsche Kultur.[27] Wirth strongly believed in matriarchy and argued that the early Germans were goddess-worshippers.[28] His "Great Mother" views particularly enraged Rosenberg: One account even claims that after Wirth left the Ahnenerbe in the late 1930s, Rosenberg tried to put him in a concentration camp.[29] Leers also seems to have been a goddess-worshipper; his wife believed that she was the reincarnation of a Bronze Age priestess.[30]

Wirth and Leers were friends of Richard Walther Darré, the Nazi minister of agriculture who is sometimes called the leader of the "Green" or ecological wing of the NSDAP. Leers first met Darré in Munich in 1927, and the two men became so close that Darré later wrote Hitler to personally vouch for Leers. Darré, who helped finance the early Ahnenerbe with funds from the Agriculture Ministry, owed much of his political success to Rudolf Hess. Both Hess and Darré were strong proponents of organic farming, so much so that they tried to protect followers of the anthroposophist leader Rudolf Steiner from the Gestapo because the anthroposophists had been in the vanguard of the German organic farming movement.

Nor was Leers' favorable opinion of Russia unique inside the Nordic Revival network. This German "new age" movement was surprisingly complex and filled with many unexpected political twists. Eugen Diederichs, the movement's leading publisher,[31] believed that America, not Russia, was Germany's real enemy. To Diederichs, "Americanism" meant "collective mass-thinking" and "the death of all independent thought and action which arises from inner spiritual principles." Americanism lacked "any higher perspective . . . It is Mammonism with its corresponding love of mere pleasure" and "the leveling shallowness of the large city, with its directionless, manipulated masses."[32]

Against America stood Russia. Like Moeller van den Bruck, Diederichs thought that Russia symbolized the rejection of modernism, rationalism, and materialism. This is why he "found much in the new, Bolshevik Russia which was a welcome alternative to the bankrupt values of the West."[33] He praised the "deeply rooted religious, mystical spirit of the Russian people" as well as "new, less materialistic attitudes towards private property which seemed to be emerging in the Soviet Union" in the early 1920s.[34] Like the Eurasians, Diederichs believed that "the coming of a new antirational era founded on intuition and the domination of Dionysus over Apollo, an age 'in which we must think irrationally, and above all, act irrationally'" would finally topple Romano-Germanic universalism.[35]

Der Weg's publisher, Dürer Verlag, had symbolic ties to the Diederichs circle. According to one scholar, Dürer Verlag was "named after a pre-war conservative-volkish literary circle in Germany and [was] in touch with its surviving members."[36] This is almost certainly a reference to the poet Ferdinand Avenarius's Dürer League. Avenarius created the journal *Der Kunstwart* (The Artistic Guardian) and the Dürer League in 1887. To Diederichs, Avenarius was more than a close friend; he was also a spiritual mentor, trusted advisor, and "one of the driving forces in the recovery of the German Volk."[37]

Another important volkish theorist with a surprising Russian twist was Artur Dinter, who achieved widespread success in 1922 with a bizarre anti-Semitic bestseller entitled *Die Sünde wider das Blut* (The Sin Against the Blood).[38] He too had occult leanings: Historian George Mosse notes that Dinter's follow-up book, *The Sin Against the Spirit*, freely mixed racial ideology with "episodes that could have been taken from Madame Blavatsky."[39] Yet Dinter opened the pages of the journal of his *Geistchristliche Religionsgemeinschaft* (Spiritual Christian Religious Community) to writers from national bolshevist groups like Ernst Niekisch's *Widerstandkreis* (Resistance), Ernst Jünger's *Kommenden* (The Vanguard), and Otto Strasser's *Revolutionäre Nationalsozialisten*. Dinter "even supported an alliance with Soviet communism," because he believed that after Trotsky's downfall, Bolshevism had evolved into "a 'Russian National Socialism.'"[40]

It was not completely surprising, then, that one of Herman Wirth's closest Ahnenerbe collaborators was a former Freikorps member and "left-wing" Conservative Revolutionary named Friedrich Hielscher. A self-proclaimed foreign policy expert, Hielscher repeatedly denounced colonialism and imperialism.[41] A talented orator with a small but influential following among Berlin's student circles, in the 1920s he "was forever organizing meetings and rallies for representatives of 'oppressed peoples'—usually African, Indian, and Chinese youths studying at German universities."[42] One of Hielscher's closest friends, SS Colonel Wolfram Sievers, actually ran the day-to-day affairs of the Ahnenerbe until its demise in 1945.[43]

Heinrich Himmler soon became the Ahnenerbe's most powerful sponsor. A utopian pastoralist of sorts, Himmler as a young man had developed close ties to the Artamenen, a 1920s utopian colony led by Willibald Hentschel. Hentschel first came to prominence in 1907 with his book *Varuna*,[44] in which he envisioned the formation of a Germanic racial utopia called Mittgart that would be nudist, land-rooted, anti-modern, and polygamous.[45] He updated his vision in a 1923 pamphlet entitled *Was soll nun aus uns werden?* (What Shall Become of Us?), in which "he called for a concerted effort to form a company of fighting knights to protect the German earth."[46] After he declared that the deity of the Aryan race was the god Artam, his movement (which called on German youth to join its peasant communes and purify themselves of the city) became known as the Artamenen. Himmler became one of the group's most ardent supporters, as did Hielscher's close friend Wolfram Sievers.[47]

Like many members of the Nordic Revival movement, Himmler particularly hated the Catholic Church. After Ahnenerbe genealogical research showed that he was related to women killed during the Great European Witch Hunt in the Middle Ages, Himmler held the Church responsible for genocide against his ancestors. In 1935 the SS leader even set up an Ahnenerbe unit called *Sonderkommando H* (Special Unit H, the H standing for *Hexen*, or *witch*) to study the question. Special Unit H had at least 20 researchers, including some scholars taken from concentration camps, as well as Himmler's cousin Wilhelm Patin, who had been a Catholic priest before joining the SS.[48] The group spent the next eight years collecting material on the witch-trial period that Himmler may have intended to use against the Catholic Church. He also hoped that the group's research would help uncover traces of the original German folk religion.

Although Nazi Agriculture Minister Richard Walther Darré actually paid for the formal creation of the Ahnenerbe in July 1935, Himmler quickly became its most powerful patron.[49] Wirth's group was incorporated into the *Abeilung für Kulturelle Forschung* (Section for Cultural Research) of Himmler's personal staff, the Personlicher Stab RISS, in November 1936. After a falling-out with Darré, Himmler appointed SS Colonel Bruno Galke as his special representative to the Ahnenerbe. Galke dismissed Wirth, who was considered Darré's eyes and ears inside the group. He was replaced as Ahnenerbe president by Dr. Walther Wüst, an SS senior colonel and dean of Munich University, where he also held the chair of Aryan Culture and Linguistics.[50]

Himmler and Darré were particularly divided over the question of German expansion to the East. Both agreed in principle that the future of Germany depended on the flourishing of its peasantry. They also were united in the idea that the German peasantry must expand east into old Germanic territory. But how far east?

Darré believed that a close bond between people and soil was fundamental.[51] He feared that German expansionism threatened to turn into a new form of nomadic "cosmopolitanism" that would destroy the German peasantry by artificially relocating it on foreign soil. Small farmers would be transformed into corrupt colonialist overlords.[52]

Like his Führer, Himmler argued that Aryan man was a natural conqueror and enslaver of inferior cultures, including the Slavs.[53] Darré's sympathetic English biographer, Anna Bramwell, believes that the basic difference between the two men "was that Darré was a racial tribalist, and Himmler an imperialist with romantic racial overtones."[54] Darré found the popular image of Aryan nomadic conquerors moving from land to land particularly abhorrent. Wasn't the quintessential nomad the rootless Jew, and wasn't Jewish communism just "a cover for nomadic exploitation of settled communities"?[55] The tragedy of Germany was that its peasantry had been dominated by a series of alien overlords, including Christianity, Charlemagne, and capitalism. As for the Catholic Church, it was little more than a "camouflaged army: The mass-murder of Saxons at Verdun was its bloody crown." Charlemagne brought Christianity to Germany by slaughtering thousands of German peasants at Altenesch, and Darré felt that Altenesch, "not the crucifixion . . . should be our holy place."[56]

Darré also praised the radical Peasant Revolt of 1525. Nor was his glorification of the Peasant Revolt a personal quirk. Otto Strasser's Black Front "flew the black flag of the postmedieval Peasants' Wars," which Arthur Moeller van den Bruck had proclaimed "the banner of Germany's reawakening."[57] Nor were peasant revolts a relic of Germany's distant past. There had been a massive uprising of farmers who battled both police and landlords in Schleswig-Holstein during the late 1920s, and at times the movement bordered on insurrection. Many Conservative Revolutionaries endorsed the uprising, and government buildings were bombed to support the revolt.[58]

Darré, much like the Eurasians, despised the Teutonic Knights. He was so opposed to the notion that the Third Reich should follow in the footsteps of the Teutonic Knights that he wrote the introduction to a book called *Why Colonies?* in opposition to unlimited Eastern expansion.

Even after the downfall of Darré's ally Herman Wirth, Wolfram Sievers continued to run the day-to-day affairs of the Ahnenerbe—an enormous undertaking. The Ahnenerbe sent teams of scholars across the world and had dozens of research bureaus, including one for runes; one for folk tales, fairy tales, and myth; a group that examined wild plant species; and another that specialized in "Volkmedizin." It even had a special unit called the *Ueberprufung des sogenannten Geheimwissenschaften* (Examination of the So-Called Occult Sciences). The Ahnenerbe studied Venus idols, medieval witch trials, and eighth-century Church councils that contained material on German folklore. In Scandinavia the Ahnenerbe examined prehistoric monuments. It also became deeply involved in cultural-political activities in Belgium and the Netherlands. It even began a comprehensive study of the famous 11th-century Bayeux tapestry that portrayed the conquest of England by the Normans.[59] In 1942, while German troops were fighting at Stalingrad, the Ahnenerbe was pressing hard for the creation of a special institute to study Tibet.[60]

The Ahnenerbe also became involved in the task of building a new culture for Nazi-controlled Europe. RSHA leaders Franz Alfred Six and Werner Best used the Ahnenerbe to help forge an ideological/cultural vision for the Waffen SS, and Six supplied Sievers with SD money for this purpose.[61] The Ahnenerbe was specifically assigned the task of "reviving and strengthening... Germanic consciousness among European groups regarded as 'ethnic' Germans"; the organization published a *Germanische Leithefte* (Germanic Guidebook) in German, Flemish, Dutch, Danish, and Norwegian for Waffen-SS volunteers.

Wolfram Sievers was tried as a major war criminal at Nuremberg and was hanged for crimes against humanity on 2 June 1948. His downfall came about because of Ahnenerbe-sponsored "scientific experiments." Under its auspices, Bolshevik political commissars captured by the Nazis and held in Auschwitz were decapitated. Their severed heads were then shipped to Munich for phrenological study by Professor Hirt of the Ahnenerbe's Institute of Scientific Research for National Defense. The Ahnenerbe was also involved in the infamous Dachau "experiments" where victims were thrown into ice cold water and timed as they froze to death so that scientists could develop better equipment for Luftwaffe pilots shot down over the North Sea.

At his trial, Sievers denied that he had anything to do with such experiments, claiming that he had merely acted as a "mailman" for orders from his superiors. Friedrich Hielscher also appeared in court to offer testimony in Sievers' defense. Between 1933 and 1944 Hielscher had helped, or tried to help, all kinds of Nazi victims; he was even in contact with some of the 20 July 1944 plotters.[62] He said that Sievers was really a member of Gruppe Hielscher, his anti-Hitler resistance network, and that Sievers had entered the Ahnenerbe as a member of Gruppe Hielscher. After Hielscher was jailed by the Gestapo in September 1944, he revealed that he was only saved from a most unpleasant fate by Sievers' intervention.

The friendship between Hielscher and Sievers was particularly striking since Hielscher had long favored a national bolshevist policy toward Russia. The Nazis even raided his house in 1933 because they thought he might be a Communist.[63] Hielscher and his friend Ernst Jünger also knew Georg Lukács, the Marxist philosopher and sometime Comintern agent. Jünger, Hielscher, and Lukács were all members of a 1920s Berlin study group called the *Arbeitskreis für Planwirtschaft* (Working Circle for Planned Economy— ARPLAN).[64] ARPLAN worked closely with the Soviet embassy in Berlin and helped organized economic research missions to the USSR. Its director, Arvid Harnack, later became a top *Rote Kapelle* (Red Orchestra) spy for Soviet military intelligence.[65]

After the leading German Communist and China expert Karl Wittfogel was placed in a concentration camp, his wife Olga Lang contacted Hielscher, who had sponsored meetings between Wittfogel, Lukács, and Jünger. He immediately agreed to help get Wittfogel out of the camp.[66] Hielscher told Lang to contact Karl Haushofer using Haushofer's son Albrecht as a go-between. Haushofer, in turn, pressured Rudolf Hess for Wittfogel's release. As Karl Wittfogel recalled:

> At the end of the Weimar period, I wrote a comprehensive book, almost eight hundred pages, *Wirtschaft und Gesellschaft Chinas*. While in the concentration camp, I heard that Haushofer, who had a great influence on Rudolf Hess at the time, had asked: "Hess, do you know that Wittfogel has written the most important book in Germany on Chinese economy? Why don't you release him?" Hess allegedly answered: "That may be so, but of all German intellectuals he has also written the worst things about the Führer. He stays put!"[67]

Wittfogel was freed only after Hielscher mobilized some of his nationalist friends inside the Nazi Party (and after Prussia's interior minister was convinced that it was astrologically correct to release him).

Olga Lang reports in her unpublished memoirs that she was even advised to approach Johann von Leers to get help for her husband's release by Russian expert Klaus Mehnert, an ARPLAN member and Strasser supporter who worked with Professor Otto Hoetzsch's East Europe Institute.[68] As a Russian, Communist, and Jew, Lang was flabbergasted. Mehnert, however, assured her that Leers was "one of those National Socialists who take socialism seriously."

Given that Sievers was in Hielscher's circle, is there any reason to believe that he was secretly "anti-Nazi"? Professor Michael Kater, a leading scholar of the Ahnenerbe, correctly points out that Himmler's "Minister of Culture" at all times acted as the perfect SS technocrat.[69] Still, *something* was going on.[70] It may also be significant that Hielscher's trail leads back to General Haushofer. Was it of no consequence that as the war ground to an end, Haushofer insisted that the future danger to Europe would come from America and not the Soviet Union? In a 1944 essay entitled "Geopolitical Latitudinal and Longitudinal Dynamics," Haushofer wrote:

> Compared to the elemental dynamic force of American imperialism, the Eurafrica idea, and the attempts of the Soviet Union to push southward to the warm ocean, drop into the background. While in East Asia the North-South development has a natural tendency to limit itself to its own sphere, America already extends rapacious hands to tropical Africa, Iran, India, and Australia. By using its Pan-American supremacy as a jumping-off point for further expansion east and west, the U.S. seeks to establish the basis for its world empire and to threaten future opponents with a third world war. This American north-south empire represents the only real danger of imperialis-

tic world domination. [Thus] the blood-soaked Caspian and Black Sea plains have become secondary theaters of war.[71]

When Leers had *Der Weg* promote both *Imperium* and the European Liberation Front, there is reason to think that he did so because of, and not in spite of, Yockey's "Russian turn."

Notes:

1. *Der Weg*, Vol. 5, No. 9. For a report on the postwar Nazi network in South America, see the January 1950 issue of the Wiener Library *Bulletin*.

2. *Der Weg's* review began: "Dieses Buch, das Liddel Hart als 'Werk eines Genius' bezeichnet und der Generalmajor J. F. C. Fuller 'das prophetischste Buch seit Spenglers *Untergang des Abendlandes*' nannte, ist in der Tat ein Lichblick in der tiefen Dunkelheit unserer Tage."

3. Philip Rees, *Biographical Dictionary of the Extreme Right Since 1890* (New York: Simon & Schuster, 1990).

4. Kurt Tauber (who called Leers "Hitler's number-one anti-Semite") cites some of his publications, including *Fourteen Years of the Jew-Republic* (1933), *Jews Are Looking at You* (1937), *History on a Racial Basis* (1934), *The Criminality of Jewry* (1937), *Blood and Race in Legislation* (1938) "and 22 others." See Kurt Tauber, *Beyond Eagle and Swastika* (Middletown, CT: Wesleyan University Press, 1967), Vol. 2, fn. 176, p. 1112.

5. In a letter to an American rightist who had asked for his photo, Leers offered a bit of his postwar biography:

> I fled from an American camp and a Russian prison. I freed friends out of the hands of the occupying forces using many different disguises in a two-year underground work in Germany after the war and so I learned that who so wants to fight Jewish world power must always be ready to disappear, and, therefore, never must give his gun and his picture away, so I am sorry I can't send you my picture. [Leers to Mana Truhill, 15 February 1954, in the Non-Sectarian Anti-Nazi League (NSANL) archives, Columbia University.]

6. Tauber, *Beyond Eagle and Swastika*, Vol. 1, p. 243.

7. When the Peróns eventually tried to take control of the funds, all four men died violent deaths. See Gerald Posner, *Mengele: The Complete Story* (New York: John Ware, 1986), p. 100. Also see Glenn Infield, *Skorzeny: Hitler's Commando* (New York: Military Heritage Press, 1981), p. 202.

8. One indication of Fritsch's role comes from a 5 March 1948 letter from a rightist living in England named G. F. Green, who published a journal called *Independent Nationalist*. Green informed his correspondent (whose name has been blanked out):

> I am asked by Fritsch to try [to] trace a small sailing ship, the *Falken*, which left Sweden about 29 January with 21 Germans on board. You can guess the how and why. No port is named and the ship's flag was not stated, nor if she is "registered." She was sailing for the Argentine. An Argentine officer named Fritz

Schultz (?) organized it all. There has been no news of her since. Fritsch urgently asks me to try [to] get data ... I have made cautious enquiries through friendly Press Attachés at one or two Embassies here. I can get no news. I am, of course, already in touch with Sweden, they are on the job ... The Russians were hot on the heels of some of the boys. [Green's letter from the John Metcalfe collection at the Hoover Institute.]

Green's correspondent may have been the New York rightist and Yockey friend Fred Weiss, because in another letter Green thanks Mrs. Weiss. Recall that Fred Weiss wrote for *Der Weg* and that H. Keith Thompson was the *Der Weg*/Dürer Verlag U.N. correspondent as well as a *Der Weg* author.

9. From an article in the October–December 1956 issue of the Buenos Aires magazine *Commentario*, the organ of the *Instituto Judio Argentino de Cultura e Informacion*, cited in the *Bulletin* of the Wiener Institute (Vol. XI, No. 1–2, 1957). Also see Ronald C. Newton, *The "Nazi Menace" In Argentina, 1931–1947* (Stanford, CA: Stanford University Press, 1992). Newton mentions *Der Weg* and the Kameradschaft network in Argentina, Brazil, and Chile on pp. 380–81.

10. Tauber, *Beyond Eagle and Swastika*, Vol. 1, p. 615.

11. Ibid., Vol. 1, p. 628.

12. Recall that Natinform smuggled anti-war crimes trials propaganda publications like General Jodl's letters to his wife back to Germany as early as 1946.

13. *Der Weg* did not hide its Eastern orientation:

Der Weg's propaganda was anti-Communist, but never anti-Soviet. The political gyration by which some German generals and even army groups had been able to spin right into the Soviet camp when Red troops occupied part of Germany was apparent in *Der Weg*. Obviously, it was "the way" by which many a still fanatically devoted Nazi could see ahead to a resurgent future, allied with the Soviet even though berating the fascism of the left, Communism. [Guenther Reinhardt, *Crime Without Punishment* (New York: Hermitage House, 1952), p. 168.]

14. These were an 1877 essay entitled "Russia and Europe" and an 1881 piece entitled "Russia and Asia."

15. In the 1930s, however, Leers helped lead the Nazi Propaganda Ministry's assault on Spengler. From Alastair Hamilton, *The Appeal of Fascism* (London: Anthony Blond, 1971), p. 155:

Johann von Leers, Leader of the Division of Foreign Policy and Information in the German High School for Politics, claimed that Spengler was a dangerous opponent of National Socialism, a reactionary who jeopardized Germany's relations with Japan by including the Japanese amongst the colored races endangering the whites in *The Hour of Decision*.

16. Leers wrote: "Als sie durch die unverzeihlichen Missgriffe in Russland, geboren aus baltischem Ressentiment der unseligen Rosenberg-Clique und aus völligem Missverstehen des russischen Menschen, erkannten."

The influence of the "Rosenberg Clique" in the Nazi Party is also described in Robert C. Williams, *Culture in Exile* (Ithaca, NY: Cornell University Press, 1972), p. 221:

> The traditional anti-Semitism of the Russian and Baltic German upper classes now was absorbed into the German attitude towards Russia. "The East" was something Asiatic, barbaric, and Jewish, a threat to the old Europe; this was the central message of Balts and Russian monarchists in emigration. But even within the Nazi party they were sometimes hard pressed to defend themselves against a rising tide of pro-Russian sentiment in Weimar Germany, on the right as well as on the left. By the mid-1920s, Rosenberg's capitalist, anti-Eastern, and colonial view of Russia was being challenged by a socialist, anti-Western, and anti-colonial view popular in the North German [Strasser] wing of the party which romanticized both Russia and Germany as part of the coming East, the new, less developed nations in revolt against the old Europe.

17. On Otto Braeutigam, see Gerald Reitlinger, *The SS: Alibi of a Nation* (New York: Viking Press, 1957), fn. 1, p. 186.

18. Letter from Leers to H. Keith Thompson. Leers had moved to Cairo and was now calling himself Prof. Dr. Omar Amin von Leers. Leers may be referring to a period when Goebbels was working in alliance with Rosenberg, around the time the Nazis organized the Anti-Komintern. See Walter Laqueur, *Russia and Germany: A Century of Conflict* (Boston: Little, Brown, 1965), p. 180.

19. Konrad Heiden, *Der Fuehrer* (Boston: Houghton Mifflin, 1944) pp. 327–28. See also Robert C. Williams, *Culture in Exile*, p. 221.

20. Moeller van den Bruck committed suicide in 1924, after suffering a nervous breakdown.

21. It also became more difficult to acquire works by Moeller as bookstores ceased to restock. In 1936 a work by Helmut Rödel that strongly condemned Moeller's views on race was published with NSDAP endorsement. See *The Scorpion*, No. 12, Winter 1988/89.

22. On Leers and sun worship, see George L. Mosse, *The Crisis of German Ideology* (New York: Schocken Books, 1981), pp. 71–72.

23. Cited in the *Bulletin* of the Wiener Institute, No. 5–6, 1956. According to this report, Leers had been arguing along these lines since his 1934 booklet *Der Kardinal und die Germanen*. Eberhard Fritsch is also cited as saying that people read *Der Weg* because "it is the old paganism that was aroused in them."

24. In *Beyond Eagle and Swastika*, Kurt Tauber writes that the German Faith Movement (*Deutsche Glaubensbewegung*) of Professor Jacob Wilhelm Hauer tried to create itself (along with the Catholics and Protestants) as the Third Church of the Third Reich, which would respect the person of Jesus while creating a Nordic-Germanic religion (Vol. 1, p. 654). "Under the leadership of Hauer, Johann von Leers, Hans F. K. Günther, Herman Wirth (the racist mythologist of 'Atlanticism'), and Count Ernst Reventlow (one of the earliest folkish Hitlerites), the German Faith Movement represented a merger of a variety of folkish, neopagan, 'Teutonic' religions." (*Beyond Eagle and Swastika*, Vol. 2, fn. 59, p. 1269.) Count Ernst zu Reventlow was a leading Volk racialist and a former member of the German Racist

Party. A one-time Strasser supporter who later went over to Hitler, he was a cautious proponent of possible German-Soviet collaboration against the West.

25. Joscelyn Godwin, *Arktos: The Polar Myth* (Grand Rapids, MI: Phanes Press, 1993), p. 56. An earlier book, entitled *The Arctic Home of the Vedas*, by an Indian nationalist scholar of the Vedas named B. G. Tilak, used astronomical evidence to argue for an original Aryan Arctic homeland.

26. James Webb, *The Occult Establishment* (La Salle, IL: Open Court, 1976), p. 322. Webb reports:

> Wirth's eccentricities were personal as well as scholarly, and visitors to his house at Doberan passed a sign reading: "Please walk softly and don't smoke: A deep breather lives here." The professor believed that his wife was a clairvoyant, and when Friedrich Hielscher called at Doberan for a vegetarian meal, he was greeted by the total silence of his hostess, who sat impassively with her brow bound by a golden fillet while Professor Wirth interpreted her thoughts by telepathy.

27. James Webb says in *The Occult Establishment* (p. 322) that Rosenberg also attacked the credibility of a document entitled the *Ura-Linda Chronicle*, which Wirth had used in his research. In *Politique et Tradition: Julius Evola dans le Siècle (1898–1974)* (Paris: Kime, 1992), Christophe Boutin presents the Ahnenerbe as Himmler's vehicle against a group of other Nazi leaders' think tanks:

> Rosenberg fondait en 1927 une association qui deviendra en 1929 le *Kampfbund für deutsche Kultur*, et dont l'un des réprésentants les plus importants fut Hans Grimm, quand Joseph Goebbels créait pour sa part en 1933 le *Reichskulturkammer*. Sous la pression de Hilter, les deux institutions durent fusionner en avril 1934 dans la *Parteiamtliche Prufung Kommission*, mais l'opposition entre deux hommes n'en demeura pas moins. Pendant ce temps, Himmler possèdait, avec Ahnenerbe, son propre organe de recherches culturelles. Ces groupes avaient des politiques culturelles differentes, qui réflétaient les choix de leurs créateurs. Goebbels par example, appréciait Van Gogh, Munch, ou Nolde, alors que Rosenberg qualifiait ce dernier de "peintre négroïde" (p. 269).

28. On Wirth's mother-cult idea, see his 1931 book *Was heisst deutsch?* Wirth's theories are cited in Jost Hermand, "All Power to the Women: Nazi Concepts of Matriarchy," in the October 1984 issue of the *Journal of Contemporary History* (Vol. 19, No. 4), fn. 67, p. 666. Herman mentions the "ideas of Herman Wirth, who had proposed highly controversial theories of the '*Allmuter Gottes*' and the '*Urgermanen Matriarchat*' in the early 1920s and had met with Hitler, Hess, and Rosenberg." Also see Godwin, *Arktos: The Polar Myth*, p. 56, and Eduard Gugenberger and Roman Schweidlenka, *Mutter Erde/Magic und Politik* (Vienna: Verlag für Gesellschaftskritik, 1987), pp. 117–23.

29. Godwin, *Arktos: The Polar Myth*, p. 56.

30. "[Leers'] wife believed herself to be the reincarnation of a Bronze Age priestess, and held regular meetings at their house, where she would wear barbaric gold jewelry. Other guests included an Austrian who had renamed himself Weisthor, the White Thor, to the irritation of some of the more aristocratic guests, who pointed out to each other that Weisthor's real name was more plebeian." (Anna

Bramwell, *Blood and Soil: Walther Darré and Hitler's "Green Party"* [Bourne End, Buckinghamshire: Kensal Press, 1985], pp. 49–50.]

"Weisthor" was "Himmler's Rasputin," Karl Maria Willigut (1866–1946), who claimed to be the last living representative of German sages or shamans from a prehistoric era. Willigut said he was in contact with them through clairvoyant memory. In September 1933 Wiligut joined the SS as "Karl Maria Weisthor." According to Nicholas Goodrick-Clarke, *The Occult Roots of Nazism* (Wellingborough, Northhamptonshire: The Aquarian Press, 1985), p. 188:

> By spring 1935 Weisthor had moved from Munich to Berlin, where he continued his work in the Chief Adjutant's office of the Reichsführer-SS Personal Staff...
> In September 1936 he was promoted SS-Brigadeführer (brigadier) in the Reichsführer-SS Personal Staff.

During this time, Weisthor's regular visitors included Leers.

For a brief critical overview of the Nazi "ecological" current, see Janet Biehl and Peter Staudenmaier, *Ecofascism: Lessons from the German Experience* (San Francisco: AK Press, 1995).

31. Diederichs also published Wirth's *The Rise of Mankind*.

32. Gary Stark, *Entrepreneurs of Ideology* (Chapel Hill: University of North Carolina Press, 1981), p. 177.

33. Ibid.

34. Ibid., p. 178. German Volk romanticism was not a unique phenomenon. Modern day Zionism, for example, was strongly influenced by German volkish ideas. See George L. Mosse, *Germans and Jews* (New York: Howard Fertig, 1970). It is also interesting to note that in 1909 Diederichs published Martin Buber's anthology of Jewish mysticism, *Ecstatic Confessions*.

35. Ibid., p. 176.

36. Newton, *The Nazi "Menace" in Argentina*, p. 380.

37. Stark, *Entrepreneurs of Ideology*, p. 79.

38. Lines in *Mein Kampf* like "The black-haired Jew-boy, with a look of satanic glee, stalks the innocent girl to violate her with his blood and rend her from her people" paid homage to Dinter's literary style.

39. George Mosse, "The Mystical Origins of National Socialism," *Journal of the History of Ideas*, January–March 1961, Vol. XXII, No. 1, p. 88.

40. From an essay by Günter Hartung called "Artur Dinter: A Successful Fascist Author in Pre-Fascist Germany" (pp. 109–10), in *The Attractions of Fascism* (New York: St. Martin's Press, 1990), edited by John Milfull.

41. On Hielscher and national bolsheviks like Ernst Niekisch, see the appendix "Three Patron Saints of Red Fascism."

42. James Joseph Ward, "Ernst Niekisch and National Bolshevism in Weimar Germany" (unpublished Ph.D. thesis, NYU, 1973), p. 138.

43. For the most detailed description of the Ahnenerbe's origin, see Michael Kater, *Das "Ahnenerbe" der SS 1935–45: Ein Beitrag zur Kulturpolitik des Dritten Reiches* (Stuttgart: Deutsche Verlag-Anstalt, 1974).

44. In *The Crisis of German Ideology*, George Mosse reports that in its time *Varuna* "was considered to be as influential as Spengler's work in the formation of a general, popular state of mind" (p. 113).

45. Hentschel set the ratio of men to women in Mittgart as one hundred men to one thousand women.

46. Mosse, *The Crisis of German Ideology*, p. 116.

47. Eric Dorn Brose, in his essay "Generic Fascism Revisited: Attitudes Toward Technology in Germany and Italy, 1919–1945," in *German Studies Review* (Vol. 10, No. 2, May 1987), calls Himmler "a former Artam functionary."

48. Cited from an article by Patricia Clough in the 22 October 1994 *Sunday Times* of London, republished in *Fortean Times*, No. 81, p. 39. Nazi hatred of the Catholic Church is well documented in *The Persecution of the Catholic Church in the Third Reich: Facts and Documents* (London: Burns Oates, 1940).

49. Robin Lumsden, *The Black Corps* (Shepperton: Ian Allan Publishing, 1992), p. 107.

50. Ibid.

51. Bramwell, *Blood and Soil*, p. 52.

52. The question of the peasantry was linked to debates over the decline of the West. A crucial figure in the debate was Leo Frobenius, head of the Research Institute for Kulturmorphologie in Frankfurt. See Robert Casillo, *The Genealogy of Demons* (Evanston, IL: Northwestern University Press, 1983), Chapter Six. Also see Suzanne Marchand, "Leo Frobenius and the Revolt Against the West," *Journal of Contemporary History*, Vol. 32, No. 2 (1997). The peasantry question also greatly concerned Heidegger, who met Darré in the 1920s.

53. Himmler, unlike Alfred Rosenberg, did not believe in breaking up the former Russian empire into German-dominated satrapies. He believed that the Slavs were little better than slaves whose only function was to serve the German colonists. He was supported in his beliefs by both Hitler and Martin Bormann.

54. Bramwell, *Blood and Soil*, pp. 130–31. On Bramwell's politics, see Nick Toczek, *The Bigger Tory Vote* (Stirling, Scotland: AK Press, 1992), pp. 5–9.

55. When Stalin announced his doctrine of "Socialism in One Country," some on the German right argued that he had finally abandoned classic Marxist doctrine for a "national socialistic Russia." See Klemens von Klemperer, "Toward a Fourth Reich? The History of National Bolshevism in Germany," in *Review of Politics*, No. 13 (1951), p. 203.

56. Hitler's Secretary Martin Bormann also hated Charlemagne. His wife Gerda told her children: "Through Charlemagne Christianity and with it Jewry got a foothold in our regions." (From a 12 September 1944 letter from Gerda to Martin Bormann. Cited in Gerald Reitlinger, *The SS: Alibi of a Nation* [New York: Viking, 1957].)

57. Tauber, *Beyond Eagle and Swastika*, Vol. 1, p. 109.

58. Hitler's reluctance to have the NSDAP support the uprising was given as further proof of his conservative nature and fear of alienating the German establishment.

59. See the essay "War-Time Activities of the SS-Ahnenerbe" by Fritz Epstein, in *On the Track of Tyranny: Essays Presented by the Wiener Library to Leonard G. Montefiore O.B.E.*, edited by Max Beloff (London: Vallentine, Mitchell, 1960).

60. This was the *Reichsinstitut für Innerasienforschung* or *Tibetforschung*, also known as the *Reichsinstitut "Sven Hedin" für Innerasienforschung*. The group was headed by Dr. Ernst Schaefer, who had led an earlier Ahnenerbe-sponsored research mission to Tibet. In *Sven Hedin's German Diary, 1935–41* (Dublin: Euphorian Books, 1951), the famous explorer writes about his meetings with Himmler and their discussions concerning Schaefer and Tibet. On 4 November 1940 Hedin visited Schaefer's Research Institute on Tibet at the University of Munich, where he was introduced in a speech by Karl Haushofer. In a later visit to Germany, in June 1942, Schaefer and University of Munich rector and Ahnenerbe President Wüst told Hedin that they were planning to found the "Reich Institute for Exploration of Central Asia 'Sven Hedin'" at the University of Munich with Heinrich Himmler's support. In January 1943 Hedin attended the opening of the Institute.

61. Lumsden, *The Black Corps*, p. 107.

62. In his *Review of Politics* essay on national bolshevism, Klemens von Klemperer reports that Count Stauffenberg (who planted the bomb that almost killed Hitler) was, like his friend Count Fritz von der Schulenburg, a disciple of Strasser and that both men flirted with the idea of a workers', soldiers', and peasants' revolution.

63. G. Ulman, *The Science of Society* (The Hague: Mouton, 1978), p. 162. Ernst Jünger's house was also raided. In the 1920s Hielscher and Jünger worked on a journal called *Arminius*, which was financed by Freikorps leader Captain Ehrhardt. See Roger Woods, *Ernst Jünger and the Nature of Political Commitment* (Stuttgart: Akedemischer Verlag Hans-Dieter Heinz, 1982). Hielscher and Jünger remained friends during World War II.

64. Jünger's *Der Arbeiter* (The Worker) should be seen in this context. It also had an impact on the thinking of Martin Heidegger. In this regard, see Pierre Bourdieu, *The Political Ontology of Martin Heidegger* (Cambridge, U.K.: Polity, 1991). Bourdieu also looks at Spengler's influence on Heidegger. An important work devoted to Jünger is John Orr, "German Social Theory and the Hidden Face of Technology," in the *Archiv. europ. sociol.*, Vol. XV, No. 2 (1974), also listed as the *European Journal of Sociology*.

65. John Costello and Oleg Tsarev, *Deadly Illusions* (New York: Crown Publishers, 1993), p. 73. Here ARPLAN is translated as *Arbeitgemeinschaft zum Studium der Sowjetrussichen*.

66. Olga Lang describes her first meeting with Hielscher this way:

> He opened the door himself. He was wearing an old-fashioned dressing-gown made of a kind of Oriental material red with a yellow pattern. His clean-shaven head was adorned with a tarkish with a tassel. A long waterpipe in his hand put the last touch to the figure of a German Spiesser (bourgeois) reminding me of Wilhelm Busch caricatures. Yet Friedrich Hielscher was not a German Spiesser. There was in him a touch of E. T. A. Hoffmann's fantastic characters, and he was

a talented, although not well known, political writer and philosopher . . . He despised me somewhat, not because of my race but because I was a woman; but he did it so openly that I really did not mind.

67. Interview with Karl Wittfogel by Matthias Greffrath, Fritz Raddatz, and Michel Korzec in *Telos*, No. 43, Spring 1980.

68. For a discussion of Hoetzsch's institute (The German Society for the Study of Eastern Europe), see Walter Laqueur, *Russia and Germany*, pp. 179–80.

69. Kater, *"Das Ahnenerbe" der SS, 1935–45*, pp. 313–38. It is also worth noting that Sievers' son is currently editor of a "New Right" journal called *Hyperborea*.

70. Hielscher's ties to Sievers are also discussed in Louis Pauwels and Jacques Bergier, *Morning of the Magicians* (New York: Stein and Day, 1964).

71. Haushofer's essay is cited in *Prevent World War III*, Vol. 1, No. 6, December 1944.

31
THE
WATCHERS

The extent and nature of Yockey's own belief in the occult remains unknown because we lack access to his writings on the subject.[1] What seems clear, however, is that occultism played a real role in his thinking, as the titles to his essays on "polarity" strongly suggest. The FBI discovered that he was carrying in his suitcase a list of book titles like *Cosmic Rays, Your Second Body*, and *Reincarnation*. His Oakland friend Alexander Scharf also recalled his alluding to paganism, telling him that he believed not in one god but in many gods.

Equally interesting is a cryptic reference to item 23 in the FBI catalog of Yockey's possessions that reads: "One page captioned *Theosophical Forum*, 6/37."[2] This was the June 1937 issue of *The Theosophical Forum*, an American journal of the Theosophy Society.[3] Although the FBI summary does not say what extract Yockey had from the publication, it was almost certainly from an essay called "Central Asia: Cradleland of Our Race" by "G. de P."—Gottfried de Purucker, the leader of the Point Loma, California, Theosophical Lodge.

The Theosophical Society was founded by the Russian-born mystic Madame Helena Petrovna Blavatsky in New York City in 1875.[4] Blavatsky published a huge book called *The Secret Doctrine* in 1888 that argued that the world had experienced the rise and fall of seven "Root Races" many times over. Now the Aryan, or fifth Root Race, dominated the world. The Aryans, however, were at the end of a karmic cycle called by Hindu doctrine the *Kali-Yuga*. The Kali-Yuga was a time of great destruction as well as the beginning of a new Sixth Root Race that would begin the ascendancy of man toward the highest, Seventh Root Race of god-men. Although Blavatsky's root races were psychic, not biological entities, her arguments had an enormous impact in the racist right in both Germany and Austria. To the volkists, Blavatsky's doctrine was proof that man had once been ruled by the highest root race, whose distant spiritual descendants were today's Aryans. *The Theosophical Forum* article elaborated on Blavatsky's theory of Aryan origin and explained that millions of years ago the Aryans emerged "from the degenerate Atlantean tribes." The Atlanteans, part of an earlier cycle some eight or nine million years ago, were themselves descended from the original god-men. It also said that the Aryan Fifth Root Race only "began to be itself" once it became "a stock separate from Atlantis," and developed independently in Russian Central Asia.

Yockey's occult interests had political ramifications.[5] He clearly saw himself as part of an underground elite, a secret new race of god-men. He even concludes *Der Feind Europas:* "We shall perform such deeds, accomplish such works, and so transform our world that our distant posterity, when they behold the remains of our buildings and ramparts, will tell their grandchildren that on the soil of Europe once dwelt a tribe of gods." His fascination with being a member of such an elite, his writings on "polarity," even his sado-masochistic inclinations, had echoes in the subterranean world of the high occult. To understand why, it is necessary to examine Baron Julius Evola, the most important and most influential fascist high-occultist in postwar Europe, and an early critic of *Imperium.*

There is another important reason to focus on Evola. By following Evola's admittedly difficult path in some detail, it becomes possible to catch a glimpse of an underground world that began taking shape during the last years of the Third Reich. Out of that world came what I will call "the Order," an elite group that I believe had its hand in *both* the "pro-Russian" and "pro-Western" factions of the postwar European far right.

Julius Cesare Andrea Evola was born in 1898 to a family of Roman aristocrats. He served as an artillery officer in the Italian army in World War I and for the rest of his life he delighted in blowing things up. He first began his assault on the bourgeois order as Italy's leading exponent of Dada.[6] He collaborated on the Dada journal *Revue Bleu*, and could be found "reading his avant-garde poetry—to the accompaniment of music by Schönberg, Satie, and Bartok—in the Cabaret Grotte dell'Augusteo," Rome's answer to Zurich's famous Dada Cabaret Voltaire. His Dada paintings were exhibited in Rome, Milan, Lausanne, and Berlin, and his *Inner Landscape 10:30 A.M.* is still displayed at Rome's Galleria Nazionale d'Arte Moderna.[7]

Evola championed Dadaism as a frontal attack on bourgeois culture. Dada was a necessary dissolution of outdated art forms—a clearing of the path, not the path itself. He discovered the path in high occultism when, in the mid-

1920s, he became part of Arturo Reghini's Gruppo di Ur, which studied magic, alchemy, and Eastern religion.[8] Reghini claimed to be a representative of the *Scuola Italica* (Italian School), a secret order that had supposedly survived the downfall of the Roman Empire and reemerged with the Hohenstaufen Emperor Frederick II. Scuola Italica was said to have inspired the Florentine poets up to Petrarch, as well as G. B. Vico's *De antiquissima Italorum sapientia*. The group later became involved in Italian Freemasonry and influenced Gabriele Rossetti's *The Mystery of Platonic Love in the Middle Ages.*

A major figure in a host of Italian theosophical and anthroposophical sects, Reghini also became a leader of the Italian Rite in Masonry. The Italian Rite, created in 1909, allied itself with the anti-clerical Piazza del Gesù branch of Masons. A fierce critic of the Vatican, Reghini in 1914 wrote an article for the journal *Salamandra* entitled "Pagan Imperialism," in which he "asserted that Roman tolerance and statecraft should be restored to the Italian nation, and Catholic influence eliminated."[9] What was most needed for Italian renewal was a return to Pagan-Roman Imperialism. To encourage Italian intervention in World War I, in May 1915 he "rallied a crowd in Piazza Venezia and launched the attack against Parliament which forced the Italian declaration of war."[10] He helped revitalize the symbol of the fasces and popularized it in the early fascist movement at a time when fascism still had what many considered to be a left-wing, secularist program hostile to the Church.[11] He also ran a series of esoteric magazines, including *Ignis* and *UR*, to which Evola contributed.[12]

In 1927 Evola published *Imperialismo pagano*, which denounced Catholicism's influence on Italian culture starting with the alliance between Church and State begun by the Roman Emperor Constantine.[13] He also unsuccessfully opposed the diplomatic agreement reached by Mussolini and the Vatican, known as the Lateran Accords, which was then still being negotiated.

The Vatican quickly took note. Father Giovanni Battista Montini, the future Pope Paul VI, wrote an article attacking *Imperialism pagano* for the June 1928 issue of the Catholic magazine *Studium*. Montini used Evola's writings to show what could happen to those who become too obsessed with a "metaphysics of obscurity, of cryptology of expression, of pseudo-mystical preciosity, of cabalistic fascinations magically evaporated by the refined drugs of Oriental erudition."[14] The Vatican-backed right-wing *Revue Internationale des Sociétés Secrètes* (RISS) in April 1928 published an article in its Partie Occultiste section called "Un Sataniste Italien: Julius Evola."[15] Pope Pius XI was so provoked by Evola's writing that he issued his 1929 encyclical *Divini illius magistri* defending Catholic education.[16]

Thanks to Reghini, Evola learned of a French Orientalist named René Guénon.[17] Born in 1886, Guénon quickly became an important figure in the

European occult underground. He eventually came to reject contemporary spiritualistic and theosophic fads in favor of more ancient spiritual traditions. After converting to Islam in 1912, he lived in Algeria and France until 1930, when he moved to Cairo. Although a Muslim, he remained close to "traditionalist" elements inside the Catholic Church, and from 1925 to 1927 was associated with a Catholic periodical called *Regnabit* (He Will Reign).[18]

In 1927 Guénon wrote *La Crise du Monde Moderne* (The Crisis of the Modern World), which described the modern age as a manifestation of the Hindu Dark Age, the Kali-Yuga. Hindu doctrine teaches that a human historical cycle (or *Manvantara*) is divided into four periods "during which the primordial spirituality becomes gradually more and more obscured." In the West, these periods correspond to the Gold, Silver, Bronze, and Iron Ages. Guénon argued that the West was now in the fourth or Iron Age, the Kali-Yuga.[19] There are four *Yugas* or ages of a cycle: the *Satya, Treta, Dvapara,* and the final age of obscurity and dissolution, the Kali-Yuga. Each age also corresponds to a caste in Hindu society. The highest age, the *Satya-Yuga,* was identified with the *Brahmin* poet/priests; the *Treta-Yuga* was the age of the aristocratic warriors, the *Kshatriya;* the *Dvapara-Yuga* corresponded to the merchant caste, the *Vaisya.* The lowest age, the Kali-Yuga, is the age of "mass man," the common worker or *Sudra,* the "casteless, the slave emancipated, the pariah glorified."[20]

To Guénon, the modern age's interest in democracy, mass culture, and materialism are all manifestations of the Kali-Yuga. The Kali-Yuga has so infected thinking that Western philosophy has become "purely human in character and therefore pertaining merely to the rational order . . . which [has been] substituted for the genuine supra-rational and non-human traditional wisdom."[21] "Truth," however, "is not a product of the human mind; the truth exists independently of ourselves, and it is for us simply to apprehend it."[22] The Renaissance and the Reformation "completed the rupture with the traditional spirit."[23] As a result, the West fell into "individualism . . . and, as a consequence, the reduction of civilization in all its departments to purely human elements."[24]

Evola embraced Guénon's argument completely. He too hated mere human "logos," and argued that it was a grave mistake to claim that the Renaissance had rediscovered pagan Greece. What the Renaissance had actually revived was the most degenerate aspect of late Greek rationalism. Evola insisted that the German economic historian Werner Sombart was correct when he mockingly called Florence "the New York of the Middle Ages."[25] Under the guise of a pagan revival, the Renaissance had ushered in the exaltation of the individual.[26] Greece, however, had reached its true zenith during the mythical Heroic Age, the time of Heracles, not Socrates.

Evola yearned for spiritual revelation, the pure shining-forth of Being he first experienced in abstract art. He was particularly inspired by the manifestation of Being described in myth and religious/occult symbolism, although he rejected the notion of a human-like "personal God."[27] His universe was ruled by a *numen:* "an immutable 'naked force,' an 'essence free of passion and change, one which creates distance with regard to everything which is merely human,' a solar realm of Olympic peace and light, of divine 'regality.'"[28] Again borrowing from Guénon, he claimed that this vision of pure being, the Hindu Satya-Yuga (*sat*, "being"; *satya*, "truth"), corresponded in the West to Hesiod's Golden Age.

As a product of the age of mass man, fascism was another expression of the Kali-Yuga. Evola fully shared Spengler's objections to Mussolini's and Hitler's pandering to the masses. Within fascism, however, he saw the possible beginnings of the new Golden Age that in Hindu theory follows the necessary dissolution of the old world in the Kali-Yuga. In that sense, fascism was an intermediate or transitional form, a kind of political Dada.

Evola was particularly concerned with the eternal struggle of polarities like Being and Becoming, Cosmos and Chaos. In his book *Revolt Against the Modern World*, he divided the world into "a physical order and a metaphysical order" or "the superior realm of Being and the inferior realm of Becoming." While Being belonged to the world of Tradition, the world of Becoming best described the modern world. Tradition was therefore forever at war with modernity.[29]

Evola believed that Nietzsche's great mistake was his uncritical acceptance of the modern age, as evidenced by his materialism. Nietzsche had confused Being (*nous*), the spirit of man, with biological energy and vitalistic life forces, and mistakenly glorified "blood, soil, the body, and its animal characteristics" while only seeing metaphysics and religion as parts of the social infrastructure that "hinder the realization of the destiny of the Übermensch." Concerned only with maximizing his individual "will to power," the modern Übermensch was the nihilistic plutocrat or stock manipulator out to increase his personal wealth at all cost.

Against Nietzsche, Evola embraced the ancient tripartite division of man into spirit, mind, and body. He also applauded the Indo-European tradition that "recognizes the fundamental divinity of Man . . . [that] God and Man are of the same stock." What was divine in man was spirit; it was "man's guiding light and the justification of his knowledge of being. The spirit is immortality itself, the basis of transcendence." Modern man, however, had deadened "the highest component of his being" and turned the concept of spirit "into an ideological, philosophical, or religious attribute."[30]

The transcendental world of Being could not be grasped by a human logos forever trapped in historical (or diachronic) time. Only symbol and myth, which exist outside time as archetypes, could successfully mirror the world of Being. Traditional societies, that is to say societies constructed around mythic (or synchronic) concepts of time, were more advanced than modern ones because they remain rooted in an atemporal dimension, "in the infinity and indeterminacy of space, forever the same." In such societies, "no quantitative measure of time is applicable, but only a representation by way of images and symbols, when numbers themselves indicate not so much quantities as rhythms."[31] Symbols and myths could not be dismissed as primitive fantasy.[32] They actually hold a great inner power, a power that can only be intuited, not learned. In *Revolt Against the Modern World*, Evola wrote that

> the truths that allow us to understand the world of Tradition are not those that can be "learned" or "discussed." They either are or are not. They can only be *remembered*, and that is possible only if one is set free from the shackles represented by various human constructions . . . and when one has awakened the capacity to *see* from the non-human standpoint, which is the same as the Traditional viewpoint.[33]

Evola's true enemy, writes Italian historian Franco Ferraresi, was "discursive thought," which "decentralizes" man by detaching him from the origins, i.e., from pure being. He instead appeals to "Memory" and the "capacity to see," supra-rational faculties similar to "a kind of Platonic anamnesis," an intellectual intuition of "the eternal, non-human realm of the spirit." In Evola's world, "Myth triumphs over history and, even more, over logos."[34] The American philosopher Thomas Sheehan suggests that Evola's metaphysics of history is best understood as "a long diatribe *against* history in the name of the ultimate primacy of the eternal, stable, suprahistorical realm of the spiritual and ontological, the 'Being of origins.'"[35] It is the world of Becoming, of Appearance, that Evola finds irrational.[36]

Despite Evola's acknowledged appropriation from Guénon, the two men became, in a certain sense, rivals. The clash stemmed from Evola's refusal to separate man from the Gods. Beginning in the 1920s, he sought to develop a voluntaristic dialectics of freedom ruled by the maxim *"Tu devi diventare Dio"* (You must become God). In his 1925 *Essays on Magical Idealism*, he wrote that "God does not exist. The Ego must create him by making itself divine."[37] It was while exploring the notion of "the individual who elevates himself to the level of absolute self-determination in the world of action," that he first discovered the power of mythology.[38]

To better understand Evola's argument, it is worth closely examining an excerpt from his 1931 book *La tradizione ermetica* (The Hermetic Tradition). In 1988, *Avaloka*, a journal devoted to Hermetic thought, translated a section from *The Hermetic Tradition* entitled "The Tree, the Serpent, and the Titan."[39] *Avaloka*'s editor, Arthur Versluis, warned his readers that "there is something Promethean, if not Luciferian, in Evola's perspective," and indeed there is.[40] Evola's "Luciferian" essay examines the dual symbolism of the Tree, namely its identification with notions of immortality and supernatural knowledge as well as its association with fatal and destructive forces like dragons, serpents, and demons. As an *axis mundi*, the tree joins two worlds, the solar world of immortality and timeless knowledge (Being) and the telluric world of Mother Earth (Becoming) that Evola associates with women, earth, and chaos symbols like dragons.

The mythological "Tree of the World" (like the Bible's tree of life and tree of knowledge) holds "an arboreal symbolism which represents the universal force." That force, usually conceived as having a feminine nature, was linked to "a store of supernatural knowledge, immortality-bestowing virtue, and power of domination." However, it also carried with it "the idea of a danger." On the one hand, "the Tree is conceived as a temptation, which brings ruin and damnation upon he who succumbs to it." Yet the Tree is also the object of conquest "which transforms he who dares to undertake it—whether it is a dragon or divine beings which he has to overcome—into a God, and, sometimes, transfers the attributes of divinity and immortality from one race of beings to another."

In Judeo-Christian mythology, Adam tried to eat of the Tree of Knowledge to become godlike. Although Adam failed, others succeeded. The chief Hindu god Indra had seized the *amrta* (*soma*, the drink of immortality) from an earlier race called the asuras. Odin (by means of a self-sacrifice at the tree known in Nordic myth as Yggdrasil) and Mithras (after eating from the fruit of the tree) also achieved a kind of parity with the gods. Heracles was another such hero. Evola then comments that these and similar legends figuratively tell us

of an undertaking which involves risk and a fundamental uncertainty. In Hesiod's *Theogony*, and typically in the legend of the King of the Woods, Gods or exceptional men are seen as taking possession of power which can pass, along with the attributes of divinity, to whoever knows how to seize it . . . But among those who make the attempt, some force a way and triumph, and others fall, paying for their daring, experiencing the fatal effects of that same [primordial female] power.

But should man even attempt to rival the gods? In mythology there were only two answers, the "magico-heroic" and the religious. According to the magico-heroic view, he who attempts to become one with the gods but fails, "is simply a being whose fortitude and good fortune were not equal to his daring." In the religious interpretation, however, such misfortune "is changed to guilt, the heroic attempt to a sacrilegious and cursed act not because of its failure, but in itself." In the religious judgment:

Adam is no longer one who fell in an undertaking in which others had prevailed: He is instead one who has sinned, and what happened to him is the only thing that could have happened to him. He has no alternative, therefore, but to seek expiation, and above all to renounce the wish which led him to that undertaking. The idea that the conquered can still think of reconquest, or intend to hold firm to the dignity which his act has earned him, appears from the religious perspective as the most reprehensible "luciferism."

But the religious view is not the only one. Nor is it at all superior to the heroic viewpoint, which also goes back to high antiquity as symbolized in the Hermetic tradition. Although Hermes is the messenger of the Gods, "he is also he who succeeds in taking from Zeus his scepter, from Venus her belt, and from Vulcan, God of the Earth's Fire, the tools of his allegorical craft." In Egyptian tradition, Hermes is elevated to "a triple greatness as Hermes Trismegistus," and "merges into the figure of one of the Kings and Masters of the primordial age who gave man the principles of a higher civilization." In mythology, Luciferian "fallen angels" first revealed the "ancient magico-hermetic sciences" to mankind, an idea Evola traces to the *Book of Enoch*:

> Among the Ben Elohim, the fallen Angels, who descended on Mount Hermon, as related in *Enoch*, is that *race of the Awakened and the Watchers* who came down to instruct mankind . . . In *Enoch*, Azazeel (or Gadreel) "who led Eve astray," taught men the use of the weapons of death—setting aside the metaphor, he infused in them the warrior spirit. In this connection, we know the myth of the Fall: the Angels were seized by the desire for the "women." However, we have already explained what the "woman" is in her relationship with the Tree . . . These Angels, then, were seized by the "desire" for power: United to it, they fell—they came down to earth, to a high place of the earth (Mount Hermon). From this union there sprang the Nephilim, a potent race (titans, as the *Papyrus of Gizeh* calls them) allegorically described as giants, but unveiled in their supernatural powers by the words of the *Book of Enoch:* "They need no food, they suffer no thirst, they escape [material] perceptions."
>
> The Nephilim, the "fallen Angels," are none other than the "titans" and "they who watch," they are the race called "glorious and warlike" in the *Book of Baruch*—the same race which lit in men the spirit of heroes and warriors, which formed their arts, which transmitted to them the mystery of magic.

It is the Nephilim, the Watchers, who teach the Royal Hermetic Art by which man can control the Gods. This notion of commanding the Gods to do one's bidding remains in fundamental conflict with the religious worldview, "which subordinates everything to devout dependence, fear of God, and morality." Concealed within the Hermetic tradition, then, is a vision of a new race of men/gods:

> The Hermetic art, then, consists of a method which has a necessary outcome, and which is exercised upon spiritual forces by supernatural means if one wishes (the symbolic Hermetic fire is often called "unnatural" or "against nature"), but always to the exclusion of every "religious," moral, absolute relationship; or in other words, it consists in a law, however unknown, of natural determinism between cause and effect. Led back by the tradition to "they who watch," to they who have despoiled the Tree and who have possessed the "woman," it is the weapon of "heroic" symbolism, acting in the spiritual world... The teaching is found in the *Corpus Hermeticum*: "Man is not made lower by having a mortal part, but on the contrary, this mortality enlarges his possibilities and his power. His double role is only possible for him because of his double nature: He is made in such a way that he embraces at the same time the earthy and the divine. Thus, we do not fear to speak the truth. A true man is higher than these (the celestial Gods), or at least equal to them. For no god leaves his sphere to come on earth, while man mounts to heaven and measures it ... Wherefore we dare to say that man is a mortal god, and that a celestial God is an immortal man."

The Hermetic Tradition was updated and reissued in 1948, the same year *Imperium* was published. To Evola, the defeat of the "Heroes" three years earlier was just that: a defeat, not a metaphysical punishment. The quest for power/knowledge, for immortality, for domination over the Tree/Female must continue. The "religious view," supremely represented by Catholicism, must not be allowed to overwhelm the Promethean magical/heroic outlook inside Europe's elite.

The desire for a new European elite also inspired René Guénon.[41] In *The Crisis of the Modern World*, Guénon wondered if there could yet arise in the West a small but powerful group "to act as guides for the mass, which would respond to its influence without requiring to know anything about its existence or about the methods by which it functioned."[42] If the elite could be formed while there was still time, "it might prepare the way for the change [of yugas or ages] so that it could take place under the most favorable circumstances, and the disturbance by which it must inevitably be accompanied would by this means be reduced to a minimum." Even if that should fail, "there would remain yet another even more important task, that of assisting in the preservation of those elements of the present world which are destined to survive and be used in building up the world that is to follow." But should the elite not come into creation in time, Western civilization "will have to die out in its entirety from lack of any surviving elements capable of contributing something towards the future, the last traces of the traditional spirit having finally disappeared."[43]

Guénon believed that only one tradition represented the necessary, irreplaceable ruling mythos for Europe.[44] In *The Crisis of the Modern World*, he argues that in the West "there is now but one organization" that "possesses a traditional character and that has preserved a doctrine capable of serving as an appropriate basis for the work in question": the Catholic Church.[45] Evola, however, was convinced that Catholic mythology was a disaster; against Jesus at the Last Supper he counterposed Heracles, who had dined at the table of the Gods.

Guénon was repelled by any attempt to weaken the separation between the world of gods and the world of men and stressed the crucial role that the priest (or Brahmin) caste played in mediating the relationship between the other world and man. Evola's Promethianism, however, denigrated the sacerdotal function represented in Europe by the Vatican, whose very name hints at its "vatic" or priestly/prophetic function. Evola argued that the prominence of the Brahmin caste was actually evidence of decline. The original high caste was the aristocratic warriors, the Kshatriya, who followed not a sacerdotal but a royal or hermetic tradition. Evola's Heraclean task was to introduce a new mythology for a new Europe-wide order of warrior magicians whose reemergence he first saw heralded in the rise of a new knightly order, Heinrich Himmler's SS.

Notes:

1. Yockey's interest in the occult may have been encouraged by his sister Vinette. According to Yockey's daughter, Dr. Francesca Yockey, Vinette had long been interested in astrological and esoteric matters. Yockey might also have been exposed to esoteric ideas through the Silver Shirt movement.

Oswald Spengler had esoteric inclinations, as did another of Yockey's favorite authors, Egon Friedell, the Viennese writer who used Spenglerian ideas in his three-volume *A Cultural History of the Modern Age*. For a brief discussion of Spengler in this regard, see Theodor Adorno, "Spengler after the Decline," in *Prisms* (Cambridge, MA: MIT Press, 1981). In *The Occult Establishment* (La Salle, IL: Open Court, 1976), James Webb notes that Friedell had expressed sympathy with Hans Hörbiger's theory of Cosmic Ice. On Hörbinger, see Robert Bowen, *Universal Ice: Science and Ideology in the Nazi State* (London: Belhaven Press, 1993).

2. FBI document SF 105-1769.

3. *The Theosophical Forum*, Vol. X, No. 6, June 1937. Yockey may have gotten this text from James Madole, a Blavatsky fan who led the National Renaissance Party.

4. For some discussion of Blavatsky's influence in the right, see James Webb, *The Occult Underground* (La Salle, IL: Open Court, 1988) and *The Occult*

Establishment (La Salle, IL: Open Court, 1988); Nicholas Goodrick-Clarke, *The Occult Roots of Nazism* (Wellingborough, Northhamptonshire, U.K.: The Aquarian Press, 1985); George L. Mosse, *The Crisis of German Ideology* (New York: Schocken Books, 1981); and Walter Kafton-Minkel, *Subterranean Worlds: 100,000 Years of Dragons, Dwarfs, the Dead, Lost Races, and UFOs from inside the Earth* (Port Townsend, WA: Loompanics Unlimited, 1989).

5. In this context it is worth noting Roger Griffin's remarks on the importance of understanding the esoteric roots of many ideas from the far right. In his essay "Revolts Against the Modern World: The Blend of Literacy and Historical Fantasy in the Italian New Right," in *Literature and History*, Vol. 11, No. 1 (Spring 1985), p. 102, he writes:

> In my own research into fascist ideology I have become convinced that the borders between literary and historical phenomena are extremely badly marked. It is important to recognize a mode of "aesthetic politics" at the level of individual experience and motivation which eludes much conventional historical analysis and is central to the question of what it meant to "be" a fascist.

6. Evola began his career around an intellectual circle tied to the Italian theorist Giovanni Papini, who published "A Nationalist Program" in 1908. Evola said he went from "decadentism, symbolism, and analogism right through to 'abstract' and dadaist composition." (Griffin, "Revolts Against the Modern World.") For a discussion of Evola's Dada period, see Richard Sheppard, "Julius Evola, Futurism and Dada: A Case of Double Misunderstanding," in *New Studies in Dada* (Driffield, U.K.: Hutton Press, 1981).

7. Richard Drake, "Julius Evola and the Ideological Origins of the Radical Right in Contemporary Italy," in *Political Violence and Terror: Motifs and Motivations*, edited by Peter Herkl (Berkeley, CA: University of California Press, 1986), p. 63.

8. On Evola's early occultism, I summarize from an article by Professor Elémire Zolla in *Gnosis*, No. 14, Winter 1990, entitled "The Evolution of Julius Evola's Thought."

9. Ibid.

10. Ibid.

11. Ibid.

12. Ibid.

13. The book also marked a final break with Reghini. In January 1929 a Reghini-controlled journal called *Ignis* showed in great detail just how much Evola had plagiarized from Reghini. The exposé discredited Evola in the eyes of his fellow occultists for some time. See Richard Drake, "Julius Evola, Radical Fascism, and the Lateran Accords," in *The Catholic Historical Review*, July 1988, pp. 412–13.

14. Ibid., p. 411.

15. Robin Wakefield, "Baron Julius Evola and the Hermetic Tradition," in *Gnosis*, No. 14, Winter 1990.

16. Thomas Sheehan, "*Diventare Dio:* Julius Evola and the Metaphysics of Fascism," in *Nietzsche in Italy* (Stanford, CA: Stanford University, 1988), edited by Thomas Harrison, p. 282.

17. Guénon may have known Reghini. In his 1927 book *Le Roi du Monde,* translated as *The Lord of the World* (Ellingstring: Coombe Spring Press, 1983), fn. 4, p. 2, Guénon says that Reghini "brought to our attention" some esoteric information.

18. Biographical background in Guénon's *The Lord of the World,* pp. 68–70.

19. René Guénon, *The Crisis of the Modern World* (London: Luzac and Company, Ltd., 1942), p. 1.

20. Thomas Sheehan, "Myth and Violence: The Fascism of Julius Evola and Alain de Benoist," in *Social Research,* Vol. 48, No. 1, Spring 1981, p. 59.

21. Guénon, *The Crisis of the Modern World,* pp. 6–7.

22. Ibid., p. 53. For Guénon, modernism "amounted to nothing less than an attempted infiltration, fortunately frustrated, of the Protestant spirit into the heart of the Catholic Church itself." *Crisis,* p. 61.

23. Ibid., p. 9.

24. Ibid., p. 51.

25. Drake, "Julius Evola and the Ideological Origins of the Radical Right in Contemporary Italy," p. 65.

26. Christophe Boutin, *Politique et Tradition: Julius Evola dans le Siècle (1898–1974)* (Paris: Kime, 1992), p. 130.

27. "For Evola, the higher realm is the (ill-defined) power of the a priori and the normative, the 'world of Being,' which alone can provide 'stability,' an underivable and unconditional principle or 'occult force,' which, when present, living, and active . . . reacts on the world of quantity by impressing upon it a form and quality. Evola's 'supernatural' [is] the 'archeological,' that is, of the ontological arche which is the origin and ordering principle of everything else, to which it is compared as form to matter." Sheehan, "Myth and Violence," p. 55.

28. Ibid., p. 56.

29. Louis Chester, "Riding the Tiger," *The Scorpion,* No. 8, p. 30.

30. Ibid., p. 31.

31. In this context see Spengler's discussion of number and myth in his chapter "The Meaning of Number" in volume one of *The Decline of the West.*

32. Franco Ferraresi, "Julius Evola: Tradition, Reaction, and the Radical Right," *Arch. europ. sociol.,* XXVIII (1987), p. 114.

33. Ibid., p. 116.

34. Ibid., pp. 117–18.

35. Thomas Sheehan believes that Evola echoes a constant theme in Western philosophy, "the primacy of *nous* over *episteme,* of *intellectus* over *ratio,* of *Vernunft* over *Verstand,* of intellectual intuition over discursive knowledge," without any mediating connection. Evola's anti-humanistic (or "more-than-human") philosophy repudiates dialogistic, discursive reasoning (*logos, ratio*) "not because he favors a descent to the irrational but because he affirms . . . the superiority of the suprarational." Spiritual intuition is the means whereby "empirical existence comes to be *really* transformed and resolved in divinity." Sheehan, "Myth and Violence," p. 51.

36. Ibid., p. 54.

37. "Evola posits a new dialect of the absolute concrete individual as freedom and will, one who makes the world be by constantly surpassing it in acts of free self-creation, which at one and the same time liberate the self and dominate the world." Sheehan, *"Diventare Dio,"* p. 284.

38. Sheehan, "Myth and Violence," pp. 52–53.

39. *Avaloka: A Journal of Traditional Religion and Culture,* Vol. III, Nos. 1–2, Winter 1988–Summer 1989. *The Hermetic Tradition* is now available in English from Inner Traditions International.

40. In the occult world a fierce war still continues between the followers of Guénon and Evola. Bulletin No. 18 of the Centro Studi Evoliani reprinted Evola's "René Guénon è la 'scolastica' guenoniana" (now available in a pamphlet by Evola entitled *René Guénon: A Teacher for Modern Times* [Edmonds, WA: Sure Fire Press, 1994]) as a riposte to an attack on Evola by the *Rivista di Studi Tradizionali,* which accused Evola of being a counterfeiter of Guénon. The RST was denounced by the Evolians as an organ of socialists and freemasons. See footnote 15 of Griffin, "Revolts Against the Modern World." For a neo-traditionalist critique of Evola, see the essay "Riding the Tiger," in Titus Burckhardt, *Mirror of the Intellect* (Albany, NY: SUNY Press, 1987).

41. The stress on elites can also be found in influential sociologists like Robert Michels and Vilfredo Pareto, as well as Lenin's argument for a professional revolutionary party in *What Is to Be Done?*

42. Guénon, *The Crisis of the Modern World,* p. 110.

43. Ibid., p. 111.

44. Guénon's turn to Rome was not unlike the decision of former radical German Romantics like Friedrich Schelling and Friedrich Schlegel, who saw Catholicism as the only appropriate mythology for Europe.

45. Guénon, *The Crisis of the Modern World,* p. 113.

32
REVOLT
AGAINST THE
MODERN WORLD

In 1934 Julius Evola published *Rivolta contro il mondo moderno* (Revolt Against the Modern World), a book that remains his perverse masterpiece. Speaking of myth in *Revolt*, he comments that "Every epoch has its own 'myth' through which it reflects a given collective climate."[1] The modern myth is "the democratic idea of evolutionism" that derives "the higher from the lower, man from animal, civilization from barbarism." Against Darwin, there stands the Traditional view "that mankind has higher origins, namely a past of light and of spirit."[2] This was a time when "'more-than-human' beings" ruled the earth.[3] In mythology, the fall of these god-like beings

> was identified with the mixing of the "divine" race with the human race, which was regarded as inferior; in some texts, that "sin" is compared to sodomy and to sexual mating with animals ... Tradition, in more recent eras, developed a variety of myths referring to races as bearers of civilization and to the struggles between divine races and animal, cyclopic, or demonic races. They are the *Aesir* against the *Elementarwesen*; the Olympians and the heros against giants and monsters of the darkness, the water, and the earth. They are the Aryan *deva* fighting against the *asura*, "the enemies of the divine heroes"; they are the Incas, the dominators who impose their solar laws on the aborigines who worshipped "Mother Earth."[4]

Evola's own mythmaking centered around Hyperborea, the original Arctic homeland, also known as Thule, the sacred island. Evola's Hyperborea was as much a vision of Being (or what he calls a "framework of an ontology") as a historic fact.[5] The sacred figure in Hyperborea was the king, conceived not simply as the ruler of a warrior aristocracy but as a "God/man"—a living link to the divine much like the Japanese emperor or Egyptian pharaoh.[6] King, not high priest, was the true pontifex who united the natural and supernatural dimensions.

From Hyperborea (or Ultima Thule), the sun-worshipping Boreal Race migrated in two directions. One group went to northern Europe, where it preserved its solar symbolism in the swastika. A second migration went first to Atlantis and then into the Americas and Western Europe. Remnants of Hyperborean culture had also been preserved by the Aryans, who originally entered India from the far north.

During their vast migrations, the Hyperboreans encountered many indigenous cultures. Although the northern European branch kept itself relatively pure, the "Atlanteans" allowed intermarriage with the aboriginal races of the south. These encounters with "inferior races, which were enslaved to the chthonic cult of demons and mixed with animal nature," gave rise to "memories of struggles that were eventually expressed in mythological form."[7] In these myths geography took on symbolic meaning. The chaotic, fertile sea was female. Mountains, as fixed "elevated places" (and the traditional seat of the Gods), were the masculine opposite of the "contingency of the 'waters.'"[8] Another symbolic north/south dividing line involved burial ritual: In solar cults the dead are incinerated, while in the south the dead are placed in graves and returned to Mother Earth.

The south's religions, the cults of Earth and Sea, were matriarchal.[9] Out of them came pantheistic naturalism, sensuality, promiscuity, and a passive mystical and contemplative nature.[10] The south also gave rise to egalitarianism by dethroning the original ruling warrior caste and replacing it with the sacerdotal or priest caste. Any society governed by such a priest caste was inherently "feminine in its attitude to the spirit" because kingship had been reduced to a purely material function. Before the decay, the dominant warrior caste had followed the northern solar-worshipping religion without need of priestly mediation. The elevation of the Brahmins above the Kshatriyas therefore marked the beginning of the Silver Age.[11] Now the priests determined the divinity of the king.

The north/south struggle was mythologically symbolized by the clash between the sun-god principle of the north that stood for "the superior invisible realm of being" and the moon goddess of the south whose domain was the "inferior realm of becoming." Evola believed that the Italian personality was split along a north/south archetypal axis, where "Nordic elements coexisted in perpetual anarchy with Africo-Mediterranean elements," causing an absence of "psychic equilibrium" critical to an understanding of Italy's complex, infuriating history.[12] He rethought world history as well, declaring that the Mayans were a telluric race, while the Aztecs and Incas followed the solar north. Japan was a model solar civilization whose aristocratic bushido warrior code best preserved Tradition. In Greece, the *Eumenides* symbolized the victory of the masculine north over matriarchy.

With Heracles the West had its first great mythic hero. In his book *Metaphysics of Sex*, Evola called Heracles the embodiment of solar masculinity who became legendary both as a conqueror of the Amazons, and as "a foe of the Mother (of Hera, just as Roman Hercules was the foe of Bona Dea), from whose bonds he freed himself."[13] Heracles dominated the Tree/Female life force principle by obtaining "Hebe, everlasting youth, as his wife in Olympus after attaining the way to the garden of Hesperides," where he plucked the golden apple, "itself a symbol linked to the Mother (the apples had been given by Gea to Hera) and to the life force."[14]

Dionysus, however, stood for a "Chthonic-Poseidon form of manhood," as he was linked to Poseidon, god of the waters, and also to Osiris, "conceived as the stream of the Nile, which waters and fertilizes Isis, the black earth of Egypt." Dionysus symbolized "the wet principle of generation related to the merely phallic concept of manhood; the god is the male considered only according to the aspect of the being who fecundates the female substance and, as such, is subordinate to her." This was why Dionysus "is always joined with female figures related to the archetype of the Great Goddess." Even as a sun god, Dionysus was still viewed "not in the aspect of pure, unchangeable light but as the star that dies and rises again." Dionysus symbolized the sun only in an inferior way, the way "the sun sets and rises again," when its light "is still not the steady, abstract light of pure being or of the pure Olympian principle."[15] As for Christianity, it was less a Jewish sect than another variant of Dionysianism from Asia Minor.

Only in its "Apollonian manifestation" does "pure manhood" fully manifest itself. Here the god Apollo becomes

> the embodiment of Olympian *nous* (perception) and of unchangeable uranic light, freed from the earthly element and also from his connection with goddesses in some spurious historical varieties of his worship. At this level Apollo, as the god of "pure form," was conceived without a mother and was "born by himself," *ametor* (without a mother) and *autophues* (self-growing), being the Doric god who "produced form geometrically." (This determination of plastic matter is proper to the male and to form, whereas the indeterminate nature of plastic matter and the limitless *apeiron*, belongs to the female.)[16]

Evola argued that the rise of Greek democracy was a victory of the peoples and cults of Asia Minor over the (northern Indo-European) Dorians. Only with Alexander the Great was there a temporary reversal of Greece's decline. The real glory of the ancient world, however, came with Rome, a culture that restored both the Olympian Gods and the imperial sun cult.

Evola's theories were significantly indebted to Johann Jakob Bachofen, the 19th-century Swiss theorist of matriarchy and author of *Das Mutterrecht* (Mother Right). He even translated and edited a selection of Bachofen's writings, *Le madri e la virilità olympica: Studi sulla storia segreta dell'antico mondo mediterraneo*, which was published in 1949. Bachofen exerted a vast, if largely covert, influence on thinkers both left and right.[17] Marx and Engels, for example, praised Bachofen's concept of primitive communism in early societies.[18] Evola, however, emphasized the Bachofen who believed that the transition of human society from matriarchy to patriarchy was the crucial moment in the evolution of human freedom.

Bachofen also supplied anthropological evidence for the symbolic war Evola had posited between Hyperborea and the cult of the Mothers. Bachofen believed that the transition of society from the maternal ("the Demeterian and Aphroditean-hetaeric") to the paternal was "the most important turning point in the history of the relations between the sexes." The female only embodied "the physical side of man" that is shared with other animals. But "the paternal-spiritual principle belongs to him alone." Through the development of the paternal principle, man "breaks through the bonds of tellurism and lifts his eyes to the higher regions of the cosmos."[19] Historical progress meant passing from female to male, from "the original divine darkness of swamp life to the final triumph of divine light, from the law of matter to that of spirit."[20]

According to Bachofen, the triumph of the male principle in the ancient world first occurred in Rome. In his 1870 work *Die Sage von Tanaquil* (The Myth of Tanaquil) he comments:

> Rome's central idea . . . the idea underlying its historical state and its law, is wholly independent of matter; it is an eminently ethical achievement, the most spiritual of antiquity's bequests to the ensuing age. And here again it is clear that our Western life truly begins with Rome. Roman is the idea through which European mankind prepared to set its own imprint on the entire globe, namely the idea that no material law but only the free activity of the spirit determines the destinies of peoples.[21]

Bachofen believed that all human culture emerges from conflict. "It is no paradox," he wrote, "but a great truth borne out by all history that human culture advances only through the clash of opposites." For Rome, the clash was between the female Oriental principle[22] and "the austerity of a race inspired to create, under the sign of reason, a world empire of illuminated law." Rome's destruction of Dido's Carthage was a spiritual struggle, "a clash primarily of *Grundanschauungen*, spiritual ideals, and not of merely economic and political interests."[23]

The historian of religion Joseph Campbell describes *The Myth of Tanaquil* as Bachofen's great argument that the effort of European man "to achieve the proprietorship and rational control of his own destiny, releasing himself from the domination of cosmic-physical forces and a primitive philosophy of existence," had its first enduring victory in Rome.[24] Victory, however, was only gained "at the cost of a ruthless suppression and subordination of the claims and allures of the natural world—the more cruel and ruthless, the greater the allure."[25]

Bachofen asserted that Christianity and other Oriental cults that swept late Imperial Rome were not merely foreign incursions: "On the contrary, [they] marked the re-emergence of an attitude to nature, history, and the state that had always been there but that Rome had tried to suppress"—namely, its underlying matriarchy.[26] Rome's fundamental war was with "the enemy in itself—the principle of its own natural religion, which constantly rises up to oppose the idea of the state and can never be completely subordinated." The ultimate danger to Rome was the "Asiatic nature principle in itself," the temptation to abandon the sword for "the blandishments of the soft, luxuriant Orient." Only the "incursion of the noble and pure Northern barbarians" saved the West from complete reversion to Oriental sensuality.[27]

Evola believed that the high point of post-Imperial Rome was the brief domination of Europe by the Hohenstaufen Holy Roman Emperor Frederick Barbarossa. In the Guelph-Ghibelline split,[28] when the "northern" element challenged the hegemony of the Papacy, Evola identified with Dante, a Ghibelline supporter of Barbarossa.[29] Contra Guénon, he stressed that any "identification of *our* tradition with the Christian and Catholic Church is the *most absurd of all errors*."[30] He also studied medieval chivalric orders, especially the Knights Templar, which had been destroyed in the early 1300s by the French monarchy working in close alliance with the Papacy.[31] He viewed orders like the Knights Templar as attempted revivals of the Kshatriyas' royal tradition in the West, and in 1937 devoted a book entitled *Il mistero del Graal e la tradizione ghibellina dell'Imperio* to this theory.[32]

Evola saw the beginning of a new return of the Kshastriyas (or what he also called "the royal order of Melchizedek") with the emergence of a new order of "Black Monks," Himmler's SS. Fascism could act as a possible midwife for the rebirth of an elite-ruled, all-powerful state, a new Sparta-Rome-Prussia: "a heroic-sacral world, where a severe ethos prevailed, together with love for discipline, a virile bearing, an austere, commanding soul."[33]

Evola's reservations about Hitler were the same as Spengler's. Because it was based on a kind of Rousseauist Volk ideal and Führerprinzip, the Third Reich was little more than a popular dictatorship that relied on a kind of collective psychic hypnosis. Nazism was, in short, a form of "romantic-telluric Dionysianism."[34] As biological racists, the Nazis (like Nietzsche before them) were too accepting of the materialistic mythology of the modern world. Against Nazi race theory, Evola argued that the "Nordics" represented a spiritual, not racial, civilization. There were "Nordic" elements in ancient China, India, Persia, Egypt, Greece, Rome, Mexico, and the Mediterranean. Rome was not built by a "race" but by a merger of various tribes and clans. To argue that culture was racially determined was to engage in a form of Protestant predeterminism dressed up in pseudo-Darwinian jargon.[35]

Evola codified his ideas in a 1941 book called *Sintesi di dottrina della razza* (Synthesis of the Doctrine of Race) that Mussolini declared fascism's definitive statement on the subject. While Evola did not ignore race, he framed it in a context far different from the Nazis. As historian Richard Drake explains: "Although biology did, in fact, matter to Evola, his precise position was that race must not be understood *solely* as a biological condition; it was a spiritual condition as well."[36] "Aryan" qualities like loyalty, faith, and courage were not limited to a single race, but were ideals held by an elite.[37] Sounding very much like Yockey, Evola claimed that "only of an elite may one say that 'it is of a race,' 'it has race': The people are only people, mass."[38]

As for the "Jewish question," Evola believed that Jewish culture had a "corrosive irony" and that Jewish intellectuals were in the vanguard of those who denounced Tradition by reducing human activity to materialist economic (Marx) and sexual (Freud) motives. Conspiracy theories about the Jews, however, were demagogic aberrations absurdly inadequate to explain Europe's crisis. If Jews were prominent in Western institutions, this was a symptom of modern decadence, not a cause. The ideological hegemony of rationalism and materialism that began with the Renaissance was the real problem.

In December 1937 and June 1938, Evola lectured on his ideas to the German-Italian Society in Berlin.[39] SS Brigadier Karl Maria Wiligut (a volkist fanatic also known as Karl Maria Weisthor) was chosen by Himmler to evaluate Evola's theories.[40] Wiligut concluded that Evola was best described as a "Roman reactionary," and argued that the SS should hinder his contacts in Germany. One SS study complained:

> Evola's doctrine is neither national socialist nor fascist . . . What separates him in particular from the national socialist worldview is his radical neglect of the concrete, historical fact of our national past in favor of an abstract spiritual Utopia based on fantasy.[41]

The Correspondence Administrative Department of Himmler's personal staff also issued a report arguing against Evola's plans to "establish a secret international order," and warned:

The ultimate and secret goal of Evola's theories and projects is most likely an insurrection of the old aristocracy against the modern world which is foreign to the idea of nobility. Thus the first German impression, that he was a "reactionary Roman," was correct: His overall character is marked by the feudal aristocracy of old. His learnedness tends toward the dilettante and pseudoscientific.

Hence it follows that National Socialism sees nothing to be gained by putting itself at the disposal of Baron Evola. His political plans for a Roman-Germanic Imperium are utopian in character and moreover likely to give rise to ideological entanglements. As Evola has also only been tolerated and hardly supported by fascism, there is not even a tactical need to assist him from our side. It is therefore suggested:

1. Not to give any concrete support to Evola's present efforts to establish a secret international order and a special publication intended for that purpose.

2. To stop his public effectiveness in Germany, after the lecture series, without deploying any special measures.

3. To prevent him from advancing to leading departments in party and state.

4. To have his propagandistic activity in neighboring countries carefully observed.[42]

Himmler concurred. An SS letter about Evola dated 11 August 1938 states: "Reichsführer Heinrich Himmler has taken note of the opinions expressed in the report on Baron Evola's lectures and strongly agrees with the ideas and proposals set forth in the final paragraph."[43]

After the outbreak of World War II, with the Rome-Berlin axis a reality, some of Evola's texts were published in 1940 by the Ahnenerbe, including *Über das Problem des arischen Naturwissenschaft* and *Die Juden und die Mathematik*, which appeared in the *Nationalsozialistiche Monatshefte*.[44] Despite the war, little had changed in the volkish faction of the SS. The German Racial Policy Office in 1942 declared that Evola's ideas were illustrative of "the low spiritual level of modern Italy due to racial decline."

Evola had to look elsewhere inside Himmler's Black Order for support. He found his SS connection not with the Wotanists inside Himmler's inner circle but with the pan-Europeanist elements inside both the Waffen SS and the Reich Security Main Office (RSHA), Nazi Germany's CIA.

Notes:

1. The political importance of myth was also central to the theories of the philosopher and social critic Georges Sorel, whose work Evola was familiar with.

2. Julius Evola, *Revolt Against the Modern World* (Rochester, VT: Inner Traditions International, 1995), p. 183. This is not a translation of the original edition, but an updated version published in 1969.

3. Ibid., p. 178.

4. Ibid., pp. 178–79.

5. Thus, when talking about the original hermaphrodite in Plato's theory of love, Evola writes:

The primordial beings whom Plato has described, even recounting their physical features, ought not, of course, to be conceived as actual members of some pre-historic race whose remains or fossils we would expect to find. Instead, we should conceive of a *state*, a spiritual condition of origins, not so much in the historical sense as in the framework of an ontology, of a doctrine of the manifold states of being. [From *Metafisica del Sesso*, translated as *Eros and the Mysteries of Love: Metaphysics of Sex* (Rochester, VT: Inner Traditions International, 1991), p. 43. In the rest of this book I shall refer to it as *Metaphysics of Sex*.]

Guénon also argued the case for Thule on the grounds of "initiatic science" rather than archéology.

6. In the notion of the pharaoh, "stability appears as an essential attribute that complements the attribute of 'power-life' already present in the sovereign." Evola claimed that the hieroglyphic *djed* particularly conveys "the stability of the 'solar gods resting on pillars or on light beams.'" Evola, *Revolt Against the Modern World*, p. 18. In *Lord of the World* (Ellingstring: Coombe Spring Press, 1983), Guénon also examines the issue of the sacred king. James Frazer's *The Golden Bough* first made the issue of the sacred nature of kingship a subject of modern investigation.

7. Evola, *Revolt Against the Modern World*, p. 196.

8. Ibid., p. 188. Evola also wrote *Meditation du Haut des Cimes* (Meditation of the Mountaintops) about mountains as a challenge to man's heroic nature.

9. In German there is *Mutter* (mother), *Moder* (decaying matter), *Moor* (bog), *Marsch* (marsh), and *Meer* (ocean).

10. Christophe Boutin, *Politique et Tradition: Julius Evola dans le Siècle (1898–1974)* (Paris: Kime, 1992), p. 112.

11. Joscelyn Godwin, *Arktos: The Polar Myth* (Grand Rapids, MI: Phanes Press, 1993), pp. 21, 57–61.

12. Richard Drake, "Julius Evola and the Ideological Origins of the Radical Right in Contemporary Italy," in *Political Violence and Terror: Motifs and Motivation*, edited by Peter Herkl (Berkeley, CA: University of California Press, 1986), p. 71.

13. Evola, *Metaphysics of Sex*, p. 133. For an interesting modern interpretation of Heracles, see Nicole Loraux, "Herakles: The Super-Male and the Feminine," in *Before Sexuality: The Construction of Erotic Experience in the Ancient Greek World*, edited by D. Halperin, J. Winkler, and F. Zeitlin (Princeton, NJ: Princeton University Press, 1990).

14. Ibid., pp. 133–34.

15. Ibid., p. 133.

16. Ibid., p. 134.

17. On Bachofen, I have relied on the English edition of his selected writings, entitled *Myth, Religion and Mother Right* (Princeton, NJ: Princeton University

Press, 1967). Also see two articles on Bachofen by Lionel Grossman: "Basle, Bachofen, and the Critique of Modernity in the Second Half of the Nineteenth Century," in the *Journal of the Warburg and Courtauld Institute* (Vol. 47, 1984), and "Orpheus Philologus: Bachofen versus Mommsen on the Study of Antiquity," in *Transactions of the American Philosophical Society* (Vol. 73, Part 5, 1983). Also see Jonathan Fishbane, "Johann Jakob Bachofen as a Historical Theorist," in *Continuity* (Fall 1983), and Robert Casillo, *The Genealogy of Demons* (Evanston, IL: Northwestern University Press, 1983), Chapter Seven.

18. In *The Origin of the Family, Private Property, and the State*, Engels gives Bachofen's theories high praise. Also see Erich Fromm, *The Crisis of Psychoanalysis* (New York: Henry Holt, 1991).

19. Joseph Campbell, introduction to *Myth, Religion and Mother Right*, p. xlvii.

20. Grossman, "Orpheus Philologus," p. 63.

21. Campbell, introduction to *Myth, Religion and Mother Right*, p. l.

22. Namely "the Aphroditic, Demetrian, and Dionysian legacies of the Sabines and Etruscans, Hellenistic Carthage, and, finally, Cleopatra's Hellenistic Egypt."

23. Campbell, introduction to *Myth, Religion and Mother Right*, p. xlviii. In *The Myth of Tanaquil*, Bachofen writes:

> The crucial meeting in Carthage shows the parting of the cultural ways. Dido is the Oriental king-woman, planning to enslave the man by her harlot's arts. She seeks to dominate Aeneas as Omphale dominated Heracles, Semiramis Ninus, Deliah Samson. She strives to embody the power which Asia gave the hetaeric queen over the life and throne of her husband . . . But Aeneas represents the new view of life to which Rome was destined to elevate mankind. . . . Under the impact of the Roman national hero, the throne of the Oriental hetaera, which Cleopatra-Isis would like to erect anew, sinks into ruins . . . Asia's sensual maternity never reaches the land which the *Weltgeist* has chosen as the birthplace of a new era.

24. Ibid., p. xlviii.

25. Ibid.

26. Grossman, "Basle and Bachofen," p. 175.

27. Ibid., fn. 164, p. 182.

28. During the conflict between Emperor and Pope there was a virtual civil war in Italy's city-states, with the Imperial faction dubbed Ghibelline after the Hohenstaufen castle of Weibeling. The Guelfs derived their name from the Welf Saxon dynasty backed by the Papacy against the Hohenstaufens.

29. "Le guelfisme représente donc en fait une victorie de las caste sacerdotale et du principle lunaire sur la caste guerriere et le principle solaire. Ce seront alors les peuples germaniques, restés plus proches, selon notre auteur, de la tradition nordico-aryenne, qui entameront, au travers du gibelinisme et la Chevalerie, la lutte pour la restauration de l'idéal impérial roman." (Boutin, *Politique et Tradition: Julius Evola dans le Siècle (1898–1974)*, p. 126.)

30. Drake, "Julius Evola and the Ideological Origin of the Radical Right in Contemporary Italy," p. 69. Evola also described fascism as a "laughable revolution" after Mussolini signed the Lateran Accords with the Vatican.

31. Evola had in mind the attack by Philippe le Bel (Philip the Fair) against the Templar Order in the early 1300s, when Philip seized the Templar treasury and executed many knights, including the Grand Master of the Order, Jacques de Molay. Philip claimed that the Knights had adopted a secret heretical and satanic religion and that in destroying the Order (and taking its wealth) he was doing God's work.

32. Available in English as *The Mystery of the Grail* (Rochester, VT: Inner Traditions International, 1997). Evola's glorification of the Hohenstaufen was influenced by Ernst Kantorowicz's famous book *Frederick the Second, 1194–1250* (London: Constable, 1931).

33. Franco Ferraresi, "Julius Evola: Tradition, Reaction, and the Radical Right," *Arch. europ. sociol.,* XXVIII (1987), p. 118.

34. Thomas Sheehan, "Myth and Violence: The Fascism of Julius Evola and Alain de Benoist," *Social Research,* Vol. 48, No. 1, Spring 1981, p. 51.

35. Evola's opposition to biological anti-Semitism was also rooted in aristocratic elitism. Modern racism and anti-Semitism have "mass" leveling qualities. The Volk concept not only separated the "Aryan" from the "Jew"; it also blurred the separation of noble from commoner, since the essence of "Aryan man" was genetic and not grounded in history, wealth, rank, or genealogy.

36. Drake, "Julius Evola," p. 70.

37. Ibid.

38. Ferraresi, "Julius Evola," p. 124. Ferraresi adds his own critique of Evola's anti-Semitism, which is also directed against the well-known historian of Italian fascism Renzo de Felice, who gave some grudging acknowledgement that Evola rejected orthodox anti-Semitism:

> That Evola was a racist cannot be doubted, among other reasons because he claims it to his own credit. In his opinion, the myth of race was to be an important weapon for Fascism's struggle against the chief evils of modern society: universalism, individualism, rationalism, evolutionism, and for the reconstruction of Italian society. But he scorned purely biological notions of race in favor of a "spiritual" concept: This inner character, however, was to be in harmony with somatic traits. The pattern of Evola's argument (and ambiguity) on this point is very similar to the one that emerges in other, connected areas of his doctrine: The superiority of a group, a caste, an elite, etc., is claimed on purely spiritual grounds, but then it is blood that transmits such "spiritual" features; States must be ruled by elites bound by purely spiritual values, but then it is to old aristocracies that he looks for providing such elites; virility is a spiritual, not a biological quality, but a virile woman would be against nature; etc . . . The rejection of a purely physical notion of racial purity is at the origin of Evola's critique of biological racism and, during Fascism, it provoked a series of attacks on him by "orthodox" racists . . . In his postwar writings, Evola claims that it enabled him to keep his distance from "vulgar anti-Semitism" on the ground that there is no necessary correspondence between Jewish blood and Jewish spirit, nor, for that matter, between physical and spiritual "aryanism."
>
> The trouble with this distinction between the "spiritual" and the "physical" dimension of race, however, is that, within its framework, the Jewish spirit is

constantly depicted as the negative pole, the destructive, disgregating force, against whatever is positive, solar, virile, etc., typically represented by the Aryans ... Believing that such spirit may be embodied also by Gentiles can hardly be considered a pro-Jewish attitude.

In "Myth and Violence," Thomas Sheehan points out that

Evola prided himself on developing a theory of races that went beyond the merely biological (a racism of the blood à la Nazism) to the spiritual. What constitutes a superior race for Evola is the *spiritual* orientation of a given stock, the subsumption of the requisite biological material (and that did mean the Aryan races) under a qualitatively elevating form, namely reference to the realm of the spirit. But in fact all that Evola's theory does is to promote biological-ethnic racism a step higher. There are enough references in his works to the "inferior, non-European races," to the "power of inferior strata and races," to disgusting "Negro syncopations" in jazz, to "Jewish psychoanalysis"—and enough adulation of the Aryans—for us to divine that Evola's "spiritual" racism may have had something other than disinterested Apollonian origins.

Evola shared Yockey's hatred of black people. Thomas Sheehan notes that in Evola's 1941 *Sintesi di dottrina della razza*, the "utter imbecility" of his racial ideas was revealed by his discussion of a "limit case" called "telegenesis." Evola writes: "A [white] woman whose sexual relations with a black man have been over for years can, nonetheless, in union with a white man give birth to a black baby" through "subconscious influences." See Thomas Sheehan, "*Diventare Dio:* Julius Evola and the Metaphysics of Fascism," in *Nietzsche in Italy* (Stanford, CA: Stanford University, 1988), edited by Thomas Harrison, p. 281.

39. Evola's *Pagan Imperialism* was published in German in 1933, and *Revolt Against the Modern World* appeared in a 1935 German edition.

40. Nicholas Goodrick-Clarke, *The Occult Origins of the Third Reich* (Wellingsborough, Northhamptonshire: The Aquarian Press, 1985), p. 179.

41. Roger Griffin, "Revolts Against the Modern World: The Blend of Literary and Historical Fantasy in the Italian New Right," in *Literature and History*, Vol. 11, Spring 1985, p. 109.

42. Cited from p. xviii of the introduction by "H. T. Hansen" (reportedly Hans Thomas Hakl) to the Inner Traditions International edition of *Revolt Against the Modern World*. It is possible that the SS document cited by Griffin and this report are actually excerpts from the same document. Griffin cites the Bundesarchiv material relating to Evola as the "Himmler file, orange folder, drawer II, folder 126." The report cited in Hansen's footnote says it comes from "dossier document AR-126," which leads me to suspect that the two authors may be citing from the same report.

43. Ibid., p. xviii.

44. Boutin, *Politique et Tradition*, fn. 172, 173, p. 299.

33

THE

ORDER

In early September 1943, Julius Evola and Heinrich Himmler briefly found themselves unlikely neighbors at the "Wolf's Lair," Hitler's headquarters in Rastenburg, East Prussia.[1] Evola helped welcome Mussolini to Hitler's compound on 14 September 1943, after Il Duce's daring rescue by German airborne commandos from a mountaintop jail in Italy. Evola's curious ascent to the Nazi inner sanctum, just a few years after the SS's attack on him, was intimately related to the German defeat at Stalingrad. By late 1943 it was clear that if Germany had any chance to survive, it had to mobilize all of conquered Europe against its enemies. Military reality necessitated a power shift inside the SS from the volkists to the pan-Europeans.

Evola, however, identified most closely with the old political and economic ruling elites. Reflecting on a speech he delivered in 1934 to Berlin's Herrenklub, the more aristocratic successor to Moeller van den Bruck's Juniclub, he wrote:

> Here I found my natural habitat. From then on a cordial and fruitful friendship was established between myself and the club's president, Baron Heinrich von Gleichen... That was also the basis for certain activity in Germany, grounded on common interests and objectives.[2]

When the volkist wing of the SS accused Evola of trying to revive the old nobility, the criticism may have taken into account his ties to the Herrenklub.

Despite the SS attack, as well as his own hesitation about Hitler, Evola spent World War II working for a section of SS intelligence called the

Sicherheitsdienst des Reichsführers-SS (Security Service of the Reichsführer-SS, or SD) in Rome, Berlin, and Vienna. He may even have collaborated with the SD in Romania in the late 1930s. Founded in June 1931 by Reinhard Heydrich, the SD initially spied on the Nazi Party's domestic political opponents. It also ran a press and information service headed by Franz Alfred Six. After the Nazi seizure of power, the SD branched out into foreign intelligence operations. It developed a reputation for recruiting some of Germany's "best and brightest" lawyers, economists, and academics into its ranks. At the outbreak of the war, the SD became part of the *Reichssicherheitshauptamt* (Reich Security Main Office, or RSHA), which was established in September 1939 to consolidate all SS intelligence operations into one super-agency.

Evola's SD connections began in the 1930s, when his main Italian patron was Roberto Farinacci, the most powerful voice inside Italian fascism favoring close diplomatic relations with Nazi Germany. A past secretary general of the Fascist Party and a member of the Fascist Grand Council, Farinacci maintained his own power base as *ras* (boss) of the northern province of Cremona.[3] A former radical socialist, he spent much of the early 1930s on the fringes of power. His extreme anti-clerical views clashed with Mussolini's detente with the Holy See; he had also attacked Mussolini for being too soft on the "Jewish question."

Farinacci held a financial interest in *Vita Italiana*, a fiercely anti-Semitic monthly founded by Giovanni Preziosi. Farinacci and Preziosi published an Italian edition of *The Protocols of the Elders of Zion* in October 1937 with an introduction by Evola. Preziosi first introduced Evola to his future patron after he came across a journal that Evola had created in 1930 called *Torre* (The Tower). In it, Evola demanded "a fascism more radical, more intrepid, a truly absolute fascism, made of pure force, inaccessible to any compromise."[4] After five months *Torre* collapsed, but during that time Evola managed to alienate enough fascist higher-ups that he felt compelled to maintain a group of bodyguards. Preziosi, however, admired *Torre*. Thanks to his help, Evola was given a page to edit in Farinacci's Cremona-based paper, *Regima fascita*, called "Diorama filosofico." Some contributors to his page included Paul Valéry, Gottfried Benn, Sir Charles Petrie, Prince Karl Anton Rohan, and Othmar Spann.[5]

When the Rome-Berlin Axis was formed in October 1936, Mussolini again turned to Farinacci because of his excellent relations with Goebbels and Himmler, and in 1937 Farinacci led the Italian delegation to the Nazi Party Congress at Nuremberg. During the war, Farinacci regularly fed information to the German embassy—in particular to the SD's top man in Rome, SS Colonel Eugen Dollmann.[6] He did so in the hope that if Mussolini stumbled, the Nazis would back him as Italy's new leader. Through his SD and military connections, he too was brought to Rastenburg after the Fascist Grand Council deposed Mussolini.[7]

Evola was engaged in a project in Romania in the 1930s that may also have involved the SD. Romania's importance could be summed up in one word: oil. During World War II, Romania supplied the Reich with one-third of its oil imports. Romania was equally important to Italy for political reasons: Fascist movements in Romania, Hungary, and Greece were potential allies in an Italian-dominated "southern fascist axis" that opposed Nazi racial doctrine for obvious reasons.

Evola's link to Romania was through an elite fascist sect called the Romanian Legion of the Archangel Michael. The Legion created a political party called the *Garda de Fier* (Iron Guard) in the 1930s. The Iron Guard, in turn, was regularly represented in meetings of the *Comitati d'azione per l'Universalità di Roma* (Action Committee for Roman Universality, or CAUR), a government-backed group that networked with fascist organizations across Europe that looked to Italy for political guidance and financial support. Eventually Italian Foreign Minister Count Ciano decided that CAUR was a waste of time and money and ordered the group shut down in 1936.[8]

The Legion of the Archangel Michael and the Iron Guard, however, continued to maintain links to some of the most extreme elements in Italian fascism, including Evola. Evola went to Bucharest in 1937 and met the Legion's founder, Corneliu Zelea Codreanu (dubbed "the Captain"). The Iron Guard became the third-strongest party in Romania that same year, winning some 478,000 ballots, or 16 percent of the total vote.[9] With the growth in its political strength, there came Legion-sanctioned assassinations. Iron Guard "death teams" were formed in April 1936 to "avenge the nation" and "punish traitors and scoundrels who would exterminate the Captain and his movement." Members of such units greeted each other with cries of "Long live death! Long live the Legionary Triumph!"[10]

Evola enthusiastically embraced the fanatically anti-Semitic Legion, and in 1938 wrote a series of articles in *Guardia* that were never reprinted in his lifetime. He praised Codreanu's struggle against "the Judaic horde" and said that since his earliest days, "Codreanu had a clear idea of what a communist takeover of Romania would mean . . . the country's enslavement . . . to 'the filthiest tyranny, the talmudic, Israelite tyranny.'"[11] His encomium concluded:

> Codreanu saw clearly that Judaism has been able to dominate the world via Freemasonry, and Russia via communism. Mussolini, who has destroyed communism and masonry—Codreanu says—has implicitly declared war also on Jewry . . . The recent anti-Semitic turn of Fascism proves that Codreanu was entirely right.[12]

Evola wrote his articles during a time of crisis. Codreanu's Legion had grown so powerful that Romania's King Carol II launched a series of savage attacks on it.[13] In November 1938, 14 Legion men (including Codreanu) were taken out of their prison cells, strangled with ropes, and then reported shot in the back while trying to escape.[14] One Legion supporter who managed to avoid execution was Mircea Eliade, the world-famous scholar of religion and one of Evola's closest Romanian friends. After being picked up during the 1938 crackdown, he managed to get himself released from jail and transferred to a sanitorium. His escape from death was ironic given that there is evidence that he had helped develop the Legion's notorious "Long Live Death!" ideology.[15] Eliade first read Evola during his student days. Highly impressed with *Revolt Against the Modern World*, he compared it favorably to *The Decline of the West*. The two men finally met in Bucharest in 1937, on the same day that Evola was introduced to Codreanu.[16]

Eliade's University of Bucharest mentor was the theology and philosophy professor Nae Ionescu, who ran a right-wing newspaper called *Cuvantul*.[17] Ionescu was a member of the Lausanne-based *Centre International d'Études sur le Fascisme* (CINEF), which promoted fascist ideas inside elite circles.[18] According to a 1974 book on the Iron Guard, Ionescu served as Codreanu's emissary in Germany and helped launder money from I. G. Farben to the Legion of the Archangel Michael.[19] In articles for the popular press, his protégé Eliade called on the "Romanian race" to "put an end to a life exhausted by poverty and syphilis, invaded by Jews, and debilitated by foreigners. The revolution of the Legionaries must achieve its supreme goal: the redemption of the race."[20] He proclaimed that the Legion had gone beyond mere politics to a far greater task, the total spiritual transformation of man. Many Legion ideas were identical to Eliade's, and even his sympathetic American biographer admits that "Codreanu's handbook for nest [cell] leaders reads almost as though it were a selection from one of Eliade's columns in *Vremea*."[21]

The Iron Guard maintained excellent ties to the SD. By the autumn of 1940, when Romania was solidly in the Axis camp, the role of the SD in Legion affairs became particularly pronounced. The key German operative in Romania, Baron Otto von Bolschwing, had joined the SD in 1932 and quickly became caught up in both the "Jewish question" and the Mideast political situation with Adolf Eichmann.[22] Once World War II began, Bolschwing was made the SD's "man in Bucharest."

King Carol II abdicated the throne on 6 September 1940, after he was unable to prevent portions of northern Transylvania being taken from Romania by another Axis ally, Hungary. Before abdicating, the King appointed General Ion Antonescu to govern the country as regent for Carol's son, King Michael. In an attempt at national unity, Antonescu made surviving Iron Guard leader Horia Sima his deputy prime minister. Iron Guard militants were also released from prison, and Guardists in exile were invited back to Romania to join a new "Party of the Nation."[23] Despite Hitler's decision to give full diplomatic support to Antonescu, in January 1941 the SD backed an Iron Guard coup against him.[24] From 21 to 23 January 1941 the Iron Guard took over much of Bucharest and went on an insane killing spree, especially against Bucharest's Jews.[25] After the Romanian army crushed the revolt, Bolschwing helped smuggle leading Guardists into Germany, where they were interned under extremely mild conditions. The Iron Guard also had a protector in the Vatican, which saw it as part of the "southern tier" of Vatican-backed fascism that included Croatia's Ustaschi.[26]

As the war turned increasingly difficult for Germany, elements inside the RSHA began demanding a more sophisticated occupation policy. The need for a new line may explain an article Evola wrote for the Nazi-backed journal *European Review*. Founded in 1941, the magazine was supported by Grossraum advocate Franz Alfred Six, the high-ranking SD officer who now served as propaganda overlord for occupied Europe. Evola's "Reich and Imperium as Elements in the European New Order" defended Roman law against the argument that it was "mechanistic" and "universalistic." Rome's legal system had also provided the theoretical basis for the medieval idea of the Reich. No doubt with groups like the Iron Guard and Ustaschi in mind, he pointed out that within southern Europe there was a community of "Aryan peoples" where the "anti-Jewish idea" played an important role. He also argued that the Greeks and Russians could play a positive role within the New Order if only they were allowed.[27]

Historian Robert Herzstein believes that Evola was attempting to justify southern fascism to the Germans by "aryanizing" it. He further reports that in 1942 certain Italian diplomats became interested in Evola's arguments and hoped to create "a bloc consisting of Italy, Romania, Hungary, and perhaps other nations" that would conclude "a compromise peace and build some form of European confederation."[28] But who was Evola really speaking for? The Italian Foreign Ministry? Or Grossraumordnung elements inside the Waffen SS and the SD?[29]

After Mussolini's fall from power in late July 1943, Evola fled to Germany with SD help.[30] Once in Berlin, he went to work for the SD's Italian section.[31] Evola and Farinacci left Berlin on 18 September 1943, and returned to Rome to organize an SD-backed political group called the Movimento per la Rinascita dell'Italia.[32] After a visit by American intelligence agents to his apartment, Evola decided once again to pack his bags and return north. This time, however, he headed to Vienna.

Evola's SD work at the end of the war is shrouded in mystery. Historian Richard Drake says that while he was in Vienna, "Evola performed vital liaison services for the SS as Nazi Germany sought to recruit a European army for the defense of the Continent against the Soviet Union and the United States."[33] According to his own account, Evola spent his time living incognito while doing "intellectual" research. But what kind of research?

While Evola was in Vienna, the SD supplied him with a series of arcane texts plundered from private libraries and rare book collections.[34] The SD bureau that provided him with these documents was Amt VII,[35] an obscure branch that served as an RSHA research library.[36] With this precious archive, Evola closely studied masonic rituals and translated certain "esoteric texts" for a book called *Historie Secrète des Sociétés Secrètes*. It never appeared because Evola claimed that all his documents were lost during the Russian bombardment.[37]

But why would the SD actively involve itself in Evola's arcane research at a time when hundreds of thousands of Russian soldiers were sweeping into the Reich? And why would Evola choose to live in Vienna under a false name and devote his time to such a strange project? Could the answer to this question be found in the cryptic reference to Evola's "efforts to establish a secret international order" in the 1938 SS report?

I believe that Evola's Vienna project was intimately linked to the development of what I will call "the Order," a new kind of Knights Templar designed to successfully function sub rosa. Well before the end of World War II, the intelligence and financial networks of the Third Reich were hard at work preparing underground networks to survive the coming Allied occupation. Escape lines to South America and the Middle East were organized. Bank accounts were created in Switzerland and other neutral nations to finance the underground with plunder the Nazis had looted from occupied Europe. But how was this secret empire to be managed, except by a virtually invisible "government in exile"?

For years Evola had been fascinated by knightly orders as expressions of the Kshatriya caste of warrior aristocrats. In the formal structure of the SS, he saw the precursor to a new *Ordenstaat*, a State ruled by an Order.[38] He also understood the great advantages provided by medieval orders of chivalry due to their transnational composition. Crusading orders, like the Knights Templar and the Knights of Saint John of Jerusalem, were pan-European, with separate "national" sections (*"langues,"* or tongues) unified through a Council presided over by a Grand Master. After the collapse of fascist state power, a new Order, an "invisible college" of sorts, was needed not only to manipulate bank accounts and travel schedules but to have policy-making functions. Nor could it simply be run under the auspices of the Vatican, since Evola believed that Rome's downfall had been caused by the acceptance of Christianity by the dominant faction of the Roman elite.[39] The Emperor Constantine's official embrace of the "gentle Nazarene" in 313 A.D. had culminated, a hundred years later, in Alaric's sack of Rome. With the American chewing-gum imperialists threatening in the West, and the new Huns sweeping in from the East, was the situation in 1945 really so different? The Order was a vessel for those "Hermetic" elements of the Conservative Revolution, old ruling class, and new Nazi elite not entirely beholden to the political, cultural, and religious "Guelf" wing of the European aristocracy, which remained ideologically loyal to the continued propagation of the ruling Christian mythology.

This account of the origins of the Order is obviously speculative, and I advance it as hypothesis, not fact. Yet if I am correct the SD really did have a need for Evola's unique talents. With his extensive knowledge of matters esoteric and occult; his fascination with secret societies and knightly Orders; his Waffen SS transnationalism; his ties to some of the highest figures in fascism, Nazism, and movements like the Iron Guard; and his loyal service to the SD, Baron Evola was a perfect candidate to help theorize a new underground Order. As the SD's equivalent of Albert Pike, the former Confederate Army general who designed the rituals for the Scottish Rite Masons in the late 1800s, Evola's task was to help create the inner organizational and ritual structure for the Grand Masters of a secret Shamballah whose financial nerve center was carefully hidden away in Swiss bank accounts.

With the war rapidly coming to an end, however, the Order lacked the time to implement its plans. With support from the top RSHA leadership, a deception game was begun with both Allied intelligence and the Catholic Church. Utilizing Wall Street and Vatican fears of communism, some of Himmler's top cronies, like SS General Karl Wolff, became Damascus-road converts to a "kindler, gentler" SS eager to establish friendly relations with both the Americans and the Holy See.

A strange game also developed inside the SD that had a peculiar occult twist. It appears likely that one of Evola's SD helpers during his Vienna period was an obscure SS major named Werner Goettsch. Born in Kiel in 1912, Goettsch had been recruited into the SD in 1932. He was arrested in Alt Ausee, Austria, by the 80th detachment of the U.S. Army CIC on 11 May 1945,[40] and later interrogated by U.S. Army Intelligence, which issued a report on him on 24 July 1945.[41]

Goettsch told the CIC about his SD activities, including his role in the 1935 murder of Otto Strasser's "Black Front" radio operator Rudolf Formis, an operation made possible by Alfred Franke-Gricksch.[42] After the Formis affair he requested a discharge from the SD, but he did not get one until late 1936. He then "opened an insurance agency in BERLIN in partnership with his friend [Otto] von BOLSCHWING, but the agency failed within a short time." SD chief Reinhard Heydrich next

> ordered GOETTSCH back into the SD in 1937 and sent him to the Sipo Fuehrer Schule, from which he was graduated in 1938. GOETTSCH was

assigned to Amt VI of the RSHA, under O(ber)/Fuehrer JOST, and sent in 1939 . . . to organize an intelligence service in the Balkans. GOETTSCH made contacts with German businessmen and also helped organize the German minority groups in the Sudetenland and Czechoslovakia. He travelled through Bulgaria and Hungary . . . In the fall of 1939, GOETTSCH became the head of VI-E and began selecting key men for work in the Balkans . . . He also secured . . . permission to operate secret W/T stations in the Balkan countries.[43]

After November 1939 Goettsch "was increasingly hampered by tuberculosis." Despite his illness, he visited Bolschwing in Bucharest in 1940 and helped set up an SD transmitter network. As his health worsened he spent a good deal of his time under medical care "reading political theory, history, and publications on mysticism." Then, in early 1943,

> while deep in this reading which changed his feelings towards Nazi ideology, GOETTSCH was appointed liaison officer between Amt VI and the Propaganda Ministry. Because of continued illness and a changed ideological point of view, GOETTSCH asked KALTENBRUNNER to transfer him to Amt VII, where he was able to read publications and books available only in the library of Amt VII. Later he sought the acquaintance of Dr. DOPPLER, a Freemason in VIENNA, who later advised him concerning the evacuation of Amt VII's library.[44]

"Kaltenbrunner," who reassigned Goettsch, was Ernst Kaltenbrunner, the director of the RSHA and the number-two man in the SS. An Austrian boyhood friend of Adolf Eichmann's with a doctorate in law, the nearly seven-foot-tall Kaltenbrunner organized Nazi espionage networks as minister for state security in Austria after the Anschluss. Himmler named him head of the Reichssicherheitshauptamt in January 1943, after Reinhard Heydrich's assassination.[45]

After joining Amt VII in the winter of 1943, Goettsch heard about a group called the "Free Austria" movement. He then "formed an independent group of influential RSHA members who wanted to free Austria from Nazi rule. Efforts to make English or American contacts were unsuccessful at first, but in January 1945 HOETTL met Dr. LESLIE, a U.S. representative in Switzerland." "Hoettl" was SS Colonel Willi Hoettl, the Gestapo chief of intelligence for southeast Europe and Italy, who joined the SS with Kaltenbrunner after the Anschluss.[46] Baron Otto von Bolschwing may have been another member of Free Austria. After successfully escaping Hitler's wrath for the SD's failed Iron Guard coup, Bolschwing returned to Vienna in 1943. Even before the fighting ended, he was feeding the U.S. information about German rocket scientists. After the war he became one of the highest-ranking CIA contract employees in Europe.[47]

Nor did Goettsch bother to keep his seemingly treasonous activity secret from Kaltenbrunner:

In December 1944 GOETTSCH . . . broached the matter of a Free Austria to KALTENBRUNNER, who agreed to tolerate the movement but refused to join it. In April another meeting was held with KALTENBRUNNER. Dr. NEUBACHER, whose views carried weight with KALTENBRUNNER, tried to persuade him to open negotiations with the Western Powers. At first KALTENBRUNNER refused, but later he agreed to confer with General KESSELRING. GOETTSCH does not know any further details.

Kaltenbrunner, along with SS General Karl Wolff, had already been involved with trying to work out a secret deal with both the Vatican and the Americans, who were represented in Switzerland by Allen Dulles from the Office of Strategic Services (OSS).[48] In September 1943 Wolff was appointed German military governor of northern Italy and plenipotentiary to Mussolini. An SS *Oberstgruppenführer* (General) like Kaltenbrunner, Wolff was outranked only by Himmler as *Reichsführer-SS* (Supreme Commander).

The Wolff-Dulles negotiations, codenamed "Operation Sunrise" by the OSS, were ostensibly organized to negotiate the surrender of German forces in northern Italy. If so, the talks were a dismal failure. Months of negotiation only resulted in the surrender of German forces in Italy on 2 May 1945, just five days before the final German capitulation at Rheims. Reports on the Dulles-Wolff talks angered the Soviets, who feared that a deal was being hatched between the Americans and the SS for a separate peace in the West.

One of Wolff's top men in the talks was SS Colonel Eugen Dollmann, the SD agent who was Roberto Farinacci's and Evola's friend inside the German embassy in Rome. Wolff used Dollmann's excellent Vatican connections to arrange a meeting with the Pope. Pius XII and Wolff held a private discussion in the Vatican on 9 September 1943.[49]

Wolff and Dulles both knew that the American government was locked into a policy of unconditional surrender. What was really on the table for negotiation was the future of Europe beginning the day after the surrender. In addition to having extensive financial connections to Germany as a partner at the New York law firm Sullivan and Cromwell, Dulles had earlier worked for the State Department, so he was acutely aware of how the harsh policy imposed by the Allied powers at Versailles had caused enormous instability in Germany and encouraged the spread of communism. Did Wolff offer Dulles cooperation from SS intelligence networks in postwar anti-Soviet operations in return for certain concessions? In short, had Wolff used Operation Sunrise to hammer out a private understanding with elements of the American elite represented by Dulles?

In one of his youthful poems, Evola wrote about "Black monks who will burn the city," and who "when the time is full . . . will guide the forces of the resurrection."[50] In Vienna, amid occult texts and Russian bombs, Evola helped conjure a new Order of "black monks" to guide "the forces of the resurrection." At the same time, the black monks of the SS were furiously attempting to reach an accommodation with future CIA head Allen Dulles. If they succeeded, a new Order of Knights Templar would flourish long after the Führerbunker went up in flames.

Notes:

1. Christophe Boutin, *Politique et Tradition: Julius Evola dans la Siècle* (Paris: Kime, 1992), p. 243.

2. Franco Ferraresi, "Julius Evola: Tradition, Reaction, and the Radical Right," *Arch. europ. sociol.*, XXVIII (1987), p. 107.

3. I have relied on Harry Fornari's biography *Mussolini's Gadfly* (Nashville, TN: Vanderbilt University Press, 1971) for background information on Farinacci.

4. Richard Drake, *The Revolutionary Mystique and Terrorism in Contemporary Italy* (Bloomington, IN: Indiana University Press, 1989), p. 119.

5. Ibid.

6. Dollmann, the SD's top Italy expert, scored an intelligence coup by warning that Mussolini was in danger with the Fascist Grand Council. When Mussolini was deposed on 25 July 1943, the Germans were taken by surprise. The German Ambassador to Italy, Mackensen, was dismissed from his job for sending a report to the Foreign Office two days earlier that Mussolini's position was better than ever. Dollmann, however, had tried to warn Mackensen that Mussolini was in trouble. See Allen Dulles, *The Secret Surrender* (New York: Harper and Row, 1966), pp. 57–58.

7. While at Rastenburg, Farinacci badly alienated Hitler with his severe personal criticism of Mussolini.

8. Michael Ledeen, *Universal Fascism: The Theory and Practice of the Fascist International* (New York: Howard Fertig, 1972), especially the chapter entitled "The Fascist International."

9. The Iron Guard had begun rapidly expanding its base a year earlier:

Authoritative sources agree that 1936 was the year of much growth and success for the Legion, functioning with considerable freedom under a tolerant government. While its greatest activity was in the villages (engaging in public works projects, building churches, harvesting crops, etc.), in 1935–36 it stepped up operations in the cities . . . The Corps of Legionary Workers, a kind of labor union, was organized in 1936 also, and soon it reported 6,000 members in Bucharest alone . . . The Legion's growth can be gauged from these statistics: In 1935 there were 4200 nests; by January 1937 there were 12,000. But the increase in 1937 was simply phenomenal: At the end of the year there were reportedly 34,000 nests. [From Mac Linscott Ricketts, *Mircea Eliade: The Romanian Roots* (Boulder, CO: East European Monographs, 1988), Vol. 2, pp. 919–20.]

10. Ibid., p. 919.

11. Ferraresi, "Julius Evola: Tradition, Reaction, and the Radical Right," p. 129.

12. Ibid. In his memoirs, *Il Cammino del cinabro*, Evola writes that Codreanu was "one of the most illustrious and spiritually oriented figures that I ever met among the national movements of the day."

13. Carol was the son of King Ferdinand and Queen Marie of Romania. After marrying Queen Helen of Greece and producing a son, he deserted his family and ran off with his Jewish mistress to Paris. At the age of six, his son Michael became King Michael of Romania. Carol then successfully plotted his return to power and two years later he retook the throne from his son.

14. Ricketts, *Mircea Eliade*, Vol. 2, p. 1081.

15. Roger Griffin reports that Eliade "had been a leading light in the occultist right-wing circles" in Bucharest, and he believes that Eliade helped create the Iron Guard's esoteric "religion of death" ideology. See his "Revolts Against the Modern World," in *Literature and History*, Vol. 11, Spring, 1985, p. 115.

16. Ricketts, *Mircea Eliade*, Vol. 2, p. 849.

17. From "Fascism and Religion in Romania," Adriana Berger's review of Vol. 2 of Eliade's *Autobiography* (Chicago, IL: University of Chicago Press, 1988), and Mac Linscott Ricketts' two-volume biography of Eliade in *Annals of Scholarship*, Vol. 6, No. 4, 1989, pp. 456–57. Berger was a research consultant for Eliade's papers.

18. Ledeen, *Universal Fascism*, p. 87.

19. Mihai Fatu and Ion Spalatelul, *Garda de Fier—organizatie terorista de tip fascist* (Bucuresti: Ed. Politica, 1974), as cited in Berger, fn. 6, p. 463.

20. Griffin, "Revolt Against the Modern World," p. 117. Eliade especially celebrated the Legion's "Long Live Death" ideology as expressed in a Legion oath:

> Instead of swearing vengeance on his enemies and calling for *their* deaths, the Legionary vows his readiness to give up his *own* life at any moment! This orientation of the Legion toward preparation for death, Eliade says, is a Christian ascetic orientation, more appropriate to monks than to heroes. By vowing to forsake earthly joys, sever ties of human love, and be ready to die, the Legionary adopts a monastic ideal. It is a *tragic* vision of life, but not a *pessimistic* one in Eliade's judgment, because it is the reflex of the joyous faith in eternal love and life in Christ in heaven. [Ricketts, *Mircea Eliade*, Vol. 2, p. 924.]

21. Ricketts, *Mircea Eliade*, Vol. 2, pp. 920–21. In 1940 Eliade became a member of the Romanian embassy in London. According to reports from the British Foreign Office cited by Adriana Berger, he was considered the most Nazi member of the embassy and was reported to have been working for the Germans. See "Fascism and Religion," p. 459. For a strong attack on Berger's use of British sources, see Bryan Rennie, *Reconstructing Eliade* (Albany, NY: SUNY Press, 1996).

22. For Eichmann's description of his SD duties, see *Eichmann Interrogated: Transcripts from the Archives of the Israeli Police* (New York: Farrar, Straus & Giroux, 1983). Bolschwing is called "a certain Ernst von Bollschwingh" in the transcript (p. 25).

23. For a discussion of the situation in Romania, see F. L. Carsten, *The Rise of Fascism* (Berkeley, CA: University of California Press, 1967).

24. Bolschwing's maneuvers were part of a factional battle inside the Third Reich. His boss, SD General Walter Schellenberg, thought a successful SD-backed coup in Romania by the devoutly pro-German Iron Guard would score points with Hitler. More important, he wanted the SS to maintain de facto control over Romania's oil fields.

25. One Legion member named Rachmistriuc tried to attack Romanian General Antonescu. He later came to the United States and changed his name to Alexander Ronnett. Ronnett became a prominent Iron Guard spokesman in America and author of *Romanian Nationalism: The Legionary Movement* (Chicago, IL: Loyola University Press, 1974). He also wrote for Willis Carto's *Journal of Historical Review*. Ronnett was Eliade's personal physician and dentist for twenty years when Eliade was teaching at the University of Chicago. See Ted Anton, *Eros, Magic, and the Murder of Professor Culianu* (Evanston, IL: Northwest University Press, 1996), p. 117. Also see Russ Bellant, *Old Nazis, the New Right, and the Republican Party* (Boston: South End Press, 1991) for more on Ronnett.

26. The Iron Guard endeared itself to the Vatican by supplying volunteers to fight for Franco in the Spanish Civil War. One Iron Guard leader that Bolschwing smuggled out of Bucharest, Constantin Papanace, a former Romanian Minister of Economics, became the leader of the Vatican-backed *Forul Legionaire* group in Rome. For background on Romania and Bolschwing, see Charles Higham, *American Swastika* (New York: Doubleday, 1985) and Christopher Simpson, *Blowback* (New York: Weidenfeld and Nicholson, 1988).

27. Christophe Boutin also cites Evola:

> L'important—écrit Evola—c'est que dans cette situation, un certain changement de perspective eut lieu. On cessa d'identifier l'"aryanité" à la "germanité." On voulait combattre non pour un national-socialisme expansionniste reposant sur un racisme unilatéral, non pour un pangermainisme, mais pour une idée supérieure de l'Europe et pour un "Ordre Nouveau" européen. [Boutin, *Politique et Tradition*, pp. 276–77.]

28. Robert Herzstein, *When Nazi Dreams Came True* (London: Sphere, 1982), pp. 166–67.

29. As early as 1943, SD intelligence chief Walter Schellenberg was making overtures to Allen Dulles, who ran the OSS station in Berne, Switzerland. Schellenberg's agent was Prince Max-Egon von Hohenlohe, who owned vast estates in the borderland between Germany and Bohemia and claimed to have some 30 places of residence in Europe and Latin America. An American intelligence report called him "a very dangerous person" who "gives a convincing appearance of being neutral and is always engaged in some obscure peace-making activities, counting very frequently on the assistance of religious organizations and noble families in Europe." Peter Grose, *Gentleman Spy: The Life of Allen Dulles* (Amherst, MA: University of Massachusetts Press, 1996), pp. 156–57. Schellenberg also backed a failed attempt to topple Nazi Foreign Minister Joachim von Ribbentrop, who stood in the way of peace negotiations. See Christopher R. Browning, "Unterstaatkretaer Martin Luther and the Ribbentrop Foreign Office," *Journal of Contemporary History*, 12 (1977), pp. 327–29, 332–39.

30. Evola entered Germany disguised as a soldier in a German Waffen SS unit.

31. Boutin, *Politique et Tradition*, p. 243.

32. Richard Drake, "Julius Evola and the Ideological Origins of the Radical Right in Contemporary Italy," in *Political Violence and Terror: Motifs and Motivations*, edited by Peter Herkl (Berkeley, CA: University of California Press, 1986), p. 67.

33. Drake, *The Revolutionary Mystique*, p. 120.

34. The SD's occult library contained several hundred thousand rare books looted from private collections across Europe. From the American Counter Intelligence Corps' (CIC) interrogation of SD Major Werner Goettsch:

> Early in 1943 HIMMLER ordered that all books and publications about occultism, astrology, and mysticism be transferred to the "Ahnenerbe" (Ancestral Heritage), but the librarian of Amt VII, Stubaf BURMEESTER, secretly kept duplicates and put them at GOETTSCH's disposal. Later in 1943, STRECK-ENBACH, the acting Leiter of the RSHA, ordered Amt VII to evacuate its books and archives. At first, only the books and archives and personnel papers remained in BERLIN until the order was given to bring all papers and documents to the Sudetenland, where they were kept in SCHLEISIER SEE, FORT NIMES, and PER-STEIN. One box, called the Schweden Kiete, was filled with the rarest papers and documents and kept by Dr. DITTL in a shelter at BERLIN SW 68, Wilhelmstr 102. No one except Dr. DITTL had access to the box.

35. In Robin Wakefield's "Baron Julius Evola" essay in *Gnosis* (No. 14, Winter 1990), he seems to say that Evola actually worked for AMT VII: "Evola spent most of World War II in Germany, employed by a branch of the SS as a translator of the archives of various Masonic and other secret societies which were proscribed in Nazi-dominated Europe."

36. Amt VII maintained the RSHA's library, the Freemasonry museum, and other archives. Himmler even got Amt VII involved in the study of witchcraft during the Middle Ages.

A 24 July 1945 CIC report on Amt VII gives its background:

> When the SD moved from BERLIN to MUENCHEN late in 1934, it included Zentral Abteilung II and the Presse Abteilung. The former was divided into two Haupt Abteilungen specializing in enemy ideologies. Haupt Abteilung I dealt with Jewry, Freemasonry, and Catholicism; Haupt Abteilung II with Marxism, Reactionary movements, and the LUDENDORFF movement.

After Franz Alfred Six, who headed the Press Department, decided he wanted not just to spy on the German press but to influence it, he made a power play to take over Zentral Abteilung II:

> SIX succeeded in having himself made chief of this department in 1936 and then wrote articles about Freemasonry, Catholicism, and Judaism, which were sometimes published by the Nordische Verlag in HAMBURG.
>
> After a time there was friction between the Gestapo and Zentral Abteilung II. Both agencies often issued reports which were mutually contradictory. A re-organization of Zentral Abteilung II took place. It was officially dissolved, its papers

and files of operational value were sent to the Gestapo, and what was left of Zentral Abteilung II became Amt VII of the RSHA. [From *The Final Solution of the Abwehr*, Volume 13 of *Covert Warfare* (New York: Garland Publishing, 1989).]

37. Boutin writes in *Politique et tradition* (p. 245):

C'est à Vienne, ville où vit "incognito sous un nom d'emprunt," qu'Evola travaille à son ouvrage sur les sociétés secrètes et leur influence, grâce à des documents mis à sa disposition par les Allemands (sans doute la SS). "J'avais simplement été chargé—écrira-t-il—d'étudier des rituels maçonniques . . . et de superviser la traduction de certains textes à caractère ésotérique." Mais son *Historie secrète des sociétés secrètes* ne verra jamais le jour, et tous ces documents disparaitront dans le [Russian] bombardement.

38. Nor were Evola's views unique. Spengler saw Prussia as an example of an Ordenstaat ruled by a grand-master/king.

39. Evola also identified with Julian the Apostate, the Emperor of Rome who tried to reinstate paganism. Julius Evola, *The Path of Enlightenment in the Mithraic Mysteries* (Edmond, WA: The Alexandrian Press/Holmes Publishing Group, 1994).

40. Alt-Aussee was the site of the final headquarters of Ernst Kaltenbrunner, the head of the RSHA.

41. That report is reprinted in *Covert Warfare 13: The Final Solution of the Abwehr*.

42. Goettsch said he entered Formis's room just after Alfred Naujocks murdered him. Naujocks was a leading SD "dirty tricks" expert. After World War II, Naujocks was said to have played an important role in ODESSA. See Robert Wistrich's entry on Naujocks in *Who's Who in Nazi Germany* (London: Routledge, 1982).

43. Goettsch's friend Bolschwing was on an almost identical track. When war broke out in Europe, Bolschwing was drafted into the SS and assigned by the SD's Walter Schellenberg to Amt VI, the foreign intelligence service. Charles Higham, *American Swastika*, p. 235.

44. It is also curious that towards the end of the war, Himmler ordered an easing up of the SS attack on freemasonry. One of the SS's leading anti-masonic fanatics, *Standartenführer* (colonel) Grigorii Schwarz-Bostunich, was told by Himmler that the official line on freemasonry had been modified and that Schwarz-Bostunich's lectures on freemasonry were now subject to SS censorship. He also would not be allowed to wear an SS uniform when giving his talks. Walter Laqueur, *Russia and Germany* (Boston: Little, Brown, 1965), pp. 124–25.

45. Wistrich, *Who's Who in Nazi Germany*.

46. On Hoettl, see Gerald Reitlinger, *The SS: Alibi of a Nation* (New York: Viking Press, 1957), p. 20. Under the name "Louis Hagen," Hoettl wrote a series of books after the war on intelligence matters. In his discussion of the Operation Sunrise negotiations in his book *The Secret Surrender* (New York: Harper & Row, 1966), p. 50, Allen Dulles writes that at the end of February 1945

an Austrian agent arrived in Bern from Vienna, having been sent by Kaltenbrunner himself, chief of the RSHA, and the most powerful man in the SS after Himmler. The Austrian had been acquainted with Wilhelm Hoettl, one of Kaltenbrunner's intelligence officials in Austria, and through him had met Kaltenbrunner.

Goettsch also created his own Free Austria group inside the SD that included Hoettl:

> The group consisted of Hans BETTIG, HOETTL, Stubaf VANECK, O/Stubaf ZEIS-CHKA, H/Stuf HANDL, and SS Mann FEHLAND. Another large group was led by Dr. NEUBACHER, Stufaf KRAUS, and GOERING's assistant MUEHLMANN. GOETTSCH's group held conferences with Rafael SPANN, Prof. HEINRICH, and Dr. Karl WINKLER, and decided to contact the British through Prof. HEINRICH's friend, Major CHRISTIE, at the Traveller's Club in LONDON. . . . Through General MIHAILOVICH, contact was made with the American legation in BEL-GRADE . . . In January 1945 the German industrialist von WESTEN brought Dr. HOETTL to Switzerland to meet the US representative LESLIE. [From *The Final Solution of the Abwehr*.]

47. According to Christopher Simpson, Bolschwing was so valued by the CIA that in 1949 he was allowed to set up his own spy network to penetrate the CIA-financed Gehlen Org, which he claimed was being infiltrated by Soviet agents. Bolschwing's secret intelligence agency even ran its own East Bloc infiltration operations. Nor did the CIA forget about his Iron Guard connections. In a sworn deposition cited in *Blowback* (p. 256), Bolschwing said that

> in the summer of 1948, at the height of the Civil War in Greece, I was asked by my American courier officer to make contact with the Romanians, who might influence the Greek situation . . . In the course of that endeavor, I visited with Mr. Constantine Papanace . . . who was residing under the presumed auspices of the Vatican in or near Rome.

48. Due to Wolff, Evola's Ahnenerbe opponent, Karl Maria Wiligut ("Weisthor"), had been forced to resign from the SS; this happened to occur shortly after his negative critique of Evola. In February 1939 Wolff brought to Himmler's attention the fact that Wiligut had spent 1924 to 1927 in a Salzburg mental asylum. As for Kaltenbrunner, at his war crimes trial at Nuremberg he told the court that he had negotiated with Dulles in person. (Kaltenbrunner was later convicted and hanged.) Charles Higham, *American Swastika*, p. 198. For an overview of the Free Austria movement (codenamed "Operation Herzog") and Kaltenbrunner, see Peter R. Black, *Ernst Kaltenbrunner: Ideological Soldier of the Third Reich* (Princeton, NJ: Princeton University Press, 1984), Chapter VII.

49. For an interesting account of the meeting and the events surrounding it, see Constantine, Prince of Bavaria, *The Pope: A Portrait From Life* (London: Wingate, 1954), pp. 235–47.

50. Drake, "Julius Evola and the Ideological Origins of the Radical Right in Contemporary Italy," p. 79.

34
STRATEGY
OF TENSION

In 1945 Julius Evola was badly wounded during a Russian bombardment of Vienna and was partially crippled for the rest of his life.[1] During the attacks, he had refused to go to a bomb shelter and instead worked in his office or walked through the streets in order to "question his fate."[2] After spending time in an Austrian hospital, he returned to Rome in 1948 and became a *maéstro ségreto* (secret master) to youthful extremists of the hard right. He told his acolytes that "iron and fire" must be used against Italy's Communists because "violence is the only possible and reasonable solution." He also attacked the MSI for supporting "capitalist piracy and cynical, antisocial plutocracy."[3]

Evola and members of the radical fascist group Fasci d'Azione Rivoluzionaria (FAR) were arrested in April 1951 and charged with plotting to overthrow the state. The crackdown was orchestrated by Christian Democratic Interior Minister Mario Scelba in conjunction with SIFAR, Italy's postwar secret service. After six months in jail, Evola was charged with being "the spiritual father" of FAR.[4] Although ultimately acquitted of the charges, his arrest had clearly been a warning from the Christian Democratic establishment, as well as the CIA, to get in line.

Two years later Evola published *Gli uomini e la rovine* (Men Among the Ruins), in which he seemingly abandoned his anti-American stance. He now argued that "the immediate task is that of 'reinforcing the State,' while *malgré soi* [in spite of oneself] keeping it within the Western alliance (*malgré soi* because American materialism is as much an enemy of the traditional values as Russian totalitarian collectivism)."[5]

What did Evola mean by "reinforcing the state"? And why did he now argue for keeping Italy "within the Western alliance"? Had he yielded to American pressure? Or did his decision have something to do with the fact that *Men Among the Ruins* was published in 1953, shortly after Allen Dulles became the new director of the CIA? One clue comes from the man who wrote the introduction to the book, Prince Junio Valerio Borghese, the "Black Prince" of Italian far-right politics.[6]

A modern condottiere, Borghese was one of Italy's most innovative and daring naval strategists, and headed an elite naval sabotage unit called Decima Flottiglia MAS (or X-MAS) during World War II. His use of midget submarines against the British caught the attention of Grand Admiral Karl Dönitz, who arranged for Borghese to train German naval sabotage units. After the collapse of Mussolini's government in 1943, Borghese's men continued to fight for Germany under the overall command of SS General Karl Wolff. His unit now became a brutal anti-partisan army that targeted the Communist-dominated Resistance movement in northern Italy. It also fought against American Rangers and Canadian troops on the Anzio front.[7] Decima Mas even had a spy outfit headquartered in Switzerland that worked closely with the SD.

At the end of the war Borghese opened up contact with the OSS's James Jesus Angleton. Angleton, who later became one of the CIA's most powerful officials, ran the OSS's "X-2" counterintelligence branch for Italy during the war. He personally saved Borghese from certain partisan execution by dressing him up in an American uniform and driving him south to Rome for interrogation. Although Borghese was convicted of war crimes, the Italian Supreme Court of Appeals ordered him released from jail in 1949. After regaining his freedom, the Black Prince became a hero for MSI hardliners.[8]

Borghese was also courted by the American embassy, the Vatican, and the Christian Democrats. All of them wanted him to become the leader of a new pro-NATO "national front" because the MSI was still considered an unreliable "hotbed of anti-American and anti-Atlantic sentiment" that could hinder Italian integration into the Western alliance "unless the party's moderates were able to obtain control and enforce internal discipline."[9] Given his reputation, the CIA believed that Borghese was the perfect candidate to lead the new front.[10] The MSI, however, was terrified of losing him. Some Salò veterans visited his castle at Artena to warn him about "reactionary forces" behind the "national front" and begged him to join the MSI. MSI Secretary Augusto De Marsanich even offered to make him the group's honorary president. The Evolians also hoped that he would help in the struggle against the MSI's parliamentary "softs." Borghese officially joined the MSI in November 1951, and one month later, on 2 December 1951, he became the MSI's honorary president.[11]

Borghese's importance for the CIA went beyond politics. The CIA-backed SIFAR spy agency began organizing secret squadrons (many composed of ex-officers of the SID, Mussolini's secret police) for espionage and "counter-espionage" operations against the left in 1949. The CIA then created an underground army of ex-fascist combat veterans in an operation codenamed "Operation Gladio" (Gladio being the name for a Roman double-edged sword). Gladio, however, couldn't succeed without Borghese's tacit approval.

Operation Gladio was first made public in August 1990, when then–Prime Minister Giulio Andreotti admitted its existence to the Italian Parliamentary Committee on Terrorism. To this day much about Gladio remains mysterious. It seems that planning for the operation began to take shape in 1951, around the time Borghese was being actively courted by the CIA. Gladio was incorporated into Office "R" of SIFAR in 1956. On paper, Gladio was a NATO-backed "Stay Behind" operation: Any Soviet attack on Italy would encounter a pre-established resistance network, a militarily-trained underground with access to secret arms caches hidden across the country. To implement Gladio, SIFAR established a sabotage training school in Sardinia in 1954. Technically, Gladio was made up of two principal branches: 40 S/B (Stay Behind) units trained in guerrilla warfare, and five rapid deployment units with names like Alpine Star, Sea Star, Rhododendron, and Azalea. American-supplied weapons, including hand grenades, sniper rifles, and explosives were also buried in 139 hiding spots.[12]

The Italian government initially claimed that Gladio was part of a general agreement within NATO. NATO, however, officially denied any involvement. Revelations that Gladio-type organizations existed in non-NATO nations like Austria, Spain, and Switzerland further eroded the NATO cover story. Gladio really seems to have been what its name means: a double-edged sword to be used against both the Soviets and any elements inside Italy, from either the left or the right, that might try to take Italy out of NATO. Gladio also served as the backdrop for the "strategy of tension," which repeatedly destablized Italian politics with bombings and other terrorist acts. Popular fear of terrorism, from either the "left" or "right," could then be used to justify a suspension of constitutional law or even, in a worst-case scenario, a military-backed Pinochet-like "white coup" to insure Italy's continued allegiance to the West.

The suspension of constitutional law and a "legal" military seizure of power to restore public order were both practical postwar applications of Carl Schmitt's constitutional theories. Recall that Schmitt first became famous in Germany for his "theory of the exception" that justified the suspension of parliamentary democracy in an emergency.[13] Schmitt argued that the distinction between state and civil society had been rendered obsolete in the modern world by the clash of hostile interest groups, as evidenced by the class struggle. By pretending otherwise, classical liberalism had neutralized and depoliticized conflict and tried to turn every social struggle into a debating game. The correct response to the liberal ideal of state neutralism and non-intervention was the "total state." Writing in the 1920s, Schmitt justified the total state by arguing that it was the best way to defend democracy.[14] For Schmitt sovereignty lay not in constitutional norms but in the very existence of the state itself. In a crisis, the key issue was always "determining which particular agency has the capacity—outside of law—to impose an order which, because it is political, can become legal."[15] Sovereignty is exercised in a situation of conflict involving public safety and order when the "exception" demands resolution by force. Political crisis legally justified the extra-legal suspension of the old constitutional order by the strong state.

The CIA was haunted by the specter of a democratic electoral victory by a Moscow-allied Communist Party. In Europe this fear was most pronounced in Italy, where the Communists had come extremely close to entering coalition governments with the Socialists and the left wing of the Christian Democrats. Both the CIA and the right had to make sure that mechanisms were in place to keep the "state" safe from any ballot box misdeeds by its citizens. Before any radical shift in power occurred through voting or protest in the streets, there had to be the ability to engineer either a right-wing military-backed coup d'état or a suspension of parliamentary norms under the guise of restoring "order."

Seen in this context, the fact that Prince Borghese wrote the introduction to *Men Among the Ruins* takes on special significance. Franco Ferraresi's commentary on Evola's idea of the State as expressed in the book also takes on an added level of meaning:

> The notion of using the forces of the "true Right" for the defense of the State against subversion corresponds to a lasting concern of Evola's. Industrial society has made the State a hostage in the hands of trade unions and organized masses, which can jam the whole machinery with strikes and sabotage. The Army and the police, "given the level reached in Italy by the communist gangrene," might not be able to provide an adequate defense. Hence the need, for the right, to gradually organize a close network of task forces, "ready to quickly intervene against all possible emergencies," in order first and foremost to uphold "against the rabble, the State and its authority (even when it is an 'empty State')."[16]

Evola's Gladio-like notion of "reinforcing the State," even an "empty state," operated on two levels. Networks of fascist loyalists in the armed forces and intelligence services now pushed closer and closer to centers of power, using the "imminent" danger of communism or terrorism (from either the "left" or "right") as justification for their rise. These networks also sponsored far-right paramilitary shock-troops to intervene in crisis situations. The most important of these groups was Giuseppe "Pino" Rauti's *Ordine Nuovo* (New Order, or ON), which had split from the MSI after its 1956 congress chanting, "Fewer double-breasted suits and more cudgels." Rauti's move was ideologically inspired by Evola, whom Rauti worshipped.[17] Rauti also maintained close ties to Italian military intelligence:[18] Organizations like Ordine Nuovo were regularly employed as street fighters against the left; they also engaged in bombings and killings, and helped create a popular climate for more repressive measures against "anarchy" from either the right or left—a kind of political yin/yang that justified the flourishing of the secret state. As part of the strategy of tension, rightist operatives and police agents used left and anarchist groups that they had created, or legitimate sects that had been infiltrated. By the 1970s the social crisis in Italy had also given rise to an entire independent subculture of armed sects on both the left and the right.

Behind the strategy of tension there lurked what appears to have been a devil's pact between the Order and Allen Dulles. Until Dulles was named CIA director by President Eisenhower (and his brother, John Foster Dulles, became secretary of state), operational links to the Nazi underground came primarily from the Office of Policy Coordination (OPC), headed by Dulles protégé Frank Wisner, the former chief of OSS operations in Bucharest, Romania. After the war, Dulles, Wisner, Angleton, and the OPC's Carmel Offie virtually ran covert operations in Italy as their own private affair.

The OPC's budget was $4.7 million in 1949. Three years later, when Dulles was still only CIA deputy director, it had reached $82 million. OPC personnel had jumped from 302 to 6,954.[19] OPC was officially incorporated into the CIA in 1952 as the Agency's Directorate of Plans.[20] In 1956, after President Eisenhower established the Killian Commission to investigate the Agency, it was discovered that more than half of the CIA's personnel and 80 percent of its budget had been devoted not to intelligence-gathering but to psychological and political warfare programs.[21] Throughout this entire time, the Dulles network was intimately involved in complex deals with factions inside the postwar SS.[22]

Did Dulles offer to protect elements of the SS in return for its support for CIA-backed anti-Soviet operations in Europe and the Third World? Did he think that granting the Order a certain amount of autonomy was a small price to pay for bringing it into the American camp? Might he even have been personally compromised in some way, or manipulated by the Dulles family psychiatrist, Carl Jung?[23] *Men Among the Ruins*, then, may have been less a concession by Evola to American power than a signal that some sort of understanding reached by Dulles and Wolff at the end of the war was now fully operational.

For 40 years the strategy of tension was an astonishing success. Countless investigations of right-wing terrorism were called off when evidence disappeared or magistrates were assassinated. Nor was the strategy confined to Italy. In Central and South America, for example, CIA-supported military and security elites with links to far-right and neo-fascist movements took power in Bolivia, Argentina, Brazil, and Chile, among other countries.

With elements of the Italian intelligence services behind them, Evola-inspired groups like Ordine Nuovo were encouraged to embrace violence and terror as spiritual acts. To the Evolians, violence had its own metaphysical justification. Action was celebrated as a heroic end in itself as long as it was rooted in the higher values of the Kshatriya. Believing combat an existential duty, the far right idolized the Iron Guard's legacy of the "political soldier" and its mystique of death.[24]

Evola glorified the Iron Guard and the SS as models for an ideal Order, "a 'male society' carrying in their hands the principle of *imperium* and holding ... that loyalty is the basis of their honor."[25] To the members of a group like Ordine Nuovo, the goal was more than political: "The aim is to strive for transcendence via a process of veritable ontological rupture carrying the individual to supreme identity with himself, hence with absolute being."[26] For this reason, Evola praised the Islamic idea of the "'dual war'— the 'small,' material one waged against the enemy or the infidel ('small holy war'); and the 'great holy war,'" namely "the struggle of the supra-human element of man against all that is instinctive, passionate, subject to natural forces."[27] According to *Men Among the Ruins*, a man must especially love "the most destructive situations because, being elementary, they offer him the chance to reach the stage that could be called of 'the absolute Being.'"[28] An Order could also replicate at a micro-level Traditional society, where the individual is an organic part of a hierarchical state governed by a caste of warrior-priests. Such a state "cultivates life as an essentially initiatic experience from which the degenerative forces of secularism, egalitarianism, and individualism are kept at bay by ritual and the iron rule of law and caste."[29]

Evola's cult of heroic violence permeated the culture of the ultra-right. Some of Italy's leading young fascists were also extremely knowledgeable occultists. A leading left-wing Italian freemason named Francesco Siniscalchi (who unsuccessfully tried to expose P-2 Grand Master Licio Gelli in the 1970s) encountered some of Italy's top fascists, whom he described as skilled "left-hand path" occultists.[30] In his book *Puppet Masters*, Philip Willan observed that the "remarkable control exercised by the leaders of the extreme right over some of their teenage followers" could in part be explained by "their dabbling in black magic and esotericism."[31] Roger Griffin, another student of the Italian right, believes that the Evolian elite required acts of violence by members as part of their initiation ritual. He also sees similarities

between this process and the left-hand path of Tantric Hinduism that produced the Thugees, another group Evola much admired.[32] Nor was Evola a
novice in such matters: His *Lo Yoga della potenza: Saggio sui Tantra* (The
Yoga of Power) is an important study of Tantric texts.[33]

To rise in such an Order one has to go through a process of initiation and
grades. Seemingly secular acts (like beatings, bombings, and killings) were
conceived as "political" only on a "lower," almost vulgar level; to the initiate, political violence was part of a spiritual path. By tapping into methods
used in the occult and Traditional world, Evola developed extremely powerful
MKULTRA-like thought-control techniques.

Some hint of Evola's method can be found in *The Yoga of Power*, where he
writes that all those who choose to follow an initiatic path must surrender
themselves totally to their spiritual teacher "and obey his orders without
questioning, whether they are reasonable, fair, or humane."[34] In an essay
called "The Way of the Samurai," he glorifies the kamikaze for realizing that
"one's individual existence is unreal" and that death is merely the "sacrifice
of the ephemeral and limited part of himself in favor of the 'Higher Self,'
which participates in the so-called 'Great Liberation.'"[35] In his most important postwar book, *Metaphysics of Sex*, Evola examines groups like the
Assassins and cites a French scholar who wrote:

> Before reaching the point where all pleasure was allowed to them, [the
> Assassins] underwent very hard trials; their life was that of the strictest
> orders; they aspired to break their own will and eliminate their own person
> so as to find it again as pure glory in divine splendor. . . . They had to pray,
> to meditate, and exercise themselves in the deeds that disgust us most. But
> as soon as they had reached the freedom of the spirit, everything was per-
> mitted.[36]

In *Metaphysics of Sex* Evola poses "a complete concept [in which] three
aspects are distinguished and confirmed in creation: the power that creates,
the power that preserves, and the power that destroys, and these three correspond to the well-known Hindu triad, Brahma, Vishnu, and Shiva."[37] Given
his political agenda, the old Dadaist was particularly interested in the "Shiva"
aspect of life, the power that destroys:

> Both the western pre-Orphic worship of Dionysus and the religion of
> Zagreus as the "Great Hunter who overthrows everything," and the Eastern
> worship of Shiva and Kali, Durga, and other "fearful" divinities, are equally
> characterized by the acknowledgment and glorification of destruction, vio-
> lation, and incitement: They admit expression of a liberating frenzy, very
> often strictly linked to orgiastic experience in a ritual, sacrificial, and trans-
> figuring framework.[38]

The Shiva left-hand path, in Evola's interpretation, was especially dear to the Kshatriya caste:

> The *Bhagavad Gita* . . . tells us that the Divinity in his supreme form . . . can only be the infinite, and that the infinite can only represent the crisis, the destruction, and the breaking of everything that has a finite, conditioned, mortal character . . . At this level, time, understood as the force that alters and destroys, is said to embody in a certain way this transcendent aspect of divinity . . . just at the moment of every destructive crisis the supreme reality can appear, the terrifying greatness which transcends all manifestation. The *Bhagavad Gita* adopts this view . . . to metaphysically sanction warlike heroism against humanitarianism and sentimentality. God himself exhorts the warrior Arjuna not to hesitate to fight and strike . . . In his heroic onslaught, which takes no account of his own life or that of others, and which shows faithfulness to his own nature as a son of the warrior caste, Arjuna will reflect the awful and majestic power of the transcendent which breaks and overwhelms everything, thus foreshadowing absolute freedom . . . this state of active and transfiguring exaltation lived and shone, even at the highest moments of the sacrificial experience, in those performing bloody sacrifices, especially if they were done under the sign of "fearful" divinities or aspects of divinity.[39]

Through esoteric initiation and violent acts, one could become a Heracles-like immortal. As Evola puts it: "Knighthood did not necessarily have a hereditary character: It was possible to become a knight as long as the person wishing to become one performed feats that could demonstrate both his heroic contempt for attachment to life as well as . . . faithfulness."[40]

Following their spiritual master, the would-be knights of the Ordine Nuovo broke with the MSI-supported Malmö International in 1956. They then joined the Neue Europaïsche Ordnung (New European Order) led by René Binet and Guy Amaudruz.[41] The NEO was a highly unusual political formation with a powerful esoteric bent. According to the book *Fascism Today*, between 1955 and 1961 "especially among those neo-Nazis who were still dreaming of Orders, initiation ceremonies, aristocracies, and solar civilizations," the NEO "achieved a certain amount of success . . . by exalting not only Hitler's Europe, but also the blood myths, Nietzsche's superman, and Bachofen's theory of the struggle between 'telluric' and 'Olympian' civilizations."[42] The NEO maintained its fascination with far-right racial mythology throughout the 1960s and 1970s. At its 1969 Madrid conference, the organization created the Institut Supérieur des Sciences Psychosomatiques, Biologiques, et Raciales. The Institut, in turn, set up offices in Montreal, including a publishing house called Editions Celtiques. Another branch in Argentina was tied to Professor Jacques de Mahieu, the head of the University of Buenos Aires and president of NEO's Institute for the Science of Man.[43]

The NEO press regularly churned out a strange series of works on mythology and ancient history. It also republished the biopolitical writings of its co-founder, René Binet. As for Evola, Europe's modern Hassan-i-Sabbah died in 1974 at age 76. His disciples scattered his ashes in the Italian Alps.

Notes:

1. H. T. Hansen, introduction to Julius Evola, *Revolt Against the Modern World* (Rochester, VT: Inner Traditions International, 1995).

2. Ibid., p. xxii.

3. Richard Drake, *The Revolutionary Mystique and Terrorism in Contemporary Italy* (Bloomington, IN: Indiana University Press, 1989), p. 126.

4. Evola successfully claimed he was a writer without any organized political affiliation.

5. Franco Ferraresi, "Julius Evola: Tradition, Reaction, and the Radical Right," *Arch. europ. sociol.*, XXVIII (1987), p. 131.

6. My discussion of Prince Borghese's political history comes almost exclusively from Jeffrey Bale's 1994 University of California at Berkeley Ph.D. dissertation, "The 'Black' Terrorist International: Neo-Fascist Paramilitary Networks and the 'Strategy of Tension' in Italy, 1968–1974." Yockey may also have met with Borghese sometime in the mid-1950s. According to H. Keith Thompson: "He [Yockey] certainly knew of Evola, and he may have said that he met him.... I knew Prince Borghese and gave FPY a letter of introduction... I also referred FPY to Marshal Rodolfo Graziani, active in the MSI (he died in 1955). To what extent FPY followed up on these I don't know." (H. Keith Thompson's response to my questionnaire.)

7. After the Italian surrender in 1943, Borghese took 1,300 of his men to fight on the German side and then recruited another 4,000 volunteers to become the naval forces of the Salò Republic.

8. Other top fascists freed by Italy's courts included: Dino Grandi (one of the most influential fascist leaders and a former ambassador, minister of justice, minister of foreign affairs, and president of the Chamber of Fasces and Corporations), Giovanni Giuriati (a senator, minister, president of the Chamber of Deputies, and member of the Fascist Grand Council), Augusto Turati (longtime secretary of the Fascist Party), and Paolo Orano (member of the Grand Council, second-in-command of the militia, secretary of the interior, president of the Chamber of Fasces and Corporations). One of the most notorious cases of amnesty involved Guido Leto, the former head of the OVRA (Mussolini's secret police), who also served as deputy chief of police in the Salò Republic. Franco Ferraresi, "The Radical Right in Postwar Italy," in *Politics and Society*, March, 1988, pp. 108–09.

9. Bale, "The 'Black' Terrorist International," p. 258.

10. Ibid., p. 260. As we shall see later, the CIA had similar designs in Germany for General Heinz Guderian.

11. His decision may have actually appealed to the CIA, which may have felt that Borghese could only reinforce the MSI's pro-Atlanticist orientation. See Bale, "The 'Black' Terrorist International," p. 261.

12. Franco Ferraresi, "A Secret Structure Codenamed Gladio," in *Italian Politics, a Review*, Vol. 7. On the origin of "Gladio-type" networks in Europe, see Sallie Pisani, *The CIA and the Marshall Plan* (Lawrence, KS: University Press of Kansas, 1996), p. 74.

13. Paul Hirst, "Carl Schmitt's Decisionism," *Telos*, No. 72, Summer 1987, p. 16.

14. Mark Neocleous, "Perpetual war, or 'war and war again': Schmitt, Foucault, fascism," in *Philosophy and Social Criticism*, Vol. 22, No. 2, 1996, pp. 48–49.

15. Hirst, "Carl Schmitt's Decisionism," p. 19.

16. Ferraresi, "Julius Evola," p. 131.

17. Rauti's book *Le idee che mossero il mondo* blatantly plagiarized from Evola. See Thomas Sheehan, "Myth and Violence: The Fascism of Julius Evola and Alain de Benoist," in *Social Research*, Vol. 48, No. 1, Spring 1981, fn. 9, p. 50.

18. Rauti's connections to Italian military intelligence are also known. In the mid-1960s, Rauti and another murky ON "journalist" named Guido Giannettini became members of the "brain trust" of the Defense Chief of Staff, the highest military authority in Italy. In May 1965 Ordine Nuovo's leaders attended a famous conference in Rome headed by the military-sponsored Instituto di Studi Storici e Militari "Alberto Pollio" to discuss "revolutionary war." This wing of the Italian military and secret service was especially close to one faction of the Italian General Staff centered around General Giuseppe Aloja, who was locked in a bitter factional struggle with General Giovanni De Lorenzo over the use of special elite "counter subversion" units. The Aloja faction had Rauti (also a journalist for *Il Tempo*) co-write a book with Giannettini. The book (in part an argument for the Italian military to buy German "Leopard" tanks against those like De Lorenzo who wanted the American M-60) was to include a section written by Rauti "promoting the creation of 'politicized' elite units capable of defending the nation against communist subversion." Rauti and Giannettini's book,

> *Le mani rosse sulle Forze armate*, was completed in just over one week. After a few copies were distributed to military commands, Aloja was persuaded that it would be better to recall the book, which accused De Lorenzo of being a virtual communist, so as not to create an irreparable schism within the armed forces. He duly asked Rauti to suspend the diffusion of the book, which the ON leader agreed to do provided that he was adequately compensated. [Bale, "The 'Black' Terrorist International," pp. 155–56.]

In his essay on the radical right in *Politics and Society*, Franco Ferraresi reports that Rauti was given $1,500.

19. David Binder, "Agents of CIA Recall Postwar Resistance Groups in Europe," in the 17 November 1990 *New York Times*.

20. Although Wisner became CIA deputy director for plans in 1951, the merger of OPC with the CIA's Office of Special Operations was not accomplished until 1952. Evan Thomas, *The Very Best Men* (New York: Simon & Schuster, 1975), p. 351. Also see Pisani, *The CIA and the Marshall Plan*, pp. 78–79.

21. Peter Grose, *Gentleman Spy: The Life of Allen Dulles* (Amherst, MA: University of Massachusetts Press, 1996), p. 445.

DREAMER OF THE DAY

22. As I shall show later in this book, Eugen Dollmann, Evola's chief SD contact in the German embassy in Rome, also functioned as a top liaison man between Dulles and the Order.

23. Jung also treated Dulles's wife, Clover, for years. One of Jung's assistants, Mary Bancroft, was an OSS operative in Switzerland as well as Allen Dulles's mistress. Like Evola, Jung was an expert in myth, symbol, and psyche with a complex and ambiguous relationship to the Third Reich.

24. Ferraresi, "Julius Evola and the Radical Right," p. 138.

25. Ibid., p. 126.

26. Ibid., p. 132.

27. Ibid., p. 139.

28. Ibid., p. 122.

29. Roger Griffin, "Revolts Against the Modern World," *Literature and History*, Vol. 11, Spring 1985, p. 104.

30. Called "left hand" to distinguish it from more orthodox or "right-hand" sects. Left (*vama*) can also mean "woman" and relates to the sexual and sensual nature of the "left-hand path" as opposed to the austerity practiced by the followers of the "right-hand path."

31. Philip Willan, *Puppet Masters: The Political Use of Terrorism in Italy* (London: Constable, 1991), p. 43.

32. Griffin, "Revolt Against the Modern World," p. 110.

33. Now available in English as *The Yoga of Power: Tantra, Shakti, and the Secret Way* (Rochester, VT: Inner Traditions International, 1992). Evola continued his study of the East and mysticism all through the postwar era. He was closely affiliated with the Instituto Italiano per il Medio ed Estremo Orienta headed by Giuseppe Tucci, one of the world's leading Tibet scholars. The Institute published a journal called *East and West*. Another member of the Institute who was also a close friend of Evola's was Prince Boris de Rachewilz, a right-wing Egyptologist, head of the Ludwig Keimer Foundation, and Ezra Pound's son-in-law. (See Renato Del Ponte, *Julius Evola: Lettere 1955–1974* [Finale Emillia: La Terra degli Avi, 1995] as well as de Rachewiltz's essay "Uno 'Kshatriya' nell'Età del Lupo," in Gianfranco De Turris, *Testimonianze su Evola* [Rome: Edizioni Mediterranee, 1973].) Some of Evola's writings also appeared in the journal *Antaios: Zeitschrift für eine Freiwelt*, edited by Ernst Jünger and Mircea Eliade. Eliade also lectured at the Instituto Italiano; his collection of essays *Occultism, Witchcraft, and Cultural Fashions* (Chicago, IL: University of Chicago Press, 1976) is dedicated to Giuseppe Tucci. Evola wrote the introduction to the Italian edition of Eliade's book on shamanism, *Lo sciamanismo e le technic dell'estasi* (Milan: Bocca, 1957).

34. Evola, *The Yoga of Power*, p. 99.

35. Julius Evola, *Zen: The Religion of the Samurai* (Edmonds, WA: Sure Fire Press/Holmes Publishing Group, 1994), pp. 22–23.

36. Julius Evola, *Metaphysics of Sex* (Rochester, VT: Inner Traditions International, 1991), p. 229.

37. Ibid., p. 108.

38. Ibid., p. 109.

39. Ibid.

40. Evola, *Revolt Against the Modern World*, pp. 79–80.

41. Rauti's ON rowdies were not the first members of a defeated MSI faction to align with the NEO. A few years earlier, the MSI "left wing" broke with both the party and the Malmö International and threw in with the NEO. The MSI left included Giorgio Pini, an undersecretary of the interior in the Salò Republic who later became the leader of the Salò veterans organization, the Federazione Nazionale Combattenti Reppublicani Sociale Italiani, which was later taken over by Prince Borghese. Pini quit the MSI in 1952 because it was "a reactionary party without a future."

The NEO "left" included René Binet's French comrade Marc Augier (also known as Saint-Loup). A former member of the French Socialist Party, Augier had fought for the Waffen SS Charlemagne Division on the Eastern Front after becoming convinced that the only way socialism could be achieved in Europe was through National Socialism. After hiding out in Austria after the war, he made his way to South America and briefly served as a lieutenant-colonel in the Argentine army. He then returned to France, where he hooked up with Binet (also a veteran of the Charlemagne Division), and together they published *Combattant Européen*.

42. Angelo del Boca and Mario Giovana, *Fascism Today* (New York: Pantheon, 1969), p. 86.

43. Serge Dumont, *Les Brigades Noires* (Brussels: EPO, 1983), pp. 35–36. Jacques Maria de Mahieu was an expert in medieval philosophy who had fought with the Nazis during World War II. In the early 1950s he was part of the Buenos Aires–based *Centro de Estudios Economicos Sociales*, which published a journal called *Dinamica Social*. For a brief discussion of the group, see *Europa Nazione*, Vol. 1, No. 2, 1951.

I believe the Montreal and Buenos Aires groups were branches of the NEO's Institut. The NEO's Guy Amaudruz was the secretary general of what I believe was the official umbrella group based in Lausanne called the Institut Supérieur des Sciences Psychosomatique, Biologiques, et Raciales. There was also a German branch called the Akademie für Psychosomatik, Biologie, und Rassenkunde. For more on the NEO's occult worldview, see the appendix "Nos."

35

DOES MARS
NEED WOMEN?

More than any other mass mass movement that has arisen in the 20th century, Nazism still retains an eerie, mythic quality. To historian Saul Friedländer, Nazism remains "a footprint, an echo of lost worlds, haunting an imagination invaded by excessive rationality and thus becoming the crystallization point for thrusts of the archaic and of the irrational."[1] According to Susan Sontag, Nazism "fascinates in a way other iconography staked out by the Pop sensibility (from Mao Tse-tung to Marilyn Monroe) does not."[2] Michel Foucault wondered:

> How is it that Nazism—which was represented by shabby, pathetic, puritanical characters, laughably Victorian old maids, or at best smutty individuals—how has it now managed to become, in France, in Germany, in the United States, in all pornographic literature throughout the world, the ultimate symbol of eroticism? Every shoddy erotic fantasy is now attributed to Nazism.[3]

The continuing appeal of the mythic, erotic, visionary, hyper-masculinized "otherness" of Nazism resists conventional historical analysis.

Fascism's sexual mystique was quite important to Yockey. At the time of his death he appears to have been working on a text entitled *America's Destiny* that had a significant sexual-political content. Yockey first attacked American culture as feminine in *Imperium*; in *America's Destiny* he planned to elaborate on his argument.[4] He was apparently taking notes for this project, because the FBI found "two pages of materials from *Social Justice in England*

and America by H. G. Wells and *Sex and Character* by Otto Weininger" in his suitcase.

Yockey's interest in Otto Weininger, one of the strangest figures in 20th-century intellectual history, is particularly striking. Weininger is best known as the author of *Geschlecht und Charakter* (Sex and Character), first published in 1903. *Sex and Character* claimed that cultures and races were either "feminine" or "masculine" and could be interpreted along a spectrum whose antipodes were "Absolute Manhood" and "Absolute Womanhood." Shortly after the book's publication, Weininger committed suicide in Beethoven's house in Vienna.

Like Bachofen, Weininger influenced European culture in oblique ways. In a 1919 essay for *The Little Review*, Ford Maddox Ford recalled:

> The most important, as it is the most singular, of contributions to modern literature on the sex question is an extraordinary work called in English *Sex and Character*. This book is noteworthy because it had an immense international vogue . . . I remember sitting with a table full of overbearing intellectuals in that year [1906], and they at once began to talk—about Weininger. It gave me a singular feeling because they all talked under their breaths.[5]

Julius Evola was especially affected by *Sex and Character*. He edited and wrote an introduction to the 1956 Italian edition of the book (*Sesso e carattere*),[6] and was inspired by Weininger to write *Metaphysics of Sex* in 1958.[7] Ludwig Wittgenstein also considered *Sex and Character* important because it explored the relationship between logic and ethics.[8] *Sex and Character* even occupied a prized place on Adolf Hitler's bookshelf. While it is not known whether Hitler actually *read* the book, he certainly learned about Weininger's ideas from Dietrich Eckhart. Hitler once remarked that "Dietrich Eckhart told me that in all his life he had known just one good Jew: Otto Weininger, who killed himself on the day when he realized that the Jew lives upon the decay of peoples."

Sex and Character argues that each individual is torn between following Kant's Categorical Imperative and the heteronomic pursuit of sensual pleasure and gratification at the expense of others. Weininger biologically grounded his idea by arguing for a universal human bisexuality. While the ideal Masculine type is associated with rational conduct and morality, the ideal Feminine embodies the non-rational in a way similar to Kant's notion of "radical evil" in human nature. Because all humans are bisexual, everyone is to some degree or another "guilty" of letting their irrational passions defy reason's dictate.[9]

Although all individuals share traits of "Absolute Manhood" and "Absolute Womanhood," Absolute Womanhood is most pronounced in women because they are closer to nature. "Woman" not only lacks a higher spiritual capacity; she also lacks an ego or "being" since Weininger's "ego" is modeled on Kant's transcendental ego, which transcends empirical reality.[10] Absolute Manhood, however, has ontological links to the transcendental ego. The human capacity for memory also enters into the mix because memory is a synthetic function. Logic is associated with Being's resistance to phenomena. Absolute Womanhood, however, lacks being, memory, logic, and ethics understood in a transcendental sense.[11]

Commenting on Weininger's ideas in *Metaphysics of Sex*, Evola writes:

> We are not dealing with everyday logic, which woman, when necessary, knows how to use "instrumentally" with undoubted ability and ingenuity . . . Instead, we are dealing with logic as a love of pure truth and inward coherence, which leads to a strict and impersonal style of thought that constitutes a sort of inner imperative for the absolute man. Woman is almost incapable of this logic, and it does not interest her . . . Woman, insofar as she is woman, will never know ethics in the categorical sense of pure inner law detached from every empirical, eudemonistic, sensitive, sentimental, and personal connection. Nothing in woman that may have an ethical character can be separated from instinct, sentiment, sexuality, or "life"; it can have no relationship with pure "being."[12]

For anyone not imbued with Absolute Manhood, *Sex and Character* remains a difficult book. Its method calls to mind the joke about the Englishman, the Frenchman, and the German who were studying the camel:

> The Frenchman went to *Jardin des Plantes*, spent half an hour there, questioned the guard, threw bread to the camel, poked it with the point of his umbrella, and, returning home, wrote an article for his paper full of sharp and witty observations.
>
> The Englishman, taking his tea basket and a good deal of camping equipment, went to set up camp in the Orient, returning after a sojourn of two or three years with a fat volume, full of raw, disorganized, and inconclusive facts which, nevertheless, had real documentary value.
>
> As for the German, filled with disdain for the Frenchman's frivolity and the Englishman's lack of general ideas, he locked himself in his room and there he drafted a several-volume work entitled: *The Life of the Camel Derived from the Concept of the Ego.*[13]

Weininger argues that he is discussing absolute types (polarities) of Manhood and Womanhood, not actual men and women.[14] Yet he insists that

> women have no existence and no essence; they are not, they are nothing. Mankind occurs as male or female, as something or nothing. Woman has no share in ontological reality, no relation to the thing-in-itself, which, in the deepest interpretation, is the absolute, is God. Man in his highest form, the

genius, has such a relation ... Woman has no relation to the idea, she neither affirms nor denies it; she is neither moral nor anti-moral; mathematically speaking, she has no sign; she is purposeless, neither good nor bad, neither angel nor devil, never egotistical (and therefore has often been said to be altruistic); she is as non-moral as she is non-logical. But all existence is moral and logical existence. So woman has no existence.

Woman is untruthful. An animal has just as little metaphysical reality as the actual woman, but it cannot speak, and consequently it does not lie. In order to speak the truth one must *be* something; truth is dependent on an existence, and only that can have a relation to an existence which is itself something ... So that woman always lies, even if, objectively, she speaks the truth.[15]

The meaning of woman is to be meaningless. She represents negation, the opposite pole from the Godhead, the other possibility of humanity. And so nothing is so despicable as a man become female, and such a person will be regarded as the supreme criminal even by himself. And so also is to be experienced the deepest fear of man; the fear of the woman, which is the fear of unconsciousness, the alluring abyss of annihilation ... Immorality is the will towards negation, the craving to change the formed into the formless, the wish for destruction. And from this comes the intimate relation between femaleness and crime.[16]

Not only do women and homosexuals ("a man become female") partake in criminality, so do certain races. "What shall we make" of the Chinese "feminine freedom from internal cravings and their incapacity for every effort? One might feel tempted to believe in the complete effeminacy of the whole race." As for blacks: "A genius has perhaps scarcely ever appeared amongst the negroes, and the standard of their morality is almost universally so low that it is beginning to be acknowledged in America that their emancipation was an act of imprudence."[17]

Perhaps because he was from a Jewish family that had converted to Christianity, the Jews attracted Weininger's special scrutiny, although he claims in his discussion of Judaism that he was neither attacking "a race nor a people nor a recognized creed" but "a tendency of the mind."[18] To Weininger, Judaism was "saturated with femininity" to the point that "the most manly Jew is more feminine than the least manly Aryan."[19] "Greatness," both the "greatness of morality" and the "greatness of evil," was absent from both Jews and women, although in "Aryan man, the good and bad principles of Kant's religious philosophy are ever present, ever in strife."[20] As for sex: "The Jew is always more absorbed by sexual matters than the Aryan," although Jews were "notably less potent sexually and less liable to be enmeshed in a great passion."[21] The Jew was also "an inborn communist."[22] Socialism, on the other hand, "is Aryan (Owen, Caryle, Ruskin, Fichte)."[23] Judaism had also ruined science:

The Aryan feels that the effort to grasp everything, and to refer everything to some system of deductions, really robs things of their true meaning; for him, what cannot be discovered is what gives the world its significance. The Jew has no fear of these hidden and secret elements, for he has no consciousness of their presence. He tries to take a view of the world as flat and commonplace as possible, and to refuse to see all the secret and spiritual meanings of all things. His view is non-philosophical rather than anti-philosophical.[24]

It is the Jew and the woman who are the apostles of pairing to bring guilt to humanity. Our age is not only the most Jewish but the most feminine.[25]

The homosexual played a role analogous to the Jew and the female because Weininger believed that "in all cases of sexual inversion" there was an "anatomical approximation to the opposite sex." The choice, then, was between "Judaism and Christianity, between business and culture, between male and female, between the race and the individual, between unworthiness and worth . . . between negation and the God-like . . . There are only two poles, and there is not a middle way."[26]

Through Lanz von Liebenfel's racialist/occultist publication *Ostara*, Hitler was given a "sci-fi," comic-book version of Weininger's war of absolute polarities. Here humanity was divided "into two races: the *Aesir*, the 'Nordic Gods of Light,' including all blond hero-types, and the *Vanir*, the 'creatures of the darkness,' including *Tschandalas*, dark-haired runts, and apelike perverts who try to cloak their inherent inferiority in a pious and otherworldly phraseology."[27] In the war between the Gods of Light and the Vanir we also see Hyperborea against the South, the Kshatriya against the Mothers, Male against Female, Aryan against Jew.

Another striking influence on Yockey was an obscure German intellectual named Hans Blüher—one of the most important figures in one faction of the early German gay liberation movement. Evidence of Yockey's strong interest in Blüher comes from Elsa Dewette, who reports that Yockey was so enthusiastic about Blüher's *Die Rolle der Erotik in der männelichen Gesellschaft* (The Role of the Erotic in Male Societies) that in March 1950 he translated the entire second volume into English for her because her German "had gotten a little hazy from lack of practice."[28] She also cited a passage from Blüher that Yockey had translated:

The LEAGUE is the proselyte for that way of life that the GREEKS called ETHOS. This word has something to do with the MAN. It gives notice that the man has already pledged his best to the man. Our most essential, superabundant, purest, and as they say, most selfless performances are, in one way or another, born in the light of a superior man who gave the stimulus to them. Whoever is in the League cannot sink: All are sustained by this utter certainty.

Women strive constantly WHOLLY to possess a man. That trap-door to oblivion which lies hidden in a well-guarded secret place in her being, demands a sacrifice: In this way, most men go to ruins through their wives.

Yockey then commented: "I have always said this. My phrase was and remains: Nearly all women bring out the worst in men: the economic and the social."[29]

Unlike Weininger, Blüher attacked the notion that homosexuals were an intermediate or "third" sex. The originator of the "third sex" or "Uranian" theory (from Plato's discussion in the *Symposium* on homosexual love as belonging to the "Muse Urania") was the German writer Karl Heinrich Ulrichs. Ulrichs believed that the male homosexual was a type of androgyne—a female soul trapped in a male body.[30] His argument greatly influenced the first gay liberation organization in Germany, Doctor Magnus Hirschfeld's Scientific Humanitarian Committee. Hirschfeld's Committee published the *Jahrbuch für sexuelle Zwischenstufen* (Yearbook for Intermediate Sexual Types). Needless to say, the Nazis hated Hirschfeld, who was first assaulted by anti-Semites in 1920 in Munich. He was again attacked in 1921 and left for dead with a fractured skull. There was yet another assassination attempt in Vienna in 1923.[31] As soon as the Nazis took power they looted the Berlin headquarters of Hirschfeld's Institute for Sexual Science and burned some 12,000 books from the then-greatest library on sexuality in the world. Heartbroken, Hirschfeld died in exile in 1935.

Within the German homosexual community, there was a different kind of opposition to the biological "third sex" paradigm adopted by Hirschfeld. In 1896, *Der Eigene* (The Self-Owner) was founded as the first homosexual journal in Germany. Its creator, Adolf Brand, also created the *Gemeinschaft der Eigenen* (Community of Self-Owners) that for a brief period was dominated by the anarchist philosophy of Max Stirner.[32] For the Gemeinschaft, the idea that homosexuals were feminine was an abomination.[33]

Before directly examining Blüher, it is necessary to better understand the Gemeinschaft der Eigenen. Although Blüher never formally joined the group, he was very close to one of its founders and financiers, Wilhelm Jansen. Although he was an adult, Jansen became a leader of the Wandervogel youth movement until he was expelled for promoting homosexuality.[34] The Gemeinschaft's main theorist was a wealthy Jewish private scholar named Benedict Friedländer, who wrote *Renaissance des Eros Uranios* in 1904. In it, he called for "erotic" (but not "sexual") relations between men and boys (*Männer und Jünglingsliebe*) and opposed any attempt to medicalize homosexuality along the "third sex" model. He also claimed that most medical theories about homosexuality were modern versions of Christian superstition led by priests and supported by women.[35]

To the Gemeinschaft, "homosexual and heterosexual behavior was predominantly determined culturally . . . and the same was true of masculinity and femininity . . . the association of homosexuality with effeminate men was also a consequence of social processes."[36] While the Gemeinschaft conceded that sex with women was necessary for procreation, it celebrated the aesthetic superiority of pedophile relations between men and boys. Non-bisexuals were ridiculed as *Kümmerlinge* (atrophied or puny beings).[37]

Friedländer was obsessed with the notion that the rise of female power in culture and politics was destroying Western civilization. He turned to Bachofen's *Das Mutterrecht* to prove that the growth of democratic society, with its "slave morality," foreshadowed a reversion to a "matriarchate" when male spirituality had been crushed by primitive communism and superstition. Progress in society was only made possible once groups of secret male societies (*Männerbünde*) broke the chains of matriarchy through a series of wars that subjugated both women and "inferior races."

In his 1906 *Male and Female Culture*, Friedländer, like Weininger before him, divided world cultures into male and female. Muslim countries and Japan met with his approval. The United States, England, and France, however, had become too feminine, thus bringing the continued world supremacy of the white race into question. In *Seven Propositions*, written a few weeks before his death in 1908, he also warned against the coming "yellow peril."[38] Friedländer begins *Seven Propositions*: "The white race is becoming even sicker under the curse of Christianity, which is foreign to it and mostly harmful. That is the genuinely bad 'Jewish influence,' an opinion that has been proven true, especially through the conditions in North America."[39]

Friedländer drew up a "Synopsis of Some Characteristics of Persons of Predominantly Male and Predominantly Female Culture," which is reminiscent of Yockey's list of opposites in *Der Feind Europas*, at times even in style. Some of his polarities (Male Culture versus Female Culture) include:

[Male] Correct estimate of woman as spouse, housewife, and mother.
[Female] Exaggerated superstitious veneration of woman as a being equal by
    birth in every respect, in extreme cases as superior.
[Male] Wealth little respected.
[Female] Wealth highly respected; something already emphasized by Aristotle.
[Male] Small danger of a plutocracy.
[Female] Danger of a plutocracy very great.
[Male] Heroic national defensive wars against overpowering attackers.
[Female] Predatory and exploitative wars against powerless nations with the
    goal of enriching the plutocracy.
[Male] Sexual candor and openness.
[Female] Sexual hypocrisy and prudery.

[Male] National art of an original kind, which participates in the intimate, living part of the people.

[Female] Private art of luxury and show, predominantly imitative.

[Male] Esteem for the beauty of youths.

[Female] Woman considered the beautiful sex.

[Male] Main model from antiquity, Hellas before and at its golden period.

[Female] Main model from antiquity, Egypt, as well as Rome from the beginning of its downfall; yet here more penetrating cultural studies are still required.

[Male] Main modern example Japan. (Of the half-civilized peoples apparently many Muslim nations.)

[Female] Main modern example the United States of America. (Of half-civilized peoples apparently Tibet.)

[Male] Recognition, high position, and encouragement of genius.

[Female] Recognition, high position, and encouragement of advanced narrow-mindedness and related careerism.[40]

In the 1920s, journals like *Der Eigene* and *Eros* continued Friedländer's polemics against the corrupting influence of America in particular, because American consumerism was said to be even more of a threat to Germany than Bolshevik Russia.[41] Only a war-oriented homoerotic culture could save Germany from impending decadence.[42]

In 1902, under the inspiration of Heinrich Schurtz's then-current bestseller *Altersklassen und Männerbünde: Eine Darstelling der Grundformen der Gesellschaft* (Age Groups and Male Societies: A Presentation of the Origin of Society), the Gemeinschaft began a close study of secret, all-male societies called Männerbunds as the possible vehicle for the revival of "male culture." Schurtz argued that men had two primal drives, the sexual and the social or state-building. Women, however, only had a sexual drive. Civilization therefore arose out of the "instinctive sympathy" between men. His argument was later expanded upon by Hans Blüher, who in 1912 wrote a bestseller about the Wandervogel youth movement entitled *Die deutsche Wandervogelbewegung als erotisches Phänomen* (The German Youth Movement as an Erotic Phenomenon), which claimed that the movement was the expression of a homoerotic attraction between men and boys. He wrote a follow-up book in 1917 entitled *Die Rolle der Erotik in der männlichen Gesellschaft* (The Role of the Erotic in Male Society), which Yockey partially translated.[43]

Blüher adopted Freud's idea about culture as a product of sexual sublimation to claim that a certain kind of male homosexual was society's most socially creative individual. Instead of spending all his energy on his family, the masculine-identified homosexual directed "his sexual energies into creative occupations," including the formation of the state.[44] The state now became more than a utilitarian organization for protection; it also represented a force for national unity around a common point of identity through a kind of male-to-male Eros.[45] Blüher soon became "one of the most important right-wing ideologues of the Männerbund, propagating a purification of German society under the guidance of all-male brotherhoods, in which members would be devoted to each other by homoeroticism and charismatic leadership."[46]

Hitler's relationship to the theorists of the Männerbund began while he was a loyal reader of Lanz von Liebenfels's *Ostara*, which was subtitled *Bücherei der Blonden und Mannesrechtler* (Library for the Blond and Male Supremacist). Liebenfels had founded his own Bund of aryosophic male supremacists called the "Templar Order." Paul Harald Grävell, a contributor to *Der Eigene*, also wrote for *Ostara*, which James Steakley characterizes as "the Nordic and male-supremacist journal which Hitler so admired."[47] Steakley believes that Hitler's views on homosexuality had "a truly striking affinity" with *Der Eigene*. The elitism of the "Community of the Special," however, challenged Hitler's ideal of a *Volksgemeinschaft*, a volkish community.[48]

Hitler's ambivalence on the question of homosexuality came out in his private conversations. He believed, for example, that homosexuality had destroyed ancient Greece by its "infectious activity" that spread "with the certainty of a natural law among the best and most masculine natures . . . it cut off from propagation precisely those whose offspring a people [Volk] depended upon."[49] It should also be recalled that for years he worked closely with Ernst Roehm, the openly homosexual head of the SA.[50]

Many Nazis were drawn to the Männerbunden model.[51] To Goebbels, National Socialism was a masculine movement by nature. Alfred Rosenberg saw the Third Reich as the result of a purposeful Männerbund, and elevated the philosopher Alfred Bäumler, a leading promoter of the Männerbund ideal, to head the Institut für politische Pädagogik at the University of Berlin in 1933. Although Bäumler joined the NSDAP only after Hitler took power, from 1929 on he had been a member of Rosenberg's *Kampfbund für deutsche Kultur* (Crusade for German Culture).[52] Yet before his conversion to the Männerbund, Bäumler had been one of Germany's leading exponents of Bachofen. He even wrote a three-hundred-page preface to a 1926 reprint of Bachofen's works entitled *Der Mythus von Orient und Occident: eine Metaphysik der Alten Welt aus den Werken von J. J. Bachofen* (The Myth of Orient and Occident: The Metaphysics of the Old World in the Work of J. J. Bachofen). Here Bäumler hailed Bachofen as the most brilliant mythologist of German Romanticism and linked his idea of matriarchy to the Volk. "The way of the Volk is the way of woman," Bäumler wrote, "anonymous, without person, producing unconsciously, at work quietly like nature." Mocking leftist intellectuals who tried to claim Bachofen as one of their own, Bäumler said that Bachofen always stressed the mythical, the metaphysical, or "maternal side of history."[53]

For Bäumler, matriarchy played a necessary role in the transition to higher forms of patriarchal society. By 1933, however, he had radically shifted toward an idealization of the Männerbunden as the crucial element in the formation of all civilization, a view similar to that first expounded by Friedländer, Blüher, and the Gemeinschaft. Although he had earlier praised Bachofen against Nietzsche, Bäumler now became a supporter of an expressly "masculine" Nietzsche.

The Männerbund model provided a perfect internal structure for Julius Evola's Order. "L'Ordre," Evola wrote, "a essentiellement le caractère d'une société virile (Männerbund)."[54] For both Yockey and Evola, Blüher's key text was his two-volume *Die Rolle der Erotik in der männlichen Gesellschaft.*[55] Here Blüher dealt with the homosexual pairs exemplified by Spartiate military figures and the sacred Seven Hundred of Thebes. He also discussed squires and knights of chivalric times, the Templars, the Freemasons, and a number of so-called "savage" or "primitive" societies.[56] He argued that all these groups had been unified through social bonds of a sexual character often camouflaged by an elaborate ritual superstructure. At the center of these societies was a group of legendary heros like Heracles, who symbolically represented a kind of homosocial/homoerotic ideal. They were, in turn, surrounded by a number of deputies or subleaders who were the hero's favorite companions.[57]

Yockey's fascination with both Weininger and Blüher is telling evidence of his mind's inner workings. In the early 1950s he also began experimenting with sado-masochism—more specifically, whipping women. Yockey's attraction to S/M was equally evident in his series of S/M-themed "John Priapus" stories, which the FBI found in his suitcase in 1960. Yet it would be wrong to reduce Yockey's inclinations to just a quirk of personality. In order to understand why, we must return one last time to Julius Evola.

Notes:

1. Saul Friedländer, *Reflections of Nazism* (Bloomington, IN: Indiana University Press, 1993), p. 49.

2. In "Fascinating Fascism," Sontag writes:

In pornographic literature, films, and gadgetry throughout the world, especially in the United States, England, France, Japan, Scandinavia, Holland, and Germany, the SS has become a referent of sexual adventurism. Much of the imagery of far-out sex has been placed under the sign of Nazism . . . But why? Why has Nazi Germany, which was a sexually repressive society, become erotic? [*A Susan Sontag Reader* (New York: Farrar Strauss Giroux, 1982), p. 323.]

3. *Foucault Live* (New York: Semiotext[e], 1989), p. 97.

4. Yockey had even clipped articles from U.S. papers with titles like "Why Does He Work So Hard?" In the late 1950s, the argument that the lack of a strong father in suburban homes, where children spent most of their time with their mother, would produce a generation unfit for the tasks demanded by the Cold War, was briefly in vogue. I suspect that Yockey's press clippings examined the growing "domestication" of the American male.

5. Bram Dijkstra, *Idols of Perversity: Fantasies of Feminine Evil in Fin-de-Siècle Culture* (New York: Oxford University Press, 1986), p. 218. The popularity of works like Max Nordau's *Degeneration* should also be recalled.

6. Otto Weininger, *Sesso e carattere* (Milan: Bocca, 1956).

7. Julius Evola, *Metafisica del sesso* (Rome: "Atanòr," 1958). Also see Evola's *La Cammino del Cinabro* (The Path of Cinabar), first published in 1963 and translated into French as *Le Chemin du Cinabre* (Milan: Editions Arché, 1982), p. 180.

8. Wittgenstein was in Vienna at the time of Weininger's suicide, and there are reports that he attended the funeral

9. Weininger's theory of original bisexuality can be traced back to Wilhelm Fliess. After *Sex and Character* was published, Fleiss wrote an angry letter to Freud claiming that Weininger had gotten some of his key ideas from a pupil of Freud's named Swoboda. (When Weininger killed himself, he left his library and papers to Swoboda.) Fliess told Freud:

> A book by Weininger has come to my attention in which I find, to my astonishment, my ideas on bisexuality and the consequent kind of sexual attraction—feminine men attract masculine women and vice versa—expounded in the first biological section. I see from one of the quotations that Weininger was in contact with Swoboda—your pupil. [Vincent Brome, *Freud and His Early Circle* (London: Heinemann, 1967), p. 7.]

10. Julius Evola, *Metaphysics of Sex* (Rochester, VT: Inner Traditions International, 1991), pp. 150–51.

11. Weininger's ideas did not emerge out of thin air. His major intellectual predecessor on the "woman question" was Schopenhauer. See in particular Schopenhauer's essay "Of Women," in his *Studies in Pessimism* (New York: Boni and Liveright, 1925). Weininger was also writing against the Viennese physicist Ernst Mach, who had revitalized Humean empiricism in psychology by, among other things, calling into question the existence of the transcendental ego.

12. Evola, *Metaphysics of Sex*, pp. 153–54.

13. Luc Ferry and Alain Renault, *French Philosophy of the Sixties* (Amherst, MA: University of Massachusetts Press, 1990). Contrast this with British Labor leader Hugh Dalton's observation that the Germans were best described as "a race of carnivorous sheep."

14. Otto Weininger, *Sex and Character* (New York: G. P. Putnam, 1906), p. 9. "Intermediate sexual forms are normal, not pathological phenomena, in all classes of organisms, and their appearance is no proof of physical decadence" (p. 253).

15. Ibid., pp. 286–87. "Women have neither this nor that characteristic; their peculiarity consists in having no characteristics at all; the complexity and terrible mystery about women comes to this; it is this which makes them above and

beyond man's understanding—man who always wants to get to the heart of things." (p. 194)

16. Ibid., pp. 297–98.

17. Ibid., p. 302.

18. Ibid., pp. 303–06.

19. Ibid., p. 306.

20. Ibid., p. 309.

21. Ibid., p. 311.

22. Ibid.

23. Ibid., p. 307.

24. Ibid., p. 314.

25. Ibid., p. 329.

26. Ibid., p. 330.

27. Jorg Hermand, "The Distorted Vision," in *Myth and Reason: A Symposium,* edited by Walter Wetzels (Austin, TX: University of Texas Press, 1973), p. 115. "Tschandala" came from the title of an August Strindberg novel. Strindberg was a member of List's society and "participated in ancient Germanic rites which Lanz von Liebenfels, with List's assistance, performed in one of his Hungarian castles." George Mosse, "The Mystical Origins of National Socialism," in *Journal of History of Ideas,* January–March 1961, p. 96.

28. Elsa Dewette, letter to Keith Stimely, 15 January 1982. In 1952 the FBI was given a copy of Yockey's Blüher translation from Warren Johnson. The FBI note reads: "'The Masculine Choice of a Wife,' from *Die Rolle der Erotik in den Mannlichen Gesellschaft,* HANS BLUHER, which contains about eighteen inserts by VARANGE. This is not pertinent." From FBI File CG 100-25647 by Agent Donald Holland.

29. Elsa Dewette, letter to Keith Stimely, 25 January 1984. Yockey may have first become aware of Blüher through a book by Samuel Igra entitled *Germany's National Vice* (London: Quality Press Ltd., 1945).

30. James Steakley, *The Homosexual Emancipation Movement in Germany* (New York: Arno Press, 1975), p. 6.

31. Ibid., p. 88.

32. "When Brand started his journal he was inspired by a kind of anarchism which should not be confused with the main current of socialist anarchism. The Stirnerian anarchism Brand felt attracted to has more in common with left-wing liberalism." (Harry Oosterhuis, "Introduction" to part V, *Journal of Homosexuality,* Vol. 22, No. 1/2, 1991, p. 183.) *Der Eigene* only promoted direct anarchist themes for two years.

James Steakley says that the Gemeinschaft was actually closer to the notorious German anti-Semite Eugen Düring: "*Der Eigene* had at first a Stirnerian anarchist editorial stance which evolved over time to an anti-Marxist 'libertarian socialism,' or 'socialitarianism,' closely reflecting Friedländer's admiration of Eugen Düring." Steakley, *The Homosexual Emancipation Movement,* p. 43. For a recent appreciation of Düring from a far-right perspective, see Alexander Jacob, *Eugen Düring on the Jews* (Brighton, U.K.: 1984 Press, 1987).

33. Harry Oosterhuis, "Introduction" to part II, *Journal of Homosexuality*, Vol. 22, No. 1/2, p. 29. This entire issue is devoted to the German right and homosexuality, and includes reprints from Friedländer and other Gemeinschaft authors. All my citations from the *Journal of Homosexuality* are from this issue. The Gemeinschaft first criticized the "medical model" paradigm for homosexuality, thus stressing "culture" over "nature." Also see Andrew Hewitt, *Political Inversions: Homosexuality, Fascism, & the Modernist Imagination* (Stanford, CA: Stanford University Press, 1996).

34. Jansen, a wealthy Hessian landowner, was also involved in nudism, sunbathing, gymnastics, and physical culture. He created his own group, the all-male *Jung-Wandervogel*, which openly endorsed the idea of the community as an erotic bond. Blüher's book on the Wandervogel was an act of special pleading by the Jansen faction. Peter Stachura, *The German Youth Movement 1900–1945* (New York: St. Martin's Press, 1981), p. 28. For a detailed look at Blüher and Jansen, as well as Blüher's conflict with Hirschfeld, see Richard Mills, "The German Youth Movement (Wandervogel)," in *Gay Roots* (San Francisco: Gay Sunshine Press, 1991), edited by Winston Leyland.

35. Harry Oosterhuis, "Introduction" to part II, *Journal of Homosexuality*, p. 33.

36. Ibid., p. 31. Hirschfeld's Committee had assigned "uranian petticoats to profound minds and heros."

37. Steakley, *The Homosexual Emancipation Movement*, p. 46.

38. Harry Oosterhuis, "Introduction" to part V, *Journal of Homosexuality*, p. 187.

39. Benedict Friedländer, "Seven Propositions," *Journal of Homosexuality*, p. 219.

40. Benedict Friedländer, "Male and Female Culture: A Causal-Historical View," *Journal of Homosexuality*, pp. 215–16. Friedländer also praises Düring in his Male Culture list: "Blossoming of the human sciences in close union of teachers and pupils. The most capable come to word and influence. The case of Socrates is basically less bad than our trio Schopenhauer, Robert Mayer, and Düring."

41. Harry Oosterhuis, "Introduction" to part V, *Journal of Homosexuality*, p. 187.

42. Ibid., pp. 187–88.

43. Walter Laqueur, *Young Germany: A History of the German Youth Movement* (London: Routledge, 1962), p. 51.

44. George Mosse, *The Crisis of German Ideology* (New York: Schocken Books, 1981), p. 213.

45. Ibid., p. 214.

46. Harry Oosterhuis, "Homosexuality and Male Bonding in Pre-Nazi Germany," *Journal of Homosexuality*, p. 123.

47. Steakley, *The Homosexual Emancipation Movement*, fn. 34, p. 67. In *The Occult Roots of Nazism* (Wellingborough, Northamptonshire: The Aquarian Press, 1985), pp. 100–0¹ Nicholas Goodrick-Clarke describes Harald Grävell van Jostennoode (1856–1932) as "the principal theosophist of Lanz's acquaintance with

the exception of Guido List." In July 1906 Grävell wrote an *Ostara* article demanding the return of the Hapsburg crown jewels to the German Reich. "The next indication of a theosophical bias in *Ostara* was Grävell's second contribution in July 1908. Here he outlined a thoroughly theosophical conception of race and a program for the restoration of Aryan authority in the world."

48. Steakley, *The Homosexual Emancipation Movement*, p. 119.

49. Harry Oosterhuis, "Male Bonding and Homosexuality in German Nationalism," *Journal of Homosexuality*, p. 249.

50. Charles Bracelen Flood, in *Hitler: The Path to Power* (Boston: Houghton Mifflin, 1989), notes of Roehm (p. 196):

> Berlin's specialized establishments included a bathhouse featuring black male prostitutes; later, one of its ardent devotees was Hitler's friend and supporter Captain Ernst Röhm, who moved from latent to overt homosexuality when he was seduced by the noted Freikorps commander Gerhard Rossbach. Röhm wrote a friend that "the steambath there is, in my opinion, the epitome of all human happiness."

51. It should also be noted that there were two important historical studies of Männerbunds published in the late 1920s and early 1930s: Lily Weiser's *Altgermanische Jünglingsweihen und Männerbünde* and Otto Höfler's *Kultische Geheimbünde der Germanen*.

52. See Hans Sluga, *Heidegger's Crisis* (Cambridge, MA: Harvard University Press, 1993), for an interesting portrait of Bäumler and Rosenberg. Also recall that Rosenberg hated the Ahnenerbe's Hans Wirth, who advocated a matriarchal conception of the German Volk.

53. Jost Hermand, "All Power to the Women: Nazi Concepts of Matriarchy," in the *Journal of Contemporary History*, October 1984, Vol. 19, No. 4.

54. Christophe Boutin, *Politique et Tradition: Julius Evola dans le Siècle (1898–1974)* (Paris: Kime, 1992), p. 345.

55. In *Gli uomini e le rovine* (p. 32), Evola also footnotes Schurtz's *Altersklassen und Männerbunde*.

56. Howard Becker, *German Youth: Bond or Free* (London: Kegan Paul, 1946), p. 64.

57. Ibid.

36

METAPHYSICS

OF THE WHIP

Yockey's interest in sado-masochism had its roots in his fascination with polarity as the clash of fixed opposites, in this case male and female. Yockey, I believe, whipped women because he saw this practice as a manifestation of a conscious "sex-pol."

Julius Evola also advocated whipping women as a form of "consciousness-raising." He outlined his reasons why in *Metaphysics of Sex*, his 1958 book directly inspired by Otto Weininger.[1] Evola saw sexuality as a bridge to the "transpsychological and transphysiological" realm of the Gods.[2] "For ordinary mankind," he wrote, "it is sex alone which, even if only in the rapture, illusion, or obscure trauma of an instant, leads to some opening through and beyond the conditionalities of merely individual existence."[3] According to Evola, the "Traditional" world had a far superior understanding of sexuality as a path to "manifold states of being" than did the hopelessly materialist Freudian West.[4] Modern scholars of religion who insisted that beliefs in gods and goddesses were anthropomorphic had gotten it wrong. Traditional man had sought "the secret and essence of sex" in the divine. Like Weininger's Absolute Man and Absolute Woman, the sexes existed as transcendental principles; before appearing in "nature," "they existed in the realm of the sacred, the cosmic, and the spiritual." The many different gods and goddesses exhibited the essence of the eternal male and eternal female. Therefore, "instead of human sex being the foundation for the understanding of the reality of sexually differentiated divine and mythological figures, it is precisely the content of these figures that will give us the key to the deepest and most universal aspects of sex in man and woman."[5]

356

The key to sexuality in Evola's system was the yin and yang of sex polarity embodied in Weininger's Absolute Manhood and Absolute Womanhood. Eros should, above all, be considered as a state "governed directly by the polarity of the sexes in the same way that the presence of positive and negative poles governs the phenomenon of magnetism and everything connected to a magnetic field."[6]

But how were the polarities of Manhood and Womanhood actually manifested? To answer this, Evola first turned to the Platonic legend of the original Hermaphrodite, or what he calls a primordial race "whose essence is now extinct" and which contained in itself both the male and female principles. This hermaphroditic race "was extraordinarily strong and brave, and they nourished in their hearts very arrogant designs, even unto an attack upon the gods themselves."[7] In other words, the hermaphrodites shared the same legendary hubris as the fallen Luciferian angels who first brought the "Hermetic royal art" to mankind.

In punishment for their rebellion, the original bisexual hermaphrodites were broken in two and made male or female, although there were some who still "retained the memory of their earlier state, and in whom the impulse to reconstitute the primordial unity was kindled."[8] At its highest level, then, Eros overcomes the original division and returns man to his elemental state:

> In its most profound aspects, eros embodies an impulse to overcome the consequences of the Fall, to leave the restrictive world of duality, to restore the primordial state, to surmount the condition of dual existentiality broken and conditioned by the "other." This is the absolute meaning of eros.[9]

Much of *Metaphysics of Sex* explores various symbols, initiation rites, rituals, and sexual practices from ancient societies (like the tantric schools of India) to modern occultists like Aleister Crowley. Evola's purpose is to argue that through both knowledge and ritual practice, the individual can overcome his materialistic, merely reproductive, or pleasurable interest in sex and use erotic passion as an ecstatic launching pad into the world of Being. The path of the spiritual lover, like that of the spiritual warrior, also bypasses the need for a mediating priest caste.

Yet behind Evola's argument, there lurked a barely concealed hatred for the female. Like Weininger, Evola thought that the female represented the principle of becoming, chaos, night, formlessness, anarchy, and the south. Existence was a cosmic struggle between the spiritual male Olympian-Uranian element of the cosmos against Titanic, demonic-feminine chaos, or between male shaping form (*Gestalt*) and female formlessness.

For this reason, Evola needed real women (not "Absolute Womanhood") for the "left-hand path" rituals he discusses in *Metaphysics of Sex*. As his analysis of the male hero's conquest of the female "Tree" in *The Hermetic*

Tradition makes clear, the female has to be conquered, not ignored. Although various esoteric paths experimented with homosexuality as a form of consciousness-alteration (exemplified in the 20th century by Crowley), Evola denounces homosexuality as useless for his purpose because "in the case of such love, it is no longer allowable to speak of the impulse of the male or female principle, as present in the primordial being, to be reunited . . . Thus the essential, which gives each myth its whole value, loses its meaning, namely, the idea of polarity."[10]

Sado-masochism (Evola-style) is a much different story. He claims that in certain aspects of sadism and masochism it is possible to find elements "that can be included in the deepest structures of heterosexual erotics, and that become perversions only when freed from limitation. No similar recognition can be given in respect to homosexuality."[11] He begins his discussion of sadism in *Metaphysics of Sex* with an interesting distinction

> between deviant sadism, a need in some neurotic or tainted individuals for cruelty as a special psychic aphrodisiac necessary to attain sexual satisfaction, and sadism understood as a natural element in eros that can be specifically aroused so as to take the possibilities beyond the usual limit.
>
> However, we must make two other distinctions. First, it is necessary to distinguish between sadism with a sexual background and sadism in the broad sense, wherein the link with sex and women may be absent or only figure in a subordinate way, and the essence of which is pleasure through cruelty, evil, and destruction per se in every form.[12]

This later form of sadism, the "perversion when one feels pleasure in carrying out acts simply because they are forbidden," Evola denounces as "Art Bakuninism." Its practitioners include Baudelaire, Byron, Wilde, Swinburne, and the Decadents who "almost like children" delight in forbidden acts of transgression.[13] There were certain practices, however, that had a mimetic relationship to the transpersonal world of the gods and could be used by "normal people":

> It is a different case, however, when sadism or masochism are magnifications of an element potentially present in the deepest essence of eros. Then the "pathological" cases represent not deviations of normal instinct but manifestations of the deepest layers of the normal instinct, which are latent in certain varieties of sexual love. This algolagnia [pleasure in inflicting or suffering pain] is not exclusively sought by perverts but is used consciously by normal people to strengthen and extend, in a transcendental and perhaps ecstatic way, the possibilities of sex.[14]

But what exactly were these practices? Evola cites two of them, one being

> certain ancient forms of the ritual violation of virgins . . . In other cases it is possible to conceive that the whipping of the woman is used as an equiva-

lent so as to produce the same liminal psychic climate. In this respect, too, practices continued secretly up to the present day in certain circles enable us to conjecture the same objective basis for ancient sexual rites also which are now misunderstood and have a bad reputation.[15]

Whipping women as a way of increasing one's own psychic power in order to enter the transpersonal realm was something Evola *advocated.* It goes almost without saying that Evola's views on women were saturated with misogyny. Only the male could represent Being. He writes that in Greece the "one," which is "in itself," complete, and self-sufficient, was regarded as masculine. The dyad, the principle of differentiation and of "other-than-self," the principle of desire and movement, was feminine.[16] A woman "could traditionally participate in the sacred hierarchical order only in a mediated fashion, through her relationship with a man." In India, "women did not have their own initiation even when they belonged to a higher caste: Before they got married they did not belong to the sacred community of the noble ones (*arya*) other than through their fathers."[17] Nor did Evola shy away from defending such "traditional" practices as the Hindu "custom" of sati. In *Revolt Against the Modern World*, he writes:

> The bride would leap into the funerary pyre in order to follow the man whom she had married into the next life. This traditional sacrifice, which was regarded as a sheer "barbarism" by Europeans and by Westernized Hindus, and in which the widow was burnt alive with the body of the dead husband, is called *sati* in Sanskrit, from the root and the prefix *sat* (being), from which the word *satya* (the truth) comes; *sati* also signifies "gift," "faithfulness," "love." Therefore this sacrifice was considered as the supreme culmination of the relationship between two beings of a different sex and as the sign of an absolute type of relationship, from the point of view of truth and superhumanity.[18]

Evola's fascination with the rebirth of Tradition in the heart of modernity, his intense interest in secret societies and sexuality, and his general penchant for the extreme, were more than just chemical imbalances in his brain. The dream of the rebirth of a Traditional society, the acute sense of the struggle of the mythic against the "Terror of History," ran deep in the minds of some of Europe's most brilliant theorists, including Evola's friend Mircea Eliade. In *The Myth of the Eternal Return* (begun in 1945), Eliade is almost in mourning for the loss of a Tradition that once held out the possibility of "creating a new man and creating him on a supra-human plane, a man-god, such as the imagination of historical man has never dreamed it possible to create."[19]

If I raise the issue of Yockey's sado-masochism, I do so only to suggest that, even here, we see evidence of a secret world that shaped his inner life. There was, in fact, little ideological difference between Evola and Yockey. Like

Yockey, Evola believed that the American cultural threat to Europe was far greater than anything the Russians could come up with. His dispute with *Imperium* was that Yockey had an overly superficial conception of what was immediately possible.

Any purely secular interpretation of the divisions in the far right between the "pro-Russian" and the "pro-American" factions of the Black International that avoids the "occult" would conclude that political differences divided the two tendencies. An Order, however, is not structured along conventional political lines. Such an organization can dictate sharp turns and reversals in seemingly fixed political logics because the "political," crudely understood, is not the motivating force.

Whether Yockey or anyone else tilted East or West, and at what time, and to what degree, and for how long, and under what conditions, was essentially a tactical question. The Order, like any intelligence agency, was a kind of octopus with many tentacles, not just a "left" and "right" one. While I believe that there were legitimate policy arguments inside the postwar underground, as might be expected, I am not at all sure that it is meaningful to conceptualize a split inside the Order along rigid "East"/"West" lines. An organization like the Order was necessary precisely to prevent the total domination of postwar Europe by either the Americans or the Russians. By playing off the U.S. and USSR against one another, the Order equally ensured its own ability to survive and prosper. In music, the basic theme can sometimes be quite simple. The real test is how well you play the complex variations.

Notes:

1. In Evola's *Le Chemin du Cinabre* (Milan: Editions Arché, 1982), p. 180, he writes that he was dissatisfied with the Italian edition of Weininger's *Sex and Character*, which he translated. This, in turn, led him to write *Metaphysics of Sex*.

2. Evola, like Ernst Jünger, was for the same reason very interested in drug use. In this context note the mention of *Antaios: Zeitschrift für eine Freiwelt*, the postwar journal edited by Ernst Jünger and Mircea Eliade, in Albert Hoffmann, *LSD: My Problem Child* (New York: McGraw-Hill, 1980).

3. Julius Evola, *Metaphysics of Sex* (Rochester, VT: Inner Traditions International, 1991), p. 273.

4. Ibid., p. 275.

5. Ibid., p. 115.

6. Ibid., p. 22. Evola also writes (p. 86): "Spengler, who considers true love between man and woman to be an effect of polarity and an identical pulsation of a metaphysical nature, says it is akin to hatred and adds that 'he who has no race does not know dangerous love.'"

7. Ibid., p. 42. The importance of bisexual consciousness was expressed in the title of Evola's autobiography, *Il cammino del cinabro* (The Path of Cinnabar). In Chinese alchemy, cinnabar derives from the union of sulfur (considered the male

principle) and mercury (the female principle). See H. T. Hansen's introduction to Evola's *The Hermetic Tradition* (Rochester, VT: Inner Traditions International, 1995), p. xii.

8. Ibid., p. 43.

9. Ibid., p. 44.

10. Ibid., p. 63.

11. Ibid., p. 66.

12. Ibid., p. 105.

13. Ibid., p. 106.

14. Ibid., p. 88.

15. Ibid., p. 89. The ever-scholarly Evola notes on p. 291:

An ancient ritual manuscript belonging to a Scottish witch, which was shown to us by Professor G. B. Gardner, director of the Museum for Witchcraft on the Isle of Man, contemplates precisely the practice of whipping a woman in the context of sexual initiation. Gardner was wondering whether this context might be linked to certain Orphic initiation scenes in the frescos of the Pompeian Villa of the Mysteries; as is known, among them is one of a young woman being beaten. This seems rather questionable because those scenes are essentially symbolic.

"Professor G. B. Gardner" was Gerald Gardner, the man most responsible for the rebirth of the modern "Wiccan" religion in England.

16. Julius Evola, *Revolt Against the Modern World* (Rochester, VT: Inner Traditions International, 1995), p. 157.

17. Ibid, p. 160.

18. Ibid., pp. 160–61. For more on Evola's ideas, see the appendix "Roll Over Bachofen."

19. Mircea Eliade, *The Myth of the Eternal Return* (Princeton, NJ: Princeton University Press, 1954), p. 159.

SHADOW REICH (1953)

The handwriting on the wall may be a forgery.

—*Ralph Hodgson*

37

THE RISE AND FALL
AND RISE OF
WERNER NAUMANN

In January 1953, just as Yockey returned to Europe, his fascist "European elite" was thrown into turmoil when Sir Ivone Kirkpatrick, the British High Commissioner for Germany, ordered the arrests of what he described as a high-level cabal of neo-Nazis intent on undermining German democracy. Kirkpatrick identified as the top conspirator a former member of the Nazi elite named Werner Naumann, whom Hitler had appointed head of the Propaganda Ministry after Goebbels' suicide. Today, however, Naumann is most remembered not for the tumultuous events of that January but for his involvement in one of World War II's great mysteries: the fate of Hitler's personal secretary, Martin Bormann. Because Bormann's story so strangely overlaps Naumann's, it is necessary to briefly examine it before directing our attention to the British crackdown on Naumann and its effect on Yockey.

Martin Bormann became politically active in an anti-French sabotage network in the Ruhr after World War I. He then joined the "Black" (illegal) Reichswehr created by the German General Staff to overcome the restrictions of the Versailles Treaty. He served as the chief of cabinet to the Office of Nazi Deputy Führer Rudolf Hess from 1933 to 1941. After Hess's strange flight to Britain, Bormann took over as head of the Nazi party apparatus. Once it became clear that Germany would lose the war, he helped prepare the postwar Nazi underground.[1] According to Allied intelligence he never got to enjoy the fruits of his clandestine labor, as he was killed during fierce street fighting in Berlin after Hitler's suicide.

Not so, claimed Naumann, who in 1953 made headlines when he reported that Bormann had survived the fighting.[2] He also said that Bormann "was a Soviet spy and he must have arranged beforehand where to meet the Red Army advance units . . . Bormann now lives in Moscow."[3] Naumann's testimony could not simply be dismissed, since he and Hitler Youth leader Arthur Axmann left the Führerbunker with Bormann's party on 30 April 1945. The fact that Naumann was alive was almost as shocking as his claim about Bormann, since Allied intelligence concluded that he had died with Bormann in the attempted breakout from Berlin. Not only had Naumann survived; he had lived clandestinely for some years before resurfacing in the late 1940s as a West German "businessman."

Naumann's story caused a temporary meltdown inside the CIA. The Agency turned to its prize German intelligence asset, the Gehlen Organization—named after its founder, General Reinhard Gehlen, a former head of German military intelligence for the Eastern Front—for answers.[4] Gehlen assured the CIA that Bormann was dead.[5] The CIA gave great weight to eyewitness testimony from Arthur Axmann, the Hitler Youth leader who swore that Bormann had been killed. Certain facts, however, called into question his credibility. Axmann, it so happened, played a critical role in the organization of escape routes for high Nazi officials; an Anglo-American counterintelligence action called "Operation Nursery" arrested Axmann in 1946 for his involvement in a huge escape network that employed groups of trucking companies to secretly transport important Nazis to safety.[6] Axmann was then classified a Group I "Major Offender" by the Allies and spent almost four years in jail.[7] His activities after his release from prison are equally interesting. According to UPI's chief German correspondent, Wellington Long, Axmann "took himself to the Soviet zone for a time, paying for his keep by writing denunciations of the West German 'spirit of revenge' for Communist newspapers."[8]

The CIA's belief in Bormann's demise had been reinforced by information supplied to the Agency's Berlin station chief by the Russians during a brief Cold War "thaw" following Stalin's death. The Soviets emphatically told the CIA that there could be no question that Bormann was dead. Some years later, however, a Soviet intelligence officer named Lev Bezymenski began his own well-publicised hunt for Bormann. According to Bezymenski, the Nazi leader had escaped Berlin and fled at least as far south as Italy.[9] A former top CIA official named Frank Wisner also became obsessed in the last year of his life with the idea that Bormann had somehow survived.[10] The Israelis, too, proved unable to resist the Bormann challenge. In 1968 Israeli journalist Michael Bar-Zohar wrote *The Avengers*, a popular book about the hunt for Nazi war criminals. Bar-Zohar claimed that agents of the French Secret Service had managed to secretly examine the baggage of an ex–SS officer at the Madrid Airport. In the luggage the spies reportedly discovered a letter from *Der Weg*'s Johann von Leers, who mentioned in passing that Bormann was in Brazil.

Naumann's claim that Bormann was alive, however, did not originate from a disinterested source. His testimony came not long after he had been arrested by British authorities and charged with plotting to subvert German democracy. British intelligence was convinced that Naumann had been chosen to lead a post-war Nazi revival by the Bruderschaft.[11]

Just 44 years old, Naumann already had an impressive career inside the National Socialist movement, which he had joined in 1928 at age 19. By 1933 he was an SA major general. After getting a degree in economics, he joined the Ministry of Propaganda in 1937 and became Goebbels' personal adjutant. After three years' service in the Luftwaffe and the Waffen SS, he returned to the Propaganda Ministry and in 1944 was named the youngest undersecretary in Hitler's regime. During the Russian siege of Berlin, he led a people's militia battalion. In gratitude, Hitler appointed him to succeed Goebbels as Minister of Propaganda.[12]

The first Bruderschaft agent to approach Naumann (as recorded in Naumann's seized diary) was none other than Arthur Axmann. Naumann next met with a host of Hitlerite generals, as well as luminaries like former Nazi finance minister Hjalmar Schacht, Bruderschaft theorist Alfred Franke-Gricksch, Luftwaffe ace Hans-Ulrich Rudel, "Hitler's Commando" Otto Skorzeny, and Wilfred von Oven, Goebbels' press secretary and a leader of the Argentine Nazi colony.[13] Another Naumann advisor was Arno Breker, Hitler's court sculptor and one of Martin Bormann's closest friends.[14]

Heinrich Malz, Naumann's "chief of information," explained to an investigator for the Anti-Defamation League why his boss was held in such high esteem by the Nazi elite. According to Malz:

[Naumann] frequently risked his skin on the Russian front . . . and was wounded a number of times. He was back in the fight in no time . . . His association with Hitler nearly cost him his life three times. Way back in the beginning, Naumann was a Brown Shirt officer, one of the four men closest to Ernst Roehm. When the assassination plot came to light, Naumann avoided the first dragnet. He escaped the firing squad but was thrown into jail. He was held four months and convinced his captors of his deep devotion to Hitler. They released him and he was read-mitted to the hierarchy . . .

His second escape from death came when Hitler's bunker fell into the hands of the Russians in the Berlin assault. Fleeing across the flaming city, Naumann stumbled and was knocked unconscious. A Hitler Youth leader [Axmann?] dragged him to safety and saved him from capture. Had any one of his comrades betrayed him, the Russians would have stuck him up against a wall and blown holes in him . . . The third escape was from the Nuremberg trials. Naumann is convinced that if he had not been in hiding he would have been hanged by the Allies. That's why Naumann has a feeling that he is destined for great things.[15]

366

The Rise and Fall and Rise of Werner Naumann

The story of the Naumann *Kreis* (Circle) began unfolding on the night of 14 January 1953, when British agents raided Naumann's villa in a Düsseldorf suburb and seized over a ton of documents. Naumann and six of his colleagues were then charged with organizing a secret Nazi cell inside the German Free Democratic Party (FDP), a moderate-right group that was part of Konrad Adenauer's coalition government.[16] Naumann's top FDP connection was Dr. Ernst Achenbach, a major corporate lawyer for a host of Ruhr "steel barons" like the Hugo Stinnes firm. He also served as a foreign-policy advisor to the FDP. In 1951 Achenbach created an organization to lobby for the release of convicted German war criminals. As its secretary he chose Dr. Werner Best, the Heidelberg-educated lawyer, SS lieutenant general, and wartime patron of Carl Schmitt. Sentenced to death by a Danish court after World War II, Best had been granted a clemency release in August 1951.

One year earlier, in August 1950, Achenbach proposed that Naumann lead a new political party of the "National Opposition." Naumann and Achenbach then decided to infiltrate the North Rhine–Westphalia branch of the Free Democratic Party after Achenbach convinced him that with two hundred dedicated men they could capture the party and make Naumann its secretary general.[17] The state party would then split from the FDP and form a new political organization freed from any direct taint of Nazi extremism.

By July 1952 the takeover of the North Rhine–Westphalia FDP was well under way, in part because the FDP branch was led by Dr. Friedrich Middelhauve, who seems to have been in on the conspiracy.[18] That same month, Middelhauve introduced his own "nationalist" *Deutsches Programm* at the local party convention. All those "wronged" by both National Socialism and "oppression by the victors and denazification" were to be compensated equally. "We absolve ourselves of the Allied judgments, which have discriminated against our people, and, in particular, its soldierhood," Middelhauve declared. At the FDP's national convention in November 1952, Middelhauve was elected one of the party's two deputy chairmen.

To those not privy to the conspiracy, Naumann appeared to be an obscure businessman who from 1950 on had acted as the manager of a Düsseldorf import-export firm named H. S. Lucht Company. H. S. Lucht was headed by Frau Lea Lucht, the daughter of a Belgian general and widow of Herbert S. Lucht, yet another Propaganda Ministry official.[19] Lea Lucht was related to one of the most remarkable military heroes of the Third Reich, Waffen SS General Leon Degrelle. A fellow Belgian, Degrelle spent his postwar years in Franco's Spain avoiding war crimes charges while helping coordinate the Nazi diaspora. Lucht's ties to Degrelle were so close that it was speculated in the press that Degrelle may have been the real head of H. S. Lucht.[20]

The company's lawyer turned out to be Ernst Achenbach, who first became Lea Lucht's friend in German-occupied Paris. Then a member of the German Foreign Service, Achenbach had served as a political advisor to the German "ambassador" to Vichy France, Otto Abetz. Abetz, in turn, worked closely with Werner Best, who coordinated the civil administration of France during the early Occupation years.[21] Although Achenbach was Abetz's deportation expert for French Jews, he somehow managed to escape prosecution. Abetz, however, was sentenced to 25 years in jail and only paroled in early 1954.[22]

Documents discovered during the British raid showed that Lucht and Naumann had turned their company into an effective mix of business, political intelligence, and intrigue. Naumann's captured diary revealed the firm's links to important Nazi exiles in Argentina as well as with leaders of Belgian, British, and French fascism.[23] It also turned out that H. S. Lucht's Madrid business manager was none other than Otto Skorzeny, whom American and British intelligence let escape from Darmstadt prison on 27 July 1948.[24] Once he was safely in Spain, Skorzeny created a mercenary unit called ADSAP (A Directorship of Strategic Assault Personnel).[25] The CIA later used Skorzeny to help supply and train Egypt's military despite the fact that the Agency "had known for some time that Skorzeny had a special employment unit established in Leipzig, East Germany, with the full knowledge of Moscow, to recruit military technicians for Egypt."[26] Skorzeny had other intriguing business ties, since his uncle by marriage was former Nazi finance minister Hjalmar Schacht.[27]

The British raid gave rise to informed speculation that the Churchill government was desperately trying to head off an emerging American alliance with Germany that it feared would be spearheaded by Eisenhower's new secretary of state, John Foster Dulles, and his brother, CIA Director Allen Dulles.[28] The Dulles' pro-German views had long caught the attention of an American organization called the Society for the Prevention of World War III, a strong supporter of denazification. The Society's January 1947 newsletter highlighted the connections between the Dulles brothers' law firm, Sullivan and Cromwell, and the J. Henry Schroder Banking Corporation in New York, a subsidiary of the Schröder banking clan that also maintained banks in London, Cologne, and Hamburg. Under Kurt von Schröder's chairmanship, the Schröder's Stein Bank of Cologne became a major financier of Himmler's SS. Allen Dulles was so upset by the charges that he hired a New York private detective to break into the Society's offices in the vain hope of finding Communist connections![29]

The Society for the Prevention of World War III had spent years warning about a postwar Nazi revival, and the British raid confirmed its worst fears. But why had London decided to act now? Jan Paulus, Washington lobbyist for the Society, believed that the British were so worried about the pro-German tilt of the new Republican administration that Anthony Eden had given the go-ahead to make public the extent of the Nazi revival in Germany. In a 28 January 1953 internal memo, Paulus wrote that

> Britain has been assembling quite a dossier on Nazi activities ever since May 6, 1952—the election in lower Saxony.[30] At that time former Foreign Minister

Herbert Morrison was much more perturbed than Britain openly revealed...
Additional evidence in Churchill's possession reveals that the Nazi movement in
Germany has reached tremendous proportions not only at home but abroad,
since their tentacles reach Argentina, Brazil, the Middle East and Far East, and
even as far as Indo-China.[31]

Paulus then reported that the British had uncovered the fact that two Russian
generals, Bulganin and Kubalov, were working closely with the Nazis; they also
found that the Russians had set up a counterpart to General Matthew Ridgeway's
SHAPE, headed by a General Shugaev, in East Germany. The British had "conclusive evidence" that the Naumann circle maintained close ties to General Vincenz
Müller, the brains behind the East German police. Paulus thought that Churchill
wanted to use this information both to warn Washington that Germany was unreliable and to gain leverage over Adenauer, even to the point of being able to topple
his government if necessary. He then said that

> Britain has an extremely extensive dossier about the Nazi activities which she
> will reveal later in case Eisenhower decides to push his broad German policy too
> far. For instance, the British have conclusive evidence that the Nazi activities
> have been financed by the Ruhr industrialists ... Additional evidence that the
> Ruhr industrialists have been collaborating very extensively with the Nazis is
> the fact that when Dr. Schacht opened his bank in Düsseldorf, the minister of
> interior and the minister of economics were present.

The British particularly feared the Naumann Circle's astonishing influence in
the Middle East. According to a March 1953 report by the Non-Sectarian Anti-
Nazi League (NSANL),[32] Dr. Gustav Scheel, a Bruderschaft leader arrested with
Naumann, maintained excellent ties to the Grand Mufti of Jerusalem. German
corporations wishing to do business in the Middle East and Africa first had to
approach Naumann, Scheel, Skorzeny, and the Grand Mufti. Scheel was especially
close to Iran's nationalist leader, Dr. Mohammad Mossadegh, and supported
Iranian efforts to nationalize Western oil companies.[33] Paul Zimmermann,
another Naumann crony arrested by the British, also had important Middle East
connections. During the Third Reich, Zimmermann had worked in the economic
and administrative department of the RSHA, where he dealt with the operation of
the concentration camps. At the time of his arrest, he was serving as an advisor to
the Iron and Steel Industry Association of the Ruhr. He also maintained close contacts with Dr. Wilhelm Voss and ex–major general Oskar Munzel, two top German
advisors to Egypt's General Naguib and Colonel Nasser.[34] Through his connections, Zimmerman managed to broker important business deals with Egypt.

The Naumann Circle's involvement with Egypt was highlighted in an article
about Egypt's Free Officers Revolution that appeared in the July 1952 issue of the
Italian fascist journal *Asso di Bastoni*. According to the story:

When the English arrested in Germany Werner Naumann... and his comrades Haselmeyer (the organizer of the first Hitler Putsch in Munich, 1923), Kaufmann, Zimmermann, and Scheel (who were all released through the intervention of the Americans), they met again in the apartment of the neo-Nazi leader Kaufmann (who, through the *Nation Europa* group in Coberg was in close contact with the English fascists of Mosley, the French Bardèche, and the Belgian Rexists of Degrelle), [they] made a photo which they dedicated to Amein el Hussein, Grand Mufti of Jerusalem, and issued a series of documents which show how the Naumann group, together with Skorzeny, Schacht, Tiefenbacher, and the fascists of Azerbeijan Dun Angiski, organized the Egyptian Revolution together with Nasser, Boghdadi, Bakouri, Sadate, Ali Maher, and Fathy Raduan, leader of the Egyptian National Socialists.[35]

When the British moved to shut Naumann down, then, they did so not just out of fear of a neo-Nazi revival in Germany but also because of the renewed German challenge to British financial and imperial interests in the Third World.

Two of Naumann's collaborators, however, were immune to arrest by British authorities. They were Yockey's friends H. Keith Thompson and Fred Weiss. Thompson explained his links to Naumann this way:

The Naumann Circle was just that, a loosely organized group of "advisors," each working on different projects but all feeding ultimately to Dr. Naumann... My essential contacts... were: Dr. Karl Henrich Peter, Dr. Heinrich Malz, Dr. Gerhard Kruger, Col. Hans-Ulrich Rudel... Another facilitator was SS Major Kurt Gross[36]... I gave FPY introductions to all these people asking that he be given any assistance possible and put to work politically where possible.[37]

Thompson said that

my own work for Malz/Peter involved not mere research in the U.S. but extensive use of governmental files. For Peter particularly, I researched deaths of German Jews in the U.S. and Canada, culling such publications as *Aufbau* in NYC, and even, with false identity, YIVO and similar Jewish archives. Peter also involved me in some legal cases. One was that of [Gestapo/RSHA counter-espionage head] Walter Huppenkoethen, a Gestapo official indicted for his work in investigating the "bomb plotters." I got into specific files in Washington, and not only got the desired info but was able to remove certain material and destroy it.[38]

Thompson's ties to Malz and Peter are especially noteworthy. Malz, a lawyer and Naumann's "coordinator of information," had been a former SA police chief in Berlin. He later became a top aide to Ernst Kaltenbrunner, who headed the RSHA from January 1943 until the end of the war.[39] Malz spent nearly three years in jail for his wartime activity. After his release, he served as a defense counsel for the SS men accused in the 1944 Malmédy massacre of American GIs. He also became Rudolf Aschenauer's number-two man and editor of *Die Andere Seite*, whose American agent was H. Keith Thompson. Peter, Thompson's other friend, became Naumann's chief researcher. After Naumann's arrest, Peter helped ghost-write his *Nau-Nau gefähdet das Empire?* (Nau-Nau Is Endangering the Empire?).[40]

Malz and Peter were important behind-the-scenes figures in the Holocaust-denial movement. According to the October–November 1954 issue of the ADL journal *Facts*, Peter and Malz wrote a preliminary memorandum on Holocaust denial called *The Big Swindle of the Six Million*. The two men also launched a project to study Jewish history and writings for their anti-Semitic propaganda. They hoped to resume the work of the Frankfurt-based Reich Institute for History of the New Germany, which had over 100,000 books and pamphlets on the Jews. Peter, while a director of the Institute, helped coordinate the looting of libraries and private collections of prominent Jews and Masonic groups in occupied Europe.[41]

Fred Weiss's role in the Naumann propaganda network is evident in a letter that Malz wrote to him:

> Just received your letter of May 14th. Thanks for your understanding of my situation. After these things are now clarified, I feel much freer to start my work for you. You will have received my long letter of May 16th. My next undertaking will be an article for C.S. [*Common Sense*]. You may expect it by the end of this month. Enclosed is the May issue [of *Die Andere Seite*]. You'll recognize some initial ideas from your material.[42]

Through Le Blanc Press and the National Renaissance Party (NRP), Weiss produced pro-Nazi hate propaganda for distribution in Germany and around the world. He also maintained close ties with leading American anti-Semites like Conde McGinley of *Common Sense*, Frank Britton of *The American Nationalist*, and Mrs. Lyrl Van Hyning from the Chicago-based *Women's Voice*. Articles prepared by Malz and Peter were often printed in the American far-right press and then republished in journals like *Der Weg* as reports from America.[43]

Another Naumann Circle supporter and close Weiss friend was the Chicago-based industrialist Arthur Koegel, owner of the Koegel Coal Company and publisher of the *Deutsch-Amerikanische Buerger Zeitung*. H. Keith Thompson knew Koegel and later recalled one meeting in New York's Empire Hotel with Koegel and Weiss to discuss financial support for the neo-Nazi publication *Nation Europa*.[44] *Nation Europa*, which first appeared in January 1951, was edited by a former Waffen SS volunteer named Arthur Ehrhardt.[45] Koegel became one of its major financial contributors as well as a member of its board of directors.[46] Werner Naumann also went to considerable lengths to raise money for it. According to the *Frankfurter Rundschau*, Naumann secured financial help for the magazine from a Paris-based fascist group that included Maurice Bardèche.[47]

The British crackdown on Naumann threw a temporary monkey wrench into the Shadow Reich's plans. It also put Yockey in a dangerous situation. He had just managed to survive detection from the FBI and the State Department in New York.

Now, only a short time after his arrival in Europe, he was on the move again. This time he headed to Egypt.

Notes:

1. Part of that planning involved a conference sponsored by the RSHA and held in the Hotel Maison Rouge in Strasbourg on 10 August 1944. Among the attendees were leaders from German industry, the Foreign Ministry, and the Ministry of Armaments. After the meeting, approximately $500 million was transferred to banks in Switzerland, Liechtenstein, Austria, Portugal, Spain, Argentina, and other neutral nations. U.S. intelligence believed the money was used to secretly acquire a controlling interest in hundreds of foreign companies in neutral nations around the world. (Angelo Del Boca and Mario Giovana, *Fascism Today* [New York: Pantheon, 1969], p. 78; their information on the meeting comes from a 1946 U.S. Treasury report.) The Canadian journalist William Stevenson estimates that the Nazis had access to some 95 tons of gold. (Stevenson, *The Bormann Brotherhood* [New York: Harcourt Brace, 1973], p. 66.)

2. Naumann, as I shall show later in this chapter, only made his revelation after his own arrest.

3. E. H. Cookridge, *Spy of the Century* (New York: Random House, 1971), p. 233.

4. The Gehlen Organization later became the *Bundesnachrichtendienst* (the Federal Intelligence Service, or BND) in 1956, after West Germany regained full sovereignty.

5. In his memoirs, however, Gehlen claimed that Bormann really was a Soviet agent who eventually wound up in Moscow, just as Naumann had said.

6. Kurt Tauber, *Beyond Eagle and Swastika* (Middletown, CT: Wesleyan University Press, 1967), Vol. 1, p. 239.

7. Ibid., Vol. 2, fn. 14, p. 1036.

8. Wellington Long, *The New Nazis of Germany* (Philadelphia: Chilton Book Company, 1968), p. 45.

9. Bezymenski believed that Bormann had made it to South America. The fate of Breslau *Gauleiter* (District Leader) Karl Hanke (the man Hitler appointed to replace Himmler as head of the SS) also remains unknown. See Walter Laqueur and Richard Breitman, *Breaking the Silence* (Hanover, NH: Brandeis University Press, 1994), pp. 110–12, 259.

10. During the 1940s Wisner headed the Office of Policy Coordination (OPC), which incorporated former Nazis into the American intelligence apparat. His Bormann mania continued right up to 29 October 1965, the day Wisner killed himself with a shotgun.

11. Bruderschaft leader Dr. Gustav Adolf Scheel, the former Gauleiter of Salzburg who had been appointed Nazi Minister of Culture in Hitler's Will, also organized a *Herrenclub* (Gentleman's Club) to support Naumann.

12. Tauber, *Beyond Eagle and Swastika*, Vol. 1, pp. 132–33.

13. Ibid., Vol. 1, p. 135.

14. Ibid. Also see Ladislas Farago, *Aftermath* (New York: Simon & Schuster, 1974), p. 115.

15. Arnold Forster and Benjamin Epstein, *Cross-Currents* (New York: Doubleday, 1956), p. 225.

16. Arrested with Naumann were Karl Kaufmann, one time Gauleiter of Hamburg; Paul Zimmermann, an SS general and official of the concentration camp branch of the SS; Gustav Scheel, designated by Hitler as the new Minister of Culture and former Gauleiter of Salzburg; Dr. Heinrich Haselmeyer, head of the National Socialist Student League; Dr. Karl Scharping, an ex-Propaganda Ministry official; and Heinz Siepen, a district leader in the Third Reich. (T. H. Tetens, *The New Germany and the Old Nazis* [London: Seeker & Warburg, 1961], p. 25.)

17. In his notes of his meeting with Achenbach, Naumann wrote:

> In order to enable National Socialists . . . to gain influence over the political events, they should join the FDP, infiltrate it, and capture its leadership. He [Achenbach] demonstrates with a few examples how easy that would be. We could inherit the entire Land executive committee organization with no more than 200 members. He wants to hire me as executive director or something like it!! He is so serious about his offer that he suggests at the end: either we accept and support him, or he'll retire from politics. [Naumann's notes cited in Tauber, *Beyond Eagle and Swastika*, Vol. 1, p. 134.]

18. Like Achenbach, Middelhauve maintained close ties to the Hugo Stinnes firm. A newspaper publisher, Middelhauve's printing firm was largely dependent on orders from Stinnes. See the analysis by Richard Lowenthal ("Germany's New Rightist Threat") in the *New Leader*, 12 January 1953.

19. Kurt Tauber gives the name of the H. S. Lucht Company as Combinel. See *Beyond Eagle and Swastika*, Vol. 2, fn. 56, p. 1042.

20. The Degrelle network may have been cryptically referenced in the April 1954 *Reporter* article on the Naumann circle's ties to H. S. Lucht, Weiss, Thompson, and Yockey. According to the *Reporter*, Bonn officials claimed that the Naumann Circle had links to "a group of former SS officers recently sentenced as Communist spies." Those former SS officers may have been part of a Belgium-based network tied to Leon Degrelle. In his book *Twice Through the Lines* (New York: Harper & Row, 1972), Otto John, the first head of the West German equivalent of the FBI, the BfV (the Federal Office for the Protection of the Constitution), mentions a group of Belgian neo-Nazis who forged European Defense Community documents for East Germany. John writes (pp. 225–26):

> It occurred to me that we might here have come across the trail of certain Belgian Nazis who were peddling intelligence both in the right-wing and left-wing extremist underground in Germany; they were also in touch with interested circles in East Berlin, to whom they passed French-language information. We had heard that they had sold to East Berlin a French text of the E.D.C. treaties—it was, in fact, a forgery . . . It soon proved that my suspicions were correct. Ulbricht had paid a considerable sum for French-language drafts of the E.D.C. treaties forged by Degrelle Nazis. The Belgians were arrested and sentenced.

21. One of the Third Reich's most important intelligence agents, Abetz was heavily involved in the creation of pro-Nazi German-French youth and cultural exchange groups before World War II. His work was sponsored by Joachim von Ribbentrop's personal foreign service research bureau. Another member of the FDP involved with the Naumann plot was Rudolf Rahn, the last Nazi ambassador to Italy. Rahn had previously

served under Otto Abetz in the Paris embassy's Culture and Propaganda section, where he helped organize anti-Masonic and anti-Jewish exhibits. (Tauber, *Beyond Eagle and Swastika*, Vol. 1, p. 285.)

22. Some four years later, on 5 May 1958, Abetz and his French-born wife died when their car exploded in Langenfeld, near Düsseldorf. See "Otto Abetz—King of Hitler's Paris," in Barbara Probst Solomon, *Horse-Trading and Ecstasy* (San Francisco, CA: North Point Press, 1989).

23. From "Where Fascism and Communism Meet," by Edmond Taylor, in the April 1954 *Reporter*. It would also be interesting to know whether H. S. Lucht had any ties to a weapons firm called Oerlikon that was represented in Germany by a Bruderschaft fellow-traveller named Major Waldemar Pabst.

24. Glenn Infield, *Secrets of the SS* (New York: Jove Press, 1990), p. 180.

25. The U.S. Army even sent some of its best men to train with Skorzeny in Spain.

26. Glenn Infield, *Skorzeny: Hitler's Commando* (New York: St. Martin's Press, 1981), p. 210.

27. Like Skorzeny, Schacht was involved in the arms trade. The New York *Aufbau* of 25 September and 2 October 1953 covered a story from the *Frankfurter Rundschau* about a weapons network (one of whose ringleaders was Schacht) that operated a bank in Liechtenstein called Octogon Trust. One Octogon official, Rudolf Ruscheweg, helped supervise the industrial looting of occupied France. Although wanted as a war criminal by the French, Ruscheweg escaped to Switzerland in 1945. Another Octogon official, Fritz Klein, was described as the brother-in-law of the late General Hans von Seeckt. As German Council-General in Shanghai during the time of Chiang Kai-shek (whose military advisor was Seeckt), Klein made huge amounts of money in the arms trade, and it was believed that he funnelled some of his profits into Octogon. In *American Swastika* (New York: Doubleday, 1985), p. 186, Charles Higham reports that Klein was a friend of the Dulles brothers.

28. Their sister Eleanor Dulles ran the State Department's Berlin desk.

29. Peter Grose, *Gentleman Spy: The Life of Allen Dulles* (Amherst, MA: University of Massachusetts Press, 1996), pp. 264–65.

30. Paulus is referring to the large vote for the extremist SRP.

31. From the archives of the Society for the Prevention of World War III in Columbia University's Butler library.

32. The NSANL was a close ally of the Society for the Prevention of World War III.

33. Fearing that any Iranian nationalization of foreign oil companies would send a dangerous message to the rest of the Third World, the CIA and British intelligence successfully organized Mossadegh's downfall.

34. Alistair Horne, *Return to Power* (New York: Praeger, 1956), p. 167.

35. From an article in the fascist publication *Asso di Bastoni* of 23 October 1955 by Daniele Gaudenzi (translated by the Non-Sectarian Anti-Nazi League). The article opens:

The story of our revolution has not been written, and among the few who were involved in it from the beginning, all are not familiar with all its details. It is believed for instance that the idea of it was born during the [1948] campaign against Israel. This is not true. When we went into that war, the plot had been in existence for already five or six years. It originated in 1942 as a result of the humiliation inflicted to Egypt by the English who forced Farouk to recall Nahas Pasha to government . . .

These specific declarations, released by Col. Gamal Abdel Nasser, dictator of the Egyptian Revolution, to the Italian journalist Indro Montanelli (*Corriere della Sera* of January 23), confirm clearly the definite fascist character of the revolutionary movement of the young officers who already in 1942, the year of the Rommel offensive towards Egypt's Alexandria, planned to overthrow the regime based on the power of the young military generation. In confirmation of this character of the National Revolution of Egypt are the statements of the Egyptian Communist Party, as reported in the magazine *Rinascita* (Rebirth) directed by P. Togliatti. These declarations, under the title of "A First Estimate of the Regime of Nasser—a Fascist Dictatorship," states textually the following . . . "The present rulers of Egypt have always been fervent admirers of fascism. Abdel-Latif al-Baghdadi, Minister of Municipal Affairs and President of the Revolutionary Tribunal, Sceicco H. Bakouri, Minister of Religious Affairs, Anwar El-Sadate, Minister of Moslem Affairs, and many other dignitaries of the regime organized, during the war, a spy network in favor of Nazi Germany. Nasser, Sadate and Bakouri, moreover, belonged to a terrorist organizations which carried out many terrorist attacks in Cairo. Faithless adventurers, these fascists worked for Germany." [*Rinascita* cites from issue #34 of the Italian Communist paper *Vie Nuove*, which used statements from the Egypt CP's paper *Rayat-I-Chaab*.]

Gaudenzi then continues:

The article shows an impressive and astounding picture of the perfect organization and the brilliant and dynamic activity of the agents of the neo-Nazi organization of Skorzeny and Bormann, jointly with the secret headquarters of the Black International and of the "Internationale of Coups d'État," which is one of its names. Various reports by the Falangist and Perónist information agencies, and a detailed document issued by the "Center of European Nationalist Forces" (the Viennese section of the "European Social Movement") enable us to get an idea of the broad and grandiose plan of action originating with the Nazis, in cooperation with the Egyptians of Nasser, to overthrow Farouk and to establish in Egypt a center of action for the whole of the Middle East, in union with Iran, Syria, and Pakistan through the tenacious and indefatigable labors of Amein el Hussein, the famous Grand Mufti of Jerusalem, a fanatic admirer of Mussolini.

In 1942, the "coup d'état" organized by Nasser's Young Egyptians to overthrow Farouk and Nahas Pasha and to open the doors of the Suez Canal to the Axis armies (in coordination with the insurrection of the Golden Guard of Iraq, a philonazist group, and the attempted "coup d'état" of Zahedi in Persia) failed in view of the ferocious repression of Great Britain and the treason of certain people sold to Farouk.

It was during the war against Israel (in which a number of ex-collaborationists from all over Europe participated as part of the Anti-Zionist Legion organized by the fascist of Azerbaijan Gatalibayli Dudanginsky, recently murdered in Monaco by the paid killers of the MVD) . . . it was then, we say, during the war of 1948 against the Jews in the Gaza desert that the nationalist officers of Egypt prepared the basis for the new and decisive coup d'état in collaboration with Otto Skorzeny and other famous Nazi leaders, leaders of the Ustachi and of the Iron Guard of Romania; through Bern, Geneva, Bressanone, and Rome, the "Black International" (whose head, it seems, was Martin

Bormann, rescued through Spain and brought first to Argentina and then to Peru) brought to Egypt ca. 600 Nazi "experts" led by the commander of the SS anti-partisan tank brigade, Dirlwanger, the SS Obergruppenfuehrer Hans Eichmann, the ex–Nazi ambassador in Spain von Stohrer (who later arranged for the re-equipment of the Egyptian Army with arms from Franco's Spain, under the direction of Otto Skorzeny, Werner Naumann, Kaufmann, Zimmermann, and Scheel). Besides these military and political technicians, there were economic experts, guided by the ex-manager of the Skoda factory confiscated by the Nazis, the engineer Voss. These Germans, to whom were added also the famous "magus" of Hitler, Hjalmar Schacht . . . were the emissaries of the . . . German banks represented by Baron Reichner. A few days after the authoritative *Daily Telegraph* gave the alarm, the Nationalist Egyptian Revolutionaries, organized in accordance with the Prussian tradition by Skorzeny and Tiefenbacher, went to the attack, and eliminated Farouk . . .

Today Tiefenbacher and the other German experts (many of whom are ex-officers of Rommel's Afrika Korps who fought with the Italians in El Alamein) are organizing the Egyptian police, the Army, and the parachutists. Voss plans large-scale electrical plants in Aswan, while a German firm is at the present time negotiating for the concession of the southern section of the Eastern desert. Naumann, for account of Allweg, plans the Cairo–Capetown railroad, Heinkel is launching his large-scale plans for jet plane factories in Egypt; Krupp has distributed his agents throughout the country; Skorzeny organizes on the basis of the SS the Egyptian Nationalist Militia (whose insignia is faithfully copied from that of the European Waffen-SS, showing a death's head, and the black flag with a silver head and a poniard between the teeth); some heads of the Hitlerjugend and a leader of the Ustachi (Croatian) Youth Movement are the instructors of the organization of the National Revolutionary Youth of Egypt; Schacht is the expert adviser and financial consultant of the Nasser government; some famous German, Croat, and Romanian journalists, expelled from their own country, direct in the Egyptian newspapers the press campaign against Israel and the Communists. Skorzeny himself has appeared in public beside Nasser during the celebration of the anniversary of the Revolution, while Heinkel, returned from Cairo, has recently stated to a Spanish Falangist group: "It has come to a point that in Egypt the English, when they wish to be well treated, claim they are Germans."

36. About Gross, Thompson explained:

I had been instrumental in springing Gross and several enlisted men (convicted in the "Dachau Fliers Case") from prison. Nothing to do with *the* Dachau, just a geographical location. Some local farmers, infuriated by Allied bombings of their villages and towns, caught some downed British airmen and killed them. Who was to blame? Well, there was an SS training school about 20 miles away commanded by Gross. Surely they must have been "guilty" of something. That's how such things went in those days.

37. H. Keith Thompson, letter to me, 3 July 1995.

38. Huppenkoethen also played a key role in the investigation of Admiral Canaris after the 20 July 1944 bomb plot.

39. Malz described his background in a letter to Fred Weiss dated 22 April 1951:

I belong to the generation of young Germans who identified themselves with National Socialism for idealistic reasons . . . I have experienced the peaks and the depths of National Socialism very consciously. During the war and afterwards I had activities which gave me very deep insight into the background of that [Hitler's] government, both in its strength and in its weakness. (At the end I was a close collaborator of the Chief of the Security Police and of the SD Intelligence Service, Dr. Kaltenbrunner, who was executed at Nuremberg.) [Malz quoted in Forster and Epstein, *Cross-Currents*, p. 222.]

As for Kaltenbrunner, the military historian Glenn Infield explains:

Kaltenbrunner was indicted on three counts . . . The judgment found him guilty of being aware of conditions in the concentration camps, arranging for the evacuation and liquidation of inmates of concentration camps as the end of the war neared, mistreatment and murder of allied POWs, ordering the SS not to interfere with attacks on Allied fliers who parachuted from their aircraft [the "Dachau fliers case"], organizing a slave labor program, and playing a leading role in the Holocaust. He was sentenced to die and was hanged on October 16, 1946, at Nuremberg. [*Secrets of the SS*, p. 213.]

40. Tauber, *Beyond Eagle and Swastika*, Vol. 1, p. 569. (Naumann got the nickname "Nau Nau" after a German journalist jokingly compared the Naumann plot to the Mau Mau uprising in Kenya.) Peter claimed only to have written the introduction to the book and to have "amplified" the original text that Naumann wrote in prison. In 1961 Peter published Kaltenbrunner's secret report to Hitler on the 20 July 1944 military conspirators. Also recall Malz's close ties to Kaltenbrunner.

41. For a brief discussion of the Nazi "research institutes," see Karl Schleunes, *The Twisted Road to Auschwitz* (Urbana, IL: University of Illinois Press, 1970).

42. Cited from the ADL publication *Facts*, Vol. 9, No. 7, October–November 1954.

43. The June 1953 (Vol. VII, No. 6) *Der Weg* article attacking the American Jewish Congress was reprinted from *Common Sense* of 1 March 1953. Malz's letter to Weiss is cited in Forster and Epstein, *Cross-Currents*, p. 241.

44. Thompson also worked with Koegel to put pressure on the State Department to admit Luftwaffe ace Hans-Ulrich Rudel to the United States.

45. Ehrhardt served a three-month prison term in 1958 for libelling the German Constitution.

46. At one point Koegel held 2.38 percent of the stock of *Nation Europa*. Another major funder of *Nation Europa* was the Swedish millionaire C. E. Carlberg.

47. Horne, *Return to Power*, p. 169. Other members of the Paris group included the New European Order's Guy Amaudruz, Jean Bauvard, Guy Lemonier, and a banker named Albertini. See the Weiner Library *Bulletin* for May–August 1953.

38

A BOMB

FOR NASSER

After Yockey vanished from the United States in early January 1953, it took American authorities seven months to pick up his trail. On 17 July 1953, "the Commander in Chief, U.S. Forces in Europe" received a message from the military attaché at the U.S. embassy in Cairo that read:

> Request available information regarding Francis Yockespallas VANDERZEE, alias Ulick VARANGE, alleged U.S. national and deserter US Army now in EGYPT. Please indicate _____.[1]

Yockey came to the embassy's attention after it learned that he had two U.S. passports and was attempting to sell one of them. One month later, on 11 August 1953, the FBI received notification from an unidentified U.S. government agency about "an American subject who is now in Cairo . . . residing at the Luna Park Hotel. Subject spends his time writing anti-Jewish articles . . . and is known to be associated with the liberation front in England."

Yockey first journeyed to the Middle East in the spring of 1953; in late February he sent a letter postmarked Beirut to a German rightist named Wolfgang Sarg.[2] His stay in Beirut had a personal angle: Yockey's ex-wife Alice had brought their two daughters, Isolde and Brünnhilde, to Lebanon to visit both their father and Alice's brother Charles, a Beirut-based oil company executive. Yockey was not impressed with Lebanon, telling Fred Weiss, "the country was quite uninteresting, totally. Just a colony, intellectually too."[3] He also seems to have visited Damascus, Syria, to meet Dr. Emil Rudolf Gelny, a "spécialiste pour les maladies névrologiques et mentales," as well as a member of the New European Order.[4] Gelny was close to Johann von Leers; in a letter from Damascus dated 24 April 1954, Gelny told Fred

378

Weiss: "Yesterday I received information that the specific Arab State to which I had submitted Prof. von Leers' exposé is seriously considering the thought to engage his services in order to bring his proposal to realization."[5]

That state was Egypt. Two months before Gelny's letter to Weiss, on 23 February 1954, General Mohammed Naguib, the titular leader of Egypt's military-led overthrow of King Farouk, resigned from the government. The real strongman behind the July 1952 revolt, Lieutenant Colonel Gamal Abdul Nasser, then took over as President. Sometime in late 1954 or early 1955, Leers moved from Argentina to Egypt, where he spent the last decade of his life as a top official in Egypt's Ministry of Information.[6]

After his visit to Lebanon and Syria, Yockey returned to Europe. By May 1953 he was living in Munich. Once back in Germany, he began looking for a translator for the manuscript that would become *Der Feind Europas*. On 26 May 1953 he informed H. Keith Thompson that he had gone to Nuremberg and given the manuscript to Naumann's aide Heinrich Malz, who had agreed to undertake the translation. A few weeks later, Yockey returned to the Middle East; this time he headed to Egypt.

On 11 June 1953 Keith Thompson received a card from Yockey postmarked the Saudi Arabian Markets, 3 sh. IBN SALAB (Kasr-31-Nilm) ("next to Metropolitan Hotel"), POB 585, Cairo.[7] Yockey also contacted Fred Weiss about his trip.[8] His 8 July 1953 letter to Weiss began:

> If I haven't written you much, there are various reasons for it. First, I didn't have much to tell. Second, I gave exact instructions to my mistress [Virginia Johnson] to tell you this and that. Thirdly, your address isn't entirely secure, no?

Despite the overthrow of King Farouk, Yockey told Weiss that Egypt remained "a colony, in the last analysis":

> They're anti-England but pro-Ami [American]. What's that? These people are terribly stupid and incorrigible (not capable of being enlightened) . . . They're simply too roasted by the sun to be able to accomplish anything. You remember the fellahin. You've been here. But then it was better. Now they've got a REVOLUTION. The name of the revolution is in Spengler's *The Hour of Decision*. A PURELY negative movement.
>
> You hate talk about "brotherhood"[9]—a few days ago an important fellahin journalist said to me, about the Jews, "I regard the Jews as cousins." And the country is now at war with the Jews. But the officials say: not against the Jews, against the ZIONISTS. Therefore *merde concentrée*. Even the Gods contend in vain against stupidity. The synagogues here are very large, and they're all on the rise. The big businesses are Jewish. On the streets the Jews can't be distinguished from the others—except in a few cases—these people come from Europe—and they say: "I'm a European." And they believe it too.

While Yockey's allusion to Weiss's time in Egypt remains a mystery, Weiss did maintain ties to the Egyptian right. When Ahmed Hussein, the head of Egypt's Green Shirt fascist party,[10] came to New York in the 1940s, he addressed a meeting sponsored by Weiss's friend Kurt Mertig, the first chairman of the National Renaissance Party.[11] Another indication of Weiss's influence comes from Otto Strasser, who contacted Weiss in the hope that he could help him get a post at Cairo University.[12] It also seems possible that Marie Weiss visited Egypt for her husband sometime in 1954.[13]

Yockey wrote Weiss to bring him up to date on a mysterious plan to have Egypt develop a new weapon of mass destruction. Yockey said that he had discussed the project with the strongman of the regime, Lieutenant Colonel Nasser:

> For two weeks I've tried to talk to the Supreme War Lord [*Allerhöchsten Kriegsherren*] about the weapon. In vain. Like the Amis, these people never say No . . . Tomorrow I'm meeting a general (presumably—here one is NEVER sure—NO ONE is reliable), who has to do with Technical Research. Privately, at his home. Maybe that will take care of something. I've already talked with the Lt. Col. He was interested, nothing more. *À propos*, the Commander in Chief of the Army is a Lt. Col.!

The "Lt. Col." and "Commander in Chief" could only have been Nasser, who, at age 35, was one year younger than his American visitor.

Yockey told the Egyptians that if they became interested in the weapon, "they must summon the genius in Amiland [Weiss]. He will talk about small matters, prices, etc." He then warned: "All these people are quite without honor; as soon as they get their hands on something, they would *never* pay for it. So we're making no progress."

What exactly was the weapon that Yockey and Weiss were trying to sell? Before examining this question, it should be noted that Weiss's scientific training had helped him become a successful patent lawyer in Germany.[14] He also had first-hand experience with weapons as an artillery officer in World War I. As for the bomb itself, it was almost certainly something Weiss had alluded to in his pamphlet *Max Planck and the Future of Western Civilization*.[15] In *Max Planck*, Weiss predicts the imminent creation of a "goose-egg bomb, capable of destroying four city blocks." This new "cobalt bomb" would soon become a "neat little weapon of death in the hands of some ten thousand shocktroopers, saboteurs, and murderers." Given its practicality in spreading anonymous terror, the cobalt bomb was destined to become the Soviet weapon of choice in the last phase of the "formless war" between East and West once some important technical problems were solved:

> Naturally, to carry safely this vest-pocket-bomb into action, presupposes the creation of a thin layer of mass, immune to the penetration of X-, gamma, or other short wave rays, hence the mobilization of the elite of scientists behind the Iron

Curtain, for the most difficult and complicated process of creating such an insulating mass.[16]

That said, it still seems highly improbable that an elderly New York landlord had managed to invent a super bomb. But was Weiss the cobalt bomb's creator? My suspicion is that Weiss and Yockey were fronting for a group of Argentina-based Nazi scientists linked to *Der Weg*.[17] After World War II, Argentina actively recruited German scientists for its military program. Perón's dictatorship attracted some leading German experts, like Kurt Tank, the chief engineer of the Focke-Wulf-Werke, who took his airplane-design team to Buenos Aires. Hans-Ulrich Rudel, the top Luftwaffe ace and a key *Der Weg* operative, worked closely with Tank. In 1948 Tank brought a young Austrian physicist named Ronald Richter to work at his aeronautical institute in Cordoba. Richter got Argentine citizenship one year later, along with his own atomic research institute on Huemul Island in Lake Nahuel Huapí. Then, in February 1951, Perón and Richter called a press conference and announced that Argentina had achieved nuclear fission using a new solar reactor called a "thermotron." When asked what material the thermotron used, Richter replied that it was a "supersecret" but that it was *not* uranium or plutonium. He also said that the substance could be found in Argentina.

Richter's announcement made headlines in the world's physics community. The famous physicist Lise Meitner recalled meeting "a strange Austrian with an Argentine visa" in Vienna in 1950 who claimed that he could create a "small" nuclear bomb in a laboratory. Although Richter managed to produce a large bang during a test, Meitner and her colleagues concluded that he had not built a mini-A-bomb, although they weren't exactly sure what he had done. Equally baffling was the fuel for Richter's device. What substance, other than uranium or plutonium, could Richter have used (or claimed to use) in his thermotron? One possible culprit was cobalt, a silver-white magnetic metallic element related to iron and nickel. Regular nuclear reactors produce cobalt 60, a heavy radioactive isotope used as a source for gamma rays. Was cobalt Richter's "supersecret"?

Richter soon came under pressure from Argentina's atomic energy commission to produce results. Although he had convinced Perón that Argentina was now in a position to produce atomic energy in liter and half-liter bottles for "family and industrial use," he failed to win over Argentina's physics community. Finally, in late 1952, he was secretly arrested.[18] Not long after his arrest, Yockey and Weiss tried to peddle their bomb to Nasser, another *Der Weg*–linked military officer turned dictator.

With the weapons project on hold, Yockey informed Weiss that he was preparing to return to Germany to check on the progress of *Der Feind Europas*. He was more than glad to go:

Please forgive me for not having written more often—there's yet another reason for it—the landscape here is so strong that it drains everything out of you. There are 20,000 Germans here and they're all slowly sinking into oblivion. In English—they're all going black. If I were to stay here, me too—I'm quite sensitive—I hate the sun, have always hated it.

Yockey may have returned to Cairo later that year, because H. Keith Thompson received a letter from him dated 4 December from Egypt. Although the year is obscured in the original letter, Thompson believes that it was 1953. He also reported that the return address was marked "Dr. Mahoud Saleh, Maadi, Egypt." Dr. Mahoud Saleh, head of Egypt's Anti-Zionist Society, was one of the most significant figures in the anti-Jewish International.[19] His network of organizations included the French-based Comité Europe-Islam, the Deutsche-Arabischen Freundschaft in Germany, the British-based Society for Combatting Zionism, and the Anti-Zionist Legion and Anti-Zionist Information Center in the United States.[20]

Despite Yockey's connections, it was not surprising that the U.S. government was able to detect his presence in Egypt. The American embassy had encouraged the July 1952 coup, and the CIA maintained a strong presence in Cairo.[21] The CIA especially looked to coup leader General Mohammed Naguib to keep more extremist elements in Egypt's Free Officers Association in line. Naguib, however, was little more than a frontman for Nasser. While Yockey was in Cairo in June 1953, Egypt was proclaimed a republic and Nasser became Deputy Premier. Then, in the spring of 1954, Naguib was forced into retirement. Not long after Nasser consolidated his hold on power, Johann von Leers moved to Cairo to help run Egypt's propaganda apparat. After converting to Islam, he changed his name to "Omar Amin von Leers."[22]

General Otto Remer also found sanctuary along the Nile. Remer fled to Egypt after being threatened with arrest in Germany for his involvement with the radical-right Socialist Reich Party (SRP). He then helped train Egyptian commandos and Algerian guerrilla fighters in a base at Abassia, Upper Egypt. In a June 1953 interview in Der Weg he called upon all "German patriotic forces" to aid in the creation of a strong Arab army.[23] Other German advisors trained Palestinian refugees for commando raids against Israel. With help from German military and technical advisors, Egypt soon became a vital support base for Algerian, Moroccan, and Tunisian guerrillas fighting against France, as well as for anti-British movements in Aden and the Mau-Mau insurgency in Kenya.

The Nazi-Nasser axis, a postwar continuation of Haushofer's policy of alliance with the "Colored World," was evident in the strange mix of fascist, geopolitical, and anti-imperialist rhetoric that flowed from Leers' pen. In an 8 August 1958 letter to H. Keith Thompson, Leers explained:

One thing is clear—more and more patriot Germans join the great Arab revolution against beastly imperialism. In Algeria half a company of German soldiers, dragging with them two French officers and two non-commissioned officers, have cut their throats in the view of the Algerian revolutionaries and have gone on the side of the Algerians and have embraced Islam.[24] That is good! To hell with Christianity, for in Christianity's name Germany has been sold to our oppressors![25] Our place as an oppressed nation under the execrable Western colonialist Bonn government must be on the side of the Arab nationalist revolt against the West. Let Adenauer be furious that honest German patriots are not extradited to him or to his British or American bosses, by those freedom-loving Arab countries. May the British swines call us "meddlers"—in a short time British meddling in the Middle East will be over, as it has finished in Iraq where the infidel servants of British imperialism are all killed. *I hamd ul Allah!* . . . the backing given by USA to the Jewish tyrants in Germany will make the German nation revolt. Indeed, for our nation there is only one hope—to get rid of Western imperialism by joining the Arab-led anti-imperialist group.

Dr. Fritz Grobba was another ally of both the Arabs and the Kremlin. A German "Lawrence of Arabia," Grobba had been the Nazi ambassador to Baghdad in 1940 when German intelligence backed an attempted anti-British revolt by Rashid Ali al-Galieni.[26] In his book *Blowback*, Christopher Simpson reports that Grobba turned his entire espionage network over to the Russians in 1945. Grobba then became a special advisor to the Soviets on Mideast affairs in 1951. According to the German press, Grobba even brokered the first meeting between Soviet emissaries and the Grand Mufti of Jerusalem.[27]

Another key figure involved in German intrigue in the Middle East was Hjalmar Schacht.[28] He first came to Egypt as General Naguib's "guest of honor" after the coup against King Farouk.[29] Schacht's most daring Middle East powerplay was the "Jiddah Agreement" between German industry and Saudi Arabia in January 1954. Under the terms of the deal, Saudi Arabia agreed to establish a fleet of supertankers (to be built in German shipyards) that would carry Saudi oil around the world. Aristotle Onassis was chosen to manage the shipping side of the operation. Besides making the Ruhr industrialists fantastically wealthy, Jiddah threatened to break the "Seven Sisters" oil companies' hegemony over the distribution of Middle East oil.[30] The Jiddah Agreement was ultimately blocked by the Western oil cartel with help from the CIA. Yet Allen Dulles's CIA was surprisingly hesitant to confront Schacht. Robert Maheu, one of the coordinators of the American attack on Jiddah, said of the CIA: "You can't imagine how hard it was to convince them that the national interest was at stake."[31]

Schacht was equally busy in the Far East. At a time when the United States was committed to the total isolation of the People's Republic of China, Schacht carried the oriflamme of German big business to Beijing. In 1957 he became a founding member of the German-China Society, which promoted business deals with the PRC.[32] The chairman of the German-China Society, Wolf Schenke, was a former chief editor of the Hitler Youth publication *Wille und Macht*, a contributor to Haushofer's *Zeitschrift für Geopolitik*, and a Far East correspondent for the

Völkischer Beobachter. After the war he became a strong advocate of an anti-American "neutralist" Germany through an organization called the Third Front. In 1951 he organized the first "West German Congress against Remilitarization" (Schenke personally supported "armed neutrality"), whose delegates included members of the Bruderschaft and SRP as well as Social Democratic and Communist-allied groups.[33]

Another prominent member of the German-China Society was Werner-Otto von Hentig, a former head of the Arab Division of Ribbentrop's Foreign Office and a close friend of Fritz Grobba. King Saud made Hentig Saudi Arabia's chief European advisor in 1955.[34] While serving as German ambassador to Indonesia, Hentig accompanied the Saudi delegation to the April 1955 Afro-Asian Conference held in Bandung, Indonesia, as a Special Counselor. He also helped broker Soviet-Arab relations in the Mideast.[35]

The idea of the "Third World" as a separate bloc between East and West first began to emerge at Bandung, where leaders like Sukarno, Nasser, Tito, Nehru, Nkrumah, and Chou En-lai met to reach some sort of understanding. Nowhere was the Third World dance between East and West more pronounced than in Egypt, where the Soviet-American struggle for political influence was played out in the arms trade. Weapons were especially difficult for Egypt to acquire since England was no longer a potential supplier. France also refused to arm a government that was aiding anti-French insurgent movements in Tunisia, Algeria, and Morocco. Caught between its traditional allies and its desire to maintain a presence in Egypt, the CIA turned to both Otto Skorzeny and the Gehlen Organization to supply Nasser with guns.

A key player in the weapons game was Dr. William Voss, who ran the famous Skoda Works armament factory during the Nazi occupation of Czechoslovakia. After King Farouk's downfall, Voss was hired to modernize Egypt's military. He soon became so powerful that the German ambassador to Egypt, Dr. Guenther Pawelke, quit in protest. In 1955 Nasser's hunger for weapons led to a stunning deal between Egypt and the now-Communist-run Skoda plant and other East Bloc suppliers. The Soviet-sanctioned agreement had major foreign policy ramifications. Until Stalin's death in 1953, Soviet propagandists had regularly denigrated non-Communist African, Asian, and Arab nationalists as either "feudal or semifeudal lords" or supporters of "petit bourgeois reformism." Not without reason, the Soviets viewed Nasser's Free Officers Association as little more than a reactionary clique with ties to the CIA.

After Bandung the Soviet line changed radically, in part because Chou En-lai lobbied the Kremlin on Nasser's behalf. The decisive factor for Moscow, however, was the Egyptian government's refusal to join a proposed U.S.-Egypt Mutual Security Pact. Equally important was Egypt's opposition to the "Baghdad Pact," a U.S. and British–sponsored effort modeled along the lines of NATO and SEATO.

Although Pakistan, Turkey, and Iraq backed the plan, the Egyptians lobbied against it with other nations, including Jordan and Lebanon.[36]

Finally, no discussion of the postwar Nazi presence in the Middle East would be complete without some mention of Haj Amin al-Husseini, the Grand Mufti of Jerusalem.[37] For years the Grand Mufti had been intimately involved in pro-German conspiracies in the Mideast, including the attempted 1940 coup in Iraq. After the coup failed, the Grand Mufti fled to Iran, where he found refuge in the Japanese embassy. He then came to Rome, in October 1941, to meet with Mussolini. That December, he traveled to Berlin and held talks with Hitler, Ribbentrop, and Grobba. Broadcasting on Berlin Radio, the Mufti called on his fellow Moslems to rise up against British, French, and Dutch colonialism. He also helped create an SD-backed propaganda and espionage network throughout the Middle East. He even organized special legions of Muslim Waffen SS volunteers that included the Bosnian "Black Legion."

After Germany's defeat, the Grand Mufti was captured by French troops. Despite demands from Yugoslavia that he be tried as a war criminal, he was allowed to escape to Egypt in 1946. From his new headquarters he continued to remain in close contact with his German comrades, including Leers.[38] Under the auspices of both the Grand Mufti and the Arab League, a series of American rightists visited the Middle East. Anti-Jewish tracts first published in America were reprinted in leading Egyptian papers like *al-Gumhuria* (The Reporter), which in 1956 featured an article from Conde McGinley's *Common Sense*.[39] Other Cairo papers translated articles from *The Cross and the Flag* and *Women's Voice*.[40]

The case of *al-Gumhuria* is particularly interesting. It was founded in December 1953 (around the time Yockey may have returned to Egypt) by Anwar el-Sadat, a Free Officer and German sympathizer who became its editor in chief. Two years later, in January 1955, Sadat became the secretary general of the Grand Mufti's World Muslim Congress (WMC). The WMC soon developed close ties to CIA-backed organizations like the Asian People's Anti-Communist League (APACL).[41] It also circulated Henry Ford's anti-Semitic writings and maintained especially good ties with Gerald L. K. Smith.[42] Such connections, however, did not prevent Sadat from playing a leading role in opposing the Baghdad Pact. In his memoirs Sadat reports that the CIA gave Saudi Arabia's King Saud a dossier alleging that he was "Soviet agent number one" in Egypt because he had attacked U.S. Secretary of State John Foster Dulles in the pages of *al-Gumhuria!*[43]

Egypt also had a staunch friend in the tiny Fred Weiss–financed National Renaissance Party (NRP). Unlike almost every other grouping on the American right, the NRP praised revolutionary Third World regimes and openly hailed Castro, Ben Bella, Sukarno, Mao, and Nasser. It regularly distributed Egyptian Ministry of Information pamphlets like *The Story of Zionist Espionage in Egypt* and Nasser's *The Philosophy of the Revolution*.[44] The Cairo–New York connection included H. Keith Thompson, who later recalled:

Following the removal of Perón in 1955, the regime in Argentina fell into the hands of leftists and "moderates." This was not a favorable development for the Duerer circles [Dürer Verlag, publisher of *Der Weg*], and they began to receive governmental attention. They gradually disbanded. Von Leers went to the Middle East, to his wide range of Arab contacts there, and he ultimately joined the Nasser forces there, receiving an appointment to the bureau of the Egyptian government dealing with anti-Zionist, anti-Israel propaganda. Von Leers was a recognized master in this field . . . During the process, I asked von Leers if he could find a spot for Yockey, not a regular desk job (which FPY would never take) but as a free-lancer in the propaganda field and possibly as a sort of courier-communicant facilitating the work of von Leers. It was in that connection that FPY functioned . . . I would say that, generally, 1953–1958 were the years during which he was "on and off" engaged in propaganda for the Arabs.

Thompson's own links to Egypt paid strange dividends. In the early 1950s he developed a close working relationship with Lyle Stuart, the maverick left-wing publisher. Stuart ran into legal difficulties with Egypt's King Farouk in 1962, after he published *Pleasure Was My Business*, the memoirs of Miami's Madame Sherry, in which she wrote that Farouk had once visited her establishment. The portly ex-despot sued Stuart, who turned to Thompson for help. According to former IHR director David McCalden, Thompson sent Stuart "an Egyptian-Nazi dossier on Farouk, which contained photographs of his majesty in various compromising situations with young ladies. The Miami suit was stopped dead in its tracks."[45]

When I asked Thompson about this, he replied:

Yes, I assisted Stuart on the Farouk matter by providing some research on his pornographic collections and sexual activities. The suit never got beyond pre-trial discovery. Stuart went to Rome and sat across the table from Farouk, who was looking for money. He never got a cent.

Stuart greatly appreciated Thompson's help. In a letter dated 3 September 1963, he wrote Thompson: "You know without my telling you how much I appreciate the initiative and effort you've exercised on behalf on my defense of the Farouk case. Nevertheless, I wanted to tell you."[46]

Notes:

1. Memo from (FBI) Liaison Representative Heidelberg to Director, FBI, 31 December 1953.

2. Yockey also wrote to H. Keith Thompson from Beirut under the name "C. R. Hanley," and wrote a letter to the German rightist Wolfgang Sarg from Beirut that is misdated 28 January 1953. It is clear that it is a mistake because Yockey says in the first line of his letter that he got Sarg's 28 January 1953 letter to H. Keith Thompson a few days earlier. Clearly he could have not gotten a letter not yet written or sent.

3. Yockey, letter to Fred Weiss, 8 July 1953.

4. H. Keith Thompson recalls getting a postcard from Yockey sent from Damascus.

5. Gelny also thanked Weiss for three registered letters from him and said he was looking forward to a possible visit from Hans-Ulrich Rudel. He sent Weiss a copy of a letter he had sent to Erich Schmidt in Dortmund-Hoerde requesting a copy of *Der Feind Europas*. Weiss had told Gelny to contact Schmidt about Yockey's book.

6. Leers died in Cairo in March 1966.

7. Misdated "1954" in Thompson's note to me.

8. Yockey's letters to Fred Weiss and H. Keith Thompson were written in German. Thompson sent me copies of the letters as well as translations.

9. Yockey was referring to a series of articles by Weiss that appeared in 1953 in the *Bulletin* of the National Renaissance Party attacking the concept of "brotherhood."

10. Hussein's party had different official names, including Misr al-Fatât in the 1930s, the Islamic National Party in 1940, and the Socialist Party in 1946. He also was the author of *Imâmi*, the Egyptian equivalent of *Mein Kampf*, and publisher of the fanatically anti-Jewish journal *al-Ichtirakya*.

11. Arnold Forster and Benjamin Epstein, *The Troublemakers* (New York: Doubleday, 1953), p. 97.

12. Arnold Forster and Benjamin Epstein, *Cross-Currents* (New York: Doubleday, 1956), p. 212.

13. There is a confusing note about the trip in the record that James Sheldon, the head of the NSANL, made of a meeting regarding Yockey and Weiss that he had with two FBI agents on 29 July 1954. An FBI agent named Edward Brandt told Sheldon that Yockey was in Canada (in fact, he was in California) and that Weiss was trying to contact him. Brandt then said that "his wife [was] in Cairo."

It is not clear whose wife Brandt was referring to. It is possible that Yockey's ex-wife Alice was in Cairo, but it is much more likely that Brandt meant Marie Weiss, since we know from a 13 April 1954 letter from Weiss's lieutenant Mana Truhill to the Swedish fascist Einer Aberg that Mrs. Weiss was planning to visit Europe. She was scheduled to meet Aberg in Gottingen on 22 April. Since Gelny had just written to Fred Weiss on 24 April 1954 about the project to relocate Leers to Cairo, it seems possible that Mrs. Weiss visited Cairo for her husband.

One other possible connection to the ring around Weiss and Thompson should be mentioned. This was a Goebbels aide named Dr. Giselher Wirsing, an SS major and virulent anti-Semite who before World War II had been the editor of the *Münichner Nueuste Nachrichten*. He had worked with Viereck in Germany's propaganda effort in America. (Viereck had been an American correspondent for Wirsing's paper.) Tom Francis (the American translator of *Der Feind Europas*) told me about postwar rumors concerning a mysterious "doctor" from Germany who was connected to the Weiss network and had ties to the Middle East. This may have been a reference to Wirsing. On Wirsing, see Kurt Tauber, *Beyond Eagle and Swastika* (Middletown, CT: Wesleyan University Press, 1967).

14. Weiss's interest in physics led him to publish three pamphlets devoted to the notion that Max Planck was a greater scientist than Einstein. These pamphlets are *Without Ullstein—No Einstein; Max Planck and the Future of Western Civilization;* and *Einstein est mort!* Weiss's pamphlets were mentioned in the 11 May 1955 issue of *Der Spiegel*. Unlike the pure Nazi line that attacked Einstein as a representative of a

false "Jewish physics," Weiss believed that Einstein was a great physicist, just not as great as Planck.

15. In February 1957 Willis Carto's *Right* cited Weiss's prediction that the Soviets were developing "goose-egg–size" atom bombs and said that he had made the prediction three years earlier. Weiss later reprinted the item and wrote that he had made the prediction in April 1954.

16. "XYZ" (Fred Weiss), *Max Planck and the Future of Western Civilization*, p. 3.

17. My discussion of the *Der Weg* science team is based on Ronald C. Newton's examination of the group in his book *The "Nazi Menace" in Argentina, 1931–1947* (Stanford, CA: Stanford University Press, 1992), pp. 375–79.

18. After Perón fled Argentina in 1955, a special parliamentary commission pronounced Richter a scientific fraud.

19. Some authors claim that Saleh was really an SS officer named Alfred Zingler. In *Dossier Néo-Nazisme* (Paris: Ramsay, 1977), Patrice Chairoff (pseudonym for Ivan-Dominique Calzi) emphatically denies that this was the case.

20. Ibid., p. 457.

21. For an extensive discussion of the German presence in Cairo, see Tauber, *Beyond Eagle and Swastika*, Vol. 2, fn. 178, 179, pp. 1113–16.

22. Leers' conversion, however, did not prevent him from working closely with Fathi er Ramle, Egypt's leading exponent of Stalinism. Walter Laqueur, *Nasser's Egypt* (London: Weidenfeld and Nicholson, 1956), p. 9.

23. Remer's links to the Arab world continued up until his death. See his 20 July 1993 interview in *Alshaab*, which was reprinted by the Louisiana-based Sons of Liberty.

24. I believe Leers was referring to Germans in the French Foreign Legion.

25. Leers' weird mix of Islam and paganism came through in a 15 November 1957 letter to H. Keith Thompson explaining his conversion:

> The Islamic bloc is today the only spiritual power in the world fighting for a real religion and human values and freedom. Besides that, it is a wonderful religion with a great philosophy and an enormous rich[ness] of wisdom. I think sometimes if my nation had got Islam instead of Christianity we should not have had all the traitors we had in World War II, two million women would not have been burnt as "witches" by the Christian churches, there would have been no Thirty Years War which destroyed Germany and killed more than half of our nation. [From the H. Keith Thompson archives at the Hoover Institute.]

26. On Grobba, see a report by Sigrid Schultz, a journalist with close ties to the Society for the Prevention of World War III, in the Society's archive.

27. See Sigrid Schultz's "Moscow's Secret Allies in the Middle East," in the Society for the Prevention of World War III archives.

28. Schacht told Canadian journalist William Stevenson that when he left prison he had "two marks and fifty pfennigs in his pocket." Then, almost overnight, Schacht "was directing a major West German bank, of which he soon became president. By the age of 74, he was masterminding a resurgence of foreign trade through private channels. A major part of that foreign trade was in the Mideast." (William Stevenson, *The Bormann Brotherhood* [New York: Harcourt, Brace, 1973], p. 120.)

29. See mention of Schacht's visit in Gilles Perrault, *A Man Apart: The Life of Henri Curiel* (London: Zed Books, 1987), p. 171. Curiel was a leader of the Communist movement in Egypt at the time, and headed up the Democratic Movement for National Liberation (DMNL), the only Marxist group to support the military uprising. All other groups, including the Egyptian Communist Party and the PCF in France, condemned the coup as fascist.

30. The Jiddah Agreement is also of interest because one of the economic advisors to the Saudi throne was St. John Philby, Kim Philby's father and a supporter of the pro-German right in England before World War II.

31. Jim Hougan, *Spooks* (New York: William Morrow, 1978), p. 293. *Spooks* contains a full description of the campaign against the Jiddah Agreement.

32. Tauber, *Beyond Eagle and Swastika*, Vol. 2, fn. 108, p. 1061.

33. Ibid., Vol. 1, pp. 173–76.

34. On Hentig, see a report from the Jewish Telegraph Agency of 16 June 1955, as reported in the Winter 1956 issue of *Prevent World War III*.

35. An article in the 21 September 1956 *Der Spiegel* discusses Hentig's relations with Moscow.

36. For a discussion of this period, see Anwar el-Sadat, *In Search of Identity: An Autobiography* (New York: Harper & Row, 1978), chapters 5 and 6.

37. In a January 1953 interview in *Der Weg*, the Grand Mufti complimented Leers on his "very important work in favor of the traditional friendship between the German and Arab nation." Cited in the Wiener Institute *Bulletin*, 1956.

38. It was through Leers that the National Renaissance Party was first put in touch with the Grand Mufti. In a letter to the NRP dated 24 March 1954, Leers said that the Grand Mufti could be contacted at 31 Sharia Muhammed Ali, Heliopolis, Cairo. Leers also asked the NRP to send the Grand Mufti a copy of *The American Nationalist*, edited by Frank Britton. An Arabic translation of Britton's book *Behind Communism* was published by Farajalla Press in Beirut.

The NRP contacted the Grand Mufti on 5 April 1954. On 17 April the Grand Mufti sent the NRP a friendly reply. See the Grand Mufti's letter in the files of the NSANL. The Grand Mufti's address on his letter was 6 Asyout Street, Heliopolis.

39. Recall that much of this material had been prepared with the help of Heinrich Malz and Karl Heinrich Peter from the Naumann network.

40. The connections between the postwar U.S. and Arab right is discussed in O. John Rogge, *The Official German Report* (New York: Thomas Yoseloff, 1961).

41. APACL was a curious blend of fanatically anti-Communist Taiwanese, Korean, and Japanese intelligence operatives. Behind them lurked badly scared Germans, light-footed priests, and CIA operatives highly skilled in the art of writing checks. It later became the World Anti-Communist League (WACL).

42. In 1988 the WMC's leader, Dr. Inamullah Khan, came under attack after winning the $396,000 Templeton Prize for Progress in Religion. On 19 April 1988 the *New York Times* ran a major exposé on Khan ("Anti-Semitism Charges Lead to Delay on Religion Prize") by Peter Steinfels; it documented the WMC's use of anti-Semitic propaganda in its publication *The Muslim World* as well as its ties to Gerald L. K. Smith and the APACL/WACL network.

43. Sadat, *In Search of Identity*, p. 149.
44. NRP *Bulletin* for February–March, 1961 (Vol. 12, Nos. 2 & 3).
45. David McCalden's *Revisionist Newsletter* #21, June 1983.
46. Stuart's letter is in the H. Keith Thompson archive at the Hoover Institute.

39
THE SPY WHO
WENT INTO
THE COLD

Yockey's activities in Egypt were tied in some way to the Bruderschaft's Alfred Franke-Gricksch, who maintained extensive Mideast connections.[1] There is a copy of a cryptic undated note to Fred Weiss in Yockey's handwriting in the ADL files.[2] Yockey told Weiss: "Have seen Schmidt. A good chap but not bright. Doesn't understand Spengler and probably not *Der Feind* either. Franke-Greis has gone to O-B [Ost/East-Berlin]. He gave me your message about Kairo but it means nothing to me."

Der Feind Europas was published in Germany sometime in the fall or winter of 1953.[3] Yockey's note, then, was most likely written in the fall of 1953, when he was back in Germany. As for "Schmidt," he was almost certainly Erich Schmidt, who helped distribute Yockey's book.[4] Schmidt was also an important conduit for money from Fred Weiss to the German right. In a letter to Hans-Ulrich Rudel dated 14 March 1954, Weiss told Rudel that if he were in financial trouble, he could "write to me to my farm immediately" or contact Schmidt in Dortmund. Weiss further reported that Schmidt would be getting a thousand Deutschmarks from him each month for the creation of a newspaper.[5]

The newspaper Weiss helped finance, Schmidt's *Der Reichsruf* (Nation's Call), later became the official paper of the Deutsche Reichs Party (DRP).[6] It began as a crude four-page weekly with articles like "England: Enemy of the White Race."[7] The paper blasted the European Defense Community (EDC) as an "instrument of Jewish imperialism," and referenced Yockey's "Prague" article when it wrote:

In American and British publications we read plainly that Beria, like Trotsky, had been an agent of Zionism. The Moscow *Pravda* writes: Zionism is a tool of American imperialism. A leaflet issued by the American [National] Renaissance Party expresses the same idea even more plainly. The EDC project will end in disaster. As far as the Jews are concerned it will be the instrument for the advance of Jewish imperialism.[8]

As for Alfred Franke-Gricksch, he had indeed "gone to O-B." In either late September or early October 1951, he crossed over into East Berlin and was never seen again. His wife Liselotte returned to Germany from a Soviet prison camp in 1955 and reported that her husband had been executed by the Russians. But was he really dead?

The mystery of Alfred Franke-Gricksch began in the summer of 1950, when Lieutenant General Vincenz Müller, the commander of the Soviet-bloc German police and chairman of the Communist Party–controlled National Democratic Party, sent a series of letters calling for a reunited Germany to important Wehrmacht officers and "ex-" Nazis living in the West.[9] In response to Müller's opening, Franke-Gricksch established contact with correspondents from ADN, the East Zone news agency. He also met Richard Scheringer, a well-known Communist Party functionary and former National Socialist, who introduced him to members of the Communist Party executive committee. Franke-Gricksch then began denouncing Western imperialism and demanding a new alliance with Russia based on an antiplutocratic "front of young peoples." On 19 January 1951 he called on Germany to abandon its military dependence on NATO and sign a new Rapallo Treaty with the USSR. He further advocated a future military nonaggression pact with the Soviet Union after Germany remilitarized.[10] His aggressive neutralism corresponded to an increase in global tensions during the Korean War, when an alliance with America could turn Germany into a future nuclear battlefield.[11]

Franke-Gricksch's overt "East turn" put him at odds with Bruderschaft founder Major Helmut Beck-Broichsitter. Franke-Gricksch spoke for the SS, Hitler Youth, and Conservative Revolutionary elements inside the "Brotherhood," while Beck-Broichsitter had the support of most Wehrmacht officers. Still, as historian Kurt Tauber notes, the ideological differences between the two camps should not be exaggerated. Beck-Broichsitter, for instance, had been asked on 25 July 1950 to sign the Communist-inspired *Stockholm Proclamation for the Outlawry of Atom Bombs*, and may well have done so.[12] He was even discovered in secret negotiations with the Soviet military authorities at Karlshorst.[13] During the talks, he assured the Russians that the Bruderschaft refused to have any dealings with a plot by U.S. military intelligence to ally the organization with the Technical Service of the League of German Youth (*Bund Deutscher Jugend*/BDJ) led by Paul Lüth.[14] The BDJ was a German branch of "Operation Gladio." With help from both the CIA and U.S. military intelligence, groups like the BDJ were trained as secret paramilitary shock troops against the left. The Social Democratic Party–led government of Hesse discovered that a neo-Nazi clique consisting of BDJ cadre had drawn up lists of SPD members to be arrested or assassinated during a Soviet invasion of Germany. German authorities learned about the BDJ's "Technical Service" branch after an ex–SS captain and Bruderschaft member named Hans Otto told Frankfurt police about its attempt to recruit him.[15]

Inside the Bruderschaft, however, Beck-Broichsitter represented those elements who were less interested in the permanent weakening of Western military power but who insisted on certain Allied concessions. They particularly detested former Nazis and Wehrmacht officers "who had agreed to collaborate with the Western allies without insisting on conditions or exacting the highest price for their collaboration."[16] One of those conditions was an end to war crimes prosecutions and the quick release of convicted war criminals from Allied jails.

Fearing that a new conflict with the Soviets might be just around the corner, American intelligence desperately wanted to reach an accommodation with the far right. U.S. agents aggressively recruited top officials from Alfred Rosenberg's Ostministerium for anti-Soviet operations. Through umbrella organizations like the Anti-Bolshevik Bloc of Nations (ABN), the CIA, in league with the Gehlen Org, reconstructed the pre-war coalition of "anti-Comintern" groups in East Europe, the Baltics, and the Ukraine, which had extensive ties to German military intelligence and the Rosenberg apparat.[17]

The U.S. was particularly interested in winning over top German military officers to NATO, especially the Bruderschaft leader and famed World War II tank commander General Heinz Guderian. American intelligence saw Guderian as a potential "Prince Borghese" tailor-made to rally the German right into the Atlanticist camp if only he were willing. An important middleman between the Bruderschaft, Guderian, and the United States was Gunther D'Alquen, an SS theorist, Werewolf leader, and editor in chief of the SS journal *Das Schwarze Korps*.[18] D'Alquen was widely suspected of being on the American payroll, and on 2 December 1948 the Swiss paper *Die Tat* filed a dispatch that cited an allegation to this effect by Fritz Saenger, the editor in chief of the British-licensed news agency DPD. Saenger claimed that D'Alquen and other Nazis, including Toni Winkelnkempner from Goebbels' Propaganda Ministry, had been in the United States working for the U.S. State Department. He said he had even seen a photo of D'Alquen standing outside the White House![19]

While D'Alquen served as the liaison for the United States, Guderian's representative was none other than Beck-Broichsitter, who initiated talks with U.S. Army Headquarters in Heidelberg after the ground had been prepared by D'Alquen. Between 11 September 1950 and 1 February 1951 Beck-Broichsitter met three times with American officials. He discussed the American overtures with Guderian at a meeting held on either 15 or 16 January 1951. Guderian decided that he would speak with the Americans only if his counterpart held an equal rank.[20]

The U.S. would also have to agree in principle with the idea of the complete equality of any future German military in terms of command responsibilities, weapons, unit size, and prestige. Finally, Guderian demanded "a psychological clearing of the air" that would occur after the West freed German war criminals held in Spandau, Landsberg, and Werl prisons.[21]

In February 1951, while he was engaged in negotiations with the U.S. on behalf of Guderian, Beck-Broichsitter managed to get Franke-Gricksch's faction expelled from the Bruderschaft. He announced that he was forming his own group called the Bruderschaft Deutschland. Franke-Gricksch countered by accusing Beck-Broichsitter of coming under the control of Allied intelligence. Beck-Broichsitter then pointed out Franke-Gricksch's own cozy ties with the Russians. The East Germans (who no doubt knew all about the "secret" talks between Beck-Broichsitter and the Americans) began denouncing the Bruderschaft in the summer of 1951 as "agents of the occupation powers in West Germany."[22]

Such was the murky political situation that continued into that fall, when Franke-Gricksch disappeared into East Berlin. According to Franke-Gricksch's son, Ekkehard:

> As a leader of the Brotherhood, my father was lured to East Berlin in late September 1951[23] where he was arrested by Soviet secret service agents. One or two days later his wife was lured into the Soviet Zone with a fabricated letter containing the message that her husband had suffered a severe colic and was laid up at his mother's in Potsdam.
>
> He died on August 18, 1953, in the Vorkuta camp in the Soviet Union. My stepmother was sentenced to 25 years forced labor, but was released in 1956.[24]

Ekkehard Franke-Gricksch's news about his father appeared in Willis Carto's *Journal of Historical Review*. The IHR's interest in Franke-Gricksch had been triggered by a book called *Hitler and the Final Solution* by the British historian Gerald Fleming, who cited a report by Franke-Gricksch on his 1943 visit to Auschwitz that gave eyewitness testimony to the presence of gas chambers.[25]

Despite his son's letter, Franke-Gricksch's fate was never clear. The Russians officially claimed that he was condemned to death in October 1951 for war crimes committed between the late summer and winter of 1942, while he was with an SS police division in Russia.[26] Given the fact that Franke-Gricksch was only in Russia for a relatively short time, as well as his previous close relationship to the Soviets, there is something highly suspicious about this explanation. If it were true, why did the Russians then lure his wife east as well? Liselotte Franke-Gricksch was sentenced to 25 years in a Russian labor camp before being permitted to return to West Germany in October 1955. Although she told German authorities that her husband had died in 1953, even she wasn't completely convinced. According to a story in Carto's *Journal of Historical Review*, Frau Franke-Gricksch inquired about her husband's fate and whereabouts in a letter dated 3

February 1969, which she sent to the Tracing Service of the German Red Cross, because she thought that he might still be alive.

Lisolette's mother, Margarette Draeger, was equally in the dark. In early 1954 the National Renaissance Party sent a letter meant for Alfred Franke-Gricksch to Frau Draeger. She replied, in a letter dated 20 February 1954, that she had forwarded the letter to Count C. Stamati, "a friend of my son-in-law," in Düsseldorf. She also added: "Our great sorrow is our solicitation regarding the fate of our son-in-law Alfred Franke-Gricksch and my daughter."[27] Yockey wrote another undated note to Weiss about Franke-Gricksch in either late 1953 or possibly late 1954. In it he reported: "Supposedly F-G, who went to Ost-Berlin to work with the Russians, was condemned to death, and his wife, who was with him, to 25 years in prison. No comment."[28]

Franke-Gricksch's odyssey should also be seen in a larger political context. He went to East Berlin in late September 1951. By the winter of 1952 the Slansky trials were underway in Prague, and by the spring of 1953 Stalin's minions had begun laying the basis for a new attack on Soviet Jews by falsely claiming that Stalin's doctors were planning to murder him. After Stalin died on 5 March 1953, his secret-police chief Lavrenti Beria, who effectively ruled the Soviet empire for a brief period, put a stop to the "Jewish Doctors' Plot" hoax. To a Beria-controlled security apparat, Franke-Gricksch may have been seen as a problem that needed liquidation. Yet it is equally possible that he was executed by an anti-Beria faction.

The Soviets attempted to disrupt America's domination of West Germany in the early 1950s with their own "neutralist" card; after Stalin's death, Beria and Wilhelm Zaisser, head of East German intelligence, escalated the game by sending clear signals that Russia would accept a reunified but neutralist Germany as a buffer state. Franke-Gricksch's call for neutralism fit into the overall Soviet game plan. Beria's policies backfired spectacularly in the summer of 1953, however, when a workers' revolt against Russian domination swept East Berlin. The uprising became a key card in the hands of Beria's Kremlin enemies, who were desperate for any excuse to topple him from power. Beria was arrested on 26 June 1953.

Yet every report about Franke-Gricksch claims that he had gotten into trouble with the Russians well before the tumultuous events of the summer of 1953. In *Beyond Eagle and Swastika*, Kurt Tauber comments that in 1955, after Frau Franke-Gricksch returned to West Germany from the Soviet Union, she explained that she and her husband had been tried in 1952 by a Russian military court "on charges of pro-Western intelligence and anti-Soviet propaganda activity." The Soviet Red Cross also informed the German Red Cross in 1957 that Franke-Gricksch had died in a labor camp on 18 August 1953, less than two months after Beria's downfall.[29]

But how could Franke-Gricksch have died in August 1953 (in Vorkuta, no less) if Yockey was in communication with him that fall or early winter? He could only have spoken to Franke-Gricksch either in early 1953 (before his own journey to

Cairo) or after the East Berlin uprising, when Yockey was back in Germany. Yockey's claim that Erich Schmidt would have trouble understanding *Der Feind Europas* suggests that he was writing Weiss after his book had been published in Germany. Yockey most likely met Schmidt after the publication of *Der Feind Europas*, when Schmidt became its distributor. Although we don't know the exact date when Weiss sent his message to Franke-Gricksch through the NRP, the fact that Franke-Gricksch's mother-in-law replied on 20 February 1954 indicates that the letter was most likely mailed sometime in January or early February 1954.[30] Clearly Weiss believed that Franke-Gricksch was alive and politically active in the winter of 1953. This again raises the possibility that Yockey wrote his message to Weiss in the fall or winter of 1953, a few months after Franke-Gricksch's official demise. Thus there remains the suspicion that Franke-Gricksch's death was faked.

Another keen student of Franke-Gricksch had difficulty with the notion that he had been arrested by the Russians. This was Otto Strasser, whose movement Franke-Gricksch had so brutally betrayed in the 1930s when he worked as an SS double agent against his Black Front comrades. In his 1953 book *The Prisoner of Ottawa*, Douglas Reed reports that Strasser had gotten conflicting information about Franke-Gricksch. Although he too had heard rumors that Franke-Gricksch had been arrested in the East Zone, Strasser remained unconvinced and pointed out that there were also reports that he had spoken at "national bolshevist" meetings in East Berlin. Strasser told Reed that he personally believed that Franke-Gricksch, while no Communist, fully supported an alliance with Moscow against the West.[31]

Most important of all for our purposes, however, is the fact that Yockey's note could only have been written at least *two years* after Franke-Gricksch crossed over into the East. Recall that Yockey first met Weiss in late 1951 and that he remained in America until January 1953. If he met Franke-Gricksch in 1953, as his note clearly indicates, it could only mean that either Franke-Gricksch had been operating undercover in the Western Zone, or that Yockey had crossed over to the East to talk with him!

It is also clear that Franke-Gricksch's line toward the East by no means vanished when he did. Even as Yockey continued his clandestine wanderings, the far-right Socialist Reich Party (SRP) brought Franke-Gricksch's East neutralist message to the German public with astonishing success.

Notes:

1. Franke-Gricksch had close ties to the Arab League. One key intermediary was reported to be Jean-Maurice Bauverd, a Swiss citizen who had worked in 1948–1949 for Radio Damascus and later transferred to the Egyptian government's press office in Cairo. Bauverd helped create Islamic press centers in Rome, Paris, and Buenos Aires. Also involved with Bauverd was a Paris-based group around the Pétainist Claude Collin that included Maurice Bardèche, René Binet, and Guy Amaudruz. See Kurt Tauber,

Beyond Eagle and Swastika (Middletown, CT: Wesleyan University Press, 1967), Vol. 1, p. 240.

2. The ADL had no understanding of the importance of Yockey's note, and there is no further discussion of it in the ADL files.

3. The Library of Congress's copy of *Der Feind Europas* shows that the book was received on 10 December 1953.

4. Recall that the Damascus-based Dr. Rudolf Emil Gelny sent a letter to Erich Schmidt in early 1954 asking for a copy of *Der Feind Europas* on the advice of Weiss.

5. Weiss's letter to Rudel in the NSANL archives.

6. On Weiss's ties to Schmidt, see "A Neo-Nazi Network," in the ADL publication *Facts*, October–November 1954. Schmidt may also have gotten money from the Chicago businessman Arthur Koegel. In a 16 February 1954 letter to Weiss quoted in *Facts*, Schmidt writes: "Koegel plans to come to Germany again next year. There is so much to talk over with him, especially what the American possibilities are for our German-oriented newspapers to get a news service for our papers."

7. "England" appeared in *Der Reichsruf*, No. 7, 20 February 1954.

8. *Der Reichsruf*, No. 6, 13 February 1954. The reference to the NRP leaflet is to Yockey's line in his "Prague" essay that while today *Pravda* is saying Zionism is an instrument of American imperialism, tomorrow *Pravda* will say American imperialism is an instrument of Zionism. The NRP issued a leaflet celebrating Beria's downfall.

9. Jan Paulus of the Committee to Prevent World War III also referred to Müller when he wrote: "The British have conclusive evidence that the seven arrested Nazis [the Naumann Circle] have been working very closely with Gen. Vincenz Müller, the brains behind the East German People's Police." Müller, a former adjutant to General Kurt von Schleicher, commanded the Wehrmacht's Army Group Center's Fourth Army during World War II. He surrendered to the Soviets in July 1944. In the 1950s Müller helped form the East German army. Kai P. Schoenhals, *The Free Germany Movement* (Westport, CT: Greenwood Press, 1989), pp. 100–01.

10. Tauber, *Beyond Eagle and Swastika*, Vol. 1, p. 167.

11. Franke-Gricksch's left turn was supported by a circle of intellectuals around Werner Naumann's friend H.-B. von Grünberg, the former director of the East Europe Institute at Königsberg. Grünberg had been a student of Professor Otto Hoetzsch, a longtime advocate of a German alliance with Russia.

12. Tauber, *Beyond Eagle and Swastika*, Vol. 1, p. 163.

13. Ibid., Vol. 1, pp. 163–64.

14. Ibid., p. 164.

15. Leo Müller, *Gladio—das Erbe des Kalten Krieges* (Reinbek bei Hamburg: Rowohlt, 1991), pp. 72–76. See also Tauber, *Beyond Eagle and Swastika*, Vol. 2, fn. 14, p. 1171; and an article by Barton Osborne and Maris Cakars entitled "Operation Ohio," which appeared in *WIN* magazine, 18 September 1975. The article discusses the CIA's involvement in the Ukrainian OUN group (Stetsko-Bandera faction), which carried out a series of assassinations in postwar Germany. It reports that "a CIA agent named Henry Sutton was putting into effect a plan to organize a paramilitary force of German youth to be thrown into action in the event of an armed confrontation with the Soviet Union . . . the CIA shipped arms to the German youth while attempting at all costs to

keep the operation a secret. The fruit of this blundered attempt is now known as the 'Black October' flap." On the murder plots and counter-plots among the Russian exiles, see "The Case of General Gulay" in the 14 April 1952 *New Leader*.

16. Tauber, *Beyond Eagle and Swastika*, Vol. 1, p. 162.

17. One operative for both the Americans and Gehlen was Eberhard Taubert, an ex–Propaganda Ministry man and mastermind of the Anti-Comintern. He, in turn, worked closely with Fritz Cramer's Committee for Information and Social Activity (CISA). Many of the groups involved with both Taubert and Cramer formed the European wing of the Asian People's Anti-Communist League (APACL).

18. Tauber, *Beyond Eagle and Swastika*, Vol. 1, pp. 123–24.

19. *Prevent World War III*, Jan.–Feb. 1949. The D'Alquen story is also cited in the *Bulletin* of the Weiner Institute.

20. This meant that Guderian would only negotiate with the commander in chief of the United States forces in Europe or General Eisenhower's chief of staff, General Alfred M. Gruenther.

21. Tauber, *Beyond Eagle and Swastika*, Vol. 1, pp. 272–73.

22. Ibid., Vol. 2, fn. 47, p. 1054.

23. Other reports say October.

24. Ekkehard Franke-Gricksch's letter cited in an article by Brian Renk called "The Franke-Gricksch 'Resettlement Action Report': Anatomy of a Fabrication," in the Fall 1991 issue of the *Journal of Historical Review*. Ekkehard Franke-Gricksch currently edits a far-right journal called CODE.

25. See the careful discussion of Franke-Gricksch's report in Jean-Claude Pressac's *Auschwitz: Techniques and Operation of the Gas Chambers* (New York: Beate Klarsfeld Foundation, 1989). Gerald Fleming mentions another document by Franke-Gricksch, entitled "From the Diary of a Fallen SS Leader," written sometime after 1948. It purported to be a discussion the "fallen SS leader" had with Himmler in the spring of 1943 about SS men who became so demoralized by their assignment at concentration camps that they committed suicide. Liselotte Franke-Gricksch later submitted this essay as evidence in the Treblinka concentration camp trial in 1965. (Gerald Fleming, *Hitler and the Final Solution* [Berkeley, CA: University of California Press, 1984], Chapter 17.)

26. Fleming, *Hitler and the Final Solution*, p. 141.

27. From the files of the NSANL.

28. From the ADL files.

29. Tauber, *Beyond Eagle and Swastika*, Vol. 2, fn. 62, p. 1055.

30. By that time Yockey had returned to the United States and could no longer be used as a courier.

31. Douglas Reed, *The Prisoner of Ottawa: Otto Strasser* (London: Jonathan Cape, 1953), pp. 247–48.

40
MOSCOW
RULES?

Yockey's *Der Feind Europas* was published in Germany in the autumn of 1953 in an edition of just two hundred copies. Because of its contents, the book could only circulate underground to avoid confiscation by Allied authorities. Nor were Yockey's problems with *Der Feind Europas* all legal. Heinrich Malz, the Naumann aide who had agreed to translate the book, failed to meet his promised deadline. In a letter to H. Keith Thompson shortly after his return from Cairo, Yockey fumed:

> Malz is an s.o.b. He solemnly and firmly promised me that he'd start right away and work at it diligently till the end. What's more he said that if I were dead, he'd treat the work as if it were his very own—he said that was his duty. A pig. A dog. A Schweinehund. A traitor. A Catholic. A Jesuit. A Freemason. Never forget that![1]

Yockey then told Thompson that he had found a new translator "quite by chance. He's a gentleman of the old school and is still unconquered, very much the right man for the job." He also asked Thompson to send him (via Weiss) DM 350 for the translation. The final version of *Der Feind Europas* seems to have been a cut-and-paste job put together by Yockey and the unknown German.[2] The chaos surrounding the book was reflected in another handwritten note Yockey sent Thompson sometime that fall:

> I've started paying the printer. He said about 1,300 DM, i.e., about $325. Half of that is about $165. The translator too still needs $45. Therefore you now owe $165 + $45 = $210. If you see the blocked account, then I'll expect an additional $210 from you for translation and printing. There will also be some postal expenses, how much I don't know. 1. Write and let me know how many copies

you want. 2. Also send me addresses of people who read German, *just a select list,* of people who should get the book. Only 200 copies will be printed. The printer is now starting. 3. Please don't forget: $210.

Fred Weiss also helped with the book's finances. According to an ADL report, Weiss met Virginia Johnson ("Madelaine Yockey") on 16 November 1953 in a diner on 42nd Street and gave her $100 in partial payment for a "book in German," clearly *Der Feind Europas.*[3]

Der Feind Europas did not come with a listed publisher or date of publication.[4] Yockey's 26 May 1953 letter to Thompson, however, mentions the book's publisher/printer Karl-Heinz Heubaum, and says that "Henbaum [sic] is 1000% better than Heinrich [Malz]." Yockey also reported in a letter from Cairo that "Haytree [Heubaum] is very good, comradely, ready to make sacrifices, brave." Heubaum published a far-right youth journal called *Der Widerhall Stimme der Jugend* (Echo of the Voice of Youth). It too had numerous problems with the law, and its August 1952 issue was suppressed for anti-Semitism.[5] Overtly volkish and anti-Christian, it was edited by Reinhard Kriszat, a leader of a postwar Nordic grouping called the *Gefährtenschaft* (Wayfarers' Fellowship). Kriszat was also a representative to an NEO conference in Paris in the spring of 1952.[6]

Yockey had been aware of *Der Widerhall* since at least 1952, and had left the May and June 1952 issues at Warren Johnson's house in Maryland. Heubaum's publishing house was just outside Munich, the city where Yockey spent much of the fall of 1953.[7] Like Yockey, Heubaum had his own curious connections to the East Bloc, and fled to East Germany sometime in the mid-1950s to avoid being jailed for anti-Semitism.[8]

The fear of a Soviet understanding with elements of the German right became especially pronounced in May 1951, when the Socialist Reich Party (SRP), a far-right group allied with the New European Order, shocked Allied occupation authorities with an astonishing electoral success.[9] That month the SRP captured 11 percent of the vote (367,000 ballots) and 16 seats in the Diet of Lower Saxony.[10] Although fiercely anti-Communist when it came to domestic policy, the SRP demanded some form of detente between a neutralist Germany and the USSR. The party's foreign-policy argument rang true to many voters, who eagerly embraced the neutralist slogan *"Ohne Mich"* (Without Me). Why should Germany ally with its American occupiers when such an alliance only made it a prime Russian target? As SRP leader General Otto Ernst Remer put it: "Instead of letting our women and children be overrun by the Russians and our men bled to death in the new Maginot Line, we should stretch out our arms so that the Russians can march as speedily as possible through Germany."[11]

Arguments like Remer's led to charges that the SRP was receiving Soviet backing. In July 1952 West Germany's interior minister reported that he had concrete evidence of Soviet funding for the party. The chairman of the SRP's Berlin branch claimed that Count Wolf von Westarp, one of the group's founders, had received substantial support from the West Kommission of East Germany's Socialist Unity Party. Fritz Dorls, the SRP's one Bundestag member, was also said to have ties to the East.[12] Little sleuthing, however, was needed to find links between the SRP and the left. In January 1951, for example, a large pro-neutralist meeting took place in Wiesbaden that included SRP leaders Dorls and Remer as well as representatives from Neutrales Deutschland, an organization closely tied to the West German Communist Party.[13]

The SRP so alarmed Allied authorities that in November 1951 the party's offices were raided. Then, on 1 July 1952, a German court issued an "interim judgment" banning all SRP propaganda. It was labeled a subversive organization and outlawed on 23 October 1952.[14] In anticipation of the ban, the SRP (under the slogan "To the Catacombs!") officially dissolved the party that September. At its last meeting, the group publicly fought over just how far East it should tilt. The SRP's "anti-Eastern" faction included Bruderschaft leader Helmut Beck-Broichsitter, who had joined the party that June.[15] Beck-Broichsitter's SRP ties, however, went back at least a year earlier, when he had recruited some SRP militants into a semi-clandestine paramilitary ring called Freikorps Deutschland (FD). The FD was formed at a secret meeting in Hamburg on 17 August 1951 by the Bruderschaft, the SRP, an SS fraternal association, and other like-minded groups.[16] Recruits went through a heavily ritualistic initiation ceremony as well as a tough physical course that included forced marches with 50-pound packs.[17] The FD had one or two thousand members divided into *Freischaren* (volunteer companies) of 113 members each.[18] Its public leaders were two ex–SS men, Hermann Lamp and Colonel Eberhard Hawranke, and a naval officer named Heinz Naumann. Behind them stood the former Vienna Gauleiter A. E. Frauenfeld, his friend and Naumann Circle–member Gustav Adolf Scheel, and Beck-Broichsitter.[19] All swore allegiance to imprisoned Grand Admiral Karl Dönitz as the legal head of Germany.

On 11 February 1953 the West German government banned Freikorps Deutschland and arrested Beck-Broichsitter. The ban scotched a wild plot to use FD members to spring Admiral Dönitz from jail. The "Free Dönitz" conspiracy was coordinated by Hans-Ulrich Rudel, who left Germany for Argentina in 1948 to run the "Rudel Club," which helped Nazis escape to South America.[20] He illegally reentered Germany for the first time in 1950.[21]

Rudel's main U.S. connection was H. Keith Thompson, who served as the American literary agent for Rudel's book *Stuka Pilot*.[22] Thompson also became involved in Rudel's plot to raid Spandau prison and free Dönitz.[23] In an article for Willis Carto's *Journal of Historical Review*, Thompson recalled:

> During 1951–53, a remarkable and fascinating plan was developed in West Germany, with roots extending to Spain, Argentina, and even the United States, for the liberation of the Spandau prisoners by a commando-type military action,

and the setting up of the Dönitz government elsewhere as a legitimate government-in-exile. Although the financing was available, and many dedicated men were involved, security was compromised in Germany and the matter became a field day for Allied journalism, resulting in a number of arrests. The full facts were never known and never will be, even though most of those involved are now deceased. Just a few years ago, I had the pleasure of burning a file on the subject which had been eagerly sought by at least four intelligence agencies for many years.[24]

Yockey played a small role in the Dönitz caper. According to Thompson: "Yockey carried some papers over for me, destined for Rudel, who was all over the place but mostly out of Germany."[25]

After the SRP breakup and the ban on Freikorps Deutschland, the German Reich Party (DRP) became Germany's leading rightist party.[26] The rise of the DRP also signaled the return of Werner Naumann, who had been released from jail on 28 July 1953, after his earlier arrest by the British authorities had been nullified by a German federal court.[27] Just 48 hours after his release, Naumann (now a right-wing folk hero) was chosen as a DRP electoral candidate. (He also helped arrange Rudel's return to Germany from Argentina to run on the DRP ticket.) Naumann was then hastily reclassified as a "Group II" offender for his role in World War II, which meant he could not legally run for office.

While it never had more than 16,000 members and a few seats in local parliaments, the DRP was the most influential far-right party in Germany in the late 1950s. Although it was headed by Adolf von Thadden, both Naumann and Rudel continued to play important roles. Despite its low profile, carefully toned-down rhetoric, and parliamentary veneer, the DRP came close to being banned several times.[28] A greatly reduced DRP merged with two other rightist groups in 1965 to become the National Democratic Party (NDP), the most important far-right party in Germany in the 1960s and the German equivalent of Britain's National Front.

Friedrich Middelhauve and Ernst Achenbach, Naumann's fellow political conspirators in the plot to take over a branch of the Free Democratic Party, also emerged undamaged. Middelhauve later became minister of economics and deputy minister president of North Rhine–Westphalia; in 1961 West Germany's president decorated him with the Grand Federal Cross of Merit with Star and Ribbon for his service to the Fatherland.[29] As for Achenbach, after serving in the Bundestag, he became a member of the European parliament and the consultative assembly of the Council of Europe in 1964. Only after Achenbach was chosen as the German member of the Committee of the European Economic Community (EEC) in 1970 did the story of his career in Paris as Otto Abetz's Jewish-deportation expert surface, thanks to the efforts of the Nazi-hunters Beate and Serge Klarsfeld.

In the early 1950s the U.S. State Department caught a brief glimpse into the Nazi underground thanks to an ex–SS officer referred to as "Kluf" in State Department documents. Kluf had contacted a State Department official in France and told him that he had been approached for recruitment by a group of ex–SS men. He then revealed the existence of a secret organization made up of former SS officers who, he said, had been partially financed by the Soviets, though the group's major source of income was German industry. The organization included two German noblewomen, Princess von Isenburg and the Countess Faber-Castell. Kluf reported that General Remer was closely cooperating with the Russians after the SRP ban.[30] Rudel was also said to have developed Soviet ties around this time.[31]

Princess Isenburg was a Catholic nun known as "Mutter Elisabeth." She ran an organization called *Stille Hilfe* (Silent Help), whose honorary president was Dr. Albert Schweitzer. Founded in 1951, Stille Hilfe provided logistical support to jailed war criminals. It is reported to have helped Dr. Hans Eisele, the chief medical officer at Buchenwald, avoid Allied capture. The group established excellent relations with some high-ranking American officials, including U.S. High Commissioner to Germany John J. McCloy, and in December 1951 it was granted tax-exempt status by the Munich tax office.[32] One of its leaders, the war-crimes trial lawyer Dr. Rudolf Aschenauer, had influential connections inside the German Ministry of Justice.

The other noblewoman mentioned by Kluf, Countess Faber-Castell, maintained especially close ties to General Remer. She even allowed him to use her hunting lodge in the Bavarian Alps as a safe house. Money from the Faber-Castell pencil manufacturing fortune was funnelled into the SRP through Remer.[33]

But what exactly was the larger organization mentioned by Kluf that *both* Princess Isenburg and Countess Faber-Castell were said to be involved with? In June 1958, three years after Germany had regained its full sovereignty, some answers were provided by the rightist journal *Deutsche Soldaten Zeitung*. It was here that Major General Hans Korte published a lengthy article describing an underground "resistance" network that had the active support of both women.[34]

Korte reported that in 1948 a group of jurists who had served in Nuremberg as defense counsels for major war criminals created a steering committee in Munich to attack the legality of the war crimes process. Two of the lawyers were Rudolf Aschenauer and Ernst Achenbach. A number of fronts or subagencies were then created, including *Die Andere Seite* and the Committee for Christian Aid to War Prisoners, whose sponsors included Cardinal Josef Frings of Cologne and Bishop Johann Neuhaeusler of Munich. The Roman Catholic Caritas organization and the Protestant Evangelisches Hilfswerk became involved as well.[35]

Cardinal Frings and a Stuttgart Protestant cleric named Theophil Wurm ran an organization called the Committee for Justice and Trade that had a mysterious bank account ("Konto Gustav") into which over 60 unidentified leaders of German big business had deposited large sums. According to the *Deutsche Soldaten Zeitung*, the Committee for Justice and Trade was closely affiliated with a propaganda center in Switzerland called Centro Europa that carried out a worldwide campaign for the early release of jailed German war criminals. Another branch of the operation, Princess Isenburg's Stille Hilfe, directed its propaganda and fundraising to members of high society and the old aristocracy, as did *Helfende Haende* (Helping Hands), a similar charity directed by Princess Stephany zu Schaumberg-Lippe. More support came from Otto Skorzeny's Kameraden Hilfe, the Rudel Club, and various German "relief," propaganda, and fundraising circles inside the United States.[36]

Another critical figure in the postwar Nazi underground not mentioned by General Korte was Eugen Dollmann, the SS colonel and SD functionary in the German embassy in Rome who served as a middleman between SS General Karl Wolff, the Vatican, and Allen Dulles during "Operation Sunrise." When I asked H. Keith Thompson about Dollmann's postwar role, he replied:

> Very important. I'm not going to spell it all out for many reasons, but there was a network performing these services and they did it effectively at much risk and cost to themselves. I figured into this work providing some funding, and actually placed some people in the U.S. and Canada.[37]

Dollmann's activity on behalf of the Nazi underground became public in the fall of 1952. On 7 October 1952, while traveling under an Italian passport as "Enrico Larcher," he was arrested in the Frankfurt airport and charged with using false papers. His suitcase was opened and documents relating to his role in the Nazi International were found.[38] Dollmann's arrest was not his first brush with the law: Earlier that same year he had been deported from Switzerland after he was found living in a villa under another false name. From this villa he made frequent trips to Germany, Austria, Italy, Spain, and Egypt.[39] On 29 January 1952 the *Basler Nachrichten* reported that Dollmann had even met with the Grand Mufti in Cairo.

Dollmann was accused of having Soviet connections by a U.S. military intelligence agent named John Valentine ("Frenchy") Grombach, who ran a semi-private, CIA-financed intelligence operation dubbed "the Pond." After a falling out with Allen Dulles, Grombach began sending hostile reports on CIA activity to right-wing senators, as well as to FBI Director J. Edgar Hoover. Grombach said that Dollmann significantly increased his work for the CIA after Allen Dulles became CIA deputy director.[40] The German press had published a series of articles in 1952 about high-ranking Nazis involved in East-neutralist groups like the SRP. Dollmann apparently had ties to some of the neutralists—ties that Grombach seized upon to try to discredit Dulles.[41]

Germany's geopolitical *Schaukelpolitik* (seesaw politics) between East and West was crudely summed up in a 1949 letter from the wealthy Chicago rightist Arthur Koegel to Fred Weiss. Koegel told Weiss:

> You will see during the next 12 months a terrific bidding on the part of both the Russians and the West to get the support of the German people. All this will mean a united Germany completely free of debt at an early date. We hope this is

correct but we can't be sure and must work hard to accomplish it. When this happens and the world is sure of peace, then there is no doubt that Germany, with the power it will then have, will have the best chances of winning a victory.[42]

It is possible, then, to see German policy after World War II as quite similar to German policy after World War I, when the threat of a "Rapallo" alliance with Russia was used to weaken the terms of the Versailles Treaty. The peculiar geopolitical position of Germany dictated political tactics that often resulted in extraordinarily byzantine alliances. Every NATO "limited nuclear war" scenario with Russia assumed Germany's total destruction. It was therefore more than just nostalgia for the little man with the toothbrush mustache that inspired many an act of intrigue inside the Shadow Reich.

Notes:

1. Yockey's letter to H. Keith Thompson is dated 14 August 1953.

2. Tom Francis, who retranslated *Der Feind Europas* into English as *The Enemy of Europe*, told me that there were numerous textual errors in German that he believed a native German speaker would not make.

3. Virginia Johnson also helped bankroll the book. An ADL report dated 1 November 1953 quoted "Madelaine" as saying about Yockey: "I go to any lengths to get money for him when he needs it. I'm now staking him for the completion of his big book."

4. As my examination of the date stamp on the Library of Congress copy of the book showed.

5. The paper ran articles promoting the *Protocols of the Learned Elders of Zion* as well as an essay by Hans-Ulrich Rudel.

6. Kurt Tauber, *Beyond Eagle and Swastika* (Middletown, CT: Wesleyan University Press, 1967), Vol. 2, fn. 33, p. 1089.

7. K-H Heubaum Verlag, 13 B, Lockham bei Munchen.

8. After twice being convicted for distributing anti-Semitic literature (and facing prison time after a third conviction), Heubaum "evaded jail by fleeing into the East Zone." Tauber, *Beyond Eagle and Swastika*, Vol. 2, fn. 94, p. 1060.

9. The SRP was also part of the New European Order; the SRP's Fritz Rössler attended the NEO's founding conference in Zurich in 1951.

10. The first SRP party congress was held in July 1950.

11. Remer is cited in a report issued by the American Jewish Committee entitled *The Recent Growth of Neo-Nazism in Europe*.

12. After the SRP was banned, Dorls met Herr Renner, a West German CP leader and former Bundestag representative. Dorls reportedly wanted the Communists to provide asylum for certain key SRP members in East Germany while also helping the group to continue to publish clandestinely. The Communists, however, issued a statement denying any such talks and declared that Renner had ordered Dorls "never to set foot in his office." Alistair Horne, *Return to Power* (New York: Praeger, 1956), pp. 44–45. The April 1954 *Reporter* (citing *Der Spiegel*) claimed that after being exposed for his "Communist ties," Dorls had been offered a job as second-in-command to Otto Skorzeny in the Madrid office of the Lucht-Naumann firm.

13. Tauber, *Beyond Eagle and Swastika*, Vol. 1, p. 173.

14. It was around this time that Remer fled to Egypt to avoid arrest for his SRP activity.

15. Tauber, *Beyond Eagle and Swastika*, Vol. 2, fn. 69, p. 1056.

16. Wellington Long, *The New Nazis of Germany* (Philadelphia: Chilton Book Company, 1968), p. 98.

17. Ibid., p. 99.

18. Horne, *Return to Power*, pp. 175–76.

19. Tauber, *Beyond Eagle and Swastika*, Vol. 2, fn. 181, p. 1116.

20. Rudel also wrote for *Der Weg*. General Remer was also involved in the illegal distribution of *Der Weg*. In April 1948, 47,000 copies of the first issue of *Der Weg* were distributed in the Western Zone and 7,000 in the East. A former Abwehr agent in Austria named Joseph Heger played a crucial role in the distribution process. See the June 1951 *ADL Bulletin*.

21. Tauber, *Beyond Eagle and Swastika*, Vol. 2, fn. 204, p. 1078.

22. See the letter dated 28 September 1952 from Rudel (Chalet "Mary"/Villa Carlos Paz/Cordoba/Argentina) to Thompson in the H. Keith Thompson collection at the Hoover Institute. Rudel's book *Stuka Pilot* had first been published in English by Euphorion Books. Thompson sent me a copy of the legal agreement between himself and Rudel (signed by Rudel on 1 July 1954 in Buenos Aires) giving him the right to negotiate for *Stuka Pilot* in America, as well as the initial agreement signed by Rudel on 28 September 1952.

23. An April 1953 poll showed that 46 percent of all Germans held a high opinion of Dönitz, whom many saw as a war hero.

As for H. Keith Thompson, see his book *Doenitz at Nuremberg* (begun in 1956 but only published in 1976 by Amber Publishing Company in New York, and reprinted by the IHR in 1983). In an article in the *Journal of Historical Review* (Vol. 4, No. 3, Fall 1983) entitled "Grand Admiral Karl Doenitz: Last President of a United Germany," Thompson recalled:

> Long before the release of Doenitz, an ad hoc committee had been formed in the United States under the direction of myself and Professor Henry Strutz, with the active assistance of a group of retired U.S. Navy admirals of high World War II rank, including T. C. Hart and Charles A. Lockwood, for the purpose of compiling testimonials for Admiral Doenitz from military and other world leaders . . . The compilation of endorsements of Doenitz enabled his lawyers to force the Bonn regime to pay him a retirement pension commensurate with his rank, whereas they had tried to pension him off as a lower-ranking officer, claiming that he owed his promotion to Hitler. Leather-bound volumes of the letters and documents were presented to Doenitz and used by him in various ways.

24. H. Keith Thompson, "Grand Admiral Karl Doenitz: Last President of a Unified Germany," in the IHR's *Journal of Historical Review* (Vol. 4, No. 3, Fall 1983).

25. H. Keith Thompson, letter to me dated 11 November 1994. In an answer to my questionnaire about whether Yockey ever met Rudel, Thompson replied: "I gave Yockey an introduction to Rudel but it was never acted upon, largely because in those

days Rudel was always on the move, to and from South America, Spain and elsewhere. He didn't sit in one place waiting for the Bonn terror regime to strike."

26. SRP founders Dorls, Krüger, and Remer had been expelled from the early DRP (then the DKP-DRP) in October 1949 for being too radical.

27. Naumann's lawyer was Ernst Achenbach. Naumann's legal team also included a British lawyer named Lane from the firm Marsh and Ferriman. Lane was sent by Sir Oswald Mosley to help in Naumann's defense. See Mosley's *My Life* (New York: Thomas Nelson, 1968) for a discussion of Naumann.

28. In 1961 the DRP suffered heavy electoral losses as well as an internal split when a more radical neutralist faction left to form the German Freedom Party.

29. On Achenbach and Middelhauve, see Tauber, *Beyond Eagle and Swastika*, Vol. 1, p. 898.

30. Glenn Infield, *Skorzeny* (New York: St. Martin's Press, 1981), pp. 211–12.

31. Former SRP leader Fritz Dorls claimed that after the ban on both the SRP and FD, Rudel had "gone over to the Soviets." Tauber, *Beyond Eagle and Swastika*, Vol. 2, fn. 204, p. 1078.

32. Stille Hilfe's members maintained extensive ties to many fascist groups. See Jeffrey Bale, "The 'Black' Terrorist International: Neo-Fascist Paramilitary Networks and the 'Strategy of Tension' in Italy, 1968–1974" (University of California at Berkeley Ph.D. thesis, 1994), pp. 58–59.

33. Tauber, *Beyond Eagle and Swastika*, Vol. 1, p. 249.

34. I am using a long English summary of Korte's article in T. H. Tetens, *The New Germany and the Old Nazis* (London: Seeker & Warburg, 1961), pp. 201–03.

35. The Evangelisches Hilfswerk published *Christ und Welt*, which regularly called for the release of war criminals.

36. Tetens, *The New Germany*, pp. 203–04. This was the same network that used both Senator Joseph McCarthy and the National Council for the Prevention of War to lobby on behalf of the SS men accused of the Malmédy massacre. It should also be noted that Fred Weiss attacked Rudolf Aschenauer for being too close to the Catholic Church and the Adenauer government. One ADL report cites Weiss as calling Aschenauer "an intriguing opportunist" who tried to give the Bishop of Munich financial control over *Nation Europa*. According to Weiss, Arthur Ehrhardt managed to block the takeover, in part with money supplied by Oswald Mosley.

37. H. Keith Thompson's reply to my questionnaire.

38. Although the *Frankfurter Rundschau* devoted considerable coverage to the case, Dollmann only spent two months in prison.

39. See Tetens, *The New Germany*, pp. 71–74, on Dollmann. In the summer of 1951 the Swiss authorities also forced former SD spy chief Walter Schellenberg to leave Switzerland.

40. In the epilogue to his book about Operation Sunrise, *The Secret Surrender* (New York: Harper & Row, 1966), Allen Dulles disingenuously writes about Dollmann (p. 252):

> Dollmann escaped from an American internment camp at Rimini in Italy but . . . did not try to get to South America. He headed for Milan. Here, reportedly, he sought out some of his old church contacts with whom he had worked during the war. Eventually

he returned to Munich, his home city, where I understand he is engaged in literary pursuits.

41. Christopher Simpson, *The Splendid Blond Beast* (New York: Grove Press, 1993), p. 243. Also see the discussion of Grombach in Simpson's book *Blowback* (New York: Weidenfeld & Nicolson, 1988); Burton Hersh, *The Old Boys* (New York: Scribner's, 1992); and Peter Dale Scott, *Deep Politics and the Assassination of JFK* (Berkeley, CA: University of California Press, 1993).

42. Koegel's 3 November 1949 letter, as quoted in the ADL publication *Facts*, October–November 1954.

41

NATINFORM

The far-right debate over ties to the Soviet Union directly affected Yockey. Shortly after the publication of his December 1952 "Prague" article, he came under attack from the Nationalist Information Bureau, better known as NATINFORM, a far-right organization with branches in England and Germany.[1] In the spring of 1953 NATINFORM distributed a special report branding Yockey a "national bolshevist."[2]

The leader of "World NATINFORM," Wolfgang Sarg, was a former SRP member who had worked for Goebbels' Propaganda Ministry during the war.[3] He was also a founding member of Helmut Beck-Broichsitter's Freikorps Deutschland and clearly part of Beck-Broichsitter's "anti-East" camp. The NATINFORM report on Yockey reflected the dispute between Franke-Gricksch and Beck-Broichsitter when it noted:

> This organization in Germany [apparently the proposed German wing of the ELF] was to be the concern of YOCKEY (at that time said to be in Germany) and it was also mentioned that agreement had been reached between F. YOCKEY and ALFRED FRANKE-GRICKSCH for collaboration and for publishing a German translation of the IMPERIUM. It was also stated that [Bruderschaft leader and Naumann-circle member Karl] KAUFMANN (Hamburg) and BECK-BROICHSIT-TER had been approached but these persons were not actively concerned in the plan as they had not agreed with all of the proposals made to them by Yockey.

Yockey got a preview of the NATINFORM report from H. Keith Thompson, who forwarded a copy of Wolfgang Sarg's 28 January 1953 letter to him about Yockey.[4] Sarg's letter included an extensive description of the 1948 meeting between Yockey and a NATINFORM informant at Baroness von Pflugl's London mansion as well as the subsequent meeting between NATINFORM's source and the ELF's Guy Chesham.

Writing from Beirut on 24 February 1953, an infuriated Yockey answered Sarg:

By an unusual chance your letter of 28 January to Keith Thompson in regard to me—the letter headed "Confidential"—so melodramatically—reached me here . . . The article on the Prague trail of Slansky et al. was indeed by me, and it foretold the Russian break with Jewry which is becoming deeper and more complete every day . . .

Yockey then told Sarg:

You misinterpret in a stupid fashion my relations with Mosley . . . When I discovered that he was pro-Churchill and pro-American and anti-Russian à *outrance*, even to the extent of mobilizing Europe to fight for American-Jewish victory over Russia, I left him . . . Most serious of all is the suggestion, which you conveyed only by innuendo, being too cowardly to state it outright, that I am a Russian agent or that the Front pursues a pro-Russian policy. To the extent that you have spread this lie, you will be required to retract it . . . The last point remains to be made on the negative side: You inserted a personal note into your vicious letter to Thompson, when you try to insult my race. You wrote to my friend, who knows me personally, that I am "small, dark, of unknown mixed races, pale . . . " My height is that of Adolf Hitler, my complexion is white, my race is exclusively European. For this stupid attempt at a personal slander, you will give me satisfaction if I am ever in your vicinity. If you refuse out of cowardice, I shall flog you before witnesses . . . [5]

In a letter to H. Keith Thompson, Sarg volleyed back:

A letter of a person, which is even frightened to put his address on the letter, cannot concern me the least. . . . Nobody in Germany—as far as Nationalists are concerned—does ever speak of the ELF or of Varange. But every genuine German Nationalist can guarantee for the fight I have been and I still am carrying out for the Nationalist, anti-Bolshevik, and anti-Jewish idea. Only one I shall name, whom you know, and who will vouch for me: General Remer . . . I would at any time be prepared to retract everything I have written to you about Varange and his Front and draw the necessary consequences. But: Before I would do so, Varange would have to *prove* me wrong . . . Mr. Varange's threats cannot worry me. My height is 1.86 meters and I have quite a good record as a soldier . . . [6]

Although Sarg was the head of World NATINFORM, the group actually began in England in the early 1950s. One of its two co-founders was Peter J. Huxley-Blythe, an early ELF member and *Frontfighter's* first editor.[7] At the outbreak of the Korean War, Huxley-Blythe was called back to the British Royal Navy and lost touch with the ELF. While in the service, he was contacted by a Royal Navy Lieutenant named Hillary Cotter. A Catholic fascist, Cotter was much taken with the plight of Hungary's Cardinal Mindszenty. After Huxley-Blythe returned to England, he and Cotter established NATINFORM as a far-right information-dissemination service.[8] They were then approached by Anthony Francis Xavier (A. F.

X.) Baron, an admirer of the British anti-Semite Arnold Leese. Baron's extensive connections with the German far right included Sarg, who seems to have been brought into NATINFORM by Baron.[9]

Huxley-Blythe later told Cotter that meeting Baron was "the worst day of our lives" because he would prove such a disruptive influence; by 1952 Baron had seized control of British NATINFORM. Baron also used his knowledge of Huxley-Blythe's earlier involvement with the ELF to try to discredit him as a secret "Yockeyite."[10] After Yockey's article on the Prague trials shocked the British far right, Baron compiled a report on Yockey's activities in England which was forwarded to Sarg at NATINFORM's less-than-palatial "world headquarters," which doubled as Sarg's home. One of Sarg's visitors recalled:

> After three hours' march through swamps, meadows, and mud, I arrived at Sarg's. Mr. Baron and a Mr. Thompson from Paris[11] were already there and ate large amounts of bacon from an indescribably dirty table. The rooms were still dirtier than they were when I had first seen them several months ago. Mrs. Sarg was filthy and terribly cross-eyed. Sarg's children were so dirty that they could hardly be recognized as children. A bed stood in the kitchen. In it lay two children, half naked. During my two days' stay they never did get out of bed. They either stood in it or fell over and slept. Mrs. Sarg is expecting her sixth child. On the wall is a large, red shield with a black eagle, the symbol of the SRP. Above it, from an almost life-size picture, General Remer looks down upon this scene and smiles. In this dirt Sarg receives his visitors from the entire world . . . Two weeks ago Rudel was here; he is a personal friend of Sarg's. The entire Remer family visits frequently.[12]

NATINFORM's primary informant on Yockey's activity in England was almost certainly John Marston Gaster, described in *Beyond Eagle and Swastika* as "a young man whose hysterical anti-Semitism was conjoined, as it was in Heinrich Himmler, with a penchant for occultism."[13] He spoke fluent German. His girlfriend Elisabeth Schnitzler, a former League of German Girls (BdM) leader,[14] played an important liaison role with NATINFORM Germany.[15] Gaster's recollection of his talks with both Yockey and Guy Chesham made up the bulk of the British section of NATINFORM's report.[16] Sarg then added his own information about Yockey's ties to Franke-Gricksch.

Not long after the publication of NATINFORM's attack on Yockey, Gaster and other NATINFORM members left the group in protest against A. F. X. Baron's dictatorial ways as well as the fear that he may have had ties to British intelligence. They then formed the European Liaison Service (ELS), which was led by John Rackam and William Ward.[17] In a letter to the National Renaissance Party explaining the split, Ward reported that Baron was

> found to be unreliable and rather disruptive in his activities. Together with other English members, I resigned. Later our opinions of him were confirmed because

he was expelled following a meeting of top NATINFORM leaders in Europe. By this time, however, we had formed our own group, the European Liberation Service,[18] and had links with German nationalist friends. Following Baron's expulsion, the ELS contacted NATINFORM Germany and a close friendship was established. Baron has since been under suspicion as working for reactionary services. Your bulletin [the NRP *Bulletin*] I have sent to Herr Wolfgang Sarg, Director of NATINFORM Germany.[19]

After Baron's downfall in the summer of 1953, Huxley-Blythe returned to what was left of British NATINFORM and became editor of the group's English-language *World Survey*.[20] He returned with Sarg's blessings, and their new friendship was bolstered by a bottle of expensive liquor that Sarg sent him as a gift.[21] Huxley-Blythe's NATINFORM also established friendly ties to Fred Weiss, H. Keith Thompson, and the National Renaissance Party. Huxley-Blythe and Thompson had been in contact since at least early 1953, when Thompson sent him a copy of the letter he had received from Wolfgang Sarg attacking Yockey. In his reply, Huxley-Blythe wrote:

> Now to Yockey. I now know for the first time of his contacts with the East, and this explains many things. In Europe his propaganda has left a decided mark, and only recently a manifestation of his pro-Communist propaganda was heard at the "National Forces of Europe" Congress in Brussels . . . by the French delegate. His propaganda must be countered and now I shall know how to proceed. Many thanks.[22]

Huxley-Blythe also requested money from Fred Weiss, and in a 4 February 1954 letter asked if Weiss could arrange to send a duplicator machine to NATINFORM.[23] Huxley-Blythe mentioned Yockey in a letter to Weiss:

> Yes! I knew that you were in touch with Yockey/Varange, as I recognized his style in the Prague release concerning the alleged Soviet anti-Semitism in Prague, Budapest, etc. I met him once and for a time was editor of *Frontfighter*. Nevertheless his assessment of the trials was wrong, as our files can prove it was an entirely bogus affair to influence the German and Arab peoples.[24]

In a follow-up letter to a National Renaissance Party member and Weiss lieutenant named Mana Truhill, Huxley-Blythe presented the East/West debate in Europe in stark terms:

> Here in Europe things are chaotic. The Nationalists are split into two groups, one of them believes our salvation lies in the Red Army because they believe that the Kremlin is now anti-Jew. The other group believes that both the Kremlin and Washington are Jew-bound.[25]

For their part, Weiss and Thompson distributed NATINFORM propaganda written by Wolfgang Sarg against Dr. Otto John (head of the West German Office for the Protection of the Constitution) inside the American far right. They also circulated Sarg's attack on Otto John to politicians hostile to both the CIA and the State Department, like Senator William Jenner.[26]

Sarg had a special reason to despise Otto John: On 24 May 1954 (just one month before John was either kidnapped or defected to East Berlin), the Adenauer government announced that NATINFORM Germany was officially banned. Sarg was charged with anti-Semitism and directing a secret organization. Soon after Otto John went East, a triumphant Sarg issued a special report blaming him for the crackdown on NATINFORM. Sarg said that John had been out to get him after he attacked John in the 13 January 1951 issue of *Deutsche Wacht*, which was then banned. John had even conspired to take over NATINFORM:

> In 1952 the German journalist MUELLER-SCHWANECK, alias EUMSCH, was introduced to Sarg by the former assistant chief of NATINFORM/Germany, KARL SMETS. MUELLER-SCHWANECK alleged to be interested in becoming a member of the NATINFORM organization but at a later date admitted to Sarg that he had been sent on behalf of Dr. ADENAUER's State Secretary BLANKENHORN, who wanted Sarg and members of NATINFORM to spy on members of his own Diplomatic Corps, and by Dr. JOHN, who wished Sarg and NATINFORM to work for his office. On learning this, all connection between MUELLER-SCHWANECK and NATINFORM was severed and the details were exposed. It was later ascertained that MUELLER-SCHWANECK had been ordered by JOHN to try and split and disorganize the anti-Communist News Service known as NATINFORM.[27]

Sarg also thought that British intelligence was plotting with John to disrupt NATINFORM and said that he "expelled in 1953 the notorious self-confessed English 'Nazi' A. F. X. Baron, and his chief German collaborator Karl Smets for attempting to seize control of the NATINFORM from within."[28] Baron and Smets then formed their own NATINFORM, which led Sarg to warn:

> It is certain these anonymous NATINFORM circulars are the work of A. F. X. BARON of Suffolk, England, and his German collaborator Municipal Inspector KARL SMETS of Koblentz, Germany. Messrs. Baron and Smets also occasionally issue NATINFORM circulars under their own names and addresses ... Baron is believed to be an agent of the British Secret Service (with whom he has admitted wartime association), while Municipal Inspector Smets is now known to have been working for Dr. Otto John.[29]

After Baron's departure, the Yockey-Sarg war-by-post more or less ended. Looking back on it today, the NATINFORM attack on Yockey shows just how the larger geopolitical debate over Russia played itself out not just in lofty theories but in the complex day-to-day micro-political intrigue that dominated the European far right in the early 1950s.

Notes:

1. NATINFORM is sometimes referred to as the "National Information Bureau." Note that NATINFORM was different from the Natinform that was established in Europe and Latin America in 1945 and circulated anti-war crimes trials propaganda. According to Huxley-Blythe, NATINFORM's name was chosen as a counter to the Communist Cominform. He said that he was completely unaware of another organization called Natinform until I informed him of its existence.

2. The NATINFORM report on Yockey was officially published in *Natinform Informationen* on 20 March 1953. An early version of the report was sent in a personal letter by Wolfgang Sarg to H. Keith Thompson in January 1953. For a passing mention of the NATINFORM March 1953 attack on Yockey, see Kurt Tauber, *Beyond Eagle and Swastika* (Middletown, CT: Wesleyan University Press, 1967), Vol. 2, fn. 207, p. 1120.

3. The September–October 1954 issue of NATINFORM's *World Survey* reported that Sarg had received a pension from the German government "for wounds received in the front line on 27th April 1945 while serving with the German Army in which he had voluntarily enlisted, though exempt in his (former) capacity of Press Official."

4. H. Keith Thompson told me that he had written to rightist contacts in Europe after the publication of Yockey's "Prague" article at Yockey's request. Thompson also supplied a copy of Sarg's letter to the FBI.

5. Yockey's letter to Wolfgang Sarg is from the H. Keith Thompson collection at the Hoover Institute.

6. Wolfgang Sarg's letter to H. Keith Thompson, dated 27 March 1953, from the H. Keith Thompson collection at the Hoover Institute.

7. My information on Huxley-Blythe comes from letters, phone calls, and a long taped reply he gave me to an extensive questionnaire that I sent him.

8. NATINFORM published Cotter's November 1950 pamphlet, *World Dictatorship by 1955?*, which had an introduction by the Canadian fascist Adrian Arcand. Cotter's piece ends: "Nationalists of All Lands Unite! You Have Nothing to Lose But Your Jews!" NATINFORM also published Cotter's *Cardinal Mindszenty* and *The Case of Douglas MacArthur*. A pamphlet called *Why Forrestal Threw Himself Out the Window* was co-written by Cotter and the Ireland-based R. de Roiste and was published by NATINFORM in 1951. British NATINFORM sold books like H. T. Mills' *Is It Too Late?*, Borge Jensen's *The UNO Fraud* and *Know Your Enemy*, various works by the Texas millionaire anti-Semite Judge Armstrong, and tracts by the Rev. Peter Nicoll, Adrian Arcand, Myron Fagen, and Robert A. Williams. NATINFORM also promoted journals like the Irish Catholic publication *FIAT;* the Irish nationalist journal *SAOIRSE;* the North America–based *Common Sense, Women's Voice, The Cross and the Flag, Intelligence Summary,* and *Attack;* the New Zealand–based *Manifesto;* and the Argentinean publication *Intransigencia,* from the Movemento Revolutionare National-Sindicalista.

The British-German NATINFORM connection led to the publication by Wolfgang Sarg of a journal called *Die Fanfare* out of Oldenburg, Germany, beginning in December 1951. One of Sarg's assistant editors was A. F. X. Baron. It was announced in the 15 February 1952 issue of *Die Fanfare* that an English-language version would be published starting in March 1952. Writers for the English edition would include Hillary Cotter, H.

T. Mills, Rev. Peter Nicoll, Borge Jensen, R. de Roiste, Michael O'Tuathail, Adrian Arcand, Elizabeth Dilling, Gerald L. K. Smith, Conde McGinley, and others including Johann von Leers and the Grand Mufti. See the Weiner Institute *Bulletin* on *Die Fanfare.*

9. British NATINFORM represented elements of the British far right disgusted by both Mosley and the ELF. Many had warm feelings for the fanatical British anti-Semite Arnold Leese.

10. By this time Huxley-Blythe's views on Russia had changed radically from his brief time with the ELF. Through Hillary Cotter he was made aware of the Russian Army of Liberation (ROA), which was composed of Russian POWs who took up arms for Germany against Stalin. (The ROA was better known as Vlasov's Army, after its leader, General Andrei Vlasov, a Soviet general captured by the Germans during the defense of Moscow.) After the war many ROA members (including Vlasov) were captured by Western forces. Thanks to an Allied agreement with Stalin, they were forcefully repatriated to certain death in Russia. Huxley-Blythe later wrote about the forced ROA repatriation in his book *The East Came West.* For more on NATINFORM, see the appendix "The Whites and the Reds."

11. This was the English inventor Norman A. Thompson, whom Huxley-Blythe described as someone interested in racial eugenics and monetary reform.

12. Tauber, *Beyond Eagle and Swastika,* Vol. 1, pp. 244–45.

13. Ibid.

14. Ibid., Vol. 2, fn. 216, p. 1121.

15. Huxley-Blythe said that Baron told him about Schnitzler's role.

16. In an undated 1953 letter to H. Keith Thompson, Huxley-Blythe confirmed Gaster's role. He also corrected a few details about the NATINFORM report before concluding: "That clears up the various inaccuracies that creep into the report prepared by Baron and compiled by John M. Gaster, a close friend of mine."

17. The ELS's German liaison was a soap salesman named Erwin Alfred Scholz, who was imprisoned for three months for distributing Nazi literature in June 1957. (Tauber, *Beyond Eagle and Swastika,* Vol. 1, pp. 252–53.)

18. Sometimes called the European Liaison Service.

19. From the NSANL archives.

20. Looking back at the British NATINFORM split today, Huxley-Blythe told me that his essential difference with Baron was that Baron was an "English nationalist" while he was a "European nationalist."

21. Although Huxley-Blythe's English NATINFORM and the ELS remained friends, the two groups maintained separate organizational identities.

22. The letter is from the H. Keith Thompson collection at the Hoover Institute.

23. See NRP member Mana Truhill's reply on behalf of Weiss to Huxley-Blythe. Truhill stated that at that time it would not be possible to send the duplicators since two had already been shipped that month to Germany. It is clear that Weiss had previously sent some financial aid to NATINFORM, because Huxley-Blythe writes: "I know you have been most generous already."

NATINFORM Germany first made contact with the NRP when Wolfgang Sarg wrote an introductory letter to NRP leader James Madole on 2 August 1952. Sarg told

Madole that he had gotten his address "from a friend of mine called Mr. A. F. X. Baron, of Framlingham, England, who reads your paper NATIONAL RENAISSANCE BUL- LETIN. I would like to arrange a regular supply of this fine paper for my Continental office of the Nationalist Information Bureau (NATINFORM)." (From the NSANL Archives.) At the time of Sarg's letter, the NRP had not yet published Yockey's article on the Prague Trials.

24. Huxley-Blythe letter to Fred Weiss, dated 2 March 1954, from the files of the NSANL. Although the addressee of the letter (which begins "Dear Comrade") is not included, it is clear from Mana Truhill's response to the letter that Huxley-Blythe had written Weiss.

25. Huxley-Blythe letter to Mana Truhill, dated 4 April 1953, from the NSANL archives.

26. See H. Keith Thompson's letter of 26 November 1954 to Senator Jenner, enclos- ing a photostat report on Otto John from Sarg; Thompson was responding to a letter of 16 November 1954 from Jenner asking for information on Otto John. Also see NATIN- FORM England's report on John, a *Common Sense* article denouncing John, and clips from Lyle Stuart's *Exposé* on the Sarg/John affair in the H. Keith Thompson archive at the Hoover Institute.

27. *NATINFORM World Survey* of September–October 1954.

28. On the fight between Baron and Sarg, see Tauber, *Beyond Eagle and Swastika*, Vol. 1, pp. 252–53. As for Baron's German ally Karl Smets, he was an important mem- ber of *Stahlhelm* (Steel Helmet).

29. *NATINFORM World Survey*, September–October 1954. Baron set up his own NATINFORM with himself as British director from his home in England. In a 22 March 1954 letter to H. Keith Thompson, Baron commented about Yockey: "There is no extra information on Frederick Yockey at the moment. Eyes and ears are being kept to the ground." Baron liked to claim ties to British intelligence, and said that NATINFORM was backed by "a former chief of British naval intelligence" as well as Field Marshals John Harding and W. J. Slim. See *Beyond Eagle and Swastika*, Vol. 2, fn. 198, p. 1119. Tauber thinks this claim highly unlikely. However, it is quite possible that Baron was in contact with former Admiral Sir Barry Domville, a former head of British naval intel- ligence and a well-known Nazi sympathizer. For more on Domville, see Richard Griffiths, *Fellow Travellers of the Right* (London: Constable, 1980).

DIE WELT—
EIN TOR
(1954-57)

Die Welt—ein Tor
Zu tausend Wüsten stumm und kalt!
(The world—a gate
To a thousand wastelands, mute and cold!)
> —*Friedrich Nietzsche,* Vereinsamt *(Isolated)*

42

NEW YORK
NUTZIS

Yockey returned to America in early 1954, a decision no doubt inspired in part by the resurgence of the far right under the banner of "McCarthyism." He also may have wanted to check on the development of the National Renaissance Party (NRP), the Fred Weiss–financed group that first published Yockey's article on the Prague trials.[1] Although tiny, the NRP regularly held street rallies in the heavily German Yorkville section of Manhattan. It even "distributed" anti-Semitic material, once by throwing leaflets off the top of the Empire State Building.[2] Today, however, if the NRP is remembered at all, it is as the personal sect of its leader, James Madole.

Abandoned by his father when he was two, Madole was raised by his mother, Grace, a crazed anti-Semite. A severe asthmatic, he spent his youth in Beacon, New York, with few if any friends. While still a teenager, he combined his love of science fiction, fantasy, lost continents, secret knowledge, "scientific eugenics," and the 1930s Technocracy movement with his mother's fierce prejudices, and concocted his own master plan. He decided that earth should be ruled by a "Phrenarch" who would lead a global "Council of Technical Integration" that would supervise everything from planetary energy distribution to marriage. Earth was just the starting point for a galactic "new worlds order" because, as Madole loved to point out: "The ultimate destiny of man lies in the stars."

Gravity was one big roadblock to the stars. An even bigger one was that "bedbug of the human family," the Jews. Madole was particularly tough on Freudianism, "this fully degenerate spasm of the Jewish mind" that he held responsible for "the pollution of more lovely young girls by hybrid garbage." Madole's invective against the inventor of the Oedipus Complex may have been fueled by personal animus, since he spent his life at the side of his beloved mother. James and Grace Madole even slept platonically in the same bed in a Manhattan apartment on West 90th Street, which they moved into in the spring of 1954 with financial help from Fred Weiss.

In 1947, while still in Beacon, Madole founded the Animist Party.[3] He propagandized for Animism in the pages of science fiction/fantasy "fanzines": His party's founding was announced in the Spring 1946 issue of *Starlight Stories*.[4] Although he attracted a few followers, Madole dissolved the sect in late 1948 after discovering that many Animists were really infiltrators from anti-fascist groups.[5] In January 1949 Madole was back in business with the National Renaissance Party, which had been founded by old rightists like William Henry MacFarland, head of the Nationalist Action League,[6] and Fred Weiss's Yorkville friend Kurt Mertig, the head of the Citizens Protective League.[7] Mertig was the NRP's first chairman, but he soon resigned because of ill health. MacFarland briefly took over the sect until Madole (also a member of the Nationalist Action League) was appointed its new chief. It was Madole's devotion to day-to-day drudge work (not his sci-fi metaphysics) that earned him his new post—that plus the fact that no one more important wanted the job.

Phrenarch at last, Madole proved to be a tireless organizer. At his Yorkville street rallies he excoriated the Jews and extolled Hitler as the "George Washington of Europe." He was equally indefatigable in trying to forge alliances with other sects, including *Common Sense*, John Hamilton's National Citizens Protective Association, the Continental League for Christian Freedom, the Christian Anti-Jewish Party, the White Circle League, and the New Confederates. Gradually the NRP began attracting a handful of followers, at first mostly elderly Irish-American ex-Coughlinites and old Bundists.

With Madole acting as his front man, Fred Weiss used the NRP for his own purposes. William Goring, a Columbia University student who infiltrated the NRP in the early 1960s, reported that while Weiss worked with Madole, "he looked down on him as an example of the shrill, vulgar type of Nazi who was useful only as a distributor of literature for intellectuals like himself."[8] When an ADL investigator questioned Weiss about Madole, he replied: "Madole is just a messenger boy for me." When he was then asked why he had sponsored Madole, Weiss explained:

> We use all kinds of characters. We have such a shortage of leaders, I would use the very Devil himself if I thought it would help get us what we are after. Madole is basically honest but fanatical and ignorant. I find him convenient to run errands and I also can put whatever I please into his *Renaissance Bulletin*. He sends the publication to a list of about a thousand names. His contributors carry half the cost and I'm saved the bother of distributing.[9]

Madole also told one of his followers that the NRP did "not want to draw the intelligent people. They want the gutter and the dirt. They leave the intelligent people to Fred Weiss."[10]

The emergence of the NRP was one small sign that the American far right was making a comeback thanks to the Cold War. H. Keith Thompson also sensed a shift in the political climate. He first established the Committee for International Justice in March 1952 in order to work "for the review of cases and release of the Axis 'war criminals,'" and "to provide humanitarian relief to destitute families of such 'war criminals.'"[11] He then formed a "Committee for the Freedom of General Remer," the SRP leader who had been under legal attack by the Bonn government, and in June 1952 he became the SRP's American agent. That same summer, Thompson, George Sylvester Viereck, and Edward Fleckenstein, head of the Yorkville-based Voters Alliance of Americans of German Ancestry (also known as the German-American Voters Alliance), attended the Republican Convention in Chicago to support Senator Robert Taft against Dwight Eisenhower.[12] Taft, a staunch critic of the war crimes trials, was a friend of Viereck. At the convention, Thompson, Viereck, and Fleckenstein socialized with Senators Dirksen and McCarthy, former Congressman Hamilton Fish, and the far-right journalist Westbrook Pegler. Viereck also spoke at the local Germania club, where he was sponsored by *Nation Europa* funder Arthur Koegel.[13]

In February 1953, about a year before Yockey returned to the United States, Thompson announced his most ambitious project of all, the "American Committee for the Advancement of Western Culture," whose members were to include Fred Weiss, Kurt Mertig, James Madole, and Edward Fleckenstein, among others.[14] The Committee was also scheduled to include an "Honorary Advisory Staff on World Affairs" made up of individuals like the SRP's Dr. Gerhard Kruger, NATINFORM leader Wolfgang Sarg, A. Raven Thomson from Mosley's Union Movement, South Africa's Hans Oswald Pirow, and many others, including King Carol II of Romania.[15] In a cover story in the NRP's April 1953 *Bulletin*, Fred Weiss enthusiastically endorsed Thompson's Committee and explained that it would serve as a "high policy-planning group for the coordination of racial nationalist activities in America, Europe, Africa, and Asia." Thompson also addressed a few NRP functions to promote his call for unity inside the right.[16]

Just as planning for the committee seemed to be picking up steam, Thompson suddenly shut it down. In a 25 August 1953 press release he explained why:

> I supervised the formation of the "American Committee for the Advancement of Western Culture," which was to be a cultural group dedicated to "the advancement of the traditional culture of our Western World against the inroads of Communism and other alien cultures." After several months of delicate negotiations, a national staff and an international advisory staff were provisionally formed. However, I was unable to gain adequate confidence in the key members of the American staff . . . I found myself continuously pressured from all sides to

convert the Committee into an anti-Semitic pressure group. This was contrary to the purpose of the Committee and, in my considered judgment, would have destroyed its effectiveness from the very beginning. In addition, the high-calibre Advisory Staff on World Affairs included prominent figures, members of parliament, judges, publishers, generals, noblemen, etc. My responsibility to them was such that I could not permit the use of their names by an American group in which I had insufficient confidence. It became evident to me that the so-called "American Nationalists" are in the main petty people lost in personal feuds and utterly incapable of unity or cooperation. Many are fine, well-meaning people. Many are not.

Thompson also feared that his Committee would be infiltrated by Jewish, left-wing, and anti-fascist groups. Thus it seems particularly ironic that one of his closest political allies was the left-wing Jewish publisher Lyle Stuart.[17] The alliance between H. Keith Thompson and Lyle Stuart dated from a December 1951 attack that Stuart had launched against the much-feared newspaper columnist Walter Winchell in the pages of Stuart's tabloid paper, *Exposé*.[18] In "The Truth about Walter Winchell," he denounced Winchell for supporting Senator Joseph McCarthy, Roy Cohn, and J. Edgar Hoover.[19]

Stuart was equally angry at the Anti-Defamation League after he discovered that some ADL leaders, including Winchell's friend and ADL legal counsel Arnold Forster,[20] had secretly met with McCarthy.[21] In the June 1952 issue of *Exposé*, Stuart claimed that the ADL had secretly subsidized anti-Jewish publications like *Common Sense* in order to keep tabs on them. He even tried to shut down the ADL's ability to monitor the fascist underground by publicly exposing Sanford ("Sandy") Griffith (a/k/a "Al Scheffer") as an undercover ADL operative. Griffith ran two innocuously named businesses, Market Analysts, Inc., and Research Survey, out of an office at 8 West 40th Street. Stuart said that Griffith's real business was as a high-class private investigator who sold the ADL information on the right. He also published Griffith's photo in *Exposé*.

Stuart's attack on the ADL brought some curious fan mail. In an October 1952 missive, Gerald L. K. Smith told him:

> I have read with interest your "Open Letter to the Directors of the Anti-Defamation League." I realize that we are poles apart when it comes to our motivation for attacking the Anti-Defamation League. I attack them because of what they have done to me. You have attacked them because they have not done enough to me. However we both agree that they are a ruthless, stupid, vicious outfit.

Stuart's campaign against the ADL led him to H. Keith Thompson, who later recalled his first meeting with Stuart:

> He asked to see me and I visited his tiny office on W. 42nd St., off Fifth. He was interested in what an "American fascist" was like; we hit it off, hence the arti-

cles and other writing I did for his *Exposé*, and later *The Independent*. I did not help finance either publication, but subscribed. Stuart and I had one thing in common: a deep, abiding hatred for "the system" (U.S.), and [we] both believed that anything which might help "bring it down" was constructive.[22]

The two men became so close that one FBI informant incorrectly told the Bureau in December 1955 that *The Independent* (which Stuart renamed *Exposé* in the mid-1950s) "was controlled and/or owned by one Harold Keith Thompson."[23] While *The Independent* was exclusively owned by Stuart, Thompson told me that "for some years, my printing plant did some of his [Lyle Stuart's] printing."[24] Thompson contributed his first article to *Exposé*, a four-part series called "I Am an American Fascist," in August 1954. Well aware of an April 1954 *Reporter* article that accused Weiss, Yockey, and himself of having Communist links, he told his readers that he intended to expose "a plan by Communists to infiltrate and control the Nationalist groups of the extreme Right Wing." By "Communist," however, he meant organizations like the Non-Sectarian Anti-Nazi League and the ADL.

Thompson also recounted his own encounters with Sanford Griffith. In the summer of 1952, after coming under FBI and press scrutiny for his involvement with the Socialist Reich Party, he said he was contacted by "Alfred Scheffer," a journalist for the *Newark Star-Ledger*, who wanted to write a sympathetic article about him. When the piece finally appeared, the article's byline was "Richard Shafer," not "Alfred Scheffer." The real Richard Shafer, a *Star-Ledger* reporter, had been told by his editor to supply his name to the story.[25]

There were other curious incidents as well. Thompson reported that Griffith/Scheffer had two women agents working for him out of an office at 192 West 10th Street. One was a memorable peroxide blond. After Thompson addressed a rightist gathering in Westchester, New York, Scheffer introduced the blond to him as his wife, forgetting that he had introduced Thompson to a completely different "Mrs. Scheffer" some weeks earlier. *New York Journal American* columnist Westbrook Pegler, who knew Thompson, also denounced Griffith in a 12 August 1954 column.[26]

For all of his thunder in *Exposé*, Thompson failed to mention one of Griffith's most prominent cronies on the far right: Fred Weiss, who also happened to be Griffith's next-door neighbor in Middletown, New York. Weiss had a pond on his farm and on the other side of the pond stood Griffith's house. For years the two men exchanged gossip, and Griffith may even have paid Weiss for some information.[27] A New York rightist named DeWest Hooker became a prominent critic of Weiss's relationship with Griffith.[28] In the July 1955 issue of his Nationalist Party *Bulletin*, Hooker published a personal affidavit stating that Weiss had arranged for himself and Griffith to meet for lunch and that Griffith had offered to help arrange publicity for the Nationalist Party. According to Hooker:

Scheffer [Sanford Griffith] would see to it that I got lots of "publicity" for my Nationalist Party movement. . . . a lot of unfavorable publicity which would be designed, however, to build me up as a "big man." Weiss pretended to me, previous to the meeting, that "Scheffer" would cooperate completely with him because he and "Scheffer" had been working together for some time and that Weiss helped supply "Scheffer" with so-called "threatening personalities," so that "Scheffer" could get a big allocation of money to fight these same "threatening personalities" . . . I cannot say for sure at this point whether Weiss is consciously working with the ADL as a paid agent . . . or whether he really believes in his "line" and is being "used" by Al Scheffer for the ADL.[29]

In Weiss's 1955 pamphlet *How West Hooker Smears Honest Patriots*, the old artillery man shot back:

Now for your accusation that I may be an agent of the ADL. Yes, I did meet the Al Scheffer you mention—you should know because you were one of the two people who introduced me to him a couple of years ago. You told me that you had seen him frequently. I relied on your recommendation and did introduce him to a couple of people. The ADL *Bulletin* did come out with attacks on me and on my friends using some letters, confidential personal letters. Perhaps you know who peddle them? . . . I did not see "Scheffer" afterwards for nearly a year. The next I heard was that you were seen with "Scheffer," even dining in public, notably at the Park Sheraton . . . So you accepted MY proposed luncheon invitation to dine with "Scheffer"? Wasn't it YOU who proposed the meeting—a sort of fishing expedition in which you had already indulged?

The murky world of Fred Weiss got a lot murkier after Hooker and Edward Fleckenstein, the head of the Voters' Alliance for Americans of German Ancestry, began spreading rumors that Weiss had gotten $16,000 from Communist sources.[30] Furious, Weiss wrote Hooker: "AND LET ME TELL YOU FURTHER; I never was offered by, nor took from, any Jewish or Communist outfit one red cent." H. Keith Thompson also came to Weiss's defense over the Communist money rumor in the October 1954 *Exposé*. Thompson blamed the allegation on James Sheldon, the head of the Non-Sectarian Anti-Nazi League (NSANL), who had used one of his NRP informers, Mana Truhill, to discredit Weiss:

Another instruction to Truhill by Sheldon was to blame all extremist activity on Frederick C. F. Weiss of Le Blanc Publications, a Nationalist, author, and active anti-Communist. Believing in the policy of supporting all Nationalists insofar as possible, Weiss had been taken in by the NRP, and smeared by Sheldon. The Anti-Nazi League was one of the agencies responsible for the circulation of the rumor that Weiss had accepted a large sum from Communist sources for the publication of his Nationalist literature.

Mana Truhill (a/k/a "Manny Truhill," and whose real name seems to have been Emmanuel Trujillo) joined the NRP in early 1953. Nicknamed "Cochise" by his motorcycle-gang cohorts, he claimed to have been born in Pennsylvania as the son of a full-blooded Apache Indian father and a French mother.[31] Orphaned and later adopted, he ran away from home and joined the Merchant Marines. He then enlisted in a U.S. Army Airborne Division in 1948, but was mustered out after getting hurt in a parachute jump. After moving to New York, he enrolled in the Communist Party–run Jefferson School of Social Science before joining the NRP.

Truhill turned his apartment on Audubon Avenue into the NRP's "Overseas Office." All day long there was a constant procession in and out of the apartment of "Communists, uniformed Nazis, motorcycle gang hoodlums, some ballet dancers Truhill had acquired in Greenwich Village, and a Jamaican medical student from Columbia University who kept parts of cadavers in the icebox."[32] He even had a picture frame with interchangeable photos of Hitler and Stalin to suit different guests. In the midst of the chaos, Truhill's call-girl girlfriend, Pat Ward, wandered aimlessly clad only in her personality. Edward Fields, who later became the leader of the National States Rights Party (NSRP), paid a surprise visit to Truhill's pad in 1954 and was not pleased with what he saw. According to Fields: "Over Truhill's desk hung the Hammer and Sickle and a picture of Joe Stalin himself. On Truhill's desk was a portrait of a Negro man, whom Truhill said was his best friend."[33]

Truhill made no secret of his ties to the Communist Party's Jefferson School to Weiss, Madole, or anyone else. When he first approached the NSANL offering to moonlight as an informer, its director James Sheldon feared he might be part of a set-up. In a 23 June 1953 letter to an attorney named Julius Goldstein, Sheldon reported:

> A man of about 28 years age phoned, and later came into the office, on Monday June 15, giving the name Emmanuel Truhill (54 Audubon Ave.—and so listed in the phone book). He described himself as a member of Madole's National Renaissance Party (the neo-Nazi group in Yorkville) and said that he wanted to help us against [the NRP], having learned that such things were bad at "the school." I asked him, on the phone, "What school?" and he replied: "Jefferson." I said: "That's a left-wing one," and was thereafter very cold, suspecting a "plant."

When the two men met later that afternoon, Truhill told Sheldon that one day, "by chance," he had heard Madole speaking at one of his Yorkville rallies. He said he had then decided to join the NRP in order to infiltrate it, and gave Sheldon a notebook filled with information on Madole's activity to prove that he was sincere. Yet Truhill kept mentioning his "Communist-front connections" to Sheldon "in such a way as to make me suspect that he may be trying to involve us [the NSANL] in something along that line." The information, however, was too good to resist. After sternly lecturing his new informer about the dangers of communism, Sheldon explained that the NSANL's policy "is always to accept any information volunteered from any source whatsoever."[34]

Truhill soon began sending in reports about Madole. One such dispatch, written on the night of 18 September 1953, detailed his first meeting with Weiss:

> At five after four we [Madole and Truhill] started down for G[rand]-C[entral]-Station . . . Got off the bus and walked into the station. Went to the Station Master's office by track 35. . . . Madole said that Weiss should be here by six P.M. I told Madole I would be right back. I went over to one of the stands in the station and was having a hamburger. About 10 minutes later, Madole came *running* over to me and said that Weiss had been there and that we were to meet him at the Sidenberg bar and grill on Third Ave. I left the hamburger with one bite out of it and went with Madole out of the station and down to Third Ave. We found the bar with ease . . . Weiss asked me who I was. I told him that I was Truhill. He told me that he has been hearing my name for the past six months and that all the things he heard were good. "Don't you ever make any mistakes?" My answer: "Mr. Weiss, I am not in the Renaissance Party to make mistakes." This he seemed to like. He took my hand in a tight grip and said: "That's what I like to hear. We need people like you."

The talk that Weiss had with Madole I could not put down word for word. But it was on three things. One was the meeting [of New York rightists]. Weiss told Madole just what he wanted to have said at the meeting. Two: He was telling us how it was he that paid for the transportation of a German flying ace of World War II from Argentina to Germany so that he could take part in the elections. This man's name was Hans Ernest Ruddel [Hans-Ulrich Rudel]. He owns a small airline now in the Argentine. I think he only has one leg. Also Madole said that Ruddel had been at one time to Beacon and that he will be coming back. And may come with another man by the name of Nowman [Werner Naumann]. Three: Weiss asked me if I was the one that was doing all the photo work for the Party. I told him that I was . . . "I want you should stay in the background at the meeting tonight. And when you see Mr. Fleckenstein, get his photo . . . Ve must have dis. Understand?" "Yes sir."[35]

Weiss next began using Truhill for a series of tasks that included contacting various Nazis around the world.[36] Weiss's ties to both the mysterious Ulick Varange and Mana Truhill inspired rumors of links between the far left and the NRP. H. Keith Thompson's friendship with Lyle Stuart also raised eyebrows. Even more shocking was the fact the NRP openly supported groups like Germany's Socialist Reich Party on the ground that they were working with the Communists against the Jews. In 1954, for example, NRP member John Marshall visited John Hamilton's St. Louis–based National Citizens Protective League. Marshall, who had been friends with Hamilton since their days in the Boston branch of the Bund in 1940, told the Protective League that the NRP "was working with the Communists, since they were fighting the same enemy."[37] Statements like that did little to comfort those on the right already inclined to look at the NRP as either Nutzis or sinister agent provocateurs. Such, then, was the stormy political climate in the spring of 1954 when Francis Parker Yockey suddenly returned to New York.

Notes:

1. The only history of the NRP that I am aware of is William Goring's "The National Renaissance Party: History and Analysis of an American Neo-Nazi Political Party," in the December 1969–January 1970 issue of the *National Information Center Newsletter* from Springfield, Massachusetts. Goring was a Columbia University student who infiltrated the NRP in the early 1960s. He also used files from the Non-Sectarian Anti-Nazi League for his study. I have relied on Goring's report as well as files on the NRP from both the ADL and NSANL. I have also tried to look at as many NRP publications from the 1950s as I could find.

2. Arnold Forster and Benjamin Epstein, *Cross-Currents* (New York: Doubleday, 1956), p. 202.

3. The name Animist was suggested to Madole by an old-time German-American pamphleteer named A. O. Tittmann, the onetime head of the Voters Alliance of Americans of German Ancestry. Tittmann said that Animist meant "spirit of the woods."

4. Madole was not the first fascist sci-fi fanatic. In 1944 Claude Degler attempted to create a right-wing sci-fi group called the "Cosmic Circle." Another fan named Michael tried to launch the "Michaelis" with little success.

5. In his pamphlet *The Bigots Behind the Swastika Spree*, rightist author Joseph Kamp claimed that Madole's Animists would never have existed on anything but paper had it not been for a Manhattan hotel owner named Vladimir Stepankowsky. Kamp said that Stepankowsky was a Communist who wanted to use the Animists as a cover to spy on other rightist groups.

6. Later called the American Flag Committee. MacFarland also maintained close ties to a Union, New Jersey, outfit called the Loyal American Group, which sponsored Conde McGinley's *Common Sense.*

7. The June 1951 *Bulletin* of the NRP was published jointly by the NRP and the Citizens Protective League.

8. Goring, "The National Renaissance Party," p. 8.

9. Forster and Epstein, *Cross Currents*, pp. 247–48.

10. Ibid., pp. 261–62.

11. H. Keith Thompson's 20 August 1953 press release was entitled "The Events of a Turbulent Year and a Clarification of My Present Position."

12. Fleckenstein also knew Fred Weiss from Yorkville politics. Thompson and Fleckenstein worked out a deal that made Thompson's Committee for the Freedom of General Remer an official committee of Fleckenstein's Voters Alliance. Thompson went to the convention as head of the "American Voters Union," a spinoff of Fleckenstein's Voters Alliance. The two men later had a bitter falling-out.

13. See H. Keith Thompson's account in the September 1954 issue of *Exposé.*

14. In the November 1954 issue of *Exposé*, H. Keith Thompson gave a list of the proposed membership of the American Committee for the Advancement of Western

Culture that included as its Honorary Chairman A. O. Tittmann. The board of directors was to include John Monk (publisher of *Grassroots* and a Weiss ally), Peter Xavier (author of *Rise America*), and E. R. Barron and Fred Polzin, both of whom were associated with Weiss. The West Coast staff was to include James White (the editor of *Reason*, who also spoke at an NRP rally in New York), Frank Moore, David Presley, Robert Keen, and Britton McFetridge. The Mid-West group would include Ross Roberts of the Nationalist Information Service, Court Asher, and Raymond Burke. In the South the NRP-allied John W. Mitchell, William Spear, and Millard Gribbs of *The American Eagle* were to be members. Guy Stephens of *The Individualist* was also to be an advisor. Eustace Mullins was to become the group's treasurer, while Edward Fleckenstein would serve as its legal council. (On Fleckenstein's discussions with H. Keith Thompson, see a 26 June 1953 letter from Fleckenstein to Fred Weiss as cited in the October–November 1954 issue of the ADL journal *Facts*.)

15. In the November 1954 issue of *Exposé*, Thompson listed proposed members of his foreign advisory board.

16. On 2 May 1953, for example, H. Keith Thompson, A. O. Tittmann, and Madole were scheduled to speak at a meeting sponsored by the NRP at a private hall at 169 East 86th Street. Thompson's topic was "Zionist Atrocities in the Holy Land," while Madole told the "True Story of Nazi Germany and Adolf Hitler, the George Washington of Europe."

17. Born Lionel Simon, he legally changed his name in 1952. In 1956 he created Lyle Stuart Inc. He recently issued a mass paperback edition of the racist and anti-Semitic book *The Turner Diaries*.

18. On Stuart and Winchell, see Neal Gabler, *Winchell: Gossip, Power and the Culture of Celebrity* (New York: Vintage, 1995).

19. Stuart also wrote *The Secret Life of Walter Winchell*, which was published in 1953 by erotica publisher Sam Roth.

20. During the Depression, Forster helped Winchell gather information on groups like the Silver Shirts, information that Winchell gave to the FBI.

21. In *Square One* (New York: Donald I. Fine, 1988), ADL legal counsel Arnold Forster gives a very interesting account of that meeting with McCarthy. According to Forster, the ADL decided it would be foolish not to accept an opportunity to talk sense to McCarthy and warn him about his supporters on the far right. Yet the meeting was completely unproductive, with McCarthy spending most of it drinking. McCarthy's camp then leaked information about the gathering to the *Capital Times* of Madison, Wisconsin, in an attempt to show that he wasn't anti-Semitic.

22. H. Keith Thompson's reply to my questionnaire.

23. From Lyle Stuart's FBI file, which Stuart copied and sent to H. Keith Thompson on 26 April 1978.

24. H. Keith Thompson, letter to me dated 13 September 1994.

25. See the September 1954 issue of *Exposé*.

26. Thompson also tried to wreck Griffith's attempts to spy on the European right. In late 1953, when Griffith went on an investigative trip to Europe, Thompson sent his European contacts a letter of warning that described Griffith and his "wives." Thompson's hatred of Griffith was more than political. During World War II Griffith's

testimony had helped put George Sylvester Viereck in jail on charges of violating the Foreign Agents Registration Act. (Viereck also made an appearance in the October and November 1956 issues of Lyle Stuart's *The Independent*; in them he published an extensive account of a visit he made to Germany in 1956, where he met with old friends like Franz von Papen and Hjalmar Schacht.)

27. The rightist author Eustace Mullins, a one-time member of the NRP whom I interviewed, remembers going with Weiss to Griffith's house. Mullins called such meetings "mental chess." The Griffith-Weiss connection came up in an amusing way when the FBI interviewed NSANL head James Sheldon on 29 July 1954. Sheldon told the FBI that Weiss sold material to "Al Scheffer" (Griffith) "which was news to the agents." Sheldon also told the FBI that Scheffer operated for the ADL. The FBI, which worked closely with the ADL, "seemed much surprised" at his knowledge.

28. His name sometimes appears as West Hooker.

29. Hooker's affidavit was cited in the September 1955 issue of John Monk's publication *Grassroots*.

30. From the ADL files.

31. Much of the little that is known about Emmanuel Truhill's background comes from a biographical "Note on the Author" at the end of Truhill's book on his relationship with the call girl Pat Ward entitled *I Love You, I Hate You: My Six Weeks of Free Love with Pat Ward*. The book was published in 1955 by the Andre Levy Company of Philadelphia, which may have been a front for erotica publisher Samuel Roth.

32. Goring, "The National Renaissance Party," p. 10.

33. Cited in *The White Sentinel*, Vol. X, No. 4, April 1960. Truhill's black friend was Doxey Wilkerson, a well-known CP functionary.

34. Sheldon's letter from the NSANL files at Columbia University.

35. From Mana Truhill's 18 September 1953 report to the NSANL.

36. Copies of some of these letters would wind up in the files of the NSANL.

37. From the April 1960 *White Sentinel*.

43

CALIFORNIA
SCHEMING

In late March or early April 1954, Edward Brandt from the FBI's New York office received important news from an unidentified informant: Francis Parker Yockey ("Frank Healy") was back in the United States.[1] The informant told Brandt that "HEALY had arrived in the United States on or about February 11th from Europe." Yockey's mistress, Virginia Johnson, had failed to show up for a party on 12 February 1954 because "her brother had recently arrived from Munich and she was visiting with him."[2] The FBI report noted that Yockey "had shown a preference for Times Square–area hotels and, when he resided in New York City in 1952, he gave the informant the following phone number: JU2-4524."

Brandt's source was almost certainly H. Keith Thompson, who gave the same phone number to the Bureau in 1952.[3] He also told the FBI that he had known Yockey as "Frank Healy."[4] Thompson and Virginia Johnson were social acquaintances, and both attended parties at George Sylvester Viereck's apartment. Thompson made it a practice to give the FBI a mix of outdated but accurate information and rumor (what he called "feeding paper"). In this way when the FBI came to question him, he was in an excellent position to determine how much the Bureau actually knew about his friend. Of course, when Thompson contacted the FBI, Yockey was long gone from New York.

Thompson's information came at a time when a major story appeared on Soviet links to the far right. The 13 April 1954 issue of *The Reporter*, one of the most influential liberal magazines of the 1950s, ran a cover story by Edmond Taylor called "Germany: Where Fascism and Communism Meet." Taylor, who served as the secretary of the Psychological Strategy Board during World War II, identified Yockey, Weiss, and Thompson as the American connection to a far-reaching neo-

Nazi network oriented East. He was particularly interested in Weiss, "a hawk-nosed, bull-necked former captain in the Kaiser's army," who served as "an important relay point in the international fascist network." After a paragraph devoted to Thompson, Taylor zeroed in on "a still stranger associate of Weiss's,"

> a small, dark, intense-looking man who usually calls himself Ulick Varange (which is supposed to signify "Ireland-Russia") but who claims to have been born Francis Parker Yockey in Chicago in 1917. Varange, who has also used the name Frank Healy, is fairly prominent in the political demimonde of international fascism, particularly in England. A book of his published in London with the title *Imperium* outlined what he considers should be the master themes of fascist strategy: anti-Americanism, neutralism for Germany, and the avoidance of any anti-Soviet activity.[5]

With the *Reporter* investigation fueling further government interest, Yockey had little choice but to go deeper underground.[6] He would do so without Virginia Johnson, who had decided to lead a more normal life. Yockey headed to California, where his sisters Vinette Coyne and Alice Spurlock were living. Both sisters had served as his co-conspirators since the late 1930s. Some indication of Vinette's complicity can be seen in a 1952 letter Yockey sent to Virginia Johnson. In it, he wrote:

> I am enclosing a letter to Vinette . . . It is written as though it comes from Warren [Johnson], in case the enemy starts reading her mail in the Roxanna Post Office. This is entirely within the realm of possibility, as is telephone tapping. Vinette, of course, will understand the letter perfectly. In it I suggest indirectly that she get herself a new mailing address, a post office box in a different place, or an arrangement with the neighbors . . . I also tell her, speaking as Warren, that I have just had a card from her brother Francis from Mexico City, saying he is en route to Buenos Aires on business.[7]

As Yockey predicted, the FBI did track down Vinette Coyne. John Kelleher from the FBI's San Francisco office interviewed Vinette and William Coyne in June 1953, when Yockey was still in Cairo. The Coynes were then living in Pacific Grove, California, where the now-divorced Alice Spurlock also sometimes stayed. They had moved to California after William Coyne was assigned to the United States Naval Post Graduate School at Monterey, where he served as a security officer before becoming Acting Executive Officer.

The Coynes told Kelleher they had not heard from Yockey for about eight months. His last letter "came from Belgium" and indicated that he "intended to go to Arabia." William Coyne then promised Kelleher that "he would willingly advise the writer [Kelleher] in the event any member of his family should receive information concerning the subject." Kelleher had no doubt about Coyne's sincerity: "Commander Coyne," he noted, "has worked very closely with Agents of the San Francisco [FBI] Office in the past, and it is believed that he is entirely cooperative in this instance, and will definitely advise an Agent of the San Francisco Office if any word is received from the subject."

Yockey showed up in the Monterey area in April 1954.[8] His stay in California was remarkably productive—not only did he get hold of another false passport, but he also fleeced a woman named Janet Buchanan Arnold out of two thousand dollars. While in Monterey, Yockey sometimes played piano for fun at a local cocktail lounge called the Gilded Cage, and it is possible that Arnold, a divorced 42-year-old music lover, first met him there.[9] At the time he was calling himself "Edward Max Price," a name he also used on his application for a new passport.[10] He used the name "Richard Allen," however, when he married Janet Arnold on 24 June 1954 at the First Church of God in Watsonville, California.[11] One of Arnold's close friends later told the FBI that "Edward" and Janet Arnold

> continued their marital relationship for approximately three months at which time EDWARD stated that he was going to Europe and that [Arnold] was not to accompany him. [Arnold] then became very hysterical but her insistence that she accompany her husband did her no good. About the time that they separated a French girl appeared on the scene who was considerably younger than [Arnold] and about the same age as EDWARD.[12] After Edward left her, [Arnold] secured an annulment allegedly in Monterey County.

The friend met Vinette and Edward Coyne at Arnold's house, where Yockey used to give piano lessons. (In a letter to Elsa Dewette about this period, Yockey joked: "I married a piano.") The source said that the relationship between "EDWARD" who "appeared to be an individual surrounded by intrigue" and a navy officer like Coyne led her and another acquaintance to become suspicious. They dubbed Vinette's husband "Bogus Coyne" and even talked about contacting the FBI to inform it about Coyne and "EDWARD"! When Yockey introduced Arnold's friend to Vinette Coyne he tried to conceal the fact that she was his sister. Because they so physically resembled each other, the source kept pressing the issue. Finally he broke down and admitted the truth.

The FBI interviewed Janet Arnold on more than one occasion, beginning in 1955. For a jilted woman she was remarkably protective of Yockey, telling agents that he "reminded her of the poet BYRON." Years after Yockey's abandonment, Arnold continued to maintain a friendship with Alice Spurlock.[13] It was only after Yockey's arrest that a worried Arnold admitted to the FBI that she and "Richard Allen" had been married.[14] She then described him as

> a megalomaniac, possessing a hatred of Jews and Negroes. YOCKEY then termed himself a Fascist. She observed that she was physically afraid of YOCKEY and that YOCKEY was very demanding in his requests, such as swimming daily in the ocean.[15]

She also said that shortly before Yockey left her on 1 October 1954, he had hit her, giving her a black eye.

While in California, Yockey made contact with an NRP supporter and attorney named James R. White.[16] H. Keith Thompson received a letter from Yockey dated 19 August 1954 with a return address given as Box 2532, Terminal Annex, Los Angeles, California, which was White's post office box.[17] A rightist named Douglas Kaye also recalls White telling him that he and Yockey had attended a local Republican Party convention where they had distributed leaflets.[18] In the summer of 1954 the far right began organizing a third-party presidential movement focused on Senator Joseph McCarthy. Yockey may have gone to the convention hoping to recruit Orange County Republicans into the McCarthy camp. McCarthy's presidential stalking horse was an organization called "Ten Million Americans Mobilized for Justice." On 29 November 1954, it held a Madison Square Garden rally organized by such far-right stalwarts as Defenders of the American Constitution leader and retired Marine Corps General Pedro del Valle. The meeting, however, only attracted 13,000 participants (including the NRP's James Madole) and was considered a failure.[19]

Yockey left California in early October 1954 with more than two thousand dollars of Janet Arnold's money as well as a new passport in the name of "Edward Max Price." He next showed up in New York, where, as "Frank Healy," he met James Madole.[20] Sometime that same month, he returned to Europe on his new passport. The FBI, however, still continued to search for him all across America. Agents even staked out a testimonial dinner for McCarthy's legal counsel Roy Cohn at the Emerson Hotel in Baltimore, Maryland.[21] While the assembled guests paid tribute to Cohn, FBI agents Ralph Vogel and John Montgomery "conducted a discreet surveillance in the vicinity of the banquet hall . . . as well as the lobby of the hotel during the hours between six P.M. and 10 P.M. on 5 October 1954" hoping to spot Yockey.[22]

Yockey's first stop in Europe appears to have been England, since John Anthony Gannon remembered last meeting him in October 1954, before Gannon moved to South America.[23] Yockey then seems to have gone to Paris from London.[24] By early December he was back in Germany. Not long after his return, Yockey's "Edward Max Price" cover fell apart. J. Edgar Hoover got a "CONFIDENTIAL" message from Army Intelligence (G-2) transmitted from the FBI Liaison Representative in Heidelberg, Germany, in January 1955 explaining just what happened:

> CIC has advised by teletype that a source reports observing subject [Yockey] in American Express Office, Stuttgart, Germany,[25] on December 3 last. Source claims to be certain of identification and says subject was using name Edward Max Price and was carrying United States Passport number 378334 issued at Washington May 19, 1954. Subject indicated plans to travel to Salzburg, Austria.

Army Counter-Intelligence Corps agent Richard Quinn, Jr., interviewed a member of the Red Cross in Stuttgart on 7 December 1954. The informant told

Quinn he first met Yockey some four years earlier at the Red Cross's St. Louis headquarters. He told his superiors at the time that Yockey should not be hired, after hearing him mention at lunch one day that the U.S. needed a "hero" like Hitler to lead it. Then:

On 3 December 1954, _____ saw SUBJECT in the offices of the American Express Company, Koenigstrasse 46, STUTTGART, Germany, located in the same building as the ARC [American Red Cross].

Thinking that he had recognized Yockey, the informant managed to speak to the teller who had serviced him, one Karl Heinz Horlacher. When Horlacher left his window to ask his manager for more cash for Yockey, the informant "intercepted HORLACHER and asked him to obtain that name of the person at his window as _____ thought he was a former ARC worker with whom _____ was acquainted."

HORLACHER returned to his window and obtained the following information from the passport SUBJECT presented for identification and gave it to _____. United States Passport No. 378334 issued 19 May 1954 at WASHINGTON, District of Columbia, USA, to Edward Max PRICE, CARMEL/HIGHLANDS, California, USA. SUBJECT was at the American Express Offices for the purpose of receiving a "Bank Transfer of Funds" from the account of W. D. COYNE, for the amount of $499.00.

The Red Cross worker returned to his office and examined Yockey's old identification card. He told Quinn that "there is no doubt that the man who presented the passport of Edward Max PRICE is SUBJECT as his voice, mannerisms, and features are exactly the same as the man _____ knows as Francis Parker YOCKEY."[26]

The CIC next interviewed Frau Lore Steinhauser, who worked in the Travel Branch of the American Express Company in Stuttgart. She told the CIC that

after inquiring for his mail, a man by the name of Edward PRICE, made inquiries ... pertaining to trains running to SALZBURG, Austria. While engaged in conversation with STEINHAUSER, PRICE mentioned that he had previously purchased a ticket from STUTTGART to SALZBURG in France. STEINHAUSER informed PRICE that he could take an afternoon train leaving STUTTGART at 1410 hours daily.

Whether Yockey went to Salzburg is unknown.[27] By January 1955, however, he was once again living in Munich, because William Coyne later admitted to FBI agents that he had sent a seven-hundred-dollar money order to that city.[28]

After the FBI realized how badly it had been duped, agents zeroed in on Yockey's "Edward Max Price" passport. They discovered that he had used the birth certificate of a real Edward Max Price who had been born in Norfolk, Virginia. The Bureau also learned that "Price," a "music teacher," had as his identifying witness on his passport application "Alice Spurlock . . . who stated she had known Price five years and was not related to him."

It was now time for the FBI to pay another visit to Yockey's relatives. On 4 February 1955 Vinette and William Coyne were asked about "Edward Max Price." Both denied knowing the name. On 10 March 1955 Alice Spurlock was interviewed by FBI agents, and she too denied knowing either the name Edward Max Price or her brother's current location. Finally, on 25 March, William Coyne was brought to the sheriff's office in Monterey for more questioning. After he again denied knowing Edward Max Price, the FBI pointed out that he had sent a money order for five hundred dollars to Price in Stuttgart. Coyne said the name now "rang a bell" but claimed that he was merely doing Alice Spurlock a favor. He then said that Yockey "had done nothing wrong, that he is misunderstood because he is so brilliant and most people are jealous of him."[29] The FBI reinterviewed Alice Spurlock on 30 March and again she denied lying about the passport application.[30]

Despite Yockey's skills as a conspirator, one chance encounter had ruined everything. A few months later, he disappeared entirely. The American government's best efforts failed to turn up any trace of him in either the United States or Europe—no trace except for an astonishing rumor that Yockey had crossed over into the Soviet zone.

Notes:

1. It is hard to tell exactly when the FBI received its information from its informant, since Brandt's report (dated 8 April 1954) included FBI interviews with other sources about Yockey. My guess is that the information most likely came to the FBI at least a week or two before the report was written. If Yockey had entered the U.S. in early or mid-February, the information came to the FBI one month later at the earliest.

2. Recall that when Yockey and Virginia were with strangers they often claimed to be brother and sister.

3. The only other place in the FBI FOIA files where I could find mention of Yockey's hotel phone number was H. Keith Thompson's earlier interview with the FBI.

4. This was an important point because Thompson had listed the name "Frank Healy" (not Yockey or "Varange") when he filed legal papers regarding his status as a registered agent for the Socialist Reich Party in 1952.

5. In his 31 March 1954 "Washington Merry-Go-Round" column hyping the *Reporter* exposé, syndicated columnist Drew Pearson also focused on Yockey.

6. Before leaving New York, Yockey may have helped write a Weiss press release dated 1 April 1954 and distributed by the NRP, entitled *Oswald Spengler, The American Jewish Committee, and Russia.*

7. Yockey even tutored Virginia on how to lie to the FBI:

In case the enemy comes to you as he probably will—after checking her [Vinette Coyne's] telephone calls—this should be your line with him: I visited you for a while, and then left, and then next you heard was the card from Mexico City. If asked about the card, naturally you destroyed it, since you do not collect post cards.

Tell Warren [Johnson] you had a call from Vinette so that he will be alerted for a visit from the enemy and will tell them the same story. Treat them distantly and firmly; make them produce their credentials, ask them directly what they want and do not be helpful at all. Show great surprise that they are seeking poor Franz, a model member of the community, etc.

8. Before coming West, Yockey may have visited Washington as well. In a 24 October 1957 FBI interview with Virginia Johnson (remarried and out of Yockey's world), she told the Bureau that the last time she had heard from Yockey was a 1954 postcard apparently sent from Washington, D.C. It is also possible that on his way to California Yockey stopped off in Carbondale, Illinois, to see his friend from Northwestern Law School, John Lannin.

9. Yockey's Gilded Cage connection comes from a friend of Janet Arnold interviewed by FBI agent Orville N. Molnen on 7 June 1959 at Carmel Valley, California. The FBI's informant thought that Yockey had a job playing piano at the bar. Molnen questioned a woman who worked at the Gilded Cage in early 1954, and she said that the bar never employed anyone named Richard Allen to play piano, although when shown a photo of Yockey she said he looked familiar. She then told the FBI that customers would play the piano at times when the featured entertainer was not performing. The Gilded Cage always used booking agents to hire pianists.

Yockey most likely met Arnold some time before May, because on 4 May 1954 Arnold and Alice Spurlock were used by Yockey as references when "E. Max Price" applied for a post office box in Pacific Grove, California. (Yockey claimed then that he was a traveling salesman for a non-existent firm called "Viking Machines" in San Francisco.) The FBI was told by the post office that Price had gotten a letter from a "Lieutenant GEORGE R. LEVY, 769 Med. Det. APO 407, New York." Who George R. Levy was (or if that was in fact his real name) remains a puzzle.

10. Arnold swore to his identity as "Edward Max Price" in May 1954, but married him as "Richard Allen" in June 1954.

11. Janet Arnold FBI interview of 13 June 1960.

12. The identity of the "French girl" remains unknown. There is a remote possibility that this could be the first appearance of the woman named "Pat Lagerstrom" or "Pat Hatch," who spoke fluent French with Yockey in New Orleans, although she was German. Recall that Yockey lived with this woman in the California area in 1959–60.

13. Although questioned earlier by the FBI with little result, Janet Arnold contacted the Bureau on 9 June 1960 (three days after Yockey's arrest) to offer information. She was interviewed by FBI agents Fred Elledge and J. Wayne Parrish on 13 June 1960. Arnold told the FBI that before Yockey left California in 1954 he convinced her to liquidate her assets so that they could go on a trip to Mexico. Arnold did partially liquidate her assets, which is how Yockey got two thousand dollars. Arnold also said that she had never witnessed or signed an application for a passport executed by Yockey but she had heard that Yockey had put her down as a reference along with Alice Spurlock. She did sign an application by Yockey for a library card.

14. A strikingly accurate ADL report from 1954 reported that Yockey was in California as of 25 September 1954 but that he had returned to Germany after fleecing a widow on the West Coast for $2,000.

435

15. Arnold's friend and FBI informant also indicated that the relationship was stormy and that Arnold often stayed at her friend's house when she and Yockey were fighting.

16. White was also one of the proposed members of H. Keith Thompson's American Committee for the Advancement of Western Culture.

17. In a list of NRP contacts published by the NSANL, White's address is the Terminal Annex post office box.

18. Douglas Kaye interview with me. Kaye misremembered the leafleting as occurring in 1952. I believe he confused the date Thompson and Viereck attended the GOP convention in Chicago with the incident told by White.

19. In *Pegler: Angry Man of the Press* (Boston: Beacon Press, 1963), Oliver Pilat reports that in November 1954 Ten Million Americans Mobilized for Justice tried to launch a mass movement for McCarthy that included the Madison Square Garden rally. The NRP also set up a front group called "Patriots for McCarthy."

Another McCarthy enthusiast wrote to the National Renaissance Party on 28 February 1954 from Argentina. This was Johann von Leers. Leers was particularly interested in information on James Sheldon and the NSANL because in December 1953 the ADL *Bulletin* reported that Mana Truhill had attempted to sell information to the ADL and that he was also feeding information to the NSANL. Leers had run a picture of Truhill with James Madole in *Der Weg* and wanted to get back at Sheldon. Leers wrote that he could place information on the NSANL in French and Arab papers:

And then, as usually, the text will be cabled to the USA and come to the attention of Mr. McCarthy, so that he may intervene against this outfit. Particularly I shall publish that all in our monthly *Der Weg* and then send it directly by a friend to Mr. McCarthy whom I don't know. We must use the wave of anticommunism existing now in the USA to destroy as many as possible of the Jewish "progressive" organizations . . .

20. A few months later, in January 1955, Madole published an article entitled "The Destiny of America" (based in part on notes from Yockey) under his own name in the NRP's *Bulletin*.

21. Senator Joseph McCarthy had also been invited to speak.

22. FBI Baltimore office report dated 6 October 1954. The false lead on Yockey apparently came from a report from the Philadelphia office of the FBI on 13 September 1954.

23. John Anthony Gannon 13 July 1980 letter to Keith Stimely. Yockey tried to talk Gannon out of leaving England but was unsuccessful. With Gannon gone, *Frontfighter* ceased publication.

24. The U.S. embassy in Paris reported that an "Edward Max Price" came to Paris from London and stayed for one day at 108 rue de Budapest and one day at 3 rue de Budapest, according to an FBI report from the Washington Field Office (WFO) dated 27 June 1956. This was based on information from the State Department. There is a problem with the Paris chronology: The dates given for Yockey's stay are from 9–11 December 1954, which makes little sense. Yockey was in Stuttgart at the American Express office on 3 December 1954. While in Stuttgart he mentioned that he had come from France and was planning to go to Austria and made inquiry about trains to Salzburg.

It seems highly unlikely that Yockey would then suddenly go to England for a few days (he had just been to England in late October) and then reenter France. My guess is that the FBI either got a wrong transmission of information from State or that the FBI made an error in its summary. The State Department could also have also gotten erroneous information from its Paris sources. However, if one substitutes "November" for "December," Yockey's schedule makes perfect sense in light of the other evidence. I believe Yockey first went to England to check on Gannon and the ELF; he then entered France and stayed in Paris for an unknown period of time before taking a train from Paris to Stuttgart in early December 1954. Examination of State Department files (specifically, dispatch 2390 dated 6 May 1955 from the U.S. embassy in Paris) might help clear up this matter.

25. At the time, Yockey may also have been using a safehouse in Pforzheim near Stuttgart. Fred Weiss had a daughter from a first marriage who lived in Pforzheim, and she may have given Yockey a place to stay.

26. The informant undoubtedly contacted the CIC about Yockey.

27. The fact that he was scheduled to visit Austria suggests the possibility that when Yockey told H. Keith Thompson about his courier work for Czech intelligence involving a meeting in Vienna, he was referring to this trip. Yockey was also a Wagnerian and he may have stopped off at Salzburg before continuing on to Vienna.

28. According to information given to the FBI by William Coyne (as well as a handwritten statement prepared by Coyne for the Office of Naval Intelligence on 25 July 1955), he sent "Price" two money orders: the $499 order in November 1954 to Stuttgart and a $700 money order in January 1955 to Munich.

29. Due to jurisdictional considerations, the FBI turned the investigation over to the Office of Naval Intelligence (ONI), which questioned William Coyne separately. In his written statement to the ONI, Coyne described Yockey this way:

> On a personal level, Mr. Yockey is unusually intelligent but tends to make enemies rather than friends. He has a quick grasp of abstract problems, an acid tongue, and a tendency to be dogmatic. He has an amazingly retentive mind, a prodigious vocabulary, and a natural gift for expressing himself succinctly. When meeting him for the first time most people seem to form immediately either an intense like or an intense dislike. Women tend to like him; men tend to dislike him.

30. When Spurlock refused to give a sample of her handwriting without consulting a lawyer, the FBI got other samples for analysis by the FBI lab. The lab was unable to definitively match Spurlock's handwriting with the writing on the passport application.

44

"LORD HAW-HAW
OF THE USSR"[1]

A year after Yockey's death, Peter J. Huxley-Blythe asked H. Keith Thompson: "Do you know in fact if Yockey did, as is generally understood here, visit the Soviet Union either in 1957 or at any other time?"[2] Rumors about Yockey's possible sojourn East first began in the mid-1950s. In his monograph on the National Renaissance Party, William Goring writes that after returning to New York "in 1955" (actually October 1954), "Frank Healy" discussed his travel plans with James Madole. According to Goring, Yockey told "the astonished Madole, who had been unaware of his identity, that he was leaving for East Germany. After visiting East Germany, he travelled through Russia, returning in 1957 or 1958."[3]

The FBI also heard that Yockey was interested in travel behind the Iron Curtain. Chicago FBI agent Lloyd Bogstad reported on 7 February 1955 that "T-1 of known reliability" told the Bureau:

> YOCKEY is traveling around West Germany and is believed to be "flirting with the Communists." Informant has heard that YOCKEY's ambition is to become the "Lord Haw-Haw of the USSR and to attack the USA." YOCKEY is believed to have a "complete loathing for the U.S." Information received by the informant indicates that YOCKEY has been in touch with Soviet authorities and he has been exploring matters connected with the cobalt bomb. The informant has learned that FREDERICK CHARLES WEISS (not further identified) has been in touch with YOCKEY in Germany on an undisclosed date. YOCKEY was in communication with WEISS from Remagen (country not indicated) about six or seven weeks previous to the last contact. WEISS indicated that YOCKEY had been in Dortmund (country not indicated) and had suddenly disappeared after having made a number of appointments which YOCKEY had not kept.[4]

There is evidence that Fred Weiss helped engineer Yockey's journey East. On 17 January 1955, Non-Sectarian Anti-Nazi League chief James Sheldon wrote down a series of notes from a conversation he had with Mana Truhill, who continued to maintain close ties with Weiss. According to Sheldon's handwritten notes:

> Weiss wants Truhill [to] prepare memorial edition of his [Weiss's] work after his death.[5] Von Leers to help. Weiss will send E.T. [Mana Truhill a/k/a Emmanuel Trujillo] to Ger. [Germany] to meet Verange (Yocki). Seems to have plan to get Verange into E. Berlin and have him do broadcasts there.

Did Yockey go East? After Yockey disappeared, Fred Weiss advanced three possible scenarios for his friend: He could either be dead or sitting in a jail cell after being captured by U.S. or West German intelligence; he could have realized his plan and entered the Soviet Bloc; or "because of his peculiar sex practice—whipping girls—Yockey may have run into one who didn't relish this kind of play and had him done in."[6] The FBI also suspected that Yockey was living in Eastern Europe: In September 1956 it had the State Department and G-2 investigate reports about a mystery man named "Frederick C. Hopkins," who had been released by the Russians on 6 September 1955, because the Bureau incorrectly suspected that Hopkins may have been Yockey.[7]

All that can be said for certain is that sometime in 1955 Yockey disappeared.[8] He also seems to have received inside information about the hunt for him. In a summary of the case written on 27 June 1956, FBI agent Kenneth J. Hauser (who reviewed State Department files on Yockey) reported that

> by dispatch 3 dated July 12, 1955, the Consulate General at Stuttgart informed the Department that it had been told by appropriate authorities on April 28, 1955, that EDWARD MAX PRICE could not be located and that he had been traced to the area between Mannheim and Frankfurt, where it was expected that he would be found but he had disappeared, and these authorities felt sure that he must have been alerted.

If Yockey did go East to avoid arrest, he was not alone. Recall that Karl-Heinz Heubaum, the printer of *Der Feind Europas*, fled into East Germany to avoid a prison term for distributing anti-Semitic literature. Heubaum's trip also caught the attention of Johann von Leers. In a letter to H. Keith Thompson dated 15 June 1957, Leers wrote:

> In Buenos Aires, M. Fritsch [from *Der Weg*] continues his work under the bad situation of the Jewish Rojas misrule. The flight of Heubaum to Eastern Germany is somehow symptomatic. The brutal Jewish tyranny in Western Germany, backed by the American government, forces more and more patriots either to emigrate, mostly to Islamic countries, or to search refuge in the Communist part of Germany. Heubaum is in no way a Communist or fellow traveller, but only anti-Jew. Therefore he has been condemned and—to avoid jail in Western Germany, where the treatment meted out is horrible—he went East. The mon-

key-love of USA government for the Jews isolates the Americans both in Germany and in the Near East. On the other hand, the Russians are clever enough to appeal to the sound anti-Jewish feeling of the peoples.[9]

Judging by the date of Leers' missive, Heubaum appears to have crossed over into the East sometime in late 1956 or early 1957. If so, it seems quite possible that Yockey had gone over before him, since he vanished in 1955.

While Yockey remained underground, Fred Weiss and H. Keith Thompson began circulating a series of Yockeyist pamphlets inside the American far right. In the summer of 1955 Weiss's Le Blanc Publications issued part one of *Russia*, an essay written by Weiss and heavily edited by Thompson. It was eventually published in three parts over the course of 1955 and 1956 by Thompson's Cooper Forms printing house.[10] Using arguments from Spengler and Yockey, *Russia* attacked "Jewish" Trotskyites and defended Stalin and Khrushchev as true sons of Mother Russia. The Russiandom of the future, *Russia* predicted, "will ultimately transform the Bolshevism of Stalin, Malenkov, Bulganin, and Khrushchev in its present-day form into an outspoken, revitalized nationalist movement." Critics might still call Russia Communist, "but what's in a name?" Weiss and Thompson attacked the idea that the oppressed Russian masses wanted to overthrow the Bolshevik yoke. In fact: "Today it is not only official Russian doctrine but also the general belief of the Russo-Mongolian masses that the unique national genius of Russia brought forth the new world of 'Communism' as the climax of its creative activity."[11] To really understand Russia, one had to realize that it was a "pre-Israelitic" pagan society:

> Today, the Russian-Mongolian movement is nothing less than a militant revival of an ancient, specifically Asiatic doctrine: a doctrine reflecting the nature and destiny of man, whose origin dates back to pre-Israelitic, as well as pre-Christian times. This old religion (for a religion it is), which received a new impetus through Dostoyevsky and other Russian thinkers, is the worship of collective human power. It holds that the individual human being can possess no individual rights above those rights of the community; that man, therefore, exists for the sake of the community. When Westerners examine their challenge—the relative importance of the interests of the community and the interest of private individuals—our own championship of individual human rights, in their eyes, appears frivolous and laughable. What is, to us, a symbol of strength is, to them, an evidence of weakness.[12]

In pamphlets like *Russia* (1955–56), *The Great Question* (1957), and *Will He Bury Us!* (1958), Weiss and Thompson criticized the far-right notion that Russia was secretly controlled by a Jewish–Wall Street–Communist cabal, and instead argued that Russia was now the most deadly enemy of international Jewry.[13] As Weiss put it in *The Great Question*:

It was not surprising that once she [Mother Russia] had taken away from her cursed Schiffs every Yiddish cultural and religious installation, the desired transformation proceeded rapidly until now there is no longer any Jewish problem in the lands of our little Mother Russia.[14]

Far from Russia being under Jewish control, "It cannot be emphasized sufficiently that the Jews, as a nation, have been finished in Russia since 1937–1938." Russia had also made huge technical and production breakthroughs: Weiss and Thompson even predict (in capital letters, no less):

WITHIN A RELATIVELY FEW YEARS, WESTERN SIBERIA AND TURKESTAN WILL BE TRANSFORMED BY SOVIET SCIENCE INTO A VERITABLE PARADISE OF WEATHER AND VEGETATION. FARMING WILL BE CONDUCTED ON A HITHERTO-UNDREAMED-OF SCALE, AND, FROM THIS POINT ON, THE SCIENTIFIC TRANSFORMATION OF THESE VAST TERRITORIES WILL INSURE AMPLE FOOD FOR AN ADDITIONAL 150,000,000 POPULATION.[15]

Great economic growth, combined with the technical expertise it acquired when it captured many of Germany's leading scientists, would soon insure Russian military supremacy. Russian prowess was already evident in the launch of the Sputnik satellite. In *The Great Question,* Weiss called Sputnik "a Russian Damocles sword in the form of a satellite dangling over our heads (without the possibility of retaliation)."[16] The Russians had even perfected Weiss's beloved cobalt bomb. In *Russia,* he writes:

According to the reports in the *New York Post,* atomic explosions were being extensively employed [in Siberia] to accomplish the river diversions [of the Ob and Jenissei Rivers] in connection with this project [the development of Turkestan]. "Atomic Satchels," capable of being transported in a small handbag, create explosions necessary for the tremendous land replacement. Formerly, equivalent explosions would have required countless trainloads of explosives.[17]

Thompson and Weiss also maintained contacts with both the American Communist Party and Russian diplomats. When I asked Thompson about his CP connections, he replied:

Yes, I had some good CP ties, even a few in CPUS[A] circles . . . Marxism aside, the CPUS people were decent and socially very conservative. The Soviet intelligence apparatus was another matter. They generally stayed clear of the CPUS because it was always under a federal magnifying glass.[18]

Thompson's real link, however, was with the Soviet diplomatic corps:

Just to more-or-less conclude the question which you raised as to my USSR contact(s) in the "war crimes" and other matters, I guess that there is no reason at this late date why I should not tell you that my connection was Valerian Zorin. A diplomat (not KGB) at the time the connection was developed, my contacts were written during the '50s as he was not in U.S. and mail drops were used.

I met Zorin personally in February 1961 at the reception for [Rockwell] Kent.[19] I'm enclosing the actual invitation which I found in my files.[20] At that time I believe that Zorin was the USSR Delegate to the U.N. Kent and [Soviet diplomat] Volsky made the introduction at the cocktail party and we talked for about 10 minutes with an interpreter to aid him . . . In the '60s the Kent connection gave me other contacts in the Ministry of Culture, etc., used primarily on Kent's business (re: gift of his art to the USSR, royalty matters, etc.).[21]

Valerian Aleksandrovich Zorin was an extremely important Soviet official. Holder of two Orders of Lenin, he was the Soviet ambassador to Czechoslovakia from 1947 to 1955,[22] a deputy minister for foreign affairs (1952–53), Soviet ambassador to West Germany (1960–62), and, in 1968, Soviet ambassador to France.[23] Thompson said he traded favors with the Russians to encourage the release of high-ranking Nazis still held by them.[24] When I questioned Thompson about this, he replied:

> You asked me about the results of arranged Soviet "quid pro quo" in re: war criminals (their term, not mine; "prisoners of war" would be more accurate) held by them. I pushed for two in case there was unsurmountable difficulty on one. They were: (1) Field Marshal Ferdinand Schoerner, who had been captured in 1945, and (2) SS General Julius Rattenhueber, security chief in the Bunker who was taken by the Russians on May 2, 1945. Schoerner was in fact released on January 24, 1955. Rattenhueber took longer, released on October 18, 1955, with a number of other officers. They liked to hang on to SS people.[25]

Thompson was a very busy man. "Keep in mind," he told me, "that I was raising money for a flood of other tasks [besides Yockey], for SRP, for Remer personally, for the defense of various 'war crimes' cases, humanitarian work, getting people out of Europe to South America, etc., etc." After estimating that he had given Yockey approximately $15,000 over the years, he noted:

> I had another fund source for use specifically in certain "war crimes" cases and to aid comrades in political difficulties. This stemmed from funds set aside for this before [the] end of World War II, some in Spain, some in Paraguay. I don't intend to get more specific on this except to say that such funds were depleted by 1980.[26]

Thompson later reported that the SS had placed about two million dollars in overseas funds for use after the war. Various individuals were given "signature control" over the accounts. Thompson said that he had "signature control over one such account with the Royal Trust in Canada. All disbursed by 1970s. There were similar accounts in Mexico, Chile, etc." He also used his printing company, Cooper Forms, to "print paper" for various accused war criminals on the run. As he put it: "I was not a printer for nothing."[27]

It was Fred Weiss, however, not Thompson, who most came under attack for alleged ties to the American Communist Party. The controversy surrounding

Weiss focused on his ongoing relationship with Mana Truhill. According to H. Keith Thompson:

> Truhill was just a thug. At least he could read and write. He was a creature of Sheldon and the various ADL operatives at the time. The CP would have run away from him; of what value would he have been to them? Crazy drug addicts are in little demand. Weiss was foolish enough to "maintain ties" with everyone on the theory that any kind of action is better than inaction ... Truhill wanted to hang with Weiss because he saw a few bucks in it, and there were always a few bucks available. Mostly damned few.[28]

Truhill's continuing ties to Weiss are not easy to understand, especially since Truhill's cover had been blown by the ADL. In a November 1953 article attacking the NRP in the ADL *Bulletin*, it was reported that Truhill had approached the ADL several months earlier and offered to sell it information about the right.[29] He shocked the ADL by saying that he was "an out-and-out Communist" who had studied at the Jefferson School.[30]

The reaction to the article inside the NRP was bizarre, since shortly after it appeared James Madole penned a response defending Truhill:

> The biggest lie in their [the ADL's] November *Bulletin* is the one pertaining to a member of the National Renaissance Party, namely Mana Truhill ... I have known Mr. Truhill for quite some time; he is one of the best workers that the National Renaissance Party has ever had ... You will find some so-called nationalists such as Mrs. Eugene Brand, Edward A. Fleckenstein, and others who wish no good fortune to the National Renaissance Party to eagerly carry this vicious, depraved Jewish lie from place to place.[31]

When the furor on the right refused to abate, Madole was forced to formally kick Truhill out of the group. As late as August 1955, however, Madole was *still* defending Truhill against his critics (including H. Keith Thompson) in the NRP *Bulletin*.[32] Undoubtedly following a line laid down by Weiss, Madole insisted that Truhill was "a professional 'soldier of fortune'" and not a spy.

The worlds of H. Keith Thompson, Fred Weiss, and Mana Truhill overlapped in the strangest ways. One example involved Sam Roth, perhaps the most famous publisher of erotica in the 1950s. Born in Austria to Orthodox Jewish parents, Roth came to America in 1904 at age nine. A freethinker and admirer of Emma Goldman, whose lectures he regularly attended, he despised Judaism with a passion—so much so that his 1934 diatribe *Jews Must Live: An Account of the Persecution of the World by Israel on All the Frontiers of Civilization* continues to be sold by far-right publishing outlets today. Roth, who made his living by publishing soft-core pornography, was continually hounded for obscenity by local police forces and the FBI. He was even hauled before the Kefauver Committee in 1955. Two years later, the U.S. Supreme Court handed down a famous decision against him that defined obscenity laws for years to come. Sentenced to jail at age

62, he spent most of the last five years of his life in prison. Roth was one of George Sylvester Viereck's "sexologist" friends, and published some of Viereck's erotica in his magazine, *American Aphrodite*. Thompson, who met Roth through Viereck, called him

> a pleasant man, a "tweedy" English gentleman type, but I'm told a literary pirate. Wrote *Jews Must Live*, which I liked and told him so. He shuddered. We met perhaps five or six times over drinks at Viereck's. [Lyle] Stuart, by then operating out of a small office at 225 Lafayette Street, bought Roth's mailing list, which enabled him to get into full-scale publishing. Marty Scheiman, lawyer for Stuart and me, defended Sam Roth on federal obscenity charges.[33]

It was through Roth that Thompson, Weiss, and Truhill became entangled with Truhill's one-time girlfriend, the call girl Pat Ward. On 10 March 1955, Truhill contacted George Washington Herz, a lawyer for Micky (Minot) Jelke, a high-society playboy arrested for running a call-girl ring that starred Pat Ward. Jelke's wealthy background, plus a clientele that included movie stars, ensured enormous press coverage. Truhill told Herz about his conversations with Ward about Jelke, and about Ward's propensity to lie. He suggested planting a tape recorder in his apartment so that the next time Ward visited he could record her statements, which could then be used to impeach her testimony against Jelke.[34] Around this same time, Pat Ward's book (*Pat Ward's Own Story!*) was published by Sam Roth.[35]

The New York tabloids heard about Ward's relationship with Truhill in late March. A photo of the leather-clad twosome (in matching motorcycle caps) even graced the front page of the *Daily News*. Hearing opportunity knock twice, Roth decided to publish Truhill's memoirs about Pat Ward. After Roth told H. Keith Thompson about his plan, a panicked Thompson alerted Weiss.[36] Both men feared that Truhill would discuss them, but when *I Love You, I Hate You: My Six Weeks of Free Love with Pat Ward* appeared there was no mention of either of them.

But why would Weiss continue to deal with Truhill, given all the furor he had caused? One possible answer is that Weiss's critics were essentially correct in suspecting an alliance between Weiss and elements of the American Communist Party. Evidence of just such a connection appeared in one of Truhill's reports to the NSANL. In August 1955 (the same month that Madole's defense of Truhill appeared in the NRP *Bulletin*), Weiss sent Truhill on a mysterious mission to Las Vegas.[37] In a letter to the NSANL's James Sheldon dated 16 August 1955, Truhill wrote:

> Am working with some friends of Weiss in Las Vegas. Am due to go to Mexico to meet a Mr. BARE sometime this week. Have no need of money as all is paid by them. Will call you as soon as I can but it is not easy as Bob (ROBERT LOWBER) is with me most of the time. Most of the people I am with are Reds—they

know Weiss for what he is and are still working with him. I see now they are just as bad as Madole and his boys. Will call or write as soon as I can.

Unfortunately, the NSANL archives contain no more information about the trip. On the letter, postmarked Las Vegas, Sheldon noted that he had not received it until 30 August 1955, after he had returned from Washington, D.C. It was impossible to determine whether Sheldon heard from Truhill again. It is also impossible to identify Mr. Bare, Robert Lowber, or the "Reds," or to determine why Weiss wanted Truhill to go to Mexico.

Equally curious is the fact that, as much as H. Keith Thompson disliked Truhill, in 1957 he tried to contact him in Canada, where Truhill was serving a jail sentence for selling drugs. In a copy of an FBI file that Lyle Stuart sent Thompson, it was reported:

_____ indicated that on 2/18/57 Keith Thompson, a former member of the National Renaissance Party (NRP), and Lyle Stewart [Stuart] allegedly had visited Emmanuel Trujillo _____ in prison in Canada, and had negotiated with him for the publication of his story about the dope business. He stated that Trujillo indicated to them that he would be released in the near future.

Thompson told me that he *did* attempt to contact Truhill:

I visited the fortress in Canada where Truhill was being held on a drug conviction, intending to interview him. The superintendent denied permission but I left a small sum of money out of sympathy for anyone who was incarcerated in that place.[38]

But why did Thompson track down Truhill? Did the Weiss network maintain ties with him even then? The mystery is all the more intriguing since, after Truhill was released, he reportedly went to Cuba to help Castro.[39]

After Yockey vanished, Weiss spent considerable energy trying to learn of his fate. He particularly feared that he may have been responsible for Yockey's capture by either the Gehlen Organization or the CIA, because he had given Yockey's address to Eugene Derzhavin-Arciuk, head of the Munich-based RONND, the Russian National Socialist Movement. Weiss worried that RONND's ties to the CIA and the Gehlen Org may have led to Yockey's being compromised.[40]

From 1955 to 1957 Weiss searched for any hint that Yockey was still alive. He even turned to Adrian Arcand in Canada for answers. According to an ADL report, H. Keith Thompson learned from Arcand during a 1956 meeting that he was in touch with Yockey, news that elated Weiss. In August 1956, when Weiss came across a handbill distributed in West Germany denouncing the presence of U.S. troops on German soil, he thought that it might have been written by Yockey for the East Germans. Weiss also turned to a Meiji University professor named Dr. Hirokichi Innami for some possible leads.[41] Innami was well connected in Japan— so much so that he arranged for Weiss to meet with the Japanese prime minister in the Waldorf Astoria on 21 June 1957.[42] Because he made frequent trips to both East and West Germany, Weiss asked Innami to make inquiries about Yockey.[43] Finally, on 1 December 1957, an ADL file reported that Weiss was jubilant because he finally had proof that Yockey was alive and well.

From at least the spring of 1955 to the winter of 1957, Yockey seemingly vanished from sight. Did he spend part of that time in East Germany and the Soviet Union? At least one well-informed source believed that Yockey had a close Russian connection. In an interview in the early 1970s with a political science professor named John George, the source ("Mr. X") discussed Yockey. The transcript of that conversation was later published in George and Laird Wilcox's book *Nazis, Communists, Klansmen, and Others on the Fringe:*

> Author: Did you know Yockey very well?
>
> X: He was a rather shadowy figure. Yes, I knew him quite well for a rather brief time. He was a remarkable guy. I did know and like Yockey as a man.
>
> Author: Why was the FBI after him so much? They had him under surveillance for about 11 years. Did he really have . . . Nazi connections in Europe, or not?
>
> X: He had Soviet connections. . . . The current bunch who exploit him don't want to hear about that angle.
>
> Author: What was he doing with the Soviets?
>
> X: I think he was a coordinator of some sort. I think the Russians, particularly in Germany, were encouraging some of those radical rightist groups and parties, for their own purposes.[44]

John George told me that H. Keith Thompson was "Mr. X."

Notes:

1. "Lord Haw-Haw" was the radio name of William Joyce, a British subject who broadcast over Berlin radio in World War II. He was later executed for treason.

2. Peter J. Huxley-Blythe, letter to H. Keith Thompson, 28 September 1961.

3. William Goring report on the NRP in the National Information Center's *Newsletter* of December 1969–January 1970, p. 4.

4. Bogstad's information almost certainly came from the ADL. When I interviewed Bogstad by phone in the summer of 1995 he told me that I should speak to the ADL's Chicago representative from the 1950s, because the Bureau relied so heavily on the ADL. It seems likely that "T-1" was the Chicago representative of the ADL who supplied the FBI with information developed by the ADL in New York.

5. At that time Weiss was quite sick.

6. ADL files.

7. FBI report dated 12 September 1955. The FBI query was triggered by a 6 September 1955 *Washington Post* article. Apparently a photo of Hopkins resembled Yockey. It was later determined that Hopkins was a German civilian named Klaus Frederic Glaubitz.

8. Sometime after he had been spotted in the American Express office in Stuttgart, Yockey altered his "Edward Max Price" passport to read "Edward Max Briceman."

9. H. Keith Thompson archives at the Hoover Institute.

10. The *Russia* series is copyrighted by both Weiss and Thompson. Thompson told me that he heavily edited the essay because Weiss was never comfortable writing in English.

11. *Russia*, part one, summer 1955.

12. Ibid. Yockey's influence was evident throughout *Russia*. In part two (subtitled *Kto Kovo—Who-Kills-Whom*) Weiss and Thompson begin their argument with a discussion of the Prague Trials that is little more than an updated version of Yockey's 1952 essay.

13. Part three of *Russia* argued this point against an unidentified rightist publisher who was almost certainly Russell Maguire from *American Mercury*.

14. In *Einstein est mort!*, Weiss writes in connection with the "Russian soul": "Their little Mother Russia; in other words: a pure National Socialism of an Asiatic type."

15. In his press release "Max Planck and the Future of Western Civilization," Weiss recommends a book called *Sibierian*, by O. C. Pfeiffer of Safari Publishers in Berlin. Weiss also says Kurt Hichle of Eisenach, Germany ("one of Hitler's outstanding 'clima-scientists'"), was the creator of the Siberian project.

16. Weiss further claimed that the Russians, thanks to a team of German scientists operating under a Doctor Schulz, had designed a rocket far superior to those used by the West. The Soviets now had the technology to launch intercontinental ballistic missiles with a range of six thousand kilometers from secret underground launch sites in Central Asia. Although U.S. B-52s could still wipe out Russia's cities, America could no longer escape a devastating counter-attack.

17. During this time Weiss also published his "Max Planck and the Future of Western Civilization" essay, which praised the development of the "goose egg"–sized mini-bombs.

18. H. Keith Thompson's reply to my questionnaire.

19. This was the famous leftist artist Rockwell Kent. Thompson was Kent's literary agent.

20. The card Thompson sent me was an invitation from the Cultural Counselor of the Soviet embassy, Mr. Volsky, and the Information and Public Relations Office of the Soviet mission to the U.N., Mr. Bourov, to a reception at the Soviet U.N. mission in honor of Rockwell Kent.

21. H. Keith Thompson, letter to me, 24 March 1995.

22. Note that during this time Yockey was said by Thompson to have had ties to Czech intelligence.

23. Zorin's biography from *Prominent Personalities in the USSR* (Metuchen, NJ: Scarecrow Press, 1968) compiled by the Munich-based Institute for the Study of the USSR.

24. In issue 22 (July 1983) of *David McCalden's Revisionist Newsletter*, McCalden writes:

> HKT also took on representation of leftist artist Rockwell Kent and managed to break the "blacklisting" of Kent among publishers. He arranged for the publication of Kent's

Greenland Journal by Ivan Obolensky of New York. It is said that as a *quid pro quo* the grateful Soviets released a "Nazi war criminal" of HKT's selection.

25. H. Keith Thompson, letter to me, 14 March 1995. In *The SS: Alibi of a Nation* (New York: Viking Press, 1957), Gerald Reitlinger dates Rattenhueber's return from Russia as 10 October 1955, the same time Lisolette Franke-Gricksch left Russia.

26. H. Keith Thompson's reply to my questionnaire.

27. H. Keith Thompson, letter to me, 6 November 1995. He explains:

Weiss had nothing to do with Yockey paperwork. As I think already discussed by letter, I handled all of this, not only for Franz but for others, exclusively political, not
criminal, people . . . In those days Argentine and Paraguayan passports, birth certificates, etc. were available in signed blanks requiring only photos, stamps, some ink
insertions, etc. I was not a printer for nothing. I don't mean by that that I did it for
profit. I never charged a cent, and it often cost me for materials, etc.

Thompson also said that Yockey's passport operation that the FBI discovered in 1960 was exclusively Yockey's own doing. My strong suspicion is that the various birth certificates, etc., were meant for Thompson.

28. H. Keith Thompson's reply to my questionnaire.

29. After contacting the NSANL in June 1953, Truhill may have made an overture to the ADL sometime in the late summer or early fall. His decision might have been inspired by Pat Ward. In *I Love You, I Hate You* (Philadelphia: Andre Levy, 1955), Trujillo cites "the Queen of Avenue D" as saying (p. 50):

Why don't you smarten up, Manny? . . . If you can't get enough money from the Anti-
Nazi League, sell the information to someone else. Why can't you sell the information
you get from the Anti-Nazi League back to the [National] Renaissance Party? You'd get
twice as much that way.

30. Thompson says in the October 1954 *Exposé* series that the FBI raided Truhill's apartment that May because it was worried about his CP links. (The FBI also interviewed the NSANL's James Sheldon about Truhill.) Thompson says Sheldon was pay-
ing Truhill some $200–$300 to help finance him on a trip to the deep South to contact rightists for the NRP. (Weiss actually proposed that Truhill take the tour.) According to Thompson: "The trip never took place, because Truhill was arrested for illegal possession of firearms and held in jail long enough for the FBI to search his apartment. The search of Truhill's apartment disclosed a quantity of Communist literature and obscene pictures."

It is hard to know why the ADL exposed Truhill. The most likely explanation may be that the ADL suspected that Truhill was trying to set it up. If the ADL gave money to a "Communist," it could be used by the far right to prove a "Communist-Jewish conspiracy." It also should be noted that the ADL article mentioned that Truhill had been selling information to a "fringe outfit," a clear reference to Sheldon's NSANL.

31. After the ADL attack, Truhill sent a letter to Ed Fleckenstein defending himself. Fleckenstein had also accused Weiss of getting CP money.

32. Madole's article is called "A Reply to Nationalist Critics of the National Renaissance Party."

33. H. Keith Thompson's reply to my questionnaire. Martin J. Scheiman was so close to Weiss that in a version of Fred Weiss's will drawn up by Weiss (later cancelled) he stated:

> In the event that my said wife, MARIE WEISS, shall decease me or in the event that she and I shall die simultaneously or nearly so . . . I give, devise and bequeath my entire residuary estate in equal shares to my friend, H. KEITH THOMPSON, JR., of 49 Ann Street, New York, N.Y., and to my friend and attorney, MARTIN J. SCHEIMAN, Time and Life Building, New York, N.Y., absolutely and forever.

Weiss also appointed Scheiman (of Scheiman, Albert & MacLean) as his executor. In an 8 May 1995 letter Thompson told me: "I even discussed some of FPY's problems with Scheiman and he thought the regime had no real case against him, passport violations being on the 'minor' list unless used to defraud someone of money."

34. Since Ward was a key government witness against Jelke, Herz was very interested. Working with Arthur Roark, a private detective from Jelke's defense team, Truhill taped a conversation with Ward but it was not allowed into the proceedings after the judge ruled that it was not relevant. The trial was actually the second trial for Jelke, who had been arrested on 16 August 1952 by the vice squad. Based on testimony from Pat Ward that she had worked as a prostitute for Jelke from September 1951 to March 1952, he was convicted. Because the press and public had been banned from the courtroom, the conviction was reversed and Jelke's new trial began on 15 March 1955. He was eventually sentenced to two to three years in prison.

35. Roth seems to have devoted at least part of the first issue of a publication called *The Earth* to Ward. A report in the files of the NSANL dated 30 June 1955 says that Arthur Roark contacted Roth about Ward. It also says that Roth offered Pat Ward a thousand dollars for her story.

36. From an NSANL report of 9 June 1955, apparently from yet another NSANL informer who knew Ward.

37. It was also at this time (the summer of 1955) that Weiss and Thompson produced the first part of the *Russia* series.

38. H. Keith Thompson's reply to my questionnaire. In a letter dated 12 June 1994, Thompson told me:

> I never met Truhill (who as I recall was on Sheldon's payroll), but it was I who appeared at a prison outside Montreal and asked to visit Truhill. After some fencing around, the warden refused me a visit, but I left him some money ($50, I think) for his incidental expenses there. He was jailed on a drug charge.

39. In his report on the NRP for the National Information Center, William Goring writes of Truhill: "He moved to Canada, where he was arrested and given a two year sentence on a narcotics charge. After getting out of jail, he is rumored to have gone to Cuba, but nothing has been heard from him since." A 7 December 1962 report in the NSANL files says that Herbert Romerstein, a professional anti-communist, thought Truhill was working with Castro.

40. See the ADL file for Weiss's concern over Yockey. In a 5 March 1956 interview with FBI agent Brandt, Weiss said the same thing. "[Weiss] further indicated that he believes YOCKEY may be avoiding any contact with him because of an incident in 1955

wherein _____ furnished the subject's address to an individual in Germany, whom _____ learned was working for American Intelligence in Germany." For more on RONND, see the appendix "The Whites and the Reds."

41. Innami's mailing address was 21 Kasugacho, Chiba City, Japan.

42. ADL files. Innami was also said to have distributed Weiss's pamphlets in Japan. Weiss dedicated his 1957 pamphlet *The Great Question* to H. Keith Thompson, Herbert Sanborn (head of department of Philosophy and Psychology, Emeritus, Vanderbilt University), John H. Monk (editor of *Grassroots*), and "Professor Dr. Hirokichi Innami, Meiji University, Tokio, Japan." As for Professor Sanborn, H. Keith Thompson told me that he was a friend of Viereck's and had nothing directly to do with Weiss or Yockey, but may have had correspondence with Weiss.

43. ADL files. H. Keith Thompson writes: "Innami was a Japanese professor, my house guest on one occasion. At the Waldorf in the '60s ['50s—K.C.] he introduced Weiss to visiting Jap prime minister. Nothing came of all this insofar as I could determine." (H. Keith Thompson's reply to my questionnaire.)

44. John George and Laird Wilcox, *Nazis, Communists, Klansmen, and Others on the Fringe: Political Extremism in America* (Buffalo: Prometheus Books, 1992), pp. 253–54.

WORLD IN FLAMES (1958-JUNE 1960)

Even if we could not conquer, we should drag half the world into destruction with us, and leave no one to triumph over Germany . . . We may be destroyed, but if we are, we shall drag a world with us—A WORLD IN FLAMES!

—Joseph Goebbels

45
HITLER AND CASTRO: UNITED IN STRUGGLE?

Yockey spent the last two years of his life almost continually on the move, traveling up and down the West Coast with known stops in Reno, Miami, New York, New Orleans, Baltimore, and Washington, D.C., as well as Mexico and Cuba. The FBI resumed its hunt for him on 13 December 1957, after the Bureau's Chicago office sent a report to J. Edgar Hoover which read:

> On December 5, 1957, _____ advised SA LLOYD O. BOGSTAD that _____ furnished the following information: [Weiss] learned that YOCKEY was alive and has found a way to contact him. _____ requested that this information be handled with the utmost discretion in order not to compromise their source.[1]

Hoover's men followed some strange leads in their hunt. On 18 and 19 June 1958 the Bureau received information from a source in New York that an unidentified rightist

> has been in correspondence with YOCKEY, who now resides in Los Angeles, and _____ recently telegraphed $20.00 to YOCKEY in Los Angeles. YOCKEY is apparently attempting to secure funds to publish another book. _____ allegedly believes that YOCKEY is living in Los Angeles as a "pimp" or as a "gigolo." YOCKEY is also alleged to have been in Los Angeles for about one month and is being "kept" by some wealthy woman.[2]

To determine whether Fred Weiss had sent Yockey money, the FBI traced the records of the Western Union office in Middletown, New York, where Weiss had his farm. Phone company records were also checked to see if there were any toll calls to the Los Angeles area between 22 July and 20 October 1958. Failing to find any sign of Yockey, the FBI contacted the LAPD's vice squad on 29 July 1958 to determine whether anyone matching his description was acting as a pimp or gigolo in the Los Angeles area.

H. Keith Thompson's post office box was also placed under mail surveillance. After a letter arrived from a "Henry Adams" of Santa Barbara, California, the Bureau interviewed Adams and discovered that he taught at the University of California at Santa Barbara and was a friend of both Thompson and Viereck.[3] The FBI also investigated mail to Thompson from an unknown correspondent whose return address was Room 328, 232 South Hill Street, Los Angeles. On 24 February 1959 the Bureau sent Agent Ewing G. Layhew to Room 328, which turned out to be the editorial office of *One,* a magazine for gay men.[4]

One real lead did emerge from Thompson's post office box after the FBI learned that he was getting mail from Box 301 in Inglewood, California: the mailing address for *The American Nationalist,* a right-extremist magazine published by Frank L. Britton.[5] In an interview with the FBI on 27 February 1959, Britton mentioned a trip he took "East." Prior to leaving, he met a man in a downtown Los Angeles cafe who wanted to travel with him. He said that after he declined to let the man go with him, the man asked him to stop at an unidentified residence to pick up some books and money. When Britton appeared at the site, "_____ was not available when he was there." So Britton "left his name and address with _____ and, subsequently, _____ corresponded with him relative to the matter." According to Britton, "the man who requested him to contact _____ resembled the picture of YOCKEY."[6] The FBI report continued:

> _____ declared that to the best of his recollection _____ [almost surely "Weiss," given the length of the blackout line] sent him three letters and a telegram money order for $20. The letters and money for the telegram _____ asserted were turned over to the unknown man. He contended that the unknown man would contact him telephonically approximately every 10 days or two weeks to inquire of mail, and _____ said that if there was mail for the unknown man, they had arranged a mutually-agreed-to meeting place or the unknown man would stop at the residence to pick up the mail. He stated that the last he heard from the man was when he gave him the $20 from the telegram. He declared that he opened the mail but that it was in German and he was unable to read it; therefore, he had no idea what the subject matter of the letters was and merely assumed that it was relative to the books and money he had made inquiry of when on his trip to the east.

Although FBI deletions make it difficult to be sure, it appears that Britton was involved in a "cut out" operation that allowed Weiss and Yockey to safely communicate through a series of fronts. Documents in Yockey's suitcase also showed that he had spent some time in southern California.

In the fall of 1958, however, Yockey abandoned Los Angeles.[7] That September, "John Forest," a self-employed "writer of radio scripts" who held a California driver's license, moved from Hollywood, California, to Bellingham, Washington, close to the Canadian border. From September to November 1958 "Jack and Joan Forest" rented an apartment in Bellingham with an "E. J. Buchanan," whom Forest gave as a reference while obtaining a library card. Buchanan (another one of Yockey's false identities?) reportedly left Bellingham that September for Juneau, Alaska, where his mail was forwarded. When the Forests left Bellingham in November (and after notifying the Post Office to send their mail to Reno, Nevada), they traveled north. The FBI's Anchorage office later discovered that the couple had spent November 1958 in Alaska, most likely Juneau.[8]

During his travels up and down the West Coast, Yockey may have been trying to illegally obtain identity documents called "Z cards" from merchant seamen. After spotting his picture in the paper, a man contacted the U.S. Navy in June 1960 to report that he had seen Yockey at the Sailors Union Hall in San Francisco. According to the source, he was offering $500 to buy Merchant Marine documents and Z cards.[9]

Yockey lived for some time in San Francisco in 1959.[10] He also spent part of that year in Reno, Nevada. Alexander Scharf, the man at whose Oakland apartment Yockey was arrested, claimed he first met Yockey ("Mike Taylor") in Reno in April 1959. Documents in Yockey's suitcase showed that "Michael Joseph Taylor" had married "Ofelia Rodriguez" in Virginia City, Nevada, on 3 September 1959. Taylor also received a letter from the Irish Consulate dated 16 June 1959 and sent to 1790 Stewart St. in Reno. Under the name "Richard Hatch," Yockey rented a musical instrument (surely a piano) from the Reno Emporium of Music, listing as his address R#3, Sparks, Nevada.

During this period, Yockey traveled with a woman who called herself "Pat Hatch," "Pat Lagerstrom," or "Ofelia Rodriguez." Although the FBI never identified her, Yockey's daughter Francesca told me that she was a German-born woman named Ingeborg. Dr. Yockey met Ingeborg only once after her father's death but remembered the encounter because Ingeborg so physically resembled her mother, Alice.[11]

Yockey also spent some time in Cuba, and his activity there seems linked to Johann von Leers' propaganda network.[12] His San Francisco cellmate Jack Fambrough told the FBI that Yockey even made a cryptic reference to Egypt:

> YOCKEY had tried to make FAMBROUGH believe that YOCKEY's source of money originated from the passport operation, but FAMBROUGH said he did not actually believe that this was true. He said he vaguely recalled a reference by YOCKEY to the Suez, but he could recall nothing specific at the time regarding the matter.

Yockey mentioned his time in Cuba to Fambrough, a light-skinned black man who Yockey erroneously thought was Cuban. According to Fambrough:

> Yockey said he had left Cuba three or four months ago and was well connected with the Castro regime. Yockey had mentioned connections in Florida and Argentina, but indicated he did not wish to divulge these connections until we were out of jail.[13]

Yockey discussed his "connections with the Castro government, and had named names which had been seen by FAMBROUGH in newspapers as being members of the Castro government," although he could not recall the names.[14] In an interview in the 22 August 1960 *San Francisco Chronicle*, Alexander Scharf said that Yockey "told me once that he had been in Cuba—it was during the spring of this year—and that he had almost gotten a very high position in the Castro government." Yockey made a similar statement to his cellmate Philip Galati, who informed the FBI "that YOCKEY spoke of going to Cuba and claimed to have been there in the recent past, stating that he had attempted to see FIDEL CASTRO but had only gotten as far as one of CASTRO's secretaries."[15]

Yockey also had Latin connections in San Francisco. Fambrough said Yockey told him that "he had contacts among Spanish persons in the San Francisco area but he did not wish to contact them at this time." One of his San Francisco landlords told the Bureau that Yockey ("Shannon") had been visited by two "Spanish types" in 1960.[16] Mark Kirstead, the career criminal who called himself "Dale Marcus" when he met Yockey in Miami, was another important source. In a 1 July 1960 interview with Immigration and Naturalization Service investigator William Boggess, Kirstead recalled meeting Yockey ("Mr. Blair") and two of his Latin associates "in the last of February or early March of 1960" at the bar of Miami's Florentine Hotel.[17] During their conversation, Yockey gave Kirstead a card with his Havana address and invited him to pay a visit. Also recall that when Yockey and Kirstead again met in a jail holding area on 15 June 1960 (two days before his suicide), Yockey told Kirstead

> that he needed help badly and asked me [Kirstead] if I would help him. I said I would and so he gave me the following information that he wanted to deliver to Emanual in the editor's office of the *Bohemian* magazine in Havana, Cuba. He (Mr. Yockey) gave me this address: A-63-27 Calle—Entre 2 y 4th Calle, Vedado, Havana, Cuba. I was to give this address to Emanual and tell him to pass it on to someone by the name of Alferd [*sic*]. He would no [know] what to do.

Yockey's Latin connections extended to Mexico City, where he received support from a network linked not to an "Alferd" but to an "Alfaro," the famous Mexican artist David Alfaro Siqueiros, a hardline Stalinist, who organized the first botched assassination attempt on Leon Trotsky in Mexico City. In August 1960, shortly after addressing the Congress of Latin American Youth in Havana,

Siqueiros was jailed for attacking Mexican president Lopez Mateos's failure to visit Cuba due to American pressure.[18]

Yockey's introduction to the Siqueiros network came from H. Keith Thompson, whose ties to CP artists included Siqueiros and Rockwell Kent.[19] After Siqueiros's arrest by the Mexican government, Thompson became active in his legal defense and wrote a long article in the August 1963 issue of Lyle Stuart's *The Independent* about the case. According to the far-right author David McCalden, Thompson's defense of Siqueiros was actually returning a favor since "at one point, Siqueiros provided a safe haven and bed for Yockey, who was yet again on the lam from the FBI." When I asked Thompson if Yockey and Siqueiros had ever met in Mexico City, he replied:

> They did not meet. Yes, Siqueiros provided the name and address of a "safe house" there . . . Siqueiros and [Rockwell] Kent certainly knew each other. My relations with Kent were mostly 1960s (post Yockey), but I was asked in the '50s to see if I could help Siqueiros out with some gallery matters and a customs problem as I recall. I became involved with the people in N.Y. working in support of Siqueiros during his troubles with the Mexican Gov't, but this was in the '60s. My relationship with S[iqueiros] began with a request from one Elizabeth Gurley Flynn [a leading member of the CPUSA], whom I knew casually. She knew of my p.r.–literary agent work, etc. We had lunch and she asked me if I could not use my circles to assist Siqueiros. I was pleased to do so. I would not know if S. was NKVD, KGB, or whatever. Probably not. I think his connections reached higher than that as he was an "international figure" of repute in art circles. I believe his contacts were diplomatic.[20]

In a 24 September 1994 letter, Thompson again said that he was sure that Yockey never met Siqueiros: "I simply gave him a name and address of a 'safe house' which came to me from S[iqueiros]." What is certain is that Yockey did spend time in Mexico, since the FBI discovered a smallpox vaccination certificate issued to "Richard Hatch" on 19 March 1960 at the Laredo, Texas, quarantine station on the United States–Mexico border.

H. Keith Thompson's links to Siqueiros, however, didn't prevent him from supporting the Cuban dictator Batista—possibly even with guns.[21] According to Thompson:

> Batista had been double-crossed by the U.S. in favor of that sweet "Agrarian Reformer" (*N.Y. Times*), and of course Batista was not sufficiently "democratic" for the ugly Washington regime which, on the one hand, talked "anti-communism" while stabbing active anti-communists in the back. While the U.S. regime was perforce anti-*Soviet*, in a global sense, it was consistently pro-socialist, favored empowering radicals, etc. While U.S. doors were being shut in his face, Batista needed some connections in the arms field to keep his military strong. Others can open doors as some shut them.[22]

After Castro's victory, Thompson says he still "remained pro-Batista. I hope that I lit a fire under [Batista's] anti-Americanism. However, insofar as Castro was anti-American, that had my support."[23]

Thompson's political affiliations did not hurt his friendship with the treasurer of the New York branch of the pro-Castro Fair Play for Cuba Committee (FPFC)—Lyle Stuart![24] Stuart, Thompson, and Fred Weiss shared yet another link—they all used Martin Scheiman of Scheiman, Albert, and MacLean as their lawyer. Scheiman also represented Ron Taber, a co-founder and executive secretary of the FPFC, when Taber was questioned by J. G. Sourwine, lead counsel for the U.S. Senate Subcommittee to Investigate the Administration of the Internal Security Act, on 10 April 1962.[25] Stuart, Thompson, and Weiss remained friends with Scheiman until 1967, when Scheiman committed suicide in his law office in the *Time-Life* Building.[26]

Lyle Stuart also had his own "Yockey connection." When Stuart went to Cuba in July 1960, shortly after Yockey's suicide, he took with him letters from Thompson concerning Yockey. On 25 August 1960, Stuart wrote Thompson: "I received and mailed those letters for you in Cuba but was unable to locate the journalist to whom you addressed the enclosed. Thus I'm returning it."[27] When I asked Thompson about this, he replied:

When I knew Stuart was there [in Cuba], I wrote him a letter asking if he could find a journalist named Rodriguez, who was a Yockey contact . . . I wrote him one letter while he was in Cuba to see if he could find that journalist who had known FPY earlier. Stuart later replied that the letter embarrassed him and that the issue was "sensitive."[28]

While Yockey remained underground, the Fred Weiss–financed National Renaissance Party began making public alliances with an unusual combination of groups that included hard-core segregationists, black separatists, and representatives from Egypt, Iraq, Cuba, and the Soviet Union.

In the late 1950s the NRP developed fraternal ties to the National States Rights Party (NSRP). Founded in 1952 as the Christian Anti-Jewish Party, the Atlanta-based NSRP was led by former KKK member J. B. Stoner and Edward Fields, a chiropractor who had ties to John Hamilton's National Citizens' Protective League.[29] Ed Fields came into contact with the NRP in 1954, when he visited Mana Truhill's apartment and found it littered with Communist propaganda and a picture of Stalin. After the NRP officially dropped Truhill, Fields grew closer to James Madole and even asked him to help sponsor a 1959 NSRP conference in New York City.

Other one-time NRP members like Eustace Mullins and Matt Koehl[30] worked closely with John Kasper, who would later become the NSRP's 1964 presidential candidate. Mullins and Koehl knew Kasper when he ran a Bleecker Street bookstore in the mid-1950s called Make It New. (The title came from Ezra Pound's advice about art.[31]) Mullins and Koehl were both poets, and Koehl had once been associated with a magazine called *Poetry Chicago*. Mullins was close to both George Sylvester Viereck and Ezra Pound, and he regularly visited Pound in Saint Elizabeth's Hospital in Washington, D.C.[32] (Both Koehl and Mullins were also frequent visitors to Weiss's farm in Middletown, New York.[33]) In 1955 Mullins, Ed Fields, and Max Nelson created the Realpolitical Institute in Chicago, and a sister group called the Institute for Biopolitics.[34] Mullins and Nelson next set up a group specializing in "political engineering" and "creative propaganda" called M & N Associates.[35]

The NRP also had contacts among black militants who favored strict racial segregation. One of its closest black collaborators was a group called the African Universal Church, headed by Archbishop Clarence C. Addison.[36] The church had a political wing known as the Nationalist Party that held joint meetings with the NRP (whites and blacks sitting in separate aisles) at the Church's headquarters at 3802 Third Avenue in the Bronx.[37] The NRP also was in touch with the United Nationalist Africa Movement as well as with Benjamin Gibbon, the editor of *The African Times* and a member of the African Nationalist Federation Council. Other black nationalists with NRP links included James Lawson, Adbul Krim, and Carlos Cooks.[38] Many of them looked to the Middle East for support against Western colonialism and were especially taken with Nasser's endorsement of the Mau-Mau rebellion against British rule in Kenya.[39]

The NRP even maintained ties with Egyptian, Iraqi, Soviet, and Cuban representatives.[40] The NSANL learned about Madole's diplomatic contacts through an informant named Joseph Rudden, a former Father Coughlin supporter code-named "27" in the NSANL reports, who often accompanied Madole to diplomatic functions. On 28 November 1958, he reported to the NSANL that he, Madole, and "Mrs. Madole" (James's mother Grace) had recently attended a reception at the Iraqi Consulate on East 79th Street.[41] At the reception, Madole "was looking for a Mr. Evanoff [Ivanov?] from the Russian Consulate whom he has met and talked to at length there. M likes this Evanoff because he also hates Jews and seemed to share in many of Madole's ideas. But he didn't see him at the party."[42]

In the late 1950s Madole frequently visited the Soviet consulate in New York.[43] He primarily served as a go-between for Weiss who, as a German national, was always concerned about deportation.[44] Madole was particularly close to a Soviet press officer named Nikolai Bourov, and in 1959 he submitted a plan to Bourov meant to interest the Russians in backing an anti-Communist and anti-Jewish group. While Madole was meeting with the Soviets, other NRP members showed up at anti-Soviet demonstrations. When Khrushchev came to New York to address the United Nations, there was a large protest outside the Soviet consulate that included a highly vocal contingent of Hungarian exiles as well as some NRP members. On 20 September 1960, Rudden reported to the NSANL:

Madole is in a frenzy. Boy, is he peeved! I went over Monday to show him the pic- ture in Monday's *Mirror* of Di Angelo, Di Milo (dark glasses), and Ryan (up front, back turned). He hadn't seen or heard of it before. He had a fit! You see, Madole was so peeved because on Saturday he had talked to this guy Lucius [Sanchez]— now you must understand this is truly CONFIDENTIAL because Madole didn't tell anyone this but me and it could be traced back only to me; he and I only know—this guy Lucius is the go-between for Madole and this guy Nikolai Bouraf [Bourov] who's, I think, the Secretary of the Russian Consulate, or something like that. I read about him in today's *News*—something in connection with the Committee for Fair Play [for Cuba]. Anyway, right after talking to this guy Lucius on Saturday about the importance of trying to get the big Russians to recognize the Jewish question like Madole sees it, his boys turn up, completely unautho- rized by him, in a picket demonstration against the Russians. Madole is fit to be tied.[45]

Madole's ties to Cuba continued after Yockey's death. On 5 March 1961 Rudden accompanied Madole to the headquarters of the Castroite 26 of July Movement on Columbus Avenue, where they were to meet a man named Lucius Sanchez and pick up a pro-Castro propaganda film for an NRP meeting. According to Rudden, "two Jews and a Christian" were there and after one of them recognized Madole, trouble broke out. To make matters worse: "[Lucius] Sanchez did not show up. The night before there was supposed to be a big Cuban meeting and dance. Lucius did not get home until very late . . . I think Sanchez is connected with the Cuban U.N. delegation."[46] Without Sanchez there to help, "Jews in FPFC" made it impossible for Madole to get his movie.

Although Madole's personal relations with the Russians and the Cubans were secret, NRP propaganda for Russia and Cuba was quite open. On 4 April 1960, for example, the NRP sent out a mailing announcing an upcoming meeting to answer the question: "Has the Soviet Union become the 'chief breeding ground for anti- Semitism,' or were American Zionists trying to foment a 'Hate Campaign against a nation which dares oppose their aggressive aims in the Middle East?'"

Less than one month before Yockey's arrest, on 14 May 1960, the NRP held a pro-Castro meeting at the Avalon Studios on 230 West 43rd Street in Manhattan. Present at the gathering as "distinguished guests" were Charles Smith from the racist magazine *Truth Seeker* and American Nazi Party leader George Lincoln Rockwell. They heard Madole praise Red China for seizing "62 million dollars in property owned by Jews in Shanghai." After hailing Indonesia's Sukarno, Madole turned to developments in Cuba, telling his audience:

Fidel Castro took over and nationalized the Jew-controlled sugar plantations. Goldman, Sachs & Co. . . . the Jewish Wall Street banker was exploiting the poor Cuban sugar workers. Goldman Sachs can go to hell too . . . Our main enemy is right here in the United States. The Nationalist China Lobby wants us to start a war, but you will never find them fighting it. We will admit Chinese, Japanese, and Negroes into the NRP, but we'll make sure the Negroes don't intermingle with our women. Chinese and Japanese do not intermarry with whites.[47]

NRP propaganda praised Castro. In the March 1960 issue of the *Bulletin*, Madole's lead article began:

The Castro Revolution in Cuba bears a marked similarity to the previous rebellions in Africa and Asia which led to the creation of the Nasser regime in the United Arab Republic, the Kassem government of the new Iraqi Republic, the military regime of Ayub Khan in Pakistan, and the Sukarno government of Indonesia. The peoples of these newly liberated nations wished to throw off the oppressive yoke of foreign colonialism just as our heroic American ancestors rebelled against the unjust taxation and repressive laws of the British Empire in 1776. The Arab, Pakistani, Indonesian, Chinese, Cuban, and Latin American peoples also intend to halt the vicious exploitation of their land, labor, and natural resources by hordes of foreign Jewish parasites operating under the protection of the French, British, American, and Dutch flags. The nefarious activities of these Jews acting as merchants, gambling and narcotics czars, businessmen, and stock speculators are largely responsible for the intense hatred of America felt by most of the people of Asia, Africa, and Latin America . . . [In Cuba] the gambling casinos of the Jewish gangster Meyer Lansky were seized. Lands and factories sold to the Cuban American Sugar Company and the United Fruit Company by greedy Batista officials were nationalized. Jewish tobacco tycoons in the United States began to groan and pound the Wailing Wall at the thought of fat profits disappearing before their very eyes. When Castro refused to purchase ships from the Israeli government for his merchant marine and then strengthened his diplomatic and economic ties with the United Arab Republic, Iraq, and the Soviet Union, IT WAS TIME FOR THE USUAL JEWISH-SPONSORED "HATE CAMPAIGN" TO BEGIN VIA THE AMERICAN PRESS, RADIO, AND TV . . . Do not be deceived, fellow-Americans. FIDEL CASTRO IS TO CUBA WHAT NASSER AND KASSEM ARE TO THE ARAB WORLD.[48]

Nor did the NRP's politics change after Yockey's death. The February–March 1961 issue of the NRP's *Bulletin* ran pictures of Nasser and Castro next to a picture of Hitler.[49] In the article that followed, Madole wrote:

Only recently has the Castro regime in Cuba begun to clear away the debris of centuries and bring freedom to these backward people by opposing the economic bondage imposed by foreign Jewish exploiters and the mental and spiritual bondage imposed by the Roman Catholic hierarchy . . . Whether or not Castro can succeed in his mission, considering the centuries of racial degeneration which have taken place in Latin America under Catholic rule, is somewhat dubious BUT WE WISH HIM WELL AND WOULD DO ALL IN OUR POWER TO HELP UPLIFT HIS PEOPLE CULTURALLY, ECONOMICALLY, AND PHYSICALLY.

The same issue of the *Bulletin* advertised Nasser's *The Philosophy of the Revolution*, Castro's *Plan for the Advancement of Latin America*, and the Cuban magazine *Obra Revolucionaria*.

The NRP also continued to promote a Yockeyist pro-Russian line. In the November–December 1962 *Bulletin*, for example, Madole wrote an article called "Soviet Russia and the Jewish Question."[50] In it, he claimed:

> While Russia is purging the majority of her Jews from government office, President Kennedy has appointed 86 to major political offices . . . If foreign communism invades any area vital to the defense of Western culture, Americans will fight it to the last drop of our blood BUT WE SHALL NOT BE MISLED INTO CONDEMNING THE SOVIET GOVERNMENT FOR DEALING HONESTLY WITH JEWISH TREASON AND CORRUPTION AS OUR OWN GOVERNMENT SHOULD BE DOING.

In this same issue the NRP informed its readers that they could now acquire:

> *IMPERIUM* written by Francis Parker Yockey, who committed suicide in a San Francisco prison cell after imprisonment by the FBI . . . This book may rate beside *MEIN KAMPF* as a philosophy of history and politics for right-wing racial nationalism.

Reading the NRP's arguments today, what is most remarkable is how prophetic they were. Starting in the early 1960s, a trickle of officially sanctioned, overtly anti-Semitic Soviet literature tried to link Russian Jews to black market activity and other crimes. After the 1967 Arab-Israeli war, the number of anti-Jewish diatribes (with "Zionist" usually used as a substitute for "Jew") dramatically increased throughout the Soviet Bloc. Arguments that first appeared in tiny publications like the NRP *Bulletin* became commonplace in Soviet journals just a decade later.

Notes:

1. Bogstad's informant was almost certainly the director of the Chicago Anti-Defamation League, since the initial ADL report that Weiss had learned that Yockey was alive is dated 1 December 1957. Four days later the FBI's Chicago office received the same news.

2. Report from the Chicago FBI office dated 24 June 1958.

3. The FBI interviewed Henry Adams on 27 February 1959. Adams later wrote a monumental biography of Franz von Papen.

4. For a brief history of *One*, see Michael Bronski, *Culture Clash: The Making of the Gay Sensibility* (Boston: South End Press, 1984).

5. It was Britton's *The American Nationalist* that Johann von Leers had the NRP send to the Grand Mufti in Cairo in 1954. Britton's writings were also published in the NRP's *Bulletin*. See the February 1953 *ADL Bulletin* for a short profile of Britton.

6. The full text of the first part of the interview reads:

After viewing a photography of YOCKEY _____ stated that he did not recognize the individual in the photograph as anyone he knew. When questioned as to whether or not he was acquainted with _____, _____ related that he made a trip to _____ in 1958 and that he stopped at _____ and talked with _____ relative to some money and books. He declared that prior to making the trip to_____, he met a man in a cafe in downtown Los Angeles.

This man, according to _____, when he learned of _____ contemplated trip to _____, desired to travel east with him. _____ stated that since he did not know the man, he refused to allow the man to accompany him on his trip. He asserted that he had seen the man several times prior to this at the cafe, the name and exact location of which he was unable to recall, and that he had engaged in conversation with the man.

_____ contended that when he refused to permit the man to accompany him on the trip east, the man asked _____ to stop at _____ residence and pick up some books and money. _____ was not available when he was there at _____ stated that he left his name and address with _____ and, subsequently, _____ corresponded with him relative to the matter. He stated that the man who requested him to contact _____ resembled the picture of YOCKEY and insisted that he could not recall the name of the man and had no information reflecting on his past or present whereabouts.

7. Yockey returned to the Los Angeles area in 1959 because the FBI discovered a rent receipt from the Du Val Apartments in L.A. to "Richard Hatch" dated 10 June 1959.

8. FBI deletions make it impossible to be completely sure.

9. The FBI document states:

On June 11, 1960, SA HARRY F. ROTE, JR., was advised by Chief Petty Officer WILLIAM M. SIMPSON, United States Navy Communications Center, Federal Office Building, San Francisco, that SIMPSON had received a telephone call during the morning of June 11, 1960, by an unidentified man. The man advised that he had recognized newspaper photographs of YOCKEY as a person he had seen at the Sailors Union Hall, San Francisco, attempting to buy Merchant Marine documents and "Z" cards. He related that Yockey was offering $500.00 for these documents . . .

On June 13, 1960, _____ telephonically advised SA WAYNE K. WELCH that he had received an anonymous telephone call on June 11, 1960, from an unknown man who stated that he was a coastguardsman from a Coast Guard facility at Wilmington, California. The man said that he had recognized YOCKEY's photograph in the newspapers as being identified with the man who had been in the Wilmington, California, area about two months ago and had offered $200.00 to purchase seaman's "Z" cards. The unidentified caller hung up without furnishing additional information, according to _____.

10. An "Ofelia Rodriguez" of 2400 Sacramento Street got a voter registration card either on 28 July or 28 August 1959. As for Yockey, "Harry Francis Shannon" registered on "7/28/59" as a supporter of the far-right Constitution Party. The difference in a month may have been a clerical error. "Shannon" lived at 925 Geary. It turned out that "Richard Hatch" of 765 Sutter Street registered two days earlier, on 26 August 1959, as a San Francisco voter. Hatch, too, listed his affiliation as the Constitution Party.

11. Dr. Yockey, who could not recall Ingeborg's last name, told me she thought Ingeborg later lived in New York City and worked in a hospital as a lab technician. While it is not possible to say with complete certainty that "Pat Hatch," "Pat Lagerstrom," "Ofelia Rodriguez," and Ingeborg were all the same woman, it seems likely.

12. Recall in this connection that while he was in New Orleans Yockey spent almost all his time in his hotel room writing. Each day he would mail his work to some unidentified address. My guess is that he was writing anti-American propaganda. Also recall that in San Francisco "Mr. Shannon" showed some of his writings to another tenant who thought them "anti-American." Shannon also boasted that he got a thousand dollars a month for writings published in South America.

13. Jack Fambrough interview with FBI agents Parrish and Welch on 13 June 1960.

14. When the FBI asked Fambrough if he thought Yockey was exaggerating, he replied

> that YOCKEY appeared to be the type of person who would attempt to minimize his ability and importance. As an example, if he felt that he could obtain $50,000.00, he would state that he could probably obtain $5,000.00. [From an FBI conversation with Fambrough on 13 June 1960.]

15. 13 June 1960 Philip Galati interview with FBI agents J. Wayne Parrish and John F. Hamaker, Jr.

16. In Yockey's address book there is a reference to a "Hector Gonzales, 69 Lapidge c/o Rivera." The FBI also found Yockey had written an address on the back of a bank statement which appeared to be "RNTA-7, Al Fondo de u 3rd Estacion, Dragones y Zulotta-6-7100."

17. Again Yockey was accompanied by two Latins, a man named Emanuel (the spelling varies), and a woman named Shena who worked at the *El Mundo* newspaper. Kirstead also described Yockey's two Miami companions. From the INS report:

> Emanuel, last name unknown, 40 to 42 years of age; five feet six inches tall; 200 pounds, stout and heavy; wearing horn-rimmed glasses and has a mustache. Shena Dietz, 30 to 32 years of age; five feet seven inches tall; dark hair, attractive. Surname could be spelled Diece or Diaz.

18. Siqueiros also believed that the Mexican CP had failed the Cuban revolution. For a CP-style biography of Siqueiros, see Philip Stein, *Siqueiros: His Life and Works* (New York: International Publishers, 1994).

19. H. Keith Thompson also become the literary agent for the blacklisted artist Rockwell Kent. See, for example, two H. Keith Thompson articles in a special Rockwell Kent issue of *American Book Collector*, Vol. XIV, No. 10, Summer 1964.

20. H. Keith Thompson's reply to my questionnaire.

21. According to David McCalden:

> In 1955–58 HKT developed a political relationship with General Fulgencio Batista, dictator of Cuba. HKT represented an Argentinean-Bolivian combine selling arms to Batista to suppress Castro's rebellion. He also aided Batista in literary representation. Thompson was acknowledged in Batista's memoirs *Respuesta*, published by Manuel

Leon Sanchez of Mexico City in 1960 (pages 213–16). [From *The Revisionist Newsletter*, Issue 21, June 1983.]

In *Respuesta*, Batista does in fact mention Thompson. When I asked Thompson about his Batista ties, he said: "If you have read McCalden on the subject, that tells it reasonably accurately. I'm not going into details." It should be noted that in the 1950s there was an Argentinean-Bolivian weapons combine whose players included Otto Skorzeny, Hans-Ulrich Rudel, and two former SD officers living in Bolivia: Friedrich Paul Schwend and Klaus Barbie.

22. H. Keith Thompson's reply to my questionnaire.

23. Ibid. Yockey seems to have been aware of Thompson's activities, since in a manuscript he wrote on New Year's Day 1960 entitled "Estimate of the World Situation" (published posthumously by Weiss and Thompson as *The World in Flames*) he remarks: "In Cuba it [the U.S. government] forbade exportation of arms to the loyal Batista and thus helped Fidel Castro; now it is committed to the overthrow of Castro."

24. Lyle Stuart's role in the FPFC caught the attention of the U.S. Senate's Committee on the Judiciary's Subcommittee to Investigate the Administration of the Internal Security Act. On 8 February 1963 the Subcommittee's counsel J. G. Sourwine tried to interrogate Stuart about his role as FPFC treasurer. See the hearings on *Castro's Networks in the United States* by the Committee on the Judiciary's Subcommittee to Investigate the Administration of the Internal Security Act (Eighty-Eighth Congress, 1st Session).

During his testimony Stuart inserted into the record a long reprint from a series he had written in *The Independent* on the FPFC. Stuart reports that he joined FPFC while he was in Havana attempting to meet with Castro. (Stuart arrived in Havana on the weekend of May Day 1960 and stayed for 13 days, then again returned in late July for three more weeks.) In January 1961 Stuart resigned his position as FPFC treasurer, although he remained a member. He resigned after the group's co-founder Richard Gibson destroyed some FPFC records "to protect the membership" without discussing it with the rest of the New York executive committee. It should be mentioned that Stuart is well known as a world-class gambler and would have had knowledge of the casino worlds in both Reno and Havana.

25. Stuart published a book on the Cuban Revolution by Ron Taber, entitled *M-26*. (M-26 was shorthand for the Movement of July 26.)

26. Scheiman makes a curious appearance on page 677 of Dick Russell's book on the Kennedy assassination, *The Man Who Knew Too Much* (New York: Carroll and Graf, 1992). Scheiman was the go-between for a man who wrote a book called *Were We Controlled?* under the name Lincoln Lawrence; it argued that Lee Harvey Oswald had been under some form of mind control. *Were We Controlled?* was published by University Books, which was founded by Felix Morrow. Morrow later sold his business to Lyle Stuart. Dick Russell reports that after Lee Harvey Oswald's mother Marguerite read *Were We Controlled?* she called a Dallas assassination researcher named Mary Ferrell and told her: "I've got to find out who wrote this book because he knew my son." At the time of the call Marguerite Oswald was in close touch with H. Keith Thompson, who served as her literary agent when she wanted to sell Lee Harvey Oswald's letters.

27. From the H. Keith Thompson files at the Hoover Institute.

28. H. Keith Thompson's reply to my questionnaire.

29. The Christian Anti-Jewish Party became the United White Party in 1956. Then, in May 1958, it became the National States Rights Party after States Rights and Constitution Party groups merged with the United White Party at a Knoxville convention. The NSRP traced its spiritual origin to a 1940s Georgia-based paramilitary group called the Columbians led by Emory Burke.

30. Koehl was even appointed a leader of the New York NRP's "fully uniformed corps." See the June 1953 NRP *Bulletin*.

31. Koehl, Kasper, and Mullins were involved in a poetry scene whose "left wing" was the Beats. Henry Strutz (co-author with H. Keith Thompson of *Doenitz at Nuremberg*) was also a poet. His 1962 poetry book *Moon Howls* was dedicated to Allen Ginsberg. *Moon Howls* came with an illustration and a short commentary by Rockwell Kent.

32. Mullins wrote a biography called *This Difficult Individual Ezra Pound* (New York: Fleet Pub., 1961). On Mullins, see his two books *A Writ for Martyrs* (Staunton, VA: O.T.U. Christ Church, 1985) and *My Life in Christ* (Staunton, VA: Faith and Service Books, Aryan League of America, 1968).

33. Mana Truhill reported to the NSANL on 5 September 1953 that after one such visit Koehl had to leave New York:

> Kohl [*sic*] has left the City because he was involved in an incident. It seems that Kohl has a gun and was shooting it out of his car, and he shot at or toward a Jewish man wearing a skull cap, somewhere near Middletown, New York. The police started to investigate and were about to catch up to him, so he went back to stay with his family in Wisconsin.

34. Max Nelson (Maynard Orlando Nelson) first called attention to himself in the 1950s when, as a student at the University of Minnesota, he dressed up in a Nazi uniform. In *A Writ for Martyrs*, Mullins reports that the FBI tried to have Nelson put in a mental institution.

35. M & N Associates distributed poetry, including one ditty called "Goodbye!" that began:

> Goodbye nigger, goodbye Jew . . .
> And goodbye Puerto Rican too

It concluded:

> Goodbye junkies, do-gooders, and half-asses
> AND WELCOME EICHMANN AND HIS AUSCHWITZ GASSERS!

36. The Church (whose main publication was called *African Defender*) had been founded in 1927 by Laura Kofey, a Garveyite dissident who was assassinated one year later.

37. An ADL report notes a joint NRP/African Universal Church rally held on 15 December 1963 in the Bronx. Also present at the meeting were Dr. Josef ben Johannan and James Thronhill, the vice president of African Nationalists, Inc. Madole and James Cassidy represented the NRP.

38. Cooks, a famous Harlem street-corner agitator, ran the African Pioneering Syndicate, Inc., in the 1930s. He also published *The Street Speaker*. See John Roy Carlson, *Undercover* (New York: E. P. Dutton, 1943) for an attack on Cooks. On the Harlem nationalists, see Kurt Singer, *Spies and Traitors of World War II* (New York: Prentice-Hall, 1945). For a tribute to Cooks, see Robert Harris, *Carlos Cooks and Black Nationalism from Garvey to Malcolm* (Dover, MA: The Majority Press, 1992). Also see Cooks' 1955 speech praising Nasser reprinted in Harris. Volume IV of *The Marcus Garvey and Universal Negro Improvement Association Papers* (Berkeley, CA: University of California Press, 1983), edited by Robert Hill, has important references to Cooks.

An important study could be made of the way black nationalists inverted the "Yellow Peril" and Spengler's "Colored World Revolution" line and turned it into a rallying cry for their own movement. In this context, see the work of Ernest Allen, Jr.—in particular his "Waiting for Tojo: The Pro-Japan Vigil of Black Missourians, 1932–1943," in the Fall 1995 issue of *Gateway Heritage*.

39. Recall that in the mid-1950s the NRP maintained especially good ties to Egypt. The NRP also distributed propaganda from Indonesia. A pamphlet called *Revolution in Iraq*, issued by the Society of Graduates of American University in Iraq in defense of the Ba'ath uprising, was also disseminated by the NRP.

40. Madole was a regular at meetings of the Organization of Arab Students in the United States (OASUS) held at Columbia University.

41. Madole had very close ties to the Iraqis. The NSANL got one report that on 2 June 1958 Madole met with the Foreign Minister of Iraq. According to an NSANL report of 24 April 1959, the Iraqis wanted to know if Madole was willing to visit Baghdad. Madole was said to work for a Mr. Hilli and a Mr. Jewad. Jewad was reported to have been a member of the U.N. mission who was now a Foreign Ministry official in Baghdad.

42. Many of the names that appear in NSANL reports are spelled phonetically.

43. One ADL report said that Madole usually visited the Soviet "embassy" on Saturdays in 1961. A 29 April 1959 NSANL report says that Madole was interviewed by FBI Agent Edward Brandt, who wanted to know why he wasn't registered as a foreign agent.

44. During this time Weiss faced a new round of rumors accusing him of receiving political and financial support from Communist sources. On 29 April 1959 Rudden ("27") met Weiss on 86th Street in Yorkville. Weiss told him he was suing someone who had accused him of getting money from the Russians. One source for the charges that Weiss had CP ties was the anti-Communist investigator Herb Romerstein. According to a report in the files of the NSANL, Romerstein accused Madole of getting $16,000 from Soviet sources. We have come across the figure "$16,000" before because this was the amount Ed Fleckenstein had claimed that Weiss had gotten from Communist sources, so Romerstein may have been recycling old charges.

45. "Lucius" was thought by Rudden to have been originally from Peru. Rudden said that Madole had been told by the Soviet consulate that they were using Lucius as a go-between to the NRP. To make matters more confusing, Rudden (or whoever took notes

from him over the phone) transcribed the name "Lussig" when it is clear that this individual is "Lucius."

46. Madole also knew a woman at the Cuban Consulate named Dr. Plaz, who gave him copies of a Cuban pamphlet called *In Defense of National Sovereignty* to distribute.

47. From the files of the NSANL. Madole had been getting some heat from his Arab connections on his party's anti-black position. At one point he even proposed the development of a separate black wing of the NRP's "security guard."

Another report from the NSANL files about an NRP meeting held at the Henry Hudson Hotel on 27 April 1962 is almost identical to Madole's 14 May 1960 speech. According to this report, Madole

> said that Castro came into being in Cuba because all the capitalists in Cuba were foreigners; many Jews, exploiting the common people ... The Soviets and Chinese stepped into Cuba, the Middle East, in Indonesia and elsewhere, to give the people a better life.

48. The article was called "Facts Concerning the Castro Revolution in Cuba."

49. Under the pictures ran the caption: "PRESIDENT GAMAL NASSER OF THE UAR AND PREMIER FIDEL CASTRO OF CUBA ARE DESTINED TO LEAD THE PEOPLES OF AFRICA AND SOUTH AMERICA TO THE HEIGHTS OF ECONOMIC PROSPERITY AND CULTURAL ACHIEVEMENT. ADOLF HITLER'S ECONOMIC AND RACIAL DOCTRINES LAID THE FOUNDATION STONE FOR THE SURVIVAL OF ARYAN CIVILIZATION IN EUROPE AND NORTH AMERICA."

50. The article featured a cartoon entitled "Shocking Russian Anti-Semitism" that depicted a Russian soldier arresting a grotesque Jew holding a money bag. The Jew (who is trying to sneak off to Israel) says: "But comrade soldier, I'm a JEW first and a Russian second."

46

THE CARTO
CONNECTION

While Yockey continued his underground odyssey, Willis Carto, the man today most associated with Yockey, was beginning to emerge as a force inside the far right. Born in Fort Wayne, Indiana, in 1926, Carto served in the U.S. Army in World War II and earned the Purple Heart during fighting in the Philippines. After moving to San Francisco in the early 1950s, he worked for the Household Finance Corporation. Politics, however, was his true passion, and he soon became active in a conservative coalition called We the People, whose mission was to unite the disparate elements of the nativist right.[1] Carto was also the executive director of a small San Francisco–based sect called Liberty & Property that worked closely with We the People.

In the summer of 1955 Carto went on a a 7,500-mile tour across America to expand Liberty & Property's contacts with other rightists.[2] Carto first learned about Yockey when he visited St. Louis during the tour and met John W. Hamilton, a former leader of Gerald L. K. Smith's Christian Nationalist Crusade who now ran the segregationist National Citizens Protective Association. Hamilton gave Carto a copy of the rare London edition of *Imperium* that Yockey had brought to the United States in 1950 when he was working with Hamilton in Smith's CNC.[3]

Some of the ideas that made up "Yockeyism" were introduced to the American far right in Liberty & Property's no-frills newsletter, *Right: The National Journal of Forward-Looking Americanism.*[4] In its second issue, *Right* praised the Fred Weiss–H. Keith Thompson *Russia* series as "thought-provoking."[5] In March 1956, *Right* declared that the "greatest hoax of the age" was the idea that Russia was Communist. *Right* also noted that the important division over Russia inside the right was between those who claimed the Russian empire was internally weak and others, like Weiss, who argued that it was on the brink of achieving technological and military superiority over the West.[6] In *Right's* last issue (published in September 1960, just a few months after Yockey's death), the publication editorially embraced Yockey's argument that America's main enemy was the Jewish "culture distorter" and not the Soviet Union.

Carto, however, was never completely comfortable with all of *Imperium's* arguments. As a strong defender of segregation, he believed that race was the overriding issue for the American far right. His segregationist connections included the Virginia League, which was established in 1954. William Stephenson, the Virginia League's president, handled fundraising for members of the National States Rights Party (NSRP), who had been accused of bombing an Atlanta synagogue.[7] Stephenson and Carto were both on the directing committee of We the People.[8] Given these connections, it's not surprising that the February 1956 issue of the Virginia League's publication, *The Virginian*, ran an article in praise of *Right*. What *is* surprising is that in October 1956 an article by Carto that appeared in *Right* under the name "E. L. Anderson, Ph.D." extolling Marcus Garvey and black nationalism was reprinted in *The Virginian*.[9] *The Virginian* informed its readers that *Right* wanted as much information as possible on black nationalist groups in America.

Carto first became aware of black nationalism from an article in a Newport News, Virginia, publication called *Grassroots*.[10] A one-man operation, *Grassroots* was put out by Fred Weiss's friend John Monk.[11] The doyen of white racist support for black nationalism was Monk's fellow Virginian Earnest Sevier Cox, the author of books like *Teutonic Unity, White America* and *Unending Hate*.[12] Cox was also a friend of Marcus Garvey, the Jamaican-born founder of the Universal Negro Improvement Association (UNIA). Garvey thought so highly of Cox that in *Philosophy and Opinions of Marcus Garvey* he publicized his writings on race.[13] Cox, in turn, dedicated his pamphlet *Let My People Go* to Garvey.

After Garvey's deportation to Jamaica, Cox worked with a Garveyite faction called the Peace Movement of Ethiopia on a plan to voluntarily repatriate blacks to Liberia.[14] The push for African repatriation was taken up in Congress by Mississippi's racist senator Theodore Bilbo.[15] Money for Cox's plan was provided by the Pioneer Fund, founded by Col. Wickliffe Draper, a New York textile magnate and a major financier of far-right race theorists. Cox's work was also endorsed by *Right*.[16] Carto told Cox that repatriation was a valuable "flank attack" against "the inevitable niggerfication of America."[17]

Carto's connections in the segregationist right led him to join a mysterious organization called the Northern League for Pan-Nordic Friendship. Both Earnest Sevier Cox and William Stephenson were also Northern League (NL) members. Cox addressed a Northern League gathering called the Teutoburger Moot in July 1959 in Detmold, Germany; Stephenson let the southern-U.S. branch of the Northern League operate out of *The Virginian's* office and served as an assistant editor of the Northern League magazine *Northern World*.[18] (Besides *Northern World*, the NL also published *The Northlander* out of its Scotland headquarters.[19] After Carto joined, the League's West Coast headquarters became *Right*.[20])

The Northern League was officially launched in March 1958.[21] A Scotsman named Alastair Harper ran its European wing from League headquarters in Dunfermline, Scotland.[22] The League's founder and Central Organizer was Roger Pearson, an Englishman who at the time of the League's creation was living in Calcutta, India.[23] Pearson and Harper also wrote for Oswald Mosley's high-brow fascist publication *The European* in the mid-1950s.

The NL quickly established branches throughout the United States and Europe, including a cell for the western part of the United States created in 1958 through *Right*.[24] In 1959, Roger Pearson went on an extensive tour of the United States that included stops in New York, Chicago, Denver, San Francisco, Los Angeles, Houston, and New Orleans.[25] His visit to the States was part of an NL organizing drive that had already taken him to Teheran, Istanbul, Vienna, London, and Scandinavia.[26] A highlight of his American trip was the "Alphafest Moot" run by Carto, the NL's San Francisco Alpha Group Organizer.[27] The Moot was a three-day program of talks and seminars, and included an outdoor picnic in California's Redwood country.[28]

Pearson's biopolitical arguments were reflected in a 1960 essay by Carto ("E. L. Anderson, Ph.D."[29]) entitled "Cultural Dynamics: Why Do Civilizations Decline and What Can Be Done About It?"[30] Carto believed that, although *The Decline of the West* had accurately chronicled the fall of great civilizations, Spengler had failed to supply a "why" for the decline. Cultural dynamics argued that the collapse of empires was the result of an influx of alien ideals, religions, and peoples. Its adherents advanced a policy of "strict anti-imperialism" against the "disastrous trend toward cosmopolitan formlessness and disintegration of all different cultures, races, and nations."

Yet it was the vision of a noble future that most inspired Carto: In an all-italic paragraph, he wrote: *"Is man perhaps a bridge to something finer, greater, handsomer, more noble than ourselves? Yes, the dream that our genetic and cultural unit—our people—must dream began with Darwin and Nietzsche."* In another italicized sentence, he asserted: *"What assists the process of evolution is good; what assists the process of devolution is bad."* Carto, who called his mix of "ethical humanism" and genetic utopia "Evotism," concluded his essay: "I am an Evotist."

Although Evotism clearly differed from Yockey's highly spiritualized form of cultural racism, there were curious links between Yockey's world and Carto's. One link was Yockey's former European Liberation Front associate, Peter J. Huxley-Blythe, who merged British NATINFORM and *World Survey* into the NL in the late 1950s.[31] The FBI was aware of Huxley-Blythe's League ties. After he wrote to the FBI in October 1961 hoping to receive information on Yockey, the Bureau responded to his request with a form letter. An internal FBI note explained why:

> The salutation and closing of "Dear Sir" and "Very truly yours" are used in this instance since Bu[reau] files indicate that Huxley-Blythe in 1960 was an associate editor of the publication *Northland* [*The Northlander*] published in Scotland by the North [Northern] League. This organization promoted pro-Nordic friendship and was described by its representative in the U.S. as an international group dedicated to the preservation of the white race and as secretly allied with the U.S. white supremacy group the National States Rights Party.[32]

Huxley-Blythe co-published *The Northlander* with the NL's European leader Alastair Harper from League headquarters in Scotland.[33] Harper also knew another ELF member: Francis Parker Yockey. Harper reported meeting Yockey in a letter that appeared in the racist magazine *Truth Seeker*, whose book division, Truth Seeker Press, published the first American edition of *Imperium* in late 1962. In an editorial called "*Imperium*—A Controversial Book," a *Truth Seeker* editor commented:

> A Scotsman, Alastair Harper, in ordering a copy of *Imperium*, writes: Your decision to re-publish Yockey's book is a good idea. I met the man on one of my rare visits to London some years back. He was in the company of a chap called Francis X. Gannon, also an American. It is a pity that Yockey met such an end. He was intended for better things.[34]

Peter J. Huxley-Blythe, who was unaware that Harper had met Yockey until I told him, assumed that "Francis X. Gannon" must have been Harper's mistake for Yockey's British collaborator John Anthony ("Tony") Gannon. Harper, however, made it clear that Francis X. Gannon was an American, and it seems difficult to believe that he had mistaken Manchester's Tony Gannon for a Yank.[35] Also recall that Gannon had left England for South America by October 1954.

The name "Francis X. Gannon" does appear, however, in *America's Decline: The Education of a Conservative* by Professor Revilo P. Oliver, a professor of Classics at the University of Illinois.[36] Professor Oliver, who died before I could interview him, was one of the most important figures in the American radical right and a onetime Carto collaborator. In the fall of 1958, Oliver was approached by Robert Welch to become a founding member of the John Birch Society. In his discussion of the Birch Society in *America's Decline*,[37] Oliver reports that a Dr. Francis X. Gannon, who held a Ph.D. in American history, was "the most competent member" of Welch's staff and Welch's top researcher.[38]

Gannon was a protégé of Charles Callan Tansill, who taught Diplomatic History at American University in Washington, D.C., in the 1930s. Like Yockey's Georgetown friend the international law specialist Walter Jaeger, Tansill was an outspoken isolationist. After spending 1935 in Germany with support from the Carl Schurz Foundation, he became a Hitler enthusiast.[39] His pro-German views, which he expressed in numerous lectures and public forums, got him dismissed from American University.[40] He was later hired by Georgetown.

Tansill was close to both George Sylvester Viereck and H. Keith Thompson. According to Thompson:

> My Georgetown friend was Charles Callan Tansill, Prof. of History and author of many books and articles . . . Tansill was a member of the Viereck circle. I met him there frequently, visited with him in Washington, and did some favors for him in the publishing world. He was under constant pressure at Georgetown because of his views on segregation . . . I gave FPY a letter to Tansill but don't remember if they ever met.[41]

After retiring from Georgetown in 1958, Tansill began writing articles attacking integration for John Birch Society publications.

Had Tansill's protégé hooked up with Yockey and Harper in England? Unfortunately, Dr. Gannon died before I could interview him, and I was unable to locate Alastair Harper. Still, there are some important facts worth noting. Recall that the first version of Robert Welch's *The Politician* contained the famous charge that President Eisenhower was a Communist agent. General Pedro Del Valle's Washington-based Defenders of the American Constitution (DAC) and Arthur Keith Chesterton's London-based League of Empire Loyalists (LEL) had been making similar claims for some time. The DAC and LEL had direct organizational ties. As Welch's lead researcher, Gannon almost certainly had contact with both groups.

Willis Carto also had close ties to both the DAC and, for a brief period, the John Birch Society. In January 1958, around the time he became active in the Northern League, Carto created the Liberty Lobby. On 4 July 1958, the Liberty Lobby set up a research department in the Washington office of the American Council of Christian Laymen. Later that same year, Colonel Eugene C. Pomeroy, who had served as the DAC's liaison to the LEL in the winter of 1954, became the Liberty Lobby's Washington Secretary.[42] Carto briefly worked for the John Birch Society in the late 1950s and wrote an article for the Birch Society journal *American Opinion*.

I suspect that Yockey, Francis X. Gannon, and Alastair Harper may have met at some London far-right conclave linked to the LEL. Like Yockey, A. K. Chesterton was a "spiritual racist" strongly influenced by Spengler. Again like Yockey, Chesterton argued that the threat of a Soviet attack on Europe was being used "as part of an elaborate conspiracy to reduce the historic nations of Europe to economic impotence" by Wall Street and the Jews.[43]

It may also be significant that one of Chesterton's top LEL lieutenants was none other than Guy Chesham, who co-founded the ELF with Yockey and Gannon but who later had a falling-out with Yockey for personal, not political, reasons.[44] It is not impossible that the two men later resumed contact, especially given the similarity of Yockey's and Chesterton's arguments about the American threat to Europe. In his 2 October 1961 letter to the FBI soliciting information about Yockey, Peter J. Huxley-Blythe pointed out that

> Guy Chesham was instrumental in founding the British weekly newsletter *Candour,* edited by A. K. Chesterton, and its subsidiary organization THE LEAGUE OF EMPIRE LOYALISTS, both of which are virulently anti-American. When a British journalist wrote an anti-Communist article and submitted it to Chesterton he was invited to the latter's home for a weekend to discuss current politics. During the course of the weekend, Chesterton told the journalist he should refrain from attacking the Soviet Union and communism because they were not the real danger and that he should concentrate upon attacking the real enemy, the United States.

If Yockey, Francis X. Gannon, and Alastair Harper did meet, they did so after 1954, since John Anthony Gannon would certainly have been aware of an American named "Francis X. Gannon" in Yockey's circle. In his letters to Keith Stimely, Gannon failed to mention the existence of any other American, much less one with a name similar to his, during the time he knew Yockey.[45] It seems likely then that Yockey met Harper and Francis X. Gannon in London sometime after October 1954 but before he returned to the United States in late 1957 or early 1958.[46]

Fred Weiss also had his own close ties to the Northern League's East Coast outlet, *Truth Seeker* magazine. *Truth Seeker* and *Right* were so close that the two publications have been described as "the immediate antecedents of the Liberty Lobby complex."[47] It was Willis Carto's fundraising efforts, combined with Weiss's influence at *Truth Seeker,* that led Truth Seeker Press to publish the first American edition of *Imperium* in 1962.

Notes:

    1. In 1955, We the People sponsored a Constitution Day Convention in Chicago that attracted some 600 delegates.

    2. See Liberty & Property's Progress Report No. 4 (4 August 1955) on Carto's trip. During this journey Carto first conceived the idea for a centralized Washington-based lobbying organization, which became the Liberty Lobby. In August 1957 Liberty & Property's journal *Right* reported: "Liberty Lobby Being Formed" with Carto as executive secretary.

    3. Information on Carto and Hamilton from my interview with Willis Carto. In the fall of 1956 Hamilton was arrested for sodomy with a 15-year-old male. After his arrest, he was forced out of his leading position in the National Citizens Protective Association.

    4. Liberty & Property also published an extensive directory of far-right groups.

    5. *Right,* November 1955.

    6. In April 1958 *Right* ran a picture of Fred Weiss ("a disciple of Spengler") and reported that he believed that "the West is rapidly on the downgrade and that the youth-

ful USSR is to be the arbiter of the future." *Right* also ran an article by Eustace Mullins that praised Weiss. In its June 1958 issue *Right* published an article that presented Russian-style Communism as split between a nationalist "Soviet imperialist" wing and a Zionist-led form of Trotskyism. Russian support for the Arab world meant that the Soviet Union, by its "anti-Zionist foreign policy . . . had set itself in opposition to international Zionism, which has been almost inextricably bound up with international Communism since the very beginning."

7. *Common Sense,* 15 September 1958.

8. Stephenson was elected to the National Board of Directors of We the People in 1956. Carto was listed in 1957 as a regional vice president of the group. For a look at the mid-1950s right, see Arnold Forster and Benjamin Epstein, *Cross-Currents* (New York: Doubleday, 1956).

9. "E. L. Anderson, Ph.D." in the spring of 1960 was listed as an associate editor of *Northern World.*

10. Carto told me this when I met him at the Liberty Lobby's headquarters in Washington.

11. Monk printed some of Weiss's essays, including one called "American Arrogance of Thought in World Affairs" in the April 1959 issue of *Grassroots.* Monk strongly supported the Weiss-Yockey line on Russia, although in the August 1955 issue of *Grassroots* Monk denied that he was a Yockeyist. In a reply to another rightist named "Mr. B_____," Monk wrote: "I know nothing of Ulick Varange of whom you speak, whose real name you say is Francis Parker Yockey ('Field'). You are off again when you say to me ' . . . your interpretations were fashioned not by Nationalists but by the Anglo-American section of the Agitprop organization in Prague.' My interpretations are fashioned by myself, by the facts I dig out of the books I find on the shelves of the library here in Portsmouth, Va., U.S.A." "Mr. B_____" was most likely Peter J. Huxley-Blythe.

12. For background on Cox, see Ethel Hedlin's unpublished 1969 M.A. thesis from Duke University entitled "Earnest Cox and Colonization: A Study in White Racism and Black Nationalism."

13. Cited from Cox's address to the Northern League's July 1959 Teutoburger Moot in Detmold, Germany, entitled "The Monument to Herman Whom the Romans Called 'Arminius.'"

14. In its February 1957 issue *The Virginian* ran an article by Mrs. Alberta Spain, the secretary general of the Peace Movement of Ethiopia.

15. Carlos Cooks, the Harlem Garveyite, was also involved with Bilbo.

16. In 1956 the mailing address for the Joint Council for Reparation was a *Right* post office box in Sausalito, California.

17. Carto's 1955 letter to Cox is cited in the 10 September 1971 *National Review* exposé of the Liberty Lobby, by C. H. Simonds. Carto also expressed his ideas in a 1956 letter to Judge Tom Brady, a member of the Mississippi Supreme Court and a founder of the White Citizens' Councils. Carto told Brady: "THE ISSUE IS NOT IDEOLOGICAL. THE ISSUE IS ETHNOLOGICAL."

18. In October 1957 *The Virginian* ran its first ad for *Northern World.* The paper also had a column on "Nordic Culture" that featured essays by Northern League writers like

Alastair Harper, who contributed a piece to the November 1957 issue. In 1957 *The Virginian* reorganized itself as an upscale-looking publication and added to its staff General Pedro del Valle of *Task Force* and the Defenders of the American Constitution. *The Virginian* was linked to the White Citizens' Councils of America and to a sister organization called the South Carolina Grass Roots League, Inc. The director of the Virginia League was a rightist named B. M. Miller, who was also elected to a position with We the People.

19. Like *Right, The Northlander* argued that Russia was part of the "white race." In an article called "Russia versus China" in its November 1960 issue, *The Northlander* editorialized:

> History forces courses of action upon people, and Russia is going to find herself forced to admit to being a European "white" power as the world tension which she herself has so assiduously cultivated continues to rise. We shall then see what happens; but would like to make it clear that the Slav people proper, where they have not been influenced by racial admixture from the east and south, are akin closely to the Teutonic and Celtic peoples, and have no dispute with them.

Northern League activity behind the Iron Curtain came to light in a 30 August 1960 story published in the Norwegian paper *Dagbladet* entitled "Nynazistiske 'rasedyrkere' over hele Europa" (Neo-Nazi "Cultivators of Race-creed" over All of Europe). In the article, a *Dagbladet* reporter recalled his encounter with a Northern League operative. While in Wrochlaw, Poland, that summer on a writing assignment, the reporter met "an over-officious tourist with pamphlets of the organization." So strange was the incident that the reporter and another journalist wondered if the man was really a provocateur sent by the Polish secret service to entrap them. The January 1961 issue of *The Northlander,* which translated the *Dagbladet* story into English, had a different interpretation:

> We are interested to note here that instead of praising the League for its activities in Communist territory—behind the Iron Curtain in Communist-Polish occupied Germany, in fact—the *Dagbladet* calmly accepts the Russian-dictated transfer of East Germany to Poland, at the time of the seizure by Russia of Eastern Poland after the war, for Wrochlaw is really the German town of Breslau. One is left with the impression that the Communists are our friends, that Breslau is really Polish, and that the League's agents are engaged in evil, disruptive work.

20. Carto married a German woman named Elizabeth Waltrud in either 1958 or 1959.

21. On the announcement of the founding of the Northern League, see *The Northlander* of April 1958 (Vol. 1, No. 1). For an analysis of the Northern League, see Werner Smoydzin, *Hitler Lebt!* (Pfaffenhofen: Ilmgau Verlag, 1966), pp. 135–44.

22. The group maintained an office in Coventry under the guidance of Gordon Lang, and another office in Düsseldorf run by a *Northern World* editor named John P. Wardle.

23. Born in 1927, Pearson obtained his B.Sc. (honors), M.Sc., and Ph.D. from the University of London. Following commissioned service with the British Indian Army at the close of World War II, he spent some 16 years in the Far East and Africa as a company director of the Pakistan Tea Association, becoming chairman in 1954. Information

on Pearson is from a biographical sketch in the publication *South Africa—The Vital Link*, published in 1976 by Pearson's Washington, D.C.–based Council on American Affairs.

24. *The Northlander*, November–December 1958.

25. During this tour Pearson met with Gerald L. K. Smith in Los Angeles. See Smith's report in the September 1959 issue of *The Cross and the Flag*.

26. *The Northlander*, April–May 1959.

27. *The Northlander*, June–July 1959. After his American tour, Pearson returned to Germany to attend the League's Teutoburger Moot.

28. Carto's close friend Byram Campbell also attended the gathering. Campbell, who wrote for both *Northern World* and *Right*, was best known for his book *American Race Theorists* (Boston: Chapman and Grimes, 1952) attacking integration. The January–February 1959 issue of *The Northlander* had an article praising Campbell. Campbell dedicated his book *The World of Oneness* (New York: Vantage Press, 1956): "To Willis A. Carto because he is working for a sane and better society." Campbell was also close to Ralph C. Forbes, a prominent "Aryan Nations"–type leader in California. See Campbell's obituary in *Truth Seeker* for July 1965.

29. In *Power on the Right* (Palo Alto, CA: Ramparts Press, 1971), p. 152, William Turner writes of Carto's activity in the late 1950s:

> Still, Carto remained in San Francisco, where he had repaired after his falling-out with [Robert] Welch, and the late Colonel Eugene C. Pomeroy of the Defenders of the American Constitution acted as the Liberty Lobby's Washington representative. Carto worked from a small office bedecked with Nazi symbols and pictures of Hitler and cluttered with Birch Society and British Israelite literature. In one issue of *Right* he continued his anonymity by writing a "guest editorial" under the name of a "scholar" called E. L. Anderson, a name he evidently appropriated from the deceased uncle of an unpaid helper. (The helper, Norris Holt, who serviced Carto's postal boxes while he was on his frequent trips to Washington, the South, and other waypoints, told me this.)

30. Carto was so taken by the essay that he republished it 11 years later in the Summer 1971 issue of the Carto-controlled *American Mercury*.

31. In its June 1958 issue, *The Northlander* reported:

> An important step has been taken in the recent arrangement with Mr. Peter J. Huxley-Blythe by which *World Review* [*sic*] will be incorporated with *The Northlander* as from July 1958. Unity is strength and *The Northlander* is pleased to welcome Mr. Huxley-Blythe and his former associate editor, Mr. J. B. Ashworth, to the Editorial Staff.

The Northlander corrected its error. In its January–February 1959 issue the headline read: "The Northern League Northlander: Incorporating World Survey."

32. The FBI note is dated 12 October 1961.

33. See note in *The Northlander* of June–July 1959. At that time the publication came out of 23 Rolland Street in Dunfermline, Scotland. According to a notice in the January–February 1959 issue of *The Northlander*, the publication of the March 1959 issue had been shifted to England from Calcutta and would now appear "under the editorship of Mr. P. J. Huxley-Blythe, former editor of WORLD SURVEY."

34. See the February 1963 *Truth Seeker*, Vol. 90, No. 2, p. 30.

35. Harper was something of an expert on things American. In the May 1957 issue of Oswald Mosley's journal *The European*, he wrote an essay entitled "The American Film Today" examining American culture through its cinema.

36. Revilo P. Oliver, *America's Decline* (London: Londinium Press, 1981).

37. Ibid., p. 162.

38. Gannon also wrote an exposé entitled *A Biographical Dictionary of the Left* (Boston: Western Islands, 1957).

39. The German ambassador Hans Dieckhoff sent copies of Tansill's book *America Goes to War* to the Amerika Institut in Berlin, which gave it to Nazi leaders like Hermann Göring. Robert Herzstein, *Roosevelt and Hitler* (New York: Paragon House, 1989), pp. 388–89, 401.

40. On Tansill, see Warren Cohen, *The American Revisionists: The Lessons of Intervention in World War I* (Chicago, IL: University of Chicago Press, 1967).

41. H. Keith Thompson, letter to me, 31 October 1994.

42. Pomeroy also played an active role in helping to get Ezra Pound out of St. Elizabeth's Hospital. In April 1958 *Task Force* ran a story entitled "Ezra Pound Release Endorsed by Defenders [of the American Constitution]."

43. David Baker, *Ideology of Obsession: A. K. Chesterton and British Fascism* (London: I. B. Tauris, 1996), p. 195. Chesterton's views led one British rightist to conclude that he was a crypto-Communist. On Chesterton and Spengler, see chapter eight of Baker's book.

44. Recall that Tony Gannon said that Yockey wanted Chesham to divorce his wife.

45. Gannon even asked Stimely to try to discover the identity of an American called "St. Ignatius Loyola," who wrote to Yockey while he was in England in the 1940s. Gannon would have surely suggested to Stimely the name "Francis X. Gannon" to determine if he was "St. Ignatius."

46. Of course, it is possible that Yockey revisited Europe after his return to the United States, although I found no evidence that this was the case.

47. See Frank P. Mintz, *The Liberty Lobby and the American Right: Race, Conspiracy and Culture* (Westport, CT: Greenwood Press, 1985), p. 66. Mintz's book provides an excellent overview of Carto's network.

47

"WHITE MEN
OF THE WORLD,
UNITE!"

While *Right* and *The Virginian* served as Northern League contact organizations for the West and South, the League's East Coast outlet was the Manhattan-based publication *Truth Seeker*, which was edited by Charles Lee Smith, the founder of the American Association for the Advancement of Atheism and a co-founder of the National Liberal League.[1] In the mid-1950s, the Arkansas-born Smith turned *Truth Seeker* into a platform for fascist race theory.[2] Rightists like Eustace Mullins and Matt Koehl began writing regularly for Smith,[3] and *Truth Seeker* contributors spoke at the publication's "Racist Forums."[4]

Smith also worked closely with the National Renaissance Party: His 38 Park Row office became a gathering place for NRP supporters, and NRP member Frederich H. Polzin served as *Truth Seeker*'s secretary.[5] *Truth Seeker* printed NRP propaganda leaflets, which were distributed at Racist Forums along with the Northern League's *Aims and Principles* pamphlet.[6]

When the Northern League magazine *Northern World* began publishing in 1957, *Truth Seeker* (under the headline "White Men of the World, Unite!") praised it as "the only journal in the world devoted exclusively to Nordic history, culture, and problems."[7] Smith also attended the NL's California Alphafest and the League's Teutoburger Moot held in Detmold, Germany, from 27 July to 1 August 1959. Earnest Sevier Cox (the "dean of racists in North America," according to *Truth Seeker*)[8] and *Right* editor Edward Vargas were the other American delegates at Detmold.[9] All three attended a wreath-laying ceremony at the Armenius monument in the Teutoburger Wald (forest); the monument commemorated a battle fought in 9 A.D., when Armenius (or Herman) destroyed the Roman legions sent to conquer Germany.[10]

Smith then headed to England. On 4 August 1959 he addressed a London meeting presided over by Colin Jordan, a Northern League member and founder of the White Defense League (WDL) who later became the leader of the World Union of National Socialists (WUNS).[11] Jordan formed the WDL to take advantage of racial tensions unleashed during the summer of 1958, when riots between whites and immigrants from Pakistan, India, and Jamaica broke out in several London neighborhoods.[12] After returning to America, the elderly Smith became involved in NRP-sponsored anti-integration protests.[13]

Like the NRP and the WDL, the National States Rights Party (NSRP) was another Northern League–allied organization.[14] Yet a casual reader of League publications like *Northern World* would find no stormy calls to arms, pictures of Jews with long noses, blacks with thick lips, or swastikas. *Northern World* could pass for a slightly offbeat folkloric journal with a soft spot for J. R. R. Tolkien's *Lord of the Rings* trilogy; only a careful reader would be struck by an occasional notice like the one in the Winter 1960–61 issue reporting that the NSRP was willing to send a free copy of *Thunderbolt* to any *Northern World* reader.[15] The FBI believed that the Northern League and the NSRP were involved in an alliance since, in its note on NL member Peter J. Huxley-Blythe, the Bureau cited the League's "representative in the U.S." as reporting that it was "secretly allied" with the NSRP.

The NSRP was not for armchair bigots: In June 1958, the group bombed a black church in Birmingham, Alabama.[16] An Atlanta synagogue was also bombed in October 1958. Although five NSRP members were arrested, they were acquitted because the jury blamed the bombing on an FBI informant. The verdict was particularly satisfying to William Stephenson, editor of *The Virginian* and assistant editor of *Northern World*,[17] since he had handled fundraising for the accused bombers' legal defense.[18] Nor was the Atlanta bombing all that unusual since, beginning in 1957, there had been a series of bombings and attempted bombings of synagogues and Jewish educational and recreational buildings in nine American cities: Charlotte, North Carolina; Gastonia, North Carolina; Miami, Florida; Nashville, Tennessee; Jacksonville, Florida; Birmingham, Alabama; Kansas City, Missouri; Gadsden, Alabama; and another attack in Atlanta.[19]

Northern League propaganda popularized "biopolitical" arguments advocated by Neue Europäische Ordnung co-founders René Binet and Guy Amaudruz in the NEO's founding "Zurich Declaration."[20] One leading American "biopolitician" was *Truth Seeker* regular Robert Kuttner, who later wrote for Willis Carto's *American Mercury* and *Spotlight*.[21] In a March 1959 *Truth Seeker* essay entitled "Biopolitics: The Theory of Racial Nationalism," Kuttner explained that biopolitics "re-emphasizes the importance of race," especially "the basic truth that every man is part of a biological kingdom, his race, to which he owes his primary loyalty." By exciting "the kinship feeling of peoples of European stock," Kuttner argued that biopolitics could unify Europe in a way that Christianity no longer could.

The close ties between *Truth Seeker* and a figure like Weiss, who more closely identified with Yockey's neo-Spenglerian brand of spiritual racism, may appear puzzling. Yockey, however, seems to have had longstanding ties to the New European Order and may have attended the NEO's 1951 Zurich convention. More puzzling are the Northern League's links to the European Social Movement (the "Malmö International"). Northern League founder Roger Pearson's early essays appeared not in some semi-illegal, NEO-affiliated sheet, but in the much more upscale Malmö International–aligned British publication *The European*, which was sponsored by Sir Oswald Mosley.[22] *The European* also carried one of the earliest ads for the NL's *Northern World*.[23] Another NL contributor to *The European* was Alastair Harper, who had met Yockey in London.[24] Harper also knew Charles Smith: In a report on Smith's European tour, *Truth Seeker* noted that on the afternoon of 5 August 1959 he had

> met Mr. Alastair Harper from nearby Dunfermline, who took him to see Dr. Robert Gayre, author of the [Northern] League pamphlet *The Northern Face*, for an enlightening discussion. Dr. Gayre has first-hand knowledge of how the leftist-leaning Liberals and infiltrating undercover Communists gained control of the West when the war ended.

Robert Gayre was a Scottish aristocrat whose clan name was Robert Gayre of Gayre and Nigg. A physical anthropologist and heraldry expert, he founded and edited a journal of physical anthropology and race theory called *Mankind Quarterly*. After Gayre retired from *Mankind Quarterly*, Roger Pearson took over as its editor in chief and publisher.[25] Gayre may have been a guiding light behind the NL's creation, since both he and Roger Pearson were living in India at the time of the League's founding.[26] Gayre also played an important role in the Malmö International as one of four members of that organization's "study commission."[27] Another commission member was the Austrian volkish publisher Wilhelm Landig, who ran the NL's Vienna office.[28]

Robert Gayre founded *Mankind Quarterly* in 1960 to refute UNESCO-type scientific arguments for racial equality. His journal enjoyed support from such luminaries as Professor R. Ruggles Gates, the former president of the Royal Anthropological Institute in London; Professor Henry E. Garrett, a past president of the American Psychological Association; and Professor Corrado Gini of the University of Rome. All three had strong right-wing ties. Gates, for example, was a pre-war contributor to the German race journal *Zeitschrift für Rassenkunde*, while Garrett supported the White Citizens' Councils. As for Professor Gini, he had played a leading role in the formulation of orthodox Italian fascist race theory in the 1930s.

The International Association for the Advancement of Ethnology and Eugenics (IAAEE) was established in 1959, with *Truth Seeker*'s Robert Kuttner as president, to further advance the cause of biopolitics.[29] Kuttner, who became an editor of *Mankind Quarterly*, would later testify before the House Committee on the Judiciary on the evils of school desegregation as a spokesman for Willis Carto's Liberty Lobby. The IAAEE's general secretary was a former Queens College student named Donald Swan. A *Truth Seeker*/Racist Forum regular and friend of H. Keith Thompson, Swan also went by the name "Donald Walker" and "Thor Swenson." H. Keith Thompson also worked with the IAAEE:

> I did all the printing for the IAAEE, a distinguished group of ethnologists, many of international repute, examining racial differences from a scientific point of view . . . They were funded by a foundation set up by Col. [Wickliffe] Draper, and produced a series of booklets examining these matters. Their findings were used extensively in preparing defenses to *Brown v. Board of Education*, and by the White Citizens' Councils . . . [Roger] Pearson acquired Donald Swan's library on race after Swan's death from complications of diabetes. Swan's library was one of the best on the subject. I helped him to acquire some of the books from Europe.[30]

Swan also wrote for *Neue Anthropologie*, the German sister publication of *Mankind Quarterly*, and was a contributor to the South African Bureau of Racial Affairs' journal.[31] In 1966 a police raid of Swan's New York apartment turned up a Nazi flag, a German helmet, and a photograph of Swan with some followers of George Lincoln Rockwell.[32]

Truth Seeker, Right, and *Mankind Quarterly* on the one hand, and the NL and the IAAEE on the other, were interrelated wings of a close-knit political tendency. While the League and publications like *Right* and *Truth Seeker* appealed to street-level activists from the WDL, NRP, and NSRP, *Mankind Quarterly* and the IAAEE mobilized more sophisticated arguments to justify white supremacy. The NL/*Mankind Quarterly* axis was also involved in a far more covert and complex polemic inside the far right over an issue Yockey raised in *Imperium*, namely the difference between "spiritual" or "cultural" racism and biological determinism. While by no means Yockeyist, the NL/*Mankind Quarterly* network did advance a more pan-European or "Waffen SS" worldview against the pure volkists associated with what is sometimes called the German or "Black SS."

The leading Black SS ideologue was a German academic named Hans F. K. Günther, who first achieved fame in the 1920s with his book *Ritter, Tod und Teufel: Der heldische Gedanke* (The Knight, Death, and the Devil: A Heroic Thought). He went on to write other highly influential works that included *Rassenkunde des deutschen Volkes* and *The Racial Elements of European History*. Günther distinguished between three races: the "Negroids," "Mongoloids," and "Europoids." The Europoids were the superior race and the Nordics were the most

481

advanced group of Europoids. The superior nations were therefore the ones with the highest content of Nordic blood in their veins.

Robert Gayre knew Günther and in 1939 visited his Berlin laboratory. In his book *Teuton and Slav on the Polish Frontier*, Gayre reproduced photos of ideal "racial types" taken from Günther's *Rassenkunde Europas*. Gayre, however, was *not* a Günther clone. Besides being a white supremacist, he was one of Europe's leading experts in heraldry, having been the secretary general of the Sixth International Congress of Genealogy and Heraldry, secretary general of the International Orders of Commission, and *consultore pro lingua anglica* of the College of Heralds in Rome.[33] As a genealogy expert with an intimate knowledge of Europe's chivalric orders, he believed hierarchy was established through complex chains of dynastic marriages and social rank, and not by methods used to breed farm animals.[34]

Gayre's ideological co-thinkers were best represented by the Italian school of fascist race theorists led by Professor Corrado Gini.[35] The author of over 70 books, Gini was a founder and associate editor of *Mankind Quarterly*. Until his death in 1965, he headed the Institute of Statistics at the University of Rome and the University of Padua, as well as the Comitato Italiano per lo Studio dei Problemi della Popolazione. He also served as president of the International Institute of Sociology and editor of *Revue Internationale de Sociologie*.[36]

In his book *The Ideology of Italian Fascism*, Professor A. James Gregor, a world expert on Italian fascism and former secretary of the IAAEE, points out that Italian fascists consistently rejected Nordicism for "a conception of race as a dynamic constant, the ultimate product of geographic and social isolation and attendant inbreeding, natural and artificial selection, and genetic mutation." As a product of history, race was shaped far more by politics than by blood content. For the Italians, race was "the product of *politically established social isolation*, selective influences, and breeding practices which tend to stabilize specific types in specific ecological niches." Therefore, race could only be understood as "a dynamic and historic political process." With such a "dynamic view," a nation could be seen as a "race cradle," or "politically defined endogamous breeding circle." The state, "as the conscious will of the nation," could limit citizenship and establish regulations governing marriage. Against the Nordicists, the Italians

> advanced a notion of "natio-races," politically defined breeding circles, animated through the legislative enactments and the pedagogical activities of the state to produce the breeding communities for ideal racial types. The ideal type for Fascism was conceived as "Nordo-Aryan" . . . The Nordic ideal was conceived as a *tactical* device which was to foster a strictly European orientation. The designation *Mediterranean*, while technically correct, suggested to Fascists a politically inadmissible affiliation with Semites. The relationship with Nordic Europe was essentially spiritual or cultural, rather than morphological.[37]

"Race," then, was primarily determined by politics and culture, a view similar to Yockey's argument in *Imperium* as well as the NEO's 1951 "Zurich Declaration."

In July 1958, just as the Northern League was being established, a major assault on Günther and his volkish co-thinkers appeared in *The European.* The article, "National Socialism and Race," was also written by A. James Gregor. Gregor, whose father was an Italian immigrant named Antonio Gimigliano, was born in New York in 1929. After getting his Ph.D. from Columbia in social and political philosophy, he became a regional secretary of the Institut International de Sociologie headed by Professor Gini and a co-editor of the *Revue Internationale de Sociologie.* Gregor wrote extensively on Marxism and served as an editorial assistant for the American New Left publication *Studies on the Left.* He was also a member of the book review staff of the old-line Marxist journal *Science and Society* and a Regional Secretary for the Society for the Philosophical Study of Dialectical Materialism. When not writing, he conducted psychological and sociological studies of Australian aborigines and tribes in southwest Africa.[38]

Gregor's essay in *The European* was a no-holds-barred demolition of Nazi Nordicism, or what he called "the period of uncritical acceptance of 'the Nordic Hypothesis.'" Günther and his followers were to blame for the idea that (in Gregor's words)

> in almost all mental traits the Nordic Race (tall, slender, fair-skinned, blond, blue-eyed, leptoprosopic [narrow-faced], leptorrhine [narrow-nosed], dolichocephalic [long-headed]) is superior. Nordics are sage in judgment, truthful and energetic, independent, realistic, bold, courageous, clean, inventive, tenacious, prudent, steadfast in duty, competitive (only in the best sense), just, respectful of the property of others, knightly, possessed of a gift of narrative, individualistic (yet unselfish), possessed of a remarkable depth of character, a thorough-going trustworthiness, an inquiring mind devoted to natural science, a lively sense of honor, a tendency to roguish humor, a capacity for statesmanlike achievements, a gift for leadership, a talent for music, a wide range of development in the mental life as well as other endowments too numerous to mention.

Gregor then noted that by Nordicist standards Kant, Machiavelli, Dante, Coleridge, Keats, and Raphael were too short; Leibniz, Schopenhauer, Kant, Schiller, Schubert, Haydn, Beethoven, Raphael, Leplace, Napoleon, and Pascal too brachycephalic (short- or broad-headed); Ovid, Vergil, Horace, Michelangelo, Ariosto, St. Francis of Assisi, Shakespeare, Herder, Napier, Beethoven, Balzac, Zola, Raphael, Elizabeth Barrett Browning, Ibsen, Tolstoy, Faraday, Tennyson, Cromwell, and Dampier too brunet (brown pigmented). By Nordicist criteria, Mussolini was "a relatively short, barrel-chested, brown eyed, brachycephalic brunet."

Most Germans also failed the Nordic blood test, since Germany was "a compost of at least five European and two extra-European races." According to

Günther's calculations, Germany's population was at best 45–50 per cent Nordic, with only five percent of all Germans qualifying as "pure" Nordic types. The other 95 percent included Hitler, who told a 1933 Nazi gathering: "We do not conclude from a man's physical type his ability, but rather from his achievements his race." Gregor then reported that in mid-1936 the *National-socialistische Korrespondenz* "stated with clarity and authority: 'From his deeds one can recognize the Nordic man—not from the length of his nose and the color of his eyes,'" which was "a complete rejection of Guenther's Nordicism." Right-thinking Nazis only wanted to maintain Nordicism as an aesthetic ideal for Germany since "its art form was Nordic; its literature and philosophy, its music and institutions were inspired by Nordic ideals." National Socialists, therefore, should actually avoid questions "of intrinsic worth, national and racial superiority and inferiority tearing asunder the peoples of Europe" since there was "no transcendental standard by which to evaluate racial differences."

Gregor highlighted anti-Nordicist elements inside the SS, including SS Lieutenant Colonel Ludwig Eckstein, who published *Rassenleib und Rassenseele: Zur Grundlegung der Rassensellenkunde* (Racial Body and Racial Soul: Key Fundamentals of Racesoul Study) with SS approval in 1945 "even under the gathering shadows of defeat." Gregor then quoted Eckstein's conclusion to *Rassenleib*, which reads:

> While supporting our own race, and if necessary fighting against other races to protect its right to existence, we should not overlook the fact that almost all races display something in themselves that is sound and biologically resolved and therefore beautiful, natural, and valuable . . . Each race carries first of all the measure of worth in itself. When once we understand this we do not foster feelings of inferiority in others, a consequence that the hitherto existing race theories too often achieved.

In 1945 SS Colonel Alfred Franke-Gricksch was hard at work inside RSHA headquarters "even under the gathering shadows of defeat" formulating plans for a post-Nazi "sworn European community" of peoples who would retain their "individual existence" and right to form "their own political organization."[39] Was SS Lieutenant Colonel Eckstein's more "Italian" line related to Franke-Gricksch's vision of Europe's future? According to Gregor, Eckstein's ideas echoed the 1938 Italian Fascist *Race Manifesto*, which Gregor said had supplied "the germs of a worldview which makes of man a creator, a builder of future races; a philosophy which unites history, politics and race, eugenics and humanism, pride in self and respect for others, a philosophy scientifically sound and emotionally satisfying."[40]

The Northern League, then, appears to have been an activist branch of a pan-Europeanist faction inside the Fascist International. With regard to the pure Nordicists, the League's greatest victory may have been convincing Hans Günther, also a Northern League member, to moderate his views. With Roger Pearson's help, Günther published a new edition of his book *The Religious Attitudes of the Indo-Europeans*. Günther makes it clear at the very beginning of the book that he intends to emphasize the much broader category of Indo-European as opposed to the purely Nordic:

> In this work I want to advance some reflections on the religiosity of the Indo-Europeans—that is to say, the Indo-European–speaking peoples originating from a common Bronze Age nucleus—who have always exerted a significant influence on the government and spirit of predominantly Nordic races.[41]

Given the complex and confusing alignment of "Black SS" and "Waffen SS" tendencies in the same organization, a full evaluation of the Northern League remains incomplete. What does seem clear is that in the mid-1950s a powerful axis developed inside the far right around the Northern League, the IAAEE, and publications like *Right, The Virginian, Truth Seeker, Northern World, The Northlander,* and *Mankind Quarterly.* This network advocated a new biopolitical line in both crude (Carto's "I am an Evotist") and sophisticated (A. James Gregor) arguments that challenged volkish race theory.

The Northern League position, while not Yockeyist, echoed *Imperium's* call for the abandonment of crude "Darwinian materialism" in matters of race. It is interesting to note that Georgetown Professor Charles C. Tansill was a member of the IAAEE's Executive Committee along with Gayre and Gini.[42] Tansill was also an honorary board member of *Mankind Quarterly.*[43] His ties to the NL network make it even more likely that when the NL's European organizer Alastair Harper met Francis X. Gannon in Yockey's company he was indeed meeting Tansill's protégé.

Nor did Yockey's ties to the Northern League end with his death. As I shall show, in virtually every instance in both the United States and Europe where Yockey's memory was kept alive, it was due to individuals or groups that maintained strong ties to either the Northern League/*Mankind Quarterly* network or the biopoliticians of the New European Order.

Notes:

1. Smith was the author of an enormous philosophical tome entitled *Sensism: The Philosophy of the West* (New York: The Truth Seeker Co., 1956).

2. *Truth Seeker* began in 1873 as a free-thought journal. It should be noted that a path from Darwinism, atheism, and materialism to religion had been developed by the German scientist Ernst Haeckel, creator of the Monist League and the man who helped popularize Darwin in Germany. A harsh critic of conventional religion, Haeckel's book *My Church Departure* was published in English by *Truth Seeker* in 1911. Haeckel then developed a new pantheistic religion of nature involving sun-worship. One of his students, Willibald Hentschel, wrote *Varuna* and founded the Artamanen Bund. There are also reports that Haeckel was a member of the Thule Society. After World War II, Haeckel's Monist League was part of the German People's League for Religious

Freedom, which united a whole group of German "New Age" cults in its ranks. (Kurt Tauber, *Beyond Eagle and Swastika* [Middletown, CT: Wesleyan University Press, 1967], Vol. 2, fn. 70, p. 1271.) On Haeckel, see Daniel Gasman, *The Scientific Origins of National Socialism* (London: MacDonald, 1971). For a discussion of the volkists, including Johann von Leers, see Harry Westernmeyer, *The Fall of the German Gods* (Mountain View, CA: Pacific Press, 1950).

3. The August 1958 *Truth Seeker*, for example, reprinted "Report No. 1 of the Policy Committee" of Mullins' Institute for Biopolitics. *Truth Seeker* also reprinted a speech by Mullins' friend Matt Koehl.

4. NRP leader James Madole's address to a 14 November 1959 meeting of the Racist Forum is also cited in a January 1959 *Truth Seeker* article by Robert Kuttner.

5. In *Truth Seeker*'s July 1961 issue, Polzin was listed on the masthead as Secretary, while Smith remained President. Polzin Publications in Parkesburg, Pennsylvania, published Fred Weiss pamphlets like *The Great Question*. Weiss's influence was also evident in the June 1959 issue of *Truth Seeker*, which printed a Eustace Mullins article called "F. C. F. Weiss, Prophet . . . " *Right* printed the same article.

6. In his study of the NRP published in the Dec. 1969–Jan. 1970 *Newsletter* of the National Information Center, William Goring writes:

> The NRP's closest ties are with the old (founded in 1873) atheist magazine the *Truth Seeker* . . . In a sense, the *Truth Seeker* offices serve as the Nazi headquarters for New York City, since the leaders of nearly all the factions congregate there for gossip and planning. The *Truth Seeker* is also one of the main sources of funds for some of the groups. Madole gets most of his literature there at discount prices, and Whitey Mason, a *Truth Seeker* regular, pays the printing costs on most of the NRP's leaflets.

7. *Northern World* began publishing before the formation of the Northern League.

8. Charles Smith noted that "the insuppressible Fred W. Koch" gave a presentation. Koch ran a "racial and individual health propaganda center" in Kassel. A Mrs. Kathrine Norman of Norway also attended the conference.

9. Vargas also attended Carto's Alphafest. For more information, see the interview between Vargas and Burton Wolfe in the May 1960 issue of *The Californian*.

10. From the September 1959 issue of *Truth Seeker*. On the significance of the Teutoberger Forest and the shrine to Armenius (the Hermannsdenkmal), see George L. Mosse, *The Nationalization of the Masses* (New York: New American Library, 1977), pp. 75–76.

11. On Smith's tour, see his discussion in the September 1959 issue of *Truth Seeker*. On the schedule of speakers in London, see the June–July 1959 *Northlander*. The January–February 1959 issue of *The Northlander* reports that Earnest Sevier Cox and William Stephenson of *The Virginian* were scheduled to address other Northern League members in London.

12. According to the January–February 1959 issue of *The Northlander*, Jordan had agreed to affiliate the WDL with the Northern League. That same issue reported that another rightist group, the National Labour Party (NLP), had also entered into an alliance with the Northern League. The NLP was headed by John Bean and John Tyndall, both of whom would become important leaders of the British far right in the 1960s.

13. Charles Smith was arrested in Newburgh, New York, on 4 August 1961 at an NRP anti-integration demonstration on a charge of disorderly conduct. He was 73.

14. The NSRP may have had occult ties. An NSRP catalogue that listed books like *Jewish Ritual Murder, Der Stürmer,* and *The Protocols of the Learned Elders of Zion* as must-reads also included works by Dr. R. L. Clymer, head of one faction of American Rosicrucianism. Besides a Clymer pamphlet entitled *Diabolical Practices* ("Tells of U.N. plot to use birth control and other methods to exterminate the White Race"), the NSRP sold other Clymer publications, such as *Cancer the Killer* and *Poisons in Foods and Liquids.* The Clymer Rosicrucians traced their lineage back to Pascal Beverly Randolph, one of the most important American occultists of the late 19th century; Randolph was also black. (John Patrick Deveney, *Pascal Beverly Randolph* [Albany: SUNY Press, 1997].)

15. In its Winter 1960–1961 issue, *Northern World* announced that any subscriber to the NSRP's *Thunderbolt* would get a free copy of *Northern World* as well. In 1959 the *Miami News* published an article on the NSRP's J. B. Stoner, Fred Hockett, David Hawthorne, and Peter J. Crockford. Crockford is cited as representing the Northern League, which he said had members in every state. Hockett was also said to have been a member of the Northern League. That same year, *Northern World* merged with Britons Publishing House, publisher of *The Protocols of the Learned Elders of Zion.* The link-up was reported in *Northern World* in its July–August 1959 issue.

16. Only in 1980 would NSRP leader J. B. Stoner finally be convicted for his role in the bombing.

17. In October 1957 *The Virginian* ran its first ad for *Northern World.* The paper also had a column on "Nordic Culture," featuring essays by Northern League writers like Alastair Harper, who contributed a piece to the November 1957 issue of *The Virginian.*

18. *Common Sense,* 15 September 1958.

19. O. John Rogge, *The Official German Report* (New York: Thomas Yoseloff, 1961), p. 364.

20. The 1951 statement glorified heredity and demanded the strict regulation of marriage between Europeans and non-Europeans. See Guy Amaudruz, *Nous Autres Racistes* (Montreal: Les Editions Celtiques, 1971). Amaudruz reports that the NEO Zurich Declaration called for "la nécessité d'un racisme européen visant aux buts suivants: a) les mariages entre Européens et non-Européens sont soumis à une réglementation; b) des mesures médicalement et scientifiquement étudiées amélioreront les qualités héréditaires de nos peuples."

21. On Kuttner, see Michael Billig, *Psychology, Racism and Fascism* (Birmingham, U.K., 1979), a *Searchlight* pamphlet.

22. In the April 1957 issue of Mosley's *The European,* Roger Pearson, writing from Calcutta, contributed an essay entitled "Festival in Nepal." He authored another article in defense of the British racial anthropologist Sir Arthur Keith. Pearson's "Evolution and the Modern State" appeared in *The European* in April 1956.

23. See the September 1956 issue of *The European.*

24. See Alastair Harper's May 1957 essay on "The American Film Today" in *The European.*

25. *Mankind Quarterly*'s place of publication then shifted from Edinburgh to Washington, D.C.

26. In his book *Miscellaneous Racial Studies* (Edinburgh: The Armorial, 1972), Gayre reports that he spent the mid-1950s as head of the department of anthropo-geography of the University of Saugor.

27. Jeffrey Bale, "The 'Black' Terrorist International: Neo-Fascist Paramilitary Networks and the 'Strategy of Tension' in Italy, 1968–1974" (unpublished University of California at Berkeley Ph.D. thesis, 1994), p. 93.

28. In September 1958 *The Northlander* reported that the League had established a Vienna office headed by William Landig. Landig produced a journal called *Europa Korrespondenz*, which advertised in *The Northlander*. According to an exposé in the *Rheinischer Merkur* of Koblenz, a key figure behind *Europa Korrespondenz* was Johann von Leers. (Tauber, *Beyond Eagle and Swastika*, Vol. 2, fn. 177, pp. 1112–13.)

29. A biographical note in *Race and Modern Science* edited by Kuttner and published in 1967 by Social Science Press in New York (and which includes a series of contributors to *Mankind Quarterly*) reads as follows:

Robert E. Kuttner, M.A., Ph.D., is Research Associate in Biochemistry in the Department of Obstetrics and Gynecology at the University of Chicago. He joined the faculty in 1965. Before he assumed his present position, Dr. Kuttner was at Creighton University for five years, where he was also a Research Associate in Biochemistry. Before that he was engaged in brain chemistry and brain psychology research at the Institute of Living, Hartford, Conn. He has also served as a research associate at the University of Connecticut and as a member of the research staff at the Brookhaven National Laboratory, Long Island, N.Y. Dr. Kuttner is a contributing editor of the *Mankind Quarterly*...He is a member of the American Association for the Advancement of Science, the British Eugenics Society, the International Institute of Sociology, the Nebraska Academy of Science, the New York Academy of Science, and the American Eugenics Society.

30. H. Keith Thompson's reply to my questionnaire. After Swan's death, Wickliffe Draper's Pioneer Fund gave $59,000 to Roger Pearson's Institute for the Study of Man so that it could acquire Swan's books and papers.

31. On Swan, see Billig, *Psychology, Racism and Fascism*.

32. See Jack Anderson's syndicated column of 16 November 1989.

33. Around the same time that *Mankind Quarterly* was created, Gayre founded *The Armorial*, which was devoted to heraldry, titles, and knightly orders. See the introduction to Gayre's book *The Knightly Twilight*, published in Valletta, Malta, in 1973.

34. One knightly order that Gayre belonged to was the Vatican-allied Sovereign Military Order of Malta (SMOM). Although a Protestant, Gayre held a SMOM Cross of Military Merit (the Cross of Merit being open to non–Roman Catholics).

35. Gayre's ties to Italy did not end with Professor Gini. In 1943 he was assigned to Italy as an Educational Advisor to the Allied Military Government. Three years later he wrote about his experience in *Italy in Transition* (London: Faber and Faber, 1946), where he discusses his encouragement of the Sicilian separatist movement. Gayre reports that he helped found the Sicilian Anthropological Society at the University of Palermo during the war. The Anthropological Society spun off an organization called the Institute

of Social Anthropology that became a hotbed of Sicilian separatism, so much so that it was forcibly suppressed by the Italian government in 1946. What Gayre failed to mention is that elements inside the British establishment (and British intelligence) encouraged Sicilian separatism should the Communists take over northern Italy. If that did occur, the British wanted the option of turning southern Italy into a separate state. Recall that southern Italy was technically ruled by the King of Italy after the House of Savoy abandoned Mussolini and entered the war on the Allied side in 1943.

Gayre linked the issue of Sicilian separatism to the restoration of the House of Savoy. Gayre's monarchist views were summed up in the title of his 1962 book: *A Case for Monarchy—A Plea for the Maintenance and the Restoration of Monarchy with Particular Reference to the House of Savoy* (Edinburgh: The Armorial, 1962). He was also a member of the Order of Saints Maurice and Lazarus, the highest honor the House of Savoy can give to a non-Italian. Italy's pro-monarchist party merged with the MSI in the 1950s.

36. On Gini, see Billig, *Race, Psychology and Fascism.* Also see A. James Gregor, "Corrado Gini and the Theory of Race Formation," in *Sociology and Social Research* (Vol. 45, No. 2, January 1961).

37. A. James Gregor, *The Ideology of Italian Fascism* (New York: Free Press, 1969), pp. 254–55.

38. Gregor's biography primarily comes from his biographical note in Robert Kuttner, *Race and Modern Science* (New York: Social Science Press, 1967); I. A. Newby, *Challenge to the Court: Social Scientists and the Defense of Segregation 1954–1966* (Baton Rouge: Louisiana State University Press, 1967); and Gregor's fierce response to Newby ("On Learned Ignorance: A Brief Inquiry into I. A. Newby's *Challenge to the Court*"), in the second edition of Newby's book.

39. Franke-Gricksch's proposal is cited in Marlis G. Steinert, *Capitulation 1945: The Story of the Doenitz Regime* (London: Constable, 1969), pp. 5–6. It is worth noting in passing that the Strasser faction of the NSDAP advanced a foreign-policy program calling for a United States of Europe in the winter of 1925–26. Hitler rejected the proposal at the NSDAP party conference in Bamberg in 1926.

40. A. James Gregor, "National Socialism and Race," *The European,* July, 1958 (Vol. XI, No. 5), p. 288. Gregor wrote another stinging attack on Günther entitled "Nordicism Revisited" for *Phylon* (Vol. XXII, No. 4, 1961).

41. Hans F. K. Günther, *The Religious Attitudes of the Indo-Europeans* (London: Clair Press, 1966), p. 9. On the title page of the book, credit for the English translation is given to "Vivian Bird in collaboration with Roger Pearson, M.Sc. (Economics)." Note that Pearson got his M.Sc. in Economics at the University of London in the 1940s or early 1950s and then went back to get his Ph.D. in physical anthropology in the 1960s.

42. I. A. Newby, *Challenge to the Courts,* p. 134, fn. 15.

43. Ibid., p. 138.

48

"ACE IN
THE HOLE"

On New Year's Day 1960, while living in the Bay Area, Yockey finished a 12-page, single-spaced essay entitled "An Estimate of the World Situation." He had six more months to live. His daughter Bruni, who last saw her father a few months before his death when he visited Texas, recalled that he seemed as if he had "the weight of the world on his shoulders."[1] H. Keith Thompson said he last met Yockey in a Yorkville restaurant in the late 1950s. Fred Weiss and Yockey seem to have met for the final time when Yockey visited the Weiss farm a few weeks before leaving for California.[2]

In February 1961 Fred Weiss and H. Keith Thompson published Yockey's concluding political tract as a pamphlet under a new title: *The World in Flames*.[3] *The World in Flames* is the only surviving written example of Yockey's thinking in the last months of his life.[4] He begins his essay by comparing the world geopolitical situation in 1960 to 1946, when the United States seemed all powerful. Now, just 14 years later, Washington had no preponderance of power vis-à-vis the Soviet Union. "Without disturbing the Bolshevik governmental structure or ideology," the Russians had also effected "a complete revolution and deprived the Jewish leadership of all power." In contemporary Russia, the Jew had to be a Russian first: "In other words, he is not allowed to be a Jew, and is being exterminated without physical violence."

Anti-colonial revolutions were further stripping the West's power. The U.S. had already lost control of half the Arab world, while in Latin America Washington's "possessions . . . from Nicaragua to Argentina, are growing restive." The military stalemate in Korea demonstrated "that the United States infantry is inferior, and that the Zionist empire is, in the Chinese phrase, a 'paper tiger.'"[5] In America, however, the Zionists would only lose power after the nation suffered a crushing military defeat followed by economic collapse. But if Moscow and Washington were on a collision course, how would the conflict play out strategically?

> We now come to the military aspect of the Third World War. It is perfectly clear that the Washington regime has put its entire faith in "strategic bombardment." They plan to deliver the explosives to their targets by ballistic missiles, guided missiles, submarines, and airplanes, land-based and carrier-based. This faith in bombardment is just that: It is *faith*, but not rational. Faith has certain advantages, but not in the realm of technics.

The problem with bombardment was simple:

> Russia is a porous target, and rockets are effective only against dense targets. The Jewish-American citadel is far denser than the Russian citadel, and is thus vulnerable to rockets to a far greater degree. America-Jewry would be far better off if rockets did not exist. In that case its citadel would be inviolate, and it could never sustain a military disaster of the greatest magnitude, for its armies would be at the antipodes and their victory or defeat would be of minor consequence. Thus the basic Jewish-American military doctrine is one which cannot possibly give it victory.

America especially had to rely on rockets because its soldiers were "utterly worthless," since the country had "no political awareness, no significant military tradition, no military instinct, no military ambition, no moral strength, and no respect for or belief in anything whatsoever."

Russia would triumph in a future war partly because of its vast geography and partly because of its barbarian will-to-power. Yet Russia faced one insurmountable problem: It was impossible to launch a military invasion against North America. The paradox, then, was that "America-Jewry," which had placed its faith in rockets, could only defeat Russia with infantry, while Russia, "which believes in infantry, can win only with rockets." Even after the destruction of the American military presence in Europe and Asia, "there still remains the Jewish-American citadel," which would be loath to surrender power "since the very existence of Jewry is at stake, and the whole United States and its population is there to secure the existence of Jewry." With the situation now deadlocked, each side would have to rely on intercontinental missile exchanges:

> Thus the only "contact" the hostile armies can have with one another is in the limited form of an intercontinental artillery duel. By these means, it is possible for neither contestant to destroy the armies of the other, since they will be widely deployed, offering no target. The only real target for intercontinental ballistic missiles is a large city. Here the United States offers a plethora of targets, and Russia few.

491

Faced with the continued destruction of its major cities, and with a culturally weak, easily demoralized population to begin with, America might well beg for peace. But political capitulation would not necessarily ensure the cessation of the Russian assault:

> There is the distinct possibility that barbarian Russia, signatory to no treaty to mitigate the harshness of war, would continue to bombard the USA after a surrender, in order finally to eliminate it as a potential world power, by complete destruction of its industrial potential (which is almost entirely in cities). That which the Jewish-American-English-French forces did in Germany after the Second World War, destruction of industrial plants and irrational plundering of natural resources in order to destroy them, could be equally well done by Russia after the Third World War: further destruction of cities, perhaps occupation (large armies might no longer be necessary) to destroy industry systematically, on the pattern used by American-Jewish forces in Europe 1945–1950. If there was no occupation, the forest areas could be destroyed by systematic bombardment, converting most of the North American continent into desert.

Yet *The World in Flames* was not a call to nuclear war. Yockey even suggested that the ultimate U.S.-Soviet confrontation would not take place for another 15 years, because Russia had no interest in disrupting a power game in which it grew stronger every day. Then why *The World in Flames*?

The answer came in the final part of the essay, when Yockey argued that Europe must embrace a policy of anti-American neutralism. He even praised De Gaulle ("pygmy that he is") for moving France away from American control. Nor was neutralism limited to Europe, since "some 180,000,000 Latin Americans" would soon revolt against "Jewish-American economic domination."

Yockey's core concern seems to have been how the Soviet Union should best exploit its military, political, and technological prowess to encourage anti-American movements. This may be why he recommended that the main targets for Soviet missiles should be America's major cities and not its missile silos and other launch facilities. By this argument, he seemed to be encouraging a "brinkmanship" approach to Soviet foreign policy that would lead to either a gradual but increasing erosion of American power or a monumental moment of geopolitical *Ernstfall*, a life-or-death situation when a morally and psychologically "feminine" culture like the United States would politically capitulate to the virile Soviets rather than heroically accept the certain nuclear incineration of its cities. Indeed the U.S. did face such a challenge during the Cuban Missile Crisis, which occurred two years after Yockey's death.

Although *The World in Flames* was a political document, it can also be read as a meditation on Yockey's life since it revolves around war, the ultimate moment of life-or-death confrontation. Yockey lived for such moments, believing that the world was best ruled by a political/intellectual elite that regularly proved its fitness for command through acts of aristocratic daring. Nor did he develop his views in a historical vacuum. As he came to political consciousness in the 1930s, the usefulness of parliamentary democracy was being questioned throughout the West. As the historian Zeev Sternhell observes, the 1930s witnessed a "merciless criticism of liberal democracy" by both the left and right that was "directed not only against the workings of the regime—its weaknesses and institutional faults— but also against the very principles of a certain political culture."[6]

The first sophisticated modern right-wing critique of bourgeois order was advanced in Weimar Germany by the Conservative Revolutionaries. With the general crisis of democratic institutions fueled by the Great Depression, books like *The Decline of the West* and Moeller van den Bruck's *The Third Reich* now seemed like prophetic expressions of a much broader Zeitgeist. In a 1933 review of *The Third Reich*, a French critic noted how much he was drawn to its "call of pride and distress, a call of generations deeply wounded and yet virile, ready to harden themselves against decay not only through a fierce will to courage and violence but through the choice of a difficult, exacting, and perfectly disinterested task." Moeller had articulated "a deep and tragic virility, a natural tendency to heroism, a contempt for happiness, a search for sacrifice through the natural volition of one's being."[7] Similar sentiments can be found throughout Spengler's writings.

Yockey could have walked away from the "challenge of the political" many times. Like a high-stakes gambler, however, he kept raising the bet. As a result, he became Ernst Jünger's new man, the *Vanbanquespieler* or "player of dangerous games." He even used a gambling metaphor when planning his abortive escape: According to his cellmate Philip Galati, Yockey told him that if the escape failed and "I don't find a way out, I've always got an ace in the hole." I suspect that "ace" was a cyanide pill.

Once captured, Yockey had to confront his deepest fear. Would his raw desire to live overcome his self-image as a political soldier willing to die a heroic death rather than betray a sacred cause? Was he really "Ulick Varange," a martyr for a future Europa? In a sense his life had been building up to this moment when the "foe" was no longer external but the enemy within. Ultimate triumph could now only be achieved by a supreme act of self-annihilation. *Ernstfall* descended upon Yockey in a desolate San Francisco jail cell sometime in the early morning hours of 17 June 1960. I suspect that he met his final challenge with determination, peace of mind, and perhaps even with a secret last flash of knowing ecstacy.

Notes:

1. Recall that Yockey was in Texas, having crossed over from Mexico to Laredo on 19 March 1960, and that his family lived in San Antonio.

2. The rightist author Eustace Mullins told me he was present at Weiss's farm along with Matt Koehl and James Madole. Mullins said that he could not remember anything striking about Yockey, who maintained a low profile.

3. H. Keith Thompson's shop printed *The World in Flames*. A photocopy of Yockey's original manuscript, which Thompson used to produce *The World in Flames*, later showed up in the files of the NSANL.

4. A mention of a possible lost text surfaced in a report by the liberal Group Research organization in 1969. Among Yockey's writings, Group Research listed a pamphlet called *America the Enemy*, which it said was confiscated by the American government. I found no reference to such a pamphlet in the FBI files. Wes McCune, the retired head of Group Research, could not recall anything about the existence of such a pamphlet.

5. In their introduction to *The World in Flames*, Fred Weiss and H. Keith Thompson make a passing reference to China when writing about Yockey: "A man who decried the dangerous Smith Act found himself naturally opposed to the senseless exclusion from the United Nations of the People's Republic of China, representing one-fifth of mankind." They then continue:

> An undeveloped element in Yockey's evaluation is an analysis of the significance of China's competition with Russia. This challenge, spurred on by the biological pressure of some 680,000,000 Chinese and the rapid strides made by Peoples' China in science and technology, is rapidly acquiring direction and form. . . . At this point, for every Caucasian on the Eurasian Continent—*including* the Russians—the question will be how to insure for the Leucodermi [people with white skin] the greatest possible role in the final state of enforced "unification" of all the peoples of the earth. Where in America we are now taught to view this unification in terms of "Melting Pot" ideals, the Russians—as well as the British, the Germans, and other Western European nations—have different ideas about their future. Yockey knew this, and he recognized that the "Anschluss" of Russia with Europe, and particularly with Germany, was only a matter of a few years hence.

6. Zeev Sternhell, *Neither Left Nor Right* (Princeton, NJ: Princeton University Press, 1996), p. xv.

7. Ibid., pp. 233–34.

THE CULT OF SAINT FRANCIS ("YOCKEYISM" IN AMERICA)

Pro captu lectoris habent sua fata libelli. (The fortune of a book depends upon the capacity of its readers.)
—*Terantianus Marcus,* De litteris, syllabis et metris

Only where there are tombs are there resurrections.
—*Friedrich Nietzsche*

49

FLIM-FLAM

MAN?

Yockey's death doomed a full investigation into his activities. There was still, however, one key witness who might unlock at least part of the mystery—Alexander Scharf, the Czech-born Orthodox Jew, concentration camp survivor, and yeshiva principal at whose Oakland apartment Yockey had been arrested. Investigators became extremely interested in Scharf after they discovered that he had served as a witness for one of Yockey's false passports. A subpoena was issued to Scharf just three days before Yockey's suicide but, when it was served, it was discovered that he had fled San Francisco for parts unknown.

All that the government knew about Scharf at first came from the story he told the FBI at the time of Yockey's capture. He said he only knew "Richard Hatch" as a casual friend who had sent him a telegram from Washington asking if he could stay with him for a few days. Scharf told the FBI that he had first met Hatch in Reno, Nevada, in 1959, but he later gave the *San Francisco Chronicle* a somewhat different story:

> I was standing at a dice table in the Nevada Club in Reno in April 1959. My luck was very bad. I became aware that this man was watching me. Yockey smiled and asked if I wanted to have a cup of coffee—he said I was playing badly and that I better quit. I was interested. He seemed to know what he was talking about.[1]

Scharf now said that Yockey (who introduced himself as "Mike Taylor" and *not* "Richard Hatch") lent him $30 to help with his gambling debts. After Taylor moved to San Francisco, the two men would occasionally meet for lunch. Scharf said that Taylor liked me and wanted my friendship as I wanted his. He would call me up on the telephone and say "Hi, bastard" in that way Americans have of being friendly. He spoke warmly of the Jewish people. He said he admired them. And he spoke in a derogatory manner about the Germans. He said they never could have won the war, because they hated each other. He said the Jews would help each other, and he seemed to admire that.

When they did meet they spoke about many things, including "history, gambling, and the Old Testament," but never politics. Scharf also recalled:

> We were talking one day about something and he said, "Oh, you wouldn't understand that because you believe in God." He said, "I do not believe in God, but in gods, more than one." That is paganism. I shrugged. I don't argue religion with people.[2]

Taylor told Scharf he was a writer and showed him some of his work. Although he considered Taylor "a true and faithful friend," Scharf knew little about him. This seemed especially curious since Taylor

> wanted to set me up in business. I'm an educator, not a business man, but he wanted to put up the money and let me run a store on a partnership arrangement. A respectable business address would have been a foolproof front for him. That's all I offered him, I know now—respectability and camouflage. No one would ever think of looking for a fascist in the company of a teacher of Hebrew—even I didn't think that any American could be a fascist.[3]

After leaving the San Francisco area in the spring of 1960, Taylor sent Scharf postcards from New York, New Orleans, and Washington before his final telegram requesting a place to stay. When Taylor last contacted Scharf, he mentioned that he was now traveling under the name "Richard Hatch."[4] "I didn't like this, but I didn't pry," Scharf explained.[5]

But who was Alexander Scharf? In September 1959 a small item in a local Oakland paper reported that the 31-year-old Scharf, a native of Czechoslovakia and a graduate of both Columbia University and the Jewish Theological Seminary, had been named education director of Temple Beth Abraham.[6] The item also noted that he had taught in Hebrew schools in both New Jersey and California. What was not mentioned was Scharf's past in Europe, including the fact that he was a survivor of Auschwitz who still bore a bluish tatoo with his camp number on his arm.[7] (He was later moved from Auschwitz to another concentration camp, Mauthausen.[8]) When Scharf was questioned about his reason for fleeing San Francisco, he returned to his experience at Auschwitz:

> When the [FBI] agents left I was terrified—what kind of man was this? I was afraid of being liquidated by his friends, being executed. I remembered in my mind standing in the line at Auschwitz. If you went to the left you were killed, to the right you had a chance for life in a labor camp. I knew that I didn't really

know this man, Taylor or Hatch or whoever he was. Maybe he was a Communist spy. Perhaps I should have called the rabbi I worked for, but I couldn't think. I was overwhelmed with fear . . . I am astonished at even the suggestion that I am a spy for anything, or knew who this terrible man was. How could I associate with such a man knowing him to be a Nazi? The Nazis killed one of my brothers, two of my sisters, my parents, and my parents' whole family.[9]

The 20 June 1960 *San Francisco Chronicle* ran a story on Yockey and Scharf (subtitled "Fascist and a Victim") that included an interview with one of Scharf's friends, Mrs. Ezra Cohen-Sift. She described him as "not the kind of person you could get close to . . . He was very sad and very serious and even though he was likable he was always distant." She then speculated that Scharf's meeting with Yockey "must have come from something out of Europe years ago. He was a boy of 18 and wandered for many years after the war."[10] A retired Oakland man who had been a student of Scharf's recalled that he was "always looking over his shoulder . . . He is like a scared rabbit. And the thing that has made him run is what he went through in Europe."

A pupil of Scharf's named R. Harris Smith, however, painted a very different picture. Smith (author of the book *OSS*) studied with Scharf at Temple Beth Abraham as a teenager. He told me that Scharf was "the worst teacher I ever had," with "no feeling for children." Smith called Scharf a "nasty guy" with "cold eyes" and a "very cold" personality who acted "like a German" and could have been a character in the movie *Casablanca*.[11] Scharf's boss, Rabbi Harold Schulweis, also believed that he was a failure as a teacher and had made it clear that he would not be rehired.[12]

Scharf also seems to have led a complicated love-life. A search of his abandoned apartment turned up letters containing the names and addresses of 12 European women whom he later claimed were "pen-pals."[13] The Immigration and Naturalization Service learned that he had been married, but that his wife had divorced him.[14] In the 18 months preceding Yockey's arrest, Scharf had been seeing Hildegards Bohlen King, a German-born woman who worked at Reno's Cal-Neva club as a blackjack dealer.[15] Bohlen King, who came to the United States in 1956, told the *San Francisco Chronicle* that she first met Scharf on New Year's Day 1959: "We were introduced. We did not meet at the tables."[16] She too reported that Scharf "wasn't the type you meet today and become buddy-buddy with tomorrow . . . he would never become friendly with a person until he was sure he could trust them." He also "talked frequently of his experiences at the concentration camp in Auschwitz. He told me he was there about a year and that his parents were killed there."

Scharf's immigration papers, however, told a much different story. Scharf entered the United States as a resident alien from Paraguay and, according to his papers, he spent World War II not in Auschwitz, Poland, but in Asunción,

Paraguay! He was also reported to have been born in Germany, not Czechoslovakia.

According to an FBI summary of Scharf's testimony on the day of Yockey's arrest, he told the agents that he

was born in the city of Walfratshausen, Bavaria, Germany, December 12, 1923. When he was nine years old he traveled with his mother and father to Argentina, where his father died. At that time when he was about nine years old he went to Paraguay to the town of Asunción with his mother, who died in Paraguay. He went to school in Asunción, Paraguay, until he was about 15 years old, living with a family named either FERNANDEZ or HERNANDEZ. When he was about 15 years old, he left Paraguay and traveled to Rosario, Argentina. He went by himself and when he arrived in Rosario he went to work in a restaurant in the kitchen. He left Argentina in 1953 and arrived in January, 1954, at the port of New York to visit friends.[17]

While in New York, Scharf said, he first enrolled in Columbia University and later in the Jewish Theological Seminary. He further claimed that, after graduating from Jewish Theological in June 1957, he received a scholarship to study in Israel. En route to Tel Aviv, he stopped off in Paris, where he stayed until December 1957. Scharf then returned to the United States and by the beginning of 1958 was back in New York. He next visited Miami Beach, where he worked as a waiter. In April 1958 he abandoned Miami for Alaska. Scharf went first to Anchorage and then to the Aleutian Islands, where he worked in a radio station and as a waiter. Around October 1958 he headed for San Francisco and got a job as an instructor with the Bureau of Jewish Education.

Scharf's dilemma was obvious: If his papers were correct, he had been telling his friends in the Jewish community an enormous lie, a lie complete with a forged concentration camp tatoo. If his papers were false—and he *was* a concentration camp survivor—then he was living illegally in the United States. It also became clear that Scharf had known Yockey under at least three different names: "Mike Taylor," "Richard Hatch," and Yockey. The U.S. Postal Service identified Scharf's signature as a witness on Yockey's 26 June 1959 application for an Irish passport under the name Michael Joseph Taylor.[18] When FBI agents arrested Yockey, however, Scharf claimed only to know him as Richard Hatch. "But if he knew him as Hatch," Assistant U.S. Attorney William P. Clancey wondered, "what was Scharf doing signing his name on the Irish passport application for Michael Joseph Taylor?" Finally, Bohlen King reported that Scharf had referred to Yockey by his real name. She told the *San Francisco Chronicle* that when he did speak of Yockey, "it was with admiration. He greatly admired Yockey's intelligence and mentioned a few times that he had seen or heard from him."[19]

Shortly after Yockey's arrest Scharf fled the Bay Area. He was in such a panic that he failed to pack all his clothes before leaving his apartment. Fearing that it was too risky to escape by car, he abandoned his 1956 Mercury sedan on Oakland's MacArthur Boulevard and hopped on a bus headed south.[20] But where had he run to? The U.S. Attorney's Office was convinced that he was somewhere in the southwest United States since he lacked the money to travel overseas. "We're trying to blanket all escape routes and we're hoping for the best," a government source reported.[21] INS inspectors staked out Bohlen King's Reno home without any luck.[22] The government also looked at one of Scharf's friends, a former San Jose court stenographer named William Slomovich. The day before Yockey committed suicide, Slomovich left New York on the SS *Atlantic*, which was sailing to Israel. Thinking that Scharf may have been impersonating Slomovich, U.S. agents checked the *Atlantic*'s passengers when the ship stopped off in Spain to make certain that he wasn't aboard.[23] The hunt was extended farther south, thanks to a rumor that Scharf had crossed over into Mexico.[24] The rumor was half-right: Scharf had headed south of the border, but not to Mexico. After his bus reached Los Angeles, he took the first plane bound for Cuba.

Scharf's travel plans became known on 29 June 1960, when the FBI's New York office received a call from the Jewish Theological Seminary. The caller informed the Bureau that a California reporter had contacted the Seminary to check whether Scharf did in fact have a degree from Jewish Theological.[25] (According to school records, Scharf had attended Jewish Theological for two or three years but failed to graduate.[26]) The informant said that on 21 June 1960 he had received a letter from the Plante del Centro Israelito de Cuba in Santos Suarez, Cuba, wanting to verify Scharf's academic credentials.[27] Scharf, it turned out, had applied for a teaching job and had given Jewish Theological as a reference.

Scharf was no stranger to Cuba, having gone there on gambling junkets in 1956 and 1958.[28] He later told the *San Francisco Chronicle* that he had been offered a job in Havana to teach Jewish studies before graduating from Jewish Theological: "I knew they needed teachers in Cuba, my people needed them badly there, and I believed I could get a job."[29] Yet for someone who later claimed that he was trying to flee from Yockey and his friends, and not the U.S. government, Havana was a curious destination. As Scharf later explained to the *Chronicle:*

> He [Yockey] told me once that he had been in Cuba—it was during the Spring of this year [1960]—and that he had almost gotten a very high position in the Castro government. I did not like this, because I knew this man Castro was pro-Communist, but I am not a political man and I did not pry further into his affairs. The only thing he told me was that he had tried to see Castro, to convince him that he should change his policy toward the United States. He said he wanted to convince him that in the event of war the United States would invade and occupy Cuba.[30]

According to one source, around the time that Scharf was in Havana, H. Keith Thompson paid a visit to the island. The news about Thompson came to the FBI from *San Francisco Chronicle* reporter George Draper, who interviewed both Thompson and Willis Carto about Yockey.[31] According to a 9 August 1960 FBI report, Draper told James F. Cavanaugh of the State Department's Security Division in San Francisco:

> [Draper] had recently been in telephonic contact with _____ well-known Neo-Nazi, who is now in Havana, Cuba. During their conversation, _____ requested that _____ return certain papers regarding YOCKEY which _____ had previously made available to _____.[32]

H. Keith Thompson strongly denies ever visiting "Castro Cuba."[33] Despite his denial, however, one curious fact remains. Lyle Stuart, who visited Havana that August, wrote Thompson on 25 August 1960 to report that he had been unable to deliver Thompson's letter to a Cuban journalist named Rodriguez who had links to Yockey. But how did Thompson get the journalist's name in the first place if he didn't have some knowledge of Yockey's Cuban operation?[34]

Alexander Scharf's disappearance tormented the U.S. government all that summer. However, the San Francisco office of the FBI, which had spent many frustrating years on the case, was now only too eager to let the State Department and the Immigration and Naturalization Service deal with the Scharf quagmire. The San Francisco FBI warned Washington headquarters on 20 June 1960 that Scharf's case was rapidly escalating because "the press is completely intent on keeping this matter blown up." There were also "several individuals in the U.S. Attorney's Office" who were "just as intent as the press in carrying on the situation." The memo continued:

> As far as SCHARF is concerned, there is no allegation whatsoever of any substance on the surface which would appear to be worthy of getting us into the situation to locate him or to initiate investigative efforts into any inquiry along that line. We are getting heavily pressured by the USA [U.S. Attorney] to the contrary, however, and, in fact, today refused the request of AUSA WILLIAM CLANCEY for our total files concerning YOCKEY and SCHARF. I am advised by MR. CLANCEY that AUSA JAMES SCHANKE is still pushing very hard in this matter and intends to locate and arrest SCHARF and bring him before a Grand Jury on a general fishing expedition to not only elicit data concerning his relations with YOCKEY but as to his own personal activities. Thus despite the death of the substantive violator, the USA's Office intends to keep on with the situation ... It is MR. SCHANKE's idea that actually SCHARF is a Neo-Nazi posing as a Jew and, in his opinion, has been "flim-flaming" the Jewish group which has sponsored him.

All that summer the government uncovered more and more odd facts about the possible flim-flam man. According to a 29 July 1960 FBI memo, for instance, INS investigators had developed a lead that Scharf (like Yockey) had used a series of false names including "BRITT PHILLIPS," "DAVID CHAPELLE," and "BEN-JAMIN YOUNGER."

But if Scharf's flight to Havana was surprising, it was even more of a surprise when he agreed later that summer to return to the United States and testify before a San Francisco grand jury investigating the Yockey affair. Scharf decided to come back to America after reports began spreading inside Havana's Jewish community about his ties to Yockey.[35] Without friends or funds, he began talking to the *San Francisco Chronicle* from his Havana hideout and even tried to sell his exclusive story to the paper for eight hundred dollars. After assurances that there were no pending criminal charges against him, he flew from Havana to Miami on 19 August 1960. The next day he arrived in San Francisco.[36]

During four hours of grand jury testimony on 24 August 1960, Scharf claimed that he had signed Yockey's "Michael Joseph Taylor" passport application because he believed at the time that Yockey really was Mike Taylor. He insisted that he had only learned about Yockey's real name in Havana. Then, incredibly, he told the grand jury that he wasn't "Alexander Scharf"; he was really a 36-year-old man named Benjamin Junger. Junger said he was a Czech-born diamond-cutter by trade who had been interned in Auschwitz. He also said that the Nazis had killed his parents and scattered his family. After World War II he had wandered from Austria to Germany, to England, and then back to Germany.[37] He then entered the United States in 1949 from Salzburg, Austria, using the name of his real brother, Herman Junger.

"Herman Junger" then left the U.S. for Brazil. Not finding it to his liking, he went to Paraguay, where he told authorities that he was a German-born man named "Alexander Scharf" because Germans received a better reception than Czechs. After spending two years in Asunción he became a Paraguayan citizen and then returned to the U.S. to study at the Jewish Theological Seminary.

After finishing his mind-bending testimony, Junger continued to be questioned by State Department and INS investigators; that October a story appeared in the local papers that Junger may have known about a "traveler's-check swindle" carried out by Yockey. The INS tried to get Junger deported for twice entering the United States under a false name. On 30 December 1960, however, the local press reported that Junger had won his court fight to remain in America, although the INS district director vowed that the government would appeal. The Board of Immigration Appeals again ruled in Junger's favor on 13 June 1961.

Was Junger a flim-flam man? And if so, who was he flim-flamming? Had he accumulated gambling debts that made him susceptible to being used? Or was his reported background as a diamond-cutter more significant? During World War II the Nazi "diamond king" Bernet Pahbach smuggled large quantities of industrial diamonds into Germany through an international criminal underground.[38] Pahbach's men often posed as merchant seamen as a cover for their operation.[39] This underground was used to finance Nazi propaganda in places like South

America. Did the smuggling and courier operation survive World War II through the *Der Weg*/Natinform network? If Junger was a Jewish diamond-cutter, the Nazis may have recruited him in exchange for his life. Could his "semi-monthly" trips to Reno to date Bohlen King have been a cover for some kind of criminal enterprise? Recall in this context Bohlen King's remark that she and "Scharf" were "introduced" and did not meet casually. Did the report that Yockey had attempted to buy "Z cards" from American sailors also point to a courier network? Junger's Czech background is also interesting given Yockey's own reported role as a one-time courier for Czech intelligence.

It is, of course, possible that Junger really was a Nazi "flim-flamming" as a Jew. If so, he made a very convincing Jew, so much so that the ADL's Stanley Jacobs believed in his bona fides. Junger also had a scholarly knowledge of medieval Jewish religious texts. R. Harris Smith recalls that Junger did not teach Hebrew;[40] Smith said, however, that "Scharf" must have had some real knowledge of Jewish teachings because it would have been impossible to fool Rabbi Schulweis. Yet the Nazis had their Jewish-history scholars. Recall that the Naumann Circle's Karl Henrich Peter had helped run the Reich Institute for History of the New Germany, which specialized in the acquisition of exotic Jewish texts from the libraries and private collections of occupied Europe.

Another mystery involved Yockey's first encounter with Junger. Did Junger really meet Yockey in Reno in April 1959 and, if so, was their meeting really so casual? Recall that Junger claimed to have spent some time in Alaska, only leaving the state in October 1958 to move to San Francisco. He left shortly before Yockey ("Jack Forest") made his own surprising one-month visit to Alaska that November. Before moving to Alaska, Yockey notified the post office in Bellingham, Washington, to send his mail to Reno.[41] And, finally, was there any link between Yockey's presence in Reno and Mana Truhill's mysterious trip to Las Vegas for Fred Weiss four years earlier?

It is also important to consider the possibility that Junger may have been more or less what he claimed to be—an innocent set up by a clever Nazi who saw a lonely Orthodox Jew with a weakness for gambling as a perfect cover. While in jail, Yockey described his relationship with Scharf as being strictly business, and claimed that Scharf "was not connected with any of his activities but was merely an acquaintance."[42] At the time of his arrest, however, Yockey at first assumed that his friend had also been picked up by the FBI. Perhaps the most damning assault on Junger's credibility, however, came from Bohlen King's remark to the *San Francisco Chronicle* that Scharf knew Yockey by his real name. Given Yockey's modus operandi, it seems almost impossible to believe that he would reveal his true identity to anyone but a highly trusted associate.

San Francisco Chronicle reporter George Draper sent a letter to H. Keith Thompson in July 1960 about the "Scharf" puzzle. According to Draper:

Scharf created the impression here in the San Francisco Bay Area that he was pro-Zionist and positively oriented to Judaism. Furthermore, Scharf created the impression that he was a survivor of the Auschwitz concentration camp. In conversations with both yourself and Mr. Carto I obtained the impression that Scharf, conceivably, could have been anti-Zionist and that this could have been the mutual interest they shared. I could appreciate this speculative line of thinking were it not for the fact Scharf gave the impression hereabouts that he was enthusiastically pro-Zionist. Furthermore, it strikes me as unusual that a survivor of Auschwitz would gravitate to a man holding the political views, say, of yourself or Mr. Yockey.[43]

The full story of "Alexander Scharf"/Benjamin Junger may never be known. Like Yockey, his life is a complex trail of false papers and multiple identities. Appropriately enough, a brief note in the ADL files reports that, in light of all the negative publicity surrounding him, Junger said that he was seriously considering changing his name.

Notes:

1. *San Francisco Chronicle*, 22 August 1960. I want to thank the *Chronicle*'s former economics editor, Jonathan Marshall, for examining the paper's clips on Yockey and Scharf.

2. *San Francisco Chronicle*, 23 August 1960.

3. Ibid.

4. Ibid.

5. *San Francisco Chronicle*, 20 August 1960.

6. On 10 June 1960, the FBI received a report on Scharf (most likely from the Jewish Education Center) that gave this description:

Birth Date: 12/28/28. Birthplace: Czechoslovakia. U.S. Entry: Came to the United States approximately five years ago, after teaching for one year in Asunción, Paraguay. Education: Attended Columbia University, New York City, for two years; became a graduate of the Teachers Institute of the Jewish Theological Seminary in New York; taught school (not further identified) at Nutley and Passaic, New Jersey, and came to work for the Jewish Educational Center in San Francisco during January 1959.

Scharf also told an acquaintance he had come to San Francisco from Philadelphia.

7. "Seymour Fromer, director of Jewish Education in Oakland, said Scharf wears the German tattoo on his arm that proves he was a prisoner in Auschwitz, where more than two million Jews were cremated by Hitler. 'I am sure Scharf believed in Israel and Zionism,' said Fromer." (*San Francisco Sunday Chronicle*, 19 June 1960.)

8. *San Francisco Chronicle*, 22 August 1960.

9. *San Francisco Chronicle*, 23 August 1960.

10. Mrs. Cohen-Sift said that Scharf also served as an usher at her wedding to Scharf's roommate.

11. My interview with R. Harris Smith.

12. Rabbi Harold Schulweis decided to fire Scharf at the end of the school term because he thought that he was "a poor administrator." I spoke with Rabbi Schulweis in February 1996. He told me that he had little recollection of the events of that time.

13. *San Francisco Chronicle*, 22 August 1960.

14. FBI report on Scharf, 20 July 1960. The name of Scharf's former wife is blacked out.

15. The Cal-Neva had connections to organized crime. In the early 1960s Chicago mafia boss Sam Giancana attempted to take it over. Clubs like the Cal-Neva were the U.S. wing of a gambling circuit that included Havana's casinos.

16. Coincidentally, on New Year's Day, 1959, Fidel Castro took power in Cuba. For about a year, organized crime elements believed they could work out an agreement with him to continue to run the casinos.

17. Scharf's Alien Registration Card showed that he entered the U.S. in April 1955.

18. Scharf had been a guarantor or reference and had listed his address as 2401 Sacramento Street, where he lived before moving to Oakland.

19. *San Francisco Chronicle*, 23 June 1960.

20. On the police discovery of Scharf's car, see the 5 July 1960 *San Francisco Chronicle*.

21. *San Francisco Chronicle*, 22 June 1960.

22. In Scharf's apartment, the government had found a still-sealed telegram from Bohlen King to Scharf that was delivered to him on the day he disappeared. A few days after her connection with Scharf became known, Bohlen King told the press that she was reconciling with her estranged husband.

23. *San Francisco Chronicle*, 22 June 1960.

24. *San Francisco News-Call Bulletin*, 18 June 1960.

25. Although the reporter's name is blacked out, it was most likely George Draper of the *San Francisco Chronicle*, who closely investigated the story.

26. This information made Scharf's story about a scholarship to Israel after his graduation that much more interesting. This is especially so because, according to a report in the 19 June 1960 *San Francisco Chronicle*, Scharf "returned to Paraguay as a teacher" after his New York sojourn.

27. San Francisco FBI report to J. Edgar Hoover, 20 July 1960, conveying information supplied by a local INS investigator Jack Slattery concerning Scharf.

28. *San Francisco Chronicle*, 20 August 1960.

29. *San Francisco Chronicle*, 23 August 1960.

30. *San Francisco Chronicle*, 22 August 1960. The *Chronicle* then noted: "Yockey is known to have told friends in Miami that he had spent several months in Havana, 'spreading anti-American propaganda.' He also tried to get a message delivered to Cuba shortly before he committed suicide. Scharf insists that his selection of Havana as a refuge in his frantic flight was pure coincidence."

31. George Draper's 5 July 1960 letter to H. Keith Thompson in Thompson's archives at the Hoover Institute.

32. In the ADL files there is a report of an interview between Scharf and Frank Tully of the State Department (at which Stanley Jacobs of the San Francisco ADL was also

present). Scharf was asked: "Did you ever meet Harold Keith Thompson in Havana while you were there?" Scharf replied that he had not.

33. H. Keith Thompson's reply to my questionnaire.

34. Since George Draper is dead, we may never know if he was correct. It is possible that Thompson told Draper that he was trying to send a letter to some Cuban through Lyle Stuart, who was going to Cuba, and that this got garbled in such a way as to confuse Lyle Stuart's presence in Cuba with H. Keith Thompson's in the FBI report. If Thonpson did help supply weapons to Batista, it seems unlikely that he would go to Havana. Yet it should be noted that Hans-Ulrich Rudel, who was also involved in the weapons trade, was reported to have visited Havana in the early 1960s to help organize Castro's air force, according to a long profile of Rudel in the 21 October 1962 *Kolnische Rundschau*. (Kurt Tauber, *Beyond Eagle and Swastika* [Middletown, CT: Wesleyan University Press, 1967], Vol. 2, fn., 204, p. 1078.) Tauber then notes: "Uncorroborated allegations like these must, of course, be viewed with greatest caution."

35. Scharf told the *San Francisco Chronicle* (20 August 1960) that he had relied on friends in Havana "until they found out who I was a couple of weeks ago." Officials at the Jewish Theological Seminary may have informed Havana's Jewish community about Scharf's ties to Yockey.

36. *Oakland Tribune,* 20 August 1960.

37. See the 25 August 1960 *San Francisco Chronicle* article on Junger for his background.

38. According to Stanley Firmin in *They Came to Spy* (London: Hutchinson, 1946), pp. 116–17:

> Diamond smuggling was every bit as important to the German war machine as the collection of military and naval information and the working of a sabotage operation. The British Secret Service regarded the work of counteracting it as second only to the job of catching German spies. In some respects the activities of the two organizations— the spying and the diamond smuggling—were linked tightly. ·
>
> The obtaining of industrial diamonds was a matter of vital importance to German war industry. They were needed for use in cutting tools, for optical work, and a dozen other things in German factories where fine precision work was a necessity ... And to kill, as it were, two birds with one stone, the Germans decided right at the beginning that the very best method of transmitting money to their vast army of espionage and sabotage and propaganda agents in the various countries of the world was by this same method of smuggled diamonds.

39. Ibid., p. 121.

40. Smith said that students from Israel taught Hebrew.

41. From FBI report SF 105-1769, which discussed Yockey's "Jack Forest" cover during the time he was living in Bellingham, Washington; Alaska; and Reno, Nevada:

> On June 7, 1960, city directories and credit records reflected JOHN FOREST moved into 2522 Cedarwood in September 1958, coming from 6360 Bryn Mawr, Hollywood, California ... Post office records reflect FOREST moved to Reno, Nevada, in November 1958, c/o General Delivery, and BUCHANAN moved to Box 2035, Juneau, Alaska, in September 1958.

By Airtel dated June 16, 1960, in the HATCH caption, Salt Lake City advised as follows regarding FOREST:

"TED SPRINGER, Superintendent of Mails, and LEE DARAH, Clerk, General Delivery Window, U.S. Post Office, Reno, Nevada, were contacted on June 13, 1960 by SA PAUL A. BARESEL. They checked change-of-address records for 1958, 1959, and 1960. They could not locate any change of address for JACK PETER FOREST. They did locate one for JOHN and JOAN FOREST, which was dated September 22, 1958. This changed their address from General Delivery, Reno, Nevada, to 2522 Cedarwood, Bellingham, Washington."

It is noted that Seattle reported that their address was changed to General Delivery, Reno, in November 1958. In this regard, SPRINGER stated that the Reno Post Office has no change of address for JOHN and JOAN FOREST subsequent to September 22, 1958.

Recall that the FBI found out that "Forest" stayed only briefly in Bellingham and then moved to some place in Alaska (I suspect Juneau) before leaving in late November or early December 1958.

42. Report by FBI agent Keith Teeter, 14 June 1960.

43. George Draper's 5 July 1960 letter to H. Keith Thompson, from the Thompson archives at the Hoover Institute. It should be noted that there was a case of a former Nazi named Wilhelm Schmidt who actually hid out in Israel after the war, posing as a Jew who had been interned in a concentration camp in Czechoslovakia. (Michael Bar-Zohar, *The Avengers* [New York: Hawthorn Books, 1967], pp. 156–58.)

50

"WHAT'S BEHIND YOCKEYISM?"

On Friday, 17 June 1960, the day Yockey died, the National Renaissance Party held one of its regular New York meetings. The chief topic of conversation, however, was not Yockey but American Nazi Party (ANP) leader George Lincoln Rockwell, whose attempt to organize a demonstration in New York's Union Square had ignited a civil liberties debate.[1] It also put Rockwell on the front page of the *New York Times*. (Yockey's death was only mentioned in a tiny wire story in the Saturday *Times*.)

One of the ironies of the American far right is that Rockwell, a bitter foe of Yockey, is almost universally viewed as the first real postwar American Nazi. Although he never had more than a handful of followers, groups from the Aryan Nations to the White Aryan Resistance consider Rockwell their philosophical and tactical progenitor as well as a "martyred prophet of racial survival."[2]

Rockwell's fame stems in large part from his ability to play the tabloid Führer. Born on 9 March 1918 in Bloomington, Illinois, he was a natural showman whose parents had been successful vaudeville performers. Rockwell served in World War II as a Navy pilot. After being recalled to the Navy during the Korean War, he began listening to Senator Joseph McCarthy's speeches on the radio, and attended one of Gerald L. K. Smith's Christian Nationalist Crusade rallies. After reading *Mein Kampf*, he made his leap into the ultra-right.

Rockwell first created the American Federation of Conservative Organizations in 1956. He also became an assistant publisher of Russell Maguire's *American Mercury*. During this same period, he joined forces with DeWest Hooker, the New York rightist and Fred Weiss foe. With Hooker's support, Rockwell helped found both the United White Party and the National States Rights Party.[3] He then relocated to Newport News, Virginia, to work with William Stephenson of the Northern League–allied journal *The Virginian* before founding the American Nazi Party in March 1959.[4]

Although he attended NRP- and *Truth Seeker*–organized Racist Forums as an honored guest, Rockwell was clearly in the anti-Yockey wing of the right, and in the early 1960s he began warning his fellow fascists about the dangers of "Yockeyism." His attacks began not long after Fred Weiss and H. Keith Thompson published *The World in Flames*, with its vehement anti-Americanism.[5]

Rockwell's suspicions about Yockey were further confirmed by H. Keith Thompson, whom Rockwell had met in the late 1950s at the office of *American Mercury* publisher Russell Maguire.[6] In a massive survey of the far right published in the August 1962 issue of *The Independent*, Thompson argued that Yockey should not be considered part of the American right, that "vast mural of zealots and nuts, crooks and con-men; the dedicated and the phoney." Thompson described Yockey as "a colorful, FBI-pursued rightist operative with international connections," in particular the European Liberation Front, "a group doing a job for Moscow among European rightists." He then noted that Yockey "had grown to detest the American right and its mentality."[7]

As a staunch anti-Communist, Rockwell was particularly hostile to Yockey's views on Russia. Having entered the right through McCarthyism, he freely supplied information to the FBI. When an ANP member named Roger Foss told him that he had some earlier contact with Valentin Ivanoff, the first secretary of the Soviet embassy, Rockwell insisted that Foss report his contact to the FBI.[8]

Rockwell was equally critical of the National Renaissance Party. Although he praised NRP street fights against Jews, he refused to allow the ANP to have any connections with James Madole's followers.[9] Rockwell believed that the NRP had fallen "into one of the most deadly traps ever set by the scheming, villainous Hebrew: the monstrous fraud of Soviet 'anti-Semitism.'" That explained why Madole, "in all honesty," had spent the last two years preaching "that Castro is a great 'patriot' and that the Chinese Communists are really only patriotic nationalists in disguise." The NRP even claimed "that the Soviets are really the 'new barbarians' of our age, who will rout western decadence and who are, therefore, the hope of the world!"[10]

A more elaborate attack on Yockeyism as "The New Strasserism" appeared in the February 1963 issue of *The Rockwell Report*. Rockwell aide Karl Allen argued that while 90 percent of *Imperium* was sound National Socialist thinking, the "Yockey cult" was in danger of veering away from Nazism "perhaps even into an off-brand type of 'anti-Semitic communism.'" Taking note of Willis Carto's attacks on the FBI for hounding Yockey, Allen asked: "Why should an honest man object to the FBI inquiry about his activities?"

There was also a European angle to Rockwell's condemnation of Yockey. Rockwell visited England in August 1962 to help found the World Union of

National Socialists (WUNS) at a meeting held in a summer camp in Gloucestershire's Cotswold Hills.[11] His trip had been arranged by Colin Jordan, a one-time Northern League member and founder of the White Defense League, who established his own National Socialist Movement (NSM) in the early 1960s. The summer-camp gathering culminated in the "Cotswold Agreement" proclaiming Jordan the head of the WUNS and Rockwell his Deputy Führer.

Jordan, too, had strong reservations about Yockey that dated back to the early 1950s, when Jordan was a protégé of Arnold Leese, the grand old man of British anti-Semitism.[12] After World War II, Leese published a small journal called *Gothic Ripples* and gathered around him a tiny coterie led by Jordan. Leese despised Yockey for his views on both Russia and race. He also labeled the ELF "Strasserist." According to Yockey's English comrade John Anthony Gannon:

> For Leese, vertical race was everything, for FPY the horizontal aspect was the deciding issue. Perhaps Leese was too old and too rigid in his thinking to ever be expected to grasp such a new approach to race; after all, he was born in the 19th century which for FPY was, almost, a total disqualification for a true understanding of his thinking. Anyway, Leese abused FPY in his propaganda and accused him of being all sorts of a mongrel, even a Yaqui Indian . . . [13] To which FPY replied in *Frontfighter* citing Leese as "Leese or Louse."[14]

Leese made his views clear to a New York rightist hanger-on named John Langrod. In a letter dated 24 December 1953, he told Langrod that he had stopped exchanging *Gothic Ripples* with Madole after receiving the issue of the NRP *Bulletin* that featured Yockey's "What Is Behind the Hanging of the Eleven Jews in Prague?":

> I have been sending my *Gothic Ripples* (five copies each issue) to Mr. Madole . . . But I got a rude shock when I saw the *Bulletin* for December 1952, for it evidently had been written by the European Liberation Front, a poisonous group for whom I have no manner of use. On enquiry, I found that the leader of the NRP did not seem to know who the people were who had written this stuff, although the name European Liberation Front was clearly printed on p. four, first column . . . In short, there seemed to be some serious deficiency in the administration [of the NRP] . . . As to the future, if you can explain to me how your movement got included in the European Liberation Front, what steps are being taken to see that this sort of thing is past and done for, we might again exchange bulletins.[15]

After Leese died in 1956, Colin Jordan inherited his political tendency, and he was as hostile to Yockey as his mentor. In 1955 he wrote a small book called *Fraudulent Conversion: The Myth of Moscow's Change*,[16] and although Jordan does not mention Yockey by name, the book was written to refute the claim that the Soviet Union was not under Jewish control. Jordan argued that the struggle between Communism and Zionism was a Jewish family feud over the best way to rule the world. To claim otherwise was factually wrong and politically blasphemous. Thus, when Rockwell attacked Yockey he also spoke for other leading elements inside the WUNS.

Rockwell's most vitriolic polemic appeared in the 15 July 1964 issue of *The Rockwell Report* under the title "What's Behind Yockeyism?" In it, Rockwell denounced Fred Weiss's ties to the ADL operative Sanford Griffith as well as H. Keith Thompson's friendship with Fair Play for Cuba organizer Lyle Stuart. He then warned:

> There is rising all over the world, among hard-core National Socialists a new cult of what I call Yockeyism . . . I found much of interest in Yockey's book *Imperium* and actually helped promote it. But the cult founded on this man is dangerous and, I believe, in some ways downright EVIL.

Rockwell also accused Thompson of trying to infiltrate the ANP as "George Copeland," and claimed that Thompson "circulated" in New York's homosexual community and was particularly close to some "Nazi pansies . . . a group of queers who call themselves the 'real' National Socialists."[17] "Pansies," even National Socialist ones, were not Rockwell's favorite people. Although he boasted that he had saved some of his own stormtroopers from homosexuality, "a queer who is PROUD of it . . . is the foulest creature on the face of the earth."[18]

Rockwell's attack on Yockeyism was consistent with long-held feeling of uneasiness and uncertainty about Yockey's circle by many rightists. Yockey's mysteriousness, his strange death, and *Imperium*'s complexity enhanced his mystique. But that same mysteriousness, coupled with his views on race and Russia, also fueled suspicion that sinister forces really did lurk in the shadows of the cryptic cult of Yockeyism.

Notes:

1. The report on the meeting comes from the files of the NSANL.

2. From Frederick J. Simonelli, "The American Nazi Party, 1958–1967," in the Spring 1995 issue of *The Historian*. For more on Rockwell, see Frederick J. Simonelli, *American Fuehrer: George Lincoln Rockwell and the American Nazi Party* (Urbana, IL: University of Illinois Press, 1999), and William Schmaltz, *Hate: George Lincoln Rockwell & the American Nazi Party* (Washington, D.C.: Brassey's, 1999).

3. Although a co-founder of the NSRP, Rockwell felt that the group had disguised its National Socialist orientation. He also believed in separatism rather than segregation.

4. See former ANP member James Mason's book *Siege* (Denver: Storm Books, 1992), Appendix III.

5. To the race-conscious Rockwell, one passage from *The World in Flames* was especially controversial:

> No estimate would be complete which leaves two great political developments out of account, both of recent years. The first is the Arab Revolt led by a great and vigorous man, Gamal Abdul Nasser. The second is the formation of nationalist, neutralist

regimes by such brilliant statesmen as Marshal Josef Broz Tito of Yugoslavia, Nehru of India, Field Marshal Ayub Khan of Pakistan, General Ibrahim Abboud of the Sudan, Sekou Toure of Guinea, Sukarno of Indonesia, Nkrumah of Ghana, and others. These personalities embody an Idea, none are out for money or publicity. They live simply, work for and live for their ideas. One such man in a position of leadership is a world-historical force. All lead weak political units and cannot by themselves fight either of the great world powers. But all want independence for their people; Nasser, for example, for some 300,000,000 Moslems. Each is a symbol to great human masses. Their significance in each case in this Estimate is that they diminish the Jewish-American power without augmenting the Russian-Chinese power. By their Palestine policy, the Zionists may even succeed in driving the Arab world to fight for Russia.

Ironically, this was the one paragraph in the essay that Yockey did not write. Thompson and Weiss inserted it after Yockey's death to make the text more up-to-date.

6. H. Keith Thompson gave an interesting account of his relations with Rockwell to historian Frederick Simonelli. In a 12 July 1993 letter, Thompson wrote:

As to Rockwell, I had some business with J. Russell Maguire, publisher of the *American Mercury* somewhere in the mid-'50s as I recall. It concerned placing some articles by George Sylvester Viereck in that magazine. When I arrived in those offices in Manhattan, I encountered Rockwell, who was then serving as administrative assistant to Maguire. He knew very well who I was . . . some years later he [Rockwell] again approached me, this time asking to arrange a visit with Viereck, who was then recuperating in Lenox Hill Hospital. I did so, and accompanied Rockwell there for a brief visit which accomplished nothing that I could see. Thereafter Rockwell made a number of attempts to get me to join his organization in one capacity or another.

Thompson said he avoided any association "because I believed that the confrontational policies of his group were entirely counter-productive."

7. Thompson also claimed that, given his views about Russia, Fred Weiss "really doesn't belong to the right."

8. Rockwell's feelings for the FBI angered many on the right. In the August 1962 issue of *The Thunderbolt*, Ed Fields claimed that Rockwell was an FBI collaborator on the Jewish payroll. Rockwell filed a lawsuit against Fields for slander. According to a history of the far right in the October 1993 issue of *NSV Report* (Vol. 11, No. 4), Fields settled out of court, paid Rockwell, and printed a retraction in the October 1965 *Thunderbolt*.

9. See "Cautious Commendations for Madole," in the 15 June 1963 issue of *The Rockwell Report*. Rockwell also tried to court Madole. According to William Goring's monograph on the NRP for the National Information Center's *Newsletter* (December 1969–January 1970):

Genuine ideologists like Madole are rare and respected, even by those who disagree with them. Although he often attacked Madole in his bi-weekly publication *The Rockwell Report* as a leftist, the late George Lincoln Rockwell, American Nazi Party leader, had invited Madole on several occasions to join the Nazi Party as an officer and sent Madole the *Confidential Intra-Party Newsletter*, an internal ANP bulletin that went to a few outsiders, but strangely, not even to all ANP officials. As for Rockwell's open attacks on Madole, they were frequently followed by letters from Edward Fields, National States Rights Party leader, commiserating with Madole, making overtures, and complaining about what a terrible, uncouth person Rockwell is.

10. Ibid.

11. Because of immigration problems, Rockwell was smuggled into England for the occasion. Along with Jordan and Rockwell, the WUNS meeting was attended by John Tyndall (National Secretary of Jordan's National Socialist Movement), Savitri Devi, Bruno Lüdtke, and other national socialists from across Europe. On Devi, see Nicholas Goodrick-Clarke, *Hitler's Priestess: Savitri Devi, the Hindu-Aryan Myth, and Neo-Nazism* (New York: New York University Press, 1998).

Bruno Lüdtke is even more interesting for our purposes. In an August 1980 memo based on notes taken from talks with Douglas Kaye and Eustace Mullins, Yockey's would-be biographer Keith Stimely noted that "Bruno Lüdtke said in 1974 that a trunk of Yockey's effects and letters were [*sic*] given over by him to an old woman in Munich. Tried to locate her/it, but was unsuccessful." In another note in the same memo, Stimely listed as collaborators/contacts for *Der Feind Europas* "Heubaum, Bruno Lüdtke, Rudolf Aschenauer, Heinrich Malz." According to Fred Simonelli, Lüdtke was born in the greater Hamburg area on 15 November 1926. He joined the Wehrmacht in October 1944 and served in Denmark. After the war he became an active far-rightist. Lüdtke carried on an extensive correspondence with Rockwell. It should also be recalled that Marie Weiss returned to Germany in the late 1960s or early 1970s and *may* have been the "old woman."

12. Born in 1878, Leese spent many years as a veterinary surgeon in various British colonies, primarily in the Arab world. He returned to England after World War I and took up private practice in Stamford, Lincolnshire. In the 1920s he created the Imperial Fascist League (IFL), which embraced a particularly demented form of anti-Semitism. When the British Union of Fascists (BUF) emerged, Leese denounced Mosley as a political adventurer and "kosher fascist" whose first wife had Jewish blood. Leese spent three and a half years in Brixton prison under Defence Regulation 18B during World War II. In 1947 he spent another year behind bars for aiding two Dutch Nazi POWs in an attempt to escape to Argentina. See "Arnold Leese and the Imperial Fascist League: The Impact of Radical Fascism," by John Morell, in *British Fascism* (New York: St. Martin's Press, 1980), edited by Kenneth Lunn and Richard Thurlow. Also see Leese's autobiography, *Out of Step: Events in the Two Lives of an Anti-Jewish Camel-Doctor* (Guildford, 1951) and Richard Griffiths, *Fellow Travellers of the Right* (London: Constable, 1980).

13. This was Leese's joke on the name "Yockey."

14. Gannon then remarked: "Guy Chesham and I once met two of Leese's collaborators to see if any kind of co-operation were possible, but it was not." John Anthony Gannon, letter to Keith Stimely, 7 September 1980.

15. From the files of the NSANL. In a 1 December 1954 letter to Langrod, Leese commented: "I think it likely that Strasser is linked with the European Liberation Group, but cannot prove it."

16. Colin Jordan, *Fraudulent Conversion: The Myth of Moscow's Change* (London: Briton Publishing Society, 1955). Briton's address was Arnold Leese House in London.

17. In a 12 July 1993 letter to Frederick Simonelli, H. Keith Thompson commented:

Rockwell also had a fixation on homosexuality and tried to tar all his opponents with that brush. He said that he had problems with that in his own organization. He was quite aware that the mere levelling of such allegations in those days was extremely damaging and of course there was no defense save denial. But he was so rabid on the point that I often wondered if he were not himself so inclined. But I have no knowledge of that.

18. The idea that "Yockeyism" had a gay angle was not unique to Rockwell. In his monograph on the National Renaissance Party, William Goring writes:

Yockey and his European Liberation Front associates remain for the most part shadowy figures. In their devotion to super-secret conspiracies they seem to have been so secret that they accomplished practically nothing. However, their influence on postwar fascist ideology has been enormous . . . The occasional members of the European Liberation Front who show up at fascist circles and acknowledge themselves as members are usually intellectuals, not thugs, and they have many homosexual traits; they sometimes show passports indicating a lot of travel in Communist countries.

51

CARTO'S CRUSADE

In August 1960 *Right* ran a front-page story entitled "ADL Closes Its File on Yockey: Creative Genius Driven to Suicide." *Right's* hagiography was the first salvo in Willis Carto's decades-long campaign to immortalize Yockey. Yet one month after its tribute, *Right* ceased publication. It would soon be reborn as *Western Destiny*, which proudly identified itself as the "direct descendent" of *Right* and two Northern League publications, *Northern World* and *Folk*.[1] Unlike *Right*, *Western Destiny* was a well-financed and professionally produced journal. Its editorial board included Carto and Ed Vargas from *Right*, Edward Longford of *Northern World*, the American race theorist Byram Campbell, League of Empire Loyalists head A. K. Chesterton, Earnest Sevier Cox, Arthur Ehrhardt of *Nation Europa*, Robert Kuttner and Charles Smith of *Truth Seeker*, William Stevenson of *The Virginian* and the Northern League, and Jan Kruls, a Dutchman who succeeded Roger Pearson as head of the Northern League.[2]

Western Destiny was written for far-right intellectuals, and its articles frequently praised Yockey.[3] In November 1965 the journal announced that the Northern League's founder, Roger Pearson, would become its new editor.[4] Then, in April 1966, *Western Destiny* ceased publication.[5] The front cover of its last issue was a picture of Yockey being led away in handcuffs by U.S. government agents.

After *Western Destiny* closed shop, Carto took over *American Mercury*, which had fallen on hard times after the death of Russell Maguire.[6] Although *American Mercury* was now proclaimed the heir to *Northern World*, *Right*, *Folk*, and *Western Destiny*,[7] it was far cruder than the relatively highbrow *Western Destiny*. *American Mercury* had a *Reader's Digest*–like format: Diatribes like Austin App's

515

"That Elusive 'Six Million,'" impenetrable excerpts from *Imperium*, deep think tracts ("Hitler—The Greatest Spenglerian"), and Otto Skorzeny's "Rudolf Hess Was Not Insane" appeared next to articles like "Remember Penny Candy?" and "Cats Are Superior to *Some* People."

Carto's most important contribution to Yockey's legacy came in November 1962, when he persuaded Truth Seeker Press to publish the first American edition of *Imperium*.[8] When the book appeared, Yockey was still such a mystery man that Joe Rudden, James Madole's NRP lieutenant and NSANL informer, was barely aware of him. In a report to the NSANL dated 18 November 1962, Rudden wrote:

> There's a new book "IMERPIAL [sic]." Chas. Smith is behind it—also *Truth Seeker*. Jackie (?) (has something to do with it—or wrote it). Book cost $5.00. Madole bought a few. It's pushed by Weiss. Smith said Sanford Griffith of the ADL went to see Smith. Anything Jocky [sic] does is pushed by Weiss. The book is all fixed up nicely with index, etc.

The American edition of *Imperium* also came with an introduction by Carto.[9] His essay presents Yockey as an innocent lawyer-turned-philosopher made tragic victim by sinister forces that included a group "vastly more powerful" than the government, a group "so powerful, indeed, that men dare not speak its name above a whisper, unless in terms of the most groveling praise."[10] Carto, however, was less concerned with Zion's sinister hand than with *Imperium*'s ability "to formulate an ethic and faith." Couldn't *Imperium* offer "at least as much popular attractiveness as the painted lies of Marx?"[11]

Yet there were problems with *Imperium*, the most important being Yockey's take on race. Falling back on Cultural Dynamics, Carto stressed that "the genetic interpretation of race is a necessary, useful, and valid one if we are to see all of our problems clearly and accurately."[12] Yockey was much too Spenglerian for Carto, who argued that

> the very introduction of the organic concept into historical philosophizing and theorizing, plus the unparalleled mastery over Nature which the West has attained—and the infinite possibilities for this for the future—hold out the conception that the organism of the West need not suffer the same destiny as cultures which have gone before and which had none of this knowledge.

Although Spengler had predicted that the final inevitable stage of a civilization was the emergence of imperialism (Caesarism), "racists" knew better:

> Neo-Spenglerians who are attuned to the racial view of history (call them "racists" for convenience) hold that the "final" phase of a Culture—the imperialistic stage—is final *only* because the cultural organism destroys its body and kills its soul by this process.

Carto then advances a *Mein Kampf*–like argument for the role Aryans played in founding great civilizations (including those in South America and China). He also asserts that the real snake in Valhalla was imperialism "and the resulting, inevitable backwash of conquered peoples and races into the heartland as slaves, bringing exotic religions, different philosophies; in a word, cultural sophistication first, then cultural anarchy." He continues:

> We thus see the real reason underlying the "inevitable" decline and destruction of a cultural organism. It is because, at a certain stage, a Culture develops a bad case of universalism ... *It is, therefore, the natural product of universalism which kills the organism; the death of the organism itself is neither natural nor necessary!* This conclusion comes by a synthesis of the Spenglerian and the racial point of view. Each tempers the other; together a comprehensive and hopeful theory of history can be developed which holds a deep meaning to Westerners of this day. At all costs, the imperialistic phase of development must be avoided, and we must guard against the digestion of alien matter we have already partially absorbed.

Science was yet another escape route from Spenglerian decline. The West's Faustian drive to the infinite would lead to the conquest of outer space ("a Frontier that can never be dissipated") and, even more glorious, the "most noble impossibility of all," the ability to "upgrade the human species through deliberate biological mechanics."

Yockey's English comrade John Anthony Gannon was not impressed with Carto's essay; in a letter to Keith Stimely, he commented:

> As for Willis Carto, I am sure he is sincere, devoted to FPY's memory, one of us, and your friend—it is necessary to say this in view of what must now follow. I do not believe that WC has read [*Imperium*], or understood it—even if his eyes followed every single line of print in the book. How is it possible for him to write such "crap" as FPY would have certainly declaimed. It is all laughable—Cultural Dynamics, indeed! FPY would have [been] rolling on the floor in agonies of laughter at that curious mixture of Imperialist terminology and philosophical garbage. Science-worshipper, Law-worshipper—I could go on! All these types were DESPISED by FPY as having got in the way of everyone who ever wanted to do something for the Idea. Whatever excuse there may have been for such intellectual junk before [*Imperium*] was written, there never was such afterwards. You CANNOT accept *Imperium* and FEEL it or UNDERSTAND its analysis and continue to believe in that guff! ... if one could accept this old rag-bag of worn-out 19th century nostrums, how did it happen the way it did?
>
> In England, before the year 1950 there was no racially mongrelised population, and even today it is still not at the American level. If one could rely upon the FACT that every blue-eyed, fair-haired human being was a FRIEND, and that the others were probably ENEMIES, how simple and predictable life would be, and have been. Look at the degeneration of Scandinavia, where examples of non-Nordics are hard to come by! Believe me, I will go along the VERTICAL line for esthetics reasons, and certainly exclude non-Europeans from our Imperium (our colonials excepted, of course), but for all the rest it is all quite absurd when taken

to the lengths of determinism! FPY postulated that Race is what a man DOES. This means that someone who might appear to be a VERTICAL kangaroo might well be a HORIZONTAL Nordic, and vice versa. WC's ideas are a little nearer to OM's [Oswald Mosley's] as expressed in *The Alternative*, but only a little, for OM was not a Verticalist, either. I am afraid I cannot be kinder to WC than that.[13]

Just how little *Imperium* has been understood inside the U.S. right is evident by its American reception. Although the book has sold well over 20,000 copies in the U.S., there has been virtually nothing written about it inside the far right. Political scientist John George and historian Laird Wilcox are probably correct when they remark that much of *Imperium*'s "enduring reputation lies in its incomprehensibility . . . In the tiny community of neo-Nazism, *Imperium* is the 'bible' few people have thoroughly read and almost nobody understands."[14]

Given *Imperium*'s difficulty it is even more remarkable that Carto actually organized a political movement around Yockey. The high point of American Yockeyism came in 1968–69, when Carto managed to transform Youth for Wallace, the youth wing of George Wallace's presidential campaign, into a new political formation called the National Youth Alliance (NYA). The NYA's founding theoretical document was *Imperium*, which Noontide Press brought out for the first time in paperback in May 1969.[15]

The NYA was made possible in part by a strange series of events that had left the far right in chaos. On 25 August 1967 George Lincoln Rockwell was assassinated in an Arlington, Virginia, parking lot by one of his followers, John Patler. After his death, the National Socialist White People's Party (NSWPP—the former ANP) chose onetime National Renaissance Party member Matt Koehl as its new leader. Koehl's rise to power caused considerable tension among Rockwell's supporters. An insider portrait of the American far right that appeared in the October–December 1993 issue of the National Socialist Vanguard's *NSV Report* claims that after Koehl was chosen, "a group of concerned sympathizers in the New Jersey area feared that subsequent exposure of Koehl's homosexual background would be embarrassing to the NSWPP and the Movement."[16] If the *NSV Report* is to be believed, during the summer of 1970 a Koehl critic named Wilfried Kernbach approached Dr. William Pierce, a Rockwell aide who today runs the National Alliance, to warn him about Koehl. Kernbach supposedly gave Pierce incriminating evidence against Koehl "that was stolen from the home of an Anti-Defamation League (ADL) associate or member who had infiltrated the National Renaissance Party over 10 years previously." Kernbach wanted Pierce to use the information to force Koehl's resignation. Koehl, however, ordered Pierce banned from NSWPP headquarters. Pierce responded by joining forces with Carto's NYA.

The National States Rights Party (NSRP) was also in turmoil over sexual matters, although this time the allegation was that its leader was too heterosexual— at least that was the accusation leveled against Ed Fields in the pages of the March

1965 issue of *The White American*. According to the paper, Fields was draining the NSRP treasury to support "his beautiful and devoted wife" Dolores and their two children while keeping a second wife and daughter on the side.[17] The Minutemen organization was also experiencing rough times after its leader Robert DePugh was sent to jail on an illegal-gun-possession charge in 1967.

With much of his competition in shambles, Carto took advantage of the energy generated by the Wallace campaign to launch the NYA. His most prestigious co-conspirator was Professor Revilo P. Oliver, the Indo-Europeanist and University of Illinois classics professor who had made his name in the late 1950s with a series of erudite essays for William F. Buckley, Jr.'s *National Review*. Oliver first met Carto in 1956 or early 1957 at a right-wing gathering.[18] He went on to become a leading member of the John Birch Society, until he was expelled in the mid-1960s for anti-Semitism. According to Professor Oliver:

> After the election in 1968, [Carto] proposed a plan to salvage the membership of the Youth for Wallace group, which he claimed to have subsidized to the extent of $50,000 in cash in a few months, and to found a new national youth movement of the kind that I had long regarded as an indispensable part of any effective effort to preserve our nation.[19]

Oliver accepted Carto's proposal after being persuaded to do so by Louis Byers, a national organizer for Youth for Wallace and a fervent Yockeyite. Like Oliver, Byers had been purged from the John Birch Society for anti-Semitism.[20] All three men agreed that *Imperium* should become the NYA's founding philosophical text.[21] Carto next recruited John Acord, the National Chairman of Youth for Wallace, into the NYA. Youth for Wallace was officially renamed the National Youth Alliance at a Carto-chaired meeting at Washington's Army-Navy Club on 15 November 1968. Copies of *Imperium* were circulated at the gathering.[22]

With the NYA, Carto finally had the vehicle he needed to turn the American right toward Yockeyism. John Acord, who later had a bitter falling-out with Carto, attended a Pittsburgh NYA conclave where Carto gave a presentation. Accord later recalled how Carto

> spoke of his meeting with Yockey and how the movement was growing throughout the nation. He expressed his belief that political power, like that he was building in Liberty Lobby, would soon bring the "Imperium" of which all Yockeyites dream . . . In the meantime, it was necessary for Yockeyites to collect as much political power as possible within all existing political institutions and to capture the leadership of as many conservative elements as possible as the nation swings to the right. In this manner, said Carto, the FPYM [Francis Parker Yockey Movement] members will capture the nation.[23]

That night in Pittsburgh may have marked the zenith of American Yockeyism as a political movement. Just nine years after Yockey's death, Carto seemed on the brink of founding a hegemonic movement on the far right that relied on *Imperium* as its central text. One critical question, however, remained unaddressed: Did American Yockeyism have anything to do with Yockey? When George Lincoln Rockwell attacked Yockey, he zeroed in not just on Yockey's view of race but also on his anti-Americanism and support for Soviet-backed Third World movements. Carto's brand of Yockeyism, however, reflected a far more anodyne brand of orthodox far-right politics. Beginning with his introduction to *Imperium*, Carto had brilliantly marketed Yockey to the American far right. But in selling Yockey the myth, had he obliterated Yockey the man?

Notes:

1. See the June 1964 issue of *Western Destiny* for mention of its lineage. *Northern World*, the Northern League publication allied to *Right*, continued publishing into 1963. In the spring of 1963, *Northern World* ran a full-page ad for *Imperium*.

2. Austin App, the Holocaust-denying academic, was also on the board.

3. One such tribute in the October 1964 issue was entitled "Francis P. Yockey: His Genius, Our Inspiration." Another homage, in the September 1964 issue of *Western Destiny*, was written by John Sullivan, the national chairman of the U.S. Nationalist Party. Douglas Kaye also had an article in the October 1964 issue of *Western Destiny*. Sullivan and Kaye would later found the pro-Yockey zine *TRUD!*

4. Pearson may have been replacing Byram Campbell. According to an article in the September–October 1967 issue of Maurice Bardèche's *Défense de l'Occident*, *Western Destiny* had been primarily edited by Campbell, who died in July 1965.

5. After the demise of *Western Destiny*, Pearson held posts at Queens College, Charlotte, North Carolina; the University of Southern Mississippi at Hattiesburg; and was dean of academic affairs at Montana College in Butte before establishing his own think tank, the Institute for the Study of Man, in Washington, D.C.

6. The Dallas-based far-rightist General Edwin Walker took control of *American Mercury* for a brief period as publisher and managing editor.

7. *Western Destiny* readers were also put on the mailing list of *American Mercury*.

8. Carto told me that some financial support to print *Imperium* came from a Southerner no longer involved in politics. When I mentioned that Fred Weiss had strong ties to *Truth Seeker*, Carto seemed surprised.

9. Because his introduction had such an impact (far more readers of *Imperium* have completed Carto's essay than Yockey's book), some of Carto's many critics on the right claim that the real author of the introduction was University of Illinois Professor Revilo P. Oliver. Oliver, however, clearly stated that Carto wrote the introduction, although he did rely on a critique of *Imperium* prepared by Oliver. In a December 1970 letter to Colonel Curtis Dall of the Liberty Lobby, Oliver remarked: "Despite these defects, *Imperium* was by far the best doctrine that was *available*. It was basically sound, and some of the shortcomings had been corrected in the preface that Carto wrote on the basis of my critique and suggestions."

10. Carto also mentions that *Imperium* is "coded." What this means is that in two sections of the book Yockey began succeeding paragraphs with the letters of his last name. For example in the April 1983 Noontide Press paperback edition (on pp. 480–81),

Yockey codes his name into the last six paragraphs of the chapter on "The History of American Imperialism."

11. It is in this section that the influence of Professor Oliver is most apparent. I doubt that the reference to "the saprophytes among us" (saprophytes being organisms which live on dead or decaying organic matter, according to my dictionary) flowed easily from Carto's pen. Oliver, however, was famous for using ornate words.

12. The thorny problem of *The World in Flames* (alluded to by Carto's remark that "some of his later writings could have been misinterpreted as being pro-Russian") is neatly dodged with the observation: "Of course, Yockey was neither pro- nor anti-Russian; he was concerned with the health and continuity of the West, and his view of the world was at all times subjective to what he considered in the best interests of the West *at that time.*"

13. John Anthony Gannon, letter to Keith Stimely dated 15 February 1981.

14. John George and Laird Wilcox, *Nazis, Communists, Klansmen and Others on the Fringe* (Buffalo: Prometheus Books, 1992), pp. 252–53. The February 1982 issue of Wilmot Robertson's *Instauration* (perhaps the most literate journal of the racial ultraright) described *Imperium* as "much touted and much thumbed-through." It also noted that the book ("part 20th century Book of Revelations, part postscript to Oswald Spengler, part revised and updated edition of *Mein Kampf*") had turned Yockey into "a cult figure of certain hermetic elements" of the American right.

15. Carto launched Noontide Press, his publishing house, with unsold copies of the Truth Seeker edition of *Imperium.*

16. Koehl's NSWPP also produced an expensive-looking *National Socialist Review,* the first issue of which included a long essay on "National Socialism and Eros." This text identifies Adolf Hitler as a homoerotic man and praises Hans Blüher as a "proto-Nazi" who argued that Aryan man must sublimate his homoerotic impulses to the great task of culture-building. It recommends Blüher's *The Role of the Erotic in the Male Community* and discusses Otto Weininger's theory that women have "no cultural eros."

17. The Fields scandal had a strange quality of poetic justice. From May to November 1963, the month President John Kennedy was assassinated, the NSRP's *Thunderbolt* paper, which Fields edited, spread the news throughout the South that Kennedy was an adulterer.

18. R. P. Oliver's letter to Colonel Dall of the Liberty Lobby. Oliver was most likely referring to the Congress of Freedom meeting in Chicago.

19. Ibid.

20. Nor was Byers particularly shy about expressing those views. The August 1970 issue of the *Thunderbolt* cited a Byers speech to the NSRP convention (as head of the NYA, Byers was an invited guest), where he thundered: "The Jew is inbred genetically with destructive traits. He is not capable of acting for the betterment of society. He is driven by his destructive instincts to destroy even that which might protect his own status in the nation." On Byers, see a *Washington Post* profile by Paul Valentine that was reprinted in the 25 December 1969 *L.A. Times.*

21. See the June and July 1970 *Task Force* for a reprint from the NYA that cites *Imperium* as the organization's core book.

22. See C. H. Simonds' 10 September 1971 *National Review* attack on Carto. Carto and William F. Buckley, Jr., are longtime bitter rivals.

23. Ibid.

52

THINGS

FALL

When Voltaire was asked to explain the fall of the Roman Empire, he replied: "It fell because all things fall." So perhaps the collapse of the National Youth Alliance was inevitable. Still, Carto's Imperium fell a lot more quickly than Rome's. From its inception, there was a basic tension inside the NYA between the more conventional George Wallace–type racists and Carto's cadre. Weary of continual factional infighting over politics and money, Carto, Revilo P. Oliver, and Lou Byers reconstituted the NYA as a Washington-based elite movement in March 1969.[1] They also gained an important supporter in William Pierce, the former Rockwell aide whom Matt Koehl had expelled from the NSWPP.[2] But Pierce, Oliver, and Byers would themselves soon turn against Carto. Byers, who once thought Carto "Francis Parker Yockey reincarnated," now moaned: "He *says* he's a National Socialist, but he isn't—he's a French peasant turned Jewish capitalist."[3]

By 1971 the NYA had split into two factions. Oliver and Byers supported Pierce's National Alliance, which still remains active today,[4] while Carto turned to a Virginia-based sect that published a journal called *Statecraft* to rebuild his wing of the movement. *Statecraft* was filled with unbelievably crude anti-black and anti-Jewish cartoons as well as articles by authors like George Carpenter, from the *Statecraft*-allied Iron Cross Motorcycle Club, who wrote:

> Commies, Peace Creeps, and assorted radical crud! Your arch enemy, the Iron Cross, is on the loose! If there are any doubts as to our willingness to use a gun in defense of THE WHITE RACE, please note our several gunfights . . . WE, MEN OF THE IRON CROSS, shall lead our White brothers to final, brutal, and blood-soaked victory![5]

Despite such prose, Carto and *Statecraft* (renamed Youth Action in 1971) became involved in a "Strasserist" overture to the New Left.[6] Carto's NYA created We Accuse in 1971 to unite the far left and far right in a coalition to demand a new Nuremberg war crimes trial. This time, however, the accused would be William F. Buckley, Jr., David Rockefeller, Walt Rostow, Robert MacNamara, and other luminaries of Eastern Establishment groups like the Council on Foreign Relations (CFR). We Accuse argued that it was now time to "unite young activists from both the Left and Right in joint political action towards the common goal of combatting the CFR Military Industrial Complex and the super-rich international financial oligarchy." A "YOUTH ACTION War Crimes Trial" of members of the "CFR Military Industrial Complex" was held in Los Angeles on 2 September 1972. Despite a speech by Carto, entitled "The Natural Coalition," to the gathering, his Strasserist turn proved a miserable failure.[7]

The NYA breakup further marginalized Yockeyism, which was now almost exclusively identified with Carto. Nor was the National Renaissance Party capable of carrying the torch. Especially after the death of Fred Weiss, the NRP become increasingly steeped in James Madole's own peculiar brand of racist theosophy. Madole even tried to establish a relationship with Anton LaVey's Church of Satan in the late 1960s.[8] By the mid-1970s he began devoting issue after issue of the NRP *Bulletin* to tracts like "'The New Atlantis': A Blueprint for an Aryan 'Garden of Eden' in North America," which paid special homage to the Russian occultist Madame Blavatsky for bringing "the Secret Wisdom of the Aryan Race from Tibet to Europe and North America."[9] He also presented his beliefs at Herman Slater's Warlock Shop (now known as Magikal Childe) in New York on 22 August 1976.[10]

"Pure" Yockeyism was kept alive in the late 1960s by an obscure publication called *TRUD!: From the White Underground*, founded by Douglas Kaye and John Sullivan, who helped form the tiny U.S. Nationalist Party in the early 1960s with support from Fred Weiss.[11] *TRUD!* was the first American journal to publish translated extracts from *Der Feind Europas*. Nor did *TRUD!* shy away from Yockey's explicitly pro-Russian orientation.[12] Kaye and Sullivan also wrote for *Common Sense*, which, from the fall of 1970 to its demise two years later, adopted a Yockeyist outlook.[13] Kaye then published a collection of four Yockey essays: "The World in Flames," "Tragedy of Youth," "The Destiny of America," and "What is Behind the Hanging of the Eleven Jews in Prague?" in 1971. In the mid-1970s he wrote an introduction to *The Proclamation of London*, which was reprinted by the Louisiana-based Sons of Liberty.[14]

In 1981, Thomas Francis, a friend of both Louis Byers and Revilo P. Oliver, published a complete English translation of *Der Feind Europas*.[15] *The Enemy of Europe* was issued by Liberty Bell Publications, which also put out *Liberty Bell*, one of the more influential journals of the U.S. ultra-right.[16] After *The Enemy of Europe* appeared, Yockeyism appeared to have reached its absolute limit. Then Keith Stimely appeared.

Born in Connecticut in 1957 and raised on the West Coast, Stimely graduated from the University of Oregon in 1980. He also served as a reserve officer in the U.S. Army.[17] His defining political moment occurred when he was still in high school. While sitting in a barber shop, he came across an article in the men's magazine *True* that spoke of a strange neo-Nazi underground led by the sinister Willis Carto. The movement's guru was a dead mystery man named Francis Parker Yockey. Even as a child, Stimely had been fascinated by images of the Third Reich. After he discovered that remnants of the esoteric sect still survived, he threw himself into the task of learning more. In the spring of 1975, while on a high school field trip to Washington, he bought a copy of *Imperium* at the Liberty Lobby's headquarters near the Capitol Building. Describing his first encounter with *Imperium*, he recalled: "This was it! Here was hope, drama, tragedy, greatness, truth—but more important, the story of our times."[18]

Stimely decided he had to write a book on Yockey, and filed an FOIA request about him with the FBI. He revisited the East Coast to examine Carto's Yockey file at the Liberty Lobby's office and to speak with Douglas Kaye, Tom Francis, and Eustace Mullins.[19] His passion soon began to pay off in a most remarkable way. Through his ties to Carto and David McCalden, the first director of Carto's Institute for Historical Review (IHR), he learned that an Englishman named John Anthony Gannon had written the IHR to inquire if it had any plans to publish texts by or about Yockey. McCalden gave Gannon's address to Stimely and the two men began exchanging letters. Although Gannon had lost his original European Liberation Front material during his time in South America, he still had a few old mailing addresses. One was for Elsa Dewette, whom Gannon contacted on behalf of Stimley. Dewette and Stimely then began a long and impassioned correspondence about Yockey, classical music (like Yockey, Stimely was a classical pianist), and related subjects. Using his connections to the IHR, Stimely managed to approach H. Keith Thompson about Yockey. He then arranged for the IHR to issue a new edition of Thompson's *Doenitz at Nuremberg*. Thompson also spoke at the 1983 IHR conference about Admiral Dönitz, and contributed an occasional book review for the IHR's *Journal of Historical Review*.

In 1981, Carto fired David McCalden as IHR director. In revenge, McCalden set up his own "Truth Missions" and began publishing the *Revisionist Newsletter*, where he excoriated Carto and anyone else linked to the IHR, including Stimely. McCalden knew that Stimely was openly homosexual, and soon so did readers of his *Revisionist Newsletter*.[20] The *Revisionist Newsletter* also included information about H. Keith Thompson that had been gleaned in part from McCalden's earlier conversations with his then-IHR friend and colleague Stimely.

McCalden's vendetta against both Stimely and Thompson stopped after Stimely himself broke with Carto and the IHR in February 1985.[21] Stimely, who had been editor of the *Journal of Historical Review* from February 1983 to February 1985, quit because he claimed that Carto had deleted a section of an article by Holocaust-denier Robert Faurisson critical of the British historian and IHR speaker David Irving without first consulting either Faurisson or himself. He then denounced Carto as a skilled fundraiser incapable of grasping Yockey: "Carto cannot understand Yockey's historical worldview because Yockey was, at the bottom of his heart, an artist; Carto is, at the bottom of his heart, a travelling salesman."[22] Stimely was also angry that Noontide Press had failed to list *The Enemy of Europe* in its catalog because Carto found it too "anti-American."

Stimely then spent some time on the East Coast planning to create his own Francis Parker Yockey League. In a taped interview with H. Keith Thompson dated 13 March 1986, Stimely asked him:

> Supposing that a group of young, relatively young, *fascists*—not conservatives, not "populists," not reformers, not people who believe in working evolutionarily within the system, not people who believe at all in saving the system ... suppose such a group were to get together and decide to publish their own little journal on the "right," even in the modest form at first of an eight-page newsletter, entitled *Thought & Action*, which would be a very nearly explicit fascist theoretical journal working toward the explicit goal of a fascist revolution. Such a journal would explore in the realm of theory the contributions that have been made in political/social thought, and that should be taken into account by present-day revolutionaries, by such as Robert Michels, Vilfredo Pareto, Gaetano Mosca, George Sorel, even, Lawrence Dennis, Max Nomad, James Burnham, so many more ... Yockey, Spengler, Carl Schmitt, Harold Lasswell, other prime thinkers on the subjects of power and revolution and social dynamics ... and to explore all these things on a fairly high intellectual level. My question is: what is your realistic estimate of the number of people who would either understand, or be at all interested in, such a publication?

"One hundred," Thompson replied.[23]

Stimely eventually returned to the West Coast and enrolled in the graduate school program in American History at the University of Oregon at Eugene. He also discovered an interest in Yockey within the Abraxas Foundation, a Church of Satan–influenced group of "industrial culture" fans.[24] Abraxas began in San Francisco in the mid-1980s around musician Boyd Rice, Nikolas Schreck, and Schreck's girlfriend Zeena LaVey, daughter of Church of Satan founder Anton LaVey. An *épater les bourgeois* movement, Abraxas embraced taboo subjects like satanism, sadism, serial killers, Nordic mythology, and the occult aspects of the SS.[25] Another member of the scene, who later moved to the Northwest and befriended Stimely, was Adam Parfrey, owner of the publishing company Amok Press (now Feral House).[26]

In December 1992 Keith Stimely died of AIDS. As far as I can determine, he never wrote a single page of his proposed Yockey biography.

Notes:

1. The NYA was assigned a new advisory board that included Dr. Revilo P. Oliver, Admiral Crommelin, General Pedro del Valle, Austin App, and Richard Cotten, a far-right radio commentator. (William Turner, *Power on the Right* [Palo Alto, CA: Ramparts Press, 1971], p. 163.)

2. Pierce is best known as the author of *The Turner Diaries*, which depicts a bloody white nationalist revolt against an evil Zionist Occupation Government (ZOG). Lyle Stuart recently issued *The Turner Diaries* in a mass-market paperback edition.

3. Byers quoted from C. H. Simonds' 17 September 1971 *National Review* exposé of Carto.

4. Tom Francis dedicated *The Enemy of Europe* to "the founder of the Francis Parker Yockey Society, Louis T. Byers, an Aryan of the Aryans who also fought a good fight to its tragic end, 22 October 1981." As for Oliver, he returned to Carto in the early 1980s, when he became a member of the Institute for Historical Review's editorial board of advisors. After Keith Stimely asked him about his letter to Colonel Dall attacking Carto, Oliver replied in a 10 July 1985 letter: "I want to keep my letter to Dall out of circulation now because Carto, scoundrel that he is, is still the most effective force on our side, and I don't want to augment his own sabotage of his work." However, when the IHR recently went through a bitter split, Oliver sided with the anti-Carto faction, which today has legal control over the organization.

5. Turner, *Power on the Right*, p. 93.

6. Carto's attempted coalition-building strategy took place around the time Michigan KKK leader Robert Miles established Unity Now, which also sought an alliance of left and right extremes against the "Establishment." Miles was also a friend of NRP leader James Madole. A related effort to unite the left and right came from Ken Duggan, who headed his own Provisional Revolutionary Government and published a journal called *Illuminator*. Like *Statecraft*, Duggan was obsessed with both the CFR and David Rockefeller. Duggan ran C.E.D. Associates, Inc., the Industrial Enterprise Foundation, and the Interplanetary Nationalist Society. He also maintained close ties to the Michigan-based Patriot Party. Duggan was an occultist, and the Interplanetary Nationalists "developed a full line of witchcraft and attracted right-wing nationalists into their fold. Incantation, use of incense and potions, multi-colored candles, magic circles, pentagrams, and other devices became part of the I.N. repertoire," according to an article Duggan wrote for *Illuminator*. (Turner, *Power on the Right*, pp. 111–13.)

Duggan played a critical role in linking up Lyndon La Rouche's National Caucus of Labor Committees (NCLC)/U.S. Labor Party to the Liberty Lobby. A former member of the NCLC's security staff, Greg Rose, reported in an article in the 30 March 1979 *National Review:*

> As early as September 1974 the NCLC was in contact with Ken Duggan, publisher of *The Illuminator* and head of a radical rightist organization in New York known as the Provisional Revolutionary Government . . . Duggan introduced the NCLC's Scott Thompson to Willis Carto of the Liberty Lobby . . . Similar entree was provided by Duggan into Carto's National Youth Alliance and C. B. Baker's Youth Action.

The 27 October 1975 issue of the NCLC publication *New Solidarity* reported that Duggan had died while in Rikers Island, where he was being held on charges of attempted murder of another rightist, George Wilkie.

7. See the Spring 1973 *American Mercury* for a report on the conference.

8. A few Michigan-based NRP members formed their own occult/fascist sect called The Order of the Black Ram. See the NRP *Bulletin* for March–June 1974. This same issue reports that the Nazi Joe Tomassi had become an NRP organizer in California. (For more on Tomassi, see James Mason, *Siege* [Denver: Storm Books, 1992].) As for the Order of the Black Ram, Linda Blood writes in *The New Satanists* (New York: Warner Books, 1994), p. 192:

> Other examples of cross-fertilization between satanism and Nazism included the Order of the Black Ram, founded by Michael Grumboski, and John Amend's Shrine of the Little Mother. Both Grumboski and Amend are former Church of Satan members ... While it lasted, Grumboski's O.B.R. promoted a mix of satanism, occultism, and notions of Aryan racial superiority. Amend's S.L.M. courted a right-wing pagan group in Canada called the Canadian Odinist Movement, which combined admiration for the Norse gods with anti-Semitism. Amend also tried to affiliate with a neo-Nazi group called the National Renaissance Party, whose leader, James Madole, had in turn been intrigued by the Church of Satan.

9. See the NRP *Bulletin* for January and February 1976 for part of Madole's series on Atlantis. On the NRP and the occult, see Peter Levenda, *Unholy Alliance* (New York: Avon Books, 1995), pp. 319–20.

10. See the NRP *Bulletin* for July–August 1976 for a reference to Madole's talk. When Madole died in 1978, the NRP folded.

11. Both men were also contributing editors to *Western Destiny*.

12. *TRUD!* stood for Terror Removes Unwanted Democracy. It may also have been a pun on the "labor union" paper of the USSR called *Trud*. In a 1969 letter to subscribers, Kaye and Sullivan wrote: "TRUD! Listen to that word! Listen to the *sound* of TRUD! It's the sound of a police club crushing the skull of a ghetto rioter or student anarchist. TRUD! the sound of a boot kicking the backside of a pinko college professor. TRUD! the sound of a peacenik being strangled." Etc.

TRUD! was very Yockeyist in its pro-Russian stand. In *TRUD!*'s "Christmas Essay" of December 1968, the question of dissident Soviet writers is addressed this way:

> In the land of Dostoevski they have learned how to handle the bacillus that has been undermining cultures for centuries. In Prague, the Red Army found an entire underground colony of these "artists" and "writer" termites under the sponsorship of "Dr. Goldstuecker." "Goldstuecker" got away ... hundreds of these serpents, however, were caught in the nets of Marshall Gretchko and were disposed of in the usual manner (a bullet in the back of the neck).

The article continued:

> Contemporary Russian literature is healthy. It is not concerned with the morbid and obtuse "social problems" which inspire the pens of the psychopaths who turn out "OUR" literature. Russian literature is concerned with providing healthy relaxation, inspiring decent sentiments, and upholding the standards of its people.

In a March 1969 essay called "Kto Kovo?" (a reference to the 1950s *Russia* series by Fred Weiss and H. Keith Thompson), Douglas Kaye writes:

> The native White Russian gentile population has somehow managed to renew itself and has to a great extent regained control over their motherland via the military establishment. The military is beginning to usher Jewish power OUT. The exact degree of balance between Jews and Russian nationals in the higher echelons of government cannot be charted on a minute-to-minute basis. There are many Jews still to be counted in the top leadership; there are thousands of others who have been unceremoniously booted into the nearest snow drift.

TRUD! also reprinted an editorial essay from *CEDADE Information Bulletin* of Barcelona, Spain, in its 1970 issue. CEDADE (*Circulo Español de Amigos de Europa*) was the Spanish branch of the New European Order. CEDADE's Ediciones Wotan publishing house also brought out a Spanish edition of *Imperium*. One issue of *CEDADE* featured Yockey on the cover.

13. In its final issues, *Common Sense* glorified Yockey and published encomiums to the Kremlin for promoting anti-Semitism and Arab nationalism. (John George and Laird Wilcox, *Nazis, Communists, Klansmen, and Others on the Fringe* [Buffalo: Prometheus Press, 1992], pp. 301–02.)

14. *The Proclamation of London of the European Liberation Front* was reprinted by the Sons of Liberty from Metaire, Louisiana, who also published *Christian Vanguard*. The pamphlet has a short introduction by "D. T. K." (Douglas Kaye). In it, Kaye writes:

> In the early 1950s, a few cartons of remaining *Imperiums* and *Proclamations* made their way to America. These were immediately placed in the hands of knowledgeable Western Culture Thinkers by a profoundly world-wise and influential couple who were to be Yockey's mentors and sponsors for his remaining years.

The "world-wise and influential couple," Fred and Marie Weiss, would later befriend Kaye.

15. *TRUD!* had translated excerpts from the book some years earlier. See for example *TRUD!* issues #12 (July 1969) and #13–14 (August–September 1969).

16. The Tom Francis translation of Yockey's *The Enemy of Europe* came with an introduction by Dr. Revilo P. Oliver, entitled "The Enemy of Our Enemies," that was almost as long as the book. Tom Francis also wrote a brief biographical sketch of Yockey based on information supplied by Douglas Kaye. The sketch is filled with errors, including the notion that Yockey was in "G-2" during the war and that he visited Prague to attend the Slansky trials. These errors are reproduced in Martin Lee's discussion of Yockey in his book *The Beast Reawakens* (Boston: Little Brown, 1997).

17. Information on Stimely's background comes from his 1981 *Revisionist Bibliography*, published by the IHR with an introduction by then–IHR director "Lewis Brandon" (a David McCalden alias).

18. Keith Stimely, letter to Elsa Dewette, 24 November 1981.

19. Stimely also met Ed Fields and William Pierce. Fields had come to Washington to attend a conference of Pierce's National Alliance.

20. The always-stormy issue of gay Nazis had taken on a particular frenzy around this time with the emergence of a tiny, openly gay Nazi group called the National

Socialist League, which published the *NS Mobilizer*. The NSL was founded by ex-members of the NSWPP.

21. In October 1990 David McCalden died from AIDS.

22. Stimely's principal attack on Carto is his 25 February 1985 IHR resignation document called *The Problem of Willis A. Carto or Goodbye to All That!*

23. From the transcript of a 13 March 1986 taped interview in the H. Keith Thompson archives at the Hoover Institute.

24. Stimely's connection to Abraxas includes a humorous leaflet that listed him as a pianist in the 1992 "Total War" musical performance in Portland, with Abraxas music guru Boyd Rice, Michael Moynihan, and Diabolos Rex. On Abraxas, see my article "How 'Black' Is Black Metal?" in *Hit List*, Vol. 1, No. 1 (February/March 1999).

25. One of the most interesting publications of the Abraxas tendency was the music magazine *The Fifth Path*, edited by Robert Ward. Another zine from this genre, *Ohm Clock*, ran an article in its Spring 1996 issue promoting Julius Evola. A regular writer in both the music and theory orbit of Abraxas is Michael Moynihan, who has also written for the Church of Satan magazine *The Black Flame*. See Moynihan, "The Faustian Spirit of Fascism," in *The Black Flame*, Vol. 5, Nos. 1 and 2 (1994). (Moynihan's article also appeared in the February 1994 issue of *Plexus*, the theoretical journal of an Omaha group called the National Workers League.) For more on the occult links to "Yockeyism," see the appendix "The Devil and Francis Parker Yockey."

26. Parfrey also published Joseph Goebbels' novel *Michael* (New York: Amok Press, 1987). Goebbels wrote the novel in 1923, when he was a follower of the "left" Strasser wing of the NSDAP. *Michael* is in part a call to revolutionaries of the left and right to overcome their differences and overthrow the hated bourgeois order.

THE LEFT OF
THE RIGHT
("YOCKEYISM"
IN EUROPE)

Personally, I am totally indifferent to the issue of being or not being on the right. At the moment being, the ideas which it [the New Right] espouses are on the right, but they are not necessarily of the right. I can easily imagine situations where these ideas could be on the left. The extent to which these ideas can change will depend on how the political landscape will have evolved.

—Alain de Benoist

Je préfère le KGB à l'Eglise catholique.

—Jean-François Thiriart

53
NEW
RIGHT

In October 1960, four months after Yockey's death, a brief tribute to him entitled "Le Suicide d'Ulik Varange" appeared in *L'Europe Réelle*, the monthly publication of the New European Order. Yet in Europe, "Yockeyism" does not exist as a separate political current, since many of the ideas expressed in *Imperium* reflect long-held beliefs. Many European rightists, however, consider *Imperium* a classic, and in 1976, the Tübingen-based publishing house Grabert Verlag issued a German translation called *Chaos oder Imperium: Das Abendland zwischen Untergang und Neubeginn* (Chaos or Imperium: The West between Decline and Rebirth).[1] The Spanish branch of the New European Order, the Barcelona-based *Circulo Español de Amigos de Europa* (the Spanish Circle of Friends of Europe, or CEDADE), came out with a Spanish edition.[2] *Imperium* has also had a considerable influence on the British far right.[3]

Yockey's legacy has perhaps been best maintained by a group of fascist theorists known as the European "New Right," who have long argued for the need to overcome the intellectual limitations of "grandpa's fascism." The French New Right theorist Alain de Benoist may even in some sense be considered Yockey's intellectual successor. He also has a direct link to American Yockeyism dating back to 1965, when de Benoist (as "Fabrice Laroche") became a contributing editor to *Western Destiny*.[4]

In the early 1960s de Benoist was associated with a publication called *Europe-Action*, which grew out of a rightist group created in 1960 called the Fédération des Étudiants Nationalistes (FEN). FEN leader Dominique Venner was a student of *Imperium*.[5] Nor did *Europe-Action* hide its indebtedness to Yockey: One 1964 article began, "Yockey est un homme que l'on connaît peu, malgré un apport considérable à la pensée occidentale."[6]

In the late 1950s and early 1960s the French right, including the FEN, was swept up in the struggle against Algerian independence, which they overwhelmingly opposed. The downfall of French rule in Algeria, however, led FEN to adopt a more pan-European outlook. FEN leader Venner argued that the end of European colonialism also ended European colonial rivalries. The loss of Algeria meant it was now time to sublimate French nationalism to a higher form of European patriotism.[7] For this reason, *Europe-Action* also criticized German racialism. In 1963 there appeared in *Europe-Action*'s "Dictionnaire du militant" an article called "National-socialisme" that lambasted German "racisme romantique (non scientifique)." Like their co-thinkers in the *Mankind Quarterly* network, *Europe-Action* wanted a more pan-European, "biopolitical" form of racism.[8]

In the mid-1960s *Europe-Action* more or less disintegrated, and in the spring of 1966 Venner and de Benoist created another rightist sect called the Mouvement Nationaliste du Progrès (MNP). Aimed at students, the group held annual camps where recruits were given paramilitary training and courses in fascist doctrine. The MNP then organized a political party called Rassemblement Européen de la Liberté (REL) that did disastrously in the 1967 French elections.[9] After the REL electoral debacle, de Benoist became editor of a magazine named *Nouvelle École* (New School) created by a far-right intellectual circle called Groupement de Recherche et d'Etudes pour la Civilisation Européenne, or GRECE ("Grece" is also the French word for Greece).

GRECE began in November 1967 and was formally declared an official association in January 1969.[10] Unlike many French rightist currents, it rejected both royalism and Catholicism for a pagan worldview with strong emphasis on Europe's Indo-European, not Judeo-Christian, roots. From its inception, GRECE and its journal *Nouvelle École* were allied to the Northern League, *Mankind Quarterly*, and the International Association for the Advancement of Ethnology and Eugenics (IAAEE). *Nouvelle École*'s *comité de patronage* included a number of individuals closely associated with *Mankind Quarterly* and its German equivalent, Jürgen Rieger's *Neue Anthropologie*. *Mankind Quarterly*'s founder, Robert Gayre, was on the comité, as were Henry Garrett and former *Truth Seeker* writer Robert Kuttner.[11] *Nouvelle École*'s American representative was H. Keith Thompson's friend Donald Swann, who had gone from being a regular at *Truth Seeker* Racist Forums in New York to becoming a professor at the University of Southern Mississippi in Hattiesburg.[12]

De Benoist's connections also included the New European Order. French historian Pierre-André Taguieff reports that de Benoist's 1975–76 *Who's Who* lists him as a "docteur en biologie *honoris causa* de l'Institut supérieur des sciences du Québec." The Institut was founded at the 1969 CEDADE-sponsored NEO conference in Barcelona. It published works by NEO co-founders René Binet and Gaston-

Armand (Guy) Amaudruz as well as books by Jacques de Mahieu, another member of *Nouvelle École*'s comité de patronage.[13] In 1971, the Institut (through its Éditions Celtique publishing house) issued Amaudruz's *Nous Autres Racistes*, which recommended *Imperium, The Enemy of Europe, Western Destiny*, and other rightist texts to the NEO membership.[14]

Northern League founder Roger Pearson was also a member of *Nouvelle École*'s comité de patronage while serving as *Mankind Quarterly*'s editor in chief.[15] The close ties between Pearson and *Nouvelle École* became public in 1978, when Pearson hosted the 11th annual conference of the World Anti-Communist League (WACL). Present at the Washington meeting were representatives from the MSI, the Liberty Lobby, and a contingent from *Nouvelle École*.[16]

After relocating to the United States in the mid-1960s to become editor of *Western Destiny*, Pearson became involved with a leader of American Odinism.[17] He also developed a scholarly interest in all things Indo-European. In 1973, while working with Professor Donald Swann at the University of Southern Mississippi, he helped found the prestigious *Journal of Indo-European Studies*. One of the journal's co-founders was the late Marija Gimbutas. Mircea Eliade was another member of the journal's advisory board.[18]

By the late 1970s Pearson had become a player in the establishment right through his involvement with the American Security Council, where he served as editor of the ASC's *Journal of International Relations*. One of his *Journal* colleagues was James J. Angleton, the retired head of CIA Counterintelligence. Pearson even joined the editorial board of *Policy Review*, the journal of the Heritage Foundation, Washington's leading conservative think tank.[19]

De Benoist also found himself welcomed into French establishment circles in the late 1970s, and became cultural editor of *Le Figaro* magazine. His sponsor at *Le Figaro* was Louis Pauwels, the co-author of the famous book *The Morning of the Magicians*, which more or less "explained" the Third Reich as a manifestation of the European magical unconscious. GRECE also formed an alliance with the *Club de l'Horloge* (the Clock Club—named after a clock in a room of the prestigious École Nationale d'Administration), headed by Yvan Blot. The Clock Club was intent on spreading the gospel of laisse-faire economists like Friedrich Hayek. Thus in both Washington and Paris there developed curious alliances between the likes of Pearson and de Benoist and more conventional free-market cold-warriors. That alliance was made explicit in 1982 when then-President Ronald Reagan sent Pearson a letter on White House stationery praising his efforts![20]

De Benoist's new-found respectability did not prevent him from using *Nouvelle École* to extol Indo-European paganism and Conservative Revolutionary theorists like Spengler and Moeller van den Bruck. He gradually moved away from overt "biopolitics" to a more Yockey-oriented cultural critique, which he combined with a growing anti-Americanism.[21] In an essay in the April–May 1980 issue of the GRECE publication *Éléments*, de Benoist ("R. de Herte") claimed that "American oppression is neither better nor worse than Soviet oppression. It simply is not the same. Soviet Russia breaks bodies and gags mouths; the United States destroys souls and renders speech insignificant."[22] Neither "history, nor culture, nor geopolitics, nor philosophy, nor fundamental affinities" linked Europe to the United States. To de Benoist, "what is good for America is rarely good for us." Europe should be most in solidarity with "the national and popular forces of Africa, Asia, and Latin America, [who are] abusively clumped together under the label of 'Third World' and who are often used as scapegoats."[23] He further argued that the Judeo-Christian belief in egalitarianism was responsible for the decline of Europe:

> According to the classical process of the development and degradation of cycles, the egalitarian theme has entered our culture from the stage of the *myth* (equality before God), to the stage of *ideology* (equality before people); after that, it has passed to the stage of *"scientific pretension"* (affirmation of the egalitarian *fact*). In short, from Christianity to democracy, and after that to socialism and Marxism. The most serious reproach which one can formulate against Christianity is that it has inaugurated this egalitarian cycle by introducing into European thought a *revolutionary anthropology*, with a *universalist and totalitarian* character.[24]

De Benoist's Third World turn made him highly critical of Jean-Marie Le Pen's anti-immigrant National Front, which during the Cold War was strongly pro-NATO. Unlike other GRECE theorists who became Le Pen ideologues, he defended French Muslims and visited Iran in March 1987. He was accompanied on his trip by representatives of Ogmios, a far-right French book service that distributed Holocaust-denial literature, and received financial support from the Iranian embassy in Paris.[25] De Benoist also attended "The Second Green Dialogue for an Alternative World Order," sponsored by the Jamahir Society for Culture and Philosophy, which took place on 3–5 November 1995 in Tripoli, Libya.

Surprising ties have also developed between de Benoist and elements of the French Communist Party (PCF). In 1992 de Benoist spoke at a PCF think tank called the Institut de Recherches Marxistes. He then began talks on Europe's future with Marc Cohn, a former leader of the youth section of the PCF and editor of a magazine called *L'Idiot Internationale*, which features articles by authors from both the right and left.[26] *L'Idiot Internationale* was the brainchild of de Benoist's friend Jean Edern Hallier, a wealthy author and French television host who died in January 1997. In *The Terror Network*, Claire Sterling reports that Hallier told her that in 1970 he had played host to a three-day meeting with the ultra-left millionaire Italian publisher Giangiacomo Feltrinelli, Andreas Baader, Red Brigade leader Renato Curcio, and leaders of the French *Gauche Proletarienne* (Proletarian Left) "to organize European terror."[27]

The French Communist Party helped fund Hallier. In January 1990 François Hilsum, head of the PCF's Messidor publishing house (and a member of the Central Committee), signed an agreement with Hallier to publish a series of pamphlets; he gave Hallier a cash advance of 500,000 francs ($100,000) and made him a "literary advisor" to Messidor. Hallier's book of interviews with Fidel Castro was sold by PCF militants.[28] Hallier also worked with Pierre Guillaume, the leader of a weird "left anarchist," "no-holocaust" group called La Vieille Taupe (The Old Mole), which publishes the works of the IHR-allied French Holocaust-denier Robert Faurisson.[29] Guillaume and Hallier were the editors of an Editions de la Différence book collection entitled "Le Puits et le Pendule," and Hallier wrote for the GRECE publication Éléments.[30]

In April 1992, de Benoist went to Russia to meet with members of the "Red-Brown alliance," that strange coalition of Brezhnev-era hacks, young Stalinists clad in blue jeans and leather jackets, obscure ex-KGB generals, monarchists, and Mother Russia–worshippers.[31] One of his Moscow connections was the National Salvation Front's Aleksandr Prokhanov, a leading "Red-Brown" advocate. In a speech to the NSF's founding conference in 1992, Prokhanov proclaimed:

> [The NSF embodies] the end of the old and unjust civil war between the Reds and the Whites. Russia's future rests in the strong alliance between the partisans of social justice—the Reds—and of national tradition—the Whites. From now on both sides are united in the fight against globalization, cosmopolitanism, and American capitalism, as well as the social, national, and geopolitical treason of Gorbachev and Yeltsin, who serve the interests of the New World Order to the detriment of the Russian people. The common goal, beyond Left and Right, is the Third Empire.[32]

De Benoist's trip was backed by Aleksandr Dugin's far-right newspaper Dyen (The Day). Dugin, the Russian translator of both René Guénon and Julius Evola, hoped to form an alliance between Orthodox Russians and Islamic "traditionalists" against modernist subversion.[33] De Benoist, however, was not pleased with what he saw in Moscow, particularly

> the crude imperialism and Jacobinism of the vast majority of the so-called "patriots." Some of them think about nothing but the restoration of the old Russian domination over Eastern and even Central European countries. I tried to explain that they cannot solve the center's problems by dispatching tanks to the Ukraine, Poland, and the Baltic States. While I could agree with their refusal to mimic the Western liberal-market model . . . I disagreed with their conception of Russian identity and a Russian role in the world.[34]

The "Russian Question" remains today as central for "New Right" strategists as it was for Yockey. Perhaps no rightist theorist since Yockey has dwelt more on the issue of Russian integration into a Europe-wide fascist resurgence than an obscure Belgian thinker named Jean-François Thiriart. If de Benoist is today carrying the banner of *Imperium*'s plea for the political and cultural integration of Europe as a "third force," it was Thiriart above all who continued Yockey's efforts to incorporate Russia into a geopolitical axis with European fascism.

Notes:

1. Grabert Verlag, a longtime right-wing house, maintained close ties to Carto's Noontide Press.

2. On CEDADE, see Patrice Chairoff, *Dossier Néo-Nazisme*, (Paris: Ramsay, 1977), pp. 170–76.

3. For a discussion of Yockey's impact in England, see Richard Thurlow, "Destiny and Doom: Spengler, Hitler and 'British' Fascism," in *Patterns of Prejudice*, Vol. 15, No. 4, 1981. National Front leader John Tyndall is quoted as calling *Imperium* "of outstanding philosophical importance." Thurlow comments: "It is to Yockey, Hitler, and Spengler that the core of Tyndall's thought owes its greatest debt."

4. The September 1965 *Western Destiny* lists "Fabrice Laroche" as a contributing editor.

5. In *Les Mouvements d'Extrême-Droite* (Paris: Albatros, 1972), François Duprat remarks that Yockey's ideas formed "une bonne part à la base de l'idéologie d'*Europe-Action* en 1964–65" (p. 22). Duprat headed the Groupes Nationalistes Révolutionnaires (GNR) until his assassination in 1978.

6. *Europe-Action*, October 1964. In *Sur la Nouvelle Droite* (Paris: Descartes & Cie., 1994), fn. 100, pp. 146–48, Pierre-André Taguieff lists two other articles in *Europe-Action* that cite Yockey: "Les origines de l'Occident," by Pierre Lamotte from March 1964, and "Je reviens d'Amérique," by Fabrice Laroche (de Benoist) from October 1965.

7. One article in 1963 argued: "Notre volonté européiste doit sublimer notre nationalisme français en un patriotisme européen. La fin de l'Algérie a fait de nous les premiers patriotes européens." (René Monzat, *Enquêtes sur la Droite Extrême* [Paris: Le Monde, 1992], pp. 206–07.)

8. Ibid., p. 229. Also see Taguieff, *Sur la Nouvelle Droite*. An important influence on *Europe-Action*'s shift to a pan-European model was Marc Augier (Saint-Loup), who served as president of Venner's Comité France-Rhodesia. On Saint-Loup, see Monzat, *Enquêtes sur la Droite Extrême*.

9. Pierre-André Taguieff, "La stratégie culturelle de la 'Nouvelle Droite' en France (1968–1983)," in *Vous avez dit Fascismes?* (Paris: Éditions Montalba, 1984).

10. Monzat, *Enquêtes sur la Droite Extrême*, p. 208.

11. In its July–August 1972 issue, *Nouvelle École* published a letter of praise from Kuttner: "I have known of *Nouvelle École* for more than a year and I wish to tell you all the good things I think of it."

12. This is the same Donald Swann whose apartment was raided by New York police in 1966 during a crackdown on Minutemen and Nazis.

13. Taguieff, *Sur la Nouvelle Droite*, pp. 236–42.

14. In 1961 Fred Weiss sent Amaudruz and the Belgian NEO leader Robert Debbault a copy of *The World in Flames*.

15. Pearson took over *Mankind Quarterly* in 1979, when Robert Gayre became honorary editor in chief.

16. See the 28 May 1978 *Washington Post* for an exposé of the conference. According to the *Washington Post* article, members of *Nouvelle École* met informally with William Pierce, the physicist and ex–Rockwell lieutenant who created the National Alliance out of the remnants of the National Youth Alliance. Pearson came under attack from elements inside WACL, who produced a report called the "Blue Document" warning that, under Pearson, WACL was being infiltrated by hardcore Nazi organizations in Europe and Latin America. On Pearson, the Northern League, and *Nouvelle École*, see Taguieff, "La Stratégie culturelle," in *Vous avez dit Fascismes?*, pp. 116–17, 129–30. On Pearson and WACL, see John Lee Anderson, *Inside the League* (New York: Dodd Mead, 1986).

17. In the January 1966 issue of *Truth Seeker*, James H. Johnson reported on a meeting he had with Pearson, Pearson's assistant Ralph Milone (also on the board of *Western Destiny*), and James K. Warner, who was identified as "head of the Odinist religion." Warner's Sons of Liberty later republished *The Proclamation of London* with an introduction by Douglas Kaye.

The Spring 1981 issue of *Mankind Quarterly* also featured an essay on Odinism in America entitled "Revival of Germanic Religion in Contemporary Anglo-American Culture," by Stephen Flowers of the University of Texas in Austin. Professor Flowers was a close associate of Michael Aquino in a Church of Satan spinoff known as the Temple of Set. He has also translated works on Teutonic mythology and runic lore under the name "Edred Thorrson." The Temple of Set has become fascinated with the SS Ahnenerbe. According to Linda Blood, *The New Satanists* (New York: Warner Books, 1994), p. 210:

> The Temple of Set reading list notes that the complete archeological, magical, and administrative records of the Ahnenerbe are contained on microfilm in the National Archives Building of the United States. "These papers have never been sorted, indexed, and annotated in detail, but the Order of the Trapezoid has compiled a working index with brief annotations pending a more thorough study," the review notes.

Michael Aquino, the head of the Temple of Set, paid a visit to the SS headquarters at Schloss Wewelsburg in Westphalia in October 1982 to conduct a magical "working." On the general question of Odinism see Jeffrey Kaplan, *Radical Religion in America* (Syracuse, NY: Syracuse University Press, 1997). Kaplan also discusses *Imperium's* influence on elements of the Odinist movement and gives an in-depth profile of Stephen Flowers' role in Odinism, the Temple of Set, and his own Order of the Triskelion. I am, however, unaware of any evidence that links either Aquino or Flowers to fascist political movements.

18. Eliade maintained his involvement with the Iron Guard at least into the 1950s. Investigative journalist Russ Bellant found a U.S. Army intelligence CIC document that lists Eliade as a member of a Paris-based group of Iron Guardists in 1950. The group included Emile Cioran and Paul Costin-Deleanu.

19. For a description of Pearson's Washington empire, see Russ Bellant, *Old Nazis, the New Right, and the Republican Party* (Boston: South End Press, 1991), pp. 60–64.

20. Ibid., p. 62. The 28 September 1984 *Wall Street Journal* ran a piece on Reagan's 14 April 1982 letter to Pearson. The White House refused to acknowledge that it had

made a mistake, but asked that Pearson not use the letter for fundraising or promotional purposes.

21. The Club de l'Horloge broke with *Nouvelle École* over GRECE's anti-Americanism and opposition to free-market ideology. To be more precise, Yvan Blot and J. Y. Gallou of the Club de l'Horloge quit GRECE. On the split, see Pierre-André Taguieff, "From Race to Culture: The New Right's View of European Identity," in the Winter 1993–Spring 1994 issue of *Telos*, p. 100.

22. During the Soviet crackdown on Polish Solidarity, it was *Nouvelle École* that asked if it was really in Europe's best interest "to die for Gdansk."

23. De Benoist's essay ("Neither Slaves Nor Robots") was translated by M. H. Kretzschmar.

24. De Benoist, quoted from Tomislav Sunic, *Against Democracy and Equality: The European New Right* (New York: Peter Lang, 1990), p. 72. Another GRECE statement attacked the notion of "right" and "left":

> Even if many of the ideas expounded by GRECE are at this time classified as "right," can one be sure this will remain so? In fact, GRECE promotes several topics which, while once termed "right," have since been termed "left," such as regional consolidation, promotion of folk art, the protection of the environment. On the other hand, GRECE has consistently opposed the Christian ideology, nostalgia for the past, social conservatism, racism, the dominant middle-class "establishment" values, and the infiltration of the "American way-of-life." Can one then, honestly, talk about "right"? In reality, the approach taken by GRECE unites topics which raise opposition from both right and left, but above all it opens up new topics which remain impossible to classify.
>
> All the people of the earth are threatened by universalism: by the military, economic, and political universalism of Soviet Russia and its satellite states, and equally by that of the American civilization. The latter being the more dangerous because it is imperceptible. It progresses by destroying specific cultures and imposing a sole way of life, which is the American way of life ... It is this which causes the urgency for Europeans to find again their traditions and roots. These roots can be rediscovered outside the framework of Christianity and beyond it. In fact, Christianity is not our only philosophical and spiritual inheritance, and moreover it no longer unites Europe but instead instigates a one-world ideology, which in turn destroys specific cultures.
>
> Europeans will thus discover their common origins and their remotest past in the light of an Indo-European heritage ... The struggle for an identity is waged by way of the most varied means: the revival of regional languages, the protection of national languages, the promotion of popular festivities and traditions such as the celebration of the solstice, the preservation of cultural identity, the protection of the environment, the encouragement of the various forms of folk art as opposed to the society of the "show." In this way, the New Culture desires emphatically to be European.

GRECE also stressed that its neo-pagan outlook should not conflict with technology:

> In the 20th century appeared the possibility for men to transform and dominate themselves, and to go much farther than simply adapting to their surroundings in forging their own environment; the prospect of biology, electronics, genetic engineering,

telematics, astrophysics, and space research announce the coming of the "third man."
(GRECE statement translated by Denise Pesteil-Simms and Jean-Louis Pesteil.)

25. Karl Laske, *Le Banquier Noir* (Paris: Seuil, 1996), pp. 358–59.

26. *Telos*, No. 98/99, Winter 1993–Spring 1994, fn. 8, p. 35. Cohn also spoke at a GRECE-sponsored conference held in May 1992 to discuss the "recomposition of the French intellectual landscape."

27. Claire Sterling, *The Terror Network* (New York: Holt, Rinehart and Winston, 1981), p. 42.

28. The 23 June 1993 issue of the French satirical publication *Le Canard Enchainé* published an exposé of the ties between the left and right, written by Mariette Besnard and Didier Daeninckx. Their article was summarized in the 10 September 1993 issue of the U.S. Trotskyist paper *Workers Vanguard*. For a "New Right" reaction against *Le Canard Enchainé*, see an essay by Charles Champetier in *Éléments* (No. 78, September 1993). An English translation of Champetier's piece appears in *Telos*, No. 98/99, Winter 1993–Spring 1994.

29. La Vieille Taupe also joined forces with Ogmios to publish an IHR-like journal called *Annales d'Historie Revisionniste*. For more background information on La Vieille Taupe's origins, see Pierre Guillaume's essay "Debord," published in *La Vieille Taupe*, No. 1, Spring 1995, and translated into English in *NOT BORED* #28 (December 1997). Also see an anthology entitled *Négationnistes: Les Chiffonniers de l'Histoire* (Paris: Éditions Golias et Éditions Syllepse, 1997)—in particular two articles by Didier Daeninckx, "L'Obscène Alliance des Contraires" and "Le Jeune Poulpe et la Vieille Taupe."

30. In an *Éléments* article entitled "Le Droit la Différence: Pour en Finir Avec tous les Totalitarismes," Hallier denounced the United States as the "public enemy of the world." (*Telos*, No. 98/99, Winter 1993–Spring 1994, p. 172.)

31. De Benoist's visit triggered a strong protest from the French "Old Right." In the Le Penist *National Hebdo*, Roland Gaucher

attacked de Benoist, whom he suspected of harboring questionable sympathies for communists in France and Russia: "It was strange . . . to see him [Benoist] participate in a colloquium featuring intractable communists. The attitude of the French communists does not appear so strange if one knows that Benoist made contact . . . with Russian 'conservatives' . . . simply former Bolsheviks . . . and Russian nationalists like Pamiat, that anti-Semitic organization financed by the KGB under Brezhnev . . . One of the objectives shared by both nationalists and communists is to recreate a great imperialist Russia. In this context, Benoist looks a little like a 'guru.'" [*Telos*, No. 98/99, Winter 1993–Spring 1994, p. 161.]

32. Ibid., p. 162.

33. Ibid.

34. Ibid., p. 204. Dugin tried to use de Benoist to give legitimacy to a journal he created called *Elementy* in homage to GRECE. De Benoist, however, demanded that Dugin remove his name from the board of *Elementy*. According to de Benoist, Dugin had used his name without first receiving permission.

54
RED
SWASTIKA

While many of Alain de Benoist's concerns echo Yockey's vision of a culturally united Europe, the leading exponent of "Yockeyism" as pure geopolitics was the late Belgian rightist Jean-François Thiriart, who died in 1992.[1] Thiriart began his political career on the left as a member of the "Young Socialist Guard" in the 1930s, but soon turned right and joined the "Friends of the Great German Reich Association."[2] His work for the Nazis during the war led to his imprisonment as a collaborator, but he was freed from jail by 1948.[3] He went on to became a leading figure in European optometry, and owned a chain of optometry shops in Brussels called Opticon.[4]

In the 1960s Thiriart founded a group called Jeune Europe, which took its name from an organization set up by the Nazis in 1942. In his book *L'Empire Euro-Soviétique*, Thiriart noted that the original Jeune Europe emerged out of the first European Congress of Youth in Vienna and received considerable support from the Reich ambassador to Vichy France, Otto Abetz.[5] Abetz's Belgian network may have played a role in Thiriart's conversion to the far right. In the 1930s, Abetz secretly financed a leading Belgian socialist named Hendrik de Man, who became president of the Belgian Socialist Party in 1939.[6] De Man later became a leading German collaborator during the war.[7]

Thiriart began his political reemergence in 1960, during the crisis surrounding the French struggle for Algeria and Belgium's attempt to maintain control of the Congo. He served as the principal agent of the French OAS (the Secret Army Organization) in Belgium, printed OAS communiqués in his weekly paper *Nation-Europe*, found shelter for anti–de Gaulle terrorists hounded by the French police, and used Jeune Europe to mobilize support for the OAS.[8] After the secession of

Katanga Province from the Congo in 1960, Thiriart created the Comité d'Action et de Défense des Belges d'Afrique (CADBA).[9] His key role in CADBA, however, would remain secret until 1962 due to his collaborationist past. He also set up the Mouvement d'Action Civique (MAC) as a political organization inside Belgium. Thiriart's activities brought him to the attention of the Belgian authorities, who arrested him on 6 March 1962 for aiding the OAS against de Gaulle.[10] His arrest for alleged involvement in stolen passports came literally as he was exiting a plane in Brussels after attending a Venice conference of European far-right leaders.[11]

With the fall of Algeria in 1962, Thiriart and his French allies had a severe falling-out, after the OAS transformed itself into the Armée Nationale Secrète (ANS). According to Thiriart, the ANS had as "its sole aim in life" the assassination of Charles de Gaulle. But "behind this determination there was a total ideological vacuum," which made the ANS fanatics political "blockheads."[12] He also objected to the group's pro-American and pro-NATO stand, its opposition to an independent French nuclear force, and its belief that France should be the predominant European power. In 1963 Thiriart began supporting de Gaulle's attempt to distance France from American control. His turn led the French "old right" journal *Minute* to denounce "the Führer of the Belgian neo-Nazis" in a February 1964 attack.

Throughout the 1960s Thiriart argued for a united Europe. In September 1961, MAC issued a *Manifesto to the European Nation*, which called for a new Europe outside the control of both the U.S. and Soviet blocs. The *Manifesto* labeled fascist and Nazi policies "historical phenomena of yesteryear which no longer have any real political foundation."[13] It also lashed out at "narrow and small-minded nationalism, which fosters divisions between citizens of the European nation. Such nationalism must fade away, serving only as the stepping stone to a wider and richer concept of the great European nation."[14] Thiriart further developed his ideas in *Un Empire de 400 Millions d'Hommes: l'Europe*, which was translated into Italian, Spanish, Portuguese, Dutch, German, and English.

Thiriart formed Jeune Europe, which established training schools in Italy, France, Spain, Portugal, the Netherlands, and Belgium. Jeune Europe appealed to the "elite" of "European youth" who received training in psychology, propaganda, economics, militant discipline, and physical combat. His followers were taught to distinguish between a "legal Europe" under "foreign occupation" and a "legitimate Europe." Jeune Europe claimed that its "legitimacy resides in European unity, which means that any legal devices which the occupier may use are merely a matter of form as far as we are concerned."[15]

Thiriart dissolved Jeune Europe in October 1965 in favor of a new organization called the Parti Communautaire Européen (PCE). He then created a journal entitled *La Nation Européenne*, where he attacked both the Soviet Union and the United States, whom he accused of collaboration in a conspiracy to occupy Europe. As a headline in the March 1968 *La Nation Européenne* put it: "Moscou-

Washington: ennemies? non! concurrents? souvent! complices? toujours!" *La Nation Européenne* executed an opening to the New Left with cover stories like "Castro: La Revolution Continue!" It demanded that Europe leave NATO and called for "Plusieurs Viet-Nams" against the Americans.[16] Thiriart's Third World turn was endorsed by Argentina's General Juan Perón, who was living in exile in Spain when Thiriart interviewed him in the February 1969 issue of *La Nation Européenne*. In the interview both Thiriart and Perón celebrated the virtues of Fidel Castro and Che Guevara.[17] Thiriart also developed links to Communist China and met Chou en-Lai in Bucharest, Romania, in November 1966.[18] His followers were said to be working with the Chinese embassy in Brussels to help the PRC gather information on NATO and SHAPE.[19]

Thiriart's anti-Americanism led him to pen an English-language "Letter to an American Senator" in the February 1967 *La Nation Européenne*, in which he stated:

We shall speak plainly: You have been warned. Quit Europe before irreparable harm is done. If you leave Europe honorably the future may see us as allies. If you continue to occupy Europe then it will become a super-Vietnam, i.e., a super-cemetery for the soldiers of the occupying forces . . . You are a people who strangely resemble ancient Carthage with the same morals and way of life. They marched their elephants into Italy; you sail the Sixth Fleet into the Mediterranean. You know what Rome did to Carthage. You should learn that for more than 15 centuries the obsession of unity and of Roman power has activated the highest minds . . . The Guadalcanal of your history can never compare with our Salamis . . . Your imperialism is of the mercantilist Carthaginian type while ours is the Roman civilizing type. Wherever your troops land we find in their wake black markets, pornographic literature, drunkenness, and venereal diseases . . . Your military methods are barbaric. On your conscience lie the innocent people of Dresden, Hiroshima, Nagasaki, and the Vietnamese children roasted by napalm. Even the Russians, who are specialists in massacres, never matched your atrocities of Dresden—where you murdered civilians to no purpose.

While the U.S. became bogged down in Vietnam:

Europe will spring the trap . . . Then after the last warning the patriots of Europe will unleash their war of national liberation . . . Possibly your policemen of the CIA will reassure that the European nationalists are "communists" or "nazis" or both simultaneously. As they lack a modern index they are reduced to using old cliches and classification systems . . . You may try to smear us, ridicule us, ruin us, or assassinate us—all in vain. The idea has been sown. If, tomorrow, we fall beneath the blows of your CIA, 10 more will take our place. We are the avant-garde of the European idea . . . We shall be to Europe what the Jacobins were to the French republic and the Bolsheviks to Marxism—both the brains and the motor . . . You have been warned.

Thiriart then suddenly shut down his organizations and mysteriously disappeared from organized politics. His decision occurred at a highly important time for the European far right. Since the 1967 Arab-Israeli war, the far right, and Thiriart in particular, had become involved in supporting the Palestinian struggle against Israel. On 2–4 April 1969, the New European Order held its 10th congress in Barcelona, Spain. At the congress was a representative from Al Fatah. The mysterious Swiss banker François Genoud, who maintained close ties to the Arab world, also addressed the gathering.[20] Ex-Nazis–turned-mercenaries like Karl Van de Put, a Belgian member of the Afrika Korps, now went into business with Al Fatah.[21] Another leading Palestinian supporter was Jean-Robert Debbault, the Belgian NEO leader who published *L'Europe Réelle*.[22]

In 1968, as part of the rightist overture to the Middle East, Thiriart visited Cairo, where he attended the opening session of the Union Socialiste Arabe as an invited guest.[23] In the March 1968 *La Nation Européenne* he explained his policy this way: "In striving towards European nationalism, Cuba, the Arabs, and North Vietnam must be considered as tactical friends. Everyone who contrives to destroy the power of the United States helps Europe pave the way to freedom and unity." Thiriart supported the Popular Front for the Liberation of Palestine (PFLP), and PFLP leader George Habash reportedly helped finance *La Nation Européenne*.

Other European far-rightists took up the idea of "left/right" unity against "the system."[24] One leading "left rightist" was the Italian Evola-worshipper Franco Freda. Freda's 1969 tract *La disintegrazione del sistema* began as a presentation before a meeting of the European Revolutionary Front in Regensburg, West Germany, on 17 August 1969. Freda argued that "the destruction of the bourgeois world" could only be accomplished when "the nervous center of the bourgeois system" was assaulted with the utmost violence. Mimicking Evola, Freda said that "in a political soldier, purity justifies every hardness, altruism every act of cunning, while the impersonal character [of the] struggle dissolves every moralistic preoccupation." After advocating a tactical alliance with the extreme left, he insisted that terrorism was the only logical policy.[25] The Italian rightist Claudio Mutti, one of Thiriart's lieutenants in Jeune Europe, formed the "Nazi-Maoist" group Lotta di Popolo and the pro-Qaddafi Italy-Libya Association. He also ran a publishing house called Edizioni di Arte, which reprinted *The Protocols of the Elders of Zion*.[26] Other Italian rightist publications declared their solidarity with anti-capitalist Third World movements ("Che Guevara was a fascist"), the American Indians, the IRA, the Basques, and Libya. Some attempted to formulate joint strategy with left-wing extremists against "the system."[27]

Thiriart maintained his own Maoist ties through his murky dealings with a far-right "press service"/private intelligence agency, the Portugal-based Aginter Press. Aginter worked with an overtly pro-Chinese political group in Switzerland called the Parti Communiste Suisse/Marxiste-Leniniste (PCS/ML). An Aginter operative named Robert Leroy, with support from the Communist Chinese embassy in

Berne, arranged for the PCS/ML to hire Aginter operatives as "correspondents" for the group's newspaper, *L'Étincelle,* which was used to gain access to radical groups in Angola, Guinea-Bissau, and Mozambique. The head of the PCS/ML was himself most likely a member of the far right. Thiriart played a liaison role for Aginter, the PCS/ML, and the Chinese embassy.[28]

The strange ties between "red" and "black" terrorism took another twist in the early 1980s. Now thoroughly disillusioned with the Chinese, Thiriart used the rise in Cold War tensions during the Reagan administration to reemerge as a theorist of a new European/Soviet axis. A group of his disciples established a journal called *Conscience Européenne.* In its July 1984 issue the publication praised the Red Brigades, the Red Army Faction (Baader-Meinhof Group), the Revolutionary Cells (RZ), and the Belgian Cellules Communistes Combattantes (CCC) for their anti-NATO terrorist activity, calling their actions "légitime mais prématuré."[29] *Conscience Européenne* reprinted CCC communiques as well as Thiriart's tribute to Renato Curcio, who helped found Italy's Red Brigades.[30] Many of these groups also maintained ties to Soviet-bloc intelligence agencies.[31]

Nor was Thiriart's support for Euro-terrorism new. He expressed similar sentiments in a 1975 interview with a French rightist student magazine called *Cahiers du Centre de Documentation Politique et Universitaire.* In this interview, the only public expression of his political views in a decade, he argued that "exemplary anti-imperialist revolutionary tactics" would become "inevitable at some point in time." In 1975 Thiriart still felt that such action could only occur "with the solid external backing of either the Arabs or the Chinese" because "we need an inviolable sanctuary somewhere." He explained that

> it is also a question of advanced technology. Over the past 15 years European police forces have become very sophisticated from the point of view of improved techniques. European unity will come about more or less when 200 or 300 American occupiers will be killed in every corner of Europe just to prove our point. Then there will be no going back. My remark is that of a theorist. Do not take it as advice, or even a suggestion or prophecy. Communist resistance has used the "murder in cold blood" technique ever since the summer of 1941. Unimportant Germans, lieutenants, and company sergeants who never touched the French in any way were shot down in cold blood, in the back, quite arbitrarily.

He also stressed the need for an effective propaganda network:

> I think that any terrorist campaign would be useless if it is not backed by an indestructible propaganda and information network: The whole of Europe, from Stockholm to Naples, must know about each American who is killed within 48 hours of the event. Once the hundredth killing has been clocked up, the Americans will begin to crack under the weight of public opinion. The propaganda machine has an important part to play in Europe. But it does not stop there. We must also inform Americans in the USA about what is going on and

WHY. And tell them how it can be stopped. We must not kill American people or indeed anyone at all out of hatred but to exert political pressure. Americans are not better nor worse than any other people.

Thiriart then argued that the right must reach an understanding with Russia:

Europe stretches from the Azores to Siberia, including Siberia. The USSR's Eastern borders are in fact Europe's frontiers, so Russia is part of Europe. We cannot build a European state which would have two or three thousand kilometers of "military frontiers" with the USSR ... The trauma of the 1941 invasion is still very real. It is a positive psychosis in Russia. We must be clear on that. A Europe which is "against Russia" is unthinkable in historic geopolitical terms ... No enemy in the East, that should be the neo-Bismarckian axiom for a united Europe.

After paying homage to Stalin, he grumbled: "You read about the hypocrites in Paris getting worked up about camps [gulags]! As if it were possible to implant Communism without them! If you want a particular end, you have to accept the means."[32]

In the fall of 1981, Thiriart announced that he was working on a new book, which was published as *L'Empire Euro-Soviétique de Vladivostock à Dublin: L'Après-Yalta*. He now equated U.S. pressure on Russia in the 1980s with the campaign against Hitler in the late 1930s, declaring that the *"faucons"* (war hawks) from the 1930s who attacked Hitler were "les parents des actuels 'faucons' contre Andropov."[33] In the July 1984 *Conscience Européenne*, Thiriart told his disciple Luc Michel: "L'URSS est l'héritière (géopolitiquement parlant) du IIIème Reich. Les ennemis d'Hitler sont devenus les ennemis de l'URSS." He also attacked Polish Solidarity. Lech Walesa was "un marionnette de la propagande sioniste et américaine (est-il possible encore de les distinguisher?) ... Je préfère le KGB à l'Eglise catholique."[34] He then denounced NATO and claimed that Europeans played "le rôle de domestiques, de valets. Ils sont les Sénégalais de l'Armée française de 1915."

Much like Yockey in *Der Feind Europas*, Thiriart warned that if the Russians refused to reach an alliance with Europe, and instead tried to dominate it, there would be fierce resistance. Michel asked him: "Vous prônez le collaboration totale avec l'URSS?" Thiriart replied: "Totale, absolute. Mais pas inconditionnelle." After noting that Hitler was wrong to try to germanize Europe, he continued: "Si Moscou veut faire une Europe russe, je serais le premier à recommander la résistance armée à l'occupant. Si Moscou veut faire l'Europe européenne, je prône la collaboration totale à l'enterprise soviétique."

Thiriart also appealed to the geopolitical ideas of both Karl Haushofer and Ernst Niekisch,[35] telling Michel:

Plus près de nous il y a NIEKISCH et HAUSHOFER. NIEKISCH était un national-bolcheviste allemand, père du concept dit du "GRAND ESPACE

VLADIVOSTOK-FLESSINGUE." Mais il y a surtout le géopoliticien, le général HAUSHOFER et son bloc continental Mittel-Europa-Eurasie-Japon de 1941. Quelques semaines avant la malencontreuse attaque du 22 juin 1941 contre l'URSS. Rudolf HESS fut en 1914–1918 l'aide de camp du général HAUSHOFER. Mais les concepts de nation d'HITLER sont aux antipodes des miennes et de celles de HAUSHOFER. Chez HAUSHOFER l'idée de l'espace prime tout, chez HITLER c'est idée de race . . . Le pacte germano-soviétique mis au point par RIBBENTROP et MOLOTOV durant l'été 1939 représente ce qui a été fait de plus intelligent en diplomatie géopolitique depuis un siècle.

Like Yockey, Thiriart made it clear that he saw Europe as an Imperium and not a Greater Reich. In his 1975 interview with *Cahiers du Centre de Documentation Politique et Universitaire,* he said:

I think that it would be my duty as a protagonist of these former times [World War II], to denounce, in any book which I was to write, the lack of sincerity behind the move to create a German Europe between 1942 and 1945. Hitler never understood Europe. Some of his fellow travellers were conscious of Europe, but they were in the minority. The sacrifice of young and courageous men was totally foreign to the cause for which they were fighting . . . I therefore unconditionally reject the idea of building a Europe according to the aesthetic German model. Any such romanticism is to be deplored . . . The past is over and done with, and we should not try to bring it back, not even in the theater. Those who have jumped on this bandwagon are first and foremost making money, and secondly they are delighting the Israeli propaganda services.[36]

Thiriart freely discussed his Russian orientation when I met him at his flagship Opticon optometry shop in Brussels in November 1986. After telling me how he helped Otto Skorzeny "track down British and Jewish terrorists" in occupied France, we discussed his geopolitical ideas. He proudly showed me some of his writings, which had been translated into Russian and Arabic even before they were published in French. After giving me a Russian translation of *L'Empire Euro-Soviétique,* he noted that the military attaché at the Soviet embassy in Brussels had done a first-class translation. That night in my hotel room, I was strikingly reminded of Yockey when I opened one of Thiriart's essays and read:

The USSR is doomed to expand, and the only possible direction is towards Dublin. Immediately after occupying Western Europe, the present day American zone, there are two courses open to the USSR—either implanting the gulags and depending on a local communist cell which is at heart totally ineffectual, or else set[ting] about the historic task of integrating Europe. Then, and only then, there will be blue eyes and blonde hair in Dublin, Kharkov, and Vladivostok. Does anyone still remember the Varangians? Perhaps Riourik in his tomb in Novgorod is even now facing towards the West.[37]

Little could I imagine then that in just a few years Thiriart would be lecturing about his ideas not to an obscure American journalist in his posh shop in Brussels but to Soviet hardliners in Moscow.

Notes:

1. Thiriart's ideological similarity to Yockey was evident to Julius Evola, who in later editions of *Gli uomini e la rovine* included a discussion of Thiriart in his analysis of *Imperium*. Evola thought both men were too "Jacobin."

2. See the French rightist Yannick Sauveur's 1978 Mémoire pour le Diplôme d'É-tudes Approfondies of the Institut d'Études Politiques of the University of Paris, *Jean Thiriart et le National Communautarisme Européen* (which I shall refer to as Sauveur), p. 7. (The reader should keep in mind that when I cite Sauveur I am referring at times to his treatise and at times to appendices which include reprints of Thiriart's writings and biographical material.)

3. According to an English-language profile that appeared in the January–February 1967 issue of *La Nation Européenne:*

> Jean-François Thiriart was born in March [1922] of a Liège family frequently men-tioned in the history of the Kingdom. Brought up in a family of liberal tradition, Thiriart turned, at an early age, to the extreme left and became a militant communist. Later he became a collaborator with Professor Kessemaier of Hamburg, president of the Fichte Bund. Several spells in prison, for political reasons, occurred during his youth. Condemned to death "de facto" in 1943 when the Belgian service of the BBC named him as one of the "people to be eliminated"—a sad practice of those times—he was completely rehabilitated some 12 years after the war.

4. In his biography Thiriart states: "Director of the Belgian Optometry Society in 1951. Secretary General of the Belgian National Union of Opticians in 1954. Founder and president of the European Optometry Society (1967–1977)."

5. Jean Thiriart, *L'Empire Euro-Soviétique de Dublin à Vladivostock: L'après-Yalta* (Brussels: Editions Machiavel, 1983), p. 5. Thiriart was referring to the European Youth Organization (EJV) founded in Vienna on 14 September 1942. The lead speaker on the first day of the congress was Baldur von Schirach, Gauleiter of Vienna and Party leader for the Education of Youth. This was the same Baldur von Schirach who as leader of the National Socialist German Students' League (later transformed into Hitler Youth) joined Otto Abetz in forming the *Reichsbanner* in 1931. (For more on Abetz, see the appendix "Three Patron Saints of Red Fascism.") Jeune Europe sponsored a magazine called *La Jeune Europe,* which began publishing from Berlin in 1942 and carried articles by Julius Evola and Ortega y Gasset.

6. On Hendrik de Man, see Zeev Sternhell, *Neither Left Nor Right* (Princeton, NJ: Princeton University Press, 1996); Peter Dodge, *A Documentary Study of Hendrik de Man* (Princeton, NJ: Princeton University Press, 1979); and Lutz Niethammer, *Posthistorie* (London: Verso, 1992).

7. Through Abetz, the Germans financed the Belgian journal *Le Soir,* where Hendrik de Man's nephew, the literary critic Paul de Man, published some anti-Jewish articles. (John Hellman, *Emmanuel Mounier and the New Catholic Left, 1930–1950* [Toronto:

University of Toronto Press, 1981], p. 161.) Also see David Lehman, *Sign of the Times* (New York: Posidon Press, 1991).

8. Angelo del Boca and Mario Giovana, *Fascism Today* (New York: Pantheon, 1969), p. 87.

9. Frederic Laurent, *L'Orchestre Noir* (Paris: Stock, 1978), p. 102.

10. Thiriart said his arrest was the result of French pressure on the Belgian police to stop his pro-OAS activities. (Sauveur, p. 26.)

11. At Venice, Thiriart represented MAC; Sir Oswald Mosley represented the Union Movement; Adolf von Thadden, the Deutsche Reichspartei; and Count Alvisio Lordan spoke for the MSI. Their meeting led to the 4 March 1962 *European Protocol*, a largely stillborn call for the creation of a "National European Party." Thiriart, who spent a month in prison on the passport charge, was later acquitted. He remained so controversial that he was banned from Algeria, Austria, France, and England. Sauveur, p. 48.

12. Ibid., p. 77.

13. Ibid., p. 21.

14. Ibid.

15. Ibid., pp. 102–03.

16. Thiriart also wrote of Castro: "La theorie de Castro des 'plusieurs Vietnams' est juste. Mais nous ajouterons: ces Vietnams ne doivent pas nécessairement être "communistes."

17. Thiriart asked Perón: "Estimez-vous que le travail d'agitation entrepris par Fidel Castro est utile à cause latino-américaine?" Perón replied:

Absolument. Castro est un promoteur de la libération. Il a dû s'appuyer un impérialisme parce que la proximité de l'autre menaçait de l'écraser. Mais l'objectif des Cubains est bien la libération des peuples d'Amérique Latine. Ils n'ont d'autre intention que celle de constituer une tête de point pour la libération des pays continentaux. Che Guevara est un symbole de cette libération. Il a été grand parce qu'il a servi une grande cause, jusqu'à finir par l'incarner. C'est homme d'un idéal. Beaucoup de grands hommes sont passés inaperçus parce qu'ils n'avaient pas de cause noble à servir.

Thiriart also asked Perón to comment on Castro's differences with the Russians. Perón told him:

Ce rôle, les Russes ne le jouent d'ailleurs pas seulement à Cuba, mais dans d'autres pays. Ainsi Guevara, après avoir accompli sa mission à Cuba, était parti en Afrique pour entrer en contact avec ce mouvement communiste africain. Mais les responsables de ce mouvement avaient reçu l'ordre de refouler Guevara. Guevara dut quitter l'Afrique, parce que les Russes y travaillaient: un conflit opposait, au Congo, les deux impérialismes concurrents. Les deux tendances opposées qu'ils représentent peuvent, à certains moments, unir leurs forces pour dérendre la même cause: celle de l'ordre établi. C'est logique, ils défendent l'impérialisme, et non pas la liberté des peuples! [From Thiriart's 7 November 1968 interview with Perón in Spain, reprinted in the anthology *La Nation Européenne* (Brussels: Edition Machiavel)].

18. Thiriart said his contact with Chou En-lai caused the USSR to pressure Austria to expel him.

19. On the Chinese connections with Thiriart, see Patrice Chairoff, *Dossier Neo-Nazisme* (Paris: Ramsay, 1977). Thiriart's "left turn" caused considerable chaos, and some of his followers broke with him. (Jeffrey Bale, "The 'Black' Terrorist International: Neo-Fascist Paramilitary Networks and the 'Strategy of Tension' in Italy, 1968–1974" [unpublished University of California at Berkeley Ph.D. dissertation, 1994], p. 121.)

20. For more on Genoud, see the appendix "'Sheik François': Friend to Hitler and Carlos the Jackal."

21. Erna Paris, *Unhealed Wounds* (New York: Grove, 1985), p. 171.

22. Andrea Jarach, *Terrismo International* (Firenze: Vallecchi, 1979), pp. 57–59.

23. Thiriart mentions his attendance at the Congress in the November 1968 *La Nation Européenne*. In *L'Orchestre Noir* (p. 133), Frederic Laurent reports that Thiriart appeared to be working for the intelligence services of several Arab nations. On Thiriart's ties to the PFLP, see Martin Lee, *The Beast Reawakens* (Boston: Little Brown, 1997), p. 181. For more on Habash and the PFLP, see the appendix "'Sheik François'— Friend to Hitler and Carlos the Jackal."

24. Around this time the Michigan KKK leader Robert Miles created Unity Now in the United States to unite the left and right against the "establishment," while Willis Carto's wing of the National Youth Alliance also tried to link up with the New Left.

25. Richard Drake, *The Revolutionary Mystique and Terrorism in Contemporary Italy* (Bloomington, IN: Indiana University Press, 1989), pp. 130–31.

26. Jean-Marc Théolleyre, *Les Neo-Nazis* (Paris: Messidor/Temps Actuels, 1982), p. 224.

27. Franco Ferraresi, "The Radical Right in Postwar Italy," *Politics & Society*, Vol. 16, No. 1, March 1988. One Rome-based network of rightists, called Costruiamo L'Azione, tried to forge alliances with the far left until it was broken up by the police. (Leonard Weinberg, "Italian Neo-Fascist Terrorism: A Comparative Perspective," *Terrorism and Political Violence*, Vol. 7, No. 1, Spring 1995, pp. 233–34.)

28. Bale, "The 'Black' Terrorist International," pp. 140–41, fn. 223, p. 230.

29. Rene Monzat, *Enquêtes sur la Droite Extrême* (Paris: Le Monde, 1992), p. 52. Also see Bale, "The 'Black' Terrorist International," fn. 171, p. 221.

30. Monzat, *Enquêtes*, pp. 53, 73.

31. John Schmeidel, "My Enemy's Enemy: Twenty Years of Cooperation Between West Germany's Red Army Faction and the GDR Ministry for State Security," in *Intelligence and National Security*, Vol. 8, No. 4 (October, 1993). Also see H. J. Horchem's essay "Terrorism in Germany: 1985," in *Contemporary Research on Terrorism*, edited by Paul Wilkinson and Alasdair Stewart (Aberdeen: Aberdeen University Press, 1987).

32. Thiriart also said:

In my next work I shall devote a few short pages to paying tribute to leaders like Stalin or de Gaulle and castigate their spineless, wishy-washy "descendants." But for Stalin the Soviet Union would no longer exist . . . I set out on my "road," on my "search for the Political Grail" in the Communist Party when I was still very young as you know. Those were the days of Stalin. What an intoxicating atmosphere there was then in our party ranks. When you compare that with the present day Communist parties in Italy and France, composed of degenerate opportunists, vote-catching bourgeois, you immediately see that they have nothing in common.

33. Thiriart also argued: "Les campagnes de presse, ici à l'Ouest, qui veulent préparer une nouvelle croisade contre l'Union Soviétique, font irrésistiblement penser à celles des années 1937 à 1939, campagnes qui, elles, visaient à préparer la guerre contre le IIIième Reich. On retrouve d'ailleurs le même lobby." *L'Empire Euro-Sovietique*, p. 2.

34. Thiriart's atheism was evident in a September 1981 statement in which he remarked:

The creation of the Euro-Soviet Empire is indispensable, not only for historic reasons which have been adequately expounded elsewhere, but principally because we need a ground, a "sanctuary" where we can carry out applied research and work on the "superman" or "mutant man" as we have chosen to call him. Priests, pastors, and rabbis will have no place in the society which will see man mutate.

Such views fit very well with the "biopolitical" vision advanced by the IAAEE/*Mankind Quarterly* axis.

35. On Niekisch, see the appendix "Three Patron Saints of Red Fascism."

36. Another important advocate of a tilt by the right to Russia was the old SRP leader Otto Ernst Remer. In the early 1980s he created the Deutsche Freiheitbewegung to demand a new "Rapallo Pact" between Russia and Germany. For a closer look at Remer, see Martin Lee, *The Beast Reawakens*.

37. Thiriart's September 1981 introduction to the English translation of Yannick Sauveur's 1978 *Mémoire*.

55

THE MYSTERIOUS
BOOK OF VLES

The most virulent fascist movement in the world today exists not in Germany but in Russia. The collapse of the Soviet Union has led to a "Red-Brown alliance," a strange ideological coalition that has united many of Russia's fascists with powerful elements inside the old Communist Party elite and Soviet national security establishment. The Red-Brown alliance has also been encouraged by Euroright supporters of Jean-François Thiriart. In August 1992, just three months before his death, Thiriart and Michel Schneider, the editor of the now-defunct national bolshevik publication *Nationalisme et République*, visited Moscow for talks with high-ranking Soviet officials, including current Russian Communist Party boss Gennadi Zyuganov.[1]

The Red-Brown axis is supported by former GRECE member and Thiriart disciple Christian Bouchet's group Nouvelle Résistance (publisher of *Lutte de Peuple*) and the Milan-based journal *Orion*.[2] In 1991 Bouchet helped found a new European Liberation Front in homage to Yockey.[3] These same circles assisted Alain de Benoist in arranging his March 1992 trip to Moscow. De Benoist was accompanied on his visit by the Belgian Euroright theorist Robert Steuckers.[4] While in Moscow, de Benoist held discussions with Aleksandr Prokhanov, who in March 1992 founded the Red-Brown journal *Dyen* (The Day), which was later banned by the Yeltsin government. Prokhanov worked closely with Aleksandr Dugin, another *Dyen* writer, who translated and published the works of both René Guénon and Julius Evola through his publishing house AION,[5] and was a Russian correspondent for *Lutte du Peuple*. Prokhanov and Dugin both have close ties to Gennadi Zyuganov's Communist Party of the Russian Federation as well as the Red-Brown National Salvation Front (NSF).

On the NSF's initiative, a congress was held in Moscow on 2 March 1993 around the theme "The Peoples Opposed to the New American Order." A resolution from the meeting denouncing the Trilateral Commission, the Bilderberg group, and Israel was signed by Prokhanov, S. Umalatova (a former president of the Supreme Soviet), Dugin, H. Djemal from the Islamic Renaissance Party, *Orion* editor M. Battara, and C. Terracciano from the Alternative Movement.[6]

Conspicuously absent from the gathering was de Benoist, who apparently fears that the Red-Brown alliance as presently constituted is little more than a return to Great Russian nationalism under a "national bolshevik" cover. As someone who supports the notion of a decentralized "Europe of a Hundred Flags" as the constituent elements of a new Imperium, de Benoist could not embrace a Great Russian reoccupation of Ukraine, Georgia, the Baltic States, and the Chechen Republic.[7]

While de Benoist may have his doubts about the Red-Brown axis, elements inside the Soviet military/industrial/intelligence apparat have been trying to construct just such an alliance for some time.[8] During the Soviet era, many hardliners from the Communist camp embraced anti-Semitism, which was related to a broader debate over Russia's relations with the West. Although official Soviet foreign policy lauded detente, Stalinoid political formations existed just below the surface. Starting in the early 1960s, a new wave of state-sanctioned anti-Semitic tracts (often couched in "anti-Zionist" rhetoric) began appearing inside Russia.

The ideological exhaustion of the Brezhnev regime by the late 1970s resulted in a resurgence of the Russian far right, a rise sanctioned in part by elements inside the Communist Party elite. One of the most remarkable examples of this trend was an Ahnenerbe-like attempt to identify Russian culture not with Christianity but with Indo-European paganism through the promotion of a historical hoax called *The Book of Vles*. The book was said to have been composed around 875 B.C. by the Rusi (Ruthenes) people living in what is today Ukraine. In the 980s A.D. Byzantine Christianity became Russia's official religion. Yet *The Book of Vles* supposedly managed to survive and, according to an English edition of the work published in the West in 1973, was "probably taken to Novgorod, where paganism still managed to hold out."[9] (Novgorod was also the capital of the Varangian empire created by the Viking adventurer Rurik in the early 800s.) The book then vanished from history until the Russian Civil War, when a White Russian colonel named A. Izenbeck reportedly found it in the abandoned library of a plundered estate. Izenbeck, "a former artist attached to archeological expeditions into Asia," immediately recognized its importance and managed to bring it out of Russia.

In 1926 Izenbeck showed his treasure to his close friend Y. P. Miroliubov who, by a fortunate coincidence, had been planning to write either a novel or epic poem about ancient Russia. Upon seeing *The Book of Vles*, Miroliubov decided that it predated *The Lay of Igor's Host* (written around 1187 A.D. and considered the founding literary text of Russian culture), and for the next 15 years he worked on a translation. In 1941, however, Izenbeck died "and the original boards had disappeared." All Miroliubov was left with was a copy of the original script in longhand. In the 1950s, Miroliubov made *The Book of Vles* public after he saw a note in a San Francisco literary magazine published by Russian emigrés. The note's author, A. A. Kur, asked readers if they knew anything about an ancient manuscript from pagan Ruthenia. After a long letter to Kur, Miroliubov went to San Francisco to meet him. *The Book of Vles* was then published in *Zhar-Ptitza* (The Firebird), a San Francisco–based emigré magazine.

In the mid-'50s, scholarly investigation of the text was carried out by a White Russian professor named Paramonov, whose pen name was "S. Lesnoi." As Lesnoi, Paramonov wrote *Istoriya "Russov" v Neizurash Chennoy Vide* (History of the "Rus" in Undistorted Form), which was published in Paris in 1957. He then sent two papers to the Slavic Committee of the USSR Academy of Sciences: "*The Book of Vles:* The Chronicle of the Pagan Priests of the Ninth Century B.C., a New, Unexplored Historical Source" and "Were the Ancient 'Russes' Idol Worshippers and Practicers of Human Sacrifice?" The promoters of *The Book of Vles*, however, were not ivory-tower scholars. Y. P. Miroliubov, for example, wrote an article praising the German-backed "Vlasov Army," which was printed in the Vlasov paper *Russkaya Zhisn* (Russian Life).[10] Paramonov, it turned out, was an entomologist-turned–Nazi collaborator who fled Kiev with the German army.

In an analysis of *The Book of Vles* in *Jews and Jewish Topics in Soviet and East European Publications*, M. Kaganskaya underscores the remarkable impact the work would have had on Russian history *if* it were true.[11] It would have been as significant to Russian culture as Homer was to the Greeks and would demonstrate that as far back as 900 B.C., 100 years before the founding of Rome, the Russians had developed both writing and a sense of history found only in mature cultures. Nor was the document just a chronicle; it was also a collection of pagan sermons passed on from generation to generation. Russia's conversion to Christianity, as well as works like *The Lay of Igor's Host*, would now be seen as the sunset, not the beginning, of the Russian people and would mark the end of a once-great civilization. *The Book of Vles* would prove that the truly great Russian civilization came from noble Indo-European/Aryan ("Eurasian") roots, and that Russia was not a backward peasant culture that had to be "civilized" by Christianity.

The Slavic Committee of the USSR Academy of Sciences rejected *The Book of Vles* as a crude hoax in 1960. An article by L. P. Zhukovskaya of the Institute of Russian Languages published in *Voprosy Yazkoznaniya* (Linguistic Studies) was titled: "A Spurious Pre-Cyrillic Manuscript." For years it was remembered, if at all, as an interesting literary forgery.[12] Then, incredibly, in May 1976, *Nedelya* (The Week), the popular weekly supplement to *Izvestia*, ran an enormous article called "The Mysterious Chronicle: *The Book of Vles*—A Forgery or a Priceless Monument of World Culture?" The story was signed by two historians, V. Skurlatov and N. Nikolaev, Ph.D. They claimed the book was authentic and showed that Russians were "Aryans" and not Christians. The Russians were, in fact, "the most ancient Indo-European people"—*The Book of Vles* called them the descendants of "Oriy," and for that reason they were called Oryans or Aryans. The "Oryans" came from Central Asia to North India in approximately 1000 B.C. Their way of living "strongly resembled the ancient Slavo-Russes depicted in *The Book of Vles* . . . in their way of life, traditions, rituals, deities, pottery, and exterior." *Nedelya*'s story (which ignored the identity and politics of the original promoters of *The Book of Vles* as well as its 1960 refutation) began a 10-year campaign in the Soviet press to give new credence to the hoax.

One year after the *Nedelya* story, the original debunker of *The Book of Vles*, L. P. Zhukovskaya, joined forces with leading Soviet Indo-Europeanist B. A. Rybakov and V. I. Buganov (all Academicians) to publish yet another refutation of the forgery in *Voprosy Istorii* (Historical Studies), where they again pointed out that Paramonov was a Nazi collaborator.[13] None of this had the slightest impact on *The Book of Vles*'s backers, who now included L. Korneev, one of the USSR's leading "anti-Zionist" polemicists. In 1982, the Politizdat Ukrainy Publishing House published Korneev's *The Class Essence of Zionism*, which listed among Zion's numerous crimes attacks on the credibility of *The Book of Vles*. The historian L. Dymerskaya-Tsigelman believes that Korneev embraced *The Book of Vles* so he could argue that Russians were a highly civilized people whom the Jews had long hated because thousands of years ago the Oryans had a culture that rivaled Judeo-Christianity.[14]

It also turned out that *The Book of Vles*'s leading Soviet promoter, V. Skurlatov, was an extreme rightist. He first achieved notoriety while a bureaucrat in the Department of Propaganda of the Moscow Town Committee of Komsomol in the mid-1960s. Skurlatov submitted a proposal for the revival of Russia called "The Moral Statutes" to the Komsomol Central Committee, and the tract was later circulated in samizdat. The historian Alexander Yanov described the essay as a weird kind of Nietzscheanism mixed with a fascist-like worship of strength and caste. In "The Moral Statutes," Skurlatov called on the Komsomol to launch a campaign to support native, moral, and psychological values of virginity and to prevent pre-marital sexual intercourse. According to Skurlatov:

> We must not stop even at promoting ancient peasant customs: painting gates with tar, public showing of the sheet after the wedding night, corporal punishment of women who give themselves to foreigners, branding and sterilization of them . . . The whip is the best teacher. A blow on the body hardens the soul . . . There is no baser calling than to be a "thinker," an "intellectual" . . . and there is no nobler calling than to be a soldier. The intellectual is the slave of dead reason, and the soldier is the lord of life who subjects the world process to his will . . . It is necessary to resurrect and assert forever the cult which is health-giving and leads in time to immortality—the cult of the soldier.[15]

Skurlatov went on to write *Zionism and Apartheid*, which was also published by the Politizdat Ukrainy Publishing House. In it he claimed that modern racism originated in the idea that the Jews were God's chosen people. The Catholic Church elaborated on this notion by blessing the forcible conversion of "non-baptized" peoples. But the Jewish concept of "God-chosenness" (*bogoizbrannost*) was embraced even more by the bourgeoisie and its racist variant of Christianity, namely Protestantism. He then condemned the Enlightenment and "Judaism-Masonry."

The antics of Skurlatov and his friends could not have been carried out without sanction from high-level elements of the Soviet elite who were clearly willing to encourage an explicitly "Aryan" movement inside their own country. Skurlatov also became a significant figure in Soviet science fiction circles and co-edited *There Was Thunder*, an anthology of Western and Soviet sci-fi and horror writers published in 1976. (One wing of the Soviet sci-fi community wrote books with strong Russian racial, chauvinist, pagan, and theosophic elements.[16])

L. Korneev, who defended *The Book of Vles*, also promoted an Institute for Historical Review–like form of Holocaust denial. In his 1982 *Kursom Agressii i Rasizma*, he wrote:

> The infamous profiteering of Zionists makes questionable the alleged number of six million Jews which are claimed to have been annihilated during World War II. This number has no scientific foundation. The true number must be at least half or one-third of the commonly assumed estimate.

In *The Class Essence of Zionism*, Korneev cited works like *The Myth of the Six Million*, *Big Lie: Did Six Million Really Die!*, and *Die Auschwitz Luge* to support his views. He even explained Czarist pogroms as class-motivated revolts against Jewish exploiters. "Class" also played an important role in Korneev's not-so-subtle defense of Nazi policies toward the Jews:

> The anti-Semitism of German fascism was due not to some mystical reasons but to class ones . . . It is common knowledge that in the days of the Weimar Republic the power of German Judentum in the German economy and in the state administration, in the spheres of culture, science, and press was out of any proportion to its numbers in the total population. This is why it was stated in the program of the Hitler National-Socialist German Workers' Party . . . that no Jew can belong to the Germanic race and consequently cannot be a German citizen or hold any governmental positions.

Korneev also praised Henry Ford in a 1984 essay entitled "Tainaya Voina Sionizma" (The Secret War of Zionism) in *Zvezda Vostoka*. According to Korneev, Ford was "unjustly accused of anti-Semitism" for writing *The International Jew*.[17]

There were worse Soviet Bloc "experts on Zionism" than Korneev. In February 1976, the newsletter of the International Council of Jews from Czechoslovakia issued a report called "Czech Nazi Collaborators in Leading Roles." Included in the study was a profile of Svatopluk Dolejs, a/k/a "Jevgenij Jevsejev" (Yevgeni Yevseyev), who was a prominent Soviet Bloc writer on the dangers of Zionism. According to the report, Dolejs spent 1941–44 working with the Nazis in Prague and editing the anti-Semitic weekly *Arijsky Bog* (The Aryan Fight). After the war he joined the Czech secret service, and from 1960 to 1972 he ran Arab-language broadcasts from Radio Prague. He also made frequent visits to the Middle East, especially Cairo, and may well have known Johann von Leers.[18]

Elements of the Soviet elite also supported Pamyat (Memory), the first openly far-right organization in the USSR. Pamyat, formed in the early 1980s, began as "The Society for the Lovers of History and Literature," and had links to the USSR Ministry of Aviation Industry, which gave the group an office. (As Pamyat grew more explicit in its attacks on Jews and Masons—and some members began praising Czarism—the Ministry officially distanced itself from the group.) Many Pamyat members came from the right wing of VOOPIK, the All Russian Society for the Preservation of Historical and Cultural Monuments. Like the Thule Society and the Northern League, Pamyat was an ostensibly cultural organization under whose auspices the most bizarre far-right politics flourished. By the spring of 1987 Pamyat even briefly managed to capture the Moscow section of VOOPIK. Its supporters also included some leading Russian "Village School" writers.

It seems clear then that today's Russian "Red-Brown alliance" has its roots in some of the most decayed elements of the Soviet national security establishment and Communist Party elite. This ideological axis, which once seemed politically marginal, is now a significant challenge to the growth of democratic consciousness in Russia. The explosion of anti-American and anti-NATO sentiment in Russia during the recent war against Serbia will only strengthen its influence.

Notes:

1. Schneider's *Nationalisme et République* had ties to Roger Garaudy, a former Marxist turned Holocaust-denier. See the article in *Reflexes*, No. 40, Autumn 1993. An English-language version of the *Reflexes* story appeared in the British journal *Searchlight* under the heading "Abandoning the left-right distinction." Also see *Searchlight*'s March 1996 issue for a discussion of Garaudy. For an overview of the links between the Communists and the right from a conservative, anti-Communist point of view, see Ronald Gaucher and Philippe Randa, *Les "Antisémites" de Gauche* (Paris: Éditions Déterna, 1998), pp. 100–12 in particular.

2. These groups have also tried to revive the cult of Che Guevara. (Rene Monzat, *Enquêtes sur la Droite Extrême* [Paris: Le Monde, 1992], p. 74.)

3. Bouchet is also an occultist, and publishes a journal called *Thelema*. See Nicholas Goodrick-Clarke, *Hitler's Priestess: Savitri Devi, the Hindu-Aryan Myth, and Neo-Nazism* (New York: New York University Press, 1998), p. 216. For more on Bouchet, see *Searchlight*, December 1996. Also see the appendix "The Devil and Francis Parker Yockey."

4. In 1980 Steuckers published a book called *Dossier géopolitique*. Steuckers also edited a publication called *Orientations*, whose Munich correspondent was Armin Mohler, Ernst Jünger's former secretary, and an intellectual godfather of the revival of the Conservative Revolution in the European New Right. From 1964 to 1985 he directed the Siemens Foundation, based in Munich. See *Orientations*, No. 4 (November–December 1983), for Mohler's name. For more on Mohler and the question of the future of the European New Right, see Göran Dahl's important article "Will 'The Other God' Fail Again? On the Possible Return of the Conservative Revolution," in *Theory, Culture & Society*, Vol. 13, No. 1, February 1996.

5. Dugin also headed a "neo-traditionalist" group ARCTOGAIA.

6. For an extensive discussion of de Benoist and Russia, see Pierre-André Taguieff, *Sur la Nouvelle Droite* (Paris: Descartes & Cie., 1994), pp. 308–12.

7. Ibid. Also see de Benoist's discussion in *Telos* No. 98/99 (Winter 1993–Spring 1994). The far more Russian-oriented *Orion* is now denouncing Marco Tarchi, editor of *Diorama Letterario* and a close ally of Alain de Benoist. Robert Steuckers has also denounced de Benoist in his journal *Vouloir*. See *The Scorpion*, No. 19, p. 50.

8. For information on the right in Russia, see Walter Laqueur, *Black Hundred* (New York: Harper Collins, 1993); Semyon Reznik, *The Nazification of Russia* (Washington D.C.: Challenge, 1996); Alexander Yanov, *Weimar Russia* (New York: Slovo-Word Publishing House, 1997); and Martin Lee, *The Beast Reawakens* (Boston: Little Brown, 1997), pp. 304–30 in particular. In 1989–90 I wrote a long manuscript called *Red Swastika* examining this question.

9. *Vlesova Kniga (Vles Kyha)*, translated by Victor Kachur (Columbus, Ohio: 1973).

10. For more on Vlasov, see the appendix "The Whites and the Reds."

11. M. Kaganskaya, "*The Book of Vles:* The Saga of a Forgery," in *Jews and Jewish Topics in Soviet and East European Publications* (Jerusalem: Center for Research on East-European Jewry, Hebrew University), Winter 1986–1987. I owe my analysis of *The Book of Vles* almost entirely to Kaganskaya.

12. A. L. Mongait, a leading Soviet archeologist, wrote a book in 1969 that discussed *The Book of Vles* as a classic forgery.

13. *The Book of Vles* may have been part of an attempt by some White Russian Vlasov supporters to convince the Nazis that they too were Aryans and should not be treated as racially inferior to the Germans.

14. L. Dymerskaya-Tsigelman, "L. Korneev as a Phenomenon of Soviet Anti-Semitism in the 1970s–80s," in the June 1986 issue of *Jews and Jewish Topics in Soviet and East European Publications*.

15. The text of Skurlatov's "The Moral Statutes" was translated in full in *The USSR: Internal Contradictions*, Issue 6, 1982. Also see Alexander Yanov, *The Russian New Right* (Berkeley, CA: University of California Institute of International Studies Research Series, 1978).

16. For a list of such books, see the appendix to Kaganskaya's essay on *The Book of Vles*.

17. Korneev made his claims even though *The Greater Soviet Encyclopedia* identified Henry Ford as a supporter of racist and Nazi groups. *The Greater Soviet Encyclopedia* also said that Hitler killed six million Jews.

18. See the article "Czech Nazi Collaborators in Leading Roles," in the International Council of Jews from Czechoslovakia's *ICJC Newsletter* (Vol. VII, No. 1–2, February 1976). Also see the *ICJC Newsletter* for August 1976 (Vol. VII, No. 4) for a long list of Nazi collaborators who became important figures in postwar Czechoslovakia. In *The Beast Reawakens*, Martin Lee reports (p. 168) that the Soviet publication *Komsomolskaya Pravda* lifted anti-Semitic passages from a pamphlet called *America: A Zionist Colony* that had been co-authored by Johann von Leers when he was living in Cairo. Yockey's own reported ties to Czech intelligence should also be noted.

CONCLUSION: LABYRINTH'S END

Perhaps in time the so-called Dark Ages will be thought of as including our own.

—George Christoph Lichtenberg

56

LABYRINTH'S END

For the past four decades Francis Parker Yockey has remained a mysterious, largely marginal figure even inside the extremist right. What was known about him was little more than a compilation of rumor and half-truth. Indeed, if it were not for the accident of history that Willis Carto promoted *Imperium*, Yockey would now be a completely forgotten figure. The examination of his life, however, has taken us through an elaborate labyrinth the dimensions of which are barely glimpsed in conventional historical accounts.

When Yockey wrote *Imperium* he hoped to create what Moeller van den Bruck called a *Weltanschauungsgedanke* (a "thought capable of creating a conception of the world") for a new era of post-Hitler fascism. The debates within and among groups like the Malmö International, the New European Order, and the Northern League equally reflect ongoing changes in fascist ideology. Yet these complex developments are rarely analyzed, in part because the mythology of "Hitlerism" still holds sway in academia, in popular culture, and inside the far right.

The allure of Hitlerism remains particularly strong inside the American extreme right, and helps explain why George Lincoln Rockwell's tiny American Nazi Party is considered by many to be the first "real" postwar Nazi movement in America. Yockey's own brand of radical rightist politics has never found a following in the U.S.; even to many self-proclaimed fans of *Imperium*, Yockey's political ideology and actions must seem almost incomprehensible. In Europe, however, Yockey's views can easily be identified as part of a broader current inside fascism from its very beginning.

Fascism initially arose out of fin-de-siècle attemps to combine radical authoritarian elements of nationalism with strongly anti-rationalist and revolutionary currents inside socialism. Today both communism and fascism, ideologies that the French fascist Robert Brasillach once called "the two poetries" of the 20th century, seem exhausted given the triumph of multinational capitalism. Yet periods of ideological decay often breed strange new variants, such as the "Red-Brown alliance" in the former Soviet Union, which do not easily fit into conventional political-science categories of "left" and "right." As the historian Zeev Sternhell argues, an observer of early–20th-century Italian fascism would be struck as much by its "left" as by its "right" components. What is especially worrisome is that much of the left has today so deteriorated that it may well lack the capacity for understanding, much less fighting, new forms of fascism that incorporate "leftist" rhetoric and ideas. Ironically, the well-known criminal idiocies of Nutzi and skinhead elements who still fetishize the relics of "grandpa's fascism" may actually hinder the incubation of newer and more sophisticated strains of "post-Hitlerian" fascist ideology.

Nazism and communism may perhaps one day be seen as 20th-century examples of a long line of European-centered millenarian movements. As the lesson of the Holocaust reminds us over and over again, mythological thinking can be just as dangerous as the worst forms of "instrumental reason." Nor can the turn toward apocalyptic fantasy simply be dismissed as a delusion of the uneducated poor. It is equally important to remember that both apocalypse and utopia draw their real strength from the failures of the ruling political, economic, and cultural order and not simply from the hocus-pocus of the wannabe führers who litter the political and occult undergrounds. Present-day Russia is a textbook illustration of just this point.

Our collective response to some potentially difficult challenges ahead may help determine not just the future of the West but the future of the world. Spengler called his famous book *Der Untergang des Abendlandes,* or The Decline of the West. To fully understand the title, it is important to know that *Abend,* like *West,* also has the meaning "evening." *West,* for example, is related to the Latin *vesper* and the Greek *hesperos,* both meaning "evening." The "evening lands" is the place where the sun sets, which is why the Egyptians imagined the western lands as the kingdom of the dead. Spengler's title, which the English translation cannot capture, evokes an entire age or culture cycle just past sunset and heading into night. Yet the idea of the "West," particularly in America, has been linked to a sense not of closure but rather of new frontiers. Today the most important frontier is not outer but inner; it is the development of a sense of the interrelatedness of the West with the rest of the world's cultures.

The study of the past can help us develop a living sense of "world-historical" consciousnessness. Yet historical thinking will always remain a communion with all who have gone before us. The German Pietists who believed that *Gedanken ist Danken* (thinking is thanking) were right. History lets us understand our links to other peoples and times that have made us what we are, part of a vast chain stretching both backward and forward across time. To see oneself as a historical actor is to accept the responsibility to act on behalf of future generations, to accept the challenge of the heroic. It is also to enter more fully into the great dialogue between the world of Becoming and the world of Being, between the fleeting kingdom of the living and the western land to which we are all headed, the empire of our ancestors, the vast Imperium of the dead.

APPENDIX A:
NOS

In recent years a pop mixture of Julius Evola's ideas and Nazi myth has been advanced by Miguel Serrano, a well-known Chilean writer and that nation's ambassador to India (1953–62), Yugoslavia (1962–64), and Austria (1964–70).[1] Serrano's best-known work in English, *C. G. Jung and Herman Hesse: A Record of Two Friendships*, records his relationships with both men. Far less known, however, is his 1984 600-plus-page opus, *Adolf Hitler, el Último Avatāra*. In it, he argues that Hitler "is the Tenth Avatar of Vishnu, the Kalki Avatar, who has incarnated to bring about the end of the Kali Yuga and usher in a New Age."[2] *Adolf Hitler* is filled with discussions about yoga, chakras, *The Protocols of the Elders of Zion*, the membership list of the Thule Society, attacks on the "Jew Milton Friedman" and the Chicago School of Economics' role in Chile, flying saucers, Hyperborea, and the work of Herman Wirth and Evola.[3]

Serrano also cryptically refers to his ties to the New European Order in his strange mystical book *Nos: Book of the Resurrection*, which the well-known British publishing house Routledge and Kegan Paul published in 1984.[4] In *Nos*, Serrano mentions that he is "reading a book which no one else in my country has yet read, and which Père Jacques, a member of the order, will publish shortly, reproducing it from our archives."[5] "Père Jacques" was Jacques de Mahieu; an earlier de Mahieu book, *Précis de Biopolitique*, was published by the NEO's Editions Celtiques.[6] De Mahieu argues that the Aztec god Quetzalcoatl was really a Viking or Hyperborean "White God" who created both the Toltec and Mayan civilizations as well as the empire of Tiahuanacu.[7]

Serrano spends some time in *Nos* discussing his relationship with Carl Jung, whom Serrano sees as a sorceror.[8] Serrano is particularly fascinated by the magician who transcends the "Androgynous of the beginnings, in search of an absolute differentiation, the Absolute Personality."[9] Echoing Otto Weininger, Serrano argues in *Nos* that in the initiation of the magician-warriors, the aspiration is to achieve not the Androgynous but the Absolute Man. The role of the woman is also clear: "The woman dies. She is dead. She must die in order to return to life. She is the warrior's companion, existing only in his mind, in his spirit. Only with the memory of his beloved in his heart can the initiate achieve the Grail."[10]

Serrano stresses the importance of Hyperborea, where a solar race originated "from the Sun which lies on the other side of all the suns. Our star is close by and appears to the Walkers of the Dawn to show them the way." *Nos* tells the story of how the solar race "came down to live at the North Pole, on the continent of Hyperborea, which enjoyed a temperate climate during the Golden Age." After a dramatic climate shift, "the White Gods withdrew into the Interior Earth, although a few of them went to a transoceanic continent to the west, where the Sun of the Golden Age had not yet set." This is the place "where the Black Sun of the South Pole rose at the point where Arcthus, Arthos, the Hyperborean bear, became Antarctica . . . where Stonehenge, the Observatory of the Sun, became Tiahuanacu, the transmitter of Venus, the star of Lucifer." The White Gods carried "a sword, a lance, and a cauldron, together with the Soma plant. With them they also brought the stone which fell from the broken crown of *Lucifer, the King of the White Gods,* whom others have called Apollo, Abraxas, Siva, Quetzalcoatl."[11]

In both *Nos* and *Adolf Hitler*, Serrano "explains" UFOs. According to *Nos's* mythology, deep inside the earth lie the cities of Agharti, Shamballa, and the Caesars, which are inhabited by the immortal Siddhas. "There the Golden Age still exists. The Discs of Light [UFO's], covered in orichalcum, fly out from there. They carried our guide [Hitler] off to a place of safety."[12]

Nos also discusses "the Walkers of the Dawn," whose sign is the left-handed swastika, "which begins the journey back to Hyperborea, the polar homeland, and the Morning Star, Venus, the celestial point of origin of the semi-divine beings."[13] The Walkers of the Dawn are "the followers of Lucifer, of the Morning Star." They "do not beg to be allowed into heaven. They demand to be, because they feel that they have done everything possible to merit being deified." Following Evola's elevation of the warrior caste over the priest caste, Serrano continues: "At the end of our road, no fusion with God or redeemer awaits us. Our way is not the way of ecstasy of the saints but the way of separation of the magicians, of the White Gods who have become absorbed into the sources of creative energy. Creating worlds, loving each other inside and outside eternity. We do not beg, like the lunar troubadour: 'Take us back to where you took us from!'"[14]

Nos is equally interested in "holy war." According to Serrano, "We are warriors from the most holy of wars, from a mythical, eternal, cosmic war." "Purely terrestrial people," however, "do not believe in this Myth of Resurrection and Eternal Love" because they "did not fall from another planet but are the 'slaves of Atlantis.'" Then there are "those who have come from opposing stars [the Jews?

the "mud people"?], from different universes, [who] are fighting against our myth. Not all who inhabit the earth are the same. This is why we are fighting, so as to preserve a myth, a legend, which flows through the 'blood memory.'" Race mixing, or what Serrano calls "the hybridization of the 'blood memories,'" threatens to debase the mythic Archetype: "The youth of today has been influenced by black music . . . Plato has showed us that Atlantis was drowned because of an indiscriminate mingling of Archetypes" that destroyed the "blood memory."[15]

Once *Nos* is decoded, it is a remarkable glimpse into the esoteric mythology of groups like the New European Order.

Notes:

1. Serrano joined the Chilean Nazi Party in 1939. For a closer look at Serrano, see Nicholas Goodrick-Clarke, *Hitler's Priestess: Savitri Devi, the Hindu-Aryan Myth, and Neo-Nazism* (New York: New York University Press, 1990), pp. 219–22.

2. Joscelyn Godwin, *Arktos* (Grand Rapids, MI: Phanes Press, 1993), p. 70. Also see Godwin's discussion of the Romanian writer Jean Parvulesco.

3. Serrano also takes up Evola's broadsword against René Guénon's Brahmin caste in *Nos*:

Parsifal, with his "fury," or his hatred, was resisting a *participation mystique*. *Samadhi*, fusion with *Adhi*, the Primordial Being, doesn't await him at the end of his road. Because this would be the way of sainthood. What awaits him is *Kaivalya*, total separation, supreme Individuation, Absolute Personality, the ultimate solitude of the Superman. This is the way of the magician, the Siddha, the tantric hero of the Grail. The cosmic isolation of the risen Purusha.

4. Serrano also used some of the art work from *Nos* for *Adolf Hitler*.

5. *Nos*, p. 83.

6. Jacques de Mahieu, *Précis de Biopolitique* (Montreal: Editions Celtiques, 1969). Serrano emphasizes de Mahieu's argument that all great Latin American civilizations were founded by people who came from the north and who were worshipped as gods. See, for example, de Mahieu, *La Fabuleuse Épopée des Troyens en Amérique du Sud* (Puiseaux: Pardes, 1998) and *L'Agonie du Dieu-Soleil: Les Vikings en Amerique du Sud* (Paris: R. Laffont, 1974). De Mahieu's work also appeared in *Nouvelle École*.

7. De Mahieu claims the Knights Templars visited America well before Columbus. His full name is also cited on p. 186 of *Nos*.

8. In *Nos*, under the heading "Carl Gustav Jung," Serrano calls Jung "the Master of the Sphinx." He says that Jung told him: "I am not from this world. I am a Hyperborean. Like you, I am a stranger in this world, in this landscape inhabited by the 'slaves of Atlantis.'" (*Nos*, pp. 64–70.) Jung also had a great influence over Allen Dulles' entire family. On Jung and Dulles, see Peter Grose, *Gentleman Spy: The Life of Allen Dulles* (Amherst, MA: University of Massachusetts Press, 1996).

9. *Nos*, p. 1.

10. Ibid., p. 11.

11. Ibid., pp. 26–27.

12. Ibid., p. 27. UFO "Discs of Light" covered in orichalcum ("a mysterious metal referred to by Plato . . . [with] the power to neutralize gravity . . . must have been the metal which allowed the *vimanas*, the *astras*, to take off and move around the skies") play a prominent role in some right-wing cults. In his books *Messengers of Deception* (Berkeley, CA: And/Or Books, 1979) and *Revelations* (New York: Ballantine Books, 1991), Jacques Vallee discusses the relationship between the far right and certain UFO cults.

In this context, also see Christof Friedrich, *Secret Nazi Polar Expeditions* (Toronto: Samisdat Publishers, 1976) and Friedrich Mattern, *UFOs: Nazi Secret Weapon*, another Samisdat publication. Samisdat is controlled by Canadian Holocaust-denier Ernst Zundel. On UFOs and the right, see Eduard Gugenberger and Roman Schweidlenka, *Mutter Erde/Magie und Politik* (Vienna: Verlag für Gesellschaftskritik, 1987), pp. 156–63, and Walter Kafton-Minkel, *Subterranean Worlds* (Port Townsend, WA: Loompanics, 1989). For an interesting look at Nazis and Atlantis, see Manfred Nagl, "SF, Occult Sciences, and Nazi Myths," in *Science-Fiction Studies*, Vol. 1, Part 3 (Spring 1974), fn. 19, p. 195.

13. *Nos*, p. 187.

14. Ibid., p. 41.

15. Ibid., pp. 60–61.

APPENDIX B:
SECRET SOCIETIES
AND SUBVERSIVE
MOVEMENTS

Conventional wisdom has long assumed that when Hitler argued for "lebens-raum" in the East in *Mein Kampf* he took the idea from General Karl Haushofer, who had visited Hitler in jail after the Munich putsch. *Mein Kampf*, however, includes a passage that is hard not to interpret as an *attack* on Haushofer and German military intelligence support for anti-colonial movements in the Third World.

In *Mein Kampf*, Hitler complained that as far back as 1920–21, the tiny NSDAP had been approached "by various quarters" to create an alliance between it and "the movement for freedom in other countries." He specifically meant an organi-zation called the League of Oppressed Nations, whose representatives from "vari-ous Balkan states, and some from Egypt and India" had impressed Hitler "as pompous big-mouths without any realistic background." He was also disgusted by "volkish circles" who had become so "dazzled by such inflated Orientals and read-ily accepted any old Indian or Egyptian student from God-knows-where as a 'rep-resentative' of India or Egypt" that they believed "British power was on the verge of collapse in India." As a white racist, Hitler noted that "in spite of everything" he would "rather see India under British rule than under any other."[1]

Hitler's argument may have reflected earlier personal discussions he had held with both Haushofer and Moeller van den Bruck. In the spring of 1922 Rudolf Pechel, a supporter of the "left of the right," met Hitler through the initiative of Haushofer and Rudolf Hess. Pechel then arranged for Hitler to meet Moeller van den Bruck at the June Club, where Hitler addressed a small gathering. After his speech, Hitler, Moeller, and Pechel began a discussion that lasted into the morning of the next day. Hitler told them: "You have everything that I lack. You produce the intellectual tools for a renascence of Germany. I am nothing but a drummer and demagogue." But the discussion did not go well and he was merely promised copies of *Gewissen* (Conscience) and other June Club publications. After Hitler finally left, Moeller remarked: "This fellow will never understand."[2]

Hitler's antipathy to German support for anti-colonialist movements was reflected in his attack on the League of Oppressed Nations. The League had also angered many British far-rightists, including the well-known conspiracy author Nesta Webster. Best known for her book *Secret Societies and Subversive Movements*, her writings remain a fertile source for conspiracy theorists like Pat Robertson. The daughter of a Barclays Bank director and a staunch British imperialist, Webster began her career attacking Pan-Germanism. Although she supported Hitler's Germany in the late 1930s, this was not a blanket endorsement of Nazi ideology; rather, her decision reflected a common belief by British conservatives that Hitler threatened Russia, not England.[3]

If Webster was anything, she was a Francophile.[4] Her support for France led her to endorse punitive measures against Germany after World War I. She believed that Weimar Germany had secretly allied itself with Bolshevik Russia and nationalist anti-colonial movements to bring down the British Empire. In her 1931 book *Surrender of an Empire*, she attacked the League of Oppressed Nations (the *Vereinigung Vergewältister Völker*, or VVV), the same group Hitler denounced in *Mein Kampf*. Webster claimed that the VVV began in America as the "League of Small and Subject Nationalities" and was led by Dudley Field Malone, reportedly the attorney for the first Soviet representative to the United States, Ludwig Martins. A mysterious American millionaire named John de Kay supposedly helped finance both the VVV and a French pacifist paper called *La Feuille*.[5] In 1920 the group moved to Berlin, where it remained under the control of a secret society called the Druidenorden. Although the Druidenorden's official grand master was a German industrialist, Webster claims that it was really led by Count von Brockdorf-Rantzau, a former German foreign minister who served as Germany's ambassador to Moscow in the 1920s.[6] The order reportedly had ties to the "Eastern school" of German monarchists; its operatives also backed anti-British groups like the Zionist movement in Palestine and the IRA. If any of Webster's claims are even half-true, the Druidenorden sounds very much like an "off-the-shelf" German intelligence organization made necessary by the restrictions of the Versailles Treaty.

Webster also alleged that the notorious Aleister Crowley was involved with the VVV in America.[7] Crowley came under attack in the British press for his collaboration in New York with George Sylvester Viereck during World War I. In *The Confessions of Aleister Crowley*, the occultist claimed that he really was acting as a one-man unauthorized spy to help England's war effort. Crowley reports that he was recruited into Viereck's propaganda operation after a chance encounter with a "Mr. O'Brien" on a Fifth Avenue bus. O'Brien then took him to the office of Viereck's propaganda organ, *The Fatherland*.[8] But was this Crowley's first encounter with German intelligence? A leading historian of occultism named Ellic Howe (himself a former member of British intelligence during World War II) has shown that Theodor Reuss, the German leader of Crowley's sex-magic Ordo Templi Orientis (OTO), was a longtime German intelligence agent.[9]

Nesta Webster was herself in contact with another secret German order with political ambitions: Munich's Thule Society. The Thule Society was a cover organization for the Bavarian branch of a quasi-masonic, ultra-right group called the Germanenorden, which had been founded in Berlin in 1912 and had lodges in many cities.[10] Starting in April 1922, Webster launched a series of attacks against Pan-Germanism in the pages of the rightist journal *The Morning Post*. Her articles were triggered by the stunning news of the Rapallo Treaty between Germany and Communist Russia. Webster explicitly rejected any attempt to blame Rapallo on a "Jewish conspiracy." She argued instead that the Jews "from the time of Frederick the Great had frequently acted as Prussia's most faithful and efficient agents."[11] She also denounced the German General Staff for aiding the 1917 Bolshevik coup.

On 10 June 1922, *The Morning Post* ran a response from Kurt Kerlen, a Thule Society member and Hitler supporter.[12] Kerlen wrote to defend his friend General Ludendorff against charges that the German General Staff had helped the Bolsheviks. Around the same time, Ludendorff was working with the White Russian Grand Duke Kirill in an attempt to get American anti-Semites like Henry Ford to help finance the German far right.[13] In fact, the exchange between Webster and Kerlen was reprinted in America by the Beckwith Company, founded by Dr. Harris Houghton, the former head of U.S. military intelligence in New York during World War I who worked closely with Ford.[14]

Kerlen blamed German aid to Russia on a Jewish conspiracy inside the Prussian War Office. He also claimed that "Bolshevism is but another name for Jewry."[15] On 15 June 1922 Webster replied to Kerlen. She reminded him that "for over a hundred years the Jews have helped supply Prussia with munitions."[16] She then claimed that Kerlen was using the "Jews" as a cover for the real culprit, Pan-Germanism.

Given his then-close ties to Ludendorff, Hitler's encomiums to the British in *Mein Kampf*, as well as his attack on the VVV, may have been part of a deliberate strategy to court support from the Anglo-American right. But how sincere was Hitler's Anglophilia? And why did Haushofer's close friend, Thule Society member Rudolf Hess, remain Hitler's number-two man inside the NSDAP up until his own still-mysterious flight to Britain in May 1941?

Notes:

1. Adolf Hitler, *Mein Kampf,* translated by Ralph Mannheim (Boston: Houghton Mifflin, 1943), pp. 656–58.

2. Klemens von Klemperer, *Germany's New Conservatism* (Princeton, NJ: Princeton University Press, 1957), p. 193.

3. For an interesting profile of Webster, see Richard Gilman, *Behind World Revolution: The Strange Career of Nesta H. Webster* (Ann Arbor, MI: Insight Books, 1982). Also see Richard Griffiths, *Fellow Travellers of the Right* (London: Constable, 1980).

4. Webster even believed that she was the reincarnation of a late-18th-century French aristocrat, the Comtesse de Sabran, whose daughter had been imprisoned and son-in-law guillotined during the French Revolution. (Gilman, p. 26.)

5. Nesta Webster, *Secret Societies and Subversive Movements* (Hawthorne, CA: Omni Publications, 1964), p. 365.

6. In Lady Queenborough's book *Occult Theocrasy* (Pasadena, CA: Emissary Pub., 1980), the Druidenorden is described as a branch of Freemasonry. Its Sovereign Grand Master was said to be Dr. Hübbe-Schleiden, who was reported to be the Secretary General of the German Theosophical Society and a leader of several occult orders including the Black Templars, Rosicrucians, and Yggdrasil. Lady Queenborough also reprints from Nesta Webster's discussion of the VVV in *The Surrender of an Empire.*

7. Nesta Webster, *The Surrender of an Empire* (London: Boswell Printing and Publishing Co., 1931), p. 132.

8. Aleister Crowley, *The Confessions of Aleister Crowley* (New York: Hill and Wang, 1969), pp. 746–47.

9. See Ellic Howe's article (co-authored with Helmut Möller) "Theodor Reuss: Irregular Freemasonry in Germany, 1900–23," in *Ars Quatuor Coronatorum* 91 (1978). Also see Howe and Möller, *Merlin Peregrinus: Vom Untergrund des Abendlandes* (Wurzburg: Könighausen & Neumann, 1986).

10. Georg Franz, "Munich: Birthplace and Center of the National Socialist German Workers' Party," *The Journal of Modern History,* Vol. XXIX, No. 4, December 1957, p. 327.

11. *Bosche and Bolshevik* (New York: The Beckwith Company, 1923), p. 2.

12. Kerlen was the head of the Nuremberg wing of a paramilitary group formed from a coalition of German rightist groups called the Deutschvölker Schutz-und Trustbund. (Reginald H. Phelps, "'Before Hitler Came': Thule Society and Germanen Orden," *The Journal of Modern History,* Vol. XXXV, No. 3, September 1963, p. 259.)

13. For more on this issue, see the appendix "The Whites and the Reds."

14. U.S. Army and Naval Intelligence worked very closely with the British Secret Service against the Germans. Houghton was personally involved in spying activity against George Sylvester Viereck.

15. *Bosche and Bolshevik,* p. 26.

16. Ibid., p. 36.

APPENDIX C:
ROLL OVER
BACHOFEN

Few readers of D. H. Lawrence's *Lady Chatterly's Lover* or Pauline Réage's *The Story of O* approach these works intent on educating themselves about European cultural and intellectual history. Yet the ideas of Johann Jakob Bachofen, Otto Weininger, and Hans Blüher significantly influenced the authors of those two novels. In his book *The von Richthofen Sisters*, cultural historian Martin Green analyses the connections between D. H. Lawrence and a clique of bohemians from Schwabing, the "Greenwich Village" of pre-war Munich. Known as the *kosmische Runde* (Cosmic Circle), the group was composed of Ludwig Klages, Alfred Schuler, Karl Wolfskehl, and, for a time, the poet Stefan George. From 1897 to 1903, the Cosmic Circle regularly met to discuss questions of anthropology, mythology, and cultural history.

The Cosmic Circle constructed a new Weltanschauung radically opposed to what they saw as the patriarchal values of Western society. Against patriarchy, they celebrated life-values, eroticism, "the superiority of instinct and intuition to the values of science," and the primacy of the "female mode of being."[1] They based their worldview on a radical reading of Bachofen's famous book *Das Mutterrecht*. Bachofen had argued that culture passed from three stages: the tellurian, the lunar, and the solar. In its tellurian phase, society is essentially nomadic and exists through a form of hunter-gatherer economics. This period is matriarchal, with no formal marriage system. Property is organized along the lines of primitive, communitarian communism.[2] The tellurian goddess, Aphrodite, is symbolized by the bitch and the swamp. In the lunar stage, although society is still matriarchal, agriculture has replaced hunter-gathering. Now the agricultural goddess Demeter, the Great Mother Goddess, assumes primacy. Only the last solar (or

Apollonian) stage of social evolution is patriarchal; it too is brought about through changes in the mode of production, specifically by the introduction of the division of labor and individual ownership of private property. The Cosmic Circle, 1890s "modern primitives" minus piercings and tattoos, adored the tellurian. They even conducted elaborate ceremonial invocations and rites of worship to the Great Mother Earth (Erdmutter). The openly gay Alfred Schuler especially equated the oppression of both homosexuals and women with the victory of patriarchy.

The Cosmic Circle fell apart in 1903, when Klages and Schuler fell into the trap of anti-Semitism due to their hatred of Judeo-Christian culture. Schuler based his own brand of anti-Jewish hatred on the Old Testament's injunctions against sodomy and onanism. He also blamed the Jews for killing Jesus, whom he saw as a martyr for androgyny. Convinced that Jewish monotheism had destroyed matriarchy, Klages and Schuler turned against their Jewish friend and Zionist Karl Wolfskehl. Yet as odd as the Cosmic Circle must have seemed to many, its interpretation of Bachofen had an enormous impact inside the pre-war counterculture. D. H. Lawrence was someone who especially assimilated the Cosmic Circle's sexual Lebensphilosophie.

Klages and Schuler went on to combine their ideas of an Earth Mother cult with the vitalism of evolutionary biology in a kind of volkish paganism based on the mystical sacralization of "blood" (die Blutleuchte). They joined forces with the volkish publisher Eugen Diederichs and his Sera Circle, and helped encourage the German Youth Movement's turn to sun worship rituals and other expressions of neopagan spirituality.[3] Klages composed his famous essay "Mensch und Erde" (Man and Earth) for the Free German Youth Wandervogel celebration on the Meissner Heights in 1913.[4] He elaborated his ideas in Der Geist als Widersacher der Seele (The Spirit as the Adversary of the Soul), an impassioned "Green" argument against "progress." Although an anti-Semite, he refused to join the Nazis, and spent most of his life in Switzerland as a convinced anti-militarist.[5]

Nazi ideologue Alfred Rosenberg particularly detested Klages' "Asiatic" opposition to patriarchy and hatred of machine civilization. Julius Evola was another foe of both Klages and Schuler. In January 1942 he wrote an article in La Vita Italiana denouncing a book by Schuler as politically dangerous. He also accused Klages of having a "Jewish tone."[6] His attack was in keeping with his longstanding opposition to the volkish side of National Socialism. For Evola, the Cosmic Circle line on Bachofen was opposite all that he believed in.

Evola's own fascination with Otto Weininger and Hans Blüher, his enthusiasm for männerbunden, and his belief that women should find their true identity in total spiritual subjugation to men, has curious echos in The Story of O, by "Pauline Réage."[7] In the 1954 French novel, "O" is meant to represent a kind of Weininger "Absolute Woman" who lives in voluntary subjugation to an all-male sadistic secret society. Writing in Encounter, Irving Kristol summarized the book as a "Gothic tale of a woman O, who, at the instigation of her lover, becomes the slave of a freemasonry of sadists, and who finds in the indignities perpetrated upon her a perfect contentment."[8]

O is the ironic fulfillment of Weininger's dictum, "The meaning of woman is to be meaningless." The character's psychology, such as it is, could have come out of Evola's description of the true woman in an Islamic harem. In *Revolt Against the Modern World*, he writes about the harem: "It seemed natural for a woman to concentrate all her life on one man only, who was loved in such a vast and unselfish way as to allow other women to share in the same feeling and to be united with him through the same bond and the same dedication."[9] This is especially so "when the man is not perceived by her as mere husband or lover, but as her lord. The spirit animating the harem consisted in the struggle to overcome jealousy." In the harem "she experienced a true possession, an overcoming, and even a liberation because vis-à-vis such an unconditional *fides*, a man, in his human appearance, was just a means to higher ends; thus she discovered new possibilities to achieve higher goals."[10] A woman achieves "true greatness" when "she is capable of giving without asking for anything in return," which leads her to "an overcoming, even a liberation." Subjugation, therefore, becomes a "means to a higher end," as absolute negation turns into spiritual rapture.

When *The Story of O* was first published, many thought its creator was Jean Paulhan, the French literary critic, editor of *Nouvelle Revue Française* (NRF), and author of *Le Marquis de Sade et sa Complice, ou les Revanches de la Pudeur*, since he wrote the introduction to the novel. The real author, however, was Dominique Aury, an editor with Paulhan at Gallimard as well as Paulhan's mistress; she began the book first as a 60-page love letter to him. After reading the manuscript, Paulhan encouraged her to turn it into a book. An "Anglomaniac," Aury says that she worked for the French Resistance as a courier during the war. She also had a passion for uniforms, secret societies, and Gothic novels. She was particularly captivated by the idea that "destruction is inherent in creation" as well as the notion of suicide as the spirit's destruction of the body, because it is the inevitable decay of the body that will destroy all individual life. In that sense, her book is a kind of Gnostic revolt against matter.

Her lover, Jean Paulhan, had a far more curious political career. While a member of the Resistance, he simultaneously served as the "mentor" to Gerhard Heller, whom the Nazis put in charge of organizing the censorship of all books in France. Heller did so in his capacity as a member of the propaganda staff of the German ambassador to Vichy France, Otto Abetz.[11] Paulhan had a longstanding fascination with secret societies and initiatory orders. In the 1930s he became involved in the College of Sociology that had been organized by the French theorist of eroticism Georges Bataille and the scholar Roger Callois.[12] The College, an independent study group, was fascinated by männerbunden, monastic orders, and secret societies like the Knights Templar, the Teutonic Knights, the Assassins, the Jesuits, the Ku Klux Klan, and Freemasonry.[13] Like Mircea Eliade, the College saw modern society moving further and further away from the sacred, a trend they considered disastrous. To counter this, the College hoped to invent a "sacred sociology" to reactivate the presence of the sacred in the modern world.[14]

Both the College of Sociology and Bataille's *Acéphale* group became fascinated by human sacrifice, and Bataille even began planning his own religion to be based on ritual human sacrifice.[15] In his book *The Passion of Michel Foucault*, James Miller points out that in the 1930s Bataille explored the possibility of "creating a neo-pagan society, organized around sacred rituals of death and human sacrifice." Impressed with the Aztecs (one of Evola's "solar" cultures), Bataille laid plans to stage an actual sacrifice. According to Miller, his group even targeted a specific victim, although they never carried out their plan.[16] In this context it is striking that in one alternate ending of *The Story of O*, O asks permission to kill herself as an act of ultimate offering. In other words, by an act of supreme negation she has made herself into a high sacrifice worthy of the Aztecs. In this way, O fully realizes Ernst Jünger's dictum: "The greatest happiness known to man is to be sacrificed."[17]

Notes:

1. Martin Green, *The von Richthofen Sisters* (New York: Basic Books, 1974), p. 73, Martin Green, *Mountain of Truth: The Counterculture Begins: Ascona 1900–1920* (Hanover, NH: University Press of New England, 1986). Also see Richard Noll, *The Jung Cult* (Princeton, NJ: Princeton University Press, 1994), and David Clay Large, *Where Ghosts Walked* (New York: W. W. Norton, 1997), pp. 25–34.

2. In this context, see Frederick Engels, *The Origin of the Family, Private Property, and the State* (New York: Pathfinder Press, 1972).

3. Noll, *The Jung Cult*, p. 167.

4. Janet Biehl and Peter Staudenmaier, *Ecofascism: Lessons from the German Experience* (San Francisco: AK Press, 1995), pp. 11–12.

5. Klages was much admired by the leftist cultural theorist Walter Benjamin. In 1923 Benjamin wrote Klages to tell him that he found his *Vom Kosmogonischen Eros* a great book. Benjamin also admired Bachofen. (Werner Fuld, "Walter Benjamins Beziehung zu Ludwig Klages," *Akzente*, June 1981.) Otto Gross may also have been influenced by Klages. See Arthur Mitzman, "Anarchism, Expressionism, and Psychoanalysis," *New German Critique*, No. 10 (Winter 1977).

The most detailed exposition of Klages's ideas in English that I am aware of is Gunnar Alksnis's Ph.D. thesis "Ludwig Klages and his Attack on Rationalism" (unpublished, Kansas State University, 1970). Also see Joseph Pryce, "The Philosopher of the Tragic Existence: Ludwig Klages, 1872–1956," in the September 1994 issue of the neo-Nazi journal *Liberty Bell*; Georg Stauth and Byran Turner, "Ludwig Klages and the Origins of Critical Theory," in *Theory, Culture and Society*, Vol. 9, No. 3 (August 1992); Jennifer Michaels, *Anarchy and Eros* (New York: Peter Lang, 1983); Anna Bramwell, *Ecology in the 20th Century* (New Haven: Yale University Press, 1989), pp. 178–83; and the works by Green and Noll. Another essay on Klages, by F. J. Vehils, can be found in the September 1965 issue of *Western Destiny*.

6. *Gnosis*, No. 14, Winter 1990.

7. "Pauline Réage" had been identified as Dominique Aury. Aury discussed the creation of the story in a book called *Confessions of O*, by Regine Deforges, which is essentially a long interview with Aury. *Confessions of O* was published in French in 1975 and in English in 1979.

8. *Encounter*, VIII, No. 2, 1957.

9. Julius Evola, *Revolt Against the Modern World* (Rochester, VT: Inner Traditions International, 1995), pp. 161–62. See Fatna Sabbah, *Woman in the Muslim Unconscious* (New York: Pergamon Press, 1984) for a much different view.

10. Ibid., pp. 160–61.

11. In *Un Allemand à Paris: 1940–1944* (Paris: Seuil, 1981), Heller devotes a chapter entitled "Mon Maître Paulhan" to his complex relationship with Paulhan, a founder of both the Comité National des Écrivains (CRE) and the first Resistance journal *Les Lettres Française*. See also Jeffrey Mehlman, "Writing and Deference: The Politics of Literary Adulation," *Representations* 15, Summer 1986, and Michael Syrotinski, "Some Wheat and Some Chaff: Jean Paulhan and the Post-War Literary Purge in France" in *Studies in Contemporary Literature* (SICL), Vol. 16, No. 2 (Summer, 1992).

12. Bataille's College was not fascist, in part because, as worshippers of "excess" and "transgression," they felt that fascism was too bourgeois.

It should also be noted that one of the guiding intellectual influences on the College was the French Indo-Europeanist and Freemason Georges Dumézil. George Callois was a protégé of Dumézil, and Paulhan twice wrote about Dumézil's book *Mythes et dieux des Germains* in *NRF* under the pseudonym "Jean Guérin." On Dumézil and Freemasonry, see Didier Eribon, *Michel Foucault* (Cambridge, MA: Harvard University Press, 1991), pp. 73–74. For differing looks at Dumézil, see Carlo Ginzburg, "Germanic Mythology and Nazism: Thoughts on an Old Book by Georges Dumézil," in *Myths, Emblems, Clues* (London: Hutchinson Radius, 1990), and Arnaldo Momigliano, "Georges Dumézil and the Trifunctional Approach to Roman Civilization," in his *On Pagans, Jews and Christians* (Middletown, CT: Wesleyan University Press, 1987). C. Scott Littleton's *The New Comparative Mythology: An Anthropological Assessment of the Theories of Georges Dumézil* (Berkeley, CA: University of California Press, 1982) is a valuable introduction to his thought. Dumézil became a member of both the comité de patronage of *Nouvelle École* and the French Academy.

13. See Denis Hollier's collection of texts, *The College of Sociology 1937–39* (Minneapolis: University of Minnesota Press, 1988), p. xv. Callois's 19 March 1938 presentation on "Brotherhoods, Orders, Secret Societies, Churches" is reprinted in Hollier.

14. Ibid., p. xxiv. Also see Eliade's conclusion to *The Myth of the Eternal Return* (Princeton, NJ: Princeton University Press, 1965).

15. Bataille may not have been unique in his attempt to revive human sacrifice. In her book *The Nazis and the Occult* (New York: Dorset Press, 1977), pp. 99–100, Dusty Sklar writes:

A professor of anthropology at Occidental College in California, [Dumézil expert] C. Scott Littleton, provided me with astonishing details of another SS ceremony which has not been corroborated by anyone else, but which may well be true. A professor friend of his, he claims, saw original Nazi depositions taken for the Nuremberg Trials, but never included in the record, which told of a periodic sacrifice wherein a fine Aryan specimen of an SS man was beheaded and the severed head made a vehicle for communication with Secret Masters in the Caucasus.

16. James Miller, *The Passion of Michel Foucault* (New York: Simon & Schuster, 1993), pp. 86–87.

17. Roger Woods, *The Conservative Revolution in the Weimar Republic* (New York: St. Martin's Press, 1996), p. 72.

APPENDIX D:
LEFT-WING
FASCISM:
LATIN STYLE

At the time Yockey visited Cuba, it was far more common to view Fidel Castro's movement as a radical nationalist revolt than as a Communist conspiracy. It was even possible to see Castro as a left-wing Perón. In *The Fascist Persuasion in Radical Politics*, A. James Gregor points to what he sees as real similarities between Castroism and Mussolini's return to "left-wing fascism" during the Salò Republic.[1] Mussolini argued that fascism's maximalist program had been thwarted by the Church, the monarchy, wealthy capitalists, and the old aristocracy. During Salò, he tried to socialize northern Italian industry "to destroy the independent power base from which the capitalist class had resisted the totalitarian aspirations of Fascism." Gregor then suggests that in its economic views, its extreme nationalism, and its cult of the hero, Castroism had much in common with left fascist theory. Nor should Castro's lack of anti-Semitism be seen as a decisive mitigating factor. As the Israeli historian Zeev Sternhell points out, there were "innumerable Fascist Jews." Their percentage in the fascist movement was actually higher than in the Italian population as a whole.[2]

Whether one accepts Gregor's argument or not, Castroism quickly developed ties to "left-wing Perónism." Three of Perón's most trusted aides, his former foreign minister, Jeonimo Ludovico; his former interior minister, Angel Borlenghi; and John William Cooke, a top labor leader, secretly met with Che Guevara and Raul Castro in Havana in June 1960, the same month Yockey died. There they worked out an agreement to create Cuban-Perónist guerrilla training camps in

Argentina.[3] Cooke secretly returned to Argentina in 1964 to organize a guerrilla army to return Perón to power.

A strange "left wing" even emerged from one of the most violent far-right groups in Argentina, the notorious *Grupo Tacuara de la Juventud Nacional* (Tacuara Group of National Youth), also known as the Movimento Nacionalista Tacuara (MNT). The Tacuara (the word refers to a lance used by gauchos) came out of the Alianza Libertadora Nacionalista (ALN), which controlled the paramilitary wing of the right-wing student youth movement. In late 1957, after Perón's downfall, the Tacuara was formed under the ideological leadership of a bitterly anti-Semitic Jesuit priest named Julio Meinville. Then anti-Perón, it was committed to the return of religious teachings in the schools. Its ranks included many of Argentina's most privileged youths,[4] who wore the Maltese Cross in their lapels and put on uniforms for secret late-night initiation rites in Buenos Aires' Chacarita cemetery. Extraordinarily violent, the well-armed terrorists regularly attacked student meetings, liberal theater groups, and Jewish institutions while the security police looked the other way.

By the early 1960s the Tacuara "ideological line stood at some indistinct point between nazism and falangism."[5] Believed to be financed in part by the Arab League, the group carried out numerous assaults against Argentina's Jewish community. When Adolf Eichmann was captured in Argentina by the Israeli secret service, the Tacuara retaliated with synagogue bombings and other acts of terror. After Eichmann's execution, they even carved a swastika on the face of a Jewish schoolgirl named Graciela Sirota. Their rage at Eichmann's demise may have had a personal angle: In *Le Nazisme Société Secrète*, Werner Gerson claims that the real head of the Tacuara was Horst Eichmann, Adolf's son.[6]

In November 1960, however, the Tacuara split. One faction, which felt the MNT had now become too pro-Perón, formed the Guardia Restauadora Nacionalista (GRN), which remained true to Meinville's fanatic Catholicism. In 1963 the MNT split again. The Tacuara "right," led by Alberto Ezcurra Uriburu, the son of a former president of Argentina, was overtly pro–National Socialist. The Tacuara "left" became the Movimiento Nacionalista Revolucionario Tacuara (MNRT) and was headed by the Yugoslav-born José ("Joe") Baxter. Influenced by both the Cuban and Algerian Revolutions, he argued that the Tacuara should help create a mass movement to aid Perón's return. Baxter's MNRT proclaimed "an opening to the Left" and adopted slogans like "War on Imperialism!" and "On the March toward National Liberation!" Baxter denounced his old comrades as "police informers" and "shock troops of the oligarchy" whose anti-Semitism was "artificial" and "diversionary." As for Cuba, he declared in one press interview: "No one can call Fidel Castro an anti-Semite," but "as a Cuban nationalist he has done away with the exploiters and so most of the Jews had to leave."[7] Baxter also went to Cuba for guerrilla training.[8]

Baxter's MNRT had an enormous influence inside the Latin American left and inspired both the Tupamaros and Montoneros. The main theorist of Baxter's Tacuara was a former Spanish anarchist named Abraham Guillén, who had worked as a magazine editor in the Argentine Ministry of Economic Affairs during the Perón era. While there, he turned out a series of anti-American tracts with Perón's blessing. He also supported the first Perónist/Castroist guerrilla movement in northern Argentina, the *Uturuncos* (Tiger Men).

As Latin America's leading advocate of urban guerrilla warfare, Guillén argued against Che Guevara's more rural-oriented tactics. Following his lead, the MNRT and Tupamaros carried out a "series of successful bank robberies, the kidnapping and ransoming of key government and diplomatic personnel, and the continual destruction of U.S. industrial plants abroad."[9] On 29 October 1963 Baxter stole 12 million Argentine pesos from the Policlinico Bancario Buenos Aires. He used part of the money to travel to Madrid to talk with Perón. He then visited China, "Algeria, Angola, the Congo, Egypt, and North Vietnam, before ending up in Montevideo, where he shared an apartment with Violeta Setelich, a top member of the Tupamaros."[10] The MNRT tried to assassinate Argentina's General Villegas; it also raided food stores and organized handouts to the urban poor. Baxter, for his part, toured Egypt and Qaddafi's Libya in an effort to drum up financial support, only to have his efforts cut short when he was killed in a plane crash in Paris in the early 1970s.[11]

Inspired by Baxter's MNRT, groups like the Montoneros emerged out of the far right.[12] Martin Anderson notes in his book *Dossier Secreto* that while "few of the first Montoneros came from the left," as time went by "once-hostile right-wing Catholic nationalist activists found common cause with the secular, pro-Castro left under the banner of Perón." He also wonders whether elements of the Montoneros were part of some sinister intelligence operation.[13] The group's slogans, like *"Si Evita viviera, sería Montonera"* (If Evita were alive she would be a Montonero) and *"La patria socialista, sin yanquis ni marxistas"* (A Socialist nation with no Yanks or Marxists), didn't help alleviate suspicion. If anything, the Montoneros bore a striking resemblance to the wing of European fascism led by Jeune Europe boss and Perón supporter Jean-François Thiriart.[14]

Finally, after years of political instability, Juan Perón returned to Argentina in 1973. He immediately abandoned any "left" cover and launched his own "Night of the Long Knifes" under the guise of a violent "antisubversive campaign." After Perón's death in 1974, his sinister advisor Jose López Rega became a major player in Argentina's politics. An extreme anti-Semite, occultist, and member of Licio Gelli's mysterious Italian P-2 "masonic" lodge, he had lived with Perón in exile in Spain. Under López Rega's influence, Argentina's military and security services began encouraging attacks against the "Strasserist" Montoneros as well as against the Jewish community, artists, trade unionists, leftists, and other "subversives." Government-sanctioned death squads like the Alianza Anticomunista Argentina

(AAA) went into overdrive, while military helicopters dropped the bodies of thousands of the "disappeared" into the ocean. Anti-Semitic and pro-Hitler literature could also be found on almost every newsstand. To the Tacuara, Argentina must have seemed like heaven on earth.

Notes:

1. A. James Gregor, *The Fascist Persuasion in Radical Politics* (Princeton, NJ: Princeton University Press, 1974).

2. Zeev Sternhell, *The Birth of Fascist Ideology* (Princeton, NJ: Princeton University Press, 1995), p. 5.

3. For a discussion of the Perón-Castro link-up, see *Philosophy of the Urban Guerrilla: The Social and Political Philosophy of Abraham Guillén* (New York: William Morrow, 1973), edited by Donald Hodges, p. 6. For a more in-depth discussion of the meeting in Havana and its consequences, see Daniel James, *Che Guevara* (New York: Stein & Day, 1970), pp. 182–84. John William Cooke was also an admirer of Carl Schmitt. (David Rock, *Authoritarian Argentina* [Berkeley, CA: University of California Press, 1993], p. 217.)

4. See the Weiner Institute *Bulletin* of Autumn 1965 on the Tacuara. For a reference to the Tacuara that traces the group to a 1942 meeting of the ultra-right Congress of National Recuperation, see Ladislos Farago, *Aftermath* (New York: Simon & Schuster, 1974), pp. 395–96. Farago suggests that the Meinville wing of the Tacuara evolved into something called the *Movimento Sacerdote Para el Tercer Mundo* (Sacred Movement for a Third World), which he claims had "major bases" across the world and received ODESSA funds.

5. Rock, *Authoritarian Argentina*, p. 205.

6. Werner Gerson, *Le Nazisme Société Sécrète* (Paris: Productions de Paris, 1969), p. XI. Gerson's book may have been sponsored by the New European Order since its copyright reads "N.O.E." It should be recalled that a leading NEO member, Jacques Marie de Mahieu (who had come to Argentina as an exile after fighting on the Russian front in World War II) was the head of the University of Buenos Aires. De Mahieu was also an economic advisor to the Argentine government. (Rock, *Authoritarian Argentina*, p. 204.)

7. Rock, *Authoritarian Argentina*, p. 207. James Madole's NRP avidly supported Perón. See Madole's "The Attempt to Crush Argentine Nationalism," in the March–April 1962 issue of the NRP *Bulletin*. Madole wrote:

Perón was defeated by a coalition of Jewish financiers and politically minded officials of the Roman Catholic hierarchy . . . Jewish finance and their clerical allies quickly set up their usual military junta to hold down the exploited masses of the Argentine people. . . . The ARGENTINE CONFEDERATION OF LABOR NEVER ceased to rebel and agitate for the return of Colonel Perón from exile and the restoration of his economic and social reforms.

8. Hodges, *The Social and Political Philosophy of Abraham Guillén*, p. 10.

9. Ibid., p. 3.

10. Ibid., p. 10.

11. Rock, *Authoritarian Argentina*, pp. 206–07.

12. Mario Firmenich, a Montoneros leader of Croatian descent, started out as a devout Catholic student youth leader. Fernando Abal Medina, a former Tacuara member who became a Montoneros leader, also received military training in Cuba in 1967–68. (Martin Anderson, *Dossier Secreto* [Boulder, CO: Westview Press, 1993], p. 71.) Anderson believes that such groups may have acted as pawns in a larger "strategy of tension" orchestrated by the region's security services.

13. Ibid., p. 72.

14. Rock, *Authoritarian Argentina*, pp. 217–20.

APPENDIX E:
"SHEIK FRANÇOIS"—
FRIEND TO HITLER
AND CARLOS
THE JACKAL

On 30 May 1996 an obscure Swiss banker named François Genoud committed suicide in Geneva, Switzerland. From the brief mention of his death in the *New York Times*, one would not know that one of the most important figures in the history of 20th-century terrorism had died. And how many men can say that they were friends with both Adolf Hitler and Carlos the Jackal?[1]

A Swiss citizen born in Lausanne in 1915, Genoud became rabidly pro-Nazi in the early 1930s. After a trip to Germany as a teenager, he never forgot the thrill he felt shaking Adolf Hitler's hand. During World War II, Genoud became extremely close to an SD lieutenant named Paul Dickopf, who would later head the German federal police (the Bundeskriminalamt, or BKA) before being elected president of Interpol in 1968. The two men traveled together across occupied Europe. Dickopf would later claim that he had defected from the German army in August 1942 and lived clandestinely in Belgium, where he embraced the anti-Nazi cause. Curiously, the "traitor's" salary continued to be sent to his wife until January 1944.

Dickopf eventually ended up in Switzerland, where he received support from Genoud. Dickopf went there to approach Allen Dulles, head of the local OSS, pretending to be an anti-Nazi. At the time, his boss, RSHA head Ernst Kaltenbrunner, was also sanctioning the "Free Austria Movement," yet another group of "anti-Nazi" Nazis intent on befriending Dulles. Dickopf quickly established a working relationship with one of the most mysterious American spies of World War II, the

Japanese-born and Yale-educated Paul Blum, a top Dulles lieutenant who would later vouch for Dickopf's anti-Nazi credentials.

Genoud, too, was in the thick of things, having established a friendship with SS General Karl Wolff, leader of the German team in Italy that negotiated Operation Sunrise with Dulles. Shortly after the war, Genoud acquired the publishing rights to the works of Adolf Hitler, Martin Bormann, and Joseph Goebbels. He also played a major, if murky, role in aiding fugitive Nazi war criminals. Another key player in the postwar Nazi underground resident in Switzerland was SD Colonel Eugen Dollmann, General Wolff's chief lieutenant in the talks with Dulles. Besides Wolff, Dollmann and Genoud had another friend in common: Haj Amin el-Hussein, the Grand Mufti of Jerusalem. Genoud first met the Grand Mufti in Jerusalem in 1936, and again in Berlin during the war. Dollmann also maintained links to the Grand Mufti.[2]

After the 23 July 1952 Free Officers coup, Genoud established ties with an Egyptian intelligence operative named Major Fathi al-Dib. In post-coup Egypt he experienced firsthand the strange mixture of left and right, when half of Cairo's most influential weekly *Rose al Yussef* was filled with references to figures like the Soviet writer Ilya Ehrenburg and the other half carried reprints from anti-Semitic hate sheets like the American journal *Common Sense*.[3]

In 1955, with the Grand Mufti's friend Johann von Leers helping to run Egypt's Propaganda Ministry and its all-important "Institute for the Study of Zionism," Genoud began to see Egypt as a base for the anti-French FLN independence movement in Algeria. He worked in Tangier with an ex–SS officer named Hans Reichenberg to create the Arabo-Afrika import-export company, which supplied the FLN with weapons. Arabo-Afrika was actually a cover enterprise established by Werner Naumann's network, and included Genoud's friend Dr. Hjalmar Schacht.[4] In Damascus, General Otto Remer, Ernst-William Springer, and an ex–SS captain and RSHA operative named Alois Brunner created another gun-running operation, the Orient Trading Company (OTRACO), to ship arms to the FLN militants.[5]

Genoud's importance within the FLN increased when he became the group's banker. In 1952 Ahmed Ben Bella, one of the founders of the Algerian Organisation Spéciale (OS) independence movement, escaped from a French jail. After spending several months underground, he resurfaced in Cairo to be personally blessed by Nasser. In the spring of 1954 Ben Bella left Cairo and traveled to Geneva, where he and three of his OS comrades created the organizational basis for the FLN. In 1958 Genoud and a Syrian named Zouheir Mardam co-founded the Banque Commerciale Arabe in Geneva to manage the FLN's war chest.[6] One of Genoud's closest collaborators, Mohammed Khider, was secretary general of the FLN's Political Bureau. Born in 1912, Khider had been the driving force behind the Egyptian section of Mouvement pour le Triomphe des Libertés Démocratiques (MTLD), which helped launch the Algerian armed rebellion on 1 November 1954.

After Algeria won its independence, Genoud became head of the Banque Populaire Arabe in Algiers. In October 1964 (during a time of intense political infighting inside the FLN) Genoud was arrested and charged with transferring $15 million of FLN money to his Swiss bank in Khider's name. He only escaped an Algerian jail thanks to the intervention of Egypt's President Nasser. The Algerian government then spent years fighting with Genoud over the FLN treasury. Khider was assassinated in Madrid in 1967 by Algerian intelligence. Only in 1979 was the FLN "war chest" finally returned to Algeria.

During the fight for Algerian independence, Genoud came into contact with a faction of pro-FLN French leftists with links to Henri Curiel. Curiel, an Egyptian CP leader, had thrown the support of his wing of the Communist Party behind Egypt's Free Officers Association at a time when the official Communist line had labeled the Free Officers fascists. In the late 1950s Curiel helped supply the FLN militants with funds from France; it is possible that Genoud served as a financial middleman between Curiel and the Algerians. On 4 May 1978 Curiel (who had been accused by the French right of running a KGB support network for terrorists) was assassinated in the elevator of his Paris apartment building.

During the war in Algeria, Genoud met an ultra-left French lawyer named Jacques Vergès, who represented a number of FLN militants accused of terrorist bombings in Algiers' French section. Born in Thailand in 1925 to a French doctor and a Vietnamese woman, Vergès fought against the Nazis as a French Communist Party member in World War II. While a law student after the war, he continued his anti-colonialist agitation and became a good friend of Saloth Sar, a young Cambodian student better known today as Pol Pot. Vergès then spent 1951 to 1954 in Prague, where he became the director of the world Communist student group the International Union of Students. (One of his colleagues, the Stalinist youth leader Alexander Shelepin, would become head of the KGB in the late 1950s.) Vergès split with the French Communist Party because of its reluctance to support Algerian independence. He became a Maoist of sorts in the early 1960s, as well as a strong supporter of Cuba and the Tri-Continental Congress because the Cubans stressed the need for worldwide anti-colonial revolts.[7]

After the 1967 war Genoud and Vergès would reunite to support the Arab struggle against Israel. On 18 February 1969, members of the Popular Front for the Liberation of Palestine (PFLP) attacked an El Al plane on the tarmac of Zurich's Kloten airport. When the trial of three of the PFLP militants began in November 1969 in Winterthur, Switzerland, both Genoud and Vergès were in the courtroom serving as advisors to the defendants.

Genoud's closest radical Arab friend was PFLP co-founder Dr. Waddi Haddad. A Greek Orthodox Christian, Haddad fled Palestine in 1948. He then studied medicine with his fellow Greek Orthodox colleague George Habash at the American University in Beirut. In the early 1950s, Haddad and Habash founded the Arab Nationalist Movement (ANM), which published a small journal called *Vengeance*.

Although their views were considered right-wing, they received encouragement from American diplomats for their opposition to the continued British and French colonial domination of the region. In 1955, when Egypt turned to the East Bloc, the ANM followed. By 1958 the group, which by now had established small branches in Egypt, Kuwait, Yemen, Syria, and other Arab nations, was calling itself social- ist and demanding a united Arab response against Israel. The ANM's embrace of socialism eventually led to an internal factional struggle in which Haddad and Habash represented the right while Nayef Hawatmeh stood for the more ideologi- cally orthodox left.

After the 1967 war the ANM was reorganized and became the PFLP. Now the group praised Mao, Lin Piao, Che Guevara, and the Tri-Continental Congress. Habash and Haddad declared themselves leftists and embraced the Vietnamese Revolution because of U.S. support for Israel. Hawatmeh's more orthodox Marxist faction, however, believed their "left turn" was inspired less by ideology than by opportunism, and split with the PFLP to become the Popular Democratic Front for the Liberation of Palestine (PDFLP).

Waddi Haddad, who was far more a man of action than a theorist like Habash, took command of the PFLP's overseas operations. He soon attracted support from a variety of allies including the Japanese Red Army, the Baader-Meinhof Group/Red Army Faction, the Irish National Liberation Army (an IRA splinter group), and individual volunteers like Ilich Sánchez Ramirez, better known as "Carlos the Jackal." Another PFLP volunteer was a young Swiss man named Bruno Bréguet. On 23 June 1970 Bréguet was arrested in Haifa, Israel, while on a PFLP bombing mission. After his arrest, Genoud organized a campaign for his release from prison. Although he had been sentenced to 15 years, Bréguet was allowed to leave Israel in 1977. By the early 1980s he was an important member of the Carlos network in Europe. As for Haddad, he adored the Swiss banker and dubbed him "Sheik François." After Haddad's death from cancer in an East Berlin hospital on 27 March 1978, Genoud continued to maintain close ties with his terrorist net- work.

Genoud also worked with the Palestinian Liberation Organization (PLO), in particular its "Black September" terrorist network headed by Ali Hassan Salameh (the "Red Prince"), who was assassinated by the Israeli secret service on 22 November 1979. One of Genoud's intermediaries to the PLO was Fouad el- Shemali, a former student leader with the Syrian National-Social Party that had been destroyed after a failed coup attempt in Lebanon. Genoud also developed excellent ties to Libya through his Egyptian friend Fathi el-Dib, who introduced him to Abdel Moumen el-Honi, the director of the Libyan secret service. He han- dled Libyan contributions to the PLO and helped mediate relations between the Libyans and the IRA through Jean (Yann) L'Hostellier, a Breton nationalist and for- mer Waffen SS volunteer.[8]

On 5 September 1972 Black September terrorists murdered 11 Israeli athletes at the Olympic games in Munich. The head of Interpol at the time of the attack was Genoud's old friend Paul Dickopf; Genoud had lobbied the secret services of the Middle East to support Dickopf's bid to become Interpol president. Dickhopf's Interpol proved highly reluctant to get itself involved in stopping terrorism. As one Interpol spokesman argued, the Arab-Israeli conflict was a political question and Interpol was an agency designed to handle criminal, not political, matters.[9]

The early 1970s saw a series of terrorist attacks throughout Europe. Genoud's friend Jacques Vergès, however, was not involved in giving legal assistance to captured militants. One day in February 1970 he disappeared from Paris after announcing that he was going on a business trip to Spain. Then, just as mysteriously, he showed up on the streets of Paris eight years later, in the winter of 1978. Asked where he had been, he explained: "I stepped through the looking glass, where I served an apprenticeship."

In the early 1980s Genoud and Vergès returned to center-stage. On 16 February 1982 Genoud's friend Bruno Bréguet and a German woman named Magdalena Kopp were arrested in Paris after police discovered guns, hand grenades, and four kilos of explosives in their car. Kopp, it turned out, was a member of the German Revolutionary Cells created by Johannes Weinrich. She was also Carlos's common-law wife. Vergès took charge of their legal defense while Genoud paid the bills. Meanwhile, Carlos began writing threatening letters to French Interior Minister Gaston Defferre, while a series of bombs went off in different parts of the country.

The Kopp-Bréguet trial proved to be a warmup for another, even more spectacular Genoud and Vergès operation—the legal defense of Klaus Barbie, a Nazi war criminal who had been extradited from Bolivia to France in 1982. While engaged in his Arab adventures, Genoud continued to maintain excellent relations with top Nazis like General Degrelle, General Wolff, and General Remer. He was also close to New European Order founder Guy Amaudruz, who ran the NEO's main branch out of Lusanne, which happened to be Genoud's hometown. Asked his opinion of Amaudruz, Genoud said that his "grande vertu, il est extrêmement fidèle, courageux. C'est un saint."[10]

Genoud and Vergès used Barbie's trial to condemn France for its crimes against Algeria. Although Barbie was easily convicted, many questions about him remained. During his time in Bolivia, Barbie regularly fed the CIA information on the left throughout Latin America, using a contact in Bolivia's Interior Ministry. Yet Barbie and Hans-Ulrich Rudel, his partner in the weapons business, were believed to have had Cuban ties. Barbie was also reportedly involved in supplying weapons to the Italian ultra-leftist millionaire Giangiacomo Feltrinelli. It remains an open question whether Genoud helped Barbie simply out of abstract principle or because he himself had been a player in Barbie's arms and intelligence operation.[11]

Genoud became directly involved in helping Carlos after the Jackal was arrested in the Sudan by French agents on 15 August 1994. For some years after Waddi Haddad's death, Carlos operated out of bases in Hungary and other Eastern European countries. He also spent time in Damascus. After his arrest, Genoud publicly expressed his great admiration for Carlos, whom Genoud considered one of the "heros" of the Palestinian cause. He denounced the "treason" of the Arab leaders, including the Syrians and Libyans, for failing to aid him. Genoud believed that the truly "great traitor," however, was Soviet leader Mikhail Gorbachev.[12]

After his arrest, Carlos and Genoud frequently exchanged "Dear Comrade" letters. Carlos's wife Magdelena Kopp also regularly telephoned Genoud from Venezuela, where she and her daughter by Carlos lived near Carlos's parents.

Notes:

1. My analysis of Genoud is indebted to two recent major works on his life. They are Pierre Péan, *L'Extrémiste* (Paris: Fayard, 1996), and Karl Laske, *Le Banquier Noir* (Paris: Seuil, 1996). Another useful source is David Lee Preston's article "Hitler's Swiss Connection," in the 5 January 1997 *Philadelphia Inquirer*. Genoud is also discussed in John Follain's book *Jackal* (New York: Arcade Publishing, 1998).

2. On 29 January 1952 the *Basler Nachrichten* reported that Dollmann and the Grand Mufti had met secretly in Cairo shortly before the downfall of King Farouk. (T. H. Tetens, *The New Germany and the Old Nazis* [London: Seeker & Warburg, 1961], pp. 73–74.)

3. Walter Laqueur, *Nasser's Egypt* (London: Weidenfeld and Nicholson, 1956).

4. Laske, *Le Banquier Noir*, p. 250.

5. Joachim Joesten, *The Red Hand* (London: Abelard Schuman, 1962), pp. 92–93.

6. Hjalmar Schacht served as a consultant to the bank, and shortly after the FLN's victory Schacht visited Algeria.

7. The opposition of the official Latin American CPs to "Castroism" led to a series of ideological clashes, the best known being the fight between Castro and the Communist Party of Venezuela. The Tri-Continental Congress was an attempt to circumvent the intransigence of the official Communist Party apparats across Latin America to Cuban-backed (and GRU/KGB–supported?) guerrilla warfare.

8. Pean, *L'Extrémiste*, p. 341.

9. Laske, *Le Banquier Noir*, p. 278.

10. Pean, *L'Extrémiste*, p. 273. Genoud was involved in numerous other rightist publishing projects, including a new edition of Alfred Rosenberg's *The Myth of the Twentieth Century* that he wanted the right-wing Parisian book service Ogmios to issue.

11. For more on Barbie, see Magnus Linklater et al., *The Nazi Legacy* (New York: Holt, Rinehart and Winston, 1984).

12. Laske, *Le Banquier Noir*, p. 373.

APPENDIX F:
THREE PATRON
SAINTS OF
RED FASCISM

The European New Right has recently turned its attention to Ernst Niekisch, Friedrich Hielscher, and Harro Schulze-Boysen, three obscure Germans who advocated close ties between Germany and the Soviet Union in the 1920s and 1930s.[1] In 1991 New Right theorist Alain de Benoist wrote a long introduction to a French edition of Niekisch's savage 1932 polemic: *Hitler—ein deutsche Verhängnis* (Hitler—A Germany Calamity).[2] Here Niekisch attacked Hitler as a "juggler," "trickster," "drummer," and "king of the mob" who disguised his "Hapsburg instincts" with a coating of German nationalism. Hitler was "the last hope of the bourgeois world," the Nazis were "mercenary troops" of capitalism, National Socialism was "poison," a "disease" which "defends a decaying past with the slogans of the future . . . It is a product of all that is rotten in Germany," and on and on.[3] Niekisch paid a price for his views, spending many years in Nazi jails. When he was freed in 1945 he was virtually blind.

Born in 1899, Niekisch headed the leftist Workers' and Soldiers' Council during the 1918–1919 Munich revolt, and spent almost three years in jail after its collapse. In the mid-1920s he began developing his own strange mix of socialism, Eurasianism, paganism, and ruralism, which he combined with a close relationship to the German General Staff. He even worked as an intelligence agent for General Hans von Seeckt.[4]

In 1926 Niekisch created his own group (and journal) called *Widerstand* (Resistance). Widerstand held that there were two Germanies: The liberal, democratic, humanistic Germany that looked to the West was identified with the "spirit of Weimar"; the other Germany, militaristic and brutal, saw itself as part of the East. This latter Germany, symbolized by the warrior "spirit of Potsdam," was being destroyed by the pacifist, cowardly, and slavish influence of Western culture. "Prussia," the Prussia glorified by Spengler and Moeller van den Bruck, now became a catchword for a total revolt against the Western way of life.[5] Niekisch justified such a revolt with his own brand of Eurasianism:

The Asiatic way of life is summoning that of Europe to one last battle [*Entscheidungskampf*] . . . Germany will regain its freedom only when it revolts against Europe; Germany will be free only if it joins the gathering Russian-Asiatic assault against Europe . . . At this moment in history, Germany has but one burning need: The iron grasp of Europe, in which it is being strangled, must be broken. Whoever takes up the sword against Europe gives Germany hope for the future.[6]

In his 1930 work *Entscheidung* (Decision), Niekisch put forward the notion of a "Germanic-Slavic Imperium," a new Reich that would extend "from the Scheldt to Vladivostok."[7] Only such an alliance with Russia could liberate Germany from "Catholic" hegemony. Like both the Eurasians and the volkists, he argued that the German people had been victimized by Western aggression for centuries. All territory beyond the Rhine was for the West merely an object for colonization. Like Richard Walther Darré, Niekisch claimed that Charlemagne had succeeded where Caesar had failed: His military and political conquest of the Germans had been secured by the *geistigseelisch* (spiritual and mental) triumph of Christianity. Charlemagne murdered the noblest of the Saxons, dispersed the rest, and settled men of "Romanized blood" in their former territory.[8]

In the struggle against "Rome," Niekisch glorified the German peasant and claimed that the peasant or landed man "was the pre-form of the heroic":

The land, the earth, the fathers' heritage, the morals, the customs, and the faith of one's ancestors are in their entirety the super-personal force for which it can be sweet to die. The peasant values the native soil, which his ancestors tilled and which his children should yet till, more than he values himself; if it is threatened he doesn't consider his own life anymore, he has only one task—to defend the soil to his last breath, to the last drop of his blood.

In contrast, the city-dweller was "feminine":

In his most extreme form the urban-bourgeois man is the non-hero [*Nichtheld*] . . . He is too selfish, too cautious, too deliberate, too scheming, too refined, too sensitive, too shrewd, too clever, too judicious to be able to be a hero. In the climax of the peasant man is the hero, the climax of the urban man is at best the "kingly merchant"—but even behind the show of kingliness he is always only a trader . . . The more urbanized a society is, the more unmanly, cowardly, womanly it is. The cult of women belongs to fully developed traders.[9]

Through an alliance with the East, however, *Entbürgerlichung* (de-bourgeoisification) could take place: "An eastern orientation would be a return to the land, a rebellion against the city, the courage for peasant 'barbarism' and primitiveness."[10] Sounding like a Teutonic Pol Pot, Niekisch advocated

> compulsion to flee the city through economic and social policies that make life in the great cities Hell. Conscious depopulation of the cities [because they are] the seats of pacifistic cowardice and national ruination . . . Rejection of the idea of humanity. Affirmation of barbarism when necessary for the sake of national resurrection.[11]

Only by becoming more barbaric could Germans recapture their true nature. The Volk had to return to barbarianism because its strength "rests in Germania's forests; the deeper they withdraw into them, the more they find themselves. The gorges of the Teutoburg forest are needed to be able to cut off the head of the Latin South."[12] No Unabomber in lederhosen, he insisted that "the German people should not be persuaded into clubs and bearskins in a direct literal sense. Its inner attribute is crucial: that it perceive in Western civilization its abyss and in the turning away from it its salvation." For Niekisch

> the encouragement of technological advances "went without saying." The German barbarian would also support engineers, physicists, and chemists, but he would grant them "no power over the interior, the soul, the center of being." The modern barbarian would use technology as his ancestors had once used armor. He would, however, never be corrupted and worn down by its spirit. He would, rather, manage modern technology from a "barbarian-primitive essence."[13]

Niekisch was a member of an important circle called the Association for the Study of the Russian Planned Economy (ARPLAN), under whose auspices he visited the Soviet Union in 1932.[14] The Association also included Ernst Jünger, Georg Lukács, Karl Wittfogel, and Friedrich Hielscher.[15] In September 1932 Jünger published *Der Arbeiter* (The Worker), which was seen at the time as a paean to the Soviet Union. To Niekisch, the book was "an 'advance report' on the future"; he considered it a "'blueprint' for a National Bolshevik Germany."[16] Lenin's electrification campaign and Stalin's five-year plan were living expressions of Jünger's idea of "total mobilization." Soon a new warrior archetype that thrived on technology would replace the "Jesuit," symbol of the priestly-metaphysical Imperium of the Roman Church, and the "Jew," symbol of "international gold powers."[17]

After the burning of the Reichstag, Jünger, Hielscher, and Niekisch had their houses searched by the Nazis. Niekisch managed to edit *Widerstand* until December 1934, when the paper was banned. In 1935 he visited Rome and was granted a personal interview with Mussolini. He also developed ties to the Italian Consul General in Germany, whom he kept informed about opposition to Hitler. Then, in 1937, he was arrested by the Gestapo and jailed until the end of the war.[18]

After being liberated from prison, Niekisch reportedly lived in East Berlin until the 1953 workers' revolt. He then moved to West Germany, where he died in 1967.[19]

Another German now being celebrated by the European New Right is Friedrich Hielscher, yet another member of the "left of the right" wing of the Conservative Revolution.[20] An Ehrhardt Freikorp member, Hielscher was later recruited to the Berlin branch of a group called the Old Social Democratic Party of Germany. One of the group's leaders, August Winnig, later became a close ally of Niekisch. Following the Moeller van den Bruck/Haushofer line promoted by the Strasser brothers, Hielscher became an ardent foe of colonialism and imperialism. He was continually organizing meetings and rallies in Berlin for "oppressed peoples"— usually African, Indian, and Chinese youths studying at German universities. He contributed articles for *Widerstand*, although for personal reasons he and Niekisch never became close collaborators.[21] Hielscher also worked with the Artamen League, which in the late 1920s supported the peasant revolt in northern Germany, a struggle that Jünger and Niekisch endorsed. Through his connections with the northern German uprising and the Artamen League, Hielscher developed close ties to Herman Wirth and Wolfram Sievers of the Ahnenerbe. One source even claims that Hielscher founded the Ahnenerbe as a private think tank.[22]

An occultist of sorts, Hielscher created his own Nietzschean superman cult/quasi-religion. A pantheist, he believed that those members of the elite who detached themselves from the world and understood the oneness and divinity of all being were natural vessels in whom the idea of the Reich, God, or the center of eternal action was fulfilled. "Consequently they became divine themselves, acquiring the ability to exist and act for no purpose other than themselves." In his 1931 book *Das Reich*, he explained that such individuals,

> because they are unencumbered of the "world," they are the lords of the world; they are the efficacy of God himself. Therewith the humanity of these souls, their action in space and time, is raised above all other men and things.

In *Morning of the Magicians*, Jacques Bergier and Louis Pauwels claim that Hielscher accompanied the Ahnenerbe leader Wolfram Sievers to the gallows at Nuremberg so that both men could pray together one last time.[23] They also point to an entry in Ernst Jünger's Paris diary from 14 October 1943, where he remarks about Hielscher (codenamed "Bogo"):

> I thought once that he would make his mark in the history of our time as one of those people who are little known but are exceptionally intelligent. I think now he will play a more important role. Most of the young intellectuals of the generation which has grown up since the last war have come under his influence, and often been through his school . . . He has confirmed a suspicion I have had for a long time that he has founded a Church. He has now gone beyond dogma, and is mainly concerned with liturgy. He has shown me a series of songs and festivities

to celebrate the "pagan year," involving a whole system of gods, and colors and animals, food, and stones and plants.[24]

Certain elements of the New Right are particularly attracted to Hielscher's decentralist return to regionalism and tribal identities, or what is sometimes called "Europe of a Hundred Flags."[25] German New Right theorist Henning Eichberg introduced a similar idea in his 1978 book *Nationale Identität*, where he advocated "ethnopluralism."[26] To de Benoist, regionalism and ethnopluralism are the only possible forms under which a new European Imperium could successfully function.[27]

In this context it is interesting to examine Otto Abetz, another "left rightist" from the 1930s who became the German ambassador to Vichy France. Abetz is an extremely curious figure. Before World War II, he played a key role in developing links between Germany and France as the French expert for Joachim von Ribbentrop's private intelligence service inside the German Foreign Ministry. The Nazis also funded his *Deutsch-Französische Monatshefte (Cahiers Franco-Allemands)*. Yet Abetz started out as a member of the "left" Freideutsche youth movement.[28] He did not become a Nazi Party member until 1937.[29]

One of Abetz's most interesting French connections was an organization called Ordre Nouveau (ON).[30] In his book *Emmanuel Mounier and the New Catholic Left, 1930–1950*, historian John Hellman traces the ties between Abetz, Otto Strasser's Black Front, Ordre Nouveau, and the French Personalist journal *Esprit*. A central figure in this alliance was "Alexander Marc" (Alexander Lipiansky), a Russian Jew born in Odessa in 1904 whom Abetz first met in 1930. After studying at the University of Freiburg with Edmund Husserl and later at the Ecole Libre des Sciences Politiques, Marc became involved in a journal called *Plans* in 1931. *Plans* had been created by a lawyer named Philippe Lamour, who had earlier tried to form his own political party, the Parti Fasciste Révolutionnaire. Fernand Léger and Le Corbusier both participated in *Plans*. Le Corbusier, like Lamour, was also a member of George Valois's fascist "Blue Shirts."

In 1930 Ordre Nouveau issued a manifesto for a *Front Unique de la Jeunesse Européene* that advocated a new European federalism. In August 1931 Ordre Nouveau helped sponsor a youth meeting in the Ardennes. Abetz, the German organizer of the gathering, then joined forces with future Hitler Youth leader Baldur von Schirach to create Reichsbanner, a group that sought a "third way" between the Communists and the Nazis. Members of the left Conservative Revolutionary publication *Die Tat* showed up at the conference, as did Otto Strasser in his Black Front uniform. Strasser's articles were published in *Plans* and *Esprit*. He also attended the February 1932 Franco-German Youth Congress at Frankfurt-am-Main with Abetz.

Another attendee at the Frankfurt Congress was a young Conservative Revolutionary named Harro Schulze-Boysen, who directed the review *Planen*, the

German counterpart of *Plans*. He also published a journal called *Gegner* (Opponent).[31] In the late 1930s Schulze-Boysen become a top agent for the famous Soviet intelligence group codenamed Red Orchestra. His exploits amazed Walter Schellenberg, the SD spy chief, who wrote in his memoirs:

> A lieutenant colonel of the General Staff, Schulze-Boysen was also arrested [during the crackdown on the Red Orchestra]. He was the fanatical driving force of the whole espionage ring in Germany. He not only furnished secret information to the Russians, but was also active as a propagandist. On one occasion, at five o'clock in the morning, wearing a Wehrmacht uniform, he threatened a subordinate agent with a pistol in the street because the man had neglected his Communist propaganda work in a certain factory.[32]

Schulze-Boysen was executed by the Gestapo in December 1942. After the war, the East German government issued a commemorative stamp with his portrait. Today, however, his life is being celebrated in the German New Right journal *Junge Freiheit*.[33]

Clearly the European New Right hopes to use its embrace of Niekisch, Hielscher, and Schulze-Boysen to court hardline elements of fractured Communist Party elites in both Europe and Russia. The New Right desperately wants to build an ideological bridge between "the left of the right" and "anti-globalist" forces from Moscow to Tripoli. From Evola's neo-Traditionalism to Islamic fundamentalism, from hyper-statist left-wing fascism to European ethnic regionalism: All's fair in the struggle against the Yankee "New World Order."

Notes:

1. For a brief overview of this trend, see the British New Right publication *The Scorpion* (No. 4, Spring 1983), particularly Belgian New Right leader Robert Steukers' article "Neutralism and Nationalism in Germany." For background on the 1920s, see Louis Dupeux, *National Bolchevisme: Strategie Communiste et Dynamique Conservatrice* (Paris: Editions Champion, 1979).

2. Like Jean Thiriart, de Benoist also criticized Niekisch's extreme "Germanism."

3. James Ward, "Ernst Niekisch and National Bolshevism in Weimar Germany" (unpublished NYU Ph.D. thesis, 1973), pp. 310–11.

4. According to Klemens von Klemperer in *Germany's New Conservatism* (Princeton, NJ: Princeton University Press, 1957), Seeckt sent Niekisch on a mission to Moscow for talks with the Soviets (pp. 149–50).

5. Ward, "Ernst Niekisch," p. 173.

6. Ibid., p. 174.

7. Many of his arguments sound like they had come out of Yockey's *Der Feind Europas*. According to Ann Carey:

> Russia, Niekisch argued, did not understand itself. It didn't know the meaning of its own existence and had not spoken its own word. It was Germany's mission to speak the "word" valid for itself and for Russia. Moscow's unruly primitive power would

then be given direction by the German "strength of soul" and the self-transcending discipline of will. The result would be the creation of a new power center reaching from the Rhine to the Pacific, encompassing the vast expanses of northern Europe and Asia.

Within the Romano-Germanic world the German substance had always played the role of the feminine, servile, receptive element. In a Germanic-Slavic setting it would be the masculine, commanding, authoritative element. Potsdam would be the Rome and the Paris of a new eastern world reaching to the Pacific. [Ann Carey, "Ernst Niekisch and National Bolshevism in Weimar Germany" (unpublished University of Rochester, Ph.D. thesis, 1972), pp. 399–400.]

8. Ibid., p. 439.

9. Ibid., pp. 413–14.

10. Ibid., p. 417.

11. Ibid., p. 431.

12. Ibid., pp. 444–45.

13. Ibid., p. 445.

14. Recall that Arvid von Harnack, the head of ARPLAN, later became one of the leaders of the famous Soviet spy group the Red Orchestra during World War II. See the chapter "Children of the Sun."

The convergence of rightist German economic theorists with the Soviet economic model can be seen in Ferdinand Fried's *Das Ende des Kapitalismus* (1931) and the arguments of G. Wirsing. They believed that Soviet socialism had liberated productive capital from the dominance of finance capital. They also identified with Haushofer's school of geopolitics. (Kees van der Pijl, *The Making of the Atlantic Ruling Class* [London: Verso, 1984], pp. 24–25.)

15. In the summer of 1931, the KPD issued a monthly magazine called *Aufbruch* (Departure) to court the radical right. Karl August Wittfogel served on its staff for a brief period. Niekisch sat in on some *Aufbruch* meetings to discuss politics with Wittfogel and Georg Lukács. (James Ward, "Ernst Niekisch," pp. 279–82.) Also see James Ward, "Pipe Dreams or Revolutionary Politics? The Group of Social Revolutionary Nationalists in the Weimar Republic," *Journal of Contemporary History,* Vol. 15 (1980), pp. 521–22.

16. Ibid., p. 316.

17. Carey, "Ernst Niekisch," pp. 400–01.

18. Alastair Hamilton, *The Appeal of Fascism* (London: Anthony Blond, 1971), p. 166.

19. Robert Wistrich, *Who's Who in Nazi Germany* (New York: Routledge, 1995). Other reports say that Niekisch lived in West Berlin but lectured at Humboldt University in East Berlin until he was expelled in 1952 for "non-Marxist" and "idealist" theories. See *The Scorpion,* Issue No. 4 (Spring 1983).

20. Also see my discussion of Hielscher in the chapter "Children of the Sun."

21. Ward, "Ernst Niekisch," pp. 138–39. On the "Old Socialists," see Benjamin Lapp, "A 'National' Socialism: The Old Socialist Party of Saxony, 1928–32," *Journal of Contemporary History,* Vol. 30 (1995).

22. Nigel Pennick, *Hitler's Secret Sciences* (London: Neville Spearman, 1981), p. 150. Pennick also writes that Hielscher "had major connections in German occultism, for

he was an associate of the Swedish explorer Sven Hedin who was himself a friend of Karl Haushofer. Hedin lived for many years in Tibet, and brought much Tibetan occultism into the Nazi sphere." Claims like these should be viewed with extreme caution.

23. In this context, recall that Hielscher went to Nuremberg after World War II to offer testimony that the Ahnenerbe's Wolfram Sievers was part of his mysterious resistance movement against Hitler.

24. Louis Pauwels and Jacques Bergier, *The Morning of the Magicians* (New York: Stein and Day, 1963), p. 208.

25. See *Antifa Info Blatt*, No. 28, which is summarized in the English-language journal *Searchlight*. A 1959 profile of Hielscher in the Weiner Library *Bulletin* reports:

As the priest must not shirk the darkness of his age, Hielscher points now and then to his panacea for our present troubles. To him, the principal bogies are machinery and capitalism, which he hopes will be defeated by men's "turning away from inventing and exploiting." His political vision is "the undoing of the National State and the revival of the ancient tribes as members of an occidental Bund" (1947), and the State is to serve as "a community of free men, all their own masters in small workshops" (1943).

26. Hans-Georg Betz, "Deutschlandpolitik on the Margins," *New German Critique*, No. 44 (Spring–Summer 1988), pp. 130–33.

27. As de Benoist puts it:

Nation-states, whether monarchies or republics, entail closures, centralization, a national market, homogenization, destruction of regional languages and cultures, etc. On the other hand, empires always sought to establish an equilibrium between center and periphery, between sameness and diversity, unity and multiplicity. The unity was not so much political or administrative but spiritual. [*Telos*, Nos. 98/99 (Winter 1993–Spring 1994), p. 204.]

28. Walter Laqueur, *Young Germany* (London: Routledge & Kegan Paul, 1962), p. 239.

29. Ibid., p. 240.

30. Joachim von Ribbentrop was also a subscriber to Ordre Nouveau's journal.

31. John Hellman, *Emmanuel Mounier and the New Catholic Left, 1930–1950* (Toronto: University of Toronto Press, 1981), p. 6.

32. Walter Schellenberg, *Hitler's Secret Service* (New York: Jove/HBJ, 1977), p. 281.

33. See *Searchlight*, September 1995. On 5 December 1994, leftist "Autonomen" destroyed *Junge Freiheit*'s printing shop. On *Junge Freiheit* and the German New Right, see *Telos* No. 105, Fall 1995. Also see Göran Dahl, "Will 'The Other God' Fail Again? On the Possible Return of the Conservative Revolution," *Theory, Culture & Society*, Vol. 13, No. 1, February 1996.

APPENDIX G:
THE WHITES
AND THE REDS

In the 1950s NATINFORM fiercely attacked the CIA for being dominated by Wall Street Jews and penetrated by Soviet intelligence. NATINFORM was particularly upset by CIA support for a Russian exile organization called *Narodno-Trudovoy Soyuz Rossiyskikh Solidaristov* (the Popular Liberation Alliance of Russian Solidarists), better known as NTS. During World War II, NTS closely collaborated with German intelligence in the war in the East. NATINFORM, however, claimed that NTS was really a Soviet-controlled deception operation.

NTS was formed in 1930 by "second generation" White Russian emigrés primarily living in Yugoslavia and Bulgaria. Adopting a "solidarist" or corporatist worldview, it looked for ideological inspiration in its early years to Mussolini's Italy. During World War II, however, NTS collaborated most closely with the Nazis. A key connection to NTS was Dr. George Leibbrandt, who was a leading member of Alfred Rosenberg's *Ostministerium* (East Ministry). After Berlin decided to invade the USSR, Leibbrandt opened negotiations with NTS.[1] The group agreed to collaborate despite the fact that the Ostministerium wanted to dismantle Great Russia and create a number of German-dominated satrapies like an "independent" Ukraine.[2] NTS had previously opposed the balkanization of the Russian Empire, and its 1938 program insisted on the inviolability of Russia's borders.[3] By agreeing to work with Rosenberg, NTS did a 180-degree ideological turn that strongly alienated other White Russians.

Himmler's SS also opposed any semi-autonomous status for areas like the Ukraine. To Himmler, all Slavs were slaves. In September 1942 he explained that the Germans had no interest in educating the Russians. It was sufficient "(1) when the children learn the traffic signs in school so that they do not run into our automobiles, (2) when they learn the multiplication table up to 25 and can count that far, and (3) when they learn to write their own names. Anything more is unnecessary."[4] As for Hitler, when the idea arose of setting up a university to educate "free Ukrainians," he shrieked that "anyone who speaks of tending [to such needs] should be immediately thrown into a concentration camp." The Slavs needed nothing more than "kerchief, glass beads for jewelry, and whatever else colonial people might find appealing."[5]

Influence over German policy toward Russia soon shifted away from Rosenberg to Himmler, Martin Bormann, and·Bormann's friend Erich Koch. An honorary SS lieutenant general and Reich commissioner of the Ukraine from 1941 to 1944, Koch's first official act was to close all schools because "Ukraine children need no schools. What they'll have to learn later will be taught them by their German masters."[6]

Even as German policies increasingly alienated NTS, the Nazis were becoming fed up with the group. In July 1944 the Gestapo decided to clean house, and arrested the NTS leadership. NTS only avoided complete destruction thanks to the head of the security service of General Vlasov's Russian Army of Liberation (ROA), who felt its loss would be too costly when the war in the East was going so badly.

After World War II, NTS found a new patron in the CIA. The exile group and its journal *Possev* (Seed) were incorporated into the U.S.-supported Radio Free Europe/Radio Liberty complex in Munich. The CIA, British intelligence, and the Gehlen organization (later the BND) tried with mixed success to incorporate groups like NTS and the Ukrainian separatist OUN into the Anti-Bolshevik Bloc of Nations (ABN).[7] This revamped "Anti-Komintern" then became the European wing of the Asian People's Anti-Communist League (APACL), the precursor organization to the World Anti-Communist League (WACL).

In the 1950s a Munich-based White Russian monarchist organization called RONND (the Russian National Socialist Movement) spearheaded NATINFORM's campaign against NTS. NATINFORM said that RONND, which had been founded in Germany in the 1920s, was "fully responsible for unearthing the alleged secret affiliation between the NTS and the Soviet espionage in Moscow," which was publicized in RONND's newspaper, *Nabat*. During the 1930s RONND aggressively circulated the Okhrana-instigated forgery known as *The Protocols of the Learned Elders of Zion*.[8] RONND's leader, Eugene H. Derzhavin-Arciuk, worked for German intelligence in World War II. In the 1950s RONND maintained ties to the New European Order through Vsevolod Mositshkin, RONND's liaison to the NEO.[9] When Derzhavin-Arciuk and Mositshkin were sued for slandering the Jewish people, their defense was handled by Rudolf Aschenauer, the publisher of *Die Andrere Seite*.[10] Despite his help, Derzhavin-Arciuk and Mositshkin lost the case and were fined.[11]

In England and America, NATINFORM's case against the NTS was led by Peter J. Huxley-Blythe. In articles for *NATINFORM World Survey* and in pamphlets like *Betrayal: The Story of Russian Anti-Communism* and *The Paid Wreckers*, he relentlessly attacked NTS.[12] In both his pamphlets and his book *The East Came West*, he denounced the CIA and the State Department for their involvement with NTS and the "Captive Nations" movement. Huxley-Blythe also allied himself with another NATINFORM-affiliated emigré group, the Russian Revolutionary Force (RRF). The RRF claimed that America "had adopted a policy akin to that of Hitler's; that the United States government is determined to destroy Russia and replace her by small artificial states that could easily be controlled by Washington."[13]

Huxley-Blythe's attacks on NTS appeared in *Task Force*, which was published by a group of ultra-right retired U.S. military officers called the Defenders of the American Constitution (DAC). His essay in the August–September 1956 *Task Force* was described by its editors as "one of the most important articles" ever published by the journal.[14] The DAC was headed by retired Marine Corps General Pedro Del Valle; its board of directors included Colonel Eugene Pomeroy, General Bonner Fellers, and Claire Chennault. Its British cousin, the League of Empire Loyalists (LEL), was founded around the same time.[15]

The LEL's creator, Arthur Keith Chesterton, was born in England in 1899 and raised in South Africa. After breaking with Oswald Mosley in 1939, he fought for England in World War II. After the war he maintained a semi-respectable position with elements inside the Tory Party. Lord Beaverbrook even made Chesterton his personal journalist and occasional features writer for the *Daily Express* group.[16] Chesterton, however, abandoned the *Daily Express* to found the LEL in October 1954. During this same period he developed ties to Otto Strasser, whom he met in Ireland and Austria in the mid-1950s.[17]

The LEL's views were outlined in its publication *Candour* and in Chesterton's book *The New Unhappy Lords*. Chesterton attacked Anglo-American think tanks like the Royal Institute for International Affairs (RIAA), the Ford Foundation, the Council on Foreign Relations (CFR), the International Institute for Strategic Studies (IISS), the Bilderberger Group, Lazard Frères bank, and other blue-chip bastions as co-collaborators in a Jewish–One Worldist plot to strip England of its colonies. The LEL never tired in its opposition to the financial domination of England by Wall Street as well as Washington's military control of England through the "one-worldist" NATO.[18] Similar "new world order" fears led the DAC to oppose NATO.[19]

But if groups like the NTS were hopeless, were there *any* Russian movements worthy of far-right support? NATINFORM argued that the Russian resistance was best represented by men like General Arthur Smyslovsky-Holmston, the head of an obscure Buenos Aires–based group called the Suvorov Union. During the war, Holmston led some 30,000 men in the First Russian National Liberation Army, which fought a fierce war behind Red Army lines. He then spent three years in an internment camp in Liechtenstein before taking 200 of his men to Argentina, where they formed the Suvorov Union. While in Argentina, he wrote for *Der Weg*.[20] The Suvorov Union and its paper *Suvorovets* received financial support from Perón.[21] Another Buenos Aires–based ally was Johann von Leers.[22]

NATINFORM also endorsed the Russian Revolutionary Forces (RRF).[23] The RRF's political leader, a London-based emigré named George Knupffer, served as tutor to "H.I.H." the Grand Duke Vladimir, the son of the Grand Duke Kirill (Cyrill), one of the leading pretenders to the Romanov throne. A professional conspirator, Knupffer was born in St. Petersburg. His father, a member of the elite Naval Guard, fought for the Whites during the Russian Civil War. His Naval Guard commander was the Grand Duke Kirill. While in exile in London, George Knupffer became heavily involved in royalist intrigue as chairman of the Russian Supreme Monarchist Council.[24]

Knupffer's closest British ally was Chesterton's LEL, and he used the pages of *Candour* to attack the CIA and NTS.[25] Knupffer argued that the Russian Revolution was a plot financed by a cabal of New York–based Jewish bankers. Stalin, however, had ended the reign of the Jews. In revenge, the Wall Street Jews who dominated the CIA had decided to balkanize Russia until it accepted a modified form of U.N.-type "one-worldist" rule.[26] Knupffer became a mentor of sorts to Peter J. Huxley-Blythe, and through him Huxley-Blythe was initiated into the RRF. Under its Imperial Double Eagle standard, the RRF vowed: "For Faith, Tsar, and Fatherland" and against "Atheists, Communists, Separatists, NTS, Solidarists, and the dark forces behind them!" Using mimeographed journals like Huxley-Blythe's *The Free Russia* and propaganda produced by Knupffer's British-Free Russian Information Service, the RRF established an English-language outlet.[27]

Although Knupffer was the RRF's political leader, the group's top organizer was an Athens-based Russian exile named Nicholas Valenius Sheikin.[28] Born in 1909, Sheikin was a Don Cossack whose father was killed during a 1919 Cossack revolt. After his mother died of starvation in 1922, he escaped to the Middle East and became an intransigent anti-Bolshevik conspirator. While working for the Nazis in World War II as a member of the Greek Gestapo (the GFP), he regularly supplied British intelligence with information. During the Cold War, Sheikin created his own anti-Soviet network throughout the Balkans. He also became an avowed enemy of the CIA, and claimed that the Agency had secretly backed a Macedonian separatist movement to divide Greece.[29]

Under Sheikin's leadership, the RRF was primarily engaged in psychological warfare. It claimed to have broadcast into Russia through a Madrid-based radio station. It also distributed anti-Soviet leaflets to Russian sailors in Malaya, Southeast China, and Odessa. One RRF coup reportedly took place in Prague, where the group boasted that it had helped frame *Rude Pravo*'s editor "Andre Simone" (Otto Katz), one of the defendants in the Slansky trials. The RRF operation was featured in a 10 December 1952 *San Francisco News* story under the headline "Russ Exiles' Plot Hangs a Red Editor: Revolutionary Leaflets Were Slipped Into Paper, Dooming Communist."[30] A "former Red Army officer now the director of the Balkan–Middle Eastern division of the RRF" said that the group had secretly inserted over 5,000 anti-Communist leaflets inside the pages of issues of *Rude Pravo*, which were mailed to subscribers inside the Soviet Union. Once the RRF's "Prague unit" learned that anyone connected with *Rude Pravo* had come under Soviet suspicion as the Prague trials were being prepared, it began sending Simone "strange letters, some obviously in code, others congratulating him on the success of the handbill distribution, still others hinting at future dark deeds." He later received a number of "curious, cryptic telephone calls." All this was done with the knowledge that the letters and calls would be intercepted by the Soviet secret police.[31]

Like a series of matryoshka dolls, inside the elusive RRF there existed an even more mysterious organization called Young Russia (*Mladorossy*), which had about 2,000 members in the 1930s. Both Knupffer and Sheikin were leading members; the RRF also seems to have been composed of elements of the Young Russia underground reconstituted after World War II.[32] Young Russia emerged out of a Munich-based emigré student group called *Soiuz "Molodaia Rossia"* (Union of Young Russia). In 1923 Alexander Kazem-Bek became its supreme leader.[33] He transformed it into a neo-monarchist political grouping that was fanatical in its hatred of freemasonry, modernism in art, and liberal or democratic trends in the exile community.

Young Russia, however, supported the 1917 Revolution to the extent it was a national revolution that had purged Russia of foreign (Jewish) contamination. It even gave critical support to Stalin's purge of the "Jewish" Trotskyist Left Opposition. To Kazem-Bek, Stalin was a transitional figure between Jewish-inspired Marxist Bolshevism and a coming Russian nationalist revival that would culminate in a new "popular" national monarch. Mussolini's relationship with the House of Savoy provided a practical model for a future Russia led by a fascist strongman (Kazem-Bek) in an alliance with a restored monarchy. As for the monarch, Young Russia endorsed the Grand Duke Kirill (1876–1936), first cousin to Nicholas I, who proclaimed himself Czar in August 1922. Kirill said he supported a new Volksmonarchie, and in an article for Young Russia's newspaper *Mladorosskaia Iskra* he endorsed an "alliance of the Tsar and Soviets" under a "socialist" "working" monarchy that would unite the white race and prevent the restoration of Jewish rule in Russia.

Of all the claimants to the Romanov throne, the Grand Duke Kirill maintained the most intimate relations with the Nazi Party.[34] His liaison to both the NSDAP and Kazem-Bek was his chief aide-de-camp General Vasily Biskupsky, a friend of General Ludendorff, who led the most anti-Semitic wing of the exiled White Russians.[35] Biskupsky may also have channelled money from Kirill to the German far right in the early 1920s. In 1939 he told one Nazi bureaucrat that the Grand Duke Kirill had given General Ludendorff "a sum of nearly half a million gold marks in 1922–1923 for German-Russian national matters," which Biskupsky now wanted repaid.[36] The money was linked to a reported "Russian-German treaty of 1923" between Kirill's forces and Ludendorff.[37] Relations between the Nazis and Kirill began to deteriorate in the mid-1920s over the issue of Great Russia, when Biskupsky tried without success to turn the Estonia-born Alfred Rosenberg against Ukrainian separatism. The Gestapo actually jailed Biskupsky from June to September 1933, although two years later the Nazis made him the head of Russian emigration in Germany.[38]

In the 1930s Young Russia critically supported the new "Caesar," Joseph Stalin. Kazem-Bek inverted Trotsky's attack on Stalin as a "Bonapartist" and argued that a Bonapartist strong man was just what Russia needed. He openly appealed to the Russian military to finish the job begun by Stalin and make Russia's national revolution complete. Although Kazem-Bek delighted in the downfall of both Bukharin and Trotsky, he was horrified by Stalin's purge of the Red Army that resulted in the deaths of thousands of Soviet military officers. The purge ended Kazem-Bek's soft line towards Stalin. During the war, elements of Young Russia reportedly fought with the French Resistance.[39] In 1940 Kazem-Bek also fled France for America.[40] The strangest twist to the story of Young Russia, however, came in 1956, when Kazem-Bek voluntarily returned to the Soviet Union. He then became secretary to the Moscow Patriarch and a regular contributor to the journal *Zhurnal Moskovskoi Patriarkhii*. He died in Russia in 1977 at age 75.

Other elements of the Grand Duke Kirill's political network, however, continued to be active in the West. In the U.S. they operated through a mysterious group known as the Sovereign Order of Saint John of Jerusalem, Knights of Malta. The Knight's Grand Chancellor, "Colonel" Charles Thourot Pichel, lived in the small town of Shickshinny, Pennsylvania.[41] He claimed that his group, and not the wealthy Vatican-backed Sovereign Military Order of Malta (SMOM), was the legitimate heir to a chivalric order that had its origin in the early Middle Ages.

Before examining the Grand Duke Kirill's ties to Pichel, it is first necessary to describe the Shickshinny Knights' background, membership, and presence inside the U.S. far right. The group claimed descent from the Order of St. John of Jerusalem (also known as the Knights Hospitaler), which was founded in 1050 A.D. by a group of wealthy Italian laymen to aid pilgrims visiting the Holy Land. During the Crusades the Knights Hospitaler, like the Knights Templar, transformed itself into a military order of "warrior monks" to combat Islam. After being driven out of both the Holy Land and Rhodes, the Knights settled in Malta. There they built a formidable fortress-like headquarters and waged war against the Turks, while maintaining their identity as an independent transnational state comprised of separate national priories ruled by a Grand Council and presided over by a Grand Master.

In 1789 the Knights' Grand Master surrendered the group's Malta fortress to Napoleon. A year earlier Catherine the Great's son, Czar Paul I of Russia, had made it known that he wanted to become the Knights' Grand Protector. Paul, dubbed the "mad Czar" by his critics, thought that sponsorship of the Knights might help him lead a reconciliation between the Roman and Eastern Orthodox wings of the Catholic Church. Some Knights went to Russia and were given lavish financial support from Paul, whom they elected the Order's new Grand Master on 27 October 1798. After Paul I's death in 1801, his son Czar Alexander I confiscated the Order's properties. As even Pichel admits, from 1803 to 1890 the Russian Knights "remained more or less dormant."[42]

Scattered remnants of the Knights and their descendants in Germany, Russia, France, and other nations began looking to America as a place of refuge in the mid-1800s. William Lamb, a Norfolk, Virginia, businessman and former colonel in the Confederate army, encouraged the Russian Knights, now an independent chivalric order, to come to America.[43] From 1890 to 1929 the Knights allegedly held their meetings in the Waldorf-Astoria. Pichel joined the group sometime in the 1920s.

In the 1950s the Knights developed close ties to the Defenders of the American Constitution, and some DAC leaders became members of the "Military Affairs Committee" of Pichel's Knights. General Pedro Del Valle was a member of both the Supreme Court of the Knights and its Military Affairs Committee. Other members of the Military Affairs Committee included Gen. Lemuel C. Sheppard, Lieutenant General George E. Stratemeyer, Major General Charles A. Willoughby, Brigadier General Bonner Fellers, Admiral Charles M. Cooke, and seven retired U.S. Navy rear admirals. The Order's "Honorary Grand Admiral" was Admiral Sir Barry Domville, the Nazi sympathizer and former head of British Naval Intelligence who had been interned during World War II under Regulation 18B.[44] Both Willoughby and Del Valle had been close allies of General Douglas MacArthur. In order to overcome the MacArthur network's opposition to CIA activity in Asia, CIA Director Walter Bedell Smith once tried to interest Del Valle in heading up a CIA office in Tokyo, but without success.[45]

Pichel's Knights and Del Valle's DAC had ties to George Deatherage, an old Defenders "comrade in arms" whose involvement in the far right went back to the 1930s.[46] Deatherage was financed by a wealthy Knight of Malta named Tyler Kent. Kent had been a file clerk at the American embassy in London; he spent World War II in a British jail for passing information from U.S. diplomatic cables to a pro-Axis spy ring. After the war he married Clara Hyatt, heiress to the Carter's Little Liver Pills fortune. The Kents moved to Florida, where Tyler lived in luxury while squandering his wife's fortune on far-right causes. One of his closest friends was Deatherage, who ran a KKK-like group called the Knights of the White Camellia. Kent gave him an estate for life in Satsuma, Florida.

Deatherage had some interesting ideas about Russia. He contributed an article to the 1 May 1960 issue of *Common Sense* entitled "Anti-Semitism in Soviet

Russia," which argued that the Jews no longer held any power there. Yet it was Kent's suspected ties to Russia that most fascinated U.S. and British intelligence. For reasons that remain unclear, the British suspected that Kent was a Soviet spy who had been recruited while working at the American embassy in Moscow in the mid-1930s. The FBI repeatedly investigated Kent in the 1950s for possible Soviet connections, without success.[47] As late as 1970, the State Department was still concerned about Kent's supposed Soviet ties.[48]

In 1959, Kent bought a local Florida paper called the *Putnam County Weekly Sun*, which he filled with right-wing and anti-Jewish articles. After the election of John F. Kennedy, he went ballistic and issued "special bulletins" like:

KENNEDY PROCLAIMED FIRST COMMUNIST PRESIDENT OF AMERICA, (And, Friend, Don't You Smile.) BEAST KENNEDY IS GUILTY OF SEDITION AND GIVING AID AND COMFORT TO THE ENEMY WHICH IS COMMUNISM. THE KENNEDY DEMOCRATIC PARTY IS NOW THE SUBVERSIVE PARTY. A CESSPOOL OF MINORITY-TERMITES WHO SEEK TO DESTROY THE POLITICAL POWER OF THE ANGLO-SAXON WHITE PROTESTANT!"

All this time, Kent was a Knight Commander of Justice in Pichel's Knights.[49]

Pichel's Order also included Eugene Tabbutt, who in 1958 was listed as the group's "Chief Security Officer." In 1965 he became the Knights' "Security General."[50] He also served as the Imperial Director of the Klan Bureau of Investigation (KBI), the KKK's "counterintelligence" unit.[51] The Knights also had strong ties to elements inside both U.S. military intelligence and the CIA. The most prominent Knight in this regard was the Heidelberg-born Major General Charles Willoughby (who legally changed his name from Adolf Tscheppe-Weidenbach). The former head of General MacArthur's intelligence staff in World War II, Willoughby joined the Knights in the early 1960s and in 1963 served as the Order's Security General. He also ran his own International Committee for the Defense of Christian Culture.

Another Knight with intelligence ties was Colonel Philip J. Corso, a 20-year Army Intelligence operative who retired in August 1963. He seems to have spent some of his time in the military working in an Operation Gladio–type operation in Germany in the 1950s.[52] Shortly after Kennedy was assassinated, Corso, then in the employ of Senator Strom Thurmond, began telling his friends in Congress that sources inside the CIA told him that Lee Harvey Oswald had been an FBI informant.[53]

Retired CIA official Herman Kimsey (who was listed as the group's "Associate Chief of International Intelligence" in 1970) was another intriguing Knight. Although Kimsey has been described as a former Chief of Research and Analysis for the CIA,[54] his actual position inside the Agency remains unclear. Whatever he was up to, foreign heads of state showed up at his Washington funeral.[55] Kimsey championed the cause of a Knight named Michel Goleniewski.[56] Goleniewski was a Polish intelligence officer who defected to the West in January 1961. One of the CIA's most important assets, he is credited with exposing top Soviet agents like Gordon Lonsdale (a Soviet "deep cover" agent whose real name was Conon Trofimovich Molody); George Blake, a high-ranking member of British intelligence's MI6; and Heinz Felfe, one of Reinhard Gehlen's lieutenants inside the BND.[57]

Goleniewski believed that the CIA had been heavily penetrated by Soviet intelligence. He was so worried that he initially attempted to contact J. Edgar Hoover so that his defection could be handled by the FBI and not the CIA.[58] After he was safely in the United States, Goleniewski began claiming that he was really Aleksei Nicholaevich Romanov, son of Czar Nicholas II and rightful heir to the Imperial Throne.[59] He also accused Henry Kissinger of working for the KGB. His supporters claim that in 1961 he told the CIA that the Soviets had recruited Kissinger under the code name "Bor" in 1946, when Kissinger was working for U.S. military intelligence in Oberammergau, Germany.[60] Herman Kimsey and Cleve Backster, a lie-detector expert and the Knights' "Chief Interrogation Officer," took out ads to support Goleniewski. The attack on Kissinger was endorsed by another Knight, Frank Capell. Capell, a devout Catholic best known in far-right circles for his publication *The Herald of Freedom*, later broke with Pichel in a factional split inside the Knights.

To understand the presence of the Grand Duke Kirill's network in the Knights, we must examine the group's leader, Charles T. Pichel. Pichel's interest in chivalric orders went back at least to 1924, when he helped establish the American Heraldry Society in New York City.[61] By the early 1930s, he was active in the far right. On 15 July 1933 he wrote to a prominent Nazi named Ernst Hanfstaengl offering his services as a liaison between the American right and Hitler.[62] In the late 1930s he became involved in a nebulous Axis propaganda ring called "The Order of the Blue Lamoo." Pichel's ties to the Blue Lamoo surfaced in a 1939 report by a New York detective named Boris Casimir Palmer (Pilenas). A former World War I military intelligence agent, Palmer ran his own detective agency out of an office located at 170 Broadway. On 27 January 1939 he sent a letter to the Non-Sectarian Anti-Nazi League (NSANL) under the title "Subject Japanese espionage." In it, he discussed Pichel's involvement with Boris Brasol, a leading White Russian anti-Semite, intelligence operative, criminologist, literary figure, and founder of the Union of Czarist Army and Navy Officers. Brasol was said to have been a representative of a Nazi propaganda organization called the Fichte Bund, and was close to the Cossack General Grigori Semionov, who was financed by Japan.[63]

Palmer told the NSANL that a Franciscan priest, Father Peter Baptiste Duffee, claimed that Brasol also belonged to "a Nazi propaganda organization known as the Blue Lammoo [sic]. At the head of the group is Charles T. Pichel, an ex-con." Pichel, then living in Leonia, New Jersey, was said to be working "for a member of the IRA who is in the employ of the Japanese Commercial Attaché in Washington." Duffee identified the IRA man as Vincent Walsh.[64] Walsh, who later worked with the Japanese consulate in New York, was tied to Pichel, who was "said to be an Englishman, alleged drug smuggler, and Nazi spy." Duffee also reported on another Blue Lamoo'er close to Pichel, a "Count Tcherep-Spiridovich."

How well informed was Father Duffee? In his book *American Swastika*, Charles Higham reports that the priest served as Father Coughlin's liaison to Boris Brasol. Duffee was also right about the Blue Lamoo. According to the anti-fascist Friends of Democracy group, the Ancient and Noble Order of the Blue Lamoo was a White Russian fascist organization one of whose members was the "Count V. Cherep-Spiridovich."[65] The "Count" was born Howard Victor von Boenstrupp. A former patent lawyer, Boenstrupp was also known as "the Duke of St. Saba," "Colonel Bennett," and "J. G. Francis." A close associate of Silver Shirt leader William Dudley Pelley, he was indicted along with Pelley on sedition charges on 21 July 1942. Nor was this his first encounter with the law. In 1933, when he was just plain Howard, he was charged with grand larceny for allegedly stealing a valuable book and other crimes.[66] During the House Committee on Un-American Activities questioning of Fritz Kuhn, Cherep-Spiridovich's name came up in connection with two publications, *Intelligence* and *American Tribunal*. He was also linked to "the Order of the Knights of St. John of Jerusalem."[67]

Boenstrupp said he got his title after being legally adopted by a real White Russian count, Major General A. Cherep-Spiridovich, who died a suicide.[68] A friend of Boris Brasol, the count lived in America after World War I and headed the Anglo-Latino-Slav League. He was also involved in the Anti-Bolshevik Publishers Association, which published *The Gentiles' Review*. Cherep-Spiridovich was the author of a near-psychotic 1926 tract called *The Secret World Government or the Hidden Hand*, and was intimately involved in promoting *The Protocols of the Learned Elders of Zion* in the United States.

Starting in June 1922, the well-known journalist Norman Hapgood ran a series of exposés in *Hearst's International* entitled "The Inside Story of Henry Ford's Jew Mania." In it, Cherep-Spiridovich and Brasol were identified as two of the most influential figures behind Ford. According to Hapgood, Cherep-Spiridovich at one point lived in Detroit and worked for Ford.[69] He also identified another Russian friend of Brasol's involved with the *Protocols*, a former diplomat and Hereditary Knight Commander in Pichel's order named Boris Bakhmeteff.[70]

As for Brasol, his ties to Ford evolved out of his earlier connection to American military intelligence. One of his ex–military intelligence cronies was C. C. Daniels, the head of the Ford Detective Agency in New York and the brother of Secretary of the Navy Josephus Daniels. Dr. Harris Houghton, C. C. Daniels' family physician and the New York head of Army Intelligence, was also close to

Brasol. After World War I, Houghton created the Beckwith Company to publish tracts like the *Protocols*.[71]

Casimir Palmer, who worked for the Military Intelligence Division in Washington during World War I, also knew Brasol. In a signed affidavit dated 2 April 1937, he said he had first met Brasol in April 1918 when the Russian was working for the War Trade Board in New York City.[72] After telling Palmer that the downfall of the Russian monarchy had been part of a Jewish conspiracy, Brasol "mentioned something about there being in existence some sort of secret document known as the *Protocols of Zion*."[73] They next met on 29 June 1918 at Brasol's apartment on West 84th Street. Again Brasol claimed that Jewish bankers like the Warburgs were behind the Bolshevik Revolution, information that Palmer relayed "to my superior, Captain Carleton J. H. Hayes, now Professor of History at Columbia University." Palmer then reported that a copy of the *Protocols* manuscript was sent to a Congressional Committee by "a very close friend of Henry Ford, a Dr. H. A. Houghton." When Palmer met Brasol for a third time, Brasol gave him a copy of the *Protocols*, which he had gotten translated into English.

Brasol spread the *Protocols* in league with the Grand Duke Kirill. Kirill and his chief aide-de-camp General Vasily Biskupsky appear to have received financial support from Henry Ford, with Brasol serving as their intermediary. According to Robert C. Williams' book *Culture in Exile*, Kirill's wife Viktoria managed "to obtain funds for the movement from the United States."[74] In their book *Who Financed Hitler*, James and Suzanne Pool state that Brasol was Kirill's American representative at the time.[75] They report that Brasol sent money from Ford to the Grand Duke and Duchess, who in turn gave it to Ludendorff to support the Bavarian far right, including Hitler. If this information is correct, it might explain the Nazi refusal to give Biskupsky the money he claimed was due him, since the funds hadn't originated with Grand Duke Kirill in the first place.

Grand Duke Kirill had another supporter on the American far right: Charles Pichel. Pichel reports that on 13 January 1934, "the late Grand Duke Kirill, acting officially as Kirill Wladimirovich (Kirill I)" from his place of exile in Saint Briac, France, confirmed the legitimacy of Pichel's Order. Two years later, in a proclamation dated 24 November 1936, he conferred upon Pichel "the Order of St. Andrew the Apostle, First Class in Gold" for his "*zeal* in defending and helping to perpetuate the noble history of Imperial Russia and the Imperial Families of Russia." Kirill's order was "signed by the President of the Committee of Imperial Orders and the Delegate of the Emperor in the United States," presumably Brasol.[76]

Brasol also backed Kirill's son and successor, the Grand Duke Vladimir, whose tutor was the RRF's George Knuppfer. In March 1952, the English-language magazine *Russia*, published by N. P. Rybakoff (also the publisher and editor of *Rossiya*, and a member of Brasol's network since the 1920s),[77] ran an essay by H.I.H. the Grand Duke Vladimir (the official patron of the Russian Revolutionary Forces) entitled "An Appeal to the Free World." In a 15 September 1958 article for the ultra-right *Common Sense*, Brasol backed the Grand Duke Vladimir's claim to the throne. *Russia* also published articles by Brasol.[78] *Russia*'s NATINFORM connection was made clear when it ran a commentary from Peter Huxley-Blythe's *NATINFORM World Survey* attacking U.S. aid to Tito in its February 1958 issue.[79]

It seems clear that Pichel played a role in the Grand Duke Kirill's network inside the United States. Kirill's organization opposed CIA support for the "captive nations" inside the Soviet empire. In that sense, the Kirill network's polemics against both NTS and the CIA were a continuation of a debate begun in the 1920s, when General Biskupsky unsuccessfully tried to convince Alfred Rosenberg to oppose the balkanization of "Mother Russia."

Notes:

1. *NTS—The Russian Solidarist Movement*, External Research Staff, Office of Intelligence Division, Series 3, No. 76, 10 December 1951, Department of State. On NTS, see the group's booklet, *NTS: Introduction to a Russian Freedom Party* (Munich: Possev, 1979). For a Western puff-piece, see Gordon Young, *The House of Secrets* (New York: Duell, Sloan and Pearce, 1959).

2. Germany also backed an independent Ukraine in World War I.

3. *NTS—The Russian Solidarist Movement*, p. 6.

4. Jost Hermand, *Old Dreams of a New Reich* (Bloomington, IN: Indiana University Press, 1992), p. 276.

5. Ibid., p. 280.

6. See the entry on Koch in Robert Wistrich, *Who's Who in Nazi Germany* (New York: Routledge, 1982). In 1950 Koch was extradited to Poland on war crimes charges. Although he was sentenced to death, his execution was commuted to life imprisonment because he was supposedly too ill to be executed. He died in prison in November 1986 at age 90.

7. The NTS and the OUN opposed each other because the NTS had a federalist view of Russia while the OUN wanted a sovereign Ukraine.

8. It was most likely through RONND that the *Protocols* were distributed in Switzerland. (Robert C. Williams, *Culture in Exile: Russian Emigrés in Germany 1881–1941* [Ithaca, NY: Cornell University Press, 1972], p. 340.)

9. Peter J. Huxley-Blythe told me that Derzhavin-Arciuk was employed by the Germans. As for Mositshkin and the NEO, see Kurt Tauber, *Beyond Eagle and Swastika* (Middletown, CT: Wesleyan University Press, 1967), Vol. 2, fn. 41, pp. 1091–92.

10. *NATINFORM World Survey*, No. 2, July 1954. Aschenauer also asked that Johann von Leers be called to Germany to testify on behalf of RONND.

11. The case involved an article claiming that the Jews were behind Bolshevism that appeared in RONND's *Nabat*, No. 27, 4 November 1951.

12. Huxley-Blythe denounced the NTS to other rightists. In a letter dated 2 April 1954, he wrote Fred Weiss to warn him against NTS, which he labeled "a secret Communist (Malenkov-Stalin) outfit that is working against the West."

13. Peter J. Huxley-Blythe, *The East Came West* (Caldwell, ID: Caxton Printers, 1964), pp. 219–20. Also see Revilo P. Oliver's review in the May 1966 *American Opinion*.

14. Besides attacking NTS, Huxley-Blythe argued that the CIA was backing "Titoist" national communist governments in East Europe to undermine Moscow when the Russians were planning all along to recognize Gomulka in Poland and Kadar in Hungary. After the article appeared, NTS threatened to sue *Task Force* unless it was permitted a written rebuttal. In the June 1957 *Task Force*, NTS representative Alexi Malyshev said that Huxley-Blythe's attacks echoed Soviet charges that NTS was a CIA creation.

15. *Task Force's* first issue appeared in May 1954; the LEL was founded in October 1954. The December 1954 *Task Force* reported that the DAC's Colonel Pomeroy had visited London to hold political discussions with Chesterton and the LEL. The LEL also had its share of military men, including Field Marshal Lord Ironside and Lieutenant General Sir Balfour Hutchison.

16. David Baker, "A. K. Chesterton, the Strasser Brothers and the Politics of the National Front," *Patterns of Prejudice*, Vol. 19, No. 3, 1985.

17. The British author Douglas Reed was an important go-between for the two men. In a letter dated 7 February 1954 to the National Renaissance Party from his home in Paradise, Nova Scotia, Strasser wrote:

> I think it would be a good idea for you to get in touch with the very fine English nationalist publication *Candour*, published by A. K. Chesterton, who is a very good friend of [Strasser biographer] Douglas Reed. [From the files of the NSANL.]

18. George Thayer, *The British Political Fringe* (London: Anthony Blond, 1965), p. 56.

19. In the mid-1960s the LEL and the British National Party merged to form the National Front.

20. General Holmston, "Das nationale Russland," *Der Weg*, No. 1, 1954.

21. Peter J. Huxley-Blythe informed me of this.

22. In a letter to Fred Weiss dated 24 April 1954, Dr. Emile Gelny, Leers' friend in Damascus, wrote:

> An important man amongst the White Russians is General Holmston in Argentina. You can contact the White Russians in the United States through him: Prof. von Leers (Martin Haedo 863, VINCENTE LOPEZ FCNGBM, Prov. de Buenos Aires) knows him and could serve as the contact man.

23. Huxley-Blythe almost certainly became a member of the RRF. According to a biographic note to his book *The East Came West*: "In 1957 an anti-Communist Russian resistance movement not only awarded him a Special Badge and Certificate to acknowledge his work for Russia, as opposed to the Soviet Union, but paid him the unique compliment of asking him to be a member of their organization."

The RRF and RONND were not the only Eastern European groups linked to NATINFORM. NATINFORM also had ties to a Hungarian group called the White Guard. (See *NATINFORM World Survey*, June 1954.) Another Hungarian ally of NATINFORM (and Director of NATINFORM/Free Hungary) was Dr. Michael Punkosti, who spoke at a conference held in Miami in 1955 sponsored by the Guardians of Liberty. See *NAT-INFORM World Survey* No. 8, March 1955. The director of research for NATIN-FORM/Free Hungary was Mr. A. Marosvolgyi, according to the January–February 1955 *NATINFORM World Survey*, No. 7. NATINFORM's Hungarians were supporters of the exile Nazi "Hungarist" movement, and some had been followers of the executed Hungarian Nazi Ferenc Szalasi. (Tauber, *Beyond Eagle and Swastika*, Vol. 1, p. 245.)

24. On Knupffer, see the biographical summary in his book *The Struggle for World Power* (London: Plain-Speaker Pub. Co., 1963). Knupffer says that he maintained close relations with a British MP and former intelligence operative named Capt. Henry Kerby.

25. See Knupffer's articles in the December 1955 and May 1956 *Task Force.*

26. In an article in the British–Free Russian Information Service that appeared in 1956, Knupffer argued that New York Jewish bankers financed the Bolshevik Revolution. Since Stalin's time, however, "the Soviet regime is no longer an effective tool for the achievement of world domination of the materialistic messianists" (i.e., the Jews). In the mid-1960s Knupffer created the Integralist World Association in London, which published *The Plain Speaker*, whose first issue appeared in April 1965. He also promoted a fraudulent book called *Red Symphony* by a "Dr. J. Landowsky" attacking Trotsky and supporting Stalin. At the time Knupffer was pushing *Red Symphony* he was writing articles in *The Plain Speaker* denouncing Russian "agent provocateurs," including dissidents, Jews, poets, Boris Pasternak, and NTS. See *The Plain Speaker* for March 1968.

27. *The Free Russia* was established in 1956. Its editorial office was Huxley-Blythe's home.

28. In *The Free Russia* of February 1960, Sheikin's address is given as OEK No. 17, Apt. 101, New Philadelphia, Athens, and he is listed as *The Free Russia* representative for Greece and the Middle East. Huxley-Blythe, who wrote a book about Sheikin called *The Man Who Was Uncle: The Biography of a Master Spy* (London: Arthur Baker Ltd., 1975), first met him through the RRF and NATINFORM. NATINFORM also had ties to rightist elements in Greece around FYRADE (*Fili Ypodoulon Rosson Agonizomenon Di'Eleftherian*—Friends of Enslaved Russians Struggling for Freedom) one of whose leaders, Colonel George Tzavellas, was a retired member of Greek intelligence. Tzavellas, with the permission of FYRADE's Chairman, Colonel Demitri Koutsomanis, issued a document attacking the Greek section of NTS.

29. Sheikin wrote a book in Greek entitled *For This Corner of the Globe: How the Americans Are Helping to Divide Greece*, which exposed a CIA plot to back a Macedonian separatist movement called Komitadjis.

30. The article, written by Richard Starnes, was reprinted in *What Everybody Should Know About the RRF Underground*, a 1957 RRF pamphlet.

31. For an appraisal of "Andre Simone"/Otto Katz, see Stephen Koch, *Double Lives: Spies and Writers in the Secret Soviet War of Ideas Against the West* (New York: Free Press, 1994).

32. For a discussion of Sheikin's ties to Young Russia, see *The Man Who Was Uncle*. George Knupffer's ties to Young Russia are also evident in one of his pre-war works. Knupffer translated Cyril Ielita-Wilczkovski's *Before and After Stalin* (London: Selwyn

& Blount, 1939). The foreword of this book is by H.I.H. Grand Duke Dmitri of Russia, who reported that Ielita-Wilczkovski was a close associate of Young Russia's founder, Alexander Kazem-Bek. For an article by Knupffer supporting the Grand-Duke Vladimir's claims, see Knupffer and James Page's 1967 pamphlet *The Russian Claimant*, sponsored by the Monarchist Press Association for the Russian Supreme Monarchist Council.

33. My information on Young Russia comes largely from Nicholas Hayes's essay "Kazem-Bek and the Young Russian Revolution," in *Slavonic Review*, Vol. 39, No. 2, 1980.

34. Williams, *Culture in Exile*, p. 215.

35. One White Russian source claimed that Hitler once hid out in Biskupsky's Munich house. (Walter Laqueur, *Russia and Germany* [London: Weidenfeld and Nicholson, 1965], p. 108.)

36. Ibid., p. 350. Biskupsky is discussed at some length in *Culture in Exile*.

37. Despite the Kirill network's anti-Communism, a Belgrade-based Russian emigré journal called *Russkoe Delo* reported in 1922 that Biskupsky and another extremely important Russian far-rightist with Nazi ties named Scheubner-Richter had secretly met with a former Okhrana general named Komissarov in Munich. After 1917 it was reported that Komissarov was cooperating with the Bolshevik secret police. Laqueur, *Russia and Germany*, p. 121.

38. Ibid., pp. 112–13. Also see *Culture in Exile*.

39. It is quite possible that George Knupffer, like Sheikin, may have aided British intelligence. See John Costello, *Ten Days to Destiny* (New York: William Morrow, 1991).

40. In *The Man Who Was Uncle*, Huxley-Blythe reports that Sheikin arranged Kazem-Bek's escape.

41. Because Pichel lived in Shickshinny, Pennsylvania, the Pichel group is sometimes called the "Shickshinny Knights of Malta."

42. Charles Thourot Pichel, *History of the Sovereign Order of Saint John of Jerusalem, Knights of Malta* (Shickshinny, PA: Maltese Cross Press, 1970), p. 40.

43. Lamb was reportedly a descendant of General Ivan Lamb of Russia, who had been appointed by Paul I as the "Grand Preserver" of the Knights.

44. For the full list of military men (including Domville), see Pichel, *History of the Sovereign Order*, pp. 192–93. Many of the military men in the Defenders were also freemasons. See, for example, a July 1960 article in *Task Force* on the military freemasons and their relation to the far-right Constitution Party.

45. Peter Grose, *Gentleman Spy: The Life of Allen Dulles* (Amherst, MA: University of Massachusetts Press, 1996), pp. 309–10. Del Valle said the CIA tried to involve him in a plot to "get" MacArthur. (Andrew Tully, *CIA: The Inside Story* [New York: Morrow, 1962], p. 30.) Del Valle had spent the late 1940s as president of ITT for South America. He knew the Peróns but considered them too socialistic and Jewish-influenced. See Del Valle's letter to *American Mercury* (Spring 1973). Del Valle also became a good friend of American Nazi Party leader George Lincoln Rockwell.

46. *Task Force* reported Deatherage's death in its May 1965 issue.

47. A 23 November 1962 FBI file on Kent concluded:

The Bureau has conducted an investigation of Kent to determine if he was engaged in espionage or if he was sympathetic with communism. The investigation is closed and no such information was developed. Although the trial in England was conducted on the theory that information had been given to the Germans, there is an indication that Kent may have been sympathetic with the Russians.

48. On Kent's suspected ties to the Russians, see Anthony Read and Ray Bearse, *Conspirator: The Untold Story of Tyler Kent* (New York: Doubleday, 1991), as well as John Costello's *Ten Days to Destiny*. The FBI document on Kent comes from the John Toland file, which I examined at the Franklin Roosevelt Library at Hyde Park.

49. Kent's membership card in Pichel's group is in the Franklin Roosevelt Library.

50. Robert Formhal, *White Cross* (Camarillo, CA: Sanghals Press, 1979), p. 151.

51. Tabbutt is also mentioned in the 1965–66 House Committee on Un-American Activities (HCUA) hearings on the KKK.

52. Dick Russell, *The Man Who Knew Too Much* (New York: Carroll & Graf, 1992), p. 529.

53. Corso appears to have spread this rumor in conjunction with Frank Capell. (Lisa Pease, "New Orleans and the Cover-Up," *Probe*, Vol. 3, No. 6 [September–October 1996].) Also see Peter Dale Scott, *Deep Politics* (Berkeley, CA: University of California Press, 1993), and Russell, *The Man Who Knew Too Much*.

54. Kimsey is so described in an article in the 11 June 1971 New York *Daily Mirror*, cited on p. 75 of Frank Capell's book *Henry Kissinger: Soviet Agent* (Zarephath, NJ: Herald of Freedom Publications, 1974). The Defenders of the American Constitution also backed Goleniewski's charges against Kissinger. See the April 1974 issue of *Task Force* for an article on Goleniewski.

55. Kimsey also appears in Hugh McDonald's book about the Kennedy assassination, *Appointment in Dallas* (New York: Zebra Books, 1975). McDonald makes a point of noting Kimsey's ties to the Knights.

56. In his publication *The Double Eagle* (September 1980), Goleniewski said that he was a "Knight of OSA, OSG, OSJ, etc." Also see Arnaud Chaffanjon and Bertrand Galimard Flavigny, *Ordres & Contre-Ordres de Chevalerie* (Paris: Mercure de France, 1982), p. 193.

57. For a brief discussion of Goleniewski, see David Wise, *Molehunt* (New York: Random House, 1992), pp. 24–25.

58. Recall that many Eastern Europeans became highly suspicious of the CIA after American radio broadcasts into Hungary in 1956 gave a false impression that the West was willing to help the revolt. NATINFORM claimed that the CIA wanted to encourage the Hungarian underground to surface publicly so that it could be identified by the Soviet secret police for liquidation.

59. Goleniewski made his claim just before his supporters in Congress were to have him publicly testify about the extent of Soviet penetration of American intelligence operations both in Poland and elsewhere; a course that would have put him in direct conflict with the CIA. By claiming to be the Czar, Goleniewski may have been crazy like a fox. Still, if it was all a put-on, he played his part brilliantly. In his *The Double Eagle* newsletter, Goleniewski argued that England's Duke of Clarence was Jack the Ripper, who really was Adolf Hitler. Hitler was also "a member of the Satanic Society

of the Order Under the Death's Head—an ultra-secret branch of the Manichean cult inspired by the Illuminatis Order." See *The Double Eagle* (September 1980).

60. Frank Capell, *Henry Kissinger: Soviet Agent*, lays out Goleniewski's story in detail. Also see Guy Richards, *The Hunt for the Czar* (New York: Doubleday, 1970).

61. Charles Pichel, *Heraldry in America* (1928).

62. Sander Diamond, *The Nazi Movement in the United States: 1924–1941* (Ithaca, NY: Cornell University Press, 1974), fn. 26, p. 117.

63. Semionov developed a reputation as a bloodthirsty killer during the Russian Civil War.

64. Palmer mentions in his report that George Sylvester Viereck was "close to a Robert Montieth, who was an associate of Sir Roger Casement and is now close to [Father] Coughlin." Sir Roger Casement was executed for his support of Irish independence. Father Duffee wanted Palmer to meet with the IRA man Walsh, "who is seeking information on Sir William Wiseman," an important figure in British intelligence.

65. See the Friends of Democracy's pamphlet *A Confidential Statement Concerning Pro-Nazi and Anti-Semitic Organizations*.

66. *New York Times*, 18 February 1933.

67. See the HCUA questioning of Fritz Kuhn on 16 August 1939, p. 3803.

68. Not to be confused with another White Russian general named Spiridovich, who wrote a book called *History of Bolshevism*.

69. According to the Friends of Democracy report *Ford and Fascism*, Spiridovich once worked for Ford's *Dearborn Independent*. On Ford and the far right, see Leo Ribuffo, "Henry Ford and *The International Jew*," *American Jewish History*, Vol. 69, No. 4 (June 1980).

70. For mention of Bakhmeteff, see Pichel, *History of the Sovereign Order of St. John of Jerusalem*. There is a thick file in the archives of the Non-Sectarian Anti-Nazi League exploring the relationship between Bakhmeteff, Brasol, and Henry Ford in regard to the production and circulation of the *Protocols*. I believe part of this file came from Norman Hapgood's exposé.

71. For a discussion of Houghton, see the section on the *Protocols* by T. Gaster in volume four of *The Universal Jewish Encyclopedia* (1941). Also see the appendix "Secret Societies and Subversive Movements."

72. Before then, Brasol had been acting as chief of the Intelligence Division of the Russian Ministry of Munitions. I received a copy of Palmer's affidavit, as well as some of his letters, from the American Jewish Archives in Cincinnati, Ohio.

73. Palmer later unsuccessfully tried to sell a copy of the *Protocols* to the American Jewish Committee for $50,000. (Zosa Szajkowski, *Jews, Wars and Communism* [New York: Ktav Publishing, 1974], Vol. II, p. 157.)

74. Williams, *Culture in Exile*, p. 213.

75. James and Suzanne Pool, *Who Financed Hitler* (New York: Dial Press, 1978), pp. 113–16. In 1924 the Grand Duke Kirill visited New York on a fundraising drive. Williams, *Culture in Exile*, p. 288. Kirill proclaimed himself Czar on 31 August 1924. For more on Kirill, see Michael John Sullivan, *A Fatal Passion* (New York: Random House, 1997).

76. On Kirill, the Knights, and Pichel, see Pichel, *History*, p. 168, as well as Harrison Smith's *The Order of St. John of Jerusalem of Malta* (Malta: Progress Press, 1964), pp. 92–95. Kirill, who died on 13 October 1938, was the Grand Master of a Paris-based group of Russian exiles called "the Union of Hereditary Commanders and Knights of the Grand Priory of Russia of Saint John of Jerusalem."

77. According to a September 1956 story in *Russia* (the English language version of *Rossia*), Rybakoff (the publisher of *Russia*) was a former colonel in the Russian Army who came to the United States in 1923 and began working for Ford Motors.

78. Brasol's strangest contribution to *Russia* was an August 1955 review of Jennings C. Wise's *Philosophical History of Civilization* (New York: Philosophical Library, 1955). Wise's opus, a strange mishmash of occult gobbledygook and *Chariots of the Gods*-type crankish "history," purported to follow the history of different root races in the West. In promoting Wise, Brasol may have been doing a favor for a political collaborator. In his book *Father Coughlin* (Boston: Little Brown, 1973), pp. 292–93, Sheldon Marcus reports that Wise (the son of a governor of Virginia) wrote for *Social Justice* and was an associate of George Deatherage and other 1930s far-rightists. Fred Weiss and H. Keith Thompson also knew Wise. According to Thompson: "Jennings C. Wise was a Rosicrucian, and much that he wrote has to be viewed in that light." For an analysis of Wise, see Robert Wauchope, *Lost Tribes and Sunken Continents* (Chicago, IL: University of Chicago Press, 1962).

79. One year later, in February 1959, *Russia* (now renamed *Voice of Free Russia*) ran another Huxley-Blythe story about a Cossack hero named Nikolai Lazarevitch Kolakov, who fought with the Nazis under General von Panwitz in Croatia in World War II. *Voice of Free Russia*'s last issue appeared in April 1959.

APPENDIX H:
LEE HARVEY
OSWALD'S
ADDRESS BOOK

Exhibit Volume XVI of the Warren Commission Report reproduces Lee Harvey Oswald's address book as Exhibit 18. In it, Oswald noted:

Nat. Sec. Dan Burros
Lincoln Rockwell
Arlington, Virginia
American Nazi Party
(Amer. National Party)
Hollis sec. of Queens, N.Y.
(newspaper)
Nat. Socialist Bulletin

Burros' American National Party (ANP) and George Lincoln Rockwell's American Nazi Party are the only ultra-right groups mentioned in Oswald's address book.

Sometime after splitting from Rockwell, Dan Burros became a fervent Yockeyist. Why then did Oswald include both Burros and Rockwell in his address book? Fortunately this question can be easily answered by an examination of the 20 March 1961 issue of the American Communist Party paper *The Worker*, which ran a front-page story by Mike Newberry entitled "American Nazis Establish Their National Headquarters in Queens." Newberry incorrectly reported that Rockwell's American Nazi Party was planning to relocate to Queens under the "thinly disguised name of the 'American National Party.'" What Newberry had done was to confuse a splinter faction from Rockwell led by Burros and John Patler as a stalking horse for Rockwell. His mistake, however, explains why Oswald thought that Rockwell's group was the same as Burros'. Newberry also quotes from the July 1961 issue of Rockwell's *National Socialist Bulletin*.

As for Oswald's specific mention of Burros and the ANP headquarters in Hollis, Queens, *The Worker* also ran a picture of a group of Rockwell's Nazis that featured Burros, who was described as the group's "National Secretary." The caption explained that the ANP's new headquarters would be in "Hollis, Queens." The photo of Burros and his Nazi pals would have been of particular interest to Oswald because it showed them on a "Hate Bus" trip to the Deep South, which Newberry reported resulted in Burros' arrest in New Orleans, a city where Oswald had spent much of his life. At the time of the *Worker* story, Oswald was living in Minsk, Byelorussia. My best guess is that he was regularly given *The Worker* by either the Russian Red Cross or the local CP apparat, or simply read it in a local library. Thus the question of a possible "Yockeyist" tie to Oswald through his address-book note can be answered: There was none.

APPENDIX I:
THE DEVIL AND
FRANCIS PARKER
YOCKEY

A small trove of writings by Yockey recently surfaced halfway around the world. The unpublished manuscripts (23 typewritten pages in all) consist of the essays "Life as an Art" (December 1940), "Thoughts Upon Waking" (June 1950 and October 1953), "XXth Century Metaphysics" (no date but probably late 1940s), "Culture" (December 1953), and "Thoughts—Personal and Superpersonal" (most likely 1950). The essays appeared in a pamphlet entitled *Varange: The Life and Thoughts of Francis Parker Yockey*, by Kerry Bolton, a New Zealand–based rightist and self-proclaimed satanist.[1]

From a biographical point of view Yockey's most valuable essay is "Life as an Art," written when he was a 23-year-old attending Notre Dame Law School. In it he argues: "Higher men and lower men—the few called to rule and the masses born in order that the higher men may actualize a grander destiny" cannot be "comprehended otherwise than as two different species.... THESE ARE TWO SPECIES OF MEN AS DIFFERENT IN SPIRITUALITY AS LIONS AND LAMBS." "High politics" is the "supreme field" for the higher men, who all have "the same deep, unspoken feeling of the mission." Yockey concludes that the soul of the High Culture–man "IS AT BOTTOM ARTISTIC. In the deeps the will-to-power merges with the aesthetic instinct."

In "Thoughts Upon Waking," Yockey dwells on the concept of polarity and (like Otto Weininger) discusses the polarity of the sexes. He observes that "even in the highest intensity of sexual polarity, there are always the intermediate types, which leave the poles and wish to return to the middle. Diffusion, the opposite of polarity, polarity's other pole." He later notes:

> The interworkings of the poles upon one another are perfectly simple and infinitely complicated. Thus in the polarity of the sexes, in any one individual, a strong inner opposite pole to his actual sex HEIGHTENS his actual sexual polarity. Ultra-masculine figures like Caesare Borgia, Wallenstein, Oliverez, Richelieu, Napoleon, Bismarck, Hitler have NECESSARILY within them a strong feminine pole, and it is this which sharpens their feeling for the Idea of Masculinity. The limiting factor enters when the inner feminine pole is so strongly marked that it *neutralizes* the masculinity of the man. . . . The fact that no man is *purely* masculine, no woman *purely* feminine is the principle of diffusion accompanying the principle of polarity.

In his essay "Thoughts: Personal and Superpersonal," Yockey remarks: "The human race as a whole is a woman. . . . Man is thus a variation, Man is a revolt."

Yockey's hatred of the United States is also evident in these writings. In "Thoughts: Personal and Superpersonal" (some of which reads as a kind of rough draft for the January 1960 Yockey essay published under the title *The World in Flames*), he moans that the geographical position of the United States "tortures the soul" since "this mechanical thing [America] can not be tracked down to its lair and destroyed. . . . We can not have the satisfaction of standing over this misbegotten product of blind forces, sword in hand, watching its final convulsions, watching its heteroclite human material scatter like nomads over the empty landscape."

Finally, some note must be made of the Yockey revival now occurring inside elements of the occult underground. Kerry Bolton, the New Zealand–based publisher of Yockey's texts, has tried for some years to merge fascist politics with occultism. Bolton publishes a series of small journals like *Nexus* and *The Flaming Sword*, and some of his essays have appeared in the Church of Satan publication *The Black Flame*.[2] He also founded two occult groups, the Order of the Left-Hand Path (*Ordo Sinistra Vivendi*) and the Black Order, whose newsletter is *The Flaming Sword*.[3] Today, through his Renaissance Press outfit, Bolton sells copies of *Imperium* and *The Proclamation of London*,[4] and he has been linked to a white-supremacist group called the Nationalist Workers Party, which has issued Bolton-penned tracts like "Scientific Origins of Racial Nationalism."[5]

Bolton also promotes the writings of David Myatt, the British-based leader of a fascist sect called the National Socialist Movement (NSM). Myatt is the founder of the occultist Order of Nine Angles (ONA), which publishes a journal called *Fenrir*.[6] Bolton, Myatt, and the American Michael Moynihan, who heads the Portland-based Storm Publications, all write for a far-right journal called *Filosophem*, which is published in Metz, France, by a group called Blood Axis.[7]

The link between the current Yockey revival and the occult is equally clear in the case of the French "third-positionist" Christian Bouchet, who helped found a new European Liberation Front in homage to Yockey. Bouchet has been associated with the French branch of the Ordo Templi Orientis (OTO), and his occult journal is named *Thelema* in homage to Aleister Crowley.[8] He is a leading figure in Nouvelle Résistance, whose journal *Lutte du Peuple* he also edits.[9]

Bolton and Bouchet have tried to turn the "Satanic" or "black metal" music scene in a fascist direction. Bolton, for example, has helped edit an occult/black metal fanzine called *Key of Alocer*. Bouchet's group Nouvelle Résistance, meanwhile, is behind a music fanzine called *Napalm Rock*. *Napalm Rock* has embraced a leading Norwegian black metal musician named Varg Vikernes ("Count Grishnackh"), who is currently in jail for the murder of another black-metalist, Øystein Aarseth ("Euronymous").[10] When Vikernes was arrested, it was discovered that he had in his possession about 330 pounds of dynamite, some of which he claimed he was planning to use to destroy the Antifa (Anti-fascist) center Blitz House in Oslo.[11] Both *Napalm Rock* and *Filosophem* have praised Vikernes as a gallant Viking warrior.

This same rightist interest in black metal is reflected in a 1998 book on the black metal scene published by Feral House, entitled *Lords of Chaos: The Bloody Rise of the Satanic Metal Underground*, by Michael Moynihan with help from Didrik Søderlind. Moynihan has also been involved in the Abraxas Foundation, which maintains close ties to the Church of Satan.[12]

Moynihan's major outlet has been Storm, his music- and book-publishing house. Besides selling Colonel Qaddafi's *The Green Book*, Storm published *Siege: The Collected Writings of James Mason*, with an introduction by "Michael M. Jenkins" (Michael Moynihan).[13] Mason, a former member of George Lincoln Rockwell's American Nazi Party, created his own National Socialist Liberation Front (NSLF) in the 1970s. Much like Moynihan and other members of the Abraxas network like Boyd Rice, Mason became enamored of Charles Manson.[14] In *Siege*, Mason devotes a chapter to praise white racist "lone wolf" assassins who carry out attacks on racial minorities like blacks and Hispanics.[15] To Mason, such acts should be encouraged as healthy outpourings of "Viking berserker rage."

Moynihan is a leading member of an "Old Norse and Germanic religion" movement known as the Ásatrú Alliance (AA).[16] The Alliance, headquartered in Arizona, evolved out of an Odinist/Nordic revival movement in the United States known as the Ásatrú Free Assembly. The AA wing of the movement argued that Norse religion could only include people of Northern European descent, as it believes that Ásatrú is based on a racial archetype. AA leader "Valgard" (Michael) Murray was a former member of Rockwell's American Nazi Party.[17]

The AA publishes a journal called *Vor Tru*, which is edited by Robert Ward, the former editor of the rightist music and culture zine *The Fifth Path*. Another leading member of the AA is Robert Nicholas Taylor. According to a profile of Taylor in the rightist music journal *Ohm Clock:* "During a 12-year stint as a national spokesman for the Minutemen, he went on to become Director of Intelligence and set up the first guerrilla training schools ever to exist in the United States."[18] For a brief period in the early 1970s, Taylor had his own rightist folk group called Changes. Today, Moynihan's Portland-based Storm Records sells the Changes CD *Fire of Life*, which includes a song ("Twilight of the West") directly inspired by Spengler and Yockey. Moynihan is also at work on his own Blood Axis track for "a German tribute CD dedicated to the esoteric writer Julius Evola," according to *Vor Tru*.[19] The CD, *Cavalcare La Tigre*, from Eis und Licht Records, is part of Moynihan's plan to introduce the political writings of Julius Evola into the American far right. For this reason Storm is now preparing to issue an English translation of Evola's *Gli uomini e la rovine* (Men Among the Ruins).[20]

Notes:

1. The manuscripts published by Bolton most likely came from the small stash of Yockey memorabilia that Fred Weiss had, and may have later been collected by the late Keith Stimely.

2. See, for example, Bolton's essay "Eugenics and Dysgenics," in *The Black Flame*, Vol. 4, Nos. 3/4 (1993), as well as his essay "Satanic Dialectics," in *The Black Flame*, Vol. 5, Nos. 1/2 (1994). This same issue has a picture of Bolton and his young son in satanic garb (p. 38).

3. The Black Order's self-proclaimed purpose is "to (a) study the esoteric current behind National Socialism, Thule, and the occult tradition from which they are derived, (b) prepare a political and cultural infrastructure to replace the collapsing of the Old Order, (c) preserve the Dark Forces on Earth via ritual magick, study, propaganda, infiltration, and any other means deemed necessary." (*The Black Flame* Vol. 5, Nos. 1/2, pp. 18–19.) For examples of Bolton's attempt to fuse rightist theory and occultism, see two pamphlets published by Renaissance Press: *Aleister Crowley and the Conservative Revolution*, by Frater Scorpio (1996), and *Thelema Invictus*, by Siatris (1996).

4. Bolton also published a work in praise of James Madole, the leader of the National Renaissance Party. Recall that Madole tried to form an alliance with Anton LaVey's Church of Satan in the 1970s.

5. Linda Blood, *The New Satanists* (New York: Warner Books, 1994), pp. 199–200.

6. The ONA published a meditation on human sacrifice entitled *A Gift for the Prince—A Guide to Human Sacrifice*. For a spirited attack on Myatt as "the most evil Nazi in Britain," see the April 1998 *Searchlight*. Also see the November 1997 *Searchlight* article "Rocking for Satan."

7. For more on Blood Axis, see its ad in issue 4 (Spring 1996) of *Ohm Clock*, p. 31. Moynihan also uses the name Blood Axis for some of his projects.

8. Bouchet is the author of an academic thesis on Crowley and the OTO. One source reports that he was expelled from the OTO in 1992 without having passed beyond the First Degree.

9. In May 1992 the Nouvelle Résistance journal *Lutte du Peuple* published an article in solidarity with Cuba and argued that Castro was one of the last barriers against

American imperialism. In August 1992 Nouvelle Résistance members went to Moscow to establish links with the Red-Brown alliance. In the summer of 1996, *Lutte du Peuple* interviewed the hardline Stalinist Victor Anpilov, head of the Russian Communist Workers Party (RKPP), a group supported by Nouvelle Résistance and the European Liberation Front. Bouchet also published a eulogy to the deceased West German terrorist Ulrike Meinhof. For a brief look at Bouchet's activity, see Jean-Paul Bourre, *Les Profanateurs* (Paris: Le Comptoir, 1997), and *Searchlight*, December 1996. Also see the chapter "The Mysterious *Book of Vles*."

10. Vikernes took his "Count Grishnackh" moniker from a particularly evil orc in J. R. R. Tolkien's *Lord of the Rings*. Tolkien's work has also been used by members of the Italian right, who (unlike Vikernes) identify with the hobbits as part of the Volk and see the orcs as tools of International Zionist Wall Street Imperialism. In June 1980, for example, elements of the Italian far right sponsored a three-day fascist "Woodstock" in the Apennine Mountains called "Camp Hobbit." The right's attempt to use Tolkien led the head of the British Tolkien Society to issue a formal statement declaring that Frodo was no fascist fink.

11. Jeffrey Kaplan, *Radical Religion in America* (Syracuse, NY: Syracuse University Press, 1997), fn. 98, p. 212.

12. Blood, *The New Satanists*, pp. 195–96. In a 1995 interview with Kerry Bolton in *The Heretic*, Moynihan said he was "an active member" of the Church of Satan. Moynihan's work has also appeared in *The Black Flame*. See, for example, his essay "The Faustian Spirit of Fascism," in *The Black Flame*, Vol. 5, Nos. 1/2 (1994), pp. 13–16. Here, Moynihan argues that "Fascism (and National Socialism) were, at *their* core, intrinsically Faustian—in essence, Satanic."

13. James Mason, *Siege* (Denver: Storm, 1992) includes an introduction by "Michael M. Jenkins." Moynihan goes by the names "Michael Jenkins," "Michael Jenkins Moynihan," and "Michael Moynihan Jenkins." For simplicity's sake, I am calling him Michael Moynihan.

14. For more on Abraxas, see the chapter "Things Fall."

15. Mason particularly singles out former American Nazi Party member Joseph Franklin, who went around murdering interracial couples ("race traitors"); John Hinckley, the would-be assassin of President Ronald Reagan; and James Huberty, who massacred a largely Hispanic group at a McDonald's restaurant in San Diego.

16. *Ásatrú* is an Icelandic word that means "Faith of the Asir" (the old Nordic gods).

17. Kaplan, *Radical Religion in America*, p. 20.

18. *Ohm Clock*, Issue 3, Spring 1995, p. 18.

19. *Vor Tru*, Issue 58, 1998, p. 51.

20. For a detailed examination of both *Lords of Chaos* and Michael Moynihan, see my article "How 'Black' Is Black Metal?" in *Hit List*, Vol. 1, No. 1 (February/March, 1999). Also see an exchange between Feral House publisher Adam Parfrey and myself in *Hit List*, Vol. 1, No. 3 (June/July 1999). For Moynihan's reaction to my essay, see his interview in *Eye* No. 23 (September/October 1999). My response appears in *Hit List*, Vol. 1, No. 4 (September/October 1999).

INDEX

Index